# HOW TO USE YOUR *IN*... *PUBLIC SPEAKING HA*...

## Find the Content You Want Quickly

- The quick-start guide at left provides a **quick look at the contents** of this handbook. This guide is color-coded to correspond to the tabbed part dividers in the text, which divide the handbook into three key topic groups:
  - Basics of speaking in front of an audience (*Parts 1 and 2*)
  - Steps in preparing and delivering an effective speech (*Parts 3, 4, 5, and 6*)
  - Common speaking situations and strategies (*Parts 7 and 8*)
- The **full table of contents** for this handbook begins on page iii. In addition, the **tabbed dividers list the contents of each chapter within a part,** including each chapter's Speech Checklists, Speech Tips, Ethical Moment boxes, and sample speeches.
- To get you started with your first speech, a list of the **10 Steps to Entering the Public Dialogue Successfully** is featured on page xxx.
- The back of the book features a number of **useful reference aids,** including guidelines for preparing MLA and APA source citations; lists of the handbook's Speech Checklists, Speech Tips, and Ethical Moment boxes; a glossary; and an index.

## Build Your Skills and Your Confidence

- This handbook includes a number of **useful and informative features,** such as tips for speaking at work, that will help you hone your knowledge, understand the power of public speaking, and build your skills.
  See pages xvii–xxvi for detail about each of these features.
- Many of this handbook's **study resources and activities** are included in Appendix A, "Building Skills and Confidence," which begins on page A-1, just after Chapter 4. These resources include
  - Key concepts
  - Practicing the Public Dialogue Activities
  - Interactive Video Activities
  - Web Connect web links and activities

  Homework icons throughout the text let you know which of these resources and activities apply to the concepts you're learning.
- Use your **Premium Website for *Invitation to Public Speaking Handbook*** for quick access to the electronic resources that accompany this text. These resources include **study tools** (*digital glossary, key term flash cards, review quizzes*); **activities and assignments** (*Web Connect web links, Practicing the Public Dialogue activities*); and **media resources** (*Speech Builder Express 3.0, Interactive Video Activities, Speech Studio online speech review tool, downloadable Audio Study Tools*).
  For more information and access to this book's online resources, visit **academic.cengage.com/login**.

# Invitation to Public Speaking Handbook

Cindy L. Griffin
*Colorado State University*

WADSWORTH
CENGAGE Learning™

Australia • Brazil • Japan • Korea • Mexico • Singapore • Spain • United Kingdom • United States

**Invitation to Public Speaking Handbook**
**Cindy L. Griffin**

Executive Editor: Monica Eckman

Senior Development Editor: Greer Lleuad

Assistant Editor: Rebekah Matthews

Editorial Assistant: Colin Solan

Media Editor: Jessica Badiner

Marketing Manager: Bryant Chrzan

Marketing Coordinator: Darlene Macanan

Marketing Communications Manager: Christine Dobberpuhl

Content Project Manager: Corinna Dibble

Art Director: Linda Helcher

Print Buyer: Justin Palmeiro

Permissions Editor: Margaret Chamberlain-Gaston

Production Service: Elm Street Publishing Services

Text Designer: Grannan Graphic Design

Photo Manager: Jennifer Meyer Dare

Cover Designer/Image: Jun Park

Compositor: Integra Software Services Pvt. Ltd.



Library of Congress Control Number: 2009928693

ISBN-13: 978-1-4390-3586-3

ISBN-10: 1-4390-3586-5

**Wadsworth**
20 Channel Center Street
Boston, MA 02210
USA

Cengage Learning is a leading provider of customized learning solutions with office locations around the globe, including Singapore, the United Kingdom, Australia, Mexico, Brazil, and Japan. Locate your local office at: **international.cengage.com/region**.

Cengage Learning products are represented in Canada by Nelson Education, Ltd.

For your course and learning solutions, visit **www.cengage.com**.

Purchase any of our products at your local college store or at our preferred online store **www.ichapters.com**.

Printed in the U.S.A.
3 4 5 6 7 19 18 17 16

# CONTENTS

# PREFACE

Our best public speaking courses focus their efforts and energies on teaching students the skills needed to speak effectively in public settings. To accomplish this goal, public speaking texts follow a familiar and practical framework that teaches students to give informative, persuasive, and special occasion speeches. Public speaking texts are designed to expose students to the wide array of steps and components involved in public speaking and to allow students to practice these various elements in the classroom.

*Invitation to Public Speaking Handbook* not only grounds itself in this successful approach but expands it to focus on public speaking as public dialogue, encouraging students to see themselves as significant contributors to their larger communities. In this expanded context, public speaking reflects the many changes that have been taking place in our communities and our larger society; changes that call for public dialogue and an exploration of the many perspectives offered on a number of important topics (Ellinor & Gerard, 1998). When framed as a public dialogue, public speaking emphasizes the right to be heard and the responsibility to listen to others (Public Dialogue Consortium, 1998). Thus, *Invitation to Public Speaking Handbook* explores public speaking in relation to a modern definition of eloquence, in which differences, civility, narratives, visual aids, and even self-disclosure play a larger role than they tend to in traditional rhetoric.

*Invitation to Public Speaking Handbook* encourages students to see public speaking as a meaningful and useful skill beyond the classroom setting by expanding the range of venues for public speaking. The text prompts students to speak not only in required classroom speaking situations, but also when they are asked to do so (for example, in the workplace) and when they decide to do so (perhaps as voices of their communities). Thus, the text exposes them to the wide range of situations that cause us to assume the public platform and contribute to the public dialogue. It also allows instructors, if they desire, to incorporate a service learning component into their course without preventing them from teaching public speaking using the familiar required speech format. Additionally, the text's pragmatic approach—in combination with numerous dynamic, real-life examples—allows working students to design speeches with their employment settings in mind.

*Invitation to Public Speaking Handbook* also frames the act of speaking in public to emphasize the ethical and audience-centered nature of public speaking. Throughout the text, students are reminded that they speak to and for an audience, and they are encouraged to consider this audience at every step of the speechmaking process. This audience-centered approach reminds students of the responsibilities associated with speaking publicly and the importance of advance planning and preparation. It also eases some of the familiar speech anxiety students have, because it turns their attention toward speech preparation and effective communication with others and away from the performance aspect of public speaking.

Most existing texts focus primarily on informational and persuasive speaking, often also preparing students to give speeches that entertain or celebrate others. *Invitation to Public Speaking Handbook* includes this focus but also introduces students to invitational speaking, a type of speaking that is becoming increasingly common. In invitational speaking, speakers enter into a dialogue with an audience in order to clarify positions, explore issues and ideas, or share beliefs and values. When we speak to invite, we want to set the stage for open dialogue and exploration of ideas and issues—we want to come to a fuller understanding of an issue, regardless of our different positions. This speech type is introduced early in the text, when other speech types are defined and discussed, and is included in discussions of the speechmaking process throughout the text.

Finally, *Invitation to Public Speaking Handbook* emphasizes interconnections not only among each of the components of the speechmaking process but also between the speaker and the audience. In this way, the text helps students view public speaking as a layering of skills and issues rather than as a series of actions existing in isolation. Although the speaking process is presented systematically and in discrete steps, the end result is a smooth integration of material and speaking techniques. Additionally, the text's audience-centered approach, focus on ethics, and thorough integration of diversity help students better understand their audiences so they can establish credibility and communicate effectively.

## Features of This Handbook

### Easy-to-Use Handbook Format

Adapted from the third edition of the *Invitation to Public Speaking* textbook, this handbook offers a handy alternative for public speaking classes and a reference for speakers outside the classroom. Several features specific to the *Invitation to Public Speaking Handbook* make it an easy-to-use tool: The handbook is divided into color-coded sections that allow readers to easily find the information they're looking for. Each chapter stands on its own and so, if desired, can be referenced only when needed. Checklists, tips, and highlighted content throughout the book provide quick, accessible advice. And the titles of the key speeches and feature boxes in the handbook are listed on the inside back cover so readers can find and use them quickly and easily.

## Extensive Coverage of Civility and Civic Engagement

By emphasizing the "how" and the "why" of public speaking, *Invitation to Public Speaking Handbook* demonstrates the impact that participating in the public dialogue can have on students' lives and on the communities in which they live. Civility and the importance of civic engagement are emphasized throughout the handbook. For example, Civic Engagement in Action boxes, featured at the beginning of each part, highlight the ways in which students, average citizens, and celebrities have used their public speaking skills to affect the public dialogue in meaningful and satisfying ways. Students can look to these vignettes as examples of how to apply public speaking and civic engagement to their own lives as they become more active members of their communities. The text's thoughtful attention to these issues continually reminds students of the important role that public speaking plays in our diverse society.

## Focus on Skills and Confidence-Building

*Invitation to Public Speaking Handbook* prepares students to give speeches and enter the public dialogue confidently via a solid, pragmatic, skills-based foundation in public speaking. Skills and confidence-building are emphasized right from the beginning, with an overview of the public speaking process (Chapter 2, "Entering the Public Dialogue: Your First Speech") and a discussion of practical strategies for dealing with public speaking anxiety (Chapter 3, "Coping with Speech Anxiety"). Continuing through Chapter 20, "Visual Aids: Types and Formats," each chapter guides students through specific speech construction, delivery, or strategy steps. The text provides straightforward instruction in speechmaking that is based on the author's classroom experience and knowledge of students' expectations for skill training. Speech models included throughout the text are consistent with the principles presented.

Speech Checklist boxes in each chapter highlight key skills that students can apply directly to their own speeches, such as how to evaluate Internet sources. And Speech Tip boxes throughout the text highlight useful suggestions, such as tips for brainstorming speech topics.

In addition, Appendix A, "Building Skills and Confidence," appearing near the beginning of the handbook as a homework resource, offers chapter-by-chapter opportunities to build skills via key concepts review, Practicing the Public Dialogue activities, interactive video activities, and Web Connect resources. Designed specifically for skill-building, the Practicing the Public Dialogue activities frame and highlight critical instructions, exposing students to each component of the speechmaking process and giving them strategies for tackling the informative, invitational, persuasive, special occasion, and group speeches found in Chapters 21 through 26. Homework icons throughout the text let students know which of these resources in Appendix A apply to the concepts they're learning.

## Speaking Venues and Service Learning

*Invitation to Public Speaking Handbook* covers a variety of speaking venues and provides ample opportunity to incorporate a service learning component into the course. The text's flexible organization allows instructors who do not want to include service learning to easily maintain the traditional classroom-based speaking situation throughout the term.

Chapter 1, "Why Speak in Public?" offers students a comprehensive view of public speaking as public dialogue and discusses speaking when someone is asked to speak, decides to speak, or is required to speak. This allows students and instructors to step outside the speech classroom if they desire and take the public speaking skills taught and learned in the classroom into their communities. If they choose to stay with the traditional classroom speech format, the service learning information can be used to prompt students to select and deliver speeches that address larger social issues and dilemmas.

Public Speaking and Service Learning: Engaging Community boxes appear in the online resources for the handbook. Based on actual projects, these narratives reinforce for students the role and power of public speaking outside the classroom and in the public dialogue. The Instructor's Manual for *Invitation to Public Speaking Handbook* provides a definition of service learning and instruction for how to use service learning projects as a source for speech topics, speech research, and possibly an environment for delivery.

Additionally, Speaking at Work boxes throughout the handbook highlight concepts students can apply to a very specific speaking venue, the workplace. Topics featured in these boxes include the importance of listening in the workplace, the necessity of adapting speeches to involuntary workplace audiences, and the variety of informative speeches that speakers typically give at work.

## Expansive Coverage of Speech Types

Some courses emphasize particular speech types, but *Invitation to Public Speaking Handbook* was specifically developed to cover and support the entire array of public speaking types. The text's coverage of multiple speaking forms invites students to discuss audience centeredness and difference, as well as the ways in which speakers can acknowledge, incorporate, and respond to difference with respect and integrity.

Beginning in Chapter 2, "Entering the Public Dialogue: Your First Speech," the text presents a synopsis of five types of speaking: informative, invitational, persuasive, speaking on special occasions, and speaking in small groups. Each type of speech previewed in Chapter 2 is covered in depth in Chapters 21 through 26 and is given equal attention with regard to examples and tips in Chapters 3 through 20, furthering the text's goal of preparing readers for public speaking in a range of venues beyond the classroom.

The text features several full-length student speeches, presented as either a transcript, a preparation outline, or a speaking outline so that students can read the speeches in a variety of formats. These and several additional speeches are included in the *Invitation to Public Speaking Handbook* interactive video activities. All the full-length interactive video activities are accompanied by a transcript, a preparation outline, a speaking outline, sample note cards, and critical thinking questions. In addition, the interactive video activities feature dozens of clips of specific speech elements that students can read, watch, and critique.

## Coverage of Social Diversity

Through reviewer-praised examples and discussion of key concepts, the text makes a comprehensive yet subtle integration of diversity. *Invitation to Public Speaking Handbook* offers meaningful coverage of diversity by exploring culture and speaking styles, culture and listening styles, speaking to diverse audiences, and language and culture.

Rather than isolate issues of diversity into separate chapters, *Invitation to Public Speaking Handbook* presents ideas and issues of diversity in examples, discussions, Speaking Across Differences boxes, activities, and exercises throughout the text. In the process, the text provides sufficient information so that instructors do not need to do additional research in order to have meaningful conversations with their students. This "learn-as-you-go" approach benefits students and instructors as they add to their layers of knowledge about diversity.

## Coverage of Ethics

Ethical issues are discussed throughout the text to help students understand how ethical considerations affect every aspect of the speechmaking process. For example, the importance of practicing ethics in regard to listening, Internet research, interviewing, reasoning, citing sources, and in informative, invitational, and persuasive speaking are covered thoroughly. In addition, select chapters of this edition feature Ethical Moment boxes, which highlight well-known ethical dilemmas related to the public dialogue.

## Coverage of Reasoning

The text emphasizes the important skill of reasoning in informative, invitational, and persuasive speaking situations. Chapter 14, "Introduction to Reasoning," encourages students to recognize the validity of sound reasoning and evidence in any speaking context, while Chapter 24, "Persuasion and Reasoning," provides superior coverage of the critical importance of sound reasoning in persuasion.

## Resources for Students

*Invitation to Public Speaking Handbook* features an outstanding array of supplements to assist in making this course as meaningful and effective as possible.

- The **Premium Website for *Invitation to Public Speaking Handbook*** provides students with one-stop access to all the integrated technology resources that accompany the handbook. These resources include an enhanced eBook, Audio Study Tools chapter downloads, Speech Builder Express™ 3.0, InfoTrac College Edition, Public Speaking and Service Learning: Engaging Community vignettes, interactive versions of the Practicing the Public Dialogue activities, interactive video activities, Web Connect links, and self-assessments. All resources are mapped to show both key discipline learning concepts as well as specific chapter learn lists.

  **Note to faculty:** If you want your students to have access to the online resources for this handbook, please be sure to order them for your course. The content in these resources can be bundled with every new copy of the text or ordered separately. If you do not order them, your students will not have access to the online resources. *Contact your local Wadsworth Cengage Learning sales representative for more details.*
- ***Invitation to Public Speaking Handbook* interactive video activities** feature 75 video examples of student and professional

speeches, in full-length and clip form. This multimedia tool helps students prepare for their own speech performances and provide effective feedback to their peers by evaluating and critiquing introductory, informative, invitational, persuasive, and special occasion speeches. Students can compare their evaluation with the author's and, if requested, submit their response electronically to their instructor.

- Many of the Practicing the Public Dialogue activities can be completed with **Speech Builder Express 3.0 organization and outlining program**. This interactive Web-based tool coaches students through the speech organization and outlining process. By completing interactive sessions, students can prepare and save their outlines—including a plan for visual aids and a works cited section—formatted according to the principles presented in the text. Text models reinforce students' interactive practice.
- **InfoTrac College Edition with InfoMarks.** This virtual library features more than 18 million reliable, full-length articles from 5,000 academic and popular periodicals that can be retrieved almost instantly. They also have access to InfoMarks—stable URLs that can be linked to articles, journals, and searches to save valuable time when doing research—and to the InfoWrite online resource center, where students can access grammar help, critical thinking guidelines, guides to writing research papers, and much more.
- **Audio Study Tools for *Invitation to Public Speaking Handbook*.** This text's mobile content provides a fun and easy way for students to review chapter content whenever and wherever. For each chapter of the text, students will have access to a brief speech example and a five- to seven-minute review consisting of a brief summary of the main points in the text and five to seven review questions. Students can purchase the Audio Study Tools for *Invitation to Public Speaking Handbook* through iChapters (see below) and download files to their computers, iPods, or other MP3 players.
- **Cengage Learning Enhanced eBook.** This version of the handbook is a Web-based, multimedia text that offers ease of use and maximum flexibility for students who want to create their own learning experience. The enhanced eBook includes advanced book tools such as a hypertext index, bookmarking, easy highlighting, and faster searching, easy navigation, and a vibrant Web-based format. Students get access to the enhanced eBook with the printed text, or they can just purchase access to the stand-alone enhanced eBook.
- **Speech Studio Online Video Upload and Grading Program.** Speech Studio improves the learning comprehension of your public

speaking students. This unique resource empowers instructors with a new assessment capability that is applicable for traditional, online, and hybrid courses. With Speech Studio, students can upload video files of practice speeches or final performances, comment on their peers' speeches, and review their grades and instructor feedback. Instructors create courses and assignments, comment on and grade student speeches with a library of comments and grading rubrics, and allow peer review. Grades flow into a gradebook that allows instructors to easily manage their course from within Speech Studio.

- **iChapters.com.** This online store provides students with exactly what they've been asking for: choice, convenience, and savings. A 2005 research study by the National Association of College Stores indicates that as many as 60 percent of students do not purchase all required course material; however, those who do are more likely to succeed. This research also tells us that students want the ability to purchase "à la carte" course material in the format that suits them best. Accordingly, iChapters.com is the only online store that offers eBooks at up to 50 percent off, eChapters for as low as $1.99 each, and new textbooks at up to 25 percent off, plus up to 25 percent off print and digital supplements that can help improve student performance.
- **ABC News DVD: Speeches by Barack Obama.** This DVD includes nine famous speeches by President Barack Obama, from 2004 to the present day, including his speech at the 2004 Democratic National Convention; his 2008 speech on race, "A More Perfect Union"; and his 2009 inaugural address. Speeches are divided into short video segments for easy, time-efficient viewing. This instructor supplement also features critical thinking questions and answers for each speech, designed to spark class discussion.
- **ABC News DVDs: Public Speaking.** With a combination of ABC News clips, famous speeches from the last 35 years, and presidential campaign footage, these DVDs provide instructors with informative and historic footage to use within the classroom. The DVDs feature news video, including a Ted Koppel interview with a panel of White House speechwriters talking about how Presidents Bill Clinton and George W. Bush prepared for their speeches; speeches such as Al Gore's address to NYU about global climate change, Margaret Thatcher's eulogy at Ronald Reagan's funeral, and Lee Bollinger's introduction for Iranian President Mahmoud Ahmadinejad at Columbia University; and presidential campaign footage such as Barack Obama's and Mitt Romney's presidential announcements, John McCain's address to the Values Voter Summit, and the 2008 Republican and Democratic debates.

- **BBC News and CBS News DVD: Speech Communication.** This DVD provides footage of famous historical and contemporary public speeches, as well as clips that relate to current topics in speech communication. Available Spring 2010.
- **Special-Topic Instructor's Manuals.** Written by Deanna Sellnow, University of Kentucky, these three brief manuals provide instructor resources for teaching public speaking online, with a service-learning approach, and with a problem-based learning approach that focuses on critical thinking and teamwork skills. Each manual includes course syllabi; icebreakers; information about learning cycles and learning styles; and public speaking basics such as coping with anxiety, outlining, and speaking ethically.
- ***A Guide to the Basic Course for ESL Students.*** This item can be bundled and is designed to assist the nonnative speaker. The *Guide* features FAQs, helpful URLs, and strategies for accent management and speech apprehension.
- ***Service Learning in Communication Studies: A Handbook.*** An invaluable resource for students in the basic course that integrates, or will soon integrate, a service learning component. This handbook provides guidelines for connecting service learning work with classroom concepts and advice for working effectively with agencies and organizations. It also provides model forms and reports and a directory of online resources.

## Resources for Instructors

*Invitation to Public Speaking Handbook* also features a full suite of resources for instructors. To evaluate any of these instructor or student resources, please contact your local Wadsworth Cengage Learning representative for an examination copy, contact our Academic Resource Center at 800-423-0563, or visit us at http://www.cengage.com.

- **Instructor's Resource Manual**, by Cindy L. Griffin, Linda Scholz, and Jennifer Emerling Bone, all of Colorado State University. The Instructor's Resource Manual provides a comprehensive teaching system. Included in the manual are suggested public speaking assignments and criteria for evaluation, chapter outlines, and in-class activities. The manual also includes Public Speaking and Service Learning: Engaging Community vignettes. Based on actual projects, these narratives reinforce for students the role and power of public speaking outside the classroom and in the public dialogue. In addition, all of the Web Connect links and activities listed in Appendix A of the student edition are included in detail in the Instructor's Manual in the event that online access is unavailable or inconvenient. Also includes a comprehensive test bank with answer key and rejoinders, written by Sally Deuermeyer, Blinn College.

- ***The Teaching Assistant's Guide to the Basic Course.*** This guidebook is designed for today's communication teacher. Based on leading communication teacher training programs, the guide covers general teaching and course management topics, as well as specific strategies for communication instruction, such as providing effective feedback on performance, managing sensitive class discussions, and conducting mock interviews.
- **PowerLecture.** This CD-ROM contains an electronic version of the Instructor's Resource Manual, ExamView® Computerized Testing, predesigned Microsoft PowerPoint presentations, and JoinIn® classroom quizzing. The PowerPoint presentations contain text, images, and cued videos of student speeches and can be used as they are or customized to suit your course needs.
- ***Teaching the Invitational Speech Resource Guide* and Accompanying Video and DVD.** This resource, featuring an introduction by author Cindy L. Griffin, shows you how to effectively teach the invitational speech to your students.
- **Student Speeches for Critique and Analysis on Video and DVD.** These eight volumes offer a variety of sample student speeches that your students can watch, critique, and analyze on their own or in class. All of the speech types are included, as well as speeches featuring nonnative English speakers and the use of visual aids.
- **TLC technology training and support.** Get trained, get connected, and get the support you need for seamless integration of technology resources into your course with Technology Learning Connected (TLC). This unparalleled technology service and training program provides robust online resources, peer-to-peer instruction, personalized training, and a customizable program you can count on. Visit http://academic.cengage.com/tlc to sign up for online seminars, first days of class services, technical support, or personalized face-to-face training. Our online or onsite training sessions are frequently led by one of our lead teachers, faculty members who are experts in using Wadsworth Cengage Learning technology and can provide the best practices and teaching tips.
- **Flex-Text customization program.** Create a text as unique as your course: quickly, simply, and affordably. As part of our Flex-Text

program, you can add your personal touch to *Invitation to Public Speaking Handbook* with a course-specific cover and up to 32 pages of your own content, at no additional cost. Bonus chapters available now include discussions of public speaking and civic engagement, advice on conquering speech anxiety, and tips for helping ESL students master the basic course.

Contact your Wadsworth Cengage Learning representative for details or a demonstration of any of these teaching and learning resources.

## Acknowledgments

I believe that writing and scholarship are both individual and collaborative efforts. Acknowledging the individuals who assisted me throughout the process of writing this book is one small way of recognizing that collaboration and thanking those who offered invaluable assistance and endless support. To Monica Eckman, executive editor, and Greer Lleuad, senior development editor, I express my deepest and heartfelt appreciation. For their invitation to embark on this journey, their incredible vision and talent, their endless guidance, support, kindness, and laughter, I am honored and grateful. My writing process and life are richer because of the two of them. To Barbara Armentrout, development editor; Lyn Uhl, publisher; Erin Mitchell, former marketing manager; Rebekah Matthews, assistant editor; Colin Solan, editorial assistant; Jessica Badiner, technology project manager; Corinna Dibble, content project manager; Megan Lessard, photo researcher; Emily Winders, project manager at Elm Street Publishing Services; Margaret Chamberlain-Gaston, text acquisitions manager; Jennifer Meyer Dare, image acquisitions manager: I express my sincerest thanks. These amazing people shared their talents, time, and energy enhancing the book every step of the way. They also generously offered insight, wisdom, and expertise in response to my never-ending requests and questions.

To Dr. Linda Scholz, Eastern Illinois University, and Dr. Jennifer Emerling Bone, Colorado State University, friends in every way and collaborators on various aspects during various stages of this book, I am forever indebted. Their excellent ideas and insights, love and support, steady stream of laughter, smiles, and hugs, and willingness to test out the early versions of this book in their own classes are acts of courage and connection that never went unnoticed or unappreciated. The speeches of their students grace the chapters of this book, which reflects not only the talents of those students but also the extraordinary skill Linda and Jennifer possess as teachers. I am lucky to have them in my life.

My sincerest appreciation also goes to Tim Borchers at Minnesota State University Moorhead for his talent and expertise in helping to integrate technology throughout each chapter of this book. His scholarship and perspective have greatly enhanced the pedagogy of this text and have paved the way for a truly meaningful and instructive website.

To Matt Petrunia, Anne Trump, and Beth Bonnstetter, lecturers and former graduate students at Colorado State University, many, many thanks. Their hours and hours in the library, on the Internet, and in my office assisting me with research are invaluable. Working with the three of them gave me the confidence to complete this project on time and the assurance that the ideas in this book are supported by the very best of scholarship, both historical and contemporary. My colleagues at Colorado State University, Karrin Anderson, Eric Aoki, Kirsten Broadfoot, Carl Burgchardt, Martin Carcasson, Greg Dickenson, Scott Diffrient, Ann Gill, Brian Ott, Andy Merolla, Sue Pendell, Dennis Phillips, and David Vest, shared their rich knowledge about teaching public speaking, material from their own libraries, and anecdotes from their own experiences, which energized and encouraged my work. The support they offered, the confidence they expressed, and their excellent scholarship reminded me to continue to strive for the richness that is possible in teaching and writing about public speaking.

And along those lines, thanks very much to all the reviewers of this handbook for their invaluable feedback and support. They are Amy Arellano, Tarrant County College Northeast; Philip Dalton, Hofstra University; Jennifer Del Quadro, College of Southern Nevada; Jonathan Dunleavy, University of Miami; Pat Hill, University of Akron; Patricia Islas, El Paso Community College; Brenden Kendall, University of Utah; Kirstin Kiledal, Hillsdale College; Edith LeFebvre, California State University, Sacramento; Cristina Martinez, Tarrant County College; Joseph Martinez, El Paso Community College; Jean Perry, Glendale Community College; Kim Powell, Luther College; Pravin Rodriguez, Ashland University; John Saunders, Columbus State University; Cheryl Skiba-Jones, Ivy Tech Community College; Pam Speights, Wharton County Junior College; Tasha Vanhorn, Citrus College; and David Williams, Texas Tech University.

Thanks also to former and current Colorado State University lecturers, graduate students, and special-appointment faculty Cara Buckley, Kathleen Creamer, Erin Cunningham, Ian Dawe, Brian DeVeney, Alicia Ernest, Holly Gates, Bill Herman, Jeffery Ho, Lori Irwin, Keli Larson-Flewell, Jill Lippman, Katheryn Maguire, Jeremy Mellott, Beth Myers-Bass, Sonja Modesti, Kirsten Pullen, Raena Quinlivin, Virginia Ramos, Mark Saunders, Heather Scheumann, Allison Searle, Elizabeth Sink, Jamie Skerski, Kristin Slattery, Derek Sweet, Elizabeth Terry, and Toni-Lee Viney, who at various times (and sometimes without even realizing it) shared speech ideas, outlines, assignments, and stories that added to the depth and strength of this project.

Many thanks also to their students, whose speeches are found in pages of this text. And a very special thanks to Mary Triece of the University of Akron, not only for her invaluable class-test feedback, but also for so graciously providing us with the speeches of some of her students, which are also incorporated throughout this text.

And finally, a sincere thank you to my public speaking students and to the students from other parts of the country whose voices enhance this text, for their creativity, flexibility, and talents.

Without a doubt, the strongest collaborative force in my life comes from my family. My husband, Mike Harte; my son, Joseph Griffin-Harte; my sisters, Tracy Zerr and Wendy Stewart; my brother, John Griffin; my mother, Joan Christiansen; my father, John Griffin; my second mother, Betty Griffin; and my dear friend Jana Webster-Wheeler keep strong and steady the flame that fuels my energy. Their unending love and support have enriched this project and reminded me daily that the public dialogue is enhanced by our willingness to listen to others and by our commitment to speak as clearly and honestly as possible. To them, I offer my love and thanks, and the acknowledgment that their care for me gives me great strength and peace.

—Cindy L. Griffin

# 10 STEPS TO ENTERING THE PUBLIC DIALOGUE SUCCESSFULLY

Even the most eloquent, successful speeches take time and effort to create and deliver. As you read this textbook and practice giving speeches in your public speaking course, you will learn a great deal about how to give effective and interesting speeches. To get you started, here are the ten steps for giving a successful first speech.

1. **Determine whether you decided, were asked, or are required to enter this dialogue.**
   How does context affect you, your speech, and your audience?

2. **Identify your audience and their characteristics.**
   Who are they? Why are they present to listen to your speech? What is your relationship to them?

3. **Determine your topic, purpose, and thesis statement (statement of the main ideas in your speech).**
   Are they relevant, appropriate, and manageable? Have you crafted them with your audience in mind? Begin thinking about ethical choices you may have to make in order to meet your audience's needs.

4. **Formulate your main points.**
   Do the main points reflect your thesis statement and purpose? Do they follow a systematic progression? Can you manage the material you'd need to present in the time you have for the speech?

5. **Gather your materials.**
   Have you used the Internet, library, and interviews? Have you gathered material for visual aids? Is your materials relevant to your audience as well as to your topic and purpose? Have you done your research ethically and responsibly?

6. **Organize your ideas into an introduction, body, and conclusion.**
   Is your organization logical? Do the introduction, body, and conclusion fit together to make a coherent whole? Remember to incorporate connectives, which are transitions from one main idea to another that help your audience keep track of your information.

7. **Select language that enhances your ideas.**
   Are you using language that is clear and appropriate to your subject, audience, and yourself? Have you rephrased confusing or potentially offensive language? Are you clear about the reasons why you might *not* rephrase certain language?

8. **Practice your speech.**
   Have you practiced the speech three to six times? Have you practiced with your visual aids? Have you used any strategies to help with nervousness?

9. **Deliver your speech.**
   Have you visualized a successful speech beforehand? Do your notes have prompts to help you remember to make eye contact with the audience, relax, gesture naturally, breathe?

10. **Congratulate yourself on your successful first speech.**
    What did you do well? Were there any pleasant surprises? What successes and strengths will you carry over into your next speech?

PART I

# THE BASICS



## CIVIC ENGAGEMENT IN ACTION

### What's Your OrangeBand?

At lunch one day in 2003, a group of friends at James Madison University decided to try to engage students, faculty, staff, and administrators in a meaningful discussion about one important issue: the war in Iraq. They didn't want a rally, protest, or debate, "just a community-wide conversation." For one week, the students passed out simple bands of orange fabric that could be tied to a backpack or jacket to symbolize a desire to talk about the war. They wanted to spark the question "What's your OrangeBand?" and invite conversation about the war.

AP IMAGES/EVAN DYSON

Five weeks later, more than 2,000 students, professors, and community members had chosen to wear OrangeBands, attend forums, and discuss their views. Dialogue soon turned to a number of other core issues, and the question became "What's your OrangeBand today?" In 2004, the nonprofit OrangeBand Initiative, Inc., was formed. By 2006, OrangeBand had coordinated 100 forums, several Action Campaigns designed to facilitate conversations on a wide range of topics, and had inspired over 8,000 OrangeBand wearers, the support of fifty student and community organizations, members from forty different majors, and a second chapter at Eastern Mennonite University.

The organizers think that OrangeBand taps into three things that people are hungry for:

- **Civil discourse (respectful conversation).** There is desire out there to talk about issues we care about with other people and to try to learn from them when we disagree rather than dismiss and disrespect them.
- **Social capital (community).** OrangeBand is not just about having a conversation with someone but also about feeling connected to them. The group maintains that the "relationship-building aspect of

#### You Can Get Involved

To learn more about OrangeBand and to get involved, access **Web Connect P.I.1: What's Your OrangeBand?** online at your Premium Website for *Invitation to Public Speaking Handbook*. And to think more about topics you can address as a public speaker in your community and how you can go about sparking a dialogue, access **Web Connect P.I.2: Convening Public Dialogue**.

## CIVIC ENGAGEMENT IN ACTION continued

a quality conversation on an important topic" is just as important as the conversation itself.

- **Civic engagement (citizenship).** Whether we call it getting involved, citizenship, or civic responsibility, OrangeBand taps into a desire to participate in democracy. When OrangeBand conversations start up, talking quickly turns to taking action.

Skills & Confidence
Web Connect P.I.1
Web Connect P.I.2

OrangeBand chapters or groups are springing up across the nation, and the organization has only one rule: "to be successful in providing a neutral space for dialogue, the organization must remain neutral itself. We vigorously work to protect this political impartiality by inviting people of diverse perspectives to participate on staff and in our forums." OrangeBand is "not interested in advocating for any particular stance"; rather, the goal is to "generate a better understanding of why a person thinks" what she or he thinks.[1]

# THE BASICS

CHAPTER 1

# Why Speak in Public?

- The Power of Ethical Public Speaking
- Culture and Speaking Style
- What Is Ethical Public Speaking?
  - Ethical Moment: **Can Breaking the Law Be Ethical?**
- A Model of the Public Speaking Process

***In this chapter, you will learn***

- About the power of ethical public speaking
- About the importance of acting ethically as a public speaker
- About the influence of culture on speaking styles
- What makes public speaking different from other kinds of communication

Have you ever been moved by the words of a public speaker? If so, you are not alone. Most of us have left at least one public speech or lecture feeling differently about the world, the issues that concern us, and even about ourselves.

This book was designed to get you started as a public speaker. It will help you successfully and ethically add your voice to the many public conversations and debates of our democratic society. In these pages, you will learn about a range of settings in which public speaking occurs and a variety of reasons for speaking. The chapters that follow break down the components of the public speaking process into discrete steps, which you will follow in crafting your own speeches. As you gain confidence in using these techniques, you can adapt them to your own real-life speaking experiences at work and in your community. You'll find that you will speak in any number of instances to provide instructions, explain procedures, share information, encourage or influence decisions, and more.

**Speaking at Work**

*People often use their public speaking skills at work, however informally. For example, they give informative speeches (trainings, status reports), invitational speeches (dialogues to explore issues and ideas), persuasive speeches (sales pitches, arguments for or against issues), and special occasion speeches (commemorative speeches at anniversaries or going-away parties).*

Public speaking is a learned skill that gets more rewarding as our experience with it grows. No one was born a public speaker. Every speaker had to learn how to give effective speeches—even renowned speakers such Abraham Lincoln, Martin Luther King Jr., U.S. Secretary of State Hillary Clinton, and the many others you will read about in this text. The more you practice this new skill, the more quickly you will feel you are a competent speaker. With care and diligence, you will find that you can add your own voice to the public dialogue in positive ways.

This chapter introduces you to the power of ethical public speaking and thc differences between public speaking and other forms of communication. It invites you to consider the opportunities you will have to speak publicly and to recognize the importance of learning the basic skills necessary to do so successfully and effectively. When we consider the power these actions have to shape lives, we begin to get a sense of the challenges, responsibilities, and thoughtfulness that go into designing, delivering, and listening to effective public speeches.

## The Power of Ethical Public Speaking

When you speak publicly, you have the power to influence others. With every speech you give, you make choices about the kind of influence you will have. All of us are familiar with hostile public arguments and debates. We are used to politicians taking partisan stances on issues and "doing battle" with their "opponents." Such debates turn social policy questions into "wars," as groups position themselves on either side of the "dispute," offering "*the* solution" while negating the views of the "other" side. We even watch, read about, or listen to people engage in hostile or threatening exchanges over their differences.

Angry opposition may be a common style of public speaking today, but there are other ways to influence people when you give speeches. As you've watched and listened to combative exchanges, you may have heard some call for more civility in public exchanges. The word *civility* comes from a root word meaning "to be a member of a household." In ancient Greece, *civility* referred to displays of temperance, justice, wisdom, and courage. Over time, the definition has changed only slightly, and in public speaking, **civility** has come to mean care and concern for others, the thoughtful use of words and language, and the flexibility to see the many sides of an issue. To be civil is to listen to the ideas and reasons of others and to give "the world a chance to explain itself."[1] To be uncivil is to have little respect for others, to be unwilling to consider their ideas and reasons, and to be unwilling to take responsibility for the effect of one's words, language, and behaviors on others.

Deborah Tannen, author of *The Argument Culture: Moving from Debate to Dialogue*, offers one of the most compelling descriptions of many people's views about the incivility that characterizes much of our present-day public debates.[2] She explains that in an argument culture, individuals tend to approach people and situations with a me-against-you frame of mind. Since they see each issue, event, or situation as a contest, they begin with the idea that the best way to discuss any topic is by portraying it through opposing positions, rallying to one side of the cause, and attacking the other side. Although conflict and disagreement are familiar parts of most people's lives, the seemingly automatic nature of this response is what makes the argument culture so common today.

Tannen and others concerned with the argument culture recognize that there are times when strong opposition and verbal attack are called for.[3] Nevertheless, this form of communication isn't the only way people can discuss issues, offer solutions, or resolve differences. We can view public speaking not only as engaging in a public argument but also as participating in a public dialogue.

A dialogue is a civil exchange of ideas and opinions between two people or a small group of people. The **public dialogue** is the *ethical* and *civil* exchange of ideas and opinions among communities about topics that affect the public. To participate in the public dialogue is to offer perspectives, share facts, raise questions, and engage others publicly in stimulating discussions.[4] When we enter the public dialogue, we become *active and ethical citizens* who participate in our nation's democratic process and consider the needs of others in our communities as well as our own needs. The ethical dimension of our participation in the public dialogue becomes apparent when we participate in the global dialogue, speaking about issues that affect the entire world, such as human rights, hunger, access to medical care, and the environment. To be an **ethical public speaker**, you must consider the moral impact of your ideas and arguments on others when you enter the public dialogue.

Giving a speech is a natural way to enter the public dialogue because it gives us a chance to clearly state our own perspectives and to hear other people's perspectives. In this sense, giving a speech can be like participating in an ongoing conversation. Kenneth Burke describes this conversation as follows:

> Imagine that you enter a parlor. You come late. When you arrive, others have long preceded you, and they are engaged in a lively discussion, a discussion too passionate for them to pause and tell you exactly what it is about. In fact, the discussion had already begun long before any of them got there, so that no one present is qualified to retrace for you all the steps that had gone before. You listen for a while, until you decide that you have caught the tenor of the argument; then you put in your oar. Someone answers; you answer them; another perspective is shared. The hour grows late; you must depart. And you do depart, with the discussion still vigorously in progress.[5]

Throughout this book, you will encounter the power of public speaking. As you engage with this power yourself, you should always strive to give speeches that help clarify issues and stimulate thinking even as you inform, persuade, or invite others to consider a perspective. Although you may have strong views on issues, a civil and ethical approach to public speaking often is the most powerful way to present those views.

Skills & Confidence
PPD Activity 1.1
Web Connect 1.1

## Culture and Speaking Style

**Speaking across DIFFERENCES**

**Taking culture into consideration is an integral part of the public speaking process, whether you're the speaker or a member of the audience. Remember that ethnicity is just one component of a person's culture. Our culture also derives from our religious beliefs, social affiliations, political positions, environment, and so on.**

Culture has a powerful effect on communication. Whether the culture derives from our nationality, race, ethnicity, religion, work environment, peer group, or even gender, we can't ignore its effect on communication. When we give or listen to speeches, we bring our cultural styles with us. Consider a few examples of ways that culture influences public speaking:

> The traditional West African storyteller, called the *griot*, weaves a story with song and dance, and enlivens a tale with all sorts of sound effects. He or she changes the pitch to suit the characters and the action and adds all kinds of popping, clicking, clapping sounds to dramatize the events of

> the story. The members of the audience respond like a chorus. They interpose comments at convenient intervals, add their own sound effects, and sing the song of the tale along with the griot.[6]
>
> To this day, poets are held in the highest esteem in Arab societies. The Arab poet performs important political and social functions. In battle, the poet's tongue is as effective as is the bravery of the Arab people. In peace, the poet might prove a menace to public order with fiery harangues. Poems can arouse a tribe to action in the same manner as the tirade of a demagogue in a modern political campaign. Poetry frequently functions in a political context to motivate action, and, as such, it is accorded as much weight as a scholarly dissertation.[7]
>
> The late Texas governor Ann Richards's speaking style [was] dominated by the use of inductive and experiential reasoning, folk wisdom, and concrete examples and stories as the basis for political values and judgments. A favorite line she use[d] [was], "Tell it so my Mama in Waco can understand it." Her accessible style...encourage[d] audience participation and reduce[d] distance between the speaker and audience.[8]

These examples come from cultures that may be different from your own or may be familiar to you. What they suggest is that the ways we approach a public speech often reflect our cultural backgrounds.

Research on cultural styles of communication helps explain some of these differences. In general, many white males, for example, are comfortable with the direct, competitive style of interaction found in public presentations. Because historically white males have held more public offices and positions of power in the United States, it makes sense that their preferred style of communication has become the norm for public speaking. However, there are many other communication styles. African American men, for example, tend to be more comfortable with a complex style of speaking that may be competitive but is more subtle, indirect or exaggerated, intense, poetic, rhythmic, and lyrical. Hispanic or Latino males usually reject the competitive style, favoring a more elegant, expressive, or intense narrative form of public communication. Similarly, Arab American males tend to use an emotional and poetic style (poets often respond to and interpret political events in Middle Eastern countries and rely on rhythm and the sounds of words to express their ideas).[9]

Other research suggests that in most Native American cultures, framing an issue from a two-sided perspective is rare. Many Native

American cultures welcome multiple perspectives and discourage competition, preferring cooperation when discussing important matters. In addition, a more circular and flexible style of presentation is common, as is the use of stories, humor, and teasing to explain ideas or teach beliefs. In many Native American as well as some Asian and Asian American cultures, direct eye contact is a sign of disrespect, and publicly proving that someone else is wrong is considered a serious insult.[10]

The research on styles of speaking specific to women is slight. We do know that, in general, African American and Hispanic or Latina women may use a style of speech similar to the lyrical, rhythmic, or poetic style used by the males of their cultures, but it may be more collaborative than adversarial. White and Asian American women seem to share this sense of comfort with collaboration but do not often incorporate the poetic or lyrical forms into their speaking. In general, we also know that women from many different cultural backgrounds tend to incorporate a personal tone, use personal experiences and anecdotes alongside concrete examples as evidence, and establish connection and common ground with their audiences in their public speeches.[11]

In reading about these differences, you may have recognized your own culture's influence on your style of communication. These differences suggest there is more than one way to approach public speaking. Public speaking can occur when we argue with others or take sides on an issue. It can take place when we connect, collaborate, and share stories or humor with our audience. It also happens when speakers use various styles of language or delivery. To enter the public dialogue is to recognize the many different styles of speaking and to use those that fit you and the audience best.

## What Is Ethical Public Speaking?

Every day, we are bombarded with information from computers, televisions, radios, newspapers, magazines, movies, billboards, and logos on clothing and cars. Bosses, teachers, friends, and family also fill our days with words, sounds, symbols, and conversations. Researchers estimate that we spend as much as 70 to 80 percent of the day listening to others communicate. In fact, so much communication crosses our paths every day that this era has been called the *information age*. Where does public speaking fit into this environment? Consider the different sources of communication in which we can engage:

**Intrapersonal communication:** Communication with ourselves via the dialogue that goes on in our heads.

**Interpersonal communication:** Communication with other people that ranges from the highly personal to the highly impersonal. Interpersonal communication allows us to establish, maintain, and disengage from relationships with other people.

**Group communication:** Communication among members of a team or a collective about topics such as goals, strategies, and conflict.

**Mass communication:** Communication generated by media organizations that is designed to reach large audiences. This type of communication is transmitted via television, the Internet, radio, print media, and even the entertainment industry.

**Public communication:** Communication in which one person gives a speech to other people, most often in a public setting. This speech has predetermined goals and is about a topic that affects a larger community. In public speaking, one person—called the *speaker*—is responsible for selecting a topic and focus for the speech, organizing his or her ideas, and practicing his or her delivery. The speaker also is responsible for acting ethically and for responding to audience questions and feedback.

Unlike casual conversations with friends and family, public speaking contains a structure and purpose that add a level of responsibility not found in most other everyday interactions. Similarly, the ability of the audience to respond directly sets public speaking apart from mass communication. And unlike private conversations with oneself or with friends, public speaking is directed at specific groups of people and designed to be shared with those outside the immediate audience.

From these definitions, we can see that public speaking is unique because the responsibility for the organization, delivery, and flow of communication falls mostly on one person. However, if we think of public speaking as participating ethically in the public dialogue, additional differences between public speaking and other forms of communication emerge.

## Public Speaking Creates a Community

We often think of public speaking as an individual act. We imagine one person standing in front of a group of people presenting information to them. We forget that public speaking occurs because individuals belong to a community and share social relationships. We speak publicly because we recognize this connection. When we share ideas and information and consider questions and possibilities with others, we are creating a civil community. We recognize we are "members of a household," and even if we disagree with members of that household (our audience), we acknowledge that we are connected to them. We create a community when we speak, because we are talking about topics that affect us and each member of the audience.

At times, we may forget our connections to others and think our interests and needs are not important to society. However, we are members of a larger social community, and when we make our voices heard, we recognize the need to stimulate the public dialogue, to answer the claims or statements of those who have spoken before us, and to offer our audience ideas for consideration and discussion.

### Public Speaking Is Audience Centered

Public speaking also stands apart from other forms of communication because speakers recognize the central role of their audience. Speakers speak to audiences, and without them, we are not engaged in public speaking. Moreover, in public speaking, the makeup of the audience directly influences the speaker's message. Consider the following scenarios:

> Su Lin's older brother was recently almost hit by a car while riding his bike across town. Upset by motorists' lack of awareness, Su Lin wants to speak out at the next city council meeting to argue for motorist education programs.
>
> Gretchen's brother recently had a near miss while riding his bike across town. Upset by motorists' lack of awareness, Gretchen has decided to give a speech on motorist safety in her public speaking course.
>
> Arturo rides his bicycle to work every day and has persuaded many of his coworkers to do the same. He recently had a near miss with a distracted motorist, and he wants to speak to his coworkers about what they can do to stay safe while riding to work.

The audiences in these three scenarios dictate the choices each speaker will make. Each of the audiences—the city council, the public speaking class, and the other cyclists—has different positions, beliefs, values, and needs regarding cyclist safety. City councils have financial limitations, time constraints, and voter preferences that Su Lin will need to consider. Gretchen's classmates, unless they are cyclists, may not readily see the relevance of her concerns and may also resent any efforts to curb their driving habits. At Arturo's workplace, the other cyclists probably also worry about their own vulnerability and wonder whether riding to work is really worth the risk.

**Speaking at Work**
*Remaining audience centered at work is very important. When people take time out of their busy schedules to attend a meeting or a presentation, they expect the speaker to be audience centered and consider the audience's needs.*

These three examples suggest that public speaking is distinctly **audience centered**, or considerate of the positions, beliefs, values, and needs of an audience. To be audience centered is to keep your audience in your mind during every step of the public speaking process, including your research, organization, and presentation.

Public speaking also is audience centered, because speakers "listen" to their audiences during speeches. They monitor audience **feedback**, the verbal and nonverbal signals an audience gives a speaker. Audience feedback often indicates whether listeners understand, have interest in, and are receptive to the speaker's ideas. This feedback assists the speaker in many ways. It helps the speaker know when to slow down, explain something more carefully, or even tell the audience that she or he will return to an issue in a question-and-answer session at the close of the speech. Audience feedback assists the speaker in creating a connection of mutual respect with the audience.

Public speaking differs from other forms of communication not just because it is done in front of an audience, but because of the ways the speaker relates the speech's ideas to the audience.

### Public Speaking Encourages Ethical Dialogue

A final difference between public speaking and other kinds of communication is that public speaking sets the stage for the ongoing conversation Kenneth Burke described earlier in this chapter. For this conversation to be meaningful, the speaker must present ideas ethically, with fairness and honesty. This ethical aspect of speaking means that the speaker is responsible for framing the conversation, or dialogue, honestly and for laying the foundation for future discussions. Public speaking encourages ethical dialogue because speakers want the people who hear the speech to engage others—and perhaps even the speaker—in a conversation about the topic or issue after the speech is given. Public speaking encourages this ethical dialogue because the speaker is interested in presenting ideas fairly, in discussing issues openly, and in hearing more about them from the audience.

**Skills & Confidence**
PPD Activity 1.2
Web Connect 1.2
Video Activity 1.1

## Ethical Moment

### Can Breaking the Law Be Ethical?

On April 12, 1963, civil rights activist Martin Luther King Jr. and fellow activists were arrested for intentionally disobeying an Alabama Supreme Court injunction against public demonstrations. While in solitary confinement that day, King read a letter published in the Birmingham News by eight white Birmingham clergymen who asked the activists to work through the courts for the change they sought rather than protesting in the streets. In their letter, the clergy accused King and other civil rights advocates of "failing to negotiate," "using extreme measures," and "choosing an inappropriate time to act."

King responded with his "Letter from Birmingham Jail," which explained his unsuccessful attempts to negotiate with unwilling merchants and economic leaders of Birmingham, his conviction that "one has a moral responsibility to disobey unjust laws," and his unwillingness to wait any longer for freedom. In his letter, King made the point that "Injustice anywhere is a threat to justice everywhere" and went on to suggest that "We are caught in an inescapable network of mutuality, tied in a single garment of destiny. Whatever affects one directly affects all indirectly."

WHAT DO YOU THINK?

1. Do you think King acted ethically when he broke the law by disobeying the Alabama Supreme Court injunction? Why or why not?
2. Do you think the Birmingham clergy were correct in labeling King and other civil rights advocates as extremist and unwilling to negotiate? Why or why not?
3. Do you think King was right, that we are "caught in an inescapable network of mutuality"? What might be the ethical implications of this claim? How does this idea relate to the discussions about public dialogue in this chapter?

## A Model of the Public Speaking Process

Consider the following components of the public speaking process as it has been discussed thus far (Figure 1.1 can help you visualize this process):

**Speaker:** A person who stimulates public dialogue by delivering an oral message. The speaker researches the topic of the speech, organizes the material that results from the research, presents the message, and manages discussion after or, in some cases, during a speech. Throughout this process, the speaker is civil, considering the needs and characteristics of the audience.

**Message:** The information conveyed by the speaker to the audience. Messages can be verbal or nonverbal. For example, a speaker giving a speech about his recent experiences in the military would use words to describe those experiences and facial expressions and gestures to convey the emotional aspects of those experiences. Most of our messages are intentional, but sometimes we send an unintentional message, such as an unplanned pause, a sigh, or a frown that conveys an idea or a feeling we had not planned to communicate. When we speak, we convey messages by **encoding,** or translating ideas and feelings into words, sounds, and gestures. When we receive the message, we **decode** it, or translate words, sounds, and gestures into ideas and feelings in an attempt to understand the message.

**Audience:** The complex and varied group of people the speaker addresses. Because of the ethical and audience-centered nature of

**FIGURE 1.1 A model of the public speaking process**

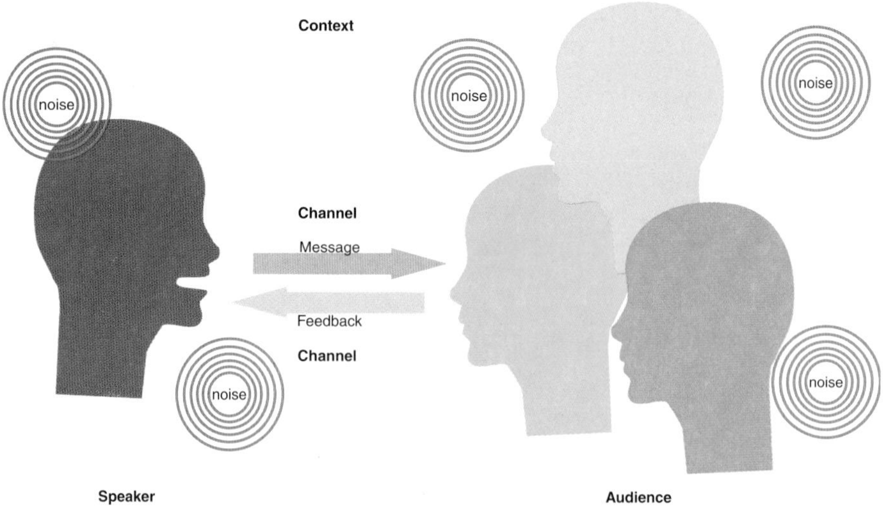

**Source:** Cengage Learning

public speaking, the speaker must consider the positions, beliefs, values, and needs of the audience throughout the design and delivery of a speech.

**Channel:** The means by which the message is conveyed. A message can be conveyed through spoken words, vocal tone and gestures, and visual aids. The channel might include technology like a microphone, a CD-ROM, a video, or PowerPoint slides.

**Noise:** Anything that interferes with understanding the message being communicated. Noise may be external or internal. External noise—interference outside the speaker or audience—might be construction work going on outside the classroom window or a microphone that doesn't work in a large lecture hall. Internal noise—interference within the speaker or audience—might be a headache that affects one's concentration or cultural differences that make it hard to understand a message.

**Feedback:** The verbal and nonverbal signals the audience gives the speaker. Feedback from an audience indicates to the speaker the need to slow down, clarify, respond to questions, alter delivery, and the like.

**Context:** The environment or situation in which a speech occurs. The context includes components such as the time of day and the place in which the speech is given, the audience's expectations about the speech, and the traditions associated with a speech. For example, a commemorative speech would likely be given in a formal setting, such as during a banquet or at a wedding reception, while a speech given as part of a service learning assignment might be given in a very informal setting, such as in your classroom or at the agency itself.

Although we describe each of these components separately, they are interconnected. Notice that the speaker is both a "speaker" and a "listener," sending a message but also attending to feedback from the audience. The audience members also have a key role, reducing external and internal noise whenever possible and listening to the message so they can contribute to the discussion that may occur when the speech is finished.

Skills & Confidence Web Connect 1.3

CHAPTER 2

# Entering the Public Dialogue: Your First Speech



*In this chapter, you will learn to*

- Identify the types of speeches most commonly given in the public dialogue
- Explain the five basic steps of preparing a speech: invention, arrangement, style, memory, and delivery
- Give your first speech

Your first speech is your entry into the public dialogue. It is your chance to develop the skills you need to speak ethically and effectively. This chapter explains the basic components of your first speech. It begins with a description of the different types of speeches common to the public dialogue. Understanding these speech types will help you identify your goals and reasons for speaking. Next, the chapter offers an overview of the speaking process, which will help you prepare and deliver your first speech. By the end of this chapter, you will be ready to give your first speech, which in a public speaking course is often a speech of self-introduction. (You may also want to consult Chapter 3, which suggests ways to reduce nervousness about public speaking.)

## Types of Public Speaking

Whether you have decided, have been asked, or are required to participate in the public dialogue, your first step is to select the type of speech you will give. There are four types of speeches: informative, invitational, persuasive, and speeches for special occasions. Each type has its own distinctive goal and character. Understanding what's expected of these different speech types is an important part of managing speech anxiety.

In this section, you'll also read about speaking in small groups. Small group speaking isn't a type of speaking but rather a speech setting. However, it is introduced here because the goals of small group speaking are often similar to those of informative, invitational, persuasive, and special occasion speaking.

### Informative Speeches

When the goal of a speech is to share information with others, the speech is informative. An **informative speech** communicates knowledge about a process, an event, a person, a place, an object, or a concept (Chapter 21), and it does so by describing, explaining, clarifying, or demonstrating information about its subject. Informative speeches are given in a wide range of situations, from informal to formal, and can vary in length depending on the situation and the audience's need.

Your ethical responsibility in an informative speech is to focus on accuracy and respect. The information you provide your audience must be factually correct and clearly presented. Your audience must also understand why that information is important to them and, if appropriate, how they can use it.

### Invitational Speeches

In an **invitational speech,** your goal is to establish a dialogue with an audience to clarify positions, explore issues and ideas, or share beliefs and values (Chapter 22). With these speeches, you seek a reciprocal exchange of ideas and information, an exchange in which your audience participates along with you in exploring the many sides of a complex issue. As a result of your invitational speech, both you and your audience leave the interaction with a better understanding of the complexities of the issue and why people hold the positions on it they do. Thus, invitational speaking most closely resembles an actual dialogue in which your speech initiates the conversation, setting the stage for an exchange of ideas and facilitating that exchange during or after the speech.

Invitational speeches are usually given in two contexts. In the first context, we want to present an issue that has many sides to it, and an invitational speech helps us explore the issue thoroughly with an audience before we decide what to do about it. In the second context, we want to articulate, or explain, our position about an issue that is controversial or that has polarized people. In this context, an invitational speech allows us and our audience to continue communicating with one another, even when we disagree profoundly. Rather than attempt to change other people, we speak invitationally to try to understand them and to help them understand us. In this context, we endeavor to share our own views and try to see the world as our audience members do, with the goal that all involved understand and are more respectful of one another's different positions and perspectives.

The primary ethical consideration in invitational speaking is your relationship to the audience. As an invitational speaker, you want to share your views, but you also want to hear the views of your audience, especially if they are very different from your own. Because of this relationship, people who speak invitationally are ethically bound to create an environment in which all the participants are able to articulate their differences, similarities, and perspectives without judgment or attempts to change them. The goal is to create an atmosphere in which people can listen to one another with respect and openness.

### Persuasive Speeches

A **persuasive speech** is one whose message attempts to change or reinforce an audience's thoughts, feelings, or actions (Chapter 23). When we speak to persuade, we act as advocates, encouraging or discouraging certain thoughts and actions. We urge our audience to accept our view or solution, take a particular action, buy a certain product, or adopt a specific proposal. When we persuade others, we defend an idea and ask our audience to agree with us rather than someone else. We seek to change or reinforce our audience's attitudes (positive or negative feelings about something), beliefs (ideas about what is real or true), or values (ideas of what is good or worthy). Attitudes, beliefs, and values are discussed more fully in Chapter 6.

Because persuasive speakers act as advocates for positions concerning complicated and often polarizing issues, their words and actions carry unique ethical responsibilities. Persuasive speakers must advocate their position without threatening, intimidating, or belittling their audience. They also must present their position without distorting or omitting important details or facts that make their case more persuasive. Finally, they must recognize the audience members' right to make their own decisions concerning the issue.

## Speaking on Special Occasions

The type of speech you give at special occasions such as award ceremonies, banquets, weddings, and retirement parties is very different from informative, invitational, and persuasive speeches. Your goal with a special occasion speech is to help your audience reflect on the special nature of a gathering. With special occasion speeches, you can introduce (yourself, someone else, or an event), commemorate (another person for his or her accomplishments), or accept (an award or special recognition).

*Introductory speeches.* When you present information with the intention of introducing yourself, another person, or an event to an audience, you are giving an **introductory speech** (Chapter 25). Introductory speeches often take place in formal settings (ceremonial events, job interviews, professional gatherings) and are usually quite short.

In an introductory speech, your goal is to give the audience a compelling perspective on yourself or another person or to welcome the audience to an event and familiarize them with it.

- *When you introduce yourself,* you share with an audience what is interesting about you and relevant to the occasion. You may describe your skills, talents, and the events in your life that have shaped who you are and what you value, but whatever you say about yourself, you want your audience to be glad they've had the opportunity to meet you.
- *When you introduce another person,* you describe his or her contributions, qualifications, or talents with the aim of stimulating the audience's recognition and interest.
- *When you introduce an event,* you set the stage for a particular program or activity. You explain the importance of the event, what's to come, and, if appropriate, offer information about how the audience can or should participate in the event.

Because a person's or an event's reputation and credibility may depend on an introductory speech, you are ethically bound to tell the truth and to create an environment that fosters awareness, appreciation, respect, and understanding.

Skills & Confidence Video Activity 2.1

*Commemorative speeches.* When you give a **commemorative speech,** sometimes called a *speech of tribute,* you praise, honor, recognize, or pay tribute to a person, an event, an idea, or an institution (Chapter 25). Commemorative speeches often take place in formal settings such as retirement parties, weddings, anniversaries, birthday parties, and memorial services.

Your goal in a commemorative speech is to share what is unique and special about someone or something and to express appreciation for special qualities and contributions. A commemorative speaking environment emphasizes values and celebrates accomplishments and contributions that have positively affected others.

Your ethical responsibility as a speaker is to tell the truth about who or what you are commemorating. You should also only share information that is appropriate and relevant to fostering recognition and appreciation in the audience for the person, event, idea, or institution.

*Acceptance speeches.* When you give an **acceptance speech,** your goal is to communicate your gratitude, appreciation, and pleasure at receiving an honor or a gift in recognition of your accomplishments (Chapter 25). Acceptance speeches are often given at formal gatherings, such as awards ceremonies or banquets, but they may also be given in more informal or casual situations, such as after a competition.

Your ethical responsibility when you give an acceptance speech is to express sincere appreciation for the recognition you are receiving. You can do this by conveying your understanding of the meaning and importance of the award. You also can do so by acknowledging those who have helped you reach your goals.

## Speaking in Small Groups

If you take a moment to consider the way you communicate in your workplace, classrooms, family get-togethers, and gatherings with friends, you will recognize that you already have experience speaking in small groups. In **small group speaking,** we give a presentation to a small collection of individuals or as part of a small group of people (Chapter 26). People generally give speeches in small groups to:

| | |
|---|---|
| introduce oneself or a team | assign tasks |
| establish the agenda for a meeting | share information |
| identify a problem | draw others into a discussion |
| generate possible solutions | resolve group conflict |
| assess the feasibility of possible solutions | build or increase group morale |

When you conduct a meeting, give a group presentation, participate in a panel discussion, present at a symposium, or give a team presentation, you are speaking in a small group.

Because we speak in small groups for so many different reasons, there is often overlap between small group public speaking and the other types of speaking. Your goals may include informing, inviting, or persuading. However, instead of formally addressing a large audience as an individual speaker, you speak within a small group, often in less formal contexts and in collaboration with other members of the group.

When you speak in a small group, you must attend to group processes and dynamics, facilitate disagreements with maturity and respect, include all members of the group in the process, and accomplish the task you have been asked or assigned to complete. Your ethical responsibilities are tied to your leadership abilities and to the different roles you and the other group members take on.

As you learn to give these various types of speeches, you will discover that each is appropriate to particular situations and requires a particular kind of environment or tone. You may find you are more comfortable with some types of speeches than you are with others. However, note that each type of speech has its place in the public dialogue, and learning to give each will help you be more successful in that dialogue once you complete your public speaking class.

## An Overview of the Speaking Process

The five basic steps of the speaking process come from scholarship on public speaking that began more than 2,000 years ago. These steps follow the classical canons of rhetoric: invention, arrangement, style, memory, and delivery. A **canon** is an authoritative list, an accepted principle or rule, or an established standard of judgment. The five canons listed here represent the accepted principles and standards of basic speech preparation.

### Invention: Choosing Your Topic and Purpose and Gathering Your Materials

The **canon of invention** provides guidelines for generating effective content for your speech. It is the first step most people take when they put together a speech. There are five parts to the canon of invention:

1. Identifying and analyzing your audience.
2. Selecting your topic.
3. Determining your purpose.
4. Deciding on your main points.
5. Collecting materials to support your ideas.

*Audience.* The first step in the invention process is to identify and analyze your audience (Chapter 6). Every choice you make from the moment you are asked, decide, or are required to speak should be made with the audience in mind. Your goal is to analyze your audience and determine the best, most ethical way to present your speech to them. You can do this by asking the following questions:

- Who is my audience?
- What are their interests, views, and experiences?
- What is the size of my audience?
- What do they know about me?
- Are they required to listen, or do they have a choice?

The audience is your reason for speaking, so you must consider them in each step of your speech preparation process.

*Topic.* Your next step in the invention process is to consider the topic, or the subject, of your speech. If you are asked or decide to speak, either your topic is given to you or you already know what you want to speak about. When you are required to speak, you often have to come up with a topic on your own. For required speeches that have no predetermined topic, Table 2.1 lists two simple techniques for selecting a topic (see also Chapter 5).

**TABLE 2.1 Two Techniques for Selecting a Speech Topic**

| | |
|---|---|
| **Develop a topic of public relevance based on your interests, hobbies, and skills** | • Do you want to know more about something (a political issue, a culturally significant craft or activity, an event in history, even a person, place, or thing)?<br>• Are you actively involved in something (an art or skill, a club or group, a blog or chat room that is politically relevant)?<br>• Are you good at some task or activity that can be linked to the public dialogue (music, electronics, sports, working with animals)? |
| **Develop a topic of public relevance by brainstorming using free association, categories, or technology** | • Sit with paper and pen or at a computer and look around the room. Pick one item and then list everything that comes to mind, whether it is related or not. Link one of those topics to a political or social issue.<br>• Jot down category headings like "events," "natural phenomena," "concepts," "objects," "problems," or "processes," and brainstorm under these categories. Write down whatever comes to mind within each of the categories. Link one of the topics to a political or social issue.<br>• Log on to a search engine (Chapter 8) and review the list of subjects displayed on the home page. Link one of these topics to the public dialogue. |

As you use these techniques, ask yourself:

- Why your audience might be interested in your topic.
- How they feel about your topic.
- What their previous experience with that topic might be.

Your goal is to stay audience centered—that is, to keep your audience in mind with each choice you make during topic selection. Remember, you are entering the public dialogue and want your audience to be interested in your subject.

*Purpose.* The third step in the canon of invention is to determine your purpose or reason for speaking (Chapter 5). Your purpose relates to the type of speech you will give and is often determined by your public speaking instructor or the person who has asked you to speak. Table 2.2 lists the most common *general purposes* for public speaking. When you select your general purpose, you are deciding what, very generally, you would like to do in your speech. Note that the general purpose of a speech is expressed as an infinitive verb (a verb used with *to,* such as *to speak*) that parallels the type of speech you're giving (for example, the general purpose of a persuasive speech is *to persuade*).

**TABLE 2.2 The Most Common General Purposes for Public Speaking**

| | |
|---|---|
| **To inform** | Share with an audience an area of expertise or body of knowledge. |
| **To invite** | Gain a fuller understanding of all perspectives by establishing a dialogue with your audience to clarify positions, explore issues and ideas, or share beliefs or values. |
| **To persuade** | Advocate or encourage an audience to adopt a particular view, position, or plan. |
| **To introduce** | Acquaint an audience with someone, something, or some event. |
| **To commemorate** | Share with an audience praise, honor, tribute, or recognition for a person, event, idea, or institution. |
| **To accept** | Express gratitude, appreciation, and pleasure at being recognized for an award or nomination. |
| **To speak in or as a small group** | Lead or facilitate a discussion with a small group of three to twelve people or speak collectively as a small group to inform, invite, persuade, or all three. |

Your next step is to identify your specific purpose and thesis statement. A *specific purpose* helps you refine your topic and speaking goal so you will be more focused as you move forward with your speech. A statement of a specific purpose includes exactly what you hope to accomplish with your audience in the time you have to speak. An example of a specific purpose is "to inform my audience of the volunteer opportunities at the American Red Cross." Your *thesis statement* is important because it allows you to state, in a single sentence, the content of your speech. The thesis statement, sometimes called the *central idea,* is more detailed than the specific purpose. It includes the main propositions, assumptions, or arguments you want to express. The thesis statement also helps you identify your main points for your speech.

Here's how Missy expressed her specific purpose and thesis statement for a required speech, "The Mysterious World of Hiccups":

| **Topic:** | **Hiccups** |
|---|---|
| General purpose: | To inform |
| Specific purpose: | To inform my audience of the "anatomy" of a hiccup. |
| Thesis statement: | Hiccups, or involuntary spasms of the diaphragm, are most often caused by food, beverages, and medicines but can be cured easily with a few simple techniques. |

Notice the use of "to inform" and "my audience" in the statement of the specific purpose. Every specific purpose statement should include these two important phrases. The infinitive phrase "to inform" (or "to accept," "to persuade," and so on) reminds you of your general purpose. The phrase "my audience" reminds you that you are speaking to a specific group of individuals and should consider them in each step of the speech. Also notice that the thesis statement is a complete sentence. This ensures that you have a fully developed thesis or argument at the very start of your speech preparation process. If you follow these guidelines, your efforts will be directed toward a specific rather than a loosely formed plan.

*Main points.* The fourth step in the invention process, identifying your main points, grows out of your specific purpose and thesis statement. Your *main points* are your most important claims, arguments, or concepts in the speech (Chapter 10). They allow you to accomplish your specific purpose and to elaborate on your thesis statement. Use your specific purpose and thesis statement to help you determine those main points. In her speech about hiccups, for example, Missy used her specific purpose and thesis statement to come up with the following main ideas:

1. Hiccups are involuntary spasms of the diaphragm that cause the space between the vocal cords to close suddenly and make a peculiar sound.
2. Hiccups are most often caused by the foods we eat, the beverages we drink, and the medicines we ingest.
3. Mild cases of hiccups can be cured with a few simple techniques.

She identified these main points by breaking her thesis down into her primary ideas (definition of hiccups, causes of hiccups, and cures for hiccups) and asking herself how she could elaborate on those ideas.

*Gathering supporting materials.* Your final step in the invention process is to gather supporting material for your speech (Chapter 7). When you need to find material to support your ideas, and almost all speakers do, focus your efforts in three places: the library, the Internet, and personal interviews. The library is the most comprehensive source of material you can use (Chapter 8). Libraries house enormous amounts of information in a variety of formats and are designed to help users find that material easily. The Internet is also a valuable source of materials, and many speakers incorporate facts from this source into their speeches (Chapter 8). The Internet makes information from around the world accessible to computer users, and it can provide you with the most current information on a topic. When you can't find the information you want in the library or on the Internet, or when you want specific, personalized information for your speech, you might conduct an interview (Chapter 9). Personal interviews can provide you with the most direct or relevant stories, facts, and examples.

As you gather materials from any of these three sources, look for the following kinds of information so that you can develop your ideas effectively (Chapter 13):

| | |
|---|---|
| **Examples:** | Specific instances used to illustrate a concept, experience, issue, or problem. Examples help you clarify a point or argument, specify the nature of something, or support your explanation. |
| **Narratives:** | Stories that recount real or fictional events. Narratives can be useful for drawing an audience into your speech. Their characters, events, and settings can help illustrate, develop, or clarify a claim you are making. Narratives can be very short, as in an anecdote, or longer. They can be told in segments over the course of the speech or told at one interval. They may even make up most or all of a speech. |

*(Continued)*

| | |
|---|---|
| **Statistics:** | Numerical summaries of facts, figures, and research findings. Statistics numerically quantify, estimate, measure, and represent events, issues, positions, actions, beliefs, and the like. |
| **Testimony:** | The opinions or observations of others. Testimony, often in the form of quotations, can come from an authority, an average person who has relevant experience with your topic, or from your own experiences. |
| **Definitions:** | Statement of the exact meaning of a word or phrase. Definitions help clarify claims and ideas, especially when new terminology is introduced or when a topic is controversial or emotional. |
| **Presentational aids:** | Materials or objects that display your ideas so the audience can see or hear your points (Chapters 19 and 20). These aids include handwritten and computer-generated images, displays, demonstrations, sound recordings, and the like. They are important because they clarify and reinforce your claims and help to stimulate the audience's interest in your speech. |

The invention process generates effective material for your speech. It involves identifying and analyzing your audience, selecting your topic, determining your purpose, deciding on your main points, and gathering material to support your ideas. It is the first step speakers take in putting together a speech.

### Arrangement: Organizing Your Ideas

The **canon of arrangement,** the next step in developing your speech, provides guidelines for ordering your ideas (Chapter 10). As you think about the structure your first speech might take, consider your audience, your thesis statement, and the ways you want to develop your main points. The three most basic components of almost every speech—an introduction, body, and conclusion—are the easiest places to start in a first speech, and they allow you to keep your audience, goal, and main ideas at the forefront of your thinking.

*Introduction.* Introductions set the stage for a speech (Chapter 12). They open up the conversation, invite or demand attention, and acquaint the audience with your topic. Even though there are a few formulas you can use to develop your introductions, speeches can begin in a variety of ways. Some speeches need elaborate and dramatic introductions. Others are much better off with a short and simple beginning. One type of introduction is not better than another, but certain types of introductions are more appropriate for particular audiences, settings, speaking goals, or even your own style.

An introduction should accomplish four objectives:

- Introduce you and your topic to the audience.
- Capture the audience's attention and get them interested in or curious about your topic.
- Establish your credibility.
- Preview the main ideas of the speech.

In her speech on hiccups, Missy followed these four principles to come up with the following introduction:

> I'm here today to share information about one of life's great mysteries. No, I'm not referring to Stonehenge or the Great Pyramids, but to something everyone in this room has experienced: hiccups! Yes, I'm talking about the mysterious world of hiccups, which seem to be a universal occurrence. However, although this mystery is universal, hiccups appear to serve no physiologic function.
>
> I recently was blessed with an overwhelming occurrence of the hiccups, and this sparked my interest and curiosity in the subject. This "blessing" caused me to do some research and investigation, during which I discovered some interesting information about hiccups. I would like to share this information with you today. Specifically, my focus will be on three aspects of hiccups that I find especially informative. First, I'll explain the anatomy of a hiccup, or what a hiccup is and how it occurs. Second, I'll explain the three most common causes of hiccups, which are food, beverages, and medicine. Third, I'll share some simple techniques for curing those milder cases of hiccups.

In this short introduction, Missy follows each of the guidelines. She introduces her topic (the class already knew her fairly well, so she didn't need to introduce herself); she catches their interest by relating her topic to the mysteries of the world, her audience, and herself; she establishes her credibility by sharing that not only has she had an

## SPEECH TIPS

### INTRODUCTION STRATEGIES

Some speakers tell a joke or a story. Others surprise their audiences with startling statistics. In the age of PowerPoint, many speakers pique an audience's interest with an interesting image.

unusual experience with her topic, but she's done some research on it as well; and she previews her main points before she begins to elaborate on any one of them.

*The body of the speech.* The body of the speech is the longest part of a speech and contains the information you have gathered to develop your main ideas (Chapter 10). There are many ways to organize this material, and your thesis statement should help you narrow your options. In public speaking courses, instructors often emphasize certain patterns over others to give students specific kinds of practice with organization. You will also notice that some speeches seem to fall naturally into one organizational pattern or another. The most common patterns are chronological, spatial, causal, problem-and-solution, and topical (Chapter 10). Other speeches are not so easy to arrange and may take careful reflection and effort to settle on an appropriate pattern. Still, there are two basic rules you can follow to organize your main ideas and subpoints.

First, identify your main ideas and arrange them according to an appropriate organizational pattern. To do this, start by asking yourself which ideas necessarily go before others. If certain ideas must be developed before you can address others, they must come first in your speech. But if there is no necessary order, ask yourself what will most interest the audience, and place those ideas up front. Your main ideas should follow a systematic, logical, or natural progression that supports and develops your thesis statement. (Chapter 11 provides advice about outlining your speech.)

Second, link your ideas together with words and phrases called *connectives.* Connectives (Chapter 10) help you transition from one point to another to introduce new points, preview or summarize ideas, and call attention to particularly important ideas.

*Conclusion.* Conclusions tend to be the shortest part of a speech, but they are very important. The conclusion of a speech brings closure to your ideas. Like introductions, conclusions can take many forms (Chapter 12). They remind the audience of the main ideas you developed in the body of your speech, and they can provide an audience with some final thoughts to reflect on. Although there is no one best way to conclude a speech, try to do two things as you bring closure to a presentation:

1. Signal to the audience that you are finished.
2. Summarize or restate your thesis statement.

Let's take a look at the conclusion to Missy's speech:

> So, now you see that there is more to learn about the mysterious world of hiccups than you might have imagined. In this speech, I've shared some very enlightening information about what a hiccup is, the reasons hiccups occur, and the process of curing

**SPEECH Checklist**

### Preparing Your First Speech

- [ ] What is my topic?
- [ ] Who is my audience?
- [ ] What is my general purpose?
- [ ] What is my specific purpose?
- [ ] What is my thesis statement?
- [ ] What is the time limit for the speech?
- [ ] Is there an identifiable introduction?
- [ ] Are the main ideas identifiable within the body of the speech?
- [ ] Is there an identifiable conclusion?

> them. Now, if someday you find yourself in the mysterious world of hiccups, you'll be well prepared to fight back with several of the remedies you've heard about today.

By stating, "In this speech, I've shared some very enlightening information," Missy signals to her audience that she is concluding her speech. She then summarizes her thesis statement and leaves her audience to ponder how they'll be able to use the information she's provided to cure their own bouts with hiccups.

## Style: Considering Language and Figures of Speech

The third step in the speech process, the **canon of style,** offers the guidelines for using language effectively, appropriately, and ethically (Chapters 15 and 17). In this step, you carefully consider the words and phrases you use in your speech.

Certain kinds of language and images are more appropriate than others for particular audiences, topics, and speaking goals (Chapter 16). At the most obvious level, you would not speak the same way to a group of children as you would to a group of adults. At more subtle levels, you will likely use different styles of speaking for supporters and opponents of a position, for those with whom you want to have a dialogue rather than a debate, and when you are commemorating or introducing people. To address such considerations, ask yourself the following questions as you select the style of language for your speech:

- What kinds of vocabulary, imagery, and rhythms best match my audience, topic, and goals?
- Have I included vocabulary, imagery, and rhythms that draw my audience into my speech and help me express my ideas vividly?
- Does any of the vocabulary, imagery, and rhythms have the potential to offend, hurt, or alienate my listeners?
- What vocabulary needs to be defined, explained, or illustrated by examples?
- Am I speaking at a level appropriate to my audience?
- Have I omitted slang, euphemisms, or other unfamiliar or inappropriate words and phrases?

As you gather materials and organize your speech, seek out language that enhances your ideas and helps you express them appropriately. Always search for ways to rephrase potentially confusing, disturbing, or offensive terms and phrases. Throughout your public speaking course, you will find that language can be one of your most important tools for entering the public conversation and for creating the right speaking environment.

### Memory: Practicing Your Speech

Two thousand years ago, the canon of memory referred to the actual memorization of a speech and the techniques for doing so. However, in your speech class, you'll be expected to give most of your assigned speeches in a conversational rather than a memorized style, or *extemporaneously.* Because of this change in preference of delivery styles, the **canon of memory,** the next step in the speech process, now refers to your efforts to rehearse your speech and the ways you prompt yourself to remember the speech as you give it (Chapter 17). Like songwriters who learn to play a song they have written by practicing it over and over again, speakers must practice their speeches to deliver them effectively. Additionally, if you are using presentational aids to support your speech, practicing with them is a must.

Later in this text, you'll learn several techniques for practicing a speech and prompting yourself as you give it. For your first speech, refer to the Speech Checklist: Practicing Your Speech, which summarizes those techniques.

### Delivery: Giving Your Speech

The **canon of delivery,** the final step in the speech process, provides guidelines for managing your voice, gestures, posture, facial expressions, and presentational aids as you give your speech (Chapters 18, 19, and 20). Follow these suggestions to aid your delivery:

**SPEECH Checklist**

## Practicing Your Speech

- ☐ Begin your practice sessions alone. *At first, practice only segments of your speech.* For example, try getting the introduction down, then the body, and then the conclusion. You may even find it useful to break the body down by practicing each main point separately.
- ☐ *Make notes on your speaking outline* to help you remember your material and delivery techniques. If you plan to use presentational aids, practice using them until you can manage them easily as you speak.
- ☐ Once you've practiced each segment of your speech individually, *practice the speech as a whole.* Try practicing in front of a mirror. Go back and *rehearse the places where you stumble* or get lost. Make sure your presentational aids work as planned.
- ☐ Before you give your speech, *practice it three to six times from start to finish,* depending on the level of spontaneity or polish you want in your speech.

**SPEECH TIPS**

### PRACTICE YOUR SPEECH IN FRONT OF AN AUDIENCE

Rehearsing your speech in front of your family or friends is a great way to gain some practice and get feedback on your presentation.

- Visualize a successful speech before you deliver it.
- Know your introduction well so you can begin your speech feeling confident.
- Use your notes as prompts and as a source of security.
- Make eye contact with audience members during the speech.
- Remember to breathe, gesture naturally, and pause as needed during your speech.

Chapter 3 discusses ways to deal with anxiety about speaking in public.

The five canons of rhetoric—invention, arrangement, style, memory, and delivery—are a part of every speech you decide, are

asked, or are required to give. Using the canons as your road map, you will be prepared to enter almost any public dialogue.

Skills & Confidence
PPD Activity 2.1
Web Connect 2.1

## STUDENT SPEECH

**with Commentary**

### *Self-Introduction*

*by Tiffany Brisco*

CENGAGE LEARNING

***Specific Purpose:*** *To introduce myself to my classmates in my public speaking course.*

***Thesis Statement:*** *I am an eighteen-year-old Southern California native whose public speaking experience over the years has prepared me well for this class and will help me fulfill my career goal of being a lawyer.*

Skills & Confidence
Speech Studio 2.1

If you have been assigned an introductory speech, such as a speech of self-introduction, a speech to introduce a classmate, or a narrative speech, you can use the following speech as a model. Use your Premium Website for the *Invitation to Public Speaking Handbook* to watch the video clip of Tiffany Brisco's speech of self-introduction. Tiffany gave this speech in an introductory public speaking class. The assignment was to give a one- to two-minute speech, and students were asked to share a bit of information about themselves so that classmates could get to know one another. Students were also asked to share any background they had in speech and why they were taking a public speaking course, besides the fact that it was required.

*INTRODUCTION*

Where to start with something so intricate? Should I start at the beginning or begin at the end and trace back? What is this intricate object that I'm going to talk to you about today, you ask? Well, my subject is, of course, myself, Tiffany Nicole Brisco, born some eighteen years ago in Southern California.

*Commentary*

*Tiffany begins with a series of questions to catch her audience's attention.*

*She reveals the subject of her speech in her introduction.*

*BODY*

I grew up an only child in a single-parent household. My mother always drove me to do my best, and at an early age I won first place in a speech contest for the reading of the poem "Little Chocolate Child." Since then, I have been in several drama classes and a few plays and have even done extra parts in movies and TV shows.

Since then, because I was very involved in school projects, I found myself on a few occasions giving speeches when running for student council offices. I was also honored to be able to do a speech at my graduation. Oddly enough, all this experience came before I had even had my first speech class, which came in my senior year in high school. It was a great class and taught me many skills and prepared me for this speech course in which I am currently enrolled. Because of my prior speaking experience, I feel very comfortable and confident when giving my speeches in this class. I decided to take this speech course at CSU because speaking skills can always come in handy, especially with the career goal of becoming a lawyer—I need to learn how to become a successful public speaker.

*Offering only a brief overview of her childhood, Tiffany describes her early years speaking in front of people. Thus, she sets the stage for her next point, her more recent speaking experience.*

*Beginning with a quick transition, she provides several examples of her speaking experiences as a teen and as an adult. She then uses these examples to help her develop her thesis: Her experiences have prepared her for a career as a lawyer.*

*CONCLUSION*

So, in a nutshell, that's me, Tiffany Nicole Brisco, an eighteen-year-old Southern California native who aspires to become a successful lawyer and, in turn, a successful public speaker.

*Tiffany signals the end of her speech with language that lets the audience know she is wrapping up. She concludes by stating her goals for the future, reminding her audience of the link between public speaking and becoming a lawyer.*

CHAPTER 3

# Coping with Speaking Anxiety

- Causes of Nervousness in Public Speaking
- Ways to Overcome Fears About Public Speaking

Ethical Moment: **Must We Listen to Others?**

*In this chapter, you will learn to*

**Understand the most common reasons for nervousness associated with giving speeches**

**Apply six techniques for reducing speech-related nervousness**

## Causes of Nervousness in Public Speaking

Many people, even the most experienced speakers, get nervous before they give a speech. One of the reasons we get anxious is that we care about our topic and our performance. We want to perform well and deliver a successful speech. Another reason we might be nervous before a speech is because we experience **communication apprehension,** "the level of fear or anxiety associated with either real or anticipated communication with another person or persons."[1]

Communication apprehension, or nervousness, can take two forms. People who are apprehensive about communicating with others in any situation are said to have **trait anxiety.** People who are apprehensive about communicating with others in a particular situation are said to have **state, or situational, anxiety.** Take a moment to consider whether you are trait anxious or state anxious in communication situations. Do you fear all kinds of interactions or only certain kinds? Most of us experience some level of state anxiety about some communication events, such as asking a boss for a raise, verbally evaluating another's performance, or introducing ourselves to a group of strangers.

In addition, most people experience some level of state anxiety about public speaking. This is called **public speaking anxiety (PSA),** the anxiety we feel when we learn we have to give a speech or take a public speaking course.[2] PSA can be alleviated with practice and by following the tips provided in this chapter. However, sometimes a few of us are extraordinarily nervous about giving speeches. If you think you are one of those people, see your instructor for special assistance about your fears.

Research on communication apprehension related to public speaking is complex, but it suggests that most people's state anxiety about public speaking exists for six reasons. Many people are state anxious because public speaking is:

- *Novel:* We don't do it regularly and lack necessary skills as a result.
- *Done in formal settings:* Our behaviors when giving a speech are more prescribed and rigid.
- *Often done from a subordinate position:* An instructor or boss sets the rules for giving a speech, and the audience acts as a critic.
- *Conspicuous or obvious:* The speaker stands apart from the audience.
- *Done in front of an audience that is unfamiliar:* Most people are more comfortable talking with people they know. Also, we fear audiences won't be interested in what we have to say.
- *A unique situation in which the degree of attention paid to the speaker is quite noticeable:* Audience members either stare at us or ignore us, so we become unusually self-focused.[3]

**Speaking at Work**

*For some people, it can be more intimidating to give a speech at work than at a family function or in a school setting. At work our performance is continually assessed, and some may feel more "on the spot" when speaking in front of their boss and coworkers.*

Research also suggests that people are usually nervous only about specific aspects of public speaking. When people ranked what they fear while giving a speech, here's what they said:[4]

| | |
|---|---|
| Trembling or shaking | 80% |
| Mind going blank | 74% |
| Doing or saying something embarrassing | 64% |
| Being unable to continue talking | 63% |
| Not making sense | 59% |
| Sounding foolish | 59% |

When this list is combined with the six reasons for state anxiety, a pattern emerges. Because public speaking is novel, and because many people are less comfortable in highly structured and formal situations, they shake or tremble. Because it is a conspicuous act, people fear their minds will go blank, they will say something embarrassing, or they will be unable to continue talking. Because it is done in front of an unfamiliar audience and speakers see themselves as being evaluated, they fear not making sense and sounding foolish.

## Ways to Overcome Fears About Public Speaking

There are several ways to ease most of the fears we have about giving speeches. The suggestions offered here should help you manage your nervousness and use it to your advantage.

### Be Prepared by Doing Your Research

One way to reduce the nervousness that comes with giving a speech is to prepare as well as you can.[5] Careful preparation will help you feel more confident about what you will say (and what others will think) and ease fears about drawing a blank or not being able to answer a question. Speakers who research their topics thoroughly before they speak feel confident. They tend to be much more relaxed and effective during their presentations.

### Practice Your Speech

Many people are nervous about giving speeches because they haven't given many before and they don't like the formal setting. If you fall into this category, practicing your speech many times before you give it can help. Here is an example of how this can be done.

> Randy was terrified to give his first speech. His instructor suggested a solution he reluctantly agreed to try. Feeling a little silly, Randy began by practicing his speech in his head. Then, when no one else was home, he began to present his speech out loud and alone in his room. He then stood in front of a mirror and delivered his speech to his own reflection. After several horrifying attempts, he began to feel more comfortable. Soon after, he began to trust his speaking ability enough to deliver his speech to his older sister, whom he trusted to be kind and constructive. First, he asked her to look interested, even if she wasn't. After doing this a few times, he asked her to give him honest nonverbal feedback. Then he asked her to share her suggestions and comments verbally. Finally, he practiced once more in the clothing he planned to wear and delivered his speech in his kitchen, which he arranged so it resembled, as closely as possible, his classroom.

When speakers practice their speeches before delivering them, they become more familiar with the process of speaking and the formality of the situation. As they gain comfort by practicing alone, they can move to rehearsals before an audience. They also have time to make changes in their presentations and to smooth out the rough spots before they actually give the speeches. This practice is part of a process known as **systematic desensitization,** a technique for reducing anxiety that involves teaching your body to feel calm and relaxed rather than fearful during your speeches. This technique can help you give successful speeches and build your confidence, thus breaking the cycle of fear associated with public speaking. Talk to your instructor if you'd like to learn more about this technique.[6]

### Have Realistic Expectations About Your Delivery

Some people fear public speaking because they have unrealistic expectations about delivery. They expect their speeches to sound like professional performances rather than speeches, and they worry about their hands shaking or their voices faltering.[7] If this is one of your fears, adjust your expectations to a more realistic level.

Remember, speakers pause, cough, rely on their notes for prompts, occasionally say "um," and even exhibit physical signs of nervousness, such as blushing or sweating. When learning to speak in public, everyone feels that the speeches they give are full of "mistakes." As we give more speeches, these "flaws" either go away, become less noticeable, or we learn to manage them effectively. Here are some realistic expectations for beginning speakers:

- Take a calming breath before you begin your speech.
- Remember your introduction.
- Strike a balance between using your notes and making eye contact with your audience.
- Make eye contact with more than one person.
- Gesture naturally rather than holding on to the podium.
- Deliver your conclusion the way you practiced it.

### Practice Visualization and Affirmations

Sometimes, when we imagine giving a speech, we see the worst-case scenario. We see ourselves trembling, forgetting what we planned to say, dropping our notes, tripping on the way to the podium, and so on. Although a speech rarely goes this badly, these negative images stay in our minds. They increase our anxiety and often set up what is called a self-fulfilling prophecy: If you see yourself doing poorly in your mind before your speech, you set yourself up to do so in the speech. There are two solutions to this negative dynamic: visualization and affirmations.

*Visualization.* **Visualization** is a process in which you construct a mental image of yourself giving a successful speech. Research on the benefits of visualization before giving a speech suggests that one session of visualization (about fifteen minutes) has a significant positive effect on communication apprehension.[8] The techniques of visualization are used by a wide range of people—athletes, performers, executives—and can range from elaborate to quite simple processes. For public speakers, the most effective process works as follows:

> Find a quiet, comfortable place where you can sit in a relaxed position for approximately fifteen minutes. Close your eyes and breathe slowly and deeply through your nose, feeling relaxation flow through your body. In great detail, visualize the morning of the day you are to give your speech.
>
> You get up filled with confidence and energy, and you choose the perfect clothing for your speech. You drive, walk, or ride to campus filled with this same positive, confident

> energy. As you enter the classroom, you see yourself relaxed, interacting with your classmates, full of confidence because you have thoroughly prepared for your speech. Your classmates are friendly and cordial in their greetings and conversations with you. You are *absolutely* sure of your material and your ability to present that material in the way you would like.
>
> Next, visualize yourself beginning your speech. You see yourself approaching the place in your classroom from which you will speak. You are sure of yourself, eager to begin, and positive in your abilities as a speaker. You know you are organized and ready to use all your visual aids with ease. Now you see yourself presenting your speech. Your introduction is wonderful. Your transitions are smooth and interesting. Your main points are articulated brilliantly. Your evidence is presented elegantly. Your organization is perfect. Take as much time as you can in visualizing this part of your process. Be as specific and positive as you can.
>
> Visualize the end of the speech: It could not have gone better. You are relaxed and confident, the audience is eager to ask questions, and you respond with the same talent you exhibited as you gave your speech. As you return to your seat, you are filled with energy and appreciation for a job well done. You are ready for the next events of your day, and you accomplish them with success and confidence.
>
> Now take a deep breath and return to the present. Breathe in, hold the breath, and release it. Do this several times as you return to the present. Take as much time as you need to make this transition.[9]

Research on visualization for public speakers suggests that the more detail we are able to give to our visualizations (what shoes we wear, exactly how we feel as we see ourselves, imagining the specifics of our speech), the more effective the technique is in reducing apprehension. Visualization has a significant effect on reducing the nervousness we feel because it systematically replaces negative images with positive ones.

*Affirmations.* Negative self-talk is often a reflection of the harsh judge many people carry within themselves. When we tell ourselves, "I'm no good at this," "I know I'll embarrass myself," or "Other people are far more talented than I," we engage in negative self-talk. We judge ourselves as inferior or less competent than others. Although it is natural to evaluate our own performances critically (it's how we motivate ourselves to improve), negative self-talk in public speaking situations is unhelpful. When our internal voices tell us we can't succeed, our communication apprehension only increases.[10]

To counter the negative self-talk that might be going on in your head before a speech, try the following technique. For every negative assessment you hear yourself give, replace it with an honest assessment, reframed to be positive. This technique, sometimes called **cognitive restructuring,** is a process that helps reduce anxiety by replacing negative thoughts with positive ones, called *affirmations.*[11] **Affirmations** are positive, motivating statements that replace negative self-talk. They are very helpful in turning our immobilizing self-doubts into realistic assessments and options. Consider the following examples:

| Negative | Positive |
|---|---|
| I'll never find an interesting topic. | I can find an interesting topic. I am an interesting person. I have creative ideas. |
| I don't know how to organize this material. | I can find a way to present this effectively. I have a good sense of organization. I can get help if I need it. |
| I know I'll get up there and make a fool of myself. | I am capable of giving a wonderful speech. I know lots of strategies for doing this. |
| I'll forget what I want to say. | I'll remember what I want to say, and I'll have notes to help me. |
| I'm too scared to look at my audience. | I'll make eye contact with at least five people in the audience. |
| I'm scared to death! | I care about my performance and will do very well. |
| I'll be the worst in the class! | I'll give my speech well and am looking forward to a fine presentation. We are all learning how to do this. |

Positive affirmations reframe negative energy and evaluations and shed light on your anxieties. To say you're terrified is immobilizing, but to say you care about your performance gives you room to continue to develop your speech. It is also a more accurate description of what is going on inside of you. Affirmations can assist you in minimizing the impact of your internal judge and, along with visualization, can reduce some of your anxieties about public speaking.

## Find Points of Connection with Your Audience

> **Speaking across DIFFERENCES**
>
> It may seem hard to find points of connection with audiences who are very different from us, but remember that we're all human. Most audience members will appreciate your efforts even if you find just a few things in common with them.

Sometimes our nervousness comes from our view of the audience (Chapter 6). When we give a speech, we possibly see the audience as a group of strangers and think of ourselves as distant from them. In the public dialogue, though, the audience really is a part of our own community. So one way to reduce some of the nervousness connected to our view of the audience is to find points of connection between ourselves and the audience.

As you prepare your speech, identify ways in which you are similar to your audience. The similarities may be as general as living in the same town or working for the same company, or as specific as sharing the same views on issues. Whatever the level of comparison, finding out about your audience reminds you that we all share many aspects of our daily lives. This helps you see that, despite differences, we do share similar views and experiences.

## Be a Good Audience Member Yourself

Some of our nervousness about audiences also comes from the fact that we don't always behave in the most supportive ways when we are members of an audience. When you are listening to a speech, do you make eye contact with the speaker? Do you sit with an attentive and alert posture, taking notes or showing interest in the presentation? Do you ask relevant questions of the speaker when the speech is over or offer constructive comments if you have the opportunity to evaluate his or her performance? Speakers who fail to behave as engaged and interested audience members often fear the very same response to their speeches.

One way to overcome this fear of disrespectful audiences is to behave as an audience member as you would want others to behave when you speak. Doing so helps establish rapport (if you are kind to a speaker, she or he will likely respond similarly to you). It also helps you learn about how to put together and deliver an effective speech.

**Skills & Confidence**
PPD Activity 3.1
Web Connect 3.1
Web Connect 3.2

The solutions offered in this section may help you reduce some of the speech anxiety so common to beginning public speakers. Preparing, practicing, being realistic, visualizing and affirming, finding connections, and modeling appropriate audience behavior are options that even experienced public speakers use. As your confidence increases, modify some of these techniques to fit your needs and the special circumstances of your speaking activities. Learning to relax while giving speeches enhances your ability to contribute to the public dialogue.

## Ethical Moment

### Must We Listen to Others?

Sometimes it's hard to listen to speakers. They may say something you don't want to hear, or they may speak about a controversial topic at a time that seems inappropriate. Although public speaking is a centuries-old practice, what feels appropriate or "right" to audiences changes over time and according to circumstance. American activist Angelina Grimke, speaking in 1838, violated many people's sense of "right." Grimke spoke at a time when it was illegal for women to speak publicly to an audience of both women and men: Women were allowed to participate in the public dialogue with women-only audiences in homes and private spaces. But Grimke violated this expectation, speaking to a mixed audience in Philadelphia about the wrongs of slavery and the importance of the vote for women—and she broke the law by doing so.

THE GRANGER COLLECTION, NEW YORK

Her actions so upset people that, even though many people supported her and came to hear her speak, hecklers also attended her speech and an angry mob gathered outside the building where she spoke. Some members of the audience were so angry that they disrupted her speech by insulting her, and the mob threw rocks at the building, threatening to hurt those inside. They also attempted to break down the doors, which were locked to protect the audience within. When Grimke began to speak, the hecklers inside began to howl, but she calmly continued, asking her audience to make links between the violence outside the building and the violence of slavery. After a few minutes of speaking, her audience calmed down and she was able to deliver one of her most important speeches on the topic of abolition and the vote.

WHAT DO YOU THINK?

1. Do you think Grimke's audience was ethical or unethical in their responses to her? Why do you think so?
2. What are some current examples of people breaking the law by speaking out, people speaking about topics that some audiences

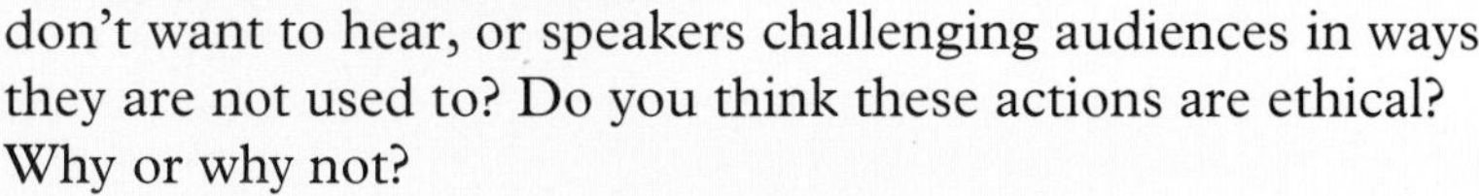


don't want to hear, or speakers challenging audiences in ways they are not used to? Do you think these actions are ethical? Why or why not?

3. How would you respond to someone speaking publicly who was saying things you didn't what to hear? Would your response be ethical? Why or why not?

CHAPTER 4

# Effective Listening

- Why Listen to Others?
- Why We Sometimes Fail to Listen
- How to Listen Carefully
  - Speech Checklist: **Listening to a Speech**
- How to Listen Critically
- How to Listen Ethically

**In this chapter, you will learn to**

- Explain why listening to others is important
- Identify the reasons we sometimes fail to listen to others
- Implement strategies for becoming a more careful listener
- Implement strategies for becoming a more critical listener
- Implement strategies for becoming a more ethical listener

You will probably spend far more time as an audience member listening to others speak than you will giving your own speeches. During one public speaking course with thirty students, you may speak for a total of perhaps twenty to thirty minutes, but you'll listen to speeches for a total of ten to fifteen hours! Similarly, in the workplace or as a member of a community group, you may speak occasionally, but you're likely to spend much more time listening to others.

**Speaking at Work**
*Because you're likely to spend more time listening at work than speaking, cultivating your listening skills is a good career move.*

Even though we do a lot of listening, the statistics on what we actually *retain* are surprising. After a ten-minute oral presentation, the average person understands and retains only 50 percent of the information presented. Forty-eight hours after the presentation, those same listeners retain only 25 percent of the information.[1]

Can you recall the last speech you heard? How much of its content do you remember? Now think of the last presentation you gave. How much of that information did you want your audience to remember? Is it inevitable that listeners lose so much information? As speakers, we want our audiences to retain more than one-quarter of the information we worked so hard to present. And as listeners, most of us want to make the time we spend listening more profitable. In this chapter, you'll learn about how you listen as an audience member, why our listening sometimes fails, and how to listen carefully, critically, and ethically. (In Chapter 17, you will learn how to adapt to your audience and help them listen to your speech more effectively.)

## Why Listen to Others?

Listening to others is one of the most powerful ways we can communicate as members of a community. When we listen to others, we confirm their humanity, presence, and worth. When we listen and **confirm,** we recognize, acknowledge, and express value for another person. So central is the act of listening that philosopher Martin Buber claimed in the 1920s, "A society may be termed human in the measure to which its members confirm one another."[2]

Listening is different from hearing. **Hearing** refers to the vibration of sound waves on our eardrums and the impulses that are then sent to the brain. When you listen to someone, you do more than simply receive sound waves—you actively engage with the information you hear.

To confirm others by listening to them is not necessarily to agree with them or even to be persuaded by them. **Listening** is simply the process of giving thoughtful attention to another person's words and understanding what you hear. By listening to another's words, you recognize those words as expressions of that person's experiences, values, and beliefs. If we are to participate in the ethical and civil public dialogue of our communities and make space for others to do so, we must listen. If we are to be effective public speakers and audiences, we must also understand why we sometimes fail to listen.

## Why We Sometimes Fail to Listen

Why do we ignore some messages but tune into others, opening ourselves up to new ideas? Why do we willingly confirm some people but refuse to consider confirming others? Similarly, why are we sometimes surprisingly good at understanding some speakers but unable to follow others? Listening researcher Michael Nichols explains that the "sustained attention of careful listening—that may take heroic and unselfish restraint. To listen well we must forget ourselves" and give our focused attention to another.[3]

Listeners fail to focus for three reasons: listener interference, speaker interference, and an inability to get beyond differences. **Interference** is anything that hinders a listener from receiving a message. Interference can be external to the listener (auditory or visual distractions) or internal (distracting thoughts or feelings).

### Listener Interference

Most listening challenges stem from poor listening habits. Have you experienced any of the following bad listening habits?

- Think you're not interested in the subject before the speech really gets going.
- Assume you know what the speaker is going to say before it's even said.
- Get so focused on the details that you miss the bigger point.
- Adopt a passive physical stance—slouching, reclining, making no eye contact.
- Adopt a defensive physical stance—turning away, crossing arms, making hostile eye contact.
- Pay attention to distractions—or create them yourself.
- Be so preoccupied with the messenger that you miss the message.
- Tune out difficult information.
- Tune out information you don't agree with or argue with the speaker's message in your own mind.
- Prepare your response while the speaker is speaking.
- Daydream or pretend you are listening when you really aren't.

At one time or another, most of us have fallen into these habits. We may think we've heard all there is to hear on a subject, so we begin daydreaming or simply pretend to listen. We become so enamored of or so frustrated with a speaker that we forget to listen to the content of a speech. We find the material too difficult to understand, so we give up listening, begin talking to the person next to us, or even start texting our friends. We even stop listening as we mentally build a counterargument to one of the speaker's points. Although we might want to blame the speaker for these lapses in listening, we really are responsible for practicing bad listening habits. Later in this chapter, we will learn how to replace these bad habits with more productive ones.

### Speaker Interference Caused by Information

Although, as speakers, we might want to blame all listening troubles on our audience, we can improve our audience's ability to listen. We can create speeches that are "listenable." A **listenable speech** is considerate and is delivered in an oral style.[4] A speech in oral style uses words meant to be heard rather than words meant to be read (written style). A **considerate speech** eases the audience's burden of processing information. One of the ways we can construct considerate speeches is by reducing interference caused by information.

Listeners generally stop listening or become frustrated when speakers present information that is too complicated, too challenging, or too simple. When we share complicated ideas, audience members can have difficulty following our line of reasoning. When our ideas challenge audience members' belief systems, they can get caught up in the differences in values and lose sight of the point we are trying to make. When we present stories or arguments that are too simple, audience members may become bored and stop listening.

The following example, an excerpt from Amy Tan's *The Kitchen God's Wife*, illustrates the speaker's dilemma when information is too complicated and too challenging for some audiences. Although Winnie, the storyteller, finally decided to share with her daughter her complicated and challenging history, she had chosen not to even attempt to explain it to others.

> For nearly forty years, I have told people Helen is my sister-in-law. But she is not. I have told people she is the wife of my brother, Kun, the one who was killed during the war. This is not the truth. But I did not say this to deceive anyone. The truth was too complicated to tell. No one would understand even if I could explain it all. In truth, he was only my half brother—related not even by blood, just by marriage. And he did not die in the war. He died before the war, his head chopped off in Changsha for selling three bolts of cloth to the revolutionaries, bragging that he cheated them by charging them a ridiculously high price, laughing that the cloth was of poor quality. But how could I ever reveal this?—that a member of my family meant to cheat his customers.... When I came to this new country, I thought I could finally forget about this half brother Kun.
>
> But then Helen wanted to come from Formosa. I had to let her come. She told me I had a debt from many years before, now I had to pay her back. So I told the U.S. immigration officials in 1953 that Helen was my sister, born to one of my father's other five wives. And once she was here, I couldn't tell our church friends that my father had five wives. How could I say that? I was the wife of a minister.[5]

Winnie has information that is too complicated for some audiences (the immigration officials, for example) and too challenging for others (members of her church, who grew up in a culture very different from hers). She struggles with a common ethical dilemma: how to bridge cultural differences while staying as close to the truth as possible. Winnie decides to communicate only the background and cultural information her audience needs to understand her story. She made this decision because she did not want to overwhelm or overly challenge her listeners by sharing the entire story. Do you think she made the best choice? Have you ever had to omit details of a story to make the information listenable?

Information can also be difficult to listen to if it is too simple. Consider this example: Katherine, a graduating senior, was the student speaker at her college graduation. Recognizing that graduation is a time of transition and uncertainty as well as excitement, she decided to read passages from one of her favorite books, Dr. Seuss's *Oh, the Places You'll Go!* After her opening remarks, she began to read:

> Congratulations! Today is your day. You're off to Great Places! You're off and away! You have brains in your head. You have feet in your shoes. You can steer yourself any direction you choose. You're on your own. And you know what you know. And YOU are the guy who'll decide where to go.[6]

If she had stopped here and continued in her own words, her speech might have been a success—most people love the messages in Dr. Seuss stories, so he is an excellent author to cite in a speech. However, Katherine continued to read passages from the book. Although it can be meaningful for adults, the book is written for children. After a while, people stopped listening because the language was too simple. They began to shift and shuffle, to lose interest, and to talk with their neighbors. Katherine's speech was too simple for college graduates and their families.

## Speaker Interference Caused by Language

Another way we can give listenable, considerate speeches is by reducing interference caused by language. Listening can fail simply because the speaker's language is unclear. The language may be too formal or technical, too casual, too noninclusive, or too cluttered.

*Formal or technical language.* Most of us are familiar with the simpler versions of the following sentences. Can you recognize them?

1. Scintillate, scintillate, asteroid minific.
2. Members of an avian species of identical plumage congregate.
3. Surveillance should precede saltation.
4. Pulchritude possesses a solely cutaneous profundity.

5. It is fruitless to become lachrymose over precipitately departed lacteal fluid.
6. Freedom from encrustations of grime is contiguous to rectitude.
7. Eschew the implement of correction and vitiate the scion.
8. It is fruitless to attempt to indoctrinate a superannuated canine with innovative maneuvers.
9. The temperature of aqueous content of an unremittingly ogled saucepan does not reach 212 degrees Fahrenheit.
10. All articles that coruscate with resplendence are not truly auriferous.[7]

You may not recognize these common sayings because they are expressed in very formal and technical language. In some situations, this style of language may be appropriate, but most audiences stop listening when the speaker's language is more formal or technical than they can understand. Here are the familiar versions of the ten sentences:

1. Twinkle, twinkle, little star.
2. Birds of a feather flock together.
3. Look before you leap.
4. Beauty is only skin deep.
5. Don't cry over spilled milk.
6. Cleanliness is next to godliness.
7. Spare the rod and spoil the child.
8. You can't teach an old dog new tricks.
9. A watched pot never boils.
10. All that glitters is not gold.

A specific type of language that is often too technical is **jargon,** language used by a special group or for a special activity. You've probably used jargon if you play sports (a *bogey* is a type of score in golf) or are a member of a specialized group (in the military, a *bogey* is an unidentified, possibly hostile, aircraft). You also may use jargon on your job to identify processes or objects specific to your occupation (truck mechanics know that a *bogie* is a

**Speaking at Work**

*Jargon is often used in the workplace. Using industry-specific jargon at work is perfectly acceptable—it helps you communicate more efficiently. But if you give a speech about your work to an audience that isn't familiar with your industry, cut back on the jargon or explain what it means.*

type of wheel assembly used in some automotive trucks). Jargon can be confusing because your audience may not know what a particular word means. As a speaker, use jargon only if it will help your audience better understand your message.

*Casual language.* Language can also be difficult to listen to if it is too casual. We often fall into our familiar, everyday language patterns, which can be too informal for an audience. Three types of commonly used casual language include slang, colloquialisms, and euphemisms. **Slang** is an informal nonstandard vocabulary, usually made up of arbitrarily changed words. A **colloquialism** is a local or regional informal dialect or expression. A **euphemism** substitutes an agreeable or inoffensive expression for one that may offend or suggest something unpleasant. When our language is too casual, audiences might not be able to follow the main ideas of the speech, or they become confused or uncomfortable. Either way, they stop listening to our message. Consider these examples:

| | |
|---|---|
| **Slang:** | Dogg, this track is off the hook! |
| | (Buddy, this song is great! I love it.) |
| | Let me drop some science. |
| | (I'll explain the facts to you; also, to "drop" or release a CD.)[8] |
| **Colloquialism:** | He done flew off his chair at the news. |
| | (He was so surprised by the news that it seemed as though he'd fall out of his chair.) |
| **Euphemism:** | I'm going to go powder my nose. |
| | (I have to use the bathroom.) |
| | Due to changing market forces, the company will be downsizing. |
| | (Because the company is not making enough profit, employees will be laid off.) |

In some settings, such as at a party with your friends, casual language is easily understood. However, in public speaking settings, translate slang, colloquialisms, and euphemisms into expressions an audience is more likely to understand. Some casual language may even be offensive to some members of an audience, causing them to stop listening or to focus on the speaker's language rather than the speaker's ideas. Or it may be very confusing to people from cultures other than your own. Remember, when your audience is confused or offended by your language, they won't hear the message you want to send.

*Noninclusive language.* Listening can break down when you use *noninclusive language*, or words that seem to refer only to certain groups of people. Such language excludes people who are not in the "in group" and who are likely to be offended by and tune out speakers who use it. A common example of noninclusive language is language that seems to describe only men, not both men and women. **Gender-inclusive language** recognizes that both women and men are active participants in the world. Using gender-inclusive language is one of the simplest ways you can improve listening, yet some people criticize and resist it. They argue that the pronoun *he* includes both women and men, and using *man* to describe all people is perfectly acceptable. For others, worrying about "gender stuff" is an issue that was resolved years ago. Yet research indicates that when we use noninclusive nouns and pronouns, listeners visualize men far more often than they do women or men and women together.

**Speaking across DIFFERENCES**

**Avoiding casual language is best when you speak to an audience made up of people from many different cultures. Slang, colloquialisms, and euphemisms don't always translate well in other languages, and some casual language may even offend people from cultures other than your own.**

If you doubt the narrowness of language that is not gender inclusive, consider the research. In 1988, researchers asked first-grade students to write a story about an average student. When the researchers used the word "he" to describe the assignment, only 12 percent of the students wrote a story about a female. When they used "he or she," 42 percent of the students wrote stories about females.[9] In 1995, to determine whether gender bias was still an issue, researchers asked college students to fill in the blanks in sentences such as, "Before a judge can give a final ruling, _____," and "Before a doctor can make a final diagnosis, _____." What pronouns did the students choose to finish the sentences? Even though women today participate in almost all aspects of public and professional life, students chose predominantly masculine pronouns to finish the sentences.[10]

Using gender-biased language prevents listeners from hearing the main arguments and ideas of a speech. Whether we mean to or not, the use of noninclusive language tends to reflect a noninclusive attitude. By using the "universal *he*," we give the impression that we do not recognize women as competent, professional individuals or that we are unaware of the research indicating that using only male pronouns serves to exclude women. Either way, listeners spend energy focusing on our use of language rather than paying attention to our arguments.

Additionally, gender-biased language can be quite ambiguous and thus confusing. When we use the "universal he" to say, "If a person wants to be treated as an adult, he must earn the respect worthy of such treatment," is the "person" a man (only), a woman (only), or a human being of either sex?[11] How is the listener to know for sure? What if Jane wants to be treated as an adult? Can she earn the respect worthy of such treatment? How would a listener know? It is easier to include Jane in the argument—and thereby reduce the work for the listener—by saying, "If people want to be treated as adults, they must earn the respect worthy of such treatment." Regardless of your own stance on the position of women in the world relative to men, avoiding noninclusive terms can help clarify ambiguous arguments or claims. It also helps listeners understand the intended message.

Another example of noninclusive language is language that does not acknowledge cultural diversity. **Culturally inclusive language** respectfully recognizes the differences among the many cultures in our society. Although it may seem obvious that we need to consider diversity when we speak to diverse audiences, at times our language does not reflect our attention to diversity.

A common example of language that is not culturally inclusive is **spotlighting,** the practice of highlighting a person's race or ethnicity (or sex, sexual orientation, physical disability, and the like) during a speech. Speakers who spotlight would, for instance, describe a lawyer as a Hispanic lawyer, a doctor as an Asian American doctor, and a friend as an African American friend. Spotlighting is most common among members of the dominant culture in a society, and it marks differences as being unusual. Consider the following examples:

> The jury includes five men and two African American women.
> The panel includes three professionals and a disabled lawyer.
> The meeting is going to be chaired by a Hispanic professor and a university administrator.
> He's a talented gay artist.[12]

None of these sentences refers specifically to whiteness, heterosexuality, or physical ability because these are all characteristics of the dominant culture in the United States. Thus, they are considered normal. Spotlighting identifies people thought to belong to a special, and hence an unusual, category. As a result of spotlighting, differences are marked as abnormal, slightly strange, or surprising. A speaker using culturally inclusive language would describe the people in these examples as five white men and two African American women (or as seven people), four professionals (including a lawyer), two employees of the university (or a Hispanic professor and a white administrator), and a talented artist.

Make sure your speech topics, source citations, and examples represent a range of cultural perspectives. Additionally, when you cite statistics, consider how culture and ethnicity have affected them. Speakers often fail to cite authorities and information from cultures other than their own. For example, we often hear that women earn approximately 81 cents to every dollar a man earns, but which women? Culturally inclusive language reveals that Asian American women earn approximately 93 cents to every dollar a white man earns, white women earn approximately 80 cents, African American women earn approximately 68 cents, and Hispanic women earn approximately 60 cents to every dollar a white man makes.[13] Noninclusive language conceals this important disparity; culturally inclusive language recognizes it.

Using culturally and gender-inclusive language communicates to an audience that you are aware of the diversity in our society and of the influence of culture. Your speech becomes more listenable because audiences gain a more holistic view of an issue. Your goal as a speaker is to connect with your audience and to share your ideas with them, so make listening as easy as possible. Using language that includes all members of your audience assists you in doing just that.

***Speaking across DIFFERENCES***

**When you use noninclusive language in a speech meant for a diverse audience, some audience members may perceive you as ignoring them and will stop listening to you. Using inclusive language is smart not because it's "politically correct," but because it helps you get your message across to *all* audience members, not just some.**

*Verbal clutter.* Sometimes audiences have a difficult time listening to a speaker because of **verbal clutter**: extra words that pad sentences and claims but don't add meaning. Even though listeners can mentally process far more words than speakers can speak per minute (the average speaker speaks at a rate of 125 to 175 words per minute, but trained listeners can process 350 to 450 words per minute), verbal clutter impedes listening because listeners must process words that are unnecessary or redundant.[14]

Examples of verbal clutter are such common words and phrases as "you know," "it's like," "I'm like," "um," "and all," "and stuff," "stuff like that," and "then I go." These small additions to a speech, although commonly used in casual conversation, distract listeners and add no useful meaning.

Similarly, strings of adjectives and adverbs act as verbal clutter. Hard to spot sometimes, we often use this type of verbal clutter when we try to create vivid descriptions. Consider the following cluttered sentences and their uncluttered alternatives:

| | |
|---|---|
| **Cluttered:** | Good, effective public speakers use carefully selected and chosen words, sentences, and phrases correctly and accurately. |
| **Uncluttered:** | Skilled speakers present their ideas clearly. |
| **What's improved?** | A few strong words are used rather than several adequate, but less focused, words. |
| **Cluttered:** | If nothing else, he was first and foremost, above all, a man of considerable honor and principled integrity. |
| **Uncluttered:** | Above all, he was a man of integrity. |
| **What's improved?** | The redundant words have been edited out (for example, honor and principled), leaving a focused message. |

Without the clutter, audiences have a far easier time listening for our main points and ideas. But how much clutter do you really want to eliminate? Notice the differences in the level of clutter in the next three examples:

| | |
|---|---|
| **Cluttered:** | At some point during the day, every single day of her life, no matter the weather or the distractions, she would make the long, steep trek three miles one way to the distant, far-off waterfall. |
| **Less cluttered:** | At some point during the day, every day of her life, she made the three-mile trek to the waterfall. |
| **Uncluttered:** | Every day, she hiked three miles to the waterfall. |

What might be called "clutter" in one speech adds richness and detail to another, setting a particular tone or mood. Go back and reread the cluttered example. If we simply took out the words "the distant, far-off," we might have a nice description for a commemorative speech or a speech of introduction. But in a persuasive or informative speech, the focus might be on the daily hike to a waterfall, not on the characteristics of the woman. Thus, the less cluttered or the uncluttered versions might make the point more effectively.

Ask yourself two questions when you want to eliminate verbal clutter. First, do the words you use help develop your argument or make more work for the listener? Second, how many words in your speech are redundant?

## Speaker Interference Caused by Differences

Differences between a speaker and an audience can also cause problems with listening. Although we are all similar in many ways, none of us exactly matches our audience in appearance, mannerisms, values, or background. When we are faced with differences, we sometimes see them in terms of a hierarchy (such as seeing a person of a certain age or sex as more trustworthy or credible than another person). When we see differences in this way, we become preoccupied with questions of right and wrong and have trouble focusing on what a speaker is saying. Here are some of the ways speakers and audiences are different and the ways those differences can prevent effective listening:

| | |
|---|---|
| **Speech style:** | Accents, tonal and rhythmic qualities, stuttering, nonnative speakers of a language, and gendered speech differences affect listening. We sometimes see these differences as strange, funny, or inappropriate and have trouble paying attention to the message. |
| **Background and occupation:** | Differences in race, ethnicity, nationality, regional upbringing, religion, education, occupation, and economic status can affect listening. When we see these differences as right or wrong, we forget to be open to the value of other experiences and influences and often stop listening. |
| **Appearance:** | Styles of dress, height, weight, hair, body adornment, and even a speaker's posture affect listening. Audiences sometimes have difficulty listening because they are so focused on the speaker's appearance that they can't focus on the message. |
| **Values:** | When a speaker holds values that are different from those of members of the audience, listening is sometimes difficult. When listeners are so convinced that certain values are "worthy" and "good" and others are "wrong" and "bad," they rarely listen to understand why an opposing position makes sense to the speaker. |

How do we minimize our differences, or explain and account for them, so audiences and speakers can more easily confirm one another? We can go a long way toward that goal by defining *difference* as meaning simply *different*—as not the same but still worth listening to. Thus, we can open up the possibility for listening that confirms others rather than listening that means we must agree with everything they say.

Although listeners are responsible for interference caused by differences, as speakers we also contribute to this listening problem. Here are a few ways we can minimize the impact of differences:

- Acknowledge and explain differences in speech styles or appearance. Act as an interpreter for the audience, explaining what those differences mean.
- Explain your background and how it affects your position or presentation of information. In this way, you become a source of information regarding your differences, not just someone unusual or unfamiliar.
- Invite others to consider your values without attempting to persuade.
- Assume an invitational stance that attempts to confirm the audience as well as offer your own perspective. (See Chapter 22 for more about invitational speaking.)

**Skills & Confidence**
PPD Activity 5.1
Web Connect 5.1

Even though differences can seem like permanent obstacles to listening, both audiences and speakers must recognize that difference is the foundation of a healthy public dialogue. Once we invite dialogue rather than monologue, we encourage the exchange of ideas, information, perspectives, and even creative solutions to many of the dilemmas we face. Both audiences and speakers are responsible for creating this healthy dialogue, and a public speaking course is an excellent place to practice listening and speaking in ways that confirm and respect differences.

## How to Listen Carefully

*Speaking across DIFFERENCES*

**Approaching your speech as a dialogue between you and your audience can help you acknowledge and respect the differences between you. And that can help you make your speech more listenable.**

As listeners, we can improve our skills and increase the amount of information we retain. In the process, we will also become better speakers. In fact, the listening strategies you'll read about in this and the next two main sections involve listening for many of the components you will incorporate later into your own speeches.

One of the most important obstacles to overcome as a listener is your own interference, or the bad habits discussed earlier in this chapter. However, if you learn to listen carefully, these bad habits are relatively easy to minimize. A **careful listener** overcomes listener interference to better understand a speaker's message. To minimize your own bad listening habits and reduce interference, try the following strategies.

### Listen for the Speaker's Purpose

Try to determine the speaker's goal. Is the speaker attempting to introduce, inform, invite, persuade, or commemorate? Can you determine who or what is being introduced and why? What information are you about to receive, and why is it important? What are you being invited to consider? What are you being persuaded to do, think, or feel?

### Listen for the Main Ideas

As the speech unfolds, identify each of the speaker's main points or arguments. Are there two, three, or more main points or arguments? Is each point clearly articulated, and do you see why it is a main point? How does the speaker connect each main point or idea? Listen to see if you can follow the development of the ideas. Listen for previews before main ideas, transitions, connectives from one idea to the next, and summaries concluding main ideas. Can you find a relationship among the main ideas?

### Listen for Supporting Evidence and Sources

What kind of evidence does the speaker use to support ideas? Identify the specific kinds of evidence used by speakers, such as narratives, personal disclosure, statistics, comparisons, and expert testimony. Does the speaker use enough evidence, and does it help the speaker make the argument?

### Listen for Consistency of Delivery and Content

Compare the speaker's style of delivery to the content of the speech. Are the two consistent? For example, if the topic is serious, does the delivery match that seriousness? How does the speaker use delivery to enhance the content or build a particular kind of environment?

### Write Down New Words, Ideas, and Questions

Take notes as you listen and jot down any unfamiliar words, phrases, or ideas. Keeping notes will help you listen for information that explains these words, phrases, and ideas and keep you focused on the content of the speech. In addition, writing down your questions will help you remember what to ask the speaker at the end of the speech.

### Offer Nonverbal Feedback

Rather than sitting passively or falling prey to distractions, listen by sitting in an upright (but relaxed) posture, and engage the speaker by making eye contact (if it is culturally appropriate). Use culturally appropriate nonverbal cues such as smiles of encouragement and head nods that signal understanding and attention. Taking notes is another nonverbal way of showing the speaker that you are listening and keeping your attention focused.

### Listen for the Conclusion

Many speeches have a distinct conclusion. Listen to see if you can discover the moment the conclusion begins. Does the speaker summarize the main points, tell a story to wrap up the speech, ask the audience to participate in some action, or do something else to bring the presentation to a close?

**SPEECH Checklist**

## Listening to a Speech

- [ ] What is the speaker's purpose?
  - — to inform
  - — to invite
  - — to persuade
  - — to introduce
  - — to commemorate
- [ ] What is the speaker's topic?
- [ ] What are the speaker's main points?
- [ ] Does the speaker connect each main point? If not, which are not connected?
- [ ] What kinds of evidence does the speaker use?
  - — narratives
  - — personal disclosure
  - — statistics
  - — comparisons/analogies
  - — expert testimony
- [ ] How does the speaker conclude the speech?
  - — summarize main points
  - — tell a story
  - — ask for audience action
  - — other
- [ ] How does the speaker's delivery enhance the content of the speech?
- [ ] What new words and interesting ideas were in the speech?
- [ ] What questions would you like to ask the speaker?

## How to Listen Critically

When you listen to a speech critically, you mentally check it for accuracy, comparing what the speaker says with what you personally know and what your own research tells you. You also listen to assess the strengths and weaknesses of the reasoning and supporting materials presented in a speech. Note that listening critically is different from listening to judge or find fault with a message. Rather, **critical listeners** listen for the accuracy of a speech's content and the implications of a speaker's message. Critical listeners benefit by remaining open to new ideas, but they also listen carefully to how speakers develop those ideas into arguments. Additionally, they consider the impact of a speaker's ideas and how they may affect immediate audiences as well as larger communities.

To help you listen to speeches critically, ask yourself the questions in Table 4.1 on page 60 and then follow the suggested guidelines. Asking these questions will help you assess a speaker's claims and arguments before you make decisions about their value or strength.

When we listen critically, we allow for dialogue because we avoid making quick decisions about good and bad, right and wrong. Listening critically encourages us to ask questions about ideas so we are better able to respond to claims and explore issues with others.

Skills & Confidence
PPD Activity 4.2
Video Activity 4.1

## How to Listen Ethically

Listening ethically encourages audiences to pay attention to the ethical implications of a message. *Ethics* refers to the study of moral standards and how those standards affect our conduct. (Or as Greek philosopher Epicurus put it, "Ethics deals with things to be sought and things to be avoided, with ways of life and with the *telos*," or the chief good, the aim, the end in life.) When we speak of ethics, we are talking about the moral principles we use to guide our behaviors and decisions. An **ethical listener,** then, considers the moral impact of a speaker's message on one's self and one's community. Ethical listeners attend to the standards and principles advocated by a speaker. To listen ethically, listeners must suspend judgment, assess the information they hear, and at times respond to the speaker's message.

### Suspend Judgment

Ethical listeners suspend judgment throughout a speech. To gather as much information as they can, they are willing to listen to a speaker's message, without assigning "right" and "wrong" to it, until the speech is complete and they've had adequate time to evaluate its arguments.

**TABLE 4.1 Guidelines for Critical Listening**

| QUESTION | GUIDELINE |
|---|---|
| • How fully has the speaker developed an idea? Is something left out, exaggerated, or understated? Does the speaker use sound reasoning? Are claims based on fact or opinion? (Chapters 14 and 24) | • Speakers must develop all major arguments fully rather than present them without explanation and development. Speakers should not exaggerate arguments or understate their importance. Major ideas should be supported by evidence in the form of examples, statistics, testimony, and the like. |
| • What sources does the speaker rely on? Are they credible? How are they related to the speaker's topic? Will the sources benefit if facts are presented in a certain way? For example, is the tobacco industry arguing that smoking isn't harmful? (Chapter 13) | • Speakers must use credible sources that are as unbiased as possible. Speakers must cite sources for all new information. Sources should be cited carefully and with enough detail so the audience knows why the source is acceptable. |
| • Are the claims the speaker makes realistic? What are the implications of those claims? Who is affected by them? In what way? Has the speaker acknowledged these effects, or are they left unstated? Are there other aspects of the issue the speaker should address? | • Speakers must make realistic and logical claims and acknowledge different perspectives. They must also acknowledge those affected by their arguments and acknowledge the effects of their proposed solutions. When speakers take a position, they must not present their position as absolute or the only one possible. |
| • How does this speech fit with what I know to be true? What is new to me? Can I accept this new information? Why or why not? | • When speakers make claims that go against your personal experience, see if you can discover why. Sometimes, the answer lies in cultural differences or in a speaker's research. Try to be open to different views of the world while at the same time assessing the speaker's evidence and reasoning objectively. Before you reject a speaker's claims, engage the speaker in a civil discussion to find out why your perspectives differ. |
| • What is at stake for the speaker? How invested is the speaker in the topic and the arguments being made? How will the speaker be affected if the audience disagrees? | • All speakers are invested in some way in their topics and arguments. However, some arguments benefit a speaker more than anyone else. Identify the speaker's motives so you can better understand why she or he is making particular claims. |

Ethical listeners consciously avoid reacting immediately to a statement they disagree with. This allows them to take in the speech's complete message and not jump to conclusions before the speaker is finished. And when they hear the complete message, they can contribute to the public dialogue in more informed ways.

Consider an example. Two students are listening to a speaker on their campus argue for free speech and the right of hate groups to say or print anything they want. Early in the presentation, the speaker says, "It's our constitutional right to express ourselves; this country was founded on that principle. Two-hundred-plus years later, I argue that we are guaranteed the right to say anything we want to anyone."

> *Listener who rushes to judgment:* "That's ridiculous. How can he say that? People don't have the right to say anything they want whenever and wherever they want. That's harassment, and we don't have the right to do that to anyone!"

By rushing to judgment, this listener may stop listening altogether or may focus on a response to the speaker rather than listening to more of what the speaker has to say. By doing so, she may miss the speaker's later claim that our right to express ourselves also guarantees that we can freely criticize hate speech, a freedom not all societies enjoy.

Now consider the speaker who listens ethically to the full message.

> *Listener who suspends judgment:* "Wow, that sounds extreme to me, but maybe he's got a reason for making that claim. Let me see if I can understand why he makes such a strong statement."

Even though this student disagrees with the speaker, he's willing to put aside his disagreement until he's heard all the speaker has to say. Thus, he'll have an easier time following the speaker's ideas, confirming them, and responding intelligently to them. Suspending judgment does not mean that we as listeners sit passively without scrutinizing whatever a speaker says. You can still question and disagree with a speaker's message. Suspending judgment is simply a tool to help you listen more effectively and take in a speaker's entire message.

### Assess Information and Respond to the Speaker's Ideas

Ethical listening also requires that listeners assess a message (listen critically) first and then respond to the speaker's ideas. When ethical listeners respond to a speaker's ideas, they participate in a constructive dialogue with a speaker. Even if they do not agree with a speaker's position, ethical listeners join the public dialogue so they can better understand a position, explore differences, and share their own views. In their attempts to understand, ethical listeners recognize, acknowledge, and show value for others, even if their positions are vastly different from the speaker's.

**Skills & Confidence**
PPD
Activity 4.3

APPENDIX A

# BUILDING SKILLS & CONFIDENCE



## Chapter 1 WHY SPEAK IN PUBLIC?

### Key Concepts

**audience** (14)
**audience centered** (12)
**channel** (15)
**civility** (6)
**context** (15)
**decoding** (14)
**encoding** (14)
**ethical public speaker** (6)
**feedback** (12)
**group communication** (10)
**interpersonal communication** (10)
**intrapersonal communication** (9)
**mass communication** (10)
**message** (14)
**noise** (15)
**public communication** (10)
**public dialogue** (6)
**speaker** (6)

### Practicing the Public Dialogue Activities

**PPD Activity 1.1 Choose a Civil, Ethical Approach to Public Speaking**
Make a list of five topics you might use for a speech in this class. How does each topic contribute to the public dialogue? Now identify how you might discuss each of these topics in a civil, ethical way. For example, would it be more ethical to approach one of your topics from a two-sided perspective and another from a multisided perspective? Why do you think so? Save these as possible topics for your in-class speeches.

**PPD Activity 1.2 Consider the Unique Aspects of Public Speaking**
Choose one of the five speech topics you identified in PPD Activity 1.1. Think about giving a speech on this topic in class.

- What are two ways in which your speech could create a sense of community with your audience?
- What are two ways in which you could stay audience centered while speaking about this topic?
- What are two ways in which your cultural background might affect your speaking style when giving a speech about this topic?
- What are two ways in which your speech could encourage dialogue with your in-class audience or with your campus community?

Save this topic and analysis to possibly use for an in-class speech later in the course.

## Interactive Video Activities

### Video Activity 1.1

Watch a video clip of a student speaker, Mike Piel, as he makes a relevant connection with his audience and remains audience centered. As you watch Mike speak, consider the strategies he uses to communicate the importance of his topic to his audience. What does Mike say to connect his topic to his audience? After you watch the video, respond to analysis questions and compare your answers to those provided by the author.

## Web Connect Resources

### Web Connect 1.1 Public Dialogue Consortium

To learn more about what the public dialogue is and how your participation in this unending conversation can help shape community, access the website of The Public Dialogue Consortium. The Consortium believes that public communication powerfully influences the world we live in and can positively affect the lives of everyday people.

### Web Connect 1.2 Thinking about Your Audience

Go to the Outloud Online website at Texas A&M University for helpful information about analyzing your audience so that you can be an audience-centered speaker.

### Web Connect 1.3 The Speaking Model

Use the American Rhetoric website, or a similar website, to find a speech. Consider the components of the public speaking model as you watch the speech, and then answer the following questions: Who is the speaker? What is the relationship between the speaker and the audience? What is the speaker's message? What do you know about the audience? Was the audience supportive or hostile to the speaker? What type of feedback do you think the audience gave the speaker?

# Chapter 2 ENTERING THE PUBLIC DIALOGUE: YOUR FIRST SPEECH

## Key Concepts

**acceptance speech** (20)
**canon** (21)
**canon of arrangement** (26)
**canon of delivery** (30)
**canon of invention** (21)
**canon of memory** (30)
**canon of style** (29)
**commemorative speech** (19)
**informative speech** (17)
**introductory speech** (19)
**invitational speech** (17)
**persuasive speech** (18)
**small group speaking** (20)

## Practicing the Public Dialogue Activities

**PPD Activity 2.1 Review the Ten Steps to Entering the Public Dialogue**

At this point in your public speaking course, you may be getting ready to give your first speech. To help you prepare, review the ten steps for entering the public dialogue listed on pages xxx-xxi of this book. Which of these steps do you think will be the easiest for you? Why do you think they'll be easiest? Which do you think will be the hardest? Why do you think they'll be hardest? For example, some people like the research process because they find it fun and interesting to read and learn new things, whereas they dread delivery because they don't like being the center of attention.

Take this opportunity to log on to Speech Builder Express, an online speech outlining and development tool that you can use to prepare your speeches for this course. Consider the steps to entering the public dialogue that you think will be hard. Can Speech Builder Express make any of those steps easier?

## Interactive Video Activities

**Video Activity 2.1**

Watch a video clip of a student speaker, Tiffany Brisco, as she gives a speech of introduction to her public speaking class. As you watch Tiffany speak, consider the content of her speech as well as her delivery. After you watch the video, respond to analysis questions and compare your answers to those provided by the author. (See the end of Chapter 2 for the transcript of her speech, with commentary.)

## Web Connect Resources

**Web Connect 2.1 What Not to Do When Giving a Speech**

For a humorous (and useful) look at what not to do when giving your speech, check out the article "What Not to Do When Making a Keynote Presentation" at SelfGrowth.com. This article is intended for keynote speakers, but you can certainly apply the tips to your own first speech.

# Chapter 3 COPING WITH SPEAKING ANXIETY

## Key Concepts

**affirmations** (40)
**cognitive restructuring** (40)
**communication apprehension** (34)
**public speaking anxiety (PSA)** (35)
**state, or situational, anxiety** (34)
**systematic desensitization** (37)
**trait anxiety** (34)
**visualization** (38)

## Practicing the Public Dialogue Activities

**PPD Activity 3.1 Reduce Any Anxiety You Feel About Giving a Speech**

With another member of your class, make a list of what makes each of you feel nervous about public speaking. Now sort this list into categories that reflect your view of yourselves as speakers, your audience, the process of developing your speech and presentational aids, and delivering your speeches. Identify which aspect or aspects of the public speaking process generate the most anxiety for each of you. Discuss which techniques for easing public speaking anxiety presented in this chapter might work best for each of you.

## Web Connect Resources

**Web Connect 3.1 Alleviating Anxiety**

If you'd like to explore some good information about speech anxiety, access the Public Speaking Anxiety/Phobia Group's website. This site provides a number of resources for people who fear public speaking (or have any social phobia), including dozens of links to helpful resources, a reading list, and a link to useful articles.

**Web Connect 3.2 Connecting with the Audience**

This site on speaking in the workplace offers three great tips for alleviating your speaking anxiety by connecting with your audience, both before and during your speech.

# Chapter 4 EFFECTIVE LISTENING

## Key Concepts

**careful listener** (56)
**colloquialism** (50)
**confirm** (45)
**considerate speech** (47)
**critical listener** (59)
**culturally inclusive language** (52)
**ethical listener** (59)
**euphemism** (50)
**gender-inclusive language** (51)
**hearing** (45)
**interference** (46)
**jargon** (49)
**listenable speech** (47)
**listening** (45)
**slang** (50)
**spotlighting** (52)
**verbal clutter** (53)

## Practicing the Public Dialogue Activities

**PPD Activity 4.1 Help Your Audience Listen to Your Speech**

Find a partner in your speech class. With your partner, choose a topic that both of you would be interested in giving a speech about. Imagine that each of you is going to give a speech to your classmates on a different aspect of this topic and that you want to ensure each speech is listenable. With your partner, identify information you could use that would be too complex for the audience. Next, identify language you could use that would be too technical, too casual, and noninclusive. What information and language could you use instead that would be more audience centered? Now, each of you write a short paragraph about your topic with as much verbal clutter included as you can. Then rewrite that paragraph, taking out the clutter. Share your paragraphs with each other. Were you each successful in reducing the clutter? What else might each of you do as a speaker to stay audience centered and create a listenable speech?

**PPD Activity 4.2 Practice Listening Critically**

Listen critically to the next speech you hear and ask yourself the questions in Table 4.1. When you listen critically, do you find that you better understand the speaker's position and retain more information than when you don't listen critically? Are you able to engage the speaker in the question-and-answer session more meaningfully?

Now listen critically to your own speech before you give it in class. Ask yourself the first two groups of questions in Table 4.1. Are you satisfied with the arguments you make and the sources you cite? How do you think your audience will respond to the last three groups of questions?

**PPD Activity 4.3 Listening Carefully, Critically, and Ethically**

Using the Speech Evaluation Worksheet for this activity (page A-6), evaluate any of the following speakers: one of your instructors, a public figure or student speaker giving one of the speeches featured in the online resources for *Invitation to Public Speaking Handbook*, or someone else speaking publicly. Bring your completed checklist to class and discuss the strategies you used to be a careful listener and the ways that listening critically and ethically helped you evaluate the strength of the speaker's ideas and claims.

You can use your Premium Website to access and print this worksheet from the Chapter 4 resources.

## Interactive Video Activities

### Video Activity 4.1

For more practice listening critically to speeches, select one or two of the political speeches featured in your online resources for *Invitation to Public Speaking Handbook* and evaluate them using the questions in Table 4.1.

## Web Connect Resources

**Web Connect 4.1 Some Notes on Gender-Neutral Language**

This University of Pennsylvania site provides information about why and how masculine pronouns have been used in the past and how to convert gender-specific language to gender-neutral language.

# Speech Evaluation Worksheet

Speaker ______________________________ Topic ______________________________

## INTRODUCTION

_____ Is the purpose of the speech clear? What is the purpose?

_____ Does the speaker establish credibility?

_____ Are the topic and purpose relevant to the audience?

_____ Does the speaker preview the speech?

_____ Does the speaker present ideas that might require me to suspend my judgment while I listen? Identify those ideas.

## BODY

_____ Are the main points clearly identified? What are the main points?

__________________________________________________________________

__________________________________________________________________

_____ Are the main points fully supported? Why or why not?

_____ What might be the moral impact of the main points on me and other people?

_____ Are the sources credible? Why or why not?

_____ Is the reasoning sound? Why or why not?

_____ Are other perspectives addressed?

_____ Is the speech listenable? Why or why not? (Consider language, organization, and interference.)

At what points do I suspend judgment to listen ethically and effectively? ____________

__________________________________________________________________

__________________________________________________________________

## CONCLUSION

_____ Does the speaker signal the end of the speech?

_____ Does the speaker summarize the main points?

_____ Does the speaker appear open to dialogue about the topic?

## DISCUSSION

What questions would I like to ask the speaker? ______________________________

__________________________________________________________________

What information would I like clarified? ______________________________

__________________________________________________________________

What would I like the speaker to talk more about? ______________________________

__________________________________________________________________

What would I like the speaker to think more about? ______________________________

__________________________________________________________________

What information do I have that I want to share with the speaker? ______________

__________________________________________________________________

__________________________________________________________________

# Chapter 5 YOUR SPEECH TOPIC AND PURPOSE

## Key Concepts

**behavioral objectives** (81)
**brainstorming** (75)
**general purpose** (80)
**specific purpose** (80)
**speech topic** (71)
**thesis statement** (84)

## Practicing the Public Dialogue Activities

**PPD Activity 5.1 Consider Why You Would Speak in Public**
Outside your public speaking classroom, when would you decide to speak publicly or agree to give a speech if you were asked? What ethical issues would you need to consider? How would the topics you'd choose to speak about contribute to Kenneth Burke's "unending conversation"? What do your answers to these questions indicate about your possible contributions to the public dialogue discussed in this chapter?

**PPD Activity 5.2 Generate a List of Possible Speech Topics**
Make a list of what you like to do or want to know more about. Make this list as detailed as you can, including what you find yourself discussing with friends or what people say you're good at. Now brainstorm additional topics using one of the techniques you read about in this chapter. Next, organize the topics you've listed by categories to help you see connections among your topics and possibly generate more. If you are doing a service learning project in your speech class, make a list of possible topics related to your volunteer experience. Choose ten possible speech topics for your next speech. Set them aside for now.

**PPD Activity 5.3 Write a General-Purpose Statement and a Specific-Purpose Statement**
With three or four other students in class, look over the lists of topics you selected in PPD Activity 5.2. Select one or two topics from each person and write a general-purpose statement and a specific-purpose statement for each. Consider whether the topics would work best as informative, invitational, persuasive, or commemorative speeches.

You can use Speech Builder Express to help you create these statements. Select "Goal/Purpose" from the left menu and follow the instructions. For short reminders about general- and specific-purpose statements, click the "Tutor" button.

**PPD Activity 5.4 Write a Thesis Statement**
In a small group or as a class, choose five of the topics you wrote purpose statements for in PPD Activity 5.2. Write a thesis statement for each. Is your thesis statement a single declarative sentence? Does it state the main ideas, assumptions, or arguments you want to express in your speech? Review the completed thesis statements and select the one for the speech you're most interested in. Why do you like this one more than the others? Does it best fit the assignment your instructor has given you, your audience, or your own personal preferences?

To create your own thesis statement, go to Speech Builder Express, select "Thesis Statement" from the left menu, and follow the instructions. For short reminders about thesis statements, click the "Tutor" button.

## Interactive Video Activities

### Video Activity 5.1

Watch examples of dividing the thesis statement into two sentences (one that states the main idea and one that previews the main points of the speech) in the persuasive speeches "No More Sugar!" and "Fat Discrimination." After you watch the videos, respond to analysis questions and compare your answers to those provided by the author.

### Video Activity 5.2

Watch the video clips of two student speakers, Rebecca Ewing and Jesse Rosser, as they deliver thesis statements. After you watch the videos, respond to analysis questions and compare your answers to those provided by the author.

### Video Activity 5.3

Watch a video clip of Ogenna Agbim as she delivers a commemorative speech about a topic she's very interested in. As you watch Ogenna speak, notice how her passion about the topic affects her delivery. After you watch the video, respond to analysis questions and compare your answers to those provided by the author.

## Web Connect Resources

### Web Connect 5.1 **Lois Gibbs**

Read more about Lois Gibbs and her experiences with public speaking. Who are some other people who have spoken to address an urgent need? What are some urgent needs in your community? Who might address them?

### Web Connect 5.2 **Joseph Welch**

Go to the American Rhetoric website to listen to a clip from Joseph Welch's speech. This clip will help you appreciate the power of his speech. What has been the impact of McCarthyism? How can speakers today avoid the extremes of the McCarthy era?

### Web Connect 5.3 **Deciding to Speak**

Go to a website that features speeches, such AmericanRhetoric.com or the White House's Briefing Room. Locate three speeches. Compare and contrast these speeches, and determine the reasons each speaker had for giving their speech. Are these people speaking on matters of importance because they have unique experiences to share, because they have questions to ask, because they are required to speak, or some combination of these reasons? In what ways do these speakers add to the public dialogue? If you've spoken in public, why did you choose to do so? What future speaking experiences do you anticipate?

**Web Connect 5.4 Brainstorming with Technology**

To brainstorm topics for your speech, go to the Yahoo! website. Choose a general category and click on it. Continue clicking on links until you find one that is relatively specific. Did this method help you find a speech topic you hadn't known about before you started clicking on links?

**Web Connect 5.5 Identifying Thesis Statements**

Go to the HeadlineSpot.com Opinions/Editorials website. Read several editorials or letters to the editor. For at least three that you read, identify the writer's specific purpose and thesis statement.

# Chapter 6 YOUR AUDIENCE AND SPEAKING ENVIRONMENT

## Key Concepts

**attitude** (96)
**audience** (93)
**audience centered** (92)
**belief** (96)
**closed-ended question** (98)
**demographic audience analysis** (97)
**dialogue** (91)
**empathy** (101)
**ethnocentrism** (97)
**master statuses** (94)
**open-ended question** (98)
**speaking environment** (101)
**standpoint** (96)
**stereotype** (99)
**value** (97)

## Practicing the Public Dialogue Activities

**PPD Activity 6.1 Conduct a Demographic Audience Analysis**

To learn about the group of people who make up your classroom audience, use the sample survey form Demographic Audience Analysis: General Survey of a Class (page A-10) to conduct a demographic analysis before your next speech. Using the information you gather, identify your audience's master statuses, standpoints, attitudes, beliefs, and values. As you prepare your speech, remain flexible about the influences of master statuses on your audience and do what you can to avoid stereotyping.

You can use your Premium Website for *Invitation to Public Speaking Handbook* to access and print this worksheet from the Chapter 6 resources.

# Demographic Audience Analysis: General Survey of the Class

**Purpose:** To assist you in analyzing the audience for your first speech.

**Instructions:** Complete the following questionnaire. You need not respond to all questions; consider what information you are willing to share with the class. In order for class members to gain a sense of the commonalties and diversities of the class, members will need to share their results with the class. This can be done as a group activity, or questionnaires can be completed and given to the teacher, who can compile the results.

1. I am:
   _____ Male
   _____ Female
2. I am currently living:
   _____ on campus
   _____ with my parents
   _____ with a spouse or a significant other
   _____ with roommates
   _____ alone
3. I am:
   _____ under 18
   _____ 18 to 25
   _____ 25 to 30
   _____ 30 to 40
   _____ 40 to 50
   _____ over 50
4. I read the front section of the newspaper or a newsmagazine at least once a week:
   _____ Yes
   _____ No
5. I watch television:
   _____ less than 4 hours a week
   _____ 4 to 10 hours a week
   _____ 11 to 20 hours a week
   _____ more than 20 hours a week
6. I am currently working:
   _____ less than 4 hours a week
   _____ 4 to 10 hours a week
   _____ 11 to 20 hours a week
   _____ more than 20 hours a week
7. I have attended a religious service or meeting at least twice in the last month:
   _____ Yes
   _____ No

8. My expectations of a reasonable starting salary after college graduation is:

   _____ under $20,000

   _____ $20,000 to $30, 000

   _____ $30,000 to $40, 000

   _____ $40,000 to $50, 000

   _____ over $50,000

9. I believe that in order for a family of four to live comfortably in America, they must earn at least:

   _____ $15,000 to $30,000 per year

   _____ $30,000 to $45,000 per year

   _____ $45,000 to $60,000 per year

   _____ $60,000 to $75,000 per year

   _____ over $75,000 per year

10. If I had to identify with an American political party, I would identify myself as a:

    _____ Democrat

    _____ Republican

    _____ Independent

    _____ Reform Party member

    _____ Libertarian

    _____ Other

11. I think of home as:

    _____ America's Northeast

    _____ America's Southeast

    _____ America's Midwest

    _____ America's Southwest

    _____ America's West

    _____ Outside America

**PPD Activity 6.2 Determine Whether Your Audience Is Voluntary or Involuntary**

Consider the audience of a speech you might give sometime in the near future. Are they a voluntary audience, present because they are interested in your topic and want to hear what you have to say? Or are they involuntary, present because they have to be? If they are a voluntary audience, adapt to your audience by identifying the various perspectives they have about your topic. If they are an involuntary audience, discover why and adapt your speech to better suit their needs. What are some ways you can communicate your empathy for them?

**PPD Activity 6.3 Consider Your Speaking Environment**

For your next speech, think about the size of your audience, the physical arrangement of the room, and the technology you want to use. What elements of your speaking environment will help you stay audience centered? What problems might come up during your speech? How could you solve them? Now consider the time of day in which you give your speech, your speaking order, and the length of your speech. How will you work with these temporal factors to stay audience centered?

## Interactive Video Activities

### Video Activity 6.1

Watch an example of a speech given by a student who used her demographic audience analysis to determine how thoroughly she needed to explain her topic to her audience. After you watch the video, respond to analysis questions and compare your answers to those provided by the author.

## Web Connect Resources

**Web Connect 6.1 Learning about Your Audience**

This website, sponsored by the University of Hawai'i Maui Community College Speech Department, provides useful tips for creating a survey you can use to analyze your audience, as well as a sample questionnaire.

**Web Connect 6.2 U.S. Census**

If you'd like to widen your exploration of demographic statistics, go to the website of the U.S. Bureau of the Census. This site is an excellent source of demographic statistics.

**Web Connect 6.3 Identifying Audiences**

Practice considering the type of a particular audience and the degree to which the speaker was able to adjust the message for the audience. Locate two speeches at a website that features speeches, such American Rhetoric.com or the White House's Briefing Room. Compare and contrast the audiences for the speeches you locate. How are the audiences similar and how are they different? To what degree does each speaker adjust to the audience?

**Web Connect 6.4 Advanced Public Speaking Institute**

This website provides a wealth of information about public speaking, including how physical location affects a speech. Click on "Room Set Up" in the table. (You don't have to subscribe to access this information.)

# Chapter 7 GATHERING SUPPORTING MATERIALS

## Key Concepts

**information overload** (118)
**preliminary bibliography** (121)
**research inventory** (116)

## Practicing the Public Dialogue Activities

**PPD Activity 7.1 Prepare Your Research Inventory**
Bring a copy of the Research Inventory Worksheet to class (a filled-in sample, Figure 7.1, is on page 117). With a partner, discuss the kinds of research you both need for your next speech, as well as the types of research you already have done. Discuss where you might find the research you need and develop a timeline for gathering this material. Consider the advantages and disadvantages of your sources for the material you might find. Remember to consider your speech goals, your audience, and the need to vary your sources of information.

You can download a blank Research Inventory Worksheet from the Chapter 7 resources in your Premium Website for *Invitation to Public Speaking Handbook*.

**PPD Activity 7.2 Prepare Your Preliminary Bibliography**
Bring to class several samples of the supporting materials you've collected for your speech, including your Internet research, library research, and interviews. Working as a class, help one another prepare your preliminary bibliography. To format your bibliography correctly, use the citation style required by your instructor. You can see samples of bibliographic entries by buying a style manual, checking one out from the library, or looking at the sample bibliographic entries in Appendix B.

You can also use Speech Builder Express to help you prepare your preliminary bibliography with whatever citation style you are assigned. Select "Works Cited" from the left menu and follow the instructions. For short reminders from this chapter about bibliographies, click the "Tutor" button.

# Chapter 8 RESEARCH ONLINE AND AT THE LIBRARY

## Key Concepts

**abstract** (130)
**bibliographic database** (129)
**Boolean operators** (129)
**database** (129)
**full-text database** (130)
**global plagiarism** (134)
**incremental plagiarism** (134)
**index** (131)
**Internet** (124)
**patchwork plagiarism** (134)
**plagiarism** (134)
**World Wide Web** (124)

## Practicing the Public Dialogue Activities

**PPD Activity 8.1 Research and Evaluate Internet and Library Sources**
Bring to class the research you've found for your speech on the Internet and at the library. Share your research with the class. Discuss whether your sources are credible, ethical, and audience centered and whether your research supports your speaking goals. Discard any information that does not seem ethical, reliable, authoritative, current, complete, relevant, consistent, or audience centered.

## Web Connect Resources

**Web Connect 8.1 Online Librarians**

Use New York Public Library's question site to call, e-mail, or chat with librarians about questions you have related to your speech topic.

**Web Connect 8.2 Understanding Call Numbers**

The site "Understanding Call Numbers," sponsored by the Honolulu Community College Library, provides a thorough explanation of how call numbers work.

**Web Connect 8.3 U.S. Government Websites and Documents**

USA.gov is a comprehensive website that lets you search U.S. government websites and documents by subject or by agency.

**Web Connect 8.4 Plagiarism: Its Nature and Consequences**

The plagiarism site of the Duke University Libraries is an excellent source of in-depth information about what plagiarism is and the consequences of plagiarizing.

# Chapter 9 CONDUCTING RESEARCH INTERVIEWS

## Key Concepts

**interview** (138)
**probe** (141)

# Chapter 10 ORGANIZING YOUR SPEECH

## Key Concepts

**causal pattern** (155)
**chronological pattern** (153)
**connective** (161)
**internal preview** (162)
**internal summary** (163)
**main points** (150)
**organization** (150)
**problem-solution pattern** (156)
**signpost** (163)
**spatial pattern** (154)
**topical pattern** (157)
**transition** (162)

## Practicing the Public Dialogue Activities

**PPD Activity 10.1 Select an Organizational Pattern for Your Speech**

As a class, brainstorm topics for speeches that could conceivably be arranged according to more than one of the organizational patterns discussed in this chapter. Choose one of these topics and then divide into five groups. Assign a different organizational pattern (chronological, spatial, causal, problem-solution, or topical) to each group. In your group, create a specific purpose, thesis statement, and up to five main points for the topic, using the organizational pattern you were assigned. Have each group present their results to the class and then, as a class, determine which organizational pattern (or patterns) worked best for the topic. Why was this pattern more successful than the others? Use what you learned from this activity to select the most appropriate pattern for your next speech.

When you're ready to organize the main points of your next speech, you can use Speech Builder Express to help you. Select "Organization" from the left menu and follow the instructions.

**PPD Activity 10.2 Prepare the Main Points and Connectives for Your Speech**

Bring your thesis statement for your next speech to class. With a partner, discuss the main points you have prepared to develop your thesis statement. Are your main points distinct? If you have combined your points, separate them. Next consider the phrasing of your main points. Have you used a parallel structure to word each one? If not, revise your wording so your points are parallel. Now consider how balanced your main points are. If you suspect you're spending too little or too much time on a point, adjust it so the coverage of each point is more balanced. Finally, identify the places within or between your main points where a connective would add clarity or help you move from one idea to the next.

You can use Speech Builder Express to help you create main points and connectives for your next speech. Select "Outline" and "Transitions" from the left menu and follow the instructions.

## Interactive Video Activities

**Video Activity 10.1**

Watch a video clip of student speaker Cindy Gardner giving a speech about how to fold an American flag. Notice how she organizes her ideas. You can use your Premium Website for *Invitation to Public Speaking Handbook* to watch the video, respond to analysis questions, and compare your answers to those provided by the author.

# Chapter 11 OUTLINING YOUR SPEECH

## Key Concepts

**coordination** (169)
**preparation outline** (166)
**speaking outline** (182)
**subordination** (173)
**subpoint** (168)
**sub-subpoint** (168)

## Practicing the Public Dialogue Activities

### PPD Activity 11.1 Build Your Preparation Outline

Using the template provided by your instructor or the sample on pages 176–181 as a guide, build a preparation outline for your next speech. Start by creating a title and indicating your specific purpose and thesis statement. Then outline your introduction, main points, subpoints, and sub-subpoints, and conclusion. Add connectives that will help you transition from one idea to the next. Finally, add a section of the works you intend to cite in your speech, following the format provided by your instructor or this book. As you prepare your outline, remember to incorporate the tips you've read in this chapter: Translate incomplete sentences or keywords into full sentences; label the introduction, body, and conclusion of your speech; use the proper symbols to indicate your main points, subpoints, and sub-subpoints; indent your points properly; and correct any imbalances you discover in your points.

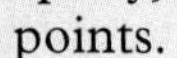

You can use Speech Builder Express to help create your outline. Select the appropriate speech parts from the left menu and follow the instructions. When you've entered all your information, click "Completing the Speech Outline" to view your preparation outline. If you like, you can then export your outline to Word to print it.

### PPD Activity 11.2 Build Your Speaking Outline

Using the template provided by your instructor or the sample on pages 186–189 as a guide, build a speaking outline for your next speech. Translate the complete sentences of your preparation outline into keywords and phrases that will help you remember key ideas as you give your speech. Review your outline to make sure your ideas are outlined and easy to follow visually. Also make sure your computer-written text or handwriting is easy to read from a distance. If it isn't, adjust your printing, fonts, or type sizes so they are clear and legible. Finally, save a copy of your outline on your computer or make a few photocopies of it.

As you practice your speech, add your delivery cues. If you find your outline is too messy after several rounds of practice and adjustments, print a new one and add only those cues that you find most helpful (or mark up one of your photocopies). Remember, your speaking outline should be legible—too many notes and changes will make it hard to read.

## Interactive Video Activities

### Video Activity 11.1

Watch a video of Katy Mazz giving her speech about the number pi. Notice how she uses her speaking outline to help her remember her main points and cite her sources accurately.

If you'd like to see more examples of preparation and speaking outlines, check out some of the other speeches in your video resources. All the full-length student speeches are accompanied by speaking (keyword) outlines, preparation (full-sentence) outlines, and note cards. As you watch a speech, let the speaking outline scroll alongside so you can see how the outline compares with the speaker's delivery.

## Web Connect Resources

### Web Connect 11.1 **MLA and APA Citation Styles**

In addition to all sorts of information about research, this site provides examples of source citations in the MLA, APA, and other common styles.

# Chapter 12 INTRODUCTIONS AND CONCLUSIONS

## Key Concepts

**preview** (192)
**rhetorical question** (192)
**summary** (204)

## Practicing the Public Dialogue Activities

### PPD Activity 12.1 **Prepare Your Introduction**

In class, generate a list of six to eight possible speech topics. Divide into groups, one for each topic. In each group, write an introduction for a speech on the topic you've chosen. Be sure to include the four parts of an introduction and one of the techniques for making it compelling. Now share this introduction with the class and get feedback on its effectiveness.

You can use Speech Builder Express to help you create your introduction. Select "Introduction" from the left menu and follow the instructions. For short reminders from this chapter about effective introductions, click the "Tutor" button. Once you've created your introduction, Speech Builder Express will save it as part of your overall outline until you are ready to complete the next step in the speech process.

### PPD Activity 12.2 **Prepare Your Conclusion**

Return to the group you worked with for the Practicing the Public Dialogue 12.1 activity and write a conclusion for the introduction you have prepared. Begin by incorporating a transition from the body of your speech to the conclusion. Then follow the steps for creating an effective and compelling conclusion. Make sure your conclusion is consistent with your introduction and the tone you want to set for the ending of your speech. Present your conclusion to the class and get feedback on your efforts.

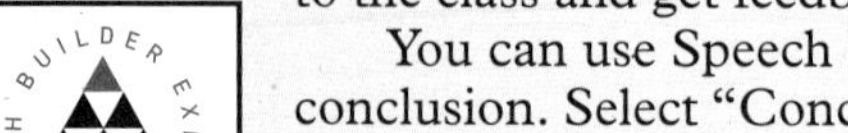


You can use Speech Builder Express to help you create your conclusion. Select "Conclusion" from the left menu and follow the instructions. For short reminders from this chapter about conclusions, click the "Tutor" button.

## Interactive Video Activities

### Video Activity 12.1

Watch a video clip of student speaker Brandi Lafferty telling a story in her introduction. After you've watched the video, respond to analysis questions and compare your answers to those provided by the author.

### Video Activity 12.2

To see a good example of a speaker who uses her conclusion to enhance her credibility, watch a video clip of student speaker Chelsey Penoyer. As you watch Chelsey speak, notice the startling statement she makes about her experience with her speech topic. How does her statement enhance her credibility? After you've watched the video, respond to analysis questions and compare your answers to those provided by the author.

### Video Activity 12.3

As you craft the introduction and conclusion of your next speech, use the excerpts from Mike Piel's speech as a model. After you watch the video, respond to the analysis questions provided and compare your answers to those provided by the author.

## Web Connect Resources

### Web Connect 12.1 **Starting with a Quotation**

To explore places on the Internet where you can find quotations for your introduction, check out this extensive list of links to quotations, organized by category.

### Web Connect 12.2 **Amusing Facts**

To find an intriguing fact that might be appropriate to include in your introduction, check out AmusingFacts.com. This website contains many interesting, unusual, and startling facts.

### Web Connect 12.3 **Ending Effectively**

Read the transcript of South African civil rights leader Nelson Mandela's address given after his release from prison in 1990. What technique did Mandela use to conclude his speech? Was his quote an appropriate way to conclude the speech? Why or why not? What are some other techniques speakers can use to conclude their speeches?

# Chapter 13 DEVELOPING AND SUPPORTING YOUR IDEAS

## Key Concepts

**bias** (236)
**brief narrative** (219)
**claim** (214)
**connotative definition** (238)
**definition** (238)
**denotative definition** (238)
**direct quotation** (233)
**etymology** (240)
**evidence** (215)
**example** (215)
**expert testimony** (233)
**extended narrative** (219)
**hypothetical example** (215)
**intertextuality** (223)
**mean** (226)
**median** (227)
**mode** (228)
**narrative** (219)
**objective** (236)
**paraphrase** (233)
**peer testimony** (233)
**personal testimony** (233)
**real example** (215)
**statistics** (224)
**testimony** (233)

## Practicing the Public Dialogue Activities

### PPD Activity 13.1 **Evaluate and Cite Your Supporting Evidence**

Bring to class the supporting materials you have gathered for your next speech. Working in pairs or with a group, separate your materials into categories: examples, narratives, statistics, testimony, and definitions. Discuss how you plan to use each type of evidence in the speech. Using the tips in this chapter to evaluate your evidence, determine whether your audience would see your evidence as credible and ethical. Why would or wouldn't they? After you've selected the evidence you believe will be appropriate for your speech, practice citing your sources aloud using the rules provided in this chapter.

## Interactive Video Activities

### Video Activity 13.1

Watch a video clip of student speaker Chelsey Penoyer as she uses narratives to bring emotion to her speech. As you watch Chelsey speak, consider how effectively she uses narratives. Do they draw you into her speech? After you watch the video, respond to analysis questions and compare your answers to those provided by the author.

## Web Connect Resources

### Web Connect 13.1 **Statistical Abstract**

The *Statistical Abstract* includes statistics related to crime, population, health, and many other topics.

**Web Connect 13.2 Word Origins**

The Word Origins website defines words and give you their original meanings. Search on the word you'd like to know about or click on "The Big List" link in the menu at the right for a list of all the words defined at this site.

**Web Connect 13.3 Avoiding Proper Meaning Superstition**

Go to Google and search on the term "feminism definition." Explore some of the sites Google uncovers to find various meanings of the word *feminism.* Which of these meanings is new to you? Which do you think is most widely held by your audience? Which source is most credible? How might knowing the differences in meanings for the concept of feminism influence a speech you might give on the topic?

# Chapter 14 INTRODUCTION TO REASONING

## Key Concepts

**analogical reasoning** (253)
**argument** (244)
**causal reasoning** (250)
**character** (260)
**competence** (260)
**conclusion** (248)
**credibility** (260)
**deductive reasoning** (248)
**ethos** (243)
**false cause** (251)
**hasty generalization** (247)
**inductive reasoning** (245)
**inferences** (244)
**logos** (243)
**major premise** (248)
**minor premise** (248)
**pathos** (243)
**reasoning by sign** (255)
**sign** (254)

## Practicing the Public Dialogue Activities

**PPD Activity 14.1 Test the Reasoning of Your Arguments**

Bring one of the main arguments in your speech to class. Present this argument to the class and determine which pattern of reasoning will help you develop this argument most fully (inductive, deductive, causal, analogical, or by sign). After each person has presented her or his argument and selected a pattern of reasoning to support it, discuss the strengths and weaknesses of each person's approach.

**PPD Activity 14.2 Apply Toulmin's Model of Reasoning to Your Arguments**

Select several of the arguments you presented in PPD Activity 14.1 and, as a class, apply Toulmin's model of reasoning to them. Identify the claims, grounds, warrant, and backing in each argument, verify the logic of these four parts, and make any adjustments in reasoning to strengthen them.

## Interactive Video Activities

### Video Activity 14.1

To see examples of two types of reasoning, deductive and causal, used in a speech, watch video clips of student speakers Lisa Alagna and Brent Erb. Consider how effectively Lisa uses deduction, paying particular attention to how she establishes the major premise of her argument. Consider how Brent makes a causal claim. Is the stated cause-and-effect relationship accurate or inaccurate? You can use your Premium Website for *Invitation to Public Speaking Handbook* to watch these videos, respond to analysis questions, and compare your answers to those provided by the author.

## Web Connect Resources

### Web Connect 14.1 **Aristotle's Forms of Proof**

To learn more about Aristotle's three forms of proof, go to the Art of Rhetoric website and read the explanations provided. Then page through a magazine and find examples of each form. Which form most persuades you? Which form is most common in the magazine you read? Why do you think that is?

### Web Connect 14.2 **Toulmin Model**

Access the Toulmin Model of Argument site for some good information about the Toulmin model and how to use it.

# Chapter 15 AUDIENCE-CENTERED LANGUAGE

## Key Concepts

**abstract language** (264)
**concrete language** (264)
**idiom** (266)
**language** (262)
**oral style** (271)
**referent** (263)
**symbol** (263)
**thought, or reference** (264)

## Practicing the Public Dialogue Activities

**PPD Activity 15.1 Evaluate Accuracy of the Language in Your Speech**
Make a list of five to ten words you think everyone in your audience will define in the same way. Exchange lists with a partner in your speech class and write definitions for each other's words, but don't use a dictionary. Share your definitions with each other and see if you agree on them. Now look up your words in a dictionary and see if your and your partner's definitions match the definitions provided in the dictionary.

**PPD Activity 15.2 Evaluate the Style of the Language in Your Speech**
Bring to class the outline and speaking notes from one of your speeches. With a partner or in a small group, discuss whether you followed an oral or a written style when you prepared this speech. (*Hint:* If you wrote out your speech word for word, you probably followed a written rather than an oral style.) If you

followed an oral style, get feedback from your partner or group about how you might strengthen your oral style to make your speech more listenable. If you followed a written style, share strategies for giving your next speech in an oral style rather than a written one.

To practice comparing an oral style to a written style, go online to watch or listen to a speech by a political figure, and then compare the speech with something this person has written. For speeches, access Web Connect 15.4. For written material, search the Internet using the search term "book excerpt" and the political figure's name. This search often yields excerpts from memoirs written by famous politicians, diplomats, heads of state, and the like.

## Interactive Video Activities

### Video Activity 15.1

To see a speaker using a casual style, watch the video clip of student speaker Brandi Lafferty giving a speech about the problems with feeding wildlife. After you watch the video, respond to analysis questions and compare your answers to those provided by the author.

## Web Connect Resources

### Web Connect 15.1 **American Heritage Dictionary**

The American Heritage Book of English Usage offers a practical guide to the sensitive use of social, racial, and ethnic terms. Scroll down the page to links that provide detailed information about the origin, use, and applicability of various names and labels, such as "Anglo" and "person of color."

### Web Connect 15.2 **Merriam-Webster Online**

This online version of the Merriam-Webster dictionary also provides a thesaurus, a link to Encyclopaedia Britannica, and more.

### Web Connect 15.3 **Words Commonly Misused**

"Words Commonly Misused" is an excellent and informative online guide to words that often give people trouble.

### Web Connect 15.4 **American Rhetoric**

AmericanRhetoric.com provides links to hundreds of speeches, including political speeches, historical speeches, and speeches from movies.

# Chapter 16 LANGUAGE AND STYLE

## Key Concepts

**alliteration** (278)
**antithesis** (278)
**metaphor** (274)
**mixed metaphor** (275)
**mnemonic device** (278)
**parallelism** (276)
**personification** (276)
**repetition** (277)
**rhythm** (276)
**simile** (274)

## Practicing the Public Dialogue Activities

**PPD Activity 16.1 Evaluate the Imagery and Rhythm of Your Speech**
As a class, select a speech topic for an imaginary speech. Prepare the general and specific purposes for the speech (Chapter 5) and the main points (Chapter 10). Break into groups and assign each of the following elements to a different group: the introduction, the conclusion, and the main points (one main point per group). In your groups, use as many of the devices for creating memorable images and appealing rhythms as you can for your part of the speech. Make sure your language is culturally inclusive and gender inclusive. Now, with your groups, deliver the parts of the speech to the class and discuss the language strategies you used in your speech part. Why did you make the choices you made? Why were they effective or not?

## Interactive Video Activities

**Video Activity 16.1**

To see a speaker use linguistic devices in her speech, watch the video clip of student speaker Stacey Newman giving a commemorative speech about fallen soldiers. Were her uses of these devices effective? Why or why not? After you watch the video, respond to analysis questions and compare your answers to those provided by the author.

# Chapter 17 METHODS OF DELIVERY

## Key Concepts

**conversational style** (286)
**delivery** (284)
**extemporaneous speech** (285)
**impromptu speech** (287)
**manuscript speech** (288)
**memorized speech** (290)

## Practicing the Public Dialogue Activities

**PPD Activity 17.1 Compare Delivery Methods**
In class, take an item out of your backpack or from your pocket. Turn to the person next to you and give an impromptu speech about this item. The speech can be informative, invitational, or persuasive and should be no longer than sixty seconds. Now find an example of something written—a paragraph in this textbook, the newspaper, or the like. Give another sixty-second "speech," reading the written material. With your partner, discuss the differences between the delivery styles. Which did you prefer to deliver? Which did you prefer to listen to?

## Interactive Video Activities

**Video Activity 17.1**

To compare the differences between a speech delivered in a conversational style and one that is read, watch the video clips of student speakers Shelley

Weibel and Eric Daley. Which style of delivery do you think is more effective? After you watch the video, respond to analysis questions and compare your answers to those provided by the author.

### Video Activity 17.2

Student speakers Brandi Lafferty, Amy Wood, Carol Godart, and Hans Erian each used a different method of delivery for her or his speech. Watch the video clips of parts of their speeches. Which delivery method do you think was most effective? After you watch the video, respond to analysis questions and compare your answers to those provided by the author.

### Video Activity 17.3

To see a student speaker attempt to gain her audience's attention in her introduction, watch the video clip of Tiffany Brisco. What does she say in her introduction that makes it easy for her audience to listen to her speech? After you watch the video, respond to analysis questions and compare your answers to those provided by the author.

## Web Connect Resources

**Web Connect 17.1 How to Give a Successful Impromptu Speech**

This online article offers insight into giving an impromptu speech. Read its advice and then consider occasions for which you have been called on to give an impromptu speech. How prepared did you feel for these occasions? Was your speech effective? How might you have improved your performance?

**Web Connect 17.2 Memorize, Read, or Extemporize?**

Read what the University of Pennsylvania's Communication Within the Curriculum website has to say about extemporaneous speaking. Think about a speech you have recently attended, such as a lecture, a sermon, a political speech, or a sales pitch. Was the speech delivered extemporaneously? Was it effective? How could it have been more effective? What can you do to improve your effectiveness as an extemporaneous speaker?

# Chapter 18 VERBAL AND NONVERBAL COMPONENTS OF DELIVERY

## Key Concepts

**articulation** (300)
**dialect** (301)
**eye contact** (304)
**facial expression** (305)
**gestures** (307)
**inflection** (298)
**monotone** (298)
**pauses** (299)
**personal appearance** (303)
**pitch** (298)
**posture** (306)
**pronunciation** (301)
**proxemics** (308)
**rate** (297)
**vocal variety** (296)
**vocalized pauses** (300)
**volume** (297)

## Practicing the Public Dialogue Activities

**PPD Activity 18.1 Refine the Verbal Components of Your Delivery**
If you'd like to get some feedback on the verbal components of your delivery, ask your public speaking class to help you. Here are some exercises you can do in front of the classroom using your classmates as you audience:

- If you are a very quiet speaker, begin speaking as softly as you can, increasing your volume until all the people at the back of the classroom nod their heads to indicate they can hear you comfortably.
- If you are a very fast speaker, begin speaking as fast as you can, decreasing your rate until your listeners nod to indicate that they are comfortable with your rate.
- If you have trouble with vocalized pauses, begin using as many of them as you can while you speak for about sixty seconds. Then continue to speak for another sixty seconds, being careful not to use a single vocalized pause.
- If you struggle with articulation, pronunciation, or dialect, begin speaking as you normally would for about sixty seconds. Then slow your speech and say each word carefully until your listeners nod to indicate that they can understand you clearly.

**PPD Activity 18.2 Refine the Nonverbal Components of Your Delivery**
As a class, discuss the differences in your styles of nonverbal delivery: Are you someone who likes to dress more formally or more casually? Do you have to make adjustments to your nonverbal style because of your cultural background? How much eye contact are you comfortable with? Do you wish you could stand closer to your audience or farther away? Would you prefer to hold the lectern, gesture, or put your hands in your pockets? Which of your personal preferences enhances your speaking presence and which might detract from it?

## Interactive Video Activities

### Video Activity 18.1

Your online resources for this book feature dozens of speeches by student and professional speakers. If you'd like to work on improving your nonverbal delivery style, watch a few of these speeches and evaluate how the speakers handle the nonverbal components of delivery. Are there things these speakers do that you'd like to incorporate into your own speech? Are there things these speakers do that you'd like to avoid?

## Web Connect Resources

**Web Connect: 18.1 Improving Vocal Variety**

Read Candice M. Coleman's Web article "Improving Vocal Variety." Use her advice to practice your next speech, paying particular attention to your vocal variety. Use a video camera or a tape recorder to hear your presentation. To what degree do you achieve vocal variety? What aspects of your delivery could be more varied?

**Web Connect 18.2 Dress for Success**

The Syms "Dress to Achieve!" website is meant to help college students dress appropriately for job interviews, but it can also give you a sense of the type of dress that is acceptable for professional presentations.

**Web Connect 18.3 Practicing Your Speech**

Go to eHow.com's "How To Deliver Effective Speeches" page and use the suggested tips to practice your next speech, paying particular attention to your gestures. Record your rehearsal with a video camera and then review the tape. Is it difficult for you to gesture effectively? Why or why not? Do you gesture too much? Not enough? Are your gestures appropriately timed?

# Chapter 19 VISUAL AIDS: PURPOSES AND CONTENTS

## Key Concepts

**bar graph** (317)
**drawing** (320)
**flow chart** (315)
**graph** (316)
**line graph** (317)
**list** (314)
**map** (322)
**organizational chart** (315)
**picture graph** (317)
**pie graph** (317)

## Practicing the Public Dialogue Activities

**PPD Activity 19.1 Identify Visual Aids to Use in Your Speech**

Identify one or two of the main points you will develop in your next speech. Outline that point (Chapter 11) and then decide what type of visual aid will help you make that point most clearly. Will it be a list, graph, photograph, video clip, or something else? Now decide how you will show the visual aid to your audience. Will you display an object before your audience or demonstrate a process? Will you show your visual aid in a handout or with a PowerPoint presentation? Discuss these choices as a class or in small groups, keeping in mind the question, "How does this visual aid help me establish my credibility and communicate more clearly?"

## Interactive Video Activities

### Video Activity 19.1

Watch a video clip of student speaker Josh Valentine as he uses visual and audio aids to illustrate and clarify points. As you watch Josh speak, consider how effectively he uses these resources. How do they enhance his delivery and credibility? After you watch the video, respond to analysis questions and compare your answers to those provided by the author.

# Chapter 20 VISUAL AIDS: TYPES AND FORMATS

## Key Concepts

**balance** (348)
**demonstration** (332)
**font** (344)
**font size** (345)
**model** (332)
**object** (332)

## Practicing the Public Dialogue Activities

### PPD Activity 20.1 Design Your Visual Aids

Begin designing your visual aids for your next speech. Make sure your visual aids follow the basic design principles of font style and size, color, and balance. Prepare at least a couple of drafts for each of your visual aids, and then check with friends or classmates about which are most effective in presenting information and promoting recall.

## Interactive Video Activities

### Video Activity 20.1

The online resources for *Invitation to Public Speaking Handbook* feature several video clips of student speakers using visual aids in their presentations. As you prepare your own visual aids for your speech, check out some of these videos to help you determine what type of visual aid might work best for you. For example,

- Consider whether Carol Godart's PowerPoint presentation helped increase her persuasiveness and credibility in her speech about fat discrimination.
- Evaluate whether Chelsey Penoyer's PowerPoint presentation on youth suicide followed the guidelines in this chapter for effective visual aids.
- Watch Cindy Gardner's demonstration speech on folding the U.S. flag.
- Watch Josh Valentine's speech on African drumming to see a speaker using photographs and audio clips.
- Evaluate Tony D'Amico's use of a poster board to display an image during his speech on Broadway musicals.

After you watch each video, respond to analysis questions and compare your answers to those provided by the author.

## Web Connect Resources

### Web Connect 20.1 Creating a PowerPoint Presentation

Most speech instructors ask their students to use PowerPoint to prepare visual aids for at least one in-class speech. If you don't already know how to use PowerPoint or would like some pointers, go to the PowerPoint in the

Classroom website and open Microsoft PowerPoint on your computer. The site is created for teachers, but it is one of the best PowerPoint tutorials available. Follow the directions to create a presentation you can use for your next speech, adding slides, images, and sounds. What difficulties did you have creating the presentation? What are the advantages of PowerPoint?

# Chapter 21 INFORMATIVE SPEAKING

## Key Concepts

**informative speaking environment** (356)
**informative speech** (356)
**speech about a concept** (362)
**speech about an event** (358)
**speech about an object** (361)
**speech about a place or a person** (360)
**speech about a process** (357)

## Practicing the Public Dialogue Activities

**PPD Activity 21.1 Select an Informative Speech Type**
As a class, brainstorm as many different informative speech topics as you can. Next, group the topics according to the five types of informative speeches you've just read about. Some might fit into several groups depending on how you phrase your thesis statement for a particular topic. Discuss which of these topics you find most interesting and why. Save this list for the next Practicing the Public Dialogue activity.

**PPD Activity 21.2 Select an Organizational Pattern for Your Informative Speech**
Return to the list of possible informative speech topics you prepared in Practicing the Public Dialogue 21.1. In groups, select a single topic and see if you can create a rough thesis statement and main points for four different informative speeches on this topic, using each of the organizational patterns you've just read about. As a class, discuss which of these speeches you would find most interesting and why. As you discuss your favorite topic and organizational pattern, consider the tips in Chapter 21 for giving effective informative speeches.

## Interactive Video Activities

### Video Activity 21.1

To consider the effectiveness of the organizational pattern one student speaker used for her informative speech, watch a video clip of Rachel Rota giving her speech about tap dancing. After you watch the video, respond to analysis questions and compare your answers to those provided by the author.

## Web Connect Resources

Web Connect 21.1 **About.com**

About.com is a terrific source for informative speech topics, offering a lot of different ways to search for or browse a wide variety of topics.

Web Connect 21.2 **A&E's *Biography***

A&E's *Biography* website is an excellent source of speech topics and information about people.

Web Connect 21.3 **The History Channel**

The History Channel is a great source for topics about places, people, and events—this resource provides information about a lot more than just World War II! Click the "Topics" link in the menu at the top of the homepage.

# Chapter 22 INVITATIONAL SPEAKING

## Key Concepts

**condition of equality** (384)
**condition of self-determination** (385)
**condition of value** (385)
**invitational environment** (382)
**invitational speaking** (381)
**multiple perspectives pattern** (396)
**speech to articulate a position** (386)
**speech to explore an issue** (389)

## Practicing the Public Dialogue Activities

**PPD Activity 22.1 Select an Invitational Speech Type**

In class, identify some of the most controversial issues we face today as a society. List these issues on the board. How many of them do you have strong feelings about? How many do you wish you could learn more about in an invitational way? Select two topics from the list and, with a partner, discuss the ways you could frame speeches about these topics invitationally. For each topic, would you want to give a speech to articulate a position or to explore an issue? How would you use equality, value, and self-determination to create an invitational speaking environment? Save this list for the next Practicing the Public Dialogue activity.

**PPD Activity 22.2 Select an Organizational Pattern for Your Invitational Speech**

Return to the list of possible invitational speech topics you prepared in Practicing the Public Dialogue 22.1. In groups, select a single topic and see if you can create a rough thesis statement and main points for four different invitational speeches on this topic, using each of the organizational patterns you've just read about. As a class, discuss which of these speeches you would find most interesting and why. As you discuss your favorite topic and organizational pattern, consider the guidelines in Chapter 22 for giving effective invitational speeches.

## Interactive Video Activities

### Video Activity 22.1

Watch a video clip of student speaker Shelley Weibel as she creates a condition of equality. How does she create this condition? After you watch the video, respond to analysis questions and compare your answers to those provided by the author.

### Video Activity 22.2

Watch a video clip of student speaker Melissa Carroll as she creates a condition of self-determination. How does she create this condition? After you watch the video, respond to analysis questions and compare your answers to those provided by the author.

### Video Activity 22.3

If you'd like to see an example of an invitational speech, watch student speaker Cara Buckley-Ott giving a speech and then exploring an issue with her audience. After you watch the video, respond to analysis questions and compare your answers to those provided by the author.

### Video Activity 22.4

Student speaker Chung-yan Man used the topical pattern of organization for her informative speech on Chinese fortune telling. Although her speech is informative, in some ways it can be considered invitational. Can you spot the ways in which the speech is invitational? After you watch the video, respond to analysis questions and compare your answers to those provided by the author.

### Video Activity 22.5

Watch Amanda Bucknam's speech on funding for HIV/AIDS in Africa and the United States. Watch for how she created the conditions of equality, value, and self-determination and remained invitational throughout her dialogue with the audience. After you watch the video, respond to analysis questions and compare your answers to those provided by the author.

## Web Connect Resources

### Web Connect 22.1 **Building a Supportive Climate**

To learn more about what qualifies as an invitational environment, sometimes called a *supportive climate*, go to the Communication Climate Inventory on the University of San Francisco website to assess the type of climate you share with your current or a past supervisor at work. (You can apply this information to the environment you foster when you give an invitational speech.) Read the commentary below the survey and score your answers accordingly. Were you surprised by how you rated? What might have been done, if anything, to improve the climate?

### Web Connect 22.2 **Invitational Speech Topics**

Because invitational speeches specifically allow for dialogue between the speaker and the audience, this speech format is well suited for controversial topics. For a list of possible topics for invitational speeches, check out "Controversial Speech Topics" at Buzzle.com.

**Web Connect 22.3** **Hecklers, Hardliners, and Heavy Questions**

The article "Hecklers, Hardliners, and Heavy Questions" at the website ExpressionsOfExcellence.com provides helpful tips on how to deal with hostile audience members.

# Chapter 23 PERSUASIVE SPEAKING

## Key Concepts

**call to action** (417)
**comparative advantages organization** (421)
**counterarguments** (426)
**fear appeal** (426)
**gain immediate action** (417)
**gain passive agreement** (417)
**Monroe's motivated sequence** (423)
**persuasive speech** (410)
**problem-cause-solution organization** (419)
**problem-solution organization** (417)
**question of fact** (411)
**question of policy** (412)
**question of value** (411)
**two-sided message** (425)

## Practicing the Public Dialogue Activities

### PPD Activity 23.1 Select a Persuasive Speech Type

As a class, brainstorm as many different persuasive speech topics as you can. Next, group the topics according to the three types of persuasive speeches you've just read about. Some might fit into more than one group, depending on how you would phrase your thesis statement for a particular topic. Discuss which of these topics you find most interesting and why. Save this list for the next Practicing the Public Dialogue activity.

### PPD Activity 23.2 Select an Organizational Pattern for Your Persuasive Speech

Return to the list of possible persuasive speech topics you prepared in Practicing the Public Dialogue 23.1. In groups, select a single topic and determine whether you want to work on a question of fact, value, or policy. See if you can create a rough thesis statement and main points for a persuasive speech on this topic using one of the organizational patterns you've just read about. Select the pattern that would best help you persuade your audience to take action or modify their thinking about a topic. As you discuss your organizational pattern, consider the guidelines for giving effective persuasive speeches in Chapter 23.

## Interactive Video Activities

### Video Activity 23.1

To see an example of a good persuasive speech, watch a video clip of Hans Erian giving his speech about the dangers of sugar. After you watch the video, respond to analysis questions and compare your answers to those provided by the author.

### Video Activity 23.2

Watch a video clip of student speaker Brent Erb giving a persuasive speech and urging immediate action from his audience. Pay attention to the solutions he proposes. Could you implement them? After you watch the video, respond to analysis questions and compare your answers to those provided by the author.

### Video Activity 23.3

Watch a video clip of student speaker Brandi Lafferty giving a persuasive speech. Did her decision to include a discussion of the problem's causes make for a more effective speech? After you watch the video, respond to analysis questions and compare your answers to those provided by the author.

### Video Activity 23.4

Watch the video clip of Courtney's speech about light pollution. Consider the effectiveness of the organizational pattern she uses for her speech. If you had given a speech on this topic, would you have used the same pattern? Why or why not? After you watch the video, respond to analysis questions and compare your answers to those provided by the author.

### Video Activity 23.5

Watch Dana Barker's speech on school dropout rates among Latinos. Consider the type of persuasive speech she chose to use and how she organized her speech, as well as the language and evidence she used. Were her choices effective? After you watch the video, respond to analysis questions and compare your answers to those provided by the author.

## Web Connect Resources

### Web Connect 23.1 **200+ Persuasive Speech Ideas**

Speech-Topics-Help.com is a thorough source of topics for persuasive speeches.

### Web Connect 23.2 **Monroe's Motivated Sequence**

This site provides an example of a speech outline that follows Monroe's motivated sequence and a checklist that can help you incorporate this pattern into a speech.

# Chapter 24 PERSUASION AND REASONING

## Key Concepts

**ad hominem fallacy** (456)
**bandwagon fallacy** (457)
**character** (442)
**common ground** (444)
**competence** (442)
**credibility** (442)
**derived credibility** (443)
**either-or fallacy** (457)
**ethos** (439)
**fallacy** (456)
**initial credibility** (443)
**logos** (439)

**mythos** (452)
**pathos** (439)
**red herring fallacy** (458)
**slippery slope fallacy** (459)
**terminal credibility** (443)

## Practicing the Public Dialogue Activities

### PPD Activity 24.1 Consider Your Credibility

As a class, make a list of people you think have strong credibility. These people can be anyone—celebrities, historical figures, people you know personally. Discuss the qualities these people have that make them credible in your eyes. Make a list of these qualities and see if they correlate with the qualities of credibility you've been reading about in this chapter. Would you find these people persuasive on all topics or only a few? What qualities do you have that make you credible? How can you use these qualities to enhance your credibility as a speaker?

### PPD Activity 24.2 Consider Appeals to Emotion and to Mythos

In small groups, discuss your preparation for the next persuasive speech you'll give in class. Identify the appeals to emotion and to mythos you plan to make in your speech. As a group, help one another strengthen these appeals and ensure that they are audience centered. Discuss whether these appeals are appropriate and how you plan to make them in an ethical way.

### PPD Activity 24.3 Considering Logical Fallacies

Using your speech topic and research for your next persuasive speech, convert the arguments you plan to make in your speech to logical fallacies. Write one example of each of the five logical fallacies you've just read about. (You'll have five different fallacies for your speech when you are finished.) Bring your fallacies to class and present each of them to your classmates. See if they can identify the type of fallacy you are committing. After every student has presented her or his fallacies, discuss which were the hardest to spot and which were the most "persuasive." Now revise those fallacies, correcting their flawed reasoning.

## Interactive Video Activities

### Video Activity 24.1

If you'd like to complete an activity similar to PPD Activity 24.1 on your own, access the videos of professional speakers included in the online resources for this book. Select two professional speakers you think are highly credible and watch their videos. Assess their initial, derived, and terminal credibility. Now select two professional speakers you think are not very credible and assess their initial, derived, and terminal credibility. How could you apply what you observed in the videos about credibility to your own speeches?

### Video Activity 24.2

To see an example of a speaker appealing to emotion in a persuasive speech, watch the video of Mary Fisher's address to the 1992 Republican National Convention. Notice how she appeals to powerful emotions but does so in an audience-centered way. After you watch the video, respond to analysis questions and compare your answers to those provided by the author.

### Video Activity 24.3

Watch Maria DiMaggio's speech on the perils of winning the lottery. Consider the persuasive reasoning Maria used in her speech and how she communicated her credibility. How solid was her reasoning? How did she establish and maintain her credibility? After you watch the video, respond to analysis questions and compare your answers to those provided by the author.

## Web Connect Resources

### Web Connect 24.1 **Appealing to Mythos**

To hear a speaker appeal to mythos, access and read or listen to American labor leader Cesar Chavez's 1984 address to the Commonwealth Club. Chavez often appealed to mythos to inspire and persuade his audiences. For example, he related the Mexican American mythos of pilgrimage, penance, and revolution to the fight for the rights of the poor. What cultural mythos can you identify in his speech?

### Web Connect 24.2 **Understanding Fallacies**

OneGoodMove.org explains some of the more common fallacies of reasoning. Choose three of the fallacies, click on their links, and read more about them. Where have you heard speakers use these fallacies? Why do audiences sometimes fall victim to a speaker's use of fallacies?

# Chapter 25 SPEAKING ON SPECIAL OCCASIONS

## Key Concepts

**acceptance speech** (478)
**commemorative speech** (474)
**introductory speech** (471)
**speech of award** (474)
**speech of tribute** (474)
**speech to entertain** (480)
**timing** (481)

## Practicing the Public Dialogue Activities

### PPD Activity 25.1 **Design a Speech of Commemoration**

Choose a person, event, idea, or institution you would like to commemorate. In class, design a one-minute speech of commemoration. Begin by making a list of the accomplishments, qualities, or influences you wish to recognize. Select two or three that you feel you can talk about comfortably, and make them the main points of your speech. Decide how you will describe these characteristics, paying special attention to the language you will use. Be sure your descriptions and praise are specific, your speech expresses sincere appreciation and respect, and your facts are accurate. Now deliver this speech to your classmates and ask them to give you feedback. Did it follow the guidelines outlined in Chapter 25?

**PPD Activity 25.2 Design a Speech of Acceptance**
Design a one- to two-minute speech of acceptance for an imaginary award you've just received—be creative (and appropriate). In your speech, express your gratitude for receiving the award, acknowledge the purpose of the award, and recognize the people who helped you achieve the award. Conclude by explaining what you will do with the award and what your future plans are. Now deliver this speech to your classmates and ask them to give you feedback. Did it follow the guidelines outlined in Chapter 25?

**PPD Activity 25.3 Design a Speech to Entertain**
Identify three local or national issues you think would be appropriate topics for a speech to entertain. Is there a lighter side to these topics, something that makes them humorous or casts them in a humorous light? Now consider a possible audience for each topic. Be sure that what you find humorous about these topics will also be funny to the audience. Select one of the three topics you feel has the strongest potential to be a successful speech to entertain and prepare a thesis statement and an outline for it. Share these with your class and ask them to give you feedback. Does the class feel your speech would be appropriate and interesting for its intended audience?

## Interactive Video Activities

### Video Activity 25.1

Watch student speaker Tara Flanagan share what is unique and special about her grandfather in a commemorative speech. (Her preparation outline appears in Chapter 25.) After you watch the video, respond to analysis questions and compare your answers to those provided by the author.

### Video Activity 25.2

To see examples of another common type of commemorative speech, a speech given at a memorial service, use your online resources to access videos of Professor Nikki Giovanni's inspiring convocation address at the memorial held for the victims of the shootings at Virginia Tech and Oprah Winfrey's eulogy for civil rights activist Rosa Parks. After you watch the videos, respond to analysis questions and compare your answers to those provided by the author.

### Video Activity 25.3

Watch Tara Flanagan's speech commemorating her grandfather. As you watch the speech, consider what examples she used to give her audience a sense of what her grandfather was like, how well she described the specific characteristics that made him special to her, and how vivid her language was in conveying what kind of person he was. After you watch the video, respond to analysis questions and compare your answers to those provided by the author.

## Web Connect Resources

**Web Connect 25.1 Tips for Making a Wedding Toast**

WeddingVendors.com provides advice about giving a common type of commemorative speech, a wedding toast.

**Web Connect 25.2 YouTube Acceptance Speeches**

To see examples of acceptance speeches for all types of occasions, access YouTube.com. When you get to the website, search on "acceptance speeches." Which of these speeches appeal to you the most? Why? Which ones followed the guidelines suggested in Chapter 25?

**Web Connect 25.3 The President Makes Fun of Himself**

Politicians often use humor to address (or deflect) issues for particular audiences. Access the White House archives website to read an example of President George W. Bush using humor at the 2001 Radio and Television Correspondents' Dinner. Why did President Bush use humor in this speech? What was the effect of his humor?

**Web Connect 25.4 Colbert Makes Fun of the President**

Humor is also often used in speeches to criticize politicians. A good example is the speech comedian and satirist Stephen Colbert gave at the 2006 White House Correspondents' Association Dinner. Why did Colbert use humor in this speech? What was the effect of his humor?

# Chapter 26 SPEAKING IN SMALL GROUPS

## Key Concepts

**agenda** (496)
**brainstorming** (495)
**groupthink** (495)
**meeting** (496)
**oral report** (491)
**panel discussion** (492)
**problem-solving session** (494)
**reflective thinking method** (494)
**small group** (489)
**small group speaking** (489)
**symposium** (493)
**team presentation** (493)

## Practicing the Public Dialogue Activities

**PPD Activity 26.1 Design a Group Presentation Speech**
In class, divide into four different small groups. Select a topic about a current issue of interest on your campus or in your local community. Assign each group one of the following small group speaking formats: a panel discussion, a symposium, a team presentation, a problem-solving session, or a meeting. Following the guidelines presented in this chapter, design a thirty-minute small group presentation on the topic you've chosen. After your presentation is planned and organized, elect one person from your group to give an oral report to the class describing your presentation. As a class, discuss the strengths, weaknesses, and ethical aspects of each type of small group presentation planned by the groups in your class. Which formats best get at the heart of your topic while remaining ethical and why?

PART II

# TOPIC AND AUDIENCE

## CIVIC ENGAGEMENT IN ACTION

### Trespassers Welcome

UNIVERSITY OF NEW ENGLAND (AUSTRALIA) PUBLIC AFFAIRS

The life story of Aboriginal philosopher and educator Jack Beetson reads like a rags-to-riches story. The son of a Wongaibon mother and an Ngemba father, he was kicked out of school at thirteen and got into trouble with the police. After spending a few years working in various unfulfilling jobs, he became a street kid in Sydney, Australia. As he neared thirty, he decided to continue his education and started attending Tranby Aboriginal College, an alternative learning environment for adult Aboriginal students. He stuck around, and several years later, he became the school's executive director. And in 2001, the Year of Dialogue among Civilizations, the United Nations presented him with an Unsung Hero Award, making him one of only twelve people in the world to receive this honor.

Today, Beetson lives on his farm, the Linga Longa Philosophy Farm, in New South Wales. A product of Beetson's lifelong efforts to bring indigenous and nonindigenous people together, the farm's workshops and forums provide a rare opportunity for people of all cultures to come together to explore their identities and differences in a friendly, informal environment. He and his wife, Shani, began the farm "so that nonindigenous Australia wouldn't have the excuse that 'there is nowhere we can go to find out'" about indigenous culture. So welcoming is Beetson that he has said he'd like to put up a "Trespassers Welcome" sign on the front gate, in the hopes that people will feel free to stop by for a conversation.

A well-respected community leader, Beetson also travels extensively, speaking out about compassion, justice, and self-determination for Aboriginal and indigenous peoples. In addition, he encourages other Aboriginals to share their culture and experiences with people in an effort to come to a mutual understanding. One of his latest endeavors is to use Aboriginal culture, philosophy, and

**You Can Get Involved**

Increase your own cultural awareness by accessing **Web Connect P.II.1: Cultural Awareness in Action** at your Premium Website for *Invitation to Public Speaking Handbook*. Use this resource to explore various cultural groups, ethnic and otherwise, and to gain an understanding of what people in these groups want to share about themselves with others.

## CIVIC ENGAGEMENT IN ACTION continued

**Skills & Confidence**
Web Connect P.II.1

ceremony to help at-risk young people embrace their indigenous heritage and reconcile with nonindigenous people. Summing up his philosophy and approach, he says, "I share this particularly with young people who come out here who are living on the street... There's not a person on the planet who's better than you are, but always remember you're no better than anybody else either. That's how I've tried to live my life."[1]

# TOPIC AND AUDIENCE

CHAPTER 5

# Your Speech Topic and Purpose



*In this chapter, you will learn to*

- Identify how context influences your speaking goals
- Choose a speech topic whether you decide to speak, are asked to speak, or are required to speak
- Develop clear statements of purpose for your speech
- Develop the thesis statement of your speech

In 2001, students from twenty-seven colleges and universities gathered in Wisconsin for the Wingspread Summit on Student Civic Engagement. The students were invited to discuss student political and civic engagement and to explore what motivated them to speak out and get involved in their local communities. The summit was called because, although students have been volunteering more than ever in recent years, they are often described as apathetic and disengaged from civic life. However, their voices tell us otherwise. They are, in fact, very engaged and have a strong desire to speak out on issues that are important to them.

Wingspread participants agreed that what motivated them was a recognition of the uniqueness of other people and a desire to promote inclusiveness. Many of the students were involved with more than one issue. For example, one student participated in the public dialogue by organizing students against sweatshops, lobbying her state legislature to replace the Native American mascot at her school, and volunteering to teach English as a second language to new immigrants.[1]

However you use public speaking skills, this chapter will help you select interesting and relevant topics for your speeches. It will also help you determine the best way to frame a topic so that you fulfill your speaking purpose, or accomplish what you want with your speech.

Successful public speaking is usually the result of careful planning rather than any so-called natural speaking ability. Although we sometimes find ourselves in front of audiences without much advance notice, we are more likely to speak on topics we care about after we've had time to prepare our ideas. Careful planning before we speak helps us choose a speech topic and then narrow it with a specific purpose and thesis statement to accommodate one of the three speaking contexts: when we decide to speak, when we have been asked to speak, and when we are required to speak.

## Goals for Different Speaking Contexts

The three basic reasons for speaking in public are (1) because we decide we must speak out about a matter of importance, (2) because we are asked to speak about our experiences or expertise, and (3) because we are required to speak in class or at work. Recognizing our context for speaking publicly helps us define and focus on our topic and our goal.

### Deciding to Speak

The most common reason for speaking is a decision to speak about an issue because it is so important or our experience is so relevant. This is also perhaps the most powerful reason people become public speakers.

Consider the story of Lois Gibbs, who, prior to 1978, described herself as a "typical American woman" with a "typical American family" living in a "typical American town." When Gibbs learned that 20,000 tons of toxic chemicals were buried beneath her home and those of her neighbors in the Love Canal section of Niagara Falls, New York, she decided to speak out.

The hazards of dioxin—the chemical poisoning her community and causing numerous illnesses, birth defects, and miscarriages in the families that lived there—were of such importance that Gibbs began giving speeches. Over a thirty-year period, she spoke about hazardous wastes and environmental activism to neighbors, friends, and homeowners. Gibbs delivered speeches to city planners, legislators, and other government officials. She even traveled internationally to speak and was a guest on a national television talk show. Gibbs is credited with bringing the issue of hazardous waste disposal to public attention and pressuring public officials to take responsibility for their actions and decisions.

When she first began to give speeches, Gibbs says she was nervous. She described herself as a "typical housewife" whose biggest decision had been "what color wallpaper to use" in her kitchen. She describes her first speaking experiences as "intimidating" attempts to understand the "jibber jabber" of officials who did not want her nosing around. She was self-conscious and everything "seemed to come out wrong."[2] After several years of speaking, she recognized her evolution as a speaker: "Fifty or sixty people came out [for a rally].... I stood up and shouted: 'Do you want out?' and they shouted back, '*Yes!*'...It was exhilarating to be in touch with the crowd in that way." Gibbs encourages others to find "the courage to change the way the government works" because, she says, "for things to change, the truth has to be understood by a large group of people who then use this knowledge to fuel their efforts to win justice."[3]

Today, people often view mass media as the voice of the public, forgetting that we still can and do insert our own voices into public discussions. We decide to speak on many occasions. In educational settings, we give class presentations and participate in student government. In social gatherings, we offer toasts and congratulations, or we debate current issues. In business and professional meetings, we discuss ideas and create plans. And in community forums, we speak about issues like the environment, population growth, education, and the like.

**Skills & Confidence** Web Connect 5.1

When people decide to speak, they generally speak about issues central to their lives and well-being. To decide to speak publicly is to decide that you can offer an audience important knowledge or a valuable perspective.

## Being Asked to Speak

To be asked to speak is probably the most flattering context for a public speaker. When we are asked to speak, we are recognized as experts, or at least as someone who has information others want. It can be exciting to think about sharing our experiences and knowledge with other people.

Ryan White was only a child when he was asked to speak and share his experiences with others. White, a hemophiliac, had received a blood transfusion at the age of thirteen that changed his life: The blood-clotting agent Hemofil contained the HIV/AIDS virus, and he became infected. In 1985, the Kokomo, Indiana, school superintendent banned him from attending the local middle school. After two years of protests and school boycotts by parents and children, court orders and injunctions that returned White to school and pulled him out again, and continual health problems, White and his family moved out of town. Shy about speaking out publicly and mistrustful of being in the spotlight, White was selective about speaking engagements. When he was sixteen, reporters described a typical speaking tour:

> "Are you afraid of dying?" asks a student at Boys Town [in Omaha]. "No," Ryan says. "If I were worried about dying, I'd die. I'm not afraid, I'm just not ready yet. I want to go to Indiana University." ... "What was it like in Kokomo?" a girl asks.... "A lot of people would back away from me on the street," Ryan says. "They'd run from me. Maybe I would have been afraid of AIDS too, but I wouldn't have been mean about it." ... Afterward, a reporter asks Ryan what was the worst thing about Kokomo. "I had no friends," Ryan says. "I was lonely. All I wanted was to go to school and fit in."
>
> White explained, "It's embarrassing.... I'm helping people, I think, and I don't want people treated like me. But now I just want to be like everyone else."[4] As a result of his willingness to share his experiences, the public education process about HIV/AIDS improved. In one of his last public appearances, in 1990, White appeared in Los Angeles with former president and first lady Ronald and Nancy Reagan to celebrate the establishment of the Ryan White National Program for AIDS Education by Athletes and Entertainers for Kids.[5] Born in 1971, White died on April 8, 1990. He never made it to Indiana University, but because of the national exposure he received and his willingness to speak publicly about his experiences, White has been described as "one of the nation's most persuasive advocates for AIDS patients' rights" and a "miracle of humanity."[6]

As you move through life, you may be asked to speak in educational settings, at service clubs, or at formal or professional gatherings. If you are asked to speak publicly, it is because people want to hear your views and ideas. But remember that although you may be considered an expert, expertise in a particular subject area does not always guarantee you are an expert at giving speeches. You'll be a more successful speaker if you follow the principles of speech preparation discussed in this book.

## Being Required to Speak

**Speaking at Work**

*At work, people are often required to speak or are asked to speak. For example, you may be required to give updates on your work at a monthly status meeting. Or you may be asked to train other employees in a procedure that you've mastered. It's not quite as common to decide to speak at work, but certainly some people decide, for example, to inform their colleagues about new industry trends or to persuade them to change a company policy.*

Occasionally, people become public speakers out of necessity. Either our jobs require us to speak, we take a course that has public speaking as a component, or we discover we are in a situation where we have no choice but to speak out. Although these can be challenging moments, when people are required to speak, they often discover they have the potential to make profound contributions to the public dialogue.

In the 1950s, Senator Joseph McCarthy campaigned ruthlessly against what he saw as a communist threat to the United States. McCarthy's efforts caught the attention of the country, and by 1953, this senator from Wisconsin had reached the height of his political power. Even President Eisenhower and his aides and cabinet officers seemed eager to please McCarthy, and McCarthy's Senate colleagues knew and feared his influence. However, in 1954, the national sentiment began to change, and people began to challenge McCarthy's abuse of power and attacks on innocent people. McCarthy's reign came to a close in the Army-McCarthy hearings when he relentlessly charged a young law clerk with communist affiliations. Joseph Welch, the military special investigator, was required to speak in response to the accusations against the law clerk. Here is what he said to McCarthy:

> Until this moment, Senator, I think I never really gauged your cruelty or your recklessness.... Let us not assassinate this lad further, Senator. You have done enough. Have you no sense of decency, sir, at long last? Have you left no sense of decency?

**Skills & Confidence** Web Connect 5.2

At the close of Welch's speech, the hearing room burst into applause, and McCarthy, "flushed and stunned, sat in silence."[7]

When you are required to speak, you must often follow strict guidelines. For example, your boss may ask you to give a presentation at a meeting and specify the topic, the amount of time, and the speaking goal. In a public speaking class, you may be asked to give an informative speech that is three minutes long, cites two sources, and includes a visual aid. Although we may not like required public speaking, learning to give speeches in a public speaking course can be invaluable as preparation for other speaking contexts. In a public speaking course, you are given structure and guidance that can help you improve your presentational skills and participate in the public dialogue.

**Skills & Confidence**
PPD Activity 5.1
Web Connect 5.3

These three contexts—deciding, being asked, and being required to speak—are the reasons people enter the public dialogue. Once you recognize why you are speaking, you can turn your attention to selecting and narrowing your speech topic and deciding on your purpose for speaking.

## Choosing Your Speech Topic

Your **speech topic** is the subject of your speech. Selecting a topic for a speech can be creative and energizing. With a little systematic thought and inventive organization, you may come up with a wide range of interesting speech topics. The steps described in this section will help you find relevant and interesting topics for your required speeches.

When you decide or are asked to speak, your topic is usually predetermined, and your task is to make sure you understand your topic fully. You can do this by asking yourself several questions, which are discussed at the end of this section.

### The Classroom Setting

Before you can select an appropriate and interesting topic for an assigned speech, you must consider the requirements of your assignment:

- *Preselected purpose.* An instructor usually tells you to give a particular type of speech, such as a speech to inform or persuade. You must select a topic compatible with the purpose.
- *Time limit.* Class size determines speech length; your instructor wants to make sure everyone in the class has time to give their speeches. Classroom speeches often last only a few minutes, and you may be penalized for going over time. You must select and narrow your topic to satisfy the assignment's time limits.
- *Required components.* You may be required to cite a specific number of outside sources, use visual aids, incorporate a specific style of language, or use a particular organizational pattern. The structure of an assigned speech often influences topic selection.

- *Instructor as an audience.* You give your classroom speeches to an instructor who is already a skilled public speaker. You must select a stimulating topic that your instructor, who has listened to many other speeches, will appreciate.
- *Class members as an audience.* Your classmates may become the best audience for you as a beginning public speaker. They're also learning the ropes of public speaking, and they'll appreciate your efforts. But they can also be a challenge because they may be interested in topics your instructor doesn't want to hear about. They're also searching for interesting topics, so try to avoid commonly used topics.

So how do you select a manageable, interesting, and dynamic topic for your required speeches? You will discover that you have a wealth of usable ideas once you organize your thoughts about who you are, what you know, and what issues and events capture your own attention.

## Choosing a Topic When You Are Required to Speak

One basic way to select a topic for a required speech is to make a list of your interests and give a speech about one of them. In this section, you'll discover how to come up with unique and exciting slants on familiar topics.

In a public speaking classroom, the first step to selecting a topic is to list all the requirements of the speech assignment. Write down your speech requirements at the top of your computer-screen page or a piece of paper. Your assignment requirements might look like this:

informative purpose
four minutes long
three or four sources
one statistic
one of the following: metaphor, analogy, narrative, or alliteration; inclusive language

The second step is to match your interests or expertise to these requirements.

*Matching your interests to a speaking assignment.* Before you can match your interests to a particular assignment, you must determine what they are. First, make three lists: (1) what you like to do, (2) what you like to talk about, and (3) what you would like to know more about.

The first list, what you like to do, can include serious activities as well as playful or silly ones. Here is a college student's list of activities paired with examples of speech topics that could come from them:

| Activity | Speech Topic |
|---|---|
| swim, run, cycle | the history of marathon running |
| spend time with my friends | gender differences in friendship styles |
| play soccer, volleyball, tennis, and Frisbee golf | how to play Frisbee golf |
| coach children in sports during the summer | how Olympic swimmers or runners train |
| ski, roller-blade, and hike | who invented roller-blades |
| get good grades | the relationship between grades and annual income |
| watch television and movies | the longest-running television sitcom |
| stay up late | medical research on optimal sleeping patterns |
| work with computers | the first chat room on the Web |
| eat pizza, hamburgers, anything barbecued, and some vegetables | the origins of pizza |

To make the list of what you like to talk about, ask yourself the following questions:

- When do I find myself participating in discussions?
- When do I feel like I have a lot to say about an issue but don't speak up?
- What topics do I raise in conversations?
- What topics do I repeatedly return to or seek more information about?

For example, if you love to talk about basketball, you could turn this broad topic into a dynamic speech by going beyond the obvious. What do you love about the sport? Is it the players' skill, the strategy of the game, the politics of athletics, or the behaviors of sports fans? You could fashion an informative, invitational, or persuasive speech out of any of these topics:

the evolution of basketball as a sport

the advantages and disadvantages of starting children in the sport at a young age

the money behind the game

the balance between athletic talent and game strategy

the role of sports fans in supporting individual teams

Issues, events, people, and ideas you are curious about also make excellent speech topics. You could give a speech that informs others of a particular event, or you could persuade them to participate in that event. If you are intrigued by a famous person, you could give a commemorative or informative speech about that person's life and accomplishments. If you are curious about a place, an idea, an object, or an animal, you could explore it with others in an informative or invitational speech. Speeches that grow out of a speaker's curiosity often capture the attention, interest, and curiosity of an audience as well.

*Matching your expertise to a speech assignment.* Almost everyone is an expert in some area of life. Some people are experts in obvious ways, such as playing a musical instrument, painting, or computer programming. Other people are experts in less obvious ways. They may have an unfailing sense of direction, know the right gift to buy for any occasion, or tell jokes that make people laugh. Dynamic speech topics can come from your own skills and talents, even ones you take for granted. Consider the following examples:

If you have a great sense of direction, you could give an informative speech on traveling and the five most important ways to avoid getting lost.

If cooking ethnic cuisines is your hobby, you could give an informative speech on the differences between traditional Mexican and Spanish foods.

If you are fluent in American Sign Language, you could give a speech persuading your audience to learn a second language.

If you come from a family of artists, you might give a speech inviting your audience to support the arts.

You can identify areas in which you may be considered an expert by asking yourself the following questions:

- What comes naturally to me?
- What runs in my family?
- Do I often get compliments when I do a particular thing?
- Do others repeatedly ask me to take the lead, take care of some situation, or solve a problem for them?
- Have I had special training or lessons?
- Have I spent years studying, practicing, or doing something?
- Do I have degrees, certifications, licenses, or other markers of my accomplishments?

You might also have expertise because of events you've witnessed or an environment you've been in. Consider these possibilities:

- Did you live or grow up in another country?
- Did you play sports in high school or college?

## SPEECH TIPS

### USING YOUR EXPERIENCES AS SPEECH TOPICS

- Be certain you can talk about the experiences easily without getting upset or revealing more than you are comfortable with.
- Although you might know a lot about a topic, you should still research it to discover aspects about which you might be unaware.

- Is there something about your family that is unique or unusual?
- Have you had unexpected or momentous experiences in your life?
- Have you been exposed to other cultures, religions, and philosophies?

**Speaking across DIFFERENCES**

**Your cultural background or interactions with other cultures can generate a number of interesting topics that are relevant to the public dialogue. For example, did you spend part of your childhood in a foreign country or have you traveled extensively? Speaking about these experiences can help audience members understand aspects of cultures that are very different from their own.**

### Brainstorming

**Brainstorming** is the process of generating ideas randomly and uncritically, without attention to logic, connections, or relevance. This process requires you to free-associate rather than plan, and it can be an effective tool for coming up with speech topics in required speaking situations. You can use this technique by yourself, in pairs, or in groups.

There are several ways to approach brainstorming: by free association, by clustering, by categories, and by technology.

*Brainstorming by free association.* Brainstorming can be as unstructured as sitting at your desk with a pencil and paper—or at your computer with a blank screen—and recording all ideas that come to your mind.

Brainstorming on a computer is especially effective because many people can type faster than they can write in longhand. When you record your ideas quickly, your thoughts will also flow quickly. You might start free-associating before turning on the computer so you will not have the pressure of filling up a blank page. At other times, seeing your ideas on

SPEECH TIPS

### SUCCESSFUL BRAINSTORMING

- Let your thoughts go where they will. Don't censor yourself or others. Allow all ideas, even those that seem trivial or odd.
- Write down your ideas quickly. Don't worry about spelling or punctuation, and abbreviate whenever you can.
- Keep your list handy over the course of several days, and add to it as new thoughts come to you.

the screen may stimulate your thinking and spur additional ideas.[8] After a minute of free-associating, your list might look like this:

> hands, keyboard, letters, movement, running, wind, kites, children, play, laughter, skinned knees, Band-Aids, nurses, hospitals, sterile, feral cats, tiger, cougars, wilderness, encroachment, farming, ranching, cows, cowboys, rodeos, circus, clowns, entertainment, containment, buckets, garage, car, war, peace, hostility, conflict, harm, warm, cold, snow skiing, skis, lifts, chairs, dining rooms, meals, holidays, families, celebration, gifts

A free association list can go on and on until you run out of ideas. When you're trying to come up with a speech topic, try to spend at least several minutes brainstorming by free association to generate as many ideas as possible. Once you've compiled your list, explore it to determine if one of your ideas might be an appropriate speech topic. The free association list here could generate the following interesting speech topics:

> the inventor of the Band-Aid
>
> what to do when you encounter a feral cat
>
> different kinds of clowns
>
> how different countries celebrate holidays or the starts of new seasons

If brainstorming by free association doesn't generate the kinds of topics you think might make an interesting speech, other brainstorming techniques might help.

*Brainstorming by clustering.* Clustering is a visual way to brainstorm. Write down an idea in the center of a piece of paper and

**FIGURE 5.1 Cluster diagram**
Scuba diving, the central idea, branches out to many additional ideas. Brainstorming by clustering gives some structure to the brainstorming process without limiting the possibilities too much.

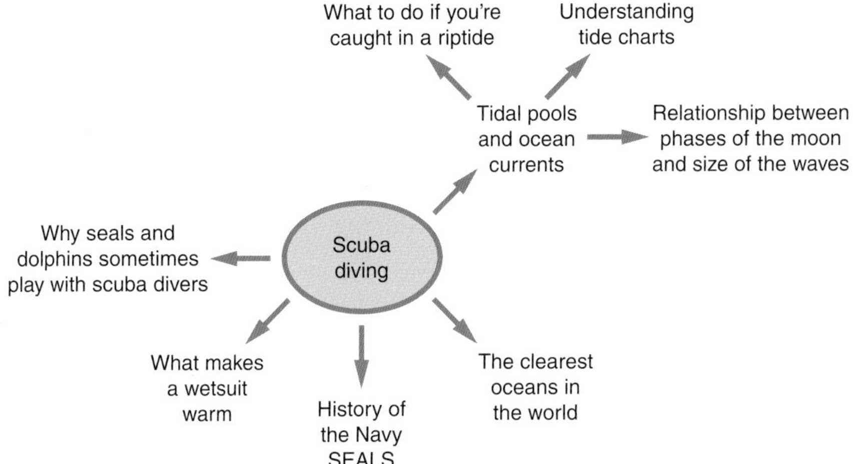


**Source:** Cengage Learning

then draw four or five lines extending from it. At the ends of these lines, write down other ideas that relate to your first idea. Then extend lines from these new ideas to even more ideas. Let's take a look at Jeret's clustering diagram. He began scuba diving at a very young age, so he used this as his general idea and developed the cluster of ideas shown in Figure 5.1.

*Brainstorming by categories.* Most speeches given in public speaking classrooms are about concepts, events, natural phenomena, objects, people, places, plans and policies, problems, and processes. Brainstorming by these categories is an excellent way to generate a speech topic, and it provides more structure than free association or clustering. To brainstorm by categories, list the following nine categories on your computer screen or a piece of paper. Then list five or six topics under each heading:

| **Concepts** | **Events** | **Natural phenomena** |
|---|---|---|
| world peace | Hurricane Katrina | aurora borealis |
| white supremacy | Sept. 11, 2001 | avalanches |
| interstellar travel | 4th of July | snow |
| immigration | quinceañera | tsunamis |
| theme dining | World AIDS Day | floods |
| cohousing | Super Bowl | earthquakes |

| **Objects** | **People** | **Places** |
|---|---|---|
| guns | Bill Gates | Mexico |
| kayaks | Barack Obama | India |
| backpacks | Hillary Clinton | my hometown |
| iPhones | Will Smith | Italy |
| coral reefs | Sarah Palin | Japan |
| laptop computers | Oprah Winfrey | Amazon rain forest |
| **Plans and policies** | **Problems** | **Processes** |
| homeland security | national budget | making wine |
| socialized medicine | global warming | suntanning |
| decreased crime | terrorism | installing a new faucet |
| eliminating unemployment | sexism | negotiating |
| quality public education | racism | developing film |

If none of the words you write down immediately strikes you as a good speech topic, select one or two and use free association or clustering to narrow your scope, generate new ideas, or frame a topic in a way that is interesting and fits the requirements of your assignment.

Similarly, if none of your brainstormed topics catches your interest, link several of them together. Can you find a connection among Mexico, India, and your hometown? What about these locations and tsunamis or earthquakes? How about laptops, global warming, and theme dining? Linking any of these topics, randomly or with purpose, gives you additional opportunities to develop interesting speech topics.

*Brainstorming with technology.* You can use technology in a number of ways to find a suitable speech topic. If you have access to the Internet, you can discover possible topics by browsing a search engine's subject index. By going to the directory pages of Yahoo! (dir.yahoo.com) or Google (www.google.com/dirhp), you can explore an array of topics or click a general subject and link to more specific subtopics until you find one that interests you and fits the requirements of your speech assignment.

Libraries also provide many online indexes for journals, newspapers, magazines, and the like. Browse through the *Reader's Guide to Periodical Literature,* InfoTrac College Edition, *The New York Times Index,* or subject-specific indexes about medicine, physics, science, or women's studies. (In Chapter 8, you'll explore how to use these types of resources more fully.)

**SPEECH Checklist**

## Narrowing Your Topic

When you decide or are asked to speak, take a moment to ask yourself, or the person who's asked you to speak, the following questions:

### About the Topic

- [ ] If you have decided to speak, what *specific* topic do you want to talk about?
- [ ] If you have been asked to speak, what *specific* topic does your audience want to hear about?

### About the Time Constraints

- [ ] Can you discuss the topic in the time allowed, or do you need to narrow or broaden your scope?
- [ ] Is there some aspect of the topic that you may be better able to cover in the time allowed?

### About the Audience

- [ ] Who is your audience?
- [ ] What is your relationship to them?
- [ ] Will your audience see you as qualified to speak about the topic? If not, could you change the topic or strengthen your qualifications in some way?
- [ ] If you have decided to speak, why are you qualified to speak about the topic?
- [ ] If you have been asked to speak, why are you qualified to speak about the topic?

## Narrowing Your Topic When You Are Asked to or Decide to Speak

When we decide to speak, we are generally responding to an issue we are interested in or concerned about. When we are asked to speak, we are usually given a topic that a specific audience wants to hear about. Even though our speech topics in these contexts are predetermined, we must be sure that we clearly understand exactly what our topic is and what's expected of us as a speaker.

The questions in the Speech Checklist will help you focus and narrow your topic so it is appropriate for your speaking situation. They'll also help you better understand why you want to speak or why

Skills & Confidence
PPD Activity 5.2
Web Connect 5.4

you've been asked to speak and what you're most qualified and prepared to speak about.

Whether you take inventory of your interests and skills, use brainstorming techniques, decide what you are motivated to speak about, or are given a topic to speak about, recognize that you are capable of generating any number of speech topics. With a little bit of creativity and organization, you can come up with speech topics that are interesting and relevant to the public dialogue.

## Articulating Your Speech Purpose

Each type of speaking has a different goal: to inform, invite, persuade, introduce, commemorate, or accept. These are the goals we focus on in this chapter. Note that as a speaker in or as part of a small group, your speaking goal generally falls into one of these six categories. We'll save the discussion of small group speaking's unique components until Chapter 26.

Speaking goals can be explained in terms of general purposes and specific purposes. The **general purpose** of a speech depends on the type of speaking: to inform; to invite, to persuade, to introduce, to commemorate, or to accept. The **specific purpose** is a focused statement that identifies exactly what a speaker wants to accomplish with a speech. Let's take a look at how you use each of these purposes to organize your thoughts about your speeches.

### General Purposes

Suppose your instructor asks you to speak about organic farming. Without knowing your purpose for the speech, it could be difficult to know where to begin. Do you describe organic farming, what it is, and who practices it (informative)? Do you ask your audience to consider the impact of organic farming on the environment and the average family's grocery bills (invitational)? Do you attempt to convince your classmates that organic farming is the most efficient type of farming (persuasive)? Do you commemorate a pioneer in organic farming or an important event in its history (commemorative)? Your first step toward answering these questions is to determine the overall goal for your speech, or your *general purpose*:

*To inform:* describe, clarify, explain, define

*To invite:* explore, discuss, exchange, understand

*To persuade:* change, shape, influence, motivate

*To introduce:* acquaint, present, familiarize

*To commemorate:* praise, honor, pay tribute

*To accept:* receive an award, express gratitude

Notice that each of these overall goals is different. For example, the goal of acquainting is different from the goal of praising, which is different from the goal of clarifying. So by determining your general purpose, you begin to find a focus for your speech.

## Specific Purposes

Once you determine your general purpose, you must then determine what exactly you want to communicate to your audience, or your *specific purpose.* A specific purpose states exactly what you want to accomplish in the speech and helps you narrow its focus. To understand the importance of a speech's specific purpose, consider Ashley's speech preparation.

For her service learning assignment, Ashley tutored fourth-graders in an after-school math homework program. This experience prompted her interest in several topics, including the Pledge of Allegiance. She decided that her general speaking purpose was to persuade her classmates to change their views on the Pledge. But how exactly did she want them to change? What did she want to persuade them to do or think? If she hadn't figured this out, she could have gone in circles as she prepared her speech and researched supporting material she didn't need.

Instead, Ashley developed a specific-purpose statement. First, she identified her **behavioral objective,** the action she wanted her audience to take at the end of her speech. After some thought, she decided that she wanted her classmates to support changes to the Pledge. She wrote on a piece of paper, "I want my classmates to believe differently about the Pledge of Allegiance." This purpose was still fairly broad, but it was more focused than her general purpose of persuading her classmates to change.

Ashley's next step was to narrow her behavioral objective even further. She defined what she meant by "believe differently." Based on her experiences in the public school and on her research, she increased her understanding of what the Pledge means, why it should be recited by children in school, and what changes she would make to it. After some thought, Ashley realized that more than just wanting her classmates to "believe differently," she wanted them to adopt her views about the Pledge.

Specifically, she wanted to persuade them to support the Pledge, but with modifications. Thus, her specific-purpose statement was "I want to persuade my audience that the Pledge should be revised and then continue to be recited in schools." With this specific idea of what she wanted to communicate to her audience, she could focus her research and the development of her speech.

**TABLE 5.1 General and Specific Speaking Purposes**

| GENERAL PURPOSE | SPECIFIC PURPOSE |
|---|---|
| **To inform:** | To inform my audience of the services offered by our campus counseling center.<br>To inform my audience of the process of planting, harvesting, and preparing organic produce. |
| **To invite:** | To invite my audience to consider the merits of the three martial arts experts who have interviewed for our school.<br>To invite my audience to consider the implications of turning part of our community park into organic gardening space. |
| **To persuade:** | To persuade my audience to use the services offered by our campus counseling center.<br>To persuade my audience to buy organic produce. |
| **To introduce:** | To introduce my audience to Maria Rodale, the editor of *Organic Gardening*.<br>To introduce my audience to today's schedule for our tour of the Martial Arts Center. |
| **To commemorate:** | To commemorate for my audience my grandparents and the values they taught me during my summers on their organic farm.<br>To commemorate for my audience Wong Fei Hung, one of the first well-known masters of the martial arts. |
| **To accept:** | To accept an award from my employer for our highly successful peer counseling program.<br>To accept the city council's "Outstanding Community Project" award for my efforts to establish organic community gardens in my neighborhood. |

Table 5.1 shows more examples of general and specific purposes. Notice the differences between the general purposes and the specific purposes. From the six general purposes, you can generate specific purposes for many different speeches.

When you state your specific speaking purpose, state it clearly and remain audience centered. Consider the following guidelines.

*State your specific speaking purpose clearly.* Begin your specific-purpose statements with the infinitive phrase stating your general purpose: *to inform, to invite, to persuade, to introduce, to commemorate,* or *to accept.* Beginning with your general purpose makes clear what you hope to accomplish with your speech. Compare the following correct and incorrect statements of purpose:

| **Correct** | **Incorrect** |
|---|---|
| To introduce Master Cho and three of his most noteworthy accomplishments to my audience. | Master Cho's talent |
| To inform my audience of the history of martial arts in the United States. | I'm going to talk about martial arts. |
| To invite my coworkers to consider supporting local community organic gardens. | Supporting community gardening |
| To persuade my audience that practicing martial arts is an excellent form of exercise. | The martial arts are good for you. |

Notice that the incorrect statements don't indicate the overall goal of the speech. Although the incorrect statements may seem to leave greater room for a speaker's creativity, they are too vague to be of much help when preparing a speech. For example, the statement "Master Cho's talent" is a speech topic rather than a statement of purpose. The statement "I'm going to talk about martial arts" won't help the speaker narrow the focus on a particular aspect of martial arts and prepare a manageable speech. Nor will it give an audience a sense of what direction the speech will take. Similarly, the phrase "Supporting community gardening" doesn't indicate the speaker's speech goal. In contrast, each of the correct statements provides a focused, solid framework from which to prepare a speech, and each lets the audience know what to expect in the speech.

*Keep your audience in the forefront of your mind.* Your specific purpose should clearly acknowledge the presence of an audience.

## SPEECH **TIPS**

### STICKING TO YOUR PURPOSE

As you begin to organize your materials about your speech, write your general and specific statements of purpose at the top of all your research notes. Like any good road map, clear statements of purpose help you select and navigate the path toward putting the final touches on your presentation.

To this end, include the words *my audience* or a more specific synonym in the statement of the specific purpose. Compare the following correct and incorrect statements of purpose:

| **Correct** | **Incorrect** |
|---|---|
| To inform my audience of the process of planting, harvesting, and preparing organic produce. | The methods of growing organic produce |
| To invite my coworkers to consider altering our current training program. | Shall we alter our training methods? |
| To persuade my audience of the importance of growing and eating organic fruit. | We should grow and eat organic fruit. |
| To commemorate for my audience Johnny Appleseed as he appears in different cultures. | Johnny Appleseed is a myth that exists in many cultures. |
| To accept and express my gratitude to the city council and my neighbors for the "Outstanding Community Project" award. | Thank you for this "Outstanding Community Project" award. |

Skills & Confidence PPD Activity 5.3

Notice how the correct examples encourage the speaker to reflect on the makeup of the audience in ways that the incorrect examples do not. The phrases "my audience," "the city council and my neighbors," and "my coworkers" encourage the speaker to focus on a specific group of people with particular traits and characteristics.

## Stating Your Thesis

The final step in the initial speech preparation process is the thesis statement, sometimes called the *central idea.* A **thesis statement** summarizes in a single declarative sentence the main ideas, assumptions, or arguments you want to express in your speech.

The thesis statement adds focus to your specific purpose because in it you state, in a single sentence, the exact content of your speech. Note that the thesis statement is closely related to the specific purpose. Recall that the specific-purpose statement indicates what you want your audience to understand or do as a result of your speech. The thesis statement helps you accomplish this goal by allowing you to state in a single sentence the specific ideas you will cover in the speech. The thesis statement helps you identify the main ideas of your speech, which will become its main points (Chapter 10).

Let's look at some specific-purpose statements to see how they relate to thesis statements (see also Table 5.2 on page 86):

**Specific purpose:** To inform my audience of the different belts in the martial arts

This statement implies that it is useful to understand the different belt levels in the martial arts. To focus on a manageable aspect of this topic, the speaker must determine exactly what he wants the audience to know about the martial arts belt systems. His thesis statement might look like this:

**Thesis statement:** In the three most common schools of martial arts in the United States—judo, karate, and tae kwon do—the black belt is the most esteemed belt level among the slightly differing belt systems.

This thesis statement takes into account how much common knowledge there is about the martial arts as well as what people are most curious about. Additionally, the thesis statement previews two main points:

1. Judo, karate, and tae kwon do are the most common schools of martial arts in the United States.
2. Each school has a slightly different belt system, but the black belt is the most esteemed belt level in all three schools.

Consider a second specific purpose and thesis statement:

**Specific purpose:** To persuade my audience to eat healthy organic fruit

This statement makes the claim that organic fruit is good for you. To persuade your audience to eat it (what you want to accomplish), you must refine this statement to explain why eating organic fruit is good for you (what you will say to accomplish your goal). In explaining why, your thesis statement begins to take shape:

**Thesis statement:** Because organic fruit does not contain the dangerous chemicals found in nonorganic fruit, it is far healthier for people to eat and better for the environment.

This thesis statement indicates that the speech will have three main points:

1. Organic fruits do not contain dangerous chemicals.
2. Organic fruits are grown in ways that make them healthier to eat than nonorganic fruits.
3. Organic fruits are grown in ways that are safe for the environment.

**TABLE 5.2 General and Specific Purposes and Thesis Statement**

| | |
|---|---|
| INFORMATIVE SPEECH | |
| **General purpose:** | To inform |
| **Specific purpose:** | To inform my audience of the three most important ways to avoid getting lost while traveling |
| **Thesis statement:** | The three simple ways travelers can avoid getting lost are to carry maps, plan out the route beforehand, and ask directions from knowledgeable sources. |
| **General purpose:** | To inform |
| **Specific purpose:** | To inform my audience about where to seek shelter during a tornado |
| **Thesis statement:** | When a tornado strikes, seek shelter in a storm cellar, a fortified storm closet, or your bathtub. |
| INVITATIONAL SPEECH | |
| **General purpose:** | To invite |
| **Specific purpose:** | To invite my audience to consider supporting the arts in our community |
| **Thesis statement:** | The arts have played a very important role in my life, enhance the quality of life in any community, and may be something my audience wants to support. |
| **General purpose:** | To invite |
| **Specific purpose:** | To invite my audience to explore the pros and cons of retaining the death penalty in the United States |
| **Thesis statement:** | I'd like to describe the benefits and drawbacks of retaining the death penalty in the United States and then explore with my audience whether this punishment is still appropriate for serious crimes. |
| PERSUASIVE SPEECH | |
| **General purpose:** | To persuade |
| **Specific purpose:** | To persuade my audience to spay or neuter their pets |
| **Thesis statement:** | Spaying or neutering pets is easy and affordable, and it helps prevent having to put down thousands of unwanted kittens and puppies each year. |
| **General purpose:** | To persuade |
| **Specific purpose:** | To persuade my audience to learn a second language |
| **Thesis statement:** | When we learn a second language, not only do we learn to appreciate the culture of the people who speak that language, but we also increase our understanding of our own culture. |

**SPEECH Checklist**

## Topic, Purpose, and Thesis Statement

- ☐ What is my topic?
- ☐ What is my general purpose?
- ☐ What is my specific purpose?
- ☐ What is my thesis statement
- ☐ What are my main points

Some instructors like to divide a thesis statement into two sentences: one that states the thesis (the main idea) and one that lists the main points of the speech (the preview). (You can read a more detailed discussion of previews in Chapter 9.)

The clarity and focus you get from developing your thesis statement and main points will guide your research efforts and choice of supporting materials, your reasoning, and your organizational patterns (Parts IV, V, and VI). Note how the thesis statement, in combination with the specific statement of purpose, helped Ogenna Agbim identify the main points in her speech.

**Skills & Confidence**
PPD Activity 5.4
Video Activity 5.1
Video Activity 5.2
Web Connect 5.5

## STUDENT SPEECH

**with Commentary**

### *This Is Dedicated . . . : A Tribute to the Women of History*

*by Ogenna Agbim*

CENGAGE LEARNING

***Specific purpose:*** *To commemorate important women in history who have come before my generation.*

***Thesis statement:*** *Throughout history, women's struggle for equality has provided opportunities for women today, and the women of the past deserve our recognition.*

**Skills & Confidence**
Video Activity 5.3
Speech Studio 5.1

If you have been assigned a speech in your class, such as an introductory, narrative, or commemorative speech, you can use the following speech as a model. Go to your Premium Website for *Invitation to Public Speaking Handbook* to watch the video clip of Ogenna Agbim's commemorative speech. Ogenna gave this speech in an introductory public speaking class. The students' assignment was to give a two- to four-minute speech commemorating an important person or important people in their lives. Notice that even though this speech was required, Ogenna chose a topic that is different enough to keep her audience engaged and listening.

*INTRODUCTION*

This is dedicated to all the women out there who have gone through the struggle: You're not going through it alone; it's our time to shine. Ladies, don't you hang your heads low. I can see you're feeling bad because you're trying to make it on your own. Ladies, it seems everything for us has gone wrong, but if you believe in me, you will find bad times will pass you on. It's our time to shine. We've been down for much too long. But we have to combine, and we have to keep moving on. We have to combine, and we have to keep moving on.

*Commentary*

*Ogenna begins her speech with a dedication, setting a tone of optimism and recognition to catch her audience's attention. She also uses rhyming language ("pass you on," "much too long") and repetition ("We have to combine, and we have to keep moving on") for effect and emphasis.*

*BODY*

I want to ask every woman gathered here today to stand up. You, you, and you. My women in front, my women in the middle, and my women in back. If no one has told you, it's your time to shine. You've been down for much too long. For the last couple of hundred years, we women: what have we not endured? We've been slaves, we've been seen through the Earth's eyes in every way but our own. We've been told how to act, and how to behave, and what makes us beautiful, and what doesn't. Hundreds of years we've spent, and decades of years, fighting for equal pay and equal opportunities and voting rights. We've supported our men, and our families, our brothers and sisters. Through it all, we haven't been appreciated. We haven't been honored, both entirely appreciated and honored enough. And without crying a river still we stand. As you stand, you represent a priceless piece of the voice that was never heard. You stand for the opportunities missed. You stand for the oppression where our happy hearts were broken and for the things that make us who we are—and made us dismissed. For what you've been through for me, and for us all, I thank you. Without you today, where would we all be?

*By identifying the women in her speaking environment specifically as members of her audience, Ogenna makes the speech relevant to them.*

*Ogenna continues to draw her audience in by tracing some of women's experiences in history, giving specific examples. She also helps her audience listen to her speech by using interesting language, such as repetition and alliteration ("priceless piece," "happy hearts"), in a way that creates pleasing rhythms.*

Now for my ladies who took a stand, take a seat for the future. As I have said, it's our time to shine. Take a front seat and count your accomplishments. Take a seat and view the laws that have been passed because of women. Take a seat and watch every seed women have planted in the concrete grow into beautiful roses. Women, we salute you. We are proud of you. You are an inspiration. You are our mentors, you are our saviors, our motivation, and I commend you. Bessie Coleman, the first African American woman to fly a plane; Zora Neale Hurston, first African American woman graduate of Barnard College; and you, Eleanor Roosevelt, who broke the rules in 1933 for women to be allowed in press conferences; Rosa Parks; Toni Morrison: With so many other women to name, the branches you have built over time will forever give me light to shine. You have

*By using specific women in history as examples, Ogenna fulfills her specific purpose and supports the claims she made in her thesis statement that women throughout history have paved the way for women today and deserve to be commemorated.*

*Ogenna brings her speech to life by using similes ("small steps are like giants in history") that evoke interesting and poetic images.*

*As she reminds her audience of the significance of past accomplishments and brings herself back into the speech, Ogenna begins to bring her speech around full*

been oppressed but have risen as organization presidents, artists, dancers, and dreamers that have led your way and mine. Women, your small steps are like giants in history. Forever you will be a heroine to those you never thought you would touch, and you will be a heroine for saving us throughout the drowning madness.

*circle, transitioning from women of history to women of today.*

Women, you motivate me in this age to become a better woman, because without your contributions, today there may not have been a history for me. There may have been no gateway for me to college, and in music, in sports, in politics, and so very much more.

*Ogenna links her conclusion to her introduction by connecting her audience to the historical women she's commemorated, reminding her audience to "Keep your head held high. You're not going through it alone."*

*CONCLUSION*

Ladies, it is your time to shine. Your efforts never go unnoticed, at least not in my eyes. Your small impacts make a huge impact on us all, even if it's one body at a time. To my women out there, if you ever find yourself going through a struggle, remember to keep your head held high. You're not going through it alone. We have been down for much too long. But like Maya Angelou once said, "We rise, we rise, we rise." And from this day forward, it is our time to shine.

*Ogenna concludes her speech with a memorable quote by a famous woman of today, author and poet Maya Angelou, who is especially appropriate because she's written extensively about her own history.*

CHAPTER 6

# Your Audience and Speaking Environment



*In this chapter, you will learn to*

- Define what an audience is
- Conduct a demographic audience analysis
- Adapt to an audience that is both a group of diverse people and a unique community
- Identify the influence of a speaking environment on an audience
- Identify strategies for adapting to audience expectations for a speech

When you give a speech, you add your voice to the public dialogue. To engage in a **dialogue** is to exchange ideas and opinions with others. When you engage in the public dialogue, you recognize that the speaker and the audience are equally important; both have opinions, feelings, and beliefs. To be a successful public speaker, you must listen

**Speaking across DIFFERENCES**

**Approaching a speech from an audience-centered perspective is an effective way to ensure that your speech appeals to a diverse group of audience members.**

carefully to your audience before, during, and after your speech.

One of the most effective ways you can listen to your audience is by adopting an audience-centered perspective. To be **audience centered** is to acknowledge your audience by considering and listening to the unique, diverse, and common perspectives of its members before, during, and after your speech. Being audience centered does not mean you must compromise your message to appeal to your audience. Nor does it mean that you can use your knowledge of the audience to manipulate its members. You don't want to say only what your audience agrees with or wants to hear. Rather, being audience centered means you understand the positions and perspectives of your audience so you can craft an appropriate, listenable message.

In Chapter 4, you learned how to listen to your audience during a speech to better respond to their needs. In this chapter, you will build on those skills and learn how to best understand your audiences. You will explore what an audience is, why there are different types of audiences, how speaking environments affect audiences, and how you can apply what you learn about your audience and speaking environment to help others listen to your speech.

## What Is an Audience?

We often use the term *audience* without much thought. We prepare our speeches with our "audience in mind," we want to "persuade our audience" of something, and we "sit in the audience" as we listen. But what does the term *audience* really mean? Who and what make up an audience, and how should speakers think about this very important group of people?

Tracing the evolution of the word *audience* helps us understand the diverse nature of audiences and gain insight into how we can best communicate with them. The word *audience* comes from the Latin root *audire*, which means "to hear." The English word *audience* was coined in the fourteenth century, when people were granted "an audience" by a sovereign or a court official, meaning they were given the privilege of having their concerns heard and, they hoped, of receiving some assistance.

People did not gather together to form "an audience," as we commonly use the term, until the eighteenth century. By that time, European and North American societies had changed a great deal.

Trade routes had opened up, cities had grown and become centers of commerce and information exchange, and groups of people had started meeting publicly to discuss their interests. The term *audience* came to mean "the hearing of one that speaks, or the Assembly of Hearers."[1]

In the nineteenth and twentieth centuries, with the advent of mass media and technologies such as offset printing, the telegraph, television, and computers, the definition of *audience* changed again. Because technology allows us to be an audience member and never leave our homes or computer screens, *audience* has come to mean "people who listen."

For the purpose of this public speaking text, **audience** is defined as a complex and varied group of people the speaker addresses. This basic definition is simple, and audiences are more complex than it suggests. Modern audiences are composed of diverse people exposed to endless messages from the media, their workplaces, their families and friends, and many other sources. Despite all these demands on their listening time, you can learn a number of skills so that your audience members will listen to you. Let's start by exploring both the individual and collective nature of audiences.

## Considering an Audience as a Group of Diverse People

Have you ever noticed that for each similarity you find you have with someone, you also find a difference? Perhaps you and a friend love action films, popcorn, and state-of-the-art theaters. Yet one of you loves bargain matinees, sitting up close, and pouring on the butter, whereas the other is happiest settling in the balcony for the late night show with no butter at all. You are similar, yet you are different.

People are unique for a variety of reasons that relate to some combination of culture, upbringing, experiences, personality, and even genetics.[2] Like you and your movie-going friend, no two people are alike. This uniqueness sets us apart and makes us interesting.

Groups of diverse people are often also similar to one another in many ways. As a public speaker, how can you give a speech that acknowledges your audience's differences and similarities? First, try to understand how your audience members view the world by analyzing their master statuses and their standpoints.

**Speaking across DIFFERENCES**

**When we consider how an audience is "diverse" or "multicultural," we are often actually considering the master statuses and standpoints of audience members.**

## Master Statuses

People who occupy the same master statuses often share common experiences, perspectives, and attitudes. **Master statuses** are significant positions a person occupies within society that affect that person's identity in almost all social situations.[3] People's master statuses can include their race or ethnicity, gender, physical ability, sexual orientation, age, economic standing, religion or spirituality, and educational level. They can also include social roles such as being a parent, child, or sibling, and being employed or unemployed. A status is a *master* status when it profoundly influences a person's identity and the way in which he or she is perceived by others.

Here's how one public speaking student described her master statuses and how they influenced her life and speaking experiences:

> I have many master statuses. I am a daughter dedicated to her family and her family values. I am forever a student, always craving new knowledge. I am a first-generation student, boldly going where no one else in my family has gone before—college. I am a Mexican American living life for my ancestors. Last but not least, I am curious, always searching for new adventures in life. All of this makes up who I am and affects every decision I make each day, from what clothes I choose to wear to the books I choose to read. It also affects what topics I choose to speak about and how effectively I listen to other speakers.

Whether we intend to or not, we often respond to other people based on one or more master statuses. For example, teenagers with rumpled and baggy clothes are often treated differently in a grocery store than neatly dressed adult mothers with children. Whether or not our assumptions about these people are correct (teenagers will cause problems, mothers are responsible and will manage their children), we categorize and respond to people based on the positions they hold in society.

Our master statuses affect our view of the world because we make judgments based on them, and hence, we see some as more valuable than others. For example, whether we are comfortable acknowledging such differences or not, American culture tends to rank whiteness, heterosexuality, and masculinity higher than dark skin colors, homosexuality, and femininity. Because the first three statuses are considered more valuable, they are generally rewarded with higher salaries, more acceptance and protections, and more personal freedoms, whereas the last three, on average, are correlated with lower salaries, less acceptance and fewer protections, and greater threats to physical safety.[4]

## **Ethical** Moment

### What's in a Master Status?

KIRKLAND/AP PHOTO

Controversial musician Marilyn Manson has made a career out of skewering icons, institutions, and events that Americans consider worthy of the greatest respect, such as Christianity and the tragic death of John F. Kennedy. Even his name is a direct attack on what fascinates America: It is an amalgam of the names of iconic actress Marilyn Monroe and reviled serial killer Charles Manson. As a result, he has been accused of being responsible for any number of destructive events, including the Columbine killings. "I definitely can see why they would pick me [to blame]," he says. "Because I think it's easy to throw my face on the TV; because in the end, I'm a poster boy for fear. Because I represent what everyone is afraid of; because I say and do whatever I want."

Manson acknowledges that his music, behavior, and image could cause people to view him in a negative light. However, he maintains that the more outrageous he is, the more the public wants to know about him: "[A]ll the little hypocrites will go and buy the magazine, read about what evil, weird people we are, and will feel better about themselves. People love to judge; as long as they have somebody else to judge, they don't have to concentrate on their own miserable lives."

But Manson has also been described as a thought-provoking artist who is smart, funny, and down to earth. His ultimate goal, he says, is not to shock people but to express himself and raise topics he feels people should be talking about, such as the shallowness of American culture. "I can't be any different, and I can't imagine being different. I am not trying to shock or enrage the people on purpose. It's not some sort of plan. It's just my personality."[5]

*(Continued)*

## Ethical Moment

WHAT DO YOU THINK?

1. What are the master statuses Marilyn Manson presents publicly? Make a list of these master statuses and then discuss why they might challenge audiences or be unfamiliar to them.
2. Do you think Marilyn Manson pushes his image too far? Why or why not?
3. Does he have an ethical obligation to tone down his image and be less shocking? Why or why not?
4. Name other public figures who challenge audiences as much as Manson does. Do you think the actions of these public figures are positive or negative? Why?

### Standpoints, Attitudes, Beliefs, and Values

The impact of unequal treatment because of master statuses can affect an individual's **standpoint,** the perspective from which a person views and evaluates society. Members of your audiences will have different standpoints. This is because they have different master statuses and thus different experiences. For example, teenagers often see life as unfairly biased against them, and mothers often see the world as expecting them and their children to behave perfectly in all situations.

Note that although people's master statuses can have a powerful influence on their view of the world, master statuses do not *determine* their standpoints. For example, not all women believe they need to have children to fully experience womanhood, just as not all men believe their masculinity is weakened if they are not the primary breadwinners for their families. Additionally, we all occupy numerous master statuses throughout our lives, and each influences us in different ways. For example, although we maintain our ethnicity throughout our lives, if we move to a new country, adapt to a new culture, and learn a different language, our sense of ethnic identity can evolve. Moreover, we all move from young to old and can experience changing family and job roles, shifting from child to parent, unemployed to employed, and so on.

Our standpoints influence our attitudes, beliefs, and values. An **attitude** is a general positive or negative feeling a person has about something. Attitudes reflect our likes and dislikes and our approval or disapproval of events, people, or ideas.[6] A **belief** is a person's idea of what is real or true or not. Beliefs are more conceptual than attitudes and reflect what we think we know about the world. A **value** is a person's idea of what is good, worthy, or important. Our values reflect what we think is an ideal world or state of being. Values help us determine whether we think a person, idea, or thing is acceptable in our worldview.[7]

Our attitudes, beliefs, and values are often strongly influenced by our cultural backgrounds. All cultures have unique ways of explaining and organizing the world. As a speaker, you must make a point of recognizing these different worldviews and guard against ethnocentrism. **Ethnocentrism** is the belief that our own cultural perspectives, norms, and ways of organizing society are superior to others. When we hold ethnocentric views, we see other cultures as odd, wrong, or deficient because they do not do things the way we do. Speakers who let ethnocentric views come through in their speeches run the risk of alienating audience members who do not hold similar views.

> *Speaking across DIFFERENCES*
>
> **Avoiding ethnocentrism will help you be a more effective and well-received speaker.**

To be audience centered, speakers must consider the master statuses, standpoints, attitudes, beliefs, and values of their audiences. When speakers take these factors into consideration, they increase their chances of giving effective speeches.

## Demographic Audience Analysis

Recognizing your audience's master statuses and standpoints can help anticipate the potential impact your speech topic and language might have on your audience. This knowledge will help you become a better, more ethical speaker. Are members of your audience first-year high school students or married graduate students? Are they of a certain ethnicity? What types of jobs do they hold? Are they grandparents? What are their educational backgrounds? How might each of these master statuses influence the standpoints of your audience members? Once you've answered these types of questions, you can better estimate the attitudes, beliefs, and values of your audience and adapt the message of your speech to them.

A common way to determine the master statuses of an audience is to conduct a **demographic audience analysis,** an analysis that identifies the traits of an audience. These traits, or demographic characteristics, include age, country of origin, ethnicity and race, physical ability or disability, family status (parent, child), religion, and gender (male or female). You can gather demographic information by interviewing your audience members personally, through a survey, or by research on the Internet. Using the Internet is best when you want to find information about a large general group of people, such as the citizens of a town, county, or region. However, to gather targeted information about your specific audience, you must interview your audience directly or conduct a survey.

You can conduct a demographic analysis before your speech by asking your audience to fill out a survey that asks about demographic information and attitudes, beliefs, and values. Surveys ask two primary types of questions: open ended and closed ended. An **open-ended question** allows respondents to answer in an unrestricted way. An example of an open-ended question is "What are your reactions to the president's policy on the economy?" People asked this question are free to respond with any answer they like. A **closed-ended question** requires respondents to choose an answer from two or more alternatives. Examples of closed-ended questions are "Do you support the president's policy on the economy?" (requires a yes or no answer) and "On a scale of 1 to 5, with 5 indicating the highest support, how do you rate the president's policy on the economy?" (requires one rating of five possible alternatives).

Skills & Confidence
PPD Activity 6.1
Video Activity 6.1
Web Connect 6.1
Web Connect 6.2

Keep your speaking goals in mind as you construct your survey and analyze your audience. What would you like your audience to do or know after you've given your speech? Do you want them to understand a concept or a process? Explore an issue? Take some action? Appreciate another person? Whatever your goals, conducting a thorough and accurate analysis of your audience will help you accomplish them in a civil and ethical manner.

Remember that your primary goal in analyzing your audience is to give an ethical, audience-centered speech. Although master statuses can be powerfully influential, we all

**SPEECH Checklist**

## Guidelines for Constructing a Survey

- ☐ Keep your survey short (one or two pages).
- ☐ Keep your questions short and focused on one idea at a time.
- ☐ Use clear and simple language.
- ☐ Keep your own biases out of the survey.
- ☐ Provide room for respondents to write their comments.

experience life differently and we grow and change over time. A pitfall when conducting demographic analyses and considering master statuses is forgetting individual differences and resorting to stereotyping. A **stereotype** is a broad generalization about an entire group based on limited knowledge or exposure to only certain members of that group. Stereotypes are harmful because they are based on incomplete information. Although it is easy to predict certain behaviors based on a stereotype, speakers need to remember that each of their audiences is a collection of people with unique experiences and personalities.

> ***Speaking across DIFFERENCES***
>
> **A demographic audience analysis can provide excellent information about audience members. However, this type of analysis tends to generate general information about a group rather than specifics about individual audience members. Keep this in mind when interpreting the results of the analysis, being sure to avoid stereotyping your audience.**

## Considering an Audience as a Community

Although audiences begin as individuals who bring various standpoints to a presentation, they rapidly become a community of people joined together in some way, if only temporarily. Understanding how an audience comes together as a temporary community helps speakers stay audience centered.

### Voluntary Audiences

Just as speakers decide something is significant enough to speak out about, people come together as audiences because they find something significant enough to listen to. These audiences are voluntary: They have chosen to be present. An example of a voluntary audience is the 1.8 million people who came to Washington, D.C., to be a part of history on January 20, 2009, Inauguration Day for President Barack Obama. Public celebrations and commemorations, such as Super Bowl victories or the return of a famous person to a hometown, also bring audiences together voluntarily. And tragedies, like the Virginia Tech school shootings, often draw people together.

The need to listen often unites people of various master statuses and standpoints. This means that not all audience members will agree with every speaker or with one another. For example, consider the vigorous debates at city council meetings about budget cuts, land development, and other controversial local topics. Despite their varied master statuses and standpoints, however, voluntary audiences usually share an active interest in the topic.. This fact certainly works to your advantage as a speaker, and staying audience centered will help you deliver your message effectively.

### Involuntary Audiences

People sometimes form an audience because they must. These audiences are involuntary: The members might prefer not to be present. Examples of involuntary audiences are students in required public speaking courses and employees in mandatory business meetings. Some involuntary audiences have little or no interest in the topic and may even display hostility toward the speaker or a disconcerting lack of attention. For example, in your public speaking class, some of your classmates would rather not hear about certain topics because of their own strong beliefs, yet they are forced to sit and listen. Others seem only to stare blankly at you. Still others ignore you and carry on e-mail or text conversations while you are speaking. Unfortunately, you may encounter the same behaviors in your professional and social worlds; some audiences attend speeches only because their jobs require it or because of family or social obligations. However, with a little forethought and effort, most involuntary audiences can be brought into the public dialogue.

For the speaker facing an involuntary audience, being audience centered may mean the difference between an ineffective and a successful speech. Before you give your speech, talk with the person who asked you to speak. Discover why your audience is required to attend. Or, at the beginning of your speech, ask your audience members why they've been asked to listen to you. Then address those issues in your speech. For example, if you are presenting to an audience that is part of a mandatory training program, ask about the rationale for the training, the goals of the training, and what your audience hopes to gain by the training. Knowing

**Speaking at Work**

*Audiences at work are often involuntary. However, the degree to which audience members want to attend a workplace speaking event varies greatly. Here's a tip: Employees like to know how the information presented will help them with their day-to-day tasks. Before you give your presentation, learn as much as you can about your audience members and how your presentation applies to them. This type of audience analysis will help ensure that the audience pays attention to what you have to say.*

this information will help you design and present a message that is relevant and useful.

Similarly, if an involuntary audience opposes your topic, learn why so you can confirm (Chapter 4) and be confirmed by audience members. Before you speak, ask your audience to write down their concerns and pass them to you, or gather this information several days earlier. The feedback you receive will help you thoughtfully address the audience's concerns, frustrations, or resistance. This audience-centered approach opens up dialogue rather than forcing ideas on people. You let your audience members know you are working to understand them as you ask them to do the same for you.

Finally, if you are speaking to an involuntary audience, use a little **empathy** by trying to understand the world as another person does. What would motivate you to listen to a topic you disagreed with or a presentation you were required to listen to? If you adopt this empathic, audience-centered approach, your involuntary audience may be pleasantly surprised by your presentation and welcome you as a speaker.

So far, you've discovered that you must consider both the individual and collective nature of audiences, you've explored why audiences come together, and you've learned how you can engage an involuntary audience. Audience-centered speakers keep all these factors in mind as they prepare and present their speeches. In the next section, you'll learn techniques to help you manage your speaking environment effectively.

**Skills & Confidence**
PPD Activity 6.2
Web Connect 6.3

## Considering Your Speaking Environment

Before audience-centered speakers give a speech, they must discover as much as they can about their **speaking environment,** or where and when they will speak, so they can manage their speaking situation with relative ease. Effective speakers must consider several situational factors: the size of the audience and the physical arrangement of the speaking site, the availability of technology, the time of day they'll be speaking, where their speech falls in a series of presentations, and the length of time they have to speak.

### Audience Size and Physical Arrangement

The size of an audience and the physical arrangement of a speaking situation can have a powerful effect on a speaking environment. You can enhance your ability to connect with your audience if you consider these matters carefully before your speech and adapt to them during your speech. Here is a description of how one speaker adapted to his speaking environment:

> I found [him] alone in an empty basketball locker room moments before he was to speak before a crowd of six thousand at Arizona State University, calmly sipping tea. "Your Holiness, if you're ready..."
>
> He briskly rose, and without hesitation he left the room, emerging into the thick backstage throng of local reporters, photographers, security personnel, and students—the seekers, the curious, and the skeptical. He walked through the crowd smiling broadly and greeting people as he passed by. Finally passing through a curtain, he walked on stage, bowed, folded his hands, and smiled. He was greeted with thunderous applause. At his request, the house lights were not dimmed so he could clearly see his audience, and for several moments he simply stood there, quietly surveying the audience with an unmistakable expression of warmth and good will. For those who had never seen the Dalai Lama before, his maroon and saffron monk's robes may have created a somewhat exotic impression, yet his remarkable ability to establish rapport with his audience was quickly revealed as he sat down and began his talk.
>
> "I think that this is the first time I am meeting most of you. But to me, whether it is an old friend or new friend, there's not much difference anyway, because I always believe we are the same; we are all human beings...."[8]

It might seem that a large audience, a group of journalists and security guards, and a wide stage would mean distance and disruption for a speaker, but not necessarily. Despite this potentially difficult physical situation, the Dalai Lama stayed audience centered by engaging with his audience personally. He asked that the house lights be left on, and he took the time to make eye contact with his audience, acknowledging a connection to each audience member. He took advantage of his setting rather than letting it control him. But how does a speaker do this?

To establish rapport with our audiences, we must consider the dynamics of audience size and physical arrangement before we speak, and we must adjust to any changes immediately before or during our speech. To stay audience centered with respect to size and place, ask yourself the questions in the Speech Checklist: Your Speaking Environment.

You probably won't be able to change the size of your audience, but you should be able to work with the physical setting to create the kind of speaking environment you want. Consider whether you want to stand or sit, where you want your audience to sit (for example, in rows, in a circle, on chairs, on the floor), and how these decisions will

**SPEECH Checklist**

## Your Speaking Environment

- [ ] How many people will be present?
- [ ] Will they stand or be seated? Where will they stand or sit?
- [ ] From where will I be speaking?
- [ ] Does this arrangement help or hinder the speaking environment I wish to create?
- [ ] What adjustments will I want to make before the presentation begins?
- [ ] What will I do if I cannot make these adjustments?
- [ ] What kinds of adjustments might I make during a presentation if I want to alter the environment?

affect your ability to connect with your audience. Ideally, you would make arrangements to establish your speaking environment ahead of time and plan to make adjustments during your speech as needed. Remember, your speaking goal is to connect with your audience before, during, and after the speech.

### Technology

Technology is the tools that speakers use to help them deliver their message. Technology can be as elaborate as a computer and LCD panel or as simple as a pen and a flip chart. Table 6.1 presents a list of technologies speakers typically use. When you're thinking of using technology for your speech, stay audience centered by asking yourself the questions in the Speech Checklist: Technology for Your Speech.

Audience-centered speakers use technology to do more than simply enhance or project their message. They also make a commitment to their audience to use that technology competently. The following example illustrates the importance of this commitment:

> Landon was a wonderful photographer and wanted to enhance his speech by showing slides of his photos. He knew there would be a slide projector in the room in which he was scheduled to speak, so he selected his slides carefully and had his carousel ready the day before the speech. The next morning, just before he was introduced to his audience, he tried to put his carousel on the projector and discovered it didn't fit—his projector and the one made available for him to use during his speech were

**TABLE 6.1 Technologies for Speakers**

| TRADITIONAL TECHNOLOGIES | ELECTRONIC TECHNOLOGIES |
|---|---|
| Podiums for notes | Microphones |
| Tables or easels for displays | Laptop computers and LCD projectors |
| Presentational aids such as posters | Overhead projectors and screens |
| Handouts | Slide projectors and screens |
| Chalk, chalkboards, and erasers | Presentational aids such as PowerPoint slides |
| Ink markers, white boards, and erasers | Televisions, VCR players, and DVD players |
| Markers, pens, and flip charts | CD-ROM and MP3 players |
| Tacks, pins, or tape | Audio cassette players |

not compatible! Undaunted, he quickly moved the slides into the available carousel. But he wasn't familiar with the projector's remote control, and several times during his speech he sent slides backward rather than forward. As a result, his presentation didn't flow the way he wanted it to, and he had to spend time studying the remote rather than connecting with his audience.

**SPEECH Checklist**

## Technology for Your Speech

- ☐ What types of technology will be available for me to use?
- ☐ Do I have time to prepare the materials I need for using that technology?
- ☐ Do I have the time to practice using the technology? Have I worked out any glitches?
- ☐ Am I prepared to speak if the technology fails?
- ☐ Am I sure that my decision to use or not use technology helps me create the kind of environment I want?
- ☐ Does the technology help me communicate my messages clearly? Does it enhance my speech or detract from it?

Landon did what he could to recover, but after his speech, he felt he didn't really create the kind of environment he wanted. He wanted people to get excited by his material, but he felt instead that they were simply patient with him.

In Chapter 20, you will learn more about presentational aids that rely on technology. Remember, although technology is a tool that can help you give a more effective speech, it has its drawbacks. If your speech relies on technology to be effective but the technology you need is not available when you arrive to speak, your presentation will be negatively affected. That's why you need to take the time to consider how to present your speech without technology. Having an alternate plan will help you stay audience centered. No matter what, you will be able to focus on delivering your message to your audience in a way that they appreciate.

### Time Factors

Audience-centered speakers also consider issues of time, sometimes referred to as *chronemics.* Three important time considerations are the time of day you'll be speaking, where your speech falls in a series of presentations (first, last, or somewhere in the middle), and how much time you'll have to speak.

*Time of day.* The time of day a speech is scheduled is significant. People's energy levels are often different in the morning than in the evening, and they are different before and after meals. Just as your level of energy is affected by the time of day, so too is the mood of an audience.

In the morning, audiences tend to be fresher, but they may also be anxious about the responsibilities they have that day. In the evening, audiences may be weary, tired from work. Around lunchtime, they are hungry and preoccupied with getting some food, or they have just eaten and may be drowsy as their bodies work to digest food rather than your message. Here are some techniques one speaker uses to adapt his message according to the time of day he speaks.

- *In the morning,* Julio begins by encouraging his audience to refill their cups of coffee and tea as he speaks. He then acknowledges the demands on their time by speaking for fifteen minutes, asking them to participate in an activity for twenty minutes, and then breaking for fifteen minutes so they can check voice mail and e-mail. When they reconvene, they follow up on the activity for about an hour.
- *After lunch,* Julio engages his audience verbally because he knows their energy will be a bit lower than it was in the morning. If he speaks for longer than half an hour or so, he

incorporates a break so audiences can check messages. If he speaks before lunch, Julio clearly defines his speaking schedule so his audience knows when they can expect to eat.

**Speaking at Work**
*The time of day has a significant effect on how well workplace audiences are able to receive your message.*

- *In the evening,* Julio acknowledges that it's the end of what was probably a busy workday. Rather than beginning by explaining the program, he immediately engages them verbally by asking them a few questions about a typical workday that they can answer by raising their hands. This strategy keeps audience members connected to him in a direct way—he knows they are probably tired, and he wants them to stay actively involved in the speech rather than sitting back passively.

Regardless of the time of day, Julio stays audience centered by acknowledging the audience's needs and by organizing his presentations accordingly.

*Speaking order.* To be audience centered, you must also consider your speaking order, or the place you occupy in a series of speakers. If you are the first speaker, you get the audience when they are fresh, listening more actively, and usually more willing to process your message. You also get to set the stage for later speakers, make the first impression, and direct the audience's energy without interference from previous speakers. Additionally, you get to connect with the audience before anyone else does, especially because audiences sometimes ask more questions of first speakers.

**Speaking at Work**
*Day-long trainings that feature a number of speakers are fairly common in the workplace. If you are asked to present at this sort of speaking event, consider your speaking order, or the place you occupy in a series of speakers.*

If you are the last speaker, or near the end of a series, your audience may be tired of processing the information presented by previous speakers. They will have had their attention pulled in lots of different directions, and they may be more inclined to tune out a speaker or to leave than to listen to another speech. Therefore, start by acknowledging previous speakers and the information they presented. Then try to use your speech to reenergize the audience and redirect their focus as needed. At the end of your speech, the audience may have asked previous speakers most of their questions, so don't be disappointed if they have few for you. Or be prepared to share the stage with previous presenters who will also be answering the audience's questions.

If you are in the middle of a series of speakers, you have the advantage of a warmed-up audience that isn't yet anxious to leave. Such an audience is also likely, however, to compare the information in your speech to the information given in previous speeches. Thus, engage the audience by making connections to previous speakers. If necessary, try to reshape the audience's mood so they're able to hear your message more effectively. At the end of your speech, keep in mind that the audience may ask questions that attempt to pull together information from prior speeches or to rectify discrepancies in claims. If you can help audiences synthesize the information from your speech and the speeches of previous speakers, you stand a better chance of sticking in their memories—people tend to remember beginnings and endings rather than what comes in the middle.

*Length of speech.* Students of public speaking often groan when an instructor sets a specific time limit to a speech and refuses to accept an infraction of that limit without penalty to the student. Why the big deal about time limits? Time limitations, although invisible to the audience, are an important structural component of a speech.

When speakers exceed the allotted time, they do several undesirable things. If they are speaking in a series, they communicate a sense of arrogance, suggesting their words are more important than those of speakers coming later. If they are the only speaker, they communicate that they don't care that audience members probably have other demands on their time. Speakers who go over time limits also suggest they cannot prioritize and organize their material efficiently; thus, they communicate an air of incompetence. In the same vein, speakers who speak for far less time than allotted also convey incompetence. A speech that is too short suggests that the speaker has not prepared fully or does not care about sharing the message with the audience. Finally, speakers whose speech exceeds the time limits risk not being able to give their entire speech.

The responsibility for staying within time constraints falls on the speaker. When you agree to speak, find out how much time you will have for your presentation and prepare your speech to fit that time frame. If your audience wants more of your information, they can ask you to elaborate or engage you later in a question-and-answer session. (Question-and-answer sessions are discussed in Chapter 26.) If you decide to speak for far less time than you have been allotted, explain to the audience that you will only deliver a short speech to allow more time for discussion with the audience. If you do not know what your time limitations are and other speakers will speak after you, do some

Skills & Confidence
PPD Activity 6.3
Web Connect 6.4

quick mental math: Divide the total time for the event by the number of speakers, allowing time for questions and discussion. Remember, audience-centered speakers manage their time efficiently and responsibly; they create an environment in which audiences feel respected and appreciated. For information about time limits and number of main points, see Chapter 10; for advice on rehearsing your speech to be sure how long it will take, see Chapter 17.

## Adapting to Audience Expectations

What expectations do you bring with you when you go to a ball game? When a friend takes you to dinner? When you listen to a new CD? We usually have certain expectations about activities and events. For example, when we attend a ball game, we expect bleachers, announcers, players, referees or umpires, rules, a scoring system, and an end to the game. We expect the game to progress in a certain way, and we know when it doesn't.

When audiences attend public speaking events, they also bring expectations with them. They expect speakers to perform in certain ways, expect public speaking events to follow a certain structure, and they base their interpretation of a speaker's message on those expectations. Audiences have expectations about the credibility of the speaker and the form of a speech. Audience-centered speakers must address these expectations because audiences use them to help decide whether or not a speaker "did a good job."

### Expectations About the Speaker

When audiences take the time to listen to a speech, they want the speaker to be competent (qualified) and credible (believable). Chapters 12 (Introductions and Conclusions), 14 (Introduction to Reasoning), and 24 (Persuasion and Reasoning) also discuss aspects of credibility, but here you'll learn how audiences use master statuses to assess whether or not a speaker is qualified and believable.

As you learned earlier in this chapter, master statuses are the positions people hold in society that affect their identities in almost all social situations. Once audience members identify a speaker's master statuses, they usually form expectations about that speaker based on their beliefs concerning those master statuses. For example, Dennis is a fifty-five-year-old white attorney. A Georgia native, he travels to law schools across the country to meet with and speak to prospective new hires for his law firm. At many presentations, he is asked about racism and sexism in the South. He is also often challenged, both overtly and

**SPEECH Checklist**

## Your Master Statuses

- [ ] Are you a woman or a man?
- [ ] What is your age and physical state?
- [ ] What is your race and ethnicity?
- [ ] Do you have an accent or a particular style of speech?
- [ ] Will you acknowledge your marital status, parental status, or sexual orientation in your speech?
- [ ] What is your educational level?
- [ ] Are you often labeled by other people in a particular way?

subtly, about whether he is able to recognize forms of discrimination that could be present in his firm. As a white male from the South, audiences often don't expect Dennis to be able to speak credibly about issues of race and gender.

To understand what an audience might expect of you as a speaker, identify your master statuses in the Speech Checklist. Your answers to questions like these will help you adjust to your audience's expectations of you as a speaker.

Carolyn Calloway Thomas, a professor in the Department of Communication and Culture at Indiana University, once asked a group of students, "What do you notice about me?" They listed a number of items—her height, dress, style of presentation, occupation, and so on. "Yes, yes," she said, "those all are significant. Go on." Finally, one student said, "You are a black woman." "Yes," she responded, "and although that affects almost every aspect of my life, as well as almost every aspect of how you respond to me, if you can't get past the fact that I am black, if that's all you see about me, we've got a communication problem. You'll get stuck there. I am a black woman, yet I also am a very complex human being."

Professor Calloway Thomas offers speakers a useful strategy for working with audience assumptions about master statuses: Simply acknowledge them. Then, help your audience move beyond master statuses because they are not the totality of who you are. Speakers can use a variety of nonthreatening phrases such as the following to help audiences move beyond assumptions about master status:

- "I'm often asked that question"
- "Audiences generally assume that…"

- "As a woman (or other master status), people expect me to..."
- "Now, you might be wondering why someone like me is speaking on this topic today."

Phrases that can help audiences shift their focus from unfamiliar styles or mannerisms include these examples:

- "Let me explain the symbolism behind the clothing I'm wearing today."
- "I'll be using an interpreter today and, as fascinating as they are to watch, I'd love it if you would look at me as I speak and ask your questions directly to me."
- "Even though I've lived in the United States for ten years now, the English language still stumps me at times. I hear it occasionally stumps some of you native speakers as well, so maybe we can help each other out with some of what we don't understand."

**Speaking across DIFFERENCES**

**It's unavoidable that audiences will judge you based on your master statuses. Part of being audience centered is doing what you can to help your audience be receptive to your positions and acknowledge you as a unique individual.**

These kinds of phrases acknowledge, directly and tactfully, that an audience's assumptions may prevent them from hearing a speaker's message. They also acknowledge differences in a positive way and encourage audiences to better understand those differences. As an audience-centered speaker, you not only want to understand the positions of your audience, but you also want your audience to understand your positions. Encourage them to move beyond simply defining you by your master statuses and ask them to recognize you as a unique individual.

### Expectations About the Form of a Speech

Communication scholar and theorist Kenneth Burke defines *form* as "the creation of an appetite" in the minds of an audience and the "adequate satisfying of that appetite." He suggests that a speech has form when one part of it leads an audience to "anticipate another part, to be gratified by the sequence."[9] In other words, audiences expect a speech to follow a certain structural progression. For audiences with a Western cultural background, it is often expected that speeches will have the following forms:

- The speaker will do most of the speaking or facilitating and share information the audience does not already have.
- The audience will listen during the speech and ask most of their questions at the end of the speech.

- Different types of speaking are typical at different types of events: At public lectures, speeches of information, invitation, or persuasion are likely; at a celebration, speeches of commemoration or acceptance are given; at business meetings, speeches take the form of presenting ideas, facilitating discussions, or gathering information; and speeches of introduction are likely at the beginning of any of these kinds of events.

**Speaking at Work**

*When you adhere to the basic form of a workplace presentation, your audience will be more receptive to your message. However, if you really feel it would be more audience-centered to violate the expected form, just be sure to explain why so audience members understand where you're coming from.*

To stay audience centered, do your best to recognize which form your audience expects for your speech. Then try to follow that form or explain your reasons for altering it. If your audience's expectations are violated, they may react negatively to your speech. For example, if you are asked to commemorate a colleague, be sure to prepare a speech that praises the person and highlights her contributions. Even if you don't feel your colleague has contributed as much as the company thinks she has, try to focus on the positive aspects of your interactions with her so your speech is appropriate for the occasion. Don't take the opportunity to give a persuasive speech that tries to convince the audience that your colleague isn't praiseworthy. By violating the form of a commemorative speech, you'll only frustrate your audience's expectations and make them feel uncomfortable. In our next example, the speaker doesn't follow the form he knows his audience expects, but he explains why he doesn't and so gives a successful speech.

> Jeff had been invited to speak to a class on communication and culture about representations of race in the media. As an Asian American who had studied the subject and was a dynamic and engaging speaker, Jeff had often been asked to give similar presentations. As a result, he was quite familiar with his material and with his audiences' expectations about how he should present it. Students expected him to lecture and present facts and research so they could take notes. But he really wanted to connect with his audience and create a dialogue, so he decided to violate his audience's expectations.

> When he began his presentation, he told the students that he knew they expected him to lecture and that they were prepared to sit back and maintain a certain distance. He said, "I'm going to make it really hard for you to stay distant, because I can't be distant from the issue of race and the media—and neither can you. You see, how the media present us as individuals, as people engaged with one another, affects us too powerfully to pretend that we can understand by simply listening to someone lecture for fifty minutes. So, I am going to tell you some of my stories, experiences, and perspectives, and I'm asking that you tell me some of yours during this time we have together."

Jeff's presentation was a huge success. His audience understood why he violated their expectations of form because he explained why. In fact, he set up new expectations—the exchange of stories and experiences. He created a new appetite, which he satisfied during his time with them.

Skills & Confidence Speech Studio 6.1

Audience-centered speakers understand that audiences have certain expectations of form for certain types of speeches. They recognize that when they choose to alter these forms, they must help their audience understand why. Remember, staying audience centered isn't saying only what the audience wants to hear; it is creating an appetite in them to hear what you have to say.

PART III

# RESEARCH

## CIVIC ENGAGEMENT IN ACTION

### "I Wanted to Understand"

UNHCR/HANDOUT/REUTERS/CORBIS

If you conduct a Google search for award-winning actor Angelina Jolie, you'll get literally millions of hits, almost all highlighting (in order) her sexy image, her relationships with famous men, and her movies. However, many people outside the reaches of Hollywood know her primarily for her humanitarian work. Through her efforts as a goodwill ambassador for the United Nations High Commissioner for Refugees (UNHCR), she has assisted the United Nations in providing relief to over 20 million refugees displaced by violence, war, and poverty around the world. Not only does Jolie engage directly with the men, women, and children who are affected, but she also assists in building shelters for refugees, has released many of her journals documenting her travel experiences, and visits U.S. detention centers so that she can more effectively advocate for the reuniting of families separated while escaping their home countries.

Angelina Jolie became interested in the plight of refugees after visiting Cambodia to film *Lara Croft: Tomb Raider*. "I started to travel and realized there was so much I was unaware of," she explains. "There were many things I hadn't been taught in school and daily global events I was not hearing about in the news. So I wanted to understand." Her belief in what the United Nations has always stood for—equality and the protection of human rights for all people—has resulted in her commitment to use her status as an A-list celebrity to learn as much as she can and speak out about the refugee crisis. For example, she says, "When I read about the 20 million people under the care of UNHCR, I wanted to understand how in this day and age that many people could be displaced."

Jolie's focus is on the humanity and heroism of those who have been forced to leave their homes and live in overcrowded and dangerous refugee camps: "What was

### You Can Get Involved

To learn more about UNHCR, access **Web Connect P.III.1: UN Refugee Assistance** at your Resource Center for *Invitation to Public Speaking Handbook*. Also check out **Web Connect P.III.2: ReliefWeb** to explore how you can get involved with global humanitarian issues. This site provides information about humanitarian emergencies and disasters around the world, including the "forgotten" ones. For a directory of organizations categorized by type, by country, and alphabetically, click the "Professional Resources" tab; then scroll down and click the "ReliefWeb Directory of Information Providers" link.

CIVIC ENGAGEMENT IN ACTION continued

Skills & Confidence
Web Connect P.III.1
Web Connect P.III.2

really shocking was that every individual person you meet will tell you that their immediate family was [affected]. Somebody's child was killed, somebody's husband. Someone was beaten.... You go to these places and you realize what life's really about and what people are really going through.... These people are my heroes."[1]

# RESEARCH

CHAPTER 7

# Gathering Supporting Materials

- Determine What Types of Information You Need
- Start with Your Personal Knowledge and Experience
- Techniques for Organizing Your Research

  Speech Checklist: **Research Inventory in Brief**

*In this chapter, you will learn to*

**Determine the types of supporting materials you need for your speech**

**Use some techniques to organize your research efforts from the start**

One of our primary responsibilities as public speakers is to provide audiences with accurate information. In addition to giving our opinions on the topics we speak about, we must also provide facts, examples, and evidence. We can find this type of information, called *supporting material,* by consulting our own experiences and knowledge, by doing research over the Internet and at the library (Chapter 8), or by interviewing the right people (Chapter 9).

Conducting research may seem intimidating at first, but if you organize your efforts, the process should be efficient and productive. In less time than you might imagine, you can fill notebooks and folders with an impressive range of supporting materials. Research will not only ensure that your ideas and arguments are accurate and that your audience is appropriately informed, but the insights it offers you on your subject can also keep you excited about your speech up until you deliver it and beyond.

This chapter will help you start collecting the supporting materials you need to enter the public dialogue successfully. You will learn how to organize your research efforts, determining what types of information you need and keeping track of what you have found. If you approach your research in an organized way, you will spend your time productively, reduce your frustration, and increase your chances of finding excellent materials to support your ideas.

## Determine What Types of Information You Need

Before you begin your research in earnest, take some time to organize your thoughts about what types of supporting material you already have and what types you still need. Start by asking yourself the following sorts of questions (in Chapter 13, examples, narratives, statistics, testimony, and definitions are discussed in detail):

- What examples and stories do I have?
- What statistics will my audience want to know?
- What kinds of testimony will they want to hear?
- What terms and phrases can I define clearly on my own?
- Is the information I already have accurate, relevant, and credible?
- How will I evaluate the accuracy, relevance, and credibility of the information I find?
- What ideas or points can I develop or support from my own experiences?

As you consider these questions, you can construct a **research inventory**, a list of the types of information you have and the types you want to find. A research inventory helps you focus your research efforts and identify areas that need special attention. It is your first step toward making the time you spend gathering materials productive.

Consider the sample research inventory in Figure 7.1. This inventory was developed for a speech on incarcerated parents and their struggles to parent from jail. The thirty minutes the student spent identifying what information she had and what she still needed saved her hours of time on the Internet, in the library, and in interviews.

In addition to saving you time, preparing a research inventory before you start to gather supporting materials helps you avoid experiencing what futurist Alvin Toffler calls *information overload.*

## FIGURE 7.1 Sample research inventory

**Speech topic:** Incarcerated parents

**General purpose:** To invite

**Specific purpose:** I want to invite my audience to consider the issues regarding incarcerated parents and when they should or shouldn't be permitted to parent.

**My audience is:** My public speaking classmates

***I currently have:***

**Examples and stories:**

A story Li wrote from the juvenile corrections facility

**Statistics:**

The number of children in the U.S. who have parents in prison, and the number of mothers and fathers released each year to return home (Sandra Enos, Mothering from the Inside, 2001)

**Testimony:**

My own experiences working with a correctional facility

**Definitions:**

**This information is relevant, accurate, and credible because:**

The story really catches the emotions and sadness of kids with incarcerated parents.

The book, Mothering from the Inside, is well researched and current.

***My audience will want to hear:***

**Examples of the following:**

Specific examples of incarcerated parents

**Statistics for the following:**

Statistics to illustrate the kinds of crimes and lengths of sentences that keep parents away from children

Statistics to illustrate the different lengths of times fathers and mothers are separated from children

**Testimony about the following:**

The experiences of mothers and fathers who are currently incarcerated

The experiences of children with incarcerated parents and of parents who have been released

**Definitions of the following:**

Kinship (who takes care of children when a parent is incarcerated)

Incarceration

Correctional facility

***The kinds of sources they will find trustworthy are:***

People who work in correctional facilities

Legal services

Periodicals and journals that publish articles on the impact of incarceration on families

**FIGURE 7.1** *(Continued)*

***I need to find the following information:***
Specific definitions
More statistics, especially about the effects on families
More testimony (from a range of perspectives)

***Sources for this information:***
Library database
InfoTrac College Edition (articles about incarceration)
Government websites (statistics)
Websites about barriers incarcerated parents face
Possibly interview a local correctional officer

In his famous book *Future Shock*,[1] Toffler explained that **information overload** happens when we take in more information than we can process but realize there is still more information we must know. Toffler goes on to offer a useful strategy for managing this overload: Classify information so it fits into manageable units. This is precisely what you do with your research inventory: organize the information for your speech into two classifications—what you have and what you need. The next step is to determine where you'll find the information you need.

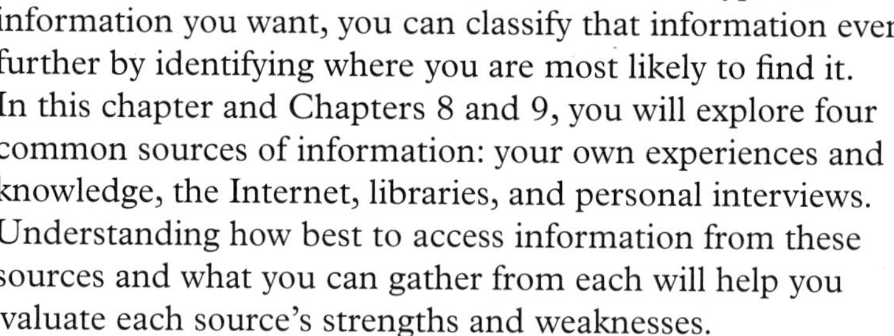

Notice that the last item on the research inventory in Figure 7.1 is "Sources for this information." Once you know what types of information you want, you can classify that information even further by identifying where you are most likely to find it. In this chapter and Chapters 8 and 9, you will explore four common sources of information: your own experiences and knowledge, the Internet, libraries, and personal interviews. Understanding how best to access information from these sources and what you can gather from each will help you evaluate each source's strengths and weaknesses.

Skills & Confidence
PPD Activity 7.1

## Start with Your Personal Knowledge and Experience

After reading Chapter 5, you probably recognized that you have firsthand knowledge about a number of subjects that would make excellent speeches. Before you begin other research, take a moment to consider what knowledge you already have about your topic. This knowledge can come from your own experiences and training, family background, hobbies, job or profession, and even from things you have read or observed.

For example, the information in Cindy's speech on folding the American flag (Chapter 21) relies on her personal experience in the military and with folding the flag during ceremonial events. Similarly, the source of research for Carol's speech on fat discrimination (Chapter 24) was her own personal experiences. If you're interested in a topic but don't have personal experience with it, you can gain experience as part of your research. For example, suppose you wanted to give a speech about a particular agency in your community. You could visit that agency and observe someone for a day to get the personal experience you need.

Your research inventory will help you figure out what information you are missing and where you need to look for it. Chapter 8 describes techniques and tools for research on the Internet and in the library. Chapter 9 explains how to gather information with personal interviews. To make the research process manageable, give yourself plenty of time and consider the following advice for organizing your research from the start. When you take time to gather and use information properly, you can enter the public dialogue with integrity.

## Techniques for Organizing Your Research

With a bit of planning, you can make the research process efficient and productive. Techniques include not only creating a research inventory but also taking notes and making copies of research material, gathering more information than you think you'll need, setting up a simple filing system, and beginning your bibliography with your first source. The time you spend doing research will be more rewarding if your approach is systematic.

### Begin by Filling Out Your Research Inventory

Take the time to fill out your research inventory so you can figure out and remember what you need. Update your inventory as you begin finding information and discovering other sources.

### Set Up a Filing System

As you gather information, you may be tempted to put it all in one folder and wait to organize it until you sit down to draft your speech. This may save time initially, but it will cost time later in the process. It is much more efficient to organize your information while you are collecting it. One of the best ways to do this is with a filing system.

Begin by organizing your materials according to your research inventory. Set up separate files for different kinds of support (such as examples and stories, statistics, testimony, and definitions), or

**SPEECH Checklist**

### Research Inventory in Brief

- [ ] What statistics, examples and stories, testimony, and definitions do I already have?
- [ ] What additional statistics, examples and stories, testimony, and definitions will my audience want to hear?
- [ ] What information do I need to find?
- [ ] What kinds of sources will my audience find trustworthy?
- [ ] What sources will I investigate for this information?

color-code your materials by type of evidence with a highlighter, or devise your own system. As you collect research, create a master list of your notes and photocopies, identifying:

- The type of evidence each one contains
- The date you found it
- The point the material makes
- Where you might use it in your speech (for example, "good for introduction")

As you continue gathering material, organize it by main points and subpoints (Chapters 5 and 10).

## Take Notes and Make Copies

Keep careful, complete notes and records of sources to ensure that you have accurate information. For Internet and library sources, include in your notes as much of the following information as you can find:

- The full name of the author
- The title of the source (book, magazine, article, document, Web page)
- The publisher (or creator or sponsor of a website)
- The place and year of publication (or posting date of a Web page)
- The page numbers where you found the information

If you access the source via the Internet, be sure to also include the exact URL of the website or page. When you record a URL, make

## SPEECH TIPS

### KEEPING TRACK OF SOURCES

On your notes from each source, be sure to record the URL or the library call number so you can easily find the source again in case you need to go back to it.

sure it is absolutely accurate. Any mistake, even a missing period or a misspelling, may lead to an incorrect site or a dead end. If the pages on which you find information have long and complicated URLs, it can be worth your time to print them out.

For interviews, record the full name of the interviewee, his or her title and place of business, and the date of the interview.

All of your notes should include the exact, complete phrases or words you are citing or quoting. In addition to taking notes, photocopy and print the pages of longer passages you may want to cite, paraphrase, or quote. Check each note for completeness by asking yourself, "If someone else wanted to go to this source, could they find it by looking at my bibliography or typing this URL?" and "If I decide to cite this in my speech, will I have all the information I need?" (For a discussion of citing sources in your speech, see Chapter 8.)

### Begin Your Bibliography with Your First Source

A bibliography is a record of each of the sources you use in your speech, and accuracy is the key to a good bibliography. Start your bibliography the moment you collect your first source. There are many different styles for bibliographies. Check with your instructor, or your employer if a work presentation requires a bibliography, for which style to follow. Start using that style with the first entry, and stick to it as you construct your bibliography. By doing so, you will have the citations you need before you log off the Internet or leave the library or the interview. And when you've finished your research, you will have a **preliminary bibliography**, a list of all the potential sources you'll use as you prepare your speech. (Figure 7.2 presents a sample of a preliminary bibliography; Appendix B provides models for citing various kinds of sources.) As you organize your speech, you'll decide which information to include or not include and remove

**Skills & Confidence**
PPD Activity 7.2

**Speaking at Work**
*If you must provide a bibliography for a presentation at work, be sure to find out what style to follow.*

**FIGURE 7.2 Sample preliminary bibliography**

Preliminary Bibliography

Enos, Sandra. Mothering from the Inside: Parenting in a Women's Prison. New York: State University of New York Press, 2001.

Every Door Closed: Facts about Parents with Criminal Records. Center for Law and Social Policy and Community Legal Services, Inc. 29 Sept 2003. Accessed 12 Oct 2006. http://www.clasp.org/publications/EDC_fact_sheets.pdf.

Poehlmann, Julie. "Children's Family Environments and Intellectual Outcomes during Maternal Incarceration." Journal of Marriage and Family 67 (2005): 1275–1285.

"The Beat Within: A Weekly Publication of Writing and Art from the Inside." Pacific News Service. Accessed 10 Oct 2006. http://thebeatwithin.org/news/view_article.html.

entries you don't need. When you finish putting your speech together, you will find that your final bibliography is complete, and you won't have to rush to finish it just before your speech.

## Gather More Material Than You Think You'll Need

We often underestimate the amount of material we need to support our ideas. Or we think we've found the perfect example, only to discover that when we put the speech together, we can't use it after all. For these reasons, gather more information than you think you'll need. Collect several possibilities for your introduction and conclusion, and if your instructor asks for three sources, gather six and use the best three. If you need one great example of what a statistic really means, ask your interviewee for a few and choose the one that best illustrates your point.

Although you probably won't use all this information in your speech, having it will help you feel more prepared and more confident. In addition, you'll be better prepared for a question-and-answer session because you'll have a deeper understanding of your topic.

CHAPTER 8

# Research Online and at the Library



*In this chapter, you will learn to*

- Search for information on the Internet
- Search for information in the library
- Evaluate the information you find
- Avoid plagiarism
- Cite your sources ethically and effectively

Your research inventory (Chapter 7) will give you a list of information you need to track down. The next question is where to look. Although the Internet may often seem the quickest route to research, it isn't always the most effective or accurate source. If you're not an expert in the subject of your speech, you can waste a lot of time on the Internet. But the Internet is better than the library for some things, such as the very latest news about a topic. Table 8.1 summarizes the differences between Internet and library research.

Recall from Chapter 6 that you increase your chances for giving a successful speech by remaining audience centered, and audiences expect information that is reliable, authoritative, current, complete, relevant, and consistent. This chapter describes the kinds of information found online and in the library, how to evaluate

**TABLE 8.1 Internet Versus Library Research**

| USE THE INTERNET WHEN YOU | USE THE LIBRARY WHEN YOU |
|---|---|
| Know what you are looking for | May want assistance with your search |
| Want the most current ideas | Want comprehensive materials |
| Want to explore less established sources | Want established sources |
| Want shortened versions of print documents | Want the full text of a document |
| Know your specific subject or URL | Want to review subject-specific databases |
| Can verify the accuracy and credibility of the information found | Can evaluate the appropriateness and relevance of the information found |

that information, and how to use researched information ethically and avoid plagiarism.

## Search for Materials on the Internet

The Internet is the most popular research tool for college students in the United States. The **Internet** links computer networks around the world, allowing users to access information from millions of sources. Most people access the Internet by using the **World Wide Web,** a system that allows users to easily navigate the millions of sites on the Internet. For public speaking students, the Internet offers information on local, regional, national, and international events and issues; it also provides a truly staggering range of ideas for supporting materials.

### The Ethics of Internet Research

Because anyone can post information on the Internet, not everything you find there is accurate. Many websites are created and regularly updated by reputable people, companies, and institutions, but just as many others are not. Many sites include information that is old, incomplete, or based on personal opinions and biases. Additionally, identifying credible Internet sites can be difficult because many sites are well designed and look professional even if they're not.

Identifying credible websites places particular ethical responsibilities on you when you use the Internet to find supporting materials. To act in good faith with your audience, use only reliable and relevant information from the Internet and accurately credit the sources in your speech. (At the end of this chapter, you'll find guidelines about citing your sources.)

### Evaluating Internet Information

How do you know whether a source found on the Internet is one you can use in your speech? As you would with any other source, evaluate the information according to the following criteria.

*Is the information reliable?* Check the domain in the URL. Is it .com (a commercial enterprise that might be trying to sell something), .org (a nonprofit organization, more interested in services and issues than in commerce), .edu (an educational institution), or .gov (a government agency)? What bias might those operating the site have about your topic? Do they make any disclaimers about the information they post on the site? What makes this information reliable?

*Is the information authoritative?* A *tilde* (~) in the URL is usually a sign that a single individual is responsible for the information. Are the person's credentials posted on the site? Can you contact the person and ask for credentials? Can you find the person's credentials in any print sources, such as a *Who's Who* reference? Regardless of whether the material was authored by a single person, an organization, an institution, or a company, is the author an expert on the subject?

*How current is the information?* Many Web pages include the date the pages were posted or last updated. If you don't see such a date on a page, you may be able to find it in your browser's View or Document menu. If you determine that the website is current, is the time frame relevant to your subject or arguments? You may find great information, but if it doesn't relate to the time frame of your speech, it's not relevant or ethical to use.

*How complete is the information?* Much of the text posted on the Internet consists of excerpts from printed material, and what is left out may change the meaning of what is included. For example, a site may contain one paragraph from a newspaper article, but that paragraph may not reflect the overall message of the article. If you want to use an excerpted portion of a printed work, you must locate the complete work to ensure you are using the material accurately.

*Is the information relevant?* Many interesting facts and stories appear on the Web, but be sure those you use as supporting material do more than just tell a great story. Your information must help develop your thesis (Chapters 13, 14, and 24). Ask yourself whether the information helps develop your main ideas, or does it take you in a different direction?

*Is the information consistent and unbiased?* Is the information you find consistent with information you find on other sites, from printed sources, or from interviews? Do other sources support the statements, claims, and facts provided by a website? If the information

**SPEECH TIPS**

### USING WIKIPEDIA

You must cross-check information you find on Wikipedia. Although Wikipedia has the form of an encyclopedia, biased and inaccurate articles have been posted on it and remained online for a long time before anyone caught them. That's why many instructors don't allow students to use Wikipedia for research. Before you use material from Wikipedia, especially if it seems questionable in any way, at least do a Web search for a couple of other sources and compare the information.

**SPEECH Checklist**

### Evaluating Internet Sources

- ☐ Is the information at an appropriate level—not too simple and not too technical?
- ☐ Is the author a known expert on the topic?
- ☐ Does the website give the author's credentials or institutional affiliation?
- ☐ Is the website sponsored by an organization or institution?
- ☐ What does the URL tell you about the website's source and goals? (For starters, does the domain name end in .edu, .gov, .com, or .net?)
- ☐ Is the publisher of the site selling a product, promoting a position, or conveying information?
- ☐ When was the site created? Has it been updated recently? Is the recency of the information important for your speech?
- ☐ Is the information supported by a bibliography or links to other websites? Are those supporting sources authoritative and credible?

is inconsistent with other sources, it may reflect new findings about a topic, or it may reflect an unfounded or unsubstantiated claim. Many sites present only one side of an issue. To guarantee a less biased presentation and a more comprehensive picture of your topic, search a number of different sites and cross-check the information against established sources such as books and other print documents. Be wary of outrageous or controversial claims that can't be checked for accuracy or aren't grounded in reasonable arguments or sources.[1]

## Research Materials at the Library

The library is your most comprehensive tool for gathering materials. There you have access to librarians, databases, indexes, journals, magazines, newspapers, books, documents, and many other useful resources, including the Internet. These materials cover an extensive range of topics and time frames. In addition, their sources are usually more reliable than those found only on the Internet, because all the materials in a library are evaluated by experts and systematically organized.

But libraries also have their weaknesses. Until you become familiar with how libraries organize their books and other materials, you can find yourself confronting what may seem like a confusing coding system and a maze of shelves. Library research can seem so difficult that—as Ernest Boyer suggested in a report for the Carnegie Foundation—about "one out of every four undergraduates spends no time in the library during a normal week."[2]

However, once you know how to use the library effectively, you can easily combine Internet research with library research to gather a wide range of useful and credible materials for your speeches.

### Library Orientations and Librarians

If you are new to library research or are unfamiliar with the library you will be using, schedule a tour of the library before you begin your research. Getting a library orientation may sound silly or boring, but it can save you countless hours wandering around a place you don't understand. Most orientations take about an hour, and they can give you the confidence you need to begin your research on the right foot.

Librarians are also excellent resources. Librarians know what is in the library and how to find it. They are trained to know how materials are cataloged and where they are located, how to search through electronic databases, and how to request materials from other libraries. These skills can be invaluable to someone who is looking for supporting materials for a speech. Surprisingly, though, many students ask a librarian for assistance only as a last resort.

SPEECH TIPS

## ASKING A LIBRARIAN'S HELP

If you find yourself spending more than half an hour searching for materials you can't find, ask for assistance.

Librarians won't do the work for you, but they can make the work you do much more efficient and fruitful. When you seek a librarian in the course of your research, consider the following advice:

Skills & Confidence Web Connect 8.1

- *Fill out your research inventory* before you begin your search and bring it with you to the library. Refer to it as you work with the librarian.
- *Ask specific questions.* For example, rather than asking, "Where can I find information on incarcerated parents?" ask where you might find statistics on the number of children with incarcerated parents, or testimony by social workers about the effects of incarceration on families, or examples of the most common problems faced by families with one or both parents incarcerated.
- *Share the specifics of your assignment with the librarian:* "It's only a four-minute speech," "My instructor wants three sources from this year and two from within the last ten years," "My audience is a potential source of funding for my proposal," "I want a really dramatic story for my introduction," and so on. Information like this will help the librarian direct you to the most useful information and will help you avoid information overload.
- *Treat the librarian with respect.* Librarians are highly trained people whose specialty is finding information. They will likely be eager to help you if you acknowledge their talents and worth.

### Library Catalogs

Online catalogs of the library's holdings can be the most user-friendly place to start your research. They allow you to search for your topic by title, author, or subject in books, journals, magazines, and other print and electronic materials in the library. Each catalog entry will also tell you whether the material is checked out or in another library and how to obtain it if it is.

You can also perform keyword searches in an online catalog. For example, if you don't know the full title of the source you want, you can search with a word that is included in the title. The computer will bring up a listing of all titles that include that word. You can then scan the list to find the specific source you want and its call number, an alphanumeric code that indicates exactly where it is stored in the library.

Skills & Confidence
Web Connect 8.2

Online subject searches allow you to find all the sources that include information about a particular topic. For example, Lin's speech topic was road rage, and she wanted to know if any recent books or magazine articles had been written about her subject. She didn't have a specific author or title, so she searched on the subject of *driving*. This search produced far too many sources to look through. She then searched on a more specific term, *road rage*. The results of this search were much more manageable. Lin later used a Boolean operator to refine her search further. **Boolean operators** are words you can use to create specific phrases that broaden or narrow your search. The most common are AND, OR, and NOT. In her search for links on road rage, Lin used the Boolean operator AND to link her topic with the broader issue of antisocial behavior. As a result, she got a listing of sites about both road rage and antisocial behavior. If she had used OR, she would have called up a listing of sites on either road rage or antisocial behavior. If she'd searched with "road rage NOT antisocial behavior," she would have gotten only links to sites about road rage that made no reference to antisocial behavior. Using Boolean operators helps focus your searches to find as much or as little information as you need.

A few libraries still use print card catalogs that you search through by hand. These are large cabinets full of small drawers containing index cards with the bibliographic information for all the items stored in the library. Entries are organized alphabetically by title, by author, and by subject. So, for example, if you wanted to find information about this textbook, you could look under "I" for *Invitation to Public Speaking Handbook*, "G" for Griffin, Cindy L., or "P" for public speaking. Each card also includes the source's call number, when it was published, who published it, and whether it contains illustrations, photographs, or maps.

The library's catalog is one way to explore the possible sources of information about your speech topic. You can also use more specific sources at the library, such as databases and indexes, government documents, and reference works.

## Databases and Indexes

**Databases** are collections of information stored electronically. A few databases are available for free on the Internet, but libraries subscribe to many others. You will find two kinds of databases in libraries. **Bibliographic databases** index publishing data for books, periodical articles, government reports, statistics, patents, research reports, conference proceedings, and dissertations. **Full-text databases** index the complete text of newspapers, periodicals, encyclopedias, research reports, court cases, books, and the like. Bibliographic databases help you find a specific source, such as the title of a particular journal article; a full-text database provides the entire text of that source.

Some databases provide abstracts of documents. An **abstract** is a summary of an article or publication. Most abstracts are about a paragraph long. You can use abstracts to quickly find out whether a document includes the information you need. However, you will need to track down the full text of the article or publication if you want to cite it in your speech. Abstracts are not sources themselves.

Databases are useful research tools for several reasons. Computer searches are quick, and they are efficient because you can search using keywords and subjects. Databases allow you to access materials from other libraries, and most can usually be accessed from any computer connected to the Internet. Sources are current because records can be entered into a computerized database as soon as they are available, and they are updated regularly. Finally, databases present information in a format that is easy to copy.

But databases also have drawbacks. The so-called logic of databases is sometimes hard to understand, so searches can yield *false hits*, or citations unrelated to your topic. For example, a search for articles on road rage may yield articles on road construction and even anger management techniques. Because full-text databases store so much text, they are especially likely to yield false hits. Additionally, some electronic databases do not include material that is more than five to ten years old. So, if you are looking for historical trends, you will need to consult other sources of information.

When you want to search through materials that are published regularly—such as magazines, newspapers, yearbooks, scholarly

**SPEECH TIPS**

### SEARCHING INDEXES

- Subject and keyword searches are crucial to finding what you want in an index, so be as specific and concise as you can.
- Indexes vary in how they classify topics, so a particular search term might not yield useful results from every index.
- You can probably find something on your topic in almost any index, so be sure you are searching indexes relevant to your topic.

journals, and proceedings from conferences—an index can be very helpful. An **index** is an alphabetical listing of the topics discussed in a specific publication, along with the corresponding year, volume, and page numbers. Many indexes are computerized, but some libraries still rely on the print versions. College libraries usually have indexes for almost every academic discipline and area of interest. Figure 8.1 presents a list of commonly used indexes.

**FIGURE 8.1 Indexes**

| | |
|---|---|
| **InfoTrac and InfoTrac College Edition** | Citations, abstracts, and full-text articles from thousands of magazines, journals, and newspapers. |
| **LEXIS/NEXIS** | Full-text database for legal, business, and current issues. Includes U.S. Supreme Court and lower court cases. |
| **Academic Search Premier** | Scholarly academic multidisciplinary database. Covers a broad range of disciplines, including general academic, business, social sciences, humanities, general sciences, education, and multicultural topics. |
| **IngentaConnect** | Indexes scholarly journals and delivers documents. A fee is charged for document delivery. |
| ***Readers' Guide to Periodical Literature*** | Indexes almost 300 popular and general-interest magazines, including *The New Yorker*, *Newsweek*, and *National Geographic Traveler*. |
| **DataTimes** | Online newspaper database, including *Washington Post*, *Dallas Morning News*, and *San Francisco Chronicle*. |
| **Christian Science Monitor** | Indexes the *Christian Science Monitor International Daily Newspaper*. |
| **New York Times Index** | Indexes the *New York Times* newspaper. |
| **NewsBank** | Web-based and microfiche collections covering current events from newspapers in over 100 cities. |
| **The Times Index (London)** | Index to the daily *Times*, the *Sunday Times*, the *Times Literary Supplement*, the *Times Educational Supplement*, and the *Times Higher Education Supplement*. |
| **Wall Street Journal Index** | Emphasizes financial news from the *Journal*. Includes *Barron's Index*, a subject and corporate index to *Barron's Business and Financial Weekly*. |
| ***Washington Post* Newspaper** | Index of the newspaper from our nation's capital. |

## Government Documents

Government documents can help you make a well-informed contribution to the public dialogue. They contain all kinds of useful information:

- Statistics on population, personal income, education, crime, health, and the like
- Information about social issues such as employment, hunger, teen pregnancy, and the environment
- Issues discussed in Congress, such as gun control, immigration, and education
- Information about historical events, such as wars and elections
- Information on local issues, such as funding for public education or charter schools, land disputes, water rights, and so on
- Research sponsored by the government
- Maps, charts, and posters that you can download or photocopy to make excellent visual aids for your speeches (Chapter 19)

You can find government documents in print, on CD-ROM or DVD, and sometimes on database indexes in the library. Most government information is also available on the Internet.

## Reference Works

Skills & Confidence Web Connect 8.3

*When and where was Oprah Winfrey born? Who was the first person to fly around the world? What was the worst hurricane in recorded history?* When you are looking for simple facts and answers to general questions like these, consult the reference works in the reference section of your library. Reference works contain useful facts and information and can provide you with quick answers, thus saving you hours of time searching the Internet or digging through indexes and abstracts. If you are unsure of exactly which reference work to consult, ask your librarian for guidance. These are some of the more commonly used references and examples of each:

- ***Almanacs:*** Collections of facts on various subjects, such as the depth of Lake Michigan (*The World Almanac and Book of Facts*).
- ***Atlases:*** Books of maps and geographical information (*The Times Atlas of World History*, *Goode's World Atlas*).
- ***Biographical dictionaries:*** Information about famous and important people (*Dictionary of American Biography*, *Who's Who*).
- ***Dictionaries:*** Compilations of words and their definitions, correct spellings and pronunciations, origins, and synonyms and

antonyms (*Oxford English Dictionary*; *Collins German-English, English-German Dictionary*).

- ***Encyclopedias:*** Overviews or surveys of a wide range of topics, such as butterflies, chemical warfare, or Toronto (*Encyclopaedia Britannica, World Book Encyclopedia*).
- ***Gazetteers and guidebooks:*** Dictionaries and descriptions of geographical places. Guidebooks contain maps; gazetteers do not (*Chambers World Gazetteer: An A–Z of Geographical Information, Baedeker Guidebooks, Fodor's Travel Guides*).
- ***Handbooks:*** Summaries or surveys of a single broad subject, such as meetings (*Robert's Rules of Order*).
- ***Manuals:*** Works that explain how to do something or how an organization operates (*United States Government Manual*).
- ***Quotation dictionaries:*** Compilations of historical and contemporary quotations (*The Oxford Dictionary of Quotations*).
- ***Reviews:*** Analyses and comments on the work of another—often authors of books, movies, plays, or other performances; artists; or people who make significant public arguments or claims (*Book Review Digest, Index to Scientific Reviews*).
- ***Yearbooks:*** Summaries of trends and events of the previous year. Can be limited to one subject or to one geographical area (*Information Please Almanac, Atlas and Yearbook*; *Americana Annual: An Encyclopedia of Events*; *Statistical Abstract of the United States*).[3]

Reference works can be helpful for a number of reasons that aren't always immediately obvious. They are quick to use and can give you a jump-start on your research efforts. They can give you an overview of a topic and get you started on gathering supporting materials. Reference sources can also help you cross-check information. They can help you

**SPEECH TIPS**

### INTERNET REFERENCE WORKS

Only a small number of the reference works on library shelves are available for free on the Internet, such as *Merriam-Webster's Dictionary* (www.merriam-webster.com/), the *Visual Dictionary* (visual.merriam-webster.com/), and *Columbia Encyclopedia* (www.bartleby.com/65/). Others, —such as *Encyclopaedia Britannica* (www.britannica.com/), are available by subscription or in a very old edition, such as the 1911 edition of *Encyclopaedia Britannica* or the 1918 edition of *Bartlett's Familiar Quotations*. The Internet is not yet a substitute for the library's reference shelves.

track down someone's credentials or give you the specific details of a person's life. Reference works tend to be timely or to provide the information you need for a specific time frame. And they are a source of ideas for other places to look for the materials you need.

### Evaluating Library Resources

Although the information in libraries is generally more reliable than materials on the Internet, you still must evaluate library sources and use them ethically. Not all the sources you find will be credible or appropriate for your particular speech and audience. Evaluate library sources by using the same strategies you use to assess Internet sources, Check that the source is:

Skills & Confidence
PPD
Activity 8.1

- Reliable
- Authoritative
- Current
- Complete
- Relevant
- Consistent with other information you have found

## Avoid Plagiarism

Once you find the information identified in your research inventory, the next challenge is to use it fairly and ethically in your speech. When you incorporate other people's ideas and words in your speech, you must give them credit in order to avoid plagiarism. **Plagiarism** is presenting another person's words and ideas as your own. That is, plagiarism is stealing someone else's work and taking credit for it. Plagiarism is a serious issue in public speaking because it's dishonest and detrimental to a healthy public dialogue. There are three types of plagiarism:

- **Patchwork plagiarism** is constructing a complete speech that you present as your own from portions of several different sources.
- **Global plagiarism** is stealing an entire speech from a single source and presenting it as your own.
- **Incremental plagiarism** is presenting select portions from a single speech as your own.

All three forms of plagiarism are extremely unethical. However, they are easy to avoid. As you do your research, avoid unintentional plagiarism by taking careful notes and accurately documenting the source of each idea. Remember to cite these sources in your speech, even if you are paraphrasing an idea or borrowing only one phrase. Sometimes you'll find, especially when researching on the Internet, that some of the basic information you need to cite a source is missing, such as the author's name. If you use the source, you must cite as much information as you can, such as the name of the site, the sponsoring organization or institution, the URL, or the name of the article. Also include as much information as you can in your bibliography. (Note that if the author's name is not included on a website, you can use the title of the article or Web page or the name of the sponsoring organization instead.)

The consequences of plagiarizing can be serious: loss of credibility, failing the assignment or course, and perhaps even expulsion from your school. The way to avoid plagiarism is simple: Do your own work and give credit to others for their ideas and words. Identify your sources in your speech, and include a Works Cited page when you hand in the outline of your speech.

Skills & Confidence Web Connect 8.4

## Citing Sources in Your Speech

As you develop your speech, each of the sources you select to support your claims must be properly cited. There are two reasons to cite sources: It is ethical and it adds credibility to your ideas.

### Citing Sources Is Ethical

In public speaking, our ideas often grow from the ideas of others. When we cite our sources, we acknowledge this debt, fulfilling our ethical responsibility to give credit to others for their work and their contributions to our thinking. If you cite your sources properly, your audience members should be able to tell which ideas are your own and which ideas come from others. If you do not cite your sources, you risk committing plagiarism, which is a serious academic offense.

### Citing Sources Adds Credibility

When you cite sources in a speech, you indicate that you have done research on your topic, have some understanding of it, and that

**SPEECH TIPS**

**KEEPING TRACK OF SOURCES**

Keeping your research notes well organized from the start makes it easy to cite sources appropriately when you give your speech.

your ideas about it have the backing of experts. Citing sources also shows your audience that you value the public dialogue and that you recognize that others have something to offer to this dialogue. When you want to bolster the credibility of a claim, cite the source so your audience recognizes the authority from which it came.

### Guidelines for Citing Sources

Although your instructor may have rules for the number and format of sources you are to cite in a speech, there are three general guidelines for citing sources. These guidelines rely on ethical principles and an audience-centered approach.

*Give credit to all sources of specific information.* When you rely on the specific ideas or words of others, give them credit during your speech. If you use someone's research, quote or paraphrase someone else, or share information from a magazine, book, newspaper, or other source, you need to name your source in your speech.

Note that you do not need to provide citations for claims based on *common knowledge*, information that most people know. For example, the statement "Eating a balanced diet is good for your health" is common knowledge and does not require a citation. But the more specific statement "Eat at least three ounces of whole grain bread, cereal, crackers, rice, or pasta every day" requires a source citation such as "according to the U.S. Department of Agriculture's food pyramid."

*Name your sources.* For your audience to feel that your claims are credible, they need to know the specific sources. General phrases such as "research shows," "evidence suggests," and "someone once said"

**SPEECH TIPS**

#### CITING SOURCES IN YOUR SPEECH

Weave the source information into your speech with phrases like the following:

- Last week's *New York Times* tells us that...
- According to the 2000 Census,...
- The director of the Center for Applied Studies in Appropriate Technology responded to my question in this way...
- The *Old Farmer's Almanac* reports that this will be the wettest year this area has experienced since 1938.
- Jane Kneller, professor of philosophy at this university, writes...

rarely substantiate a claim. If your audience is listening with care, they'll want to know your sources. They'll want specifics before they accept your claims as credible. When you cite a source in your speech, include as much of the following information as is appropriate:

- The name of the person or the publication
- The credentials of that person or publication
- The date of the study, statistic, or piece of evidence

These three items generally are enough to show your audience that your source is valid and your information is reliable and relevant to your topic. When the source is familiar to your audience, less identifying information may be necessary. For example, if your source is the U.S. Department of Agriculture's food pyramid, the agency's credentials are self-evident, and the food pyramid's date probably won't be necessary in your speech. You can usually omit details such as page numbers and place of publication from your actual speech, but you will want to include them in your list of works cited. That list should contain enough information that other people can locate your sources. (For models, see Figure 7.2, "Sample preliminary bibliography," and "Creating a Works Cited Page" in Appendix B.)

*Deliver all information accurately.* When you use a source, you must do so accurately. This means giving the name and title of the person correctly, pronouncing any unfamiliar words clearly, and delivering all statistics and quotations accurately. Mispronouncing names and titles, stumbling over dates and quotes, and leaving out important elements of a citation can reduce your credibility. It can even alter the facts you are sharing with your audience. So before you give your speech, be sure you have all your source citations recorded correctly and rehearse them until they fit smoothly into your speech. (You'll learn more about delivery in Chapters 17 and 18.)

CHAPTER 9

# Conducting Research Interviews

- Determine Who to Interview
- Schedule the Interview
- Prepare for the Interview
- Conduct the Interview
- Follow Up the Interview
- Ethical Interviewing

*In this chapter, you will learn to*

- Search for information through personal interviews
- Prepare interview questions
- Conduct an ethical and informative interview

Using the words of other people in a speech can supply important information, provide a sense of immediacy, bring abstract concepts and arguments to life, and make seemingly distant issues hit home. Therefore, including the results of an interview in your speech can be a powerful way to present your ideas. The supporting materials you gather from interviews also supplement and confirm the materials you find in your Internet and library research.

An **interview** is a planned interaction with another person that is organized around inquiry and response, with one person asking questions while the other person answers them.[1] Interviews require planning, and productive interviews involve more than simply asking a few questions. You must first decide whom you'll interview, then schedule the interview, decide on what questions to ask, conduct the interview in a professional and ethical manner, and, finally, follow up with a letter of thanks.

## Determine Who to Interview

Your first step in conducting interviews is to determine whom you want to interview. There are several criteria you can use to identify the best interview subjects for your speech:

- Who are the experts on my speech topic?
- Who has personal experience with the topic?
- Who will my audience find interesting and credible?
- Who has time to speak with me?
- Who do I have the time to contact?

As you gather other supporting materials from the Internet and the library, keep your eyes open for local people who might be excellent sources of information. If you have time, you might also consider contacting people who live outside your area via e-mail or the telephone. Choose interview subjects who have credentials and experiences relevant to your topic and so can speak intelligently about it. A good interview subject might be a well-known expert or scholar, a head of an agency or company, someone on staff or in a support position, or a member of a community group, club, or organization.

## Schedule the Interview

Most people are flattered when asked for an interview and will agree if you present yourself and your request respectfully. To ensure that a potential source sees you as credible and professional, take a moment to consider:

- Why you want the interview and why this person is an appropriate interview subject.
- What specific types of information you want to gather.
- Roughly what questions you'll ask.
- Approximately how much time you want to spend with this person.

When people are asked for an interview, they want to know the answers to all of these questions.

Before you contact someone to request an interview, rehearse what you'll say a few times (like you would a speech) so you sound organized and professional. In your request, include the following information:

- Identify who you are, providing your full name, where you're from (school, place of business), the public speaking course you're in, and your instructor's name.
- Specify the requirements of your assignment, such as its purpose, length, and topic.
- Describe why you've chosen to contact the person (for example, she's an expert in the field, he's the head of an organization).
- Request the interview, letting the person know how much time it will take and what kinds of questions you'll ask. Include two or three of your most important or engaging questions.

By describing the types of questions you'll ask, your interview subjects can determine whether they can answer them and if they need to prepare before you arrive. And by letting them know how long you need for the interview, they can schedule time for you.

## Prepare for the Interview

Preparing for interviews often takes longer than conducting them, but the payoff of careful preparation is worth the time. The two components of preparing for interviews are (1) designing your questions and (2) deciding how you will record your interview.

### Designing Interview Questions

Your interview questions are your guide for the interview. Showing up with a vague plan to "just see how it develops" may be a good strategy for meeting a new friend, but it usually does not get you what you need from an interview. Even seasoned interviewers plan their questions carefully before they begin an interview, and most of them also research their interview subjects extensively.[2]

The goal of your interview questions should be to obtain information that you couldn't find through your Internet and library research. For example, in her speech on road rage (Chapter 8), Lin couldn't find information about the personality profiles of people prone to road rage. When she interviewed a driving instructor, she asked him about his experiences with students who fell into road rage. Thus, she was able to get the information she needed.

Three kinds of questions are commonly used in interviews: open-ended questions, closed-ended questions, and probes (open-ended and closed-ended questions are also discussed in Chapter 6). *Open-ended questions* invite a wide range of possible responses. They can be as broad as "How did you become a driving instructor?" and "What are your thoughts on this most recent form of legislation?" Open-ended questions are useful for several reasons. They are usually nonthreatening and so prompt interviewees to do most of the talking. They do not restrict the form or content of an answer, and they allow interviewees to offer information voluntarily. Finally, they encourage interviewees to pull together ideas, knowledge, and experiences in interesting ways.

A *closed-ended question* prompts a brief, focused answer and allows the interviewer to keep tighter control of the direction of the conversation. A closed-ended question might be "How long have you been a driving instructor?" or "Do many of your students display road rage?" Closed-ended questions are useful because they can be answered easily and quickly, they encourage interviewees to give you specific information, and they result in shorter answers for you to process.

Most research on interviewing suggests that a combination of open-ended and closed-ended questions yields the best results in an interview. Open-ended questions give you more stories and details than closed-ended questions, but when you just need facts, there's nothing like a closed-ended question to prompt the specific answer you need.[3]

Another type of interview question is a **probe**, a question that follows up an answer to a previous question. Probes take many forms:

- Nonverbal, such as head nods or questioning eyes that indicate interest and a request to continue
- Slight vocalizations such as "Oh?" "Really?" "Um-hmm," or "Is that so?"
- Direct requests for clarification, as in "Let me see if I've got this right. Did you say . . . ?" or "Could you explain what those figures mean for our community?"
- Requests for elaboration, like "Why do you say you're angry about this new legislation?" or "When that first driver went crazy with you in the car, what was your reaction?"

Probes are excellent interview tools because they allow you to take a question further than you'd planned and get a more comprehensive answer.

## Recording the Interview

As you prepare for an interview, consider whether you want to record your conversation electronically or on paper. Both methods have advantages and disadvantages. With a recording, you have a record of your exact conversation, but you have to transcribe the whole thing to find the exact quotes you want, which can be time consuming. A recording device can also sometimes make an interviewee nervous and less prone to share stories and ideas. However, when you record an interview, you are free to relax a bit and make more extensive eye contact because you aren't busy writing things down.

When you record your interview on paper, you have the advantage of being able to make notes about nonverbal aspects of the interview that may help you when you repeat a quote in your speech. And when it is over, you already have a written transcript of your conversation. However, because you are trying to record the highlights of what is said, it can be harder to engage in a conversation with your interviewee.

Whether you plan to take notes on paper or use an electronic recording device, ask your interviewee if you have permission to record your conversation.

## Conduct the Interview

The guidelines for conducting interviews are essentially grounded in the rules of common courtesy, so they are not difficult to follow:

- Dress appropriately.
- Show up on time.
- Begin by introducing yourself to your interviewee.
- Restate the purpose of the interview and your speech assignment.
- Request permission to record the interview.
- Start with questions that will put the interviewee at ease and then follow those with your most important questions.

As the interview progresses, remember that although you are having a conversation with your interviewee, you need to listen more than you talk; you are there to get the other person's perspectives and ideas.

At the end of your interview, ask your interviewee if she or he would like to add any information. You may get a piece of information or a story you did not think to ask for directly but fits into your speech perfectly.

Finally, thank the interviewee verbally for his or her time. Before you say good-bye, be sure you have recorded names, professional titles, and addresses correctly so you can cite them accurately and send a letter of thanks.

## Follow Up the Interview

Review your notes or transcribe your recordings as soon after the interview as you can, filling in details that are fresh in your mind and spelling out abbreviations you might have used in recording words on paper. Make notes of ideas that came to you as you listened to your interviewee, such as places in your speech where particular quotes or stories might go or ways you might use some of the interview information in your opening and closing comments.

Always send formal letters of thanks to your interviewees, communicating your appreciation for their time and willingness to share information with you. You might even share with them some of the interview material you've decided to include in your speech.

## Ethical Interviewing

Ethical interviewing means preparing for interviews, asking appropriate questions, using quotes and information honestly, including only what was said and staying true to the intention of the speaker, and giving credit to interviewees for the words and ideas you include in your speech. At times, it may be tempting to alter a statement, embellish a story, or change a number or example just slightly to fit your needs. However, if the public dialogue is to function in any meaningful way, we must present material that is accurate and true. Information is inaccurate even if it's been changed only slightly, and people cannot make rational and reasonable choices if they have incorrect information.

Of course, ethics also apply to interviewees. If an interviewee provides information that seems inconsistent with what your other research supports, take the time to double-check your own research and the credentials of your interview subject. Also ask your interviewee for documentation or sources that support unusual claims. If an interviewee provides information that is highly personal or would compromise the integrity or reputation of others, do not use that information in your speech. And of course, if an individual shares something with you "off the record," that information should stay out of your speech and out of your conversations with others.

# ORGANIZATION



## CIVIC ENGAGEMENT IN ACTION

### A Boy Soldier Tells His Story

Twenty-six-year-old Ishmael Beah can not only tell the story of being in a rap band when he was eight years old but also the story of his capture and forced life as a teenaged "boy soldier" in his native Sierra Leone, Africa. In his public presentations and his discussions about his book, *A Long Way Gone*, Beah describes his life as a thirteen-year-old after his village was destroyed and he was forced to stay awake for days, popping pills, smoking marijuana, sniffing "brown-brown" (cocaine mixed with gunpowder), and killing indiscriminately. He describes a time when "taking a gun and shooting somebody had become as easy as drinking a glass of water," torture was a way of life, and leaving captivity was not a choice: "Leaving was as good as being dead." He says, "In Western culture, people have romanticized war and violence. But none of it is glorious. When you're there, it's madness. It's your life, or someone else's."

CHRISTOPHER ENA/AP PHOTO

When he was sixteen, UNICEF workers rescued Beah and other boy soldiers and took them to Freetown, Sierra Leone's capital. After a slow, torturous recovery in a rehabilitation center, he moved in with an uncle, started attending school, and even managed to enjoy life, going to pubs and soccer matches with his cousins. In 1996, he received an invitation to speak in New York City at the United Nations' First International Children's Parliament on war-affected children. There he met Laura Simms, an American author invited to the event to help the children tell their stories. Not long after he returned home, the war found its way to Freetown and an illness took his uncle's life. Desperate, Beah contacted Simms and asked her to adopt him. She agreed, and Beah emigrated to New York.

### You Can Get Involved

You can watch a video of Beah discussing his experiences with Jon Stewart on *The Daily Show* by going to ComedyCentral .com, searching on "Ishmael Beah," and clicking the link provided. You can also explore taking action to help address the exploitation of child soldiers by accessing **Web Connect P.IV.1: Amnesty International & Child Soldiers** and

(continued)

## CIVIC ENGAGEMENT IN ACTION continued

Skills & Confidence
Web Connect P.IV.1
Web Connect P.IV.2

When he decided to write a book to tell his story, he found the process difficult: "Many times I would start writing about what I did, and then have to step away and write about something easier, like my mother's cooking. What gave me the strength to continue, to face myself and relive my experiences, was reminding myself there are children living it right now." Despite the pain, he says, "I knew the importance of it, to expose what continues to happen to a lot of children. That gave me the strength to sit down and do it." He feels there are no excuses for not working to stop other children from being abducted and forced to fight in wars. Now in law school, Beah is often asked to speak about his experiences and his work advocating for children. His narratives often feature a common theme: He feels lucky to have escaped the war and lived to tell others. "For me healing is not forgetting. It's just learning to live with it, transform it."[1]

## You Can Get Involved (continued)

**Web Connect P.IV.2: Human Rights Watch & Child Soldiers** at your Resource Center for *Invitation to Public Speaking Handbook*. If you have a personal story you think might help others, consider starting a blog or using the public speaking skills you're developing in this course to speak to others in your community, such as at church or school.

# ORGANIZATION

CHAPTER 10

# Organizing Your Speech

- Organize for Clarity
- Main Points
  Speech Checklist: Main Points
- Connectives
  Speech Checklist: Connectives

*In this chapter, you will learn to*

- Identify the main points for your speech
- Determine the appropriate number of main points for your speech
- Organize your main points according to five different patterns
- Apply tips for preparing your main points effectively
- Use four different kinds of connectives in your speech

Once you've gathered the information for your speech, the next step is to organize it into a coherent presentation. There are several ways you can do this. In this chapter, you will learn about the role organization plays in clear and effective speeches, how to structure your main points, the different patterns of organization you can use, and effective ways to move from one idea to the next.[1] Once you master the fundamental steps of organization and outlining (which is covered in Chapter 11), you can branch out to more elaborate techniques. For now, use these basic frameworks to help you build speeches that are clear, interesting, and easy to follow.

## Organize for Clarity

As you've seen, public speaking is more systematic than casual conversation. Public speakers usually take considerable time to organize their ideas so that their audiences will find their message logical and easy to follow. Like many other aspects of the speechmaking process, organization is an important audience-centered responsibility. Let's look at an example that illustrates the importance of a well-organized speech. See if you can make sense of the following organization of ideas:

Take one of the corners and bring it to the center.

- The history of this process is an intriguing one.
- My mother had the flag given to her family when her brother died in the Vietnam War.

The stars on the edge of the flag are highly symbolic.

- It should never touch the ground.
- She describes the ceremony as quite beautiful and symbolic.

You need two people to fold a flag correctly.

- There is a correct way to fold a flag.
- The flag should always be displayed behind the speaker's left shoulder.

Can you follow the organizational logic? Although you begin to realize that the speech is about flags by the second subpoint, are you clear about the speaker's thesis? Is her speech informative, invitational, persuasive, or for a special occasion? Can you tell whether she was asked, required, or decided to speak?

Now consider this speech organized in a way that is more linear—not to mention more appealing—to an audience:

| | |
|---|---|
| **Specific purpose:** | To inform my audience about the rules and regulations for handling the U.S. flag. |
| **Thesis statement:** | The flag, a symbol of much that is great about this nation, should be hung, handled, and folded in a specific manner. |
| **Main points:** | I. Each part of the flag has a specific meaning or purpose dedicated to symbolizing patriotic ideas.<br>II. Because of the symbolism of each of these parts, the flag should be hung in a specific manner. |

III. Flag etiquette, more than just stories told from generation to generation, tells us how to handle a flag properly.

IV. Flags should also be folded in a specific way, with each fold representing important qualities of our country.

Skills & Confidence Video Activity 10.1

This outline gives you a much clearer sense of what the speaker, Cindy, will cover and how her ideas relate to one another. **Organization**, the systematic arrangement of ideas into a coherent whole, makes speeches listenable. It makes the speaker's ideas and arguments clear and easy to follow.

# Main Points

One of the first steps in organizing a speech is to identify your main points. **Main points** are the most important, comprehensive ideas you address in your speech. They give your speech focus and help you decide which information to include and which to leave out. They are your overarching themes or subjects.

## Identify Your Main Points

You can identify the main points of your speech in two ways. First, take stock of your speech assignment, list of ideas, and research. You will know a particular idea is a main point when you realize that if you do not develop it, your topic will seem incomplete or nonsensical, or you will not accomplish your goal for the speech.

Second, if you have already written your thesis statement, you should be able to find your main points within it. Notice in the example about folding a flag that Cindy's thesis statement defines her main points: (1) the symbolism in the U.S. flag and (2) how a flag should be hung, (3) handled, and (4) folded. Without a thesis statement (as in the first version of Cindy's outline), a speaker's ideas are simply a random collection of points.

Your thesis statement may not always be as specific as Cindy's, especially if you are giving a process, or how-to, speech. Nonetheless, you can use even a broad thesis statement to develop your main points. Notice how the four steps Candice mentions in her thesis statement become the four steps she discusses in her speech.

**Specific purpose:** To inform my audience of the process of making a scrapbook.

**Thesis statement:** There are four steps to making a quality scrapbook.

**Main points:**

I. Collect the materials you want to put into the book.

II. Decide on the order of your materials.

III. Arrange the materials in the book.

IV. Cover or bind the book.

Your thesis statement and your research should guide your selection of main points for other types of speeches as well. For an invitational speech on the problem of elder abuse, Peter developed the following specific purpose, thesis, and main points:

**Specific purpose:** To invite my audience to consider two possible solutions to the problem of elder abuse.

**Thesis statement:** The problem of elder abuse is quite widespread but may be solved by more thorough background checks of employees in care facilities and increased funding for training and salaries.

**Main points:**

I. More thorough background checks of employees in care facilities may help solve the widespread problem of elder abuse.

II. Increased funding for training and salaries may also help solve this problem.

The thesis statement identified the two primary solutions to elder abuse, and the student used his research to develop those possibilities.

### Use an Appropriate Number of Main Points

Knowing how many main points to include can be difficult, because we often gather more information than we need and our subjects can be complex. Additionally, classroom speeches often have other requirements, such as incorporating visual aids, citing a specific number of sources, and engaging in a question-and-answer discussion with the audience. So how do you determine the number of main points to include?

In any kind of speech, your time limit is your most important guideline for determining the number of main points. For even a two- to three-minute speech of introduction, you might start out with a long list of possible main points, as May did:

**Specific purpose:** To introduce myself to my audience.

**Thesis statement:** I have lived an interesting life thus far and have goals for the future.

**Main points:**

I. I was born in the air over China, so I have dual citizenship.

II. I've lived in many different cities, states, and countries.

III. I love to do anything that pertains to water.

IV. I'll graduate next June and travel with friends for the summer.

V. After that, I'll join the navy.

VI. From there, I hope to become an aquatic research scientist for a university.

Although each of these points is interesting, there are far too many to cover—even if May had ten minutes. Also notice that her thesis statement is quite vague and does not help focus her ideas.

When you have a long list of ideas for any kind of speech, recognize that you'll have to reduce your scope. Most classroom speeches are limited to two to four main points, depending on the length of your speech and your speaking goals. You can reduce your scope by returning to your thesis statement and tightening it up (as May needs to do) or by focusing on only the main points that best develop your thesis statement. Here's a solution for May's speech:

**Specific purpose:** To introduce myself to my audience.

**Thesis statement:** The first twenty-two years of my life have been nomadic ones, and I will most likely continue this lifestyle for some time.

**Main points:**

I. My nomadic lifestyle began twenty-two years ago when I was born in an airplane over an ocean near China.

II. I'll continue to nurture my nomadic spirit and love of water by joining the navy when I graduate.

By narrowing her scope and by organizing the six ideas into two main points, May can present a far more coherent and interesting speech. Her audience will be able to follow two main points easily, rather than trying to keep track of six. And by focusing and reducing the number of points, May presents a more memorable image of herself.

Remember, you want to develop your ideas fully, and trying to incorporate too many into one speech will only create problems. If you suspect you have too many main points, review your thesis statement and then consider your time limit. Ask yourself if you can reasonably cover the amount of material you have planned in the time you are allowed. (Guidelines for managing the length of your main points are offered at the end of this section.) If you have too much information, rewrite your thesis statement to narrow its scope.

### Order Your Main Points

Once you've determined the number of main points for your speech, you will want to determine the order in which you discuss them. Although there are numerous organizational patterns, the five covered here are the basic ones:

chronological
spatial
causal
problem-solution
topical

As you become more skilled at speaking, you can adjust these patterns or add to your inventory patterns that are more complex. For now, use these basic patterns to help you improve your organizational skills.

*Chronological pattern.* Speeches that trace a sequence of events or ideas follow a **chronological pattern** of organization. If the ideas in your topic extend over a period of time, you may want to use this pattern to organize your speech. In the following example, Serafina used a chronological pattern to discuss the stages of a theory:

| | |
|---|---|
| **Specific purpose:** | To inform my audience of George Kinder's theory of money maturity. |
| **Thesis statement:** | The concept of money maturity relates to a person's relationship to money during childhood, adulthood, and on into the future. |

**Main points:**

I. Kinder's first stage of money maturity focuses on the relationship to money a person acquires during childhood.

II. The second stage of money maturity addresses the relationship to money a person has as an adult.

III. The third stage of money maturity occurs when we set healthy goals for our financial security in the future.

A chronological pattern can also be used to demonstrate and explain a process, as in this example:

**Specific purpose:** To inform my audience of how to make a safe ascent during a scuba dive of less than forty feet.

**Thesis statement:** Safe ascents during scuba diving can be divided into three basic steps.

**Main points:**

I. The first step in making a safe ascent is the preparation step: Signal your buddy and check the time.

II. The second step is the "get ready" step: Raise your right hand over your head and hold your buoyancy control device (BCD) with your left hand.

III. The third step of the safe ascent is the actual ascent: Slowly rotate upward, breathe normally, and release air from your BCD as you go.

*Spatial pattern.* When ideas are arranged in terms of location or direction, they follow a **spatial pattern** of organization. For example, arranging ideas from left to right, top to bottom, or inside to outside helps your audience visualize the relationship between ideas or the structure of something. Spatial relationships can be abstract, as in the following example from a speech about eating according to the food pyramid.

**Specific purpose:** To inform my audience of some of the creative ways to eat according to the food pyramid.

**Thesis statement:** The food pyramid can be used creatively to eat interesting and healthy foods that incorporate whole grains, vegetables and fruits, protein, and even some fats and sugars.

**Main points:**

I. At the foundation of the food pyramid are the grain and vegetable servings that you can combine to make dishes from around the world, such as couscous salad with tomatoes and basil.

II. You can complement this foundation with the middle level of the pyramid—the dairy, fruit, and protein servings—by making dishes such as curried chicken with apricots.

III. The top of the pyramid includes the stuff we really like to eat, the fats and sweets that can be made into such delicacies as candied almonds.

The spatial pattern is also often used to describe real things or places, such as the geographical locations described in Demetrious's speech about five Italian villages:

**Specific purpose:** To invite my audience to visit the Cinque Terre, five villages along the Mediterranean coast of Italy that are only accessible by boat or by footpath.

**Thesis statement:** The Cinque Terre contains five villages set into a steep hillside that visitors to the Mediterranean coast of Italy may find enchanting: Monterosso, Vernazza, Corniglia, Manarola, and Riomaggiore.

**Main points:**

I. The farthest village, called Monterosso, is a popular attraction because of the huge statues carved into the rocks overlooking its beaches.

II. The next two villages, Vernazza and Corniglia, display remarkable vineyards, homes, and a central promenade and piazza.

III. A hike to the top of the fourth village, Manarola, gives you a stunning view of the sea and all five of the villages.

IV. Riomaggiore, the village of love, completes the Cinque Terre, or five villages, with its captivating display of homes and shops tucked into the final ravine of this remarkable Italian hillside.

*Causal pattern.* Speeches that describe a cause-and-effect relationship between ideas or events follow a **causal pattern** of organization. When you use this organizational pattern, you will have two main points:

one discussing the cause and the other describing its effects. You can present either the cause first or the effects first, depending on your topic and your speaking goal. The following example uses a causal pattern to organize the ideas presented in an informative speech on sibling rivalry:

**Specific purpose:** To inform my audience of the causes and most serious effects of sibling rivalry.

**Thesis statement:** Sibling rivalry is caused by competition for attention and can become quite severe if not handled properly.

**Main points:**

I. Sibling rivalry is caused by competition for positive attention from parents.

II. If ignored, sibling rivalry can turn to hatred between siblings.

If the effects have already happened, you might choose to present the effects first, followed by the cause, as in the next example. The effects of worker burnout are discussed first so that the speaker can then attempt to persuade the audience of one of burnout's possible causes.

**Specific purpose:** To persuade my audience that the rapid pace of today's workplace is leading to an unusually high level of burnout.

**Thesis statement:** Today's workers are experiencing high levels of burnout, which is caused by increased demands on their time and energy.

**Main points:**

I. Today's workers display levels of burnout that are higher than ever.

II. Today's working environments contribute to burnout through a constant demand for more output in shorter amounts of time.

You can also use the causal pattern when your topic is an event or situation and its consequences, or when you want to describe an event that might happen and what its effects might be.

*Problem-solution pattern.* Speeches that identify a specific problem and offer a possible solution follow a **problem-solution pattern** of organization. This pattern is common in persuasive speeches because we can describe a problem and follow with a call to action. The problem-solution pattern has two main points: the description of the problem followed by a description of the solution. Solutions can be general or specific. In the following example, Molly's solution is a general recommendation:

| | |
|---|---|
| **Specific purpose:** | To persuade my audience that beef by-products have invaded our lives and that awareness is the first step to becoming an educated consumer. |
| **Thesis statement:** | Becoming aware of the problem of the presence of beef by-products in such common items as deodorants, photographic film, marshmallows, gum, and candles is the first step in a solution of raising our awareness for making educated consumer choices. |
| **Main points:** | I. Without our knowledge, beef by-products are included in many of the products we put on and in our bodies, as well as in and around our houses.<br>II. The solution to this invasion is to become aware of the presence of these beef by-products so we can make informed choices about what we buy and use. |

In contrast, the next example ends in the call for a very specific solution:

| | |
|---|---|
| **Specific purpose:** | To persuade my audience to vote in favor of Bond Measure 343 in November. |
| **Thesis statement:** | Money going to support before- and after-school meal programs is at an all-time low, and this measure will ensure the improvement of these services to students in our public schools. |
| **Main points:** | I. There is currently not enough money available to provide adequate before- and after-school meal programs to students in our public schools.<br>II. Passing Bond Measure 343 will provide this necessary money. |

In Chapter 24, you'll learn more about the various types of solutions speakers can suggest to their audiences.

*Topical pattern.* Speeches that divide their topics into subtopics, each of which addresses a different aspect of the larger topic, follow a **topical pattern** of organization. When you use a topical pattern, you can organize your ideas by following a progression of ideas that suits your own style. You do this by using the principle of primacy (putting your most important idea first) or recency (putting what you most want your audience to remember last), or by arranging the ideas in other ways. In the following example, Justin arranged his ideas topically to address the two major types of phobias:

| | |
|---|---|
| **Specific purpose:** | To inform my audience of the two major types of phobias. |
| **Thesis statement:** | Although there are many specific phobias, these "irrational fears and dislikes" can be categorized in two ways: social and specific. |
| **Main points:** | I. A social phobia is a fear of appearing stupid or being shamed in a social situation.<br>II. A specific phobia is a fear of specific objects or situations, like spiders, closed spaces, and so on. |

In the following example, Alex uses a topical pattern to persuade her audience that women in "glory sports" are just as talented as the men.

| | |
|---|---|
| **Specific purpose:** | To persuade my audience that very talented women engage in what are commonly called "glory sports." |
| **Thesis statement:** | We know very little about the three most prominent women who participate in glory sports, even though they are as talented as the men who participate in the same sports. |
| **Main points:** | I. Layne Beachley is a professional surfer living in Sydney, Australia, who has held the world champion surfing title for three consecutive years.<br>II. Cara Beth Burnside resides in Southern California and is a legendary skateboarder.<br>III. Tara Dakides, also from California, is "the most progressive and influential female ever to strap on a snowboard," doing tricks "most guy pros haven't even done yet." |

Skills & Confidence
PPD Activity 10.1

Topical patterns help you organize a speech that doesn't fit into a chronological, spatial, causal, or problem-solution organizational pattern. If you try to rearrange the examples in this section into one of the other organizational patterns, you'll find that your ideas won't fit well.

## Guidelines for Preparing Main Points

There are three keys to developing your main points:

- Keep each main point separate and distinct—don't combine points.
- Word your points consistently.
- Devote appropriate coverage to each main point.

*Keep each main point separate and distinct.* To be as clear as possible, each main point should be a separate idea. Once you've identified your likely main points, double-check them to be sure you have not combined two ideas into one main point. We may be tempted to combine two ideas to cover as much information as we can. But notice what happened when Aaron combined two ideas into a single point:

| *Ineffective main points* | *More effective main points* |
|---|---|
| I. Electronic music is produced from a variety of machines that make noise electronically. | I. Electronic music is produced from a variety of machines that make noise electronically. |
| II. Electronic music has become more popular in recent years and is performed by many well-known artists. | II. Electronic music has become more popular in recent years. |
| | III. Electronic music is performed by many well-known artists. |

The points in the right column are clearer because each addresses only one idea. By separating the two points, Aaron can avoid confusing or overwhelming his audience. If electronic music's popularity and the artists who perform it are discussed in separate main points, the audience will have an easier time following the speech.

*Word your main points consistently.* Try to word your main points as consistently as possible. A parallel structure is easier to organize and remember. In the next example, Michael presented an informative speech on the reasons for stop signs. Notice how the parallel main points in the right column are clearer and more memorable than those in the left column:

| *Ineffective main points* | *More effective main points* |
|---|---|
| I. Drivers need to know who has the right of way, and a stop sign tells us that. | I. Stop signs assign the right of way to vehicles using an intersection. |
| II. Stop signs slow down drivers who are traveling at unsafe speeds. | II. Stop signs reduce the problem of speeding in certain areas. |

| | |
|---|---|
| III. Sometimes pedestrians need protection from vehicles, and stop signs give them that protection. | III. Stop signs protect pedestrians in busy intersections or near schools. |

A simple reworking of phrasing makes the main points parallel: stop signs assign, stop signs reduce, stop signs protect. Although this kind of parallel structure is not always possible, your ideas will be clearer and more memorable when you can use it.

*Devote the appropriate coverage to each main point.* Remember that your main points are your most important ideas. Therefore, each point should receive the same level of development and attention in your speech. If you find yourself spending little time developing a particular point, ask yourself whether it really is as important as you thought and whether it should be a main point in your speech. If, on the other hand, you find yourself putting a lot of development into one point, consider if you should divide it into two points. In preparing a speech on the art of batik, Martha discovered an imbalance in her main points:

**Specific purpose:** To inform my audience about batik, a beautiful and diverse art form that has been practiced for centuries.

**Thesis statement:** The art of batik has an intriguing history as well as methods of production and designs that reflect the skill and politics of the artisan.

**Main points:**

I. The history of batik (65 percent of the speech)

II. The production of batik (15 percent of the speech)

III. The designs of batik (15 percent of the speech)

IV. Where to purchase batik (5 percent of the speech)

Martha realized she had spent so much time on her first point that she didn't have time to cover her remaining points. Although the history of batik is important, it wasn't the only information she wanted to share with her audience. She also wanted to show them the production process and some of the designs she loved. After some consideration, Martha reduced the scope of her speech by dropping her fourth point (which wasn't really a part of her thesis statement), and she condensed the details of her first point. She reworked her speech as follows, saving 20 percent of her time for her introduction and conclusion:

| | |
|---|---|
| **Specific purpose:** | To inform my audience about batik, a beautiful and diverse art form that has been practiced for centuries. |
| **Thesis statement:** | The art of batik has an intriguing history as well as methods of production and designs that reflect the skill and politics of the artisan. |
| **Main points:** | I. The history of batik (30 percent)<br>II. The production of batik (25 percent)<br>III. The designs of batik (25 percent) |

Your goal, as Martha's revised main points suggest, is not necessarily to spend exactly the same amount of time on each point but to offer a balanced presentation of your ideas.

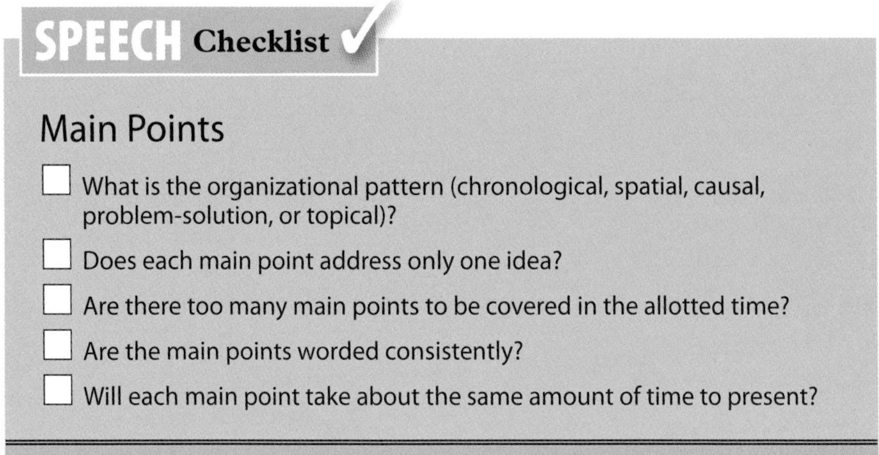
SPEECH Checklist

Main Points

- ☐ What is the organizational pattern (chronological, spatial, causal, problem-solution, or topical)?
- ☐ Does each main point address only one idea?
- ☐ Are there too many main points to be covered in the allotted time?
- ☐ Are the main points worded consistently?
- ☐ Will each main point take about the same amount of time to present?

## Connectives

Your main points are the heart of your speech. Once you have them on paper and supported with your research, you must find ways to connect them in order to enhance the audience's understanding. The words and phrases we use to link ideas in a speech are called **connectives**. They show audiences the relationship between ideas.

Before you read the descriptions of the four types of connectives, consider some of the connectives speakers use unconsciously: "all right," "next," "now," "um," "and," "so," "so then," and "ah." These words are often called *fillers* because they are words or sounds that tell the audience very little about the relationship between ideas. Fillers can be annoying, especially when the same one is repeated often in a speech. The following section offers four useful alternatives to fillers:

- Transitions
- Internal previews
- Internal summaries
- Signposts

### Transitions

**Transitions** are phrases that indicate you are finished with one idea and are moving to a new one. Effective transitions restate the idea you are finishing and introduce your next one. In the following examples, the transitions are underlined:

> Now that you understand how our childhood memories influence our relationship to money, let's explore the relationship we have to money as adults.
>
> Once you've visited Manarola, you're ready to move to the final village, Riomaggiore, also known as "the village of love."

You can consciously insert transitions such as "let's turn to," "now that you understand," "in addition to," and "that brings me to my next point." But many will come naturally as you close one point or idea and begin a new one. Use transitions to link ideas within your main points and to guide your audience from point to point as you deliver your speech.

### Internal Previews

An **internal preview** is a statement in the body of your speech that details what you plan to discuss next. Internal previews focus on what comes next in the speech rather than linking two points, as transitions do. Internal previews are very similar to the preview you offer in the introduction of a speech (covered in Chapter 12), but you use them to introduce a new point rather than the entire speech.

In the following example, Martha introduces her second point, batik production, with an internal preview:

> In discussing the production of batik, I'll explain the four steps: the preparation of the cloth, the mixing of the dyes, the application of the dye, and the setting of the image on the cloth.

After hearing this preview, the audience is ready for four steps and begins to appreciate the intricacies of the batik process. Internal previews are often combined with transitions, as in Robert's discussion of theatrical lighting:

> As you can see (*transition*), with the invention of the lightbulb came exciting and safer possibilities for theatrical lighting. And the now familiar lightbulb takes me to my third point (*internal preview*), the invention of three instruments that revolutionized lighting in the theater: the ellipsoidal, the fresnel, and the intelabeam.

Not every main point requires an internal preview, but the unfamiliar terminology in Robert's third point lends itself to a preview. Introducing new concepts or terminology before offering the details enhances your audience's understanding of your topic.

### Internal Summaries

An **internal summary** is a statement in the body of your speech that summarizes a point you've already discussed. If you've just finished an important or complicated point, add an internal summary to remind your audience of its highlights. In Jeremy's speech on sibling rivalry, he used an internal summary at the end of the speech's first point:

> To summarize, the causes of sibling rivalry—birth order, sex, parental attitudes, and individual personality traits—can cause children to compete for their parents' affection and attention.

Like internal previews, internal summaries can be combined with transitions so you can move efficiently into your next point. Here's an example from Brandon's speech:

> In short (*internal summary*), the lack of funding for before- and after-school meal programs leads to poor academic performance, increased absences, and behavioral problems. But let's see (*transition*) what this bond issue will do to remedy many of these problems.

Internal summaries are excellent tools when you want your audience to remember key points before you move on to a new idea. When combined with transitions, internal summaries can help audiences move smoothly from one idea to the next.

### Signposts

A **signpost** is a simple word or statement that indicates where you are in your speech or highlights an important idea. Signposts tell your audience where you are in the presentation of your main points and help your listeners keep track of a detailed discussion or list of items. These tools add clarity to a speech and can make it flow.

Signposts can be:

numbers ("first," "second," "third")

phrases ("the most important thing to remember is," "you'll want to make note of this")

questions you ask and then answer ("so, how do we solve this dilemma?")

In Alex's speech on women in glory sports, she asked questions to introduce each of her main points. For her first main point, she asked,

> How many of you know who Layne Beachley is?

For her second, she asked,

> So, you didn't know Layne Beachley. How about Cara Beth Burnside? Can anyone tell me her accomplishments?

And for her third, she asked,

> Okay, I'll give you one more try. Who knows Tara Dakides's contributions to the world of glory sports?

Although you don't want to overuse these kinds of questions, they can be effective in getting an audience involved in your speech. Audience members will try to answer the questions in their own heads before you say the answer.

The final use of signposts is to mark the most important ideas in your speech. When you hear or use any of the following phrases, it's a signpost asking the audience to pay close attention:

The most important thing to remember is ...

If you hear nothing else from today's speech, hear this: ...

Let me repeat that last figure for you.

This next point is crucial to understanding my arguments.

Skills & Confidence
PPD
Activity 10.2

However, you should use this kind of signpost only once in a speech. If you use it more often, the audience quickly loses confidence that what you are about to say is really "the most important thing."

**SPEECH Checklist**

## Connectives

- [ ] Are transitions needed between any of the main points, after the introduction, or before the conclusion? (Examples: "now that . . . , let's"; "let's turn to"; "in addition to"; "that brings me to my next point")
- [ ] Would any of the main points benefit from an internal preview because they are complex or unfamiliar?
- [ ] Would any of the main points benefit from an internal summary because they are complicated or especially important for the audience to remember?
- [ ] Is there anywhere that a signpost would be useful to indicate an especially important idea or where you are in your speech or in a detailed list? (Examples: "first, . . . , second, . . . , third"; "the most important thing to remember is"; "this next point is crucial")

CHAPTER 11

# Outlining Your Speech



*In this chapter, you will learn to*

- Create a preparation outline
- Prepare a speaking outline
- Prepare note cards to use as prompts during a speech

You make a positive contribution to the public dialogue when you take the time to organize your ideas carefully, and outlines are an essential step in this process. In this chapter, you will learn about outlining and how to use this technique to evaluate the organization of your speech (Chapter 10) and to prepare for its presentation.

## The Preparation Outline

The **preparation outline** is a detailed outline of your speech that helps you evaluate the organization of your ideas. The preparation outline consists of your speech's title, specific purpose, thesis statement, introduction, main points and subpoints, connectives, conclusion, and source citations. It contains enough detail for you to verify that your speech is fully organized and complete, but it does not include every word you will say. It's best to begin creating a preparation outline as soon as you begin working on your speech.

## Title, Specific Purpose, and Thesis Statement

Because a preparation outline helps focus your ideas and organize your materials, write the title of your speech, your specific purpose, and the thesis statement at the top of the outline (Chapter 5). The title of a speech usually comes from your specific purpose and thesis statement because both indicate the theme of your speech. A good title also reflects the tone of your speech. Take a look at how Brooke and Katy titled their speeches.

***Brooke:***

| | |
|---|---|
| **Title:** | The World's Fire |
| **Specific purpose:** | To inform my audience about the history and legends of the chili pepper. |
| **Thesis statement:** | The history of the chili pepper includes global, national, and personal stories. |

***Katy:***

| | |
|---|---|
| **Title:** | Why Pi? |
| **Specific purpose:** | To inform my audience about the number pi. |
| **Thesis statement:** | Pi, a fascinating number with an unusual history, has become an obsession for some people. |

Both speakers chose simple, yet appropriate, titles for their speeches. Their titles reflect the content of their speeches, which is explicitly stated in their specific purposes and thesis statements. (Katy Mazz's complete preparation outline for her speech "Why Pi?" is featured at the end of this section.)

## Introduction

You'll read much more about introductions in Chapter 12, but here we'll discuss how to incorporate this part of a speech into an outline. An introduction should do four things:

- Catch your audience's attention
- Reveal your speech topic
- Establish your credibility
- Preview your main points

Identifying these four steps in your preparation outline will help you be sure you have included each of them in your introduction.

Here's how Nathan and Brooke outlined their introductions.

***Nathan:***

I. How far do you think you can walk? (*catch attention*)

  A. A hike on the Appalachian National Scenic Trail can take you from Georgia to Maine. (*reveal topic*)

  B. I've hiked this trail twice in my life, the most recent time being last summer. (*establish credibility*)

II. Today, I'd like to share with you a brief history of this trail, some facts about the trail and how it's maintained, and stories from some people who've hiked the trail. (*preview main points*)

***Brooke:***

I. The words *chilly*, *chili*, and *Chile* refer to cold weather, spicy beans, and a country in South America. (*catch attention*)

  A. Today, I'm speaking about the chili pepper. (*reveal topic*)

  B. The Chile Today website says the chili pepper has conquered taste buds and cuisines for 10,000 years. (*catch attention and establish credibility*)

  C. To me, the chili pepper is a legend, story, and tale. (*establish credibility*)

II. The chili pepper legends I'll discuss come from a variety of stories. (*preview main points*)

  A. Some stories are found across the globe.

  B. Others are the national stories originating in our own country.

  C. My final story is a personal one about my grandfather, the person who introduced me to the chili pepper's legacy. (*also establishes credibility*)

In these examples, the speakers summarized their introductions in outline form. The outlines do not include the full text of the speeches but rather a synopsis of the main ideas. By using this format, the speakers could see that they had included the four components of a strong introduction.

## Main Points, Subpoints, and Sub-Subpoints

The most important ideas in your speech are your main points. When you want to elaborate on your main points, you use subpoints and sub-subpoints. A **subpoint** develops an aspect of a main point. A **sub-subpoint** goes deeper to develop an aspect of a subpoint. You can think of main points, subpoints, and sub-subpoints as moving from the whole to the parts, or from the general to the specific.

Here is an example of a main point, subpoints, and sub-subpoints from Kameron's speech on zebra mussels:

I. Zebra mussels cause damage to every aspect of any aquatic ecosystem they encounter.
    A. They destroy the natural balance of the ecosystem.
        1. They consume all the food available to those lower on the food chain.
        2. Larger fish no longer have smaller fish to feed on.
    B. They form large colonies that attach themselves to any solid object, making it difficult for commercial enterprises.
        1. They congregate on buoys and markers, causing them to sink.
        2. They clog intake ports by attaching themselves to anything solid.

The main point (I) is developed and supported by the two subpoints (A and B). Additionally, the subpoints are developed and supported by the sub-subpoints (1 and 2 under subpoints A and B). Also notice that the points are organized according to the principle of **coordination,** or arranging points into successive levels, with the points on a specific level having equal importance.

To summarize, a main point is the broadest, most comprehensive idea; a subpoint supports and develops the main idea; and a sub-subpoint supports and develops the subpoint.

## Conclusion

You'll read much more about conclusions in Chapter 12, but here we'll discuss how to incorporate this part of a speech into an outline. The conclusion has two goals:

- To signal the end of the speech
- To reinforce your thesis statement

As you outline your conclusion, make sure it meets these goals. Like your introduction, the outline of the conclusion isn't a word-for-word transcript. Rather, it's a summary of what you'll say. Let's take a look at how Nathan and Will outlined the conclusions to their speeches.

***Nathan:***

I. So, now do you think you could walk from New York to Chicago or from Georgia to Maine? (*bring speech to an end*)

II. Even if you're not up for the hike, many people have hiked the 2,200-mile-long footpath to raise funds, overcome disabilities, and seek out spiritual insights. (*reinforce thesis statement*)

***Will:***

I. As you've seen in these last few minutes, ideas that were once regarded as fiction may soon be reality. (*bring speech to an end*)

II. Although there are ethical questions and concerns, germ-line engineering and cloning may soon be processes that are used every day. (*reinforce thesis statement*)

## Connectives

As we discussed earlier, connectives are words and phrases used to link ideas in a speech, and they come in four varieties: transitions, internal previews, internal summaries, and signposts. Because most connectives are no more than a single sentence, simply write them out rather than outline them. By writing out your connectives, you can easily see if you're overusing a phrase (for example, "now let's" again and again), and you can also see which points you might clarify with internal previews, internal summaries, or both. In the following example from Cassie's speech on crazy lawsuits, the connective is a bridge between the introduction—which previewed the main points—and the first main point:

**Connective:** Let's begin by looking at some definitions.

I. Three terms come up in most of these cases.
   A. The first term is *tort.*
   B. The second term is *civil suit.*
   C. The third term is *frivolous lawsuit.*

Similarly, Kelly used a transition in his speech on the Japanese language to get from his first main point to his second:

**Connective:** Now that I've introduced you to some Japanese body language, I would like to discuss a little bit about spoken Japanese.

In his speech on germ-line engineering, Will incorporated an internal summary into his preparation outline and then moved on to cloning, his next main point:

**Connective:** As you've just heard, germ-line engineering combines the age-old idea of manipulating DNA strands through selective breeding of animals and the newer research that is unpacking the human DNA code. But this isn't the only radical idea around today.

## Works Cited

The final component of your preparation outline is a list of the works you cite in your speech. Follow the guidelines for citing

**SPEECH TIPS**

**CONNECTIVES IN YOUR OUTLINE**

Include connectives between the major sections of your preparation outline (introduction, body, and conclusion) and between main points to help track your transitions from one idea to the next.

sources in Chapter 7 or those required by your instructor. Your instructor might require an established format for citing sources, such as that of the Modern Language Association (MLA) or the American Psychological Association (APA). (Appendix B gives examples of MLA and APA formats.)

Skills & Confidence Web Connect 11.1

Unless your instructor indicates otherwise, include only the sources you cite orally in your speech. By listing sources, you'll see how many you relied on to build your arguments and establish your credibility. If you discover you have cited only one or two sources and think you need more, you can go back and rework sections of your speech to include additional citations. Remember, citing the work of others not only enhances your ideas and increases your credibility, but it is also ethical.

**Speaking at Work**
*The industry you work in may have an established format for citing sources. If so, being sure to use it will enhance your credibility.*

### Guidelines for the Preparation Outline

Preparation outlines are more detailed than speaking outlines because their purpose is to reveal whether your speech develops your ideas fully and clearly. Here are five techniques that will make your preparation outline most useful.

*Use complete sentences.* Always write your ideas in complete sentences. The difference between a full-sentence outline and a keyword outline is obvious when the two are compared, as in Figure 11.1 on page 172. Although you do get a sense of the topic and ideas in the keyword example, the full-sentence outline is a far more useful tool to help you prepare and track the components of your speech. A keyword outline does not show how fully developed your ideas are. In contrast, a full-sentence outline clearly shows how well your speech is organized, what the content of each point is, where there are inconsistencies, and where more development might be needed.

**FIGURE 11.1 Keyword versus full-sentence outline**

**Keyword outline (incorrect)**

I. The Tuskegee Airmen
   A. Four squadrons
   B. The elite 332nd
   C. Their names
II. Obstacles
   A. The first
   B. No officers
   C. Recognition

**Full-sentence outline (correct)**

I. The Tuskegee Airmen were an elite group of African American fighter pilots who fought during the Second World War.
   A. The first five men graduated from four different squadrons at the Tuskegee training center in Alabama.
   B. The Tuskegee Airmen were considered one of the Allies' strongest weapons.
   C. Because of their talents, the Tuskegee Airmen were given nicknames in both German and English.
II. Although history books now recognize these men as heroes, they had to overcome many obstacles to be allowed to fly.
   A. At first, they were not allowed to form a squadron because "no colored squadrons" were needed.
   B. They then were told no such unit was allowed because there were "no commissioned Negro officers" in the Air Force.
   C. Although they never lost a bomber they escorted, it wasn't until 1948 that the first African American pilot received his gold wings.

*Label the introduction, body, conclusion, and connectives.* In addition to labeling the title, specific purpose, and thesis statement in your preparation outline, label the introduction, body, conclusion, and connectives. Labeling the components of your speech encourages you to consider each one separately. It also helps you see how much time you are devoting to each section and to judge whether, for example, the introduction may be overly long or the conclusion is too abrupt.

*Use a consistent pattern of symbols and indentation.* Outlines are based on the principles of **subordination, or** ranking ideas in order from the most to the least important. The most common way to indicate subordination in an outline is to use a traditional pattern of symbols and indentations.

- Main points are labeled with capital Roman numerals (I, II, III, and so on).
- Subpoints are labeled with capital letters (A, B, C).
- Sub-subpoints are labeled with Arabic numbers (1, 2, 3).

Indentations help you visually indicate the subordination of ideas. Your main points are set farthest left, and each level of subpoints is indented progressively farther to the right.

When you indent, be sure you indent all the text that corresponds with the point, not just the first line of text. (This type of indent is called a *hanging indent.* You can use Word's numbering formatting feature or the margin tabs in the ruler at the top of your document to create hanging indents.) This will help you see the ranking of each point clearly and emphasize the relationship of subpoints to main points.

***Incorrect***

II. Although history books now recognize these men as heroes, they had to overcome many obstacles to be allowed to fly.

A. At first, they were not allowed to form a squadron because "no colored squadrons" were needed.

***Correct***

II. Although history books now recognize these men as heroes, they had to overcome many obstacles to be allowed to fly.

    A. At first, they were not allowed to form a squadron because "no colored squadrons" were needed.

In a complex outline, you may need sub-sub-subpoints and even sub-sub-sub-subpoints. Label sub-sub-subpoints with lowercase letters (a, b, c, and so on), and label sub-sub-sub-subpoints with lowercase

**FIGURE 11.2 Traditional and complex outlines**

| Traditional outline | Complex outline |
|---|---|
| I. Main point | I. Main point |
| A. Subpoint | A. Subpoint |
| 1. Sub-subpoint | B. Subpoint |
| 2. Sub-subpoint | 1. Sub-subpoint |
| 3. Sub-subpoint | a. Sub-sub-subpoint |
| B. Subpoint | i. Sub-sub-sub-subpoint |
| II. Main point | ii. Sub-sub-sub-subpoint |
| A. Subpoint | b. Sub-sub-subpoint |
| B. Subpoint | 2. Sub-subpoint |
| 1. Sub-subpoint | II. Main point |
| 2. Sub-subpoint | |

Roman numerals (i, ii, iii). Figure 11.2 gives examples of traditional and complex outlines.

*Divide points into at least two subpoints.* When you support broad ideas with more specific ideas, you divide your points. For example, in Javad's speech about the Tuskegee Airmen, he discussed the three obstacles the men overcame in his second point. He divided this main point about overcoming obstacles into three subpoints: (1) the belief that there was no need for a "colored" squadron, (2) the fact that there were no commissioned "Negro" officers in the Air Force, and (3) the fact that they were not formally recognized as pilots until 1948.

Common sense tells us that when we divide a point, we must divide it into at least two parts, because you can't divide something into only one part. But what if a point doesn't seem to divide naturally into two or more parts? For example, when Cassie began working on her speech about frivolous lawsuits, she intended to define only one legal term, not three. Thus, she wound up with only one subpoint for her main point about defining legal terms the audience might not know. To solve this dilemma, she could have folded the definition into another point. For example, she could have defined the term *tort* while describing the first crazy lawsuit. Instead, she realized there were other legal terms that might be unfamiliar, so she decided to expand her original point and ended up with three subpoints.

Be careful when you fold one point into another. Make sure you discuss only one idea in each point so that your audience can follow your discussion and reasoning easily. For example, when Shelley spoke about threatened and endangered species, she divided the two ideas "threatened" and "endangered" into separate points rather than collapsing them into one. In doing so, she was able to help her audience understand the differences between the two categories.

*Check for balance.* A speaker's goal is to offer an equal presentation of each main point, and your preparation outline will show whether your ideas are complete and balanced. If your presentation outline shows that one or two points get far more discussion than the others, reconsider your speech goals and how you have tried to accomplish them.

Suppose your preparation outline showed the structure illustrated by Figure 11.3. Note that the second main point is developed in far more detail than the first and third main points. Additionally, subpoints B and E are more fully developed than the others are. The outline shows an imbalance that needs to be corrected. Either the speech can be refocused to make the second main point the thesis statement, or some material can be eliminated from the second main point and some material added to the other two main points.

**FIGURE 11.3 Imbalanced outline**

I. Main point
II. Main point
    A. Subpoint
    B. Subpoint
        1. Sub-subpoint
        2. Sub-subpoint
        3. Sub-subpoint
    C. Subpoint
    D. Subpoint
    E. Subpoint
        1. Sub-subpoint
        2. Sub-subpoint
        3. Sub-subpoint
        4. Sub-subpoint
        5. Sub-subpoint
III. Main point
    A. Subpoint
    B. Subpoint

**SPEECH Checklist ✓**

## Your Preparation Outline

Are the following elements in your preparation outline?

- ☐ Speech title
- ☐ Specific purpose
- ☐ Thesis statement
- ☐ Introduction
- ☐ Main points and subpoints
- ☐ Connectives
- ☐ Conclusion
- ☐ Source citations

Does your preparation outline have the following characteristics?

- ☐ Complete sentences
- ☐ Labels for introduction, body, connectives, and conclusion
- ☐ Consistent pattern of symbols and indentation
- ☐ At least two supporting subpoints under each main point
- ☐ Approximately equal development of points and subpoints

# PREPARATION OUTLINE

## with Commentary

## *Why Pi?*

*by Katy Mazz*

CENGAGE LEARNING

***Specific Purpose:*** *To inform my audience about the number pi.*

***Thesis Statement:*** *Pi, a fascinating number with an unusual history, has become an obsession for some people.*

*Are you ready to build your preparation outline? Use the following outline as a model. You can use your Premium Website for* Invitation to Public Speaking Handbook *to watch a video clip of the speech Katy Mazz gave based on this outline. Katy gave this speech in an introductory public speaking class. The assignment was to give a four- to six-minute informative speech about any topic. Students were asked to create a preparation outline, to cite at least four sources, and to speak from a speaking outline or note cards. In addition, they were asked to end on a strong note. (You can read Katy's speaking outline later in this chapter.)*

**Skills & Confidence**
PPD Activity 11.1

*INTRODUCTION*

I. 3.1415926535897932384626433832795. (*catch attention*)
   A. Most of you know the name of the number I just recited.
   B. It is found in rainbows, pupils of eyes, sound waves, ripples in the water, and DNA.
   C. It is a ratio that nature and music understand but that the mind cannot comprehend.
   D. This number has sparked curiosity over the past 4,000 years.
   E. I am talking about pi—not the dessert, but the circle ratio. (*reveal topic*)

*Commentary*

*Katy labels her introduction to help keep her place as she gives her speech. The outline of her introduction is very detailed to help her account for and identify the four components of a strong introduction.*

*She writes her specific purpose and thesis statement at the beginning of her preparation outline. This helps her stay audience centered, focused on her topic, and reminded of her speech goals.*

*Katy catches her audience's attention by reciting pi to thirty-one decimal places and by getting them curious about its presence in their lives.*

*In subpoint E, she reveals the topic of her speech.*

*Katy adapts her topic to her audience by indicating she knows her audience quite well—she recognizes they are all speech majors. She establishes her credibility by indicating she has researched her topic and is personally interested in it.*

*In the last point of her introduction, Katy previews the three main points of her speech.*

II. I will try to present pi as the fascinating topic I think it is to a class of speech majors who wonder if they can survive a speech about math.
   A. I have researched this topic, finding information not only technical and historical but also fanatical. (*establish credibility*)
   B. My own interest came about when I was challenged to memorize more digits than a friend of mine.

III. I plan to inform you of what pi is, the history of pi, and how pi has created obsessions in people's lives. (*preview main points*)

*By marking the body of her speech with a heading, she can clearly see where she must shift from her introduction to her first main point.*

*Notice that she uses complete sentences for each point.*

*She divides her first main point into two subpoints. In the first one, she explains what pi is and what makes it unusual. She uses a rhetorical question in her third sub-subpoint to spark her audience's interest.*

*In her second subpoint, Katy continues to explain what pi is. Again, she presents intriguing information to help her audience appreciate pi's popularity and intrigue.*

*BODY*

I. Even if you don't know what it represents, pi is a number that almost everyone is familiar with.
   A. When you divide the circumference of a circle by its diameter, the result will always equal pi.
      1. No matter the size of the circle, this division results in what is called the circle ratio.
      2. Although we refer to pi as 3.14 or 22/7, it is actually an irrational number, meaning that it cannot be represented as a fraction.
      3. The number pi is never ending—or is it?
      4. For ages, mathematicians have puzzled, and have been almost ashamed, that it is so difficult to find another value as simple as the circle ratio.
   B. Pi is more than just the circle ratio.
      1. According to David Blatner, who wrote <u>The Joy of Pi</u>, this value can be found in all fields of math and science, architecture, the arts, and even in the Bible.
      2. The world record for calculating pi to the greatest number of decimal places is 206 billion decimal places,

calculated by Dr. Kanada at the University of Tokyo.

**Transition:** Although 206 billion digits have been calculated thus far, there was a time in antiquity when there was uncertainty of the second decimal place.

*In this transition, Katy briefly restates her last point and introduces her second point, the history of pi, with her reference to antiquity. She sets the transition off so that she can find it easily and see that she is moving on to her second main point.*

*Katy divides her second main point into three subpoints that help her develop her discussion of pi's rich history. She develops her argument chronologically, from ancient history to the present era. Notice her use of subordination and proper indentation of each new point.*

*Katy shares interesting historical facts about math that appeal to her audience of speech majors.*

II. Woven among pi's infinite digits is a rich history, ranging from the great thinkers of ancient cultures to the supercomputers of the twentieth century.
   A. Four thousand years ago, there was no decimal system, compass, paper, or pencil, yet people still found ways to calculate pi.
      1. The Egyptians used a stake, a rope, and the sand to approximate pi as a little greater than 3.
      2. The Greeks, Babylonians, Israelites, Chinese, and Mesopotamians also studied the circle ratio, yet none of them were certain of the third decimal place.
   B. Whether pi is an infinite number remained a mystery until the sixteenth century.
      1. Petr Beckmann, a former professor of engineering at Colorado University, likes to call this period the age of the digit hunters, with each generation popping out more digits than the next.
      2. Keep in mind that at this point the electronic calculator had not yet been invented.
      3. Famous mathematicians of the time continued to break records for calculating pi.

*Note her interesting language: "the age of the digit hunters" and "each generation popping out more digits." In this point, she uses her research creatively and stays audience centered.*

   C. In the twentieth century, the invention of the computer allowed mathematicians to calculate pi to 16,000 digits, confirming that pi is infinite and totally random.

*Katy brings her audience up to the present era with her third subpoint.*

**Transition:** What is the fascination with pi that has caused people to be both fascinated and obsessed?

*By asking another rhetorical question, she previews her third main point.*

*In her final point, Katy explains the obsession some people have with the number pi. In her three subpoints, she discusses a different aspect of this obsession.*

*In subpoint A, Katy tells a story of the Chudnovsky brothers and the lengths to which they went to study pi.*

III. Blatner states, "People have calculated, memorized, philosophized, and expounded on" pi more than on any number in history.
   A. The Chudnovsky brothers, Gregory and David, were both mathematicians from Russia who moved to New York to entertain their obsession with pi.
      1. In their own apartment, they built a supercomputer from scrap materials.
      2. With this computer, they were able to calculate more digits and study pi's use in various formulas.
   B. Other people try to memorize pi.
      1. Some do it for sport or to be silly, but others are more serious.
      2. Blatner states that in 1995, Hiroyuko Goto spent over nine hours reciting 42,000 digits of pi from memory, far exceeding the world record.
         a. This was a rare case, but there are methods of memorization for the average memory.
         b. Some people remember pi through poems, clever mnemonics, and songs.
         c. Some simply memorize the digits in groups of fours, which is the method I've found easiest.
   C. So many people are obsessed with pi that the number is celebrated on Pi Day every March 14, or 3/14.
      1. The website Ridiculously Enhanced Pi Page suggests that you gather with friends at 1:59 p.m. to celebrate.
      2. At this time, eat pie and share personal stories about pi.

*Katy uses Goto as an example of someone obsessed with memorizing pi and then shares some memorization methods that are easier. Notice that subpoint B is slightly more developed than subpoints A or C but that her three subpoints are still fairly evenly balanced.*

*Her third subpoint wraps up her discussion of the obsession with pi, using a lighthearted story of a tradition she learned on the Ridiculously Enhanced Pi Page website.*

*Katy includes a transition in her summary by returning to one of her questions from earlier in her speech. Also note that she marks her conclusion as a distinct part of her outline.*

**Summary and transition:** So ends my analysis of people's obsessions, but my earlier question was not fully answered.

*Katy begins her conclusion by answering her question about why pi has caused such a craze. She then summarizes her main points.*

## CONCLUSION

I. No one knows for sure why pi has caused such a craze or why several books, movies, and Web pages have been devoted to this subject. (*bring speech to an end*)

A. What inspired the Chudnovsky brothers to devote their lives to the search for pi?
B. What inspired me to write a speech on a silly number?
C. The answer lies in the mystery of pi: People explore pi because it is an adventure to do so.

II. Remember that pi is not only the circle ratio, not only the biggest influence on math over history, but also a number that has a great effect on people and an influence on everything we do. (*reinforce thesis and summarize main points*)

III. William Schaaf, in "The Nature and History of Pi," concludes that "probably no symbol in mathematics has evoked as much mystery, romanticism, misconception and human interest as the number pi."

*Notice that the outline of her conclusion includes a lot of detail. This helps her (1) make sure she has incorporated the two aspects of a strong conclusion and (2) see that her conclusion is shorter than her introduction and will take only a few moments to deliver.*

*Katy ends her speech with a quotation, leaving her audience with a strong sense of the mystique of the number pi.*

**Works Cited**

Beckmann, Petr. *A History of Pi*. New York: St. Martin's Press, 1971.

Blatner, David. *The Joy of Pi*. New York: Walker and Company, 1997.

Blatner, David. "Pi Facts and Figures." *The Joy of Pi*. Accessed September 20, 2000. http://joyofpi.com/.

Ridiculously Enhanced Pi Page. Posted 1998. *The Exploratorium*. Accessed September 23, 2000. http://www.exploratorium.edu/pi/pi98/.

Schaaf, William. "The Nature and History of Pi." *The Joy of Pi*. Accessed September 20, 2000. http://www.joyofpi.com/schaaf.htm.

Witcombe, Chris. "Notes on Pi." *Earth Mysteries*. Sweet Briar College. Accessed September 23, 2000. http://witcombe.sbc.edu/earthmysteries/EMPi.html.

*Katy includes a bibliography of the specific research she references in her speech. She prepared this speech in 2000, and note that her sources range from 1971 to 2000, indicating that she did both historical and current research. She also relies on both Internet and print sources, illustrating that she searched in several places for material rather than relying on only one kind of source.*

## The Speaking Outline

The **speaking outline,** sometimes called *speaking notes,* is a condensed form of your preparation outline that you use when speaking. You will almost never memorize a speech or read it from a manuscript. Most often, you will choose the exact words of your speech as you are giving it. A speaking outline will help you remember any specific information that you plan to include in your speech. For example, a speaking outline often includes the full text of quotations, statistics, names, and other material you want to remember exactly. It also includes delivery prompts, such as "make eye contact," "slow down," and "breathe."

The most effective speakers make frequent eye contact with their audience and speak directly to them. Their speaking outlines encourage them to do this. Because speakers do not have the full text written out in front of them, they are not tempted to read to the audience. Instead, they rely on the ideas, words, and phrases in their speaking outline to remind them of what they want to say.

Although you may feel you will give a better speech if much of it is written out fully on your speaking outline, experienced speakers have found this simply isn't so. The most dynamic speakers are those whose speaking outlines only prompt their memories and enable them to engage their audiences directly.

### Guidelines for the Speaking Outline

Speaking outlines are very personalized documents. As you gain experience speaking, you will discover what you need to include in your outline and what you can leave out. For now, use the following guidelines to help build your speaking outline.

*Use keywords and phrases.* When you write your speaking outline, use keywords and phrases or abbreviated sentences. As you prepare this outline, think carefully about what words and phrases will help

**SPEECH TIPS**

**SPEAKING OUTLINES**

You need your speaking outline for specific information you plan to use in your speech, such as quotations, statistics, and names. Many speakers also add delivery cues to their outlines to help them remember to pause, make eye contact, or use a visual aid.

you remember your complete ideas. In the example here, notice how Graham reduced his full sentences to keywords, working from the larger idea to its most essential component:

***Preparation outline***

I. Many people are not aware of what a voucher system is.
    A. Voucher programs take taxpayers' money and give it to families.
        1. Families then use money to send children to the school of their choice.
        2. The school of choice could be either a public or private school.
    B. In theory, money that normally goes to public schools now is distributed to a range of schools.
    C. The program is touted as a new solution to the old problem of inadequate public education.

***Speaking outline***

I. The voucher system
    A. Taxpayers' money to families
    B. Money normally goes to public schools
    C. New solution to old problem

The keywords capture the essence of Graham's ideas and help him remember the full thought when he looks down at his notes. The keywords call to mind the full argument or explanation. They keep him talking and prevent him from reading his speech.

*Write clearly and legibly.* Many speakers print their speaking outline from a computer because the print is more legible than their handwriting. They also use a plain, easy-to-read font, often in a larger size than normal. (Similarly, speakers who write their outline by hand print larger than they normally do.) Compare the legibility of these two font sizes:

Remind us that death is the great equalizer.

Remind us that death is the great equalizer.

Although we wouldn't use the larger font size for a paper, in a speaking outline the bigger letters make our speech much easier to deliver, especially if we're nervous.

*Add cues for delivery.* As you practice, notice where you tend to stumble, where you are too tied to the outline and forget to make eye contact, and where you move too quickly or slowly. Also notice where you have trouble with pronunciation or remembering what you want to

**SPEECH Checklist**

## Your Speaking Outline

Does your speaking outline have the following characteristics?

- ☐ Keywords and phrases only—not the full text
- ☐ Clear, legible, and large font or handwriting
- ☐ Cues for delivery, such as "make eye contact," "pause," "slow down," "look up," "show visual aid"
- ☐ Correct pronunciation of words you stumble on
- ☐ One-or-two-word prompts for stories, examples, and concepts you tend to forget

say. Add cues to help you through these rough spots. Cues are words and phrases like "slow down," "pause," "look up," "show visual aid," and "make eye contact."

Cues also include the correct pronunciation of any words that are hard for you to say, especially names, or a word or two to help you remember a complete idea, a part of a story, or an example you tend to forget. Add this final component of your speaking outline after you've written it and have practiced your speech a few times.

If you've printed your outline from a computer, handwrite your cues. If you've handwritten your speaking outline, use a different color for your cues. Be sure to keep the cues brief so they don't distract you from your audience and your speech.

## Note Cards

Some speakers prefer note cards to a speaking outline (Figure 11.4). Note cards (three-by-five or four-by-six inches) are smaller and less obvious than full sheets of paper. They also are sturdier and less likely to shake if a speaker's hands tremble. And they give us something to hold on to, sometimes making us feel a little more secure as we speak.

If you feel more comfortable with note cards, follow these guidelines:

- Use keywords and phrases and place no more than five or six lines on each card. As with speaking outlines, do not write the full text of the speech on the cards.

**FIGURE 11.4 Sample note cards**

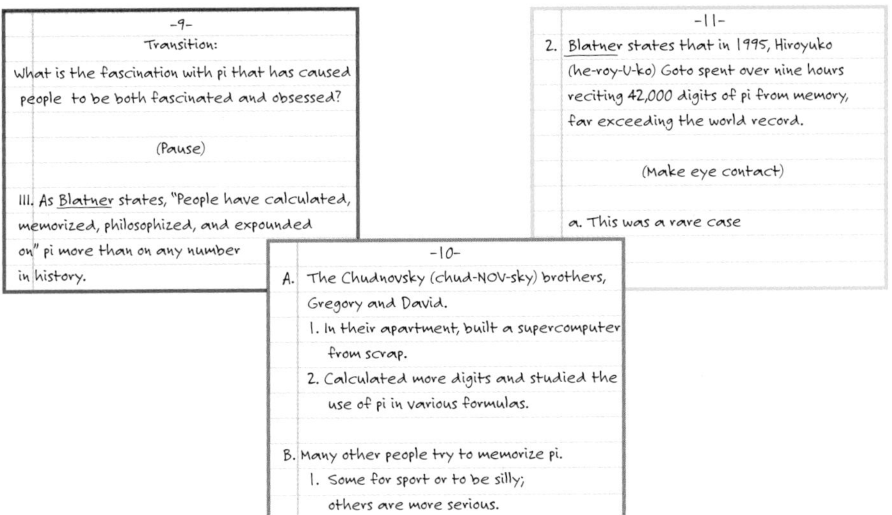


- Write clearly and legibly. Print or type directly on the card or, if you handwrite your notes, use large, clear printing that is easy to read.
- Use only one side of the card. This reduces the likelihood that cards will get out of order during the speech.
- Number each card so you can easily reorder them if they get mixed up.
- Put cues for delivery on your cards so you can see them (use separate cards or different colors for these cues).
- When you deliver the speech, the cards should have a low profile. Try not to gesture with them, play with them, or tap them on the podium. You want the audience to pay attention to you, not the note cards.

## SPEAKING OUTLINE

**with Commentary**

# *Why Pi?*

*by Katy Mazz*

CENGAGE LEARNING

**Skills & Confidence**
PPD
Activity 11.2

Are you ready to build your speaking outline? You can use the following outline as a model. Katy based her speaking outline on her preparation outline, and she modified it in places to account for problems she encountered with her delivery as she practiced her speech.

*Commentary*

*At the top of her speaking outline, Katy makes notes to herself to breathe and make eye contact with her audience. She knows she'll be nervous, so she uses these notes to remind her to take a breath and look for friendly faces. She also makes a note to pause after she recites the digits of pi and before she goes on with her introduction.*

*Note that her introduction is an abbreviated version of the introduction in her preparation outline. She gives herself just enough cues to help her remember the four goals of an introduction.*

(Breathe)

(Make eye contact)

*INTRODUCTION*

I. 3.1415926535897932384626433832795

(Pause)

- A. Most of you know the name of this number.
- B. In rainbows, pupils of eyes, sound waves, ripples in the water, and DNA.
- C. Nature and music understand, but the human mind cannot quite comprehend.
- D. 4,000 years of curiosity.

(Pause)

(Make eye contact)

- E. I am talking about pi, the circle ratio.

II. Speech majors may wonder if they can survive a speech about math.

- A. My research turned up technical, historical, and fanatical information.
- B. What sparked my own interest.

III. Today, I'll share with you what pi is, the history of pi, and how pi has created obsessions in people's lives.

*To help with her delivery, Katy reminds herself to pause and make eye contact here before stating the topic of her speech.*

*She previews her speech in point III, stating her three main points.*

## *BODY*

*Katy titles the body of her speech to remind her that she is moving to the main points. This is also a visual cue to help find her place after she makes eye contact with her audience.*

I. Pi is a symbol that most everyone is familiar with.
   A. The circumference of a circle divided by its diameter.

      (Slow)

      1. This number is also called the circle ratio.
      2. We refer to pi as 3.14 or 22/7, but it is an irrational number.
      3. Pi's mysticism is due to the fact that it's never ending—or is it?
      4. Mathematicians have long puzzled about values as simple as the ratio of a circle.
   B. Pi is more than the circle ratio.
      1. According to David Blatner, who wrote The Joy of Pi, this value can be found in all fields of math and science, architecture, the arts, and even the Bible.
      2. The world record for pi calculated to the greatest number of digits is **206 billion decimal places,** calculated by Dr. Kanada at the University of Tokyo.

*She writes "Slow" as she begins her first point to remind her to not rush through this information, which is new for many of her audience members.*

*Again, Katy gives herself enough text to remember her ideas, but not so much that she can fall prey to reading her speech to her audience.*

*Katy underlines the names of her sources and sets in bold the numbers she wants to remember so she'll deliver them correctly.*

(Pause)

Although 206 billion digits have been calculated thus far, there was a time in antiquity when there was uncertainty of the second decimal place.

*She makes a note to pause before her transition so she can shift her pace a little to signal she is moving to a new point. She also writes out her full transition to remind her to deliver it—she's concerned that her nervousness will cause her to skip it and jump into her second main point.*

II. Pi has a rich history.
   A. Four thousand years ago, people could calculate pi, even without today's resources.
      1. The Egyptians approximated pi as a little greater than 3.
      2. The Greeks, Babylonians, Israelites, Chinese, and Mesopotamians were not certain of the third decimal place.

B. The infinity of pi remained a mystery until the sixteenth century.

*As she did in her first main point, she underlines the source and sets the entire quote in bold so she can find it easily and deliver it correctly.*

1. Petr Beckmann, a former professor of engineering at Colorado University, calls this period **"the age of the digit hunters, with each generation popping out more digits than the next."**
2. Keep in mind that there was still no electronic calculator.
3. Famous mathematicians continued to break records.

C. In the twentieth century, the invention of the computer allowed mathematicians to calculate pi to **16,000 digits**.

*Again, Katy writes out her transition, this time including a signal to pause after the transition and before she begins her final main point.*

What is the fascination with pi that has caused people to be both fascinated and obsessed?

(Pause)

III. As Blatner states, **"People have calculated, memorized, philosophized, and expounded on" pi more than on any other number in history.**

*In point III, Katy adds the phonetic spelling (spelled as they should sound) of two names so she will be sure to pronounce them correctly.*

A. The Chudnovsky (**Chud-NOV-sky**) brothers, Gregory and David.
   1. In their apartment, built a supercomputer from scrap.
   2. Calculated more digits and studied the use of pi in various formulas.

B. Many other people try to memorize pi.
   1. Some for sport or to be silly; others are more serious.
   2. Blatner states that **in 1995, Hiroyuko (He-roy-U-ko) Goto spent over nine hours reciting 42,000 digits of pi from memory, far exceeding the world record**.

*Her note to make eye contact signals her to look directly at her audience after she delivers the startling statistics of nine hours and 42,000 digits. This will help emphasize her point that this feat is rare but that people really are obsessed with pi.*

(Make eye contact)

      a. This was a rare case.
      b. Some people remember pi through poems, mnemonics, and songs.
      c. Some memorize the digits in groups of fours.

C. The number is celebrated on Pi Day every March 14, or 3/14.
   1. The Ridiculously Enhanced Pi Page suggests gathering at 1:59 p.m.
   2. Eat pie and share stories about pi.

So ends my analysis of people's obsessions, but my earlier question was not fully answered.

## CONCLUSION

(Slow down!)
(Make eye contact)

*When she practiced her speech, Katy noticed she tended to rush through her conclusion. She added notes to slow down and make eye contact so she would take time wrapping up her speech.*

I. No one knows why pi has caused such a craze.
   A. What inspired the Chudnovsky brothers?
   B. What inspired me?
   C. The answer lies in the mystery and adventure.

II. The biggest influence on math over history and influences everything we do.

III. William Schaaf, in "The Nature and History of Pi," concludes that **"probably no symbol in mathematics has evoked as much mystery, romanticism, misconception and human interest as the number pi."**

*Katy ends her speech with a quote, so she underlines the source's name and sets the quote in bold so she won't stumble when she delivers the final words of the speech.*

*Source:* Adapted with permission from Katy Mazz.

CHAPTER 12

# Introductions and Conclusions



***In this chapter, you will learn to***

- Describe the four functions of an effective introduction
- Prepare a compelling introduction
- Describe the two functions of an effective conclusion
- Prepare a compelling conclusion
- Identify at least four tips for preparing both an introduction and a conclusion

Introductions, even short ones, make an audience more willing to listen a speech, think more highly of the speaker, and understand the speech better.[1] At the other end of the speech, conclusions reinforce thesis statements, remind listeners of main points, and frame the speaker's ideas and arguments in just the way he or she wants. Because the introduction and the conclusion are such important parts of a speech, they require special consideration. In this chapter, you will learn the basic techniques for developing each. As you read the following discussions, keep in mind that your introduction and conclusion frame the way you enter and exit the public dialogue.

## The Introduction

Your introduction is your first contact with your audience. In the opening words of your speech, you set the stage for what's to come, connect your audience to your topic, and establish your purpose for speaking. Introductions are like first impressions—they are important and lasting. Because of this, introductions require all of your audience analysis skills (Chapter 6). To develop an introduction that allows you to connect with your audience in the way you want, consider the four functions of any introduction:

- To catch the audience's attention
- To reveal the topic to the audience
- To establish credibility with the audience
- To preview the speech for the audience

Notice that each objective is highly audience centered. Thus, you need to design your introduction, like the body of your speech, with your audience in mind. In each of the four components of the introduction, you consider the audience's perspectives and the reason the audience is listening to your speech as well as your own goals. Let's take a closer look at each of these components and then at some techniques for implementing them with effective introductions.

### Catch the Audience's Attention

One of the most important tasks you have as a speaker is to capture the attention of your audience. You want your audience to listen to you and to be intrigued and curious about your topic. When you catch the audience's attention, you not only pique their curiosity, but you also show them how the topic relates to them. Keep in mind that however you get your audience interested in your topic, to act ethically, you must be honest, respectful, and behave in a manner consistent with the principles of an open and healthy public dialogue.

### Reveal the Topic of Your Speech

In your introduction, you also want to let the audience know the subject of your speech. Although guessing games can be fun, your audience wants to know what you will be discussing. Keeping them in suspense for a moment or two is fine, but your introduction should reveal your topic before you begin your first main point.

### Establish Your Credibility

As you've learned, to be credible is to gain the trust of your audience and to communicate to them that you have considerable knowledge of

SPEECH **TIPS**

### CREDIBILITY

Establish your credibility early in your introduction so your audience understands why you're qualified to speak on your topic. There's no need to boast or brag—simply share your qualifications with the audience. And be careful to represent your expertise accurately and ethically.

your topic. If your audience regards you as credible and competent, they will believe they have good reasons to listen to your ideas. Establishing credibility contains an ethical dimension. Audiences do not like to be lied to or misled. If you distort your credibility on a subject, your audience is less likely to believe you or be influenced by your speech.

### Preview Your Speech

The fourth component of an introduction is to preview the main points of the speech. In your **preview,** you share with your audience a brief overview of each of the main points in your speech. Previews communicate to your audience that you are organized and competent. In setting the stage for the body of the speech, previews help your audience organize their thoughts about your topic and mentally prepare for what you're going to say next.

## Preparing a Compelling Introduction

There are several creative ways to gain your audience's attention, reveal your topic, establish your credibility, and preview your speech. Let's look at some techniques that will help you prepare compelling, memorable introductions.

### Ask a Question

A question can arouse your listeners' curiosity and capture their attention. A question can also reveal the topic of your speech—the answer should relate to your topic. Sometimes speakers use a **rhetorical question,** a question, used for effect, that the audience isn't supposed to answer out loud but rather in their own minds. At other times, speakers may ask questions to solicit answers directly from the audience. In the first of the following examples, Nathan asks rhetorical questions and supplies his own answers. In the second example, Cassie solicits answers from her audience before revealing the topic of her speech:

> *"Appalachian Trail"*: Do you think you could walk from New York to just beyond Chicago? How about from Georgia to Maine? If you're up for such a hike, take the route from Georgia to Maine—that will put you on the Appalachian National Scenic Trail, a trail that stretches over 2,000 miles and traverses fourteen states. This trail is also the topic of my speech today.
>
> *"Crazy Lawsuits"*: You've heard of the game "Strange but True"? Play with me for a minute. I'll read the headline, and you tell me if it's true or not. Ready? Okay.
>
> > "Surfer Sues Surfer for Theft of Wave." True or false?
> >
> > "Deaf Bank Robber Wins Suit: Courts Say Alarm Exploited His Disability." True or false?
> >
> > "College Student Falls Out Fourth-Story Window During Mooning Prank: Sues University for Negligence." True or false?
>
> Each of these lawsuits is real, and these "crazy lawsuits" are the subject of my speech today.

Beginning a speech with a question, whether rhetorical or not, encourages active listening by your audience. Thus, questions can prevent your audience from sitting back passively as you speak. If you open your speech with a question, be sure it relates directly to your topic, and remember to pause after each question so the audience has time to answer it, either aloud or in their heads.

### Tell a Story

A second way to capture your audience's attention and reveal your topic is to tell a story. Remember from Chapter 7 that stories, or narratives, draw an audience into your speech by offering characters and dramas they can relate to. Stories also personalize topics that might seem remote or disconnected to some members of an audience. Notice how Brandi uses language creatively to draw her audience into her story:

> It seemed like such a harmless thing to do. What could be wrong with putting out a little food to help the foxes and deer make it through a hard winter? Besides, seeing wildlife in your backyard is one of the many benefits to living in Colorado. Or so thought a family who set out dog food, hamburger, and grains for foxes and deer near their home in the wooded foothills just outside Denver. But guess who also came to dinner? Tasty treats left in the family's backyard lured hungry

SPEECH TIPS

### STORIES

Most people enjoy a good story, so telling one is a particularly effective way to catch an audience's attention. What are some interesting stories from your life that you could tell in the introduction to a speech? Would one of these stories relate to the topic of your next speech?

> mountain lions into the neighborhood. Not only did the wild cats like the hamburger, but they also had their eyes on one of their favorite prey, the deer.
>
> It didn't take long for the real trouble to start. Residents' cats and dogs began disappearing from their yards. Fear and anger set in, and people began calling officials to do something about the mountain lions. What started as a well-meaning effort for deer and foxes ended in the death of one of Colorado's favorite wild animals. The mountain lion was killed in a trap set out to make the neighborhood safe again.
>
> Hi, my name is Brandi Lafferty, and today I'd like to describe some of the negative consequences associated with feeding big game wildlife and encourage you to help keep our wildlife wild.

Skills & Confidence Video Activity 12.1

If you use a story in your opening, be sure it relates directly to your topic and clearly connects to the body of your speech. Sometimes it's tempting to tell a great story just because it's a great story. Avoid this pitfall and use only stories that help introduce your topic.

### Recite a Quotation or a Poem

You can also catch your audience's interest and reveal your topic through a quotation or poem. Quotations lend your speech the credibility of someone more famous or knowledgeable than you are. They can also teach lessons or illustrate perspectives that are relevant to your speech. Quotations can be quite simple or fairly complex. In a speech on adoption, Chad began with this simple quotation:

> Dennis Rainey, author of the book *One Home at a Time*, states, "I have a wife and six children, two of which are adopted—but I can't remember which ones."

Speaking about the terrorist attacks on New York City and Washington, D.C., in September 2001, Mike began with a more complex quotation:

> Mohandas K. Gandhi said, "When I despair, I remember that all through history the way of truth and love has always won. There have been murderers and tyrants, and for a time they can seem invincible. But in the end they always fail. Think of it: always."

In the next example, Jessica begins her speech with a poem to set the tone and reveal her topic, shamrocks:

> May your thoughts be as glad as the shamrocks,
> May your heart be as light as the song.
> May each day bring you bright happy hours,
> That stay with you all year long.
> For each petal on the shamrock,
> This brings a wish your way—
> Good health, good luck, and happiness
> For today and every day.
>
> When some hear this Irish blessing, they think of a three-leaf clover. Others think of Ireland or St. Patrick. My family has its roots in Ireland, and we always think of all three. The shamrock has a long history of meaning for the Irish, and it represents the magical number 3. To fully understand the importance of the shamrock, though, you need to know how it became the symbol of Ireland. You must also understand how St. Patrick used it and how it is represented every year by St. Patrick's Day. Even if you're not Irish, a little bit of information about the shamrock will help you enjoy your next March 17 celebration or understand those who make such a big deal of it.

Notice, too, how Jessica establishes her credibility early in the introduction by referring to her family's roots in Ireland. She also connects her topic to her audience in the final sentences of the introduction.

When you use a quotation or poem, be sure it relates directly to your topic or illustrates the importance of your subject. Like stories, there are a lot of great quotations and poems, but you should only use one that sums up your topic and grabs your audience's attention. Also remember to cite the source of the quotation or poem and to deliver it so the audience knows it is a quotation or poem rather than your own words (for tips on citing sources in your speeches, see Chapter 8).

**Skills & Confidence** Web Connect 12.1

### Give a Demonstration

When you demonstrate some aspect of your topic, you can capture your audience's interest and make them want to see or hear more. In the following example, Megan began by singing. After she had captured her audience's attention, she revealed the topic of her speech: the author of her song. In the second paragraph, she previewed her speech so her audience knew exactly what she was going to cover.

> *(Begin by singing "Amazing Grace.")* Comfort is what I feel when I hear this song. No matter if I am at a funeral service or singing it in a choir, this song overwhelms me with a sense of peace. I know it has the same effect on others as well. But who was the man behind this song? And isn't it, as some say, a bit overdone? Dr. Ralph F. Wilson states that he used to think "Amazing Grace" was just that, overdone. Wilson says, "'saved a wretch like me,' come on, really now. But the author really was a wretch, a moral pariah." Wilson is the author of *The Story of John Newton*, and John Newton is the author of America's most popular hymn, "Amazing Grace."
>
> But what happened to John Newton that made him a "moral pariah"? What happened in this man's life that it was only the "grace of God" that could save him? Well, today I'm going to share with you just how a "wretch" like John Newton wrote such a well-known hymn. I'll begin by telling you a little bit about his early life. Then, I'll tell you how he came to write "Amazing Grace." Finally, I'll conclude by discussing this hymn's legacy.

Although not everyone has the talent to stand up and sing for their audiences, many speeches can be opened with some type of demonstration. Speeches about activities, sports, and art—about how to do anything—offer good possibilities for demonstrations.

When you use a demonstration to introduce your speech, make sure you can complete it in only a few minutes or even seconds. Introductions and conclusions are a relatively small part of the speech. In fact, as you will see later in this chapter, your introduction and conclusion should make up no more than 20 percent of your speech. Time your demonstration to make sure you'll have enough time for the rest of your speech. If your demonstration seems too long, think about using it in the body of your speech instead. In either case, practice your demonstration before the speech so you can make a positive impression on the audience.

### Make an Intriguing or Startling Statement

An intriguing or startling statement is an excellent way to draw your audience in with the unknown or the curious. Let's look at a few examples of this technique. The first one begins Kelly's speech about the Japanese language:

> *Ohayoo gozaimasu.* You probably don't know what I just said. I just gave you the greeting for "good morning" in Japanese,

the ninth most spoken language in the world. Having studied Japanese for over three years now, I would like to share a little bit about this intriguing language with you today. I know you're probably wondering, "Why should I care about the Japanese language when I live in the United States?" Well, according to the *Encyclopaedia Britannica,* there are currently over 125 million speakers of Japanese worldwide. In today's world, that means you're more than likely to meet a Japanese speaker at least once in your life. Wouldn't it be a good idea to know at least something about his or her language?

> Today, I'll share some of what I know about the Japanese language with you. I'll first talk about Japanese body language, which is both similar to and different from American body language. Then, I'll discuss spoken Japanese, which requires a lot of practice to learn. Finally, I'll tell you a little about the written language, which contains over 50,000 characters and three alphabets.

In this example, Kelly illustrates all four criteria for a strong introduction. He catches the audience's interest in the first few lines, establishes his credibility in the third sentence, relates the topic to his audience in his final lines of the first paragraph, and previews his speech in the second paragraph.

As you read the next example, see if you can identify all four of the criteria for a strong introduction. Notice how Katy takes a little extra time in her introduction to relate the topic, pi, to her audience and to establish her credibility:

> 3.14159265358979323846264338327795. Most of you know the name of the number I just recited. It's a number found in rainbows, pupils of eyes, sound waves, ripples in the water, and DNA—a ratio that both nature and music understand but that the human mind cannot quite comprehend. This number has sparked curiosity in many minds over the past 4,000 years. I'm talking about pi—not the dessert, but the circle ratio.

> Now, a class of speech majors is probably wondering if they can survive a six-minute speech about math. My own interest came about when I was challenged to memorize more digits than a friend of mine could. As a result of that challenge, I have researched this topic, finding information not only technical and historical but also fanatical. Today, I plan to inform you of what pi is, the history of pi, and how pi has created an obsession in people's lives.

When you choose to introduce your speech with a startling statement, use caution. You want to startle rather than offend your

Skills & Confidence Web Connect 12.2

audience. Beginning speakers sometimes fall into the trap of thinking that an offensive statement is appropriate because it will, indeed, startle. If you are thinking about using a statement that may be too graphic or inappropriate, find an acceptable alternative. Your startling statement should invite the audience to listen, not shut down communication.

### State the Importance of the Topic

Some speakers begin their speeches with clear statements of the significance or magnitude of a topic. When you state the importance of a topic, you tell the audience why they should listen. Tina used this technique to introduce a speech on the history of shoes, a topic that seems fairly ordinary but is actually quite relevant to her audience:

> Okay. Everyone look down at your feet. How many of you have shoes on? Just as I thought. Each of us has a pair of shoes or sandals on our feet. But how many know where those shoes come from? And let's be honest. How many women in the audience have shoes with heels of an inch or more? Um-hmm, don't answer. And for the men, do you steer the women in your lives toward the heels in the shoe stores? Maybe even some of you men own a pair of heels? Well, when I look in my closet, I see one pair of sneakers, two pairs of boots, and a dozen high-heeled shoes. But do I know where these shoes come from or how heels were invented? No. At least not until I did some research into my shoe fetish.
>
> Today, I'd like to share the story of shoes with you. I'd like to discuss the origination of shoes, the changes they've gone through, the invention of high heels (which originally were made for men, by the way), and the troubles those heels have caused.

In this example, Tina states the importance of her topic by reminding her audience that wearing shoes is something almost everyone does but that it can have troubling consequences for some.

You can also state the importance of a topic by showing that although a practice or phenomenon is uncommon, it has a significant impact. Will did this in his speech about germ-line engineering and cloning:

> Imagine a world filled with humans who are genetically perfect, with no flaws or birth defects—humans who are superior to what we know today. Now imagine there's no shortage of body parts for transplants or to repair what we now call "irreparable" injuries, because an exact replica of each person is available—strictly for donation. Although these two notions seem far-fetched, we may be coming closer to this imaginary world than we realize.

> The two processes I asked you to imagine are called germ-line engineering and cloning, the topic of my speech. I know most of you are familiar with these ideas from science fiction novels, movies, and television, but in the next few decades, you may be able to visit your local geneticist to create a designer baby or maybe even have yourself cloned. I realize there are serious moral and ethical concerns about genetic engineering. However, I'd like to invite you to consider that the benefits of these two forms of engineering far outweigh the disadvantages. Today, I'll describe the two processes for you, germ-line engineering and cloning, and then share the advantages of these processes. I'll then discuss two ways that those of us in this room are likely to be affected by these forms of genetic engineering, and then open the floor for discussion.

### Share Your Expertise

Although you know your qualifications for speaking on a subject, your audience may not. Sharing your expertise in an introduction is an effective way to establish your credibility quickly. Here are some credibility-establishing statements from introductions for a few student speeches:

> *"Shamrocks"*: My family has its roots in Ireland. (Jessica)
>
> *"Japanese Language"*: Having studied Japanese for over three years now, I would like to share a little bit about this intriguing language with you today. (Kelly)
>
> *"Why Pi?"*: As a result of that challenge, I have researched this topic, finding information not only technical and historical but also fanatical. (Katy)
>
> *"History of Shoes"*: Well, when I look in my closet, I see one pair of sneakers, two pairs of boots, and a dozen high-heeled shoes. But do I know where these shoes come from or how heels were invented? No. At least not until I did some research into my shoe fetish. (Tina)

Establishing your credibility often is a subtle process. In these examples, the speakers revealed their expertise by describing their qualifications to speak about their topics. They referred to family, study, research, and personal experience to communicate their competence. Use these same techniques to establish your credibility in your speeches. And remember, your credibility also comes through your research (Chapters 7 and 8), the development of your ideas (Chapter 13), your reasoning (Chapters 14 and 24), your organization (Chapter 10), and your delivery (Chapters 17 and 18).

## State What's to Come

Previewing your speech is a necessary component of your introduction. As you learned in Chapter 4, even the best listeners need help following and remembering a speaker's ideas throughout a speech. When your audience hears a preview, they will anticipate your main points, be prepared to listen to them, and not be surprised or confused.

The best previews are brief; they set the audience up for what's to come but do not go into too much detail. Here are previews from Nathan's and Cassie's speeches:

> *"Appalachian Trail"*: First, I'll give you a brief history of the trail's formation. Then, I'll share some facts with you about the trail itself and how it's maintained. Finally, I'll tell you the stories from some of those who have hiked the trail.
>
> *"Crazy Lawsuits"*: In my research, I found many crazy cases that actually have gone to court, and today, I'll discuss some of the craziest. I'll begin with some basic legal terms that come up in these cases so you can follow them more easily. Then I'll share with you some of my favorite cases and give you a sample of the kinds of things that tie up our court system. Finally, I'll persuade you that we should help those who are organizing to control these lawsuits and stop the abuses of our legal system.

In each of these examples, the speakers used variations of "first, then, finally" to identify the order of main points Although this language might seem unimaginative, spoken language is quite different from written language (Chapter 16). Audiences need extra tools to help them absorb and remember a speaker's ideas. (This is also why connectives are so helpful to audiences, as you learned in Chapter 10.) Explicit language like that used in the previews here increases the likelihood that your audience will understand your ideas, follow them throughout the speech, and remember them when the speech is over.

## Guidelines for Your Introduction

Four guidelines will help you create your introduction.

- Look for introductory materials as you do your research.
- Make the introduction brief: no more than 10 to 15 percent of the speech.
- Be creative.
- Practice the full introduction carefully before you give the speech.

*Look for introductory materials as you do your research.* As you conduct research on your speech's topic, look for stories, quotations, startling facts or statements, and other material for your introduction. If you collect a variety of material you might use in your introduction, you will have several options to choose from so that you can select the one that suits your audience and your goals best.

*Prepare and practice the full introduction in detail.* Introductions represent your first opportunity to connect with your audience, so prepare and practice the introduction completely before you give your speech.

- If you are opening with a story, practice telling the full story until you can tell it with ease and flair.
- If you are opening with a quotation, memorize it.
- If you plan to begin with a demonstration, rehearse it until you have it perfected.

Introductions set the stage for what's to come, so you want this part of the speech to go flawlessly. Use your notes as infrequently as possible, if at all, and be sure to make maximum eye contact. Practice your full introduction until you can deliver it smoothly and confidently. A well-delivered introduction will not only enhance your credibility but will also increase your confidence as you move into the body of your speech.

*Be brief.* Remember, introductions tell just a little of what's to come and set the stage for the body of the speech. Introductions should be brief, only 10 to 15 percent of the speech. If they are longer, they become tedious. They also cut into the time you need for your main points. If your planned introduction is longer than 10 to 15 percent of your speech, you probably have included too much detail. Remember, your goal is not to give your speech in the introduction but to get the audience ready to hear your speech.

*Be creative.* Creativity is one of the best ways to capture an audience's attention and reveal your topic. *Creative* doesn't necessarily mean "elaborate and artistic." In this case, creativity simply means using your imagination to come up with new ideas and perspectives on how to open your speech until you find something that works just right. Trying out several of the techniques in this chapter will help you prepare a creative and effective introduction.

Skills & Confidence
PPD
Activity 12.1

**SPEECH Checklist ✓**

### Your Introduction

- ☐ Will your introduction catch the audience's attention?
- ☐ Does your introduction reveal your topic?
- ☐ Does your introduction establish your credibility?
- ☐ Does your introduction preview the speech?
- ☐ Are you using one of the techniques for a compelling introduction?

  asking a question
  telling a story
  reciting a quotation or a poem
  giving a demonstration
  making an intriguing or startling statement
  stating the importance of the topic
  sharing your expertise
  stating what's to come
- ☐ Is your introduction no more than 10–15 percent of your speech?
- ☐ Have you practiced the full introduction carefully?

## The Conclusion

Your conclusion is your final contact with your audience. Just as the introduction represents the first impression you make on your audience, the conclusion represents your last impression, and it will linger with your listeners long after your speech is over. Take time to prepare your conclusion so you end your speech with as much care as you began it. Then practice that conclusion so you can deliver it in just the way you want. When you deliver your conclusion, you have two primary goals:

- To bring your speech to an end
- To reinforce your thesis statement

### End Your Speech

Your conclusion should signal to the audience that your presentation is over. Rather than ending abruptly or just trailing off, you want to communicate clearly that the speech is wrapping up. This signal comes through your words as well as your style of delivery. The more audience centered you are, the more effective your conclusion will be.

Like the close of a conversation, the conclusion of a speech exhibits a shift in style.[2] Generally, closure in conversations is signaled by a pause, a change in the rate of speaking, and even a different tone of voice. In speeches, we use these same nonverbal cues. When you've concluded your final main point, use these shifts in delivery to signal to your audience that you are about to wrap up.

Another effective way to signal the end of your speech is with a concluding transition. These are simple words and phrases such as "in closing," "in summary," "in conclusion," "let me close by saying," and "my purpose today has been." Although these transitions seem obvious, they alert your listeners that you are moving from the body of your speech to your conclusion. These transitions will also help you incorporate the techniques discussed in the next section.

### Reinforce Your Thesis Statement

The second function of your conclusion is to reinforce the thesis statement of your speech. Recall from Chapter 5 that your thesis statement summarizes, in a single declarative sentence, the main ideas, assumptions, or arguments you want to express in your speech. When you restate or rephrase your thesis statement in your conclusion, you remind your audience of the core idea of your speech. Notice how this reinforcement can be very succinct, as in Chad's speech on adoption, or more elaborate, as in Katy's on pi:

> *"Adoption"*: In my family, I have two parents, an older sister, and two younger brothers. One of them is adopted, but in my heart I could not tell you which one.
>
> *"Why Pi?"*: In conclusion, no one knows why pi has caused such a craze or why several books, movies, and fanatical Web pages have been produced on this subject. What inspired the Chudnovsky brothers to devote their lives to the search for pi? What inspired me to write a speech on a silly number? The answer lies in the mystery. Exploring pi is an adventure, which is why people do it. I want you to remember pi not only as the circle ratio, not only as the biggest influence on math over the course of history, but as a number that has an influence on everything we do.

Restating your thesis statement reinforces your arguments and encourages your audience to remember your speech.

## Preparing a Compelling Conclusion

There are several techniques for signaling the end of a speech and reinforcing your thesis statement. You will likely combine several of these techniques to deliver a comprehensive conclusion. As you develop your conclusion, remember to continually ask yourself, "What final ideas do I want to leave my audience with?"

### Summarize Your Main Points

An effective tool for ending your speech and restating your thesis statement is a summary of your main points. A **summary** is a concise restatement of your main points at the end of your speech. You use it to review your ideas and remind your audience of what's important in your speech. Will used a summary in his conclusion:

> As you've seen in these last few minutes, ideas that have been presented to us as fiction may soon be reality. Germ-line engineering and cloning may soon be processes that are used in our everyday life. Both techniques raise ethical questions and concerns, especially as we consider the advantages and disadvantages of each. I have shared some of my own thoughts about these issues in this presentation; I'd now like to open it up for questions and discussion.

When you summarize your main points, remember to do three things. First, offer only a summary—don't restate too much of your speech. The audience has already heard the details, and you are only trying to reinforce the key ideas and help them remember what you've said. Second, don't introduce new ideas into the summary. If you didn't bring up an idea in the body of the speech, don't raise it in the conclusion. New ideas in a conclusion will only confuse your audience. Finally, try to use the same kind of language in your summary that you used in the body of your speech. Familiar phrasing will help your audience recall your main ideas rather than forcing them to figure out what the new wording means.

### Answer Your Introductory Question

If your speech begins with questions, answer them in the conclusion. This technique reminds the audience of what they've learned in the speech. Nathan's speech about the Appalachian Trail began with questions about hiking the trail; he returned to those questions in his conclusion:

> So, now do you think you could walk from New York to Chicago or from Georgia to Maine? Well, even if you're not up for the hike, many others have been. As a result of the efforts to maintain the Appalachian Trail, individuals have hiked the 2,200-mile-long footpath to raise funds, overcome disabilities, and seek out spiritual insights. The next time someone asks you if you want to "take a hike," perhaps you'll say, "why not?"

## SPEECH TIPS

### CONCLUSIONS

Bring your speech around full circle by referring to your introduction in your conclusion. For example, if you were speaking about space exploration, you could begin your speech with the story of Galileo's first glimpse of Saturn's rings. You could then end with a description of NASA's Mars Exploration Program and its discovery of the possible presence of liquid water on the planet.

### Refer Back to the Introduction

Occasionally, a speaker opens with a word, phrase, or idea and then returns to it in the conclusion. Like answering introductory questions, this technique brings the speech full circle and provides a sense of completeness. This technique is usually combined with others, such as summarizing the main points. Kelly's speech about the Japanese language began with *Ohayoo gozaimasu*, which is "good morning" in Japanese. In the conclusion, he summarized his ideas and then returned to his opening by saying:

> Thank you for listening, or as they say in Japan, *doomo arigatoo gozaimashita*.

Reggie, who opened his speech with a story of a boy's battles with chronic health problems, finished the story in his conclusion. After restating his thesis, he said,

**Skills & Confidence** Web Connect 12.3

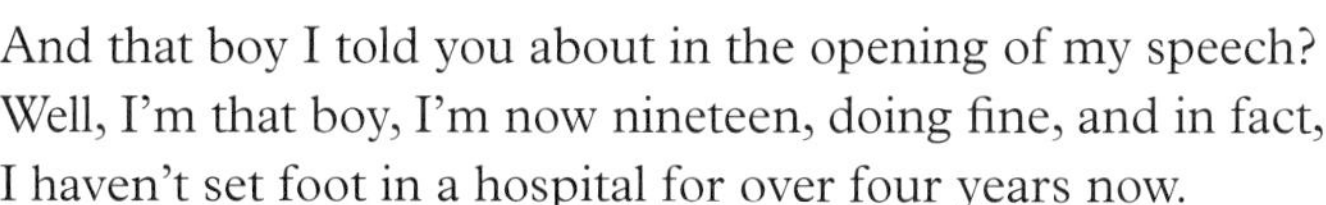

> And that boy I told you about in the opening of my speech? Well, I'm that boy, I'm now nineteen, doing fine, and in fact, I haven't set foot in a hospital for over four years now.

### Recite a Quotation

When you conclude with a quotation, you rely on someone else's words to reinforce your thesis statement. A concluding quotation should come from someone you cited in your speech or from a famous person the audience will recognize. In the following example from the speech about the history of shoes, Tina returns to a source she had cited earlier in her speech:

> As we've heard today, shoes have gone through great changes over time. What started with animal skins and then lace transformed itself into the twenty-four-inch heels worn by both men and women and on to the modern look we know today.

But as Dr. Rene Cailet says, "Shoes should protect the foot and not disturb it. Having sore feet is not normal. As in any body part, pain is a signal that something is wrong."

## Guidelines for Your Conclusion

Several guidelines will help you with your conclusion. As with the introduction, look for effective concluding materials during your research. And remember to be creative and brief. Conclusions should be no more than 5 to 10 percent of your speech. Finally, don't leave your conclusion to chance. Develop it carefully and practice it until you can deliver it with confidence.

*Look for concluding materials as you research and develop your speech.* As you research your speech, look for materials you can use in your conclusion. You may find just the right summary or technique if you keep in mind the kind of conclusion you want to create. If you find more quotations than you can use in the body of your speech, see if one will be appropriate for your conclusion. Or if a story is too long to tell in the introduction, think about saving part of it for the conclusion. As you research and develop your speech, you will come across materials that could be effective for your conclusion. Save them and then draw from these options to create an ending your audience will appreciate.

*Be creative.* Your conclusion is your last contact with your audience. Your creativity should keep your listeners interested until the very end and help them remember your ideas and arguments. A creative conclusion, like Nathan's or Reggie's, can emerge from a clear summary and a reference back to the introduction. Or it may involve sharing a quotation or finishing a story begun in the introduction. Whatever technique you use, it must suit your audience, speech goals, and the tone of your speech.

*Be brief.* Conclusions should make up only 5 to 10 percent of the total speech. Remember, conclusions don't introduce new information; they bring closure to the ideas already presented. If you find your conclusion is running too long, you may be finishing a main point you did not cover completely in the body or providing too much detail in your summary. If your conclusion is too long, reduce its scope and detail.

**Skills & Confidence**
PPD Activity 12.2
Video Activity 12.2

*Don't leave the conclusion to chance.* Take time to prepare the conclusion carefully before you deliver the speech. Your last contact with your audience should be one that enhances your credibility and strengthens your arguments. Make sure you know what you want to say, and rehearse your closing words carefully so you can make eye contact with the audience and end your speech with confidence and assurance.

**SPEECH Checklist ✓**

## Your Conclusion

- [ ] What nonverbal cues (such as a pause or a change in rate or tone) will you use to signal that your speech is concluding?
- [ ] Do you need to use a verbal transition (such as "in closing," "in summary," or "my purpose today has been")?
- [ ] Does your conclusion restate or rephrase your thesis statement?
- [ ] What ideas do you want your audience to remember?
- [ ] Are you using one or more of the techniques for a compelling conclusion?

  a brief summary of your main points
  an answer to a question in the introduction
  the end of a story begun in the introduction
  a reference to an intriguing fact in the introduction
  a relevant quotation

- [ ] Is your conclusion no more than 5 to 10 percent of your speech?
- [ ] Have you practiced the conclusion so you can deliver it with confidence and make eye contact with your audience?

# INTRODUCTION AND CONCLUSION

**with Commentary**

## *Foothills Gateway: Vote YES on Referendum 1A*

*by Mike Piel*

CENGAGE LEARNING

***Specific Purpose:*** *To persuade my audience to vote yes on Referendum 1A.*

***Thesis Statement:*** *Voting yes on Referendum 1A is a good idea because it will save Foothills Gateway, a community organization that serves people with mental disabilities at little cost to the taxpayer.*

**Skills & Confidence**
Video Activity 12.3
Speech Studio 12.1

*As you craft the introduction and conclusion of your next speech, you can use the following speech excerpts as a model. Use your Premium Website for* Invitation to Public Speaking Handbook *to watch the video clip of Mike Piel's speech. As part of a service learning assignment, Mike gave this speech in an introductory public speaking class. The assignment was to give a four- to five-minute persuasive speech about a local issue. After you watch the video, respond to the analysis questions provided and compare your answers to those provided by the author.*

*Commentary*
*Mike begins with two rhetorical questions and a compelling statistic that captures the audience's attention and relates his topic to his audience.*

*He reveals his topic and states his goal. He establishes his credibility by explicitly stating this goal and by stating that he will address the*

*INTRODUCTION*

How many of you are planning on having children? How many of you are planning on having a child with a mental disability? None?

Unfortunately, this is a reality that so many people in this world have to face day to day. In fact, one of every four people in Larimer County alone is in some way affected by someone with a mental disability. Luckily for these people, a community organization called Foothills Gateway is here to make their lives a little easier. Unfortunately, this great organization is in danger of losing its funding. The only way to prevent this from happening is to vote yes on Referendum 1A in the upcoming election. To make you more aware of the situation, I'm going to take the next few minutes to inform you of several things. I will let you know what it is exactly that Foothills Gateway does, why passing this referendum is such a good idea, and lastly, how it's going to affect you, the taxpayer.

*impact of this vote on taxpayers.*

*Mike finishes his introduction by previewing his speech. Notice how he clearly states his three main points and adapts his last point to his audience.*

*CONCLUSION*

Now, over the last few minutes, I have tried to inform you about what Foothills Gateway does, why this referendum is a good idea, and a little bit about how it's going to affect you, the taxpayer. I'll try to appeal to your good sense, your good nature as human beings—don't turn your back on people who are less fortunate than you, because if you don't take care of them, nobody else will. So please vote yes when you go to the ballot. Thank you.

*Mike signals the end of his speech with the phrase "over the last few minutes" and by restating his three main points.*

*He makes a direct appeal to his audience, reinforcing his thesis and reminding his audience of his purpose for speaking—to persuade them to vote yes on the referendum. Notice how he makes a direct, yet simple, appeal to their emotions, ending his speech on a strong note of human interest and compassion.*

PART V

# DEVELOPMENT

## CIVIC ENGAGEMENT IN ACTION

### The New Student Politics

As you read at the beginning of Chapter 5, the Wingspread Summit on Student Civic Engagement held in 2001 encouraged students to discuss their political and civic engagement and to talk about what motivated them to get involved in their communities. Here are a few of their observations about their role in the political process and civic life:

COURTESY OF CAMPUS COMPACT

- Democracy is a social responsibility, not a civic obligation. Democracy should be inclusive, meaning all should be able to participate. However, because most students will participate in the democratic process based on personal interests and experience, their participation will be individualized and seem fragmented rather than directed at a widely shared goal.
- Student political engagement cannot be measured by traditional standards. If it is, student voices and participation will be misunderstood. In the words of one student: "I don't do traditional politics, but my service [learning] work is political."
- Too many people are left out of political decisions. However, for democracy to work, access to the system is imperative. The political system must be changed by "giving the power back to the people, by educating them about the inner-workings of their political system, and helping them access it."

Fabricio Rodriguez, a student from Mesa Community College in Arizona who participated in the summit, characterized students' role in civic engagement in this way: "[W]e are a multi-tendency and cross-cultural group of citizens untangling problems on a local level that, for the first time in history, are inseparable from the global

#### You Can Get Involved

To learn more about the Wingspread Summit and how you can express your political convictions via civic engagement and service learning, access **Web Connect P.V.1: New Student Politics** at your Premium Website for *Invitation to Public Speaking Handbook*. For two good resources that allow you to participate in the more traditional political process, access

(continued)

## CIVIC ENGAGEMENT IN ACTION continued

Skills & Confidence
Web Connect P.V.1
Web Connect P.V.2
Web Connect P.V.3

critique. . . . We will be criticized for a 'lack of focus,' for being whiners, and social critics from movements past will scratch their heads as we unite for political prisoners on Monday, dispossessed indigenous persons on Tuesday, workers' rights on Wednesday, and spend the rest of the week quietly reading Howard Zinn to grade school kids." He asserts that students can use both politics and other, nontraditional means to campaign for positive change in their communities, such as participating in service learning programs in school. "Service is a small hammer. By itself it can send small chips flying. Politics act like a chisel. To its own, it can gouge the perfect surface. Together, with our hard work and inspiration, the hammer and chisel begin to carve something new, less perfect, and more human."[1]



### You Can Get Involved (continued)

**Web Connect P.V.2: Citizen Joe** and **Web Connect P.V.3: Speak Out**. These nonprofit, nonpartisan resources provide information and links you can use to send messages to elected officials, sign petitions, just talk to others about your political views, and more.

# DEVELOPMENT

CHAPTER 13

# Developing and Supporting Your Ideas

- Examples

  Speech Checklist: When to Use Examples
- Narratives

  Speech Checklist: When to Use Narratives
- Statistics

  Speech Checklist: When to Use Statistics

  Ethical Moment: What Evidence Should a Speaker Use to "Provoke a Debate"?
- Testimony

  Speech Checklist: When to Use Testimony
- Definitions

  Speech Checklist: When to Use Definitions

*In this chapter, you will learn to*

- Explain the importance of supporting materials in a speech
- Identify and provide examples of the five main types of supporting materials
- Apply tips for using each of the five types of supporting materials effectively

The public dialogue is kindled by claims. The word *claim* comes from the Latin *clamare*, which means "to call or cry out." There is something social about a claim: someone calls out to someone else. When one person asserts something, there is the expectation that another person can hear the call and understand the claim.[1]

When we enter the public dialogue, we take part in a social interaction—one person makes a claim about a topic to an audience, "calling out" to his or her listeners, and they respond to this claim in some way. In public speaking, a **claim** is an assertion that must be proved. When we make claims, we explore and exchange ideas, we respond to one another, and we clarify, refine, and revise our positions. When we communicate our claims ethically and effectively, we stimulate and enhance the public dialogue.

We prove our claims with **evidence,** the materials speakers use to support their ideas. Ethical evidence allows you to explain a process with confidence, share a perspective in a way that encourages understanding, identify a problem and pose a solution, motivate an audience to action, or acknowledge someone's accomplishments. Evidence comes from the information you already know and that you gather in your research on the Internet, at the library, and in interviews. In Chapter 8, you learned how to evaluate researched information and cite your sources. Strong evidence, which helps prove your claims, also helps build your credibility, or believability. In Chapter 14, you'll read about how you can enhance your personal credibility. Credible and ethical evidence is the foundation of the common language in the public sphere.

The five most common types of supporting material are

- Examples
- Narratives
- Statistics
- Testimony
- Definitions

You are probably familiar with these types of evidence, but you may not be sure when to use them or how to evaluate their particular strengths and weaknesses. Let's start with examples as evidence.

## Examples

**Examples** are specific instances used to illustrate a concept, experience, issue, or problem. Examples can be brief—only a word or a sentence or two—or they can be longer and richly detailed. Examples can also be real or hypothetical. A **real example** is an instance that actually took place. A **hypothetical example** is an instance that did not take place but could have. Generally, real examples are more credible and convey a sense of immediacy. Here are two real examples from student speeches:

> In her speech on binge drinking on college campuses nationwide, Eileen used a powerful example of a binge drinker by describing her friend who "consumed twelve to fifteen beers combined with shots of hard liquor each evening, and stopped only because she ran out of alcohol, time, or money."

> In his speech on the dangers of exotic pets, Kyle used an example provided by the head of his city's Pest Control and Wildlife Department: "According to the department's head, one man had a Gaboon viper, a cobra, a black-tailed rattlesnake, a copperhead, three large boas, and a full-grown alligator that acted as a 'guard dog.'" Kyle explained to his audience that these pets were hazardous because the owner was "bitten by his Gaboon viper and died from the bite. The remaining so-called pets? They went to the Humane Society to be adopted by other people or to be euthanized."

These students used examples to help clarify exactly what they meant when they used the terms *binge drinker* and *hazardous pets.*

Occasionally, you can clarify a point with a hypothetical example. A hypothetical example usually begins with words like *imagine, suppose*, or *let's say that.* For example, when Clara addressed a group of teenagers in an after-school program on proper eating for her service learning project, she could have simply said, "Skipping breakfast isn't good for you." Instead, to be a more effective speaker, she supported her claim with a hypothetical example:

> Suppose you skipped breakfast this morning. Let's see what that would do to your energy level by about 9 or 10 o'clock—that's during second period, right? If you haven't eaten by then, you'll probably feel bored or restless, and maybe sad or unmotivated. You might also feel angry or irritable, kind of grouchy and crabby. And maybe you'll feel a little lightheaded or dizzy if you stand up fast. You might have a headache. You'll definitely have trouble concentrating on your schoolwork because your blood sugar is low or because all you can think about is how hungry you are. Sound familiar to any of you?

Clara's hypothetical example, although not real itself, grew out of research that was grounded in real experience and helped her audience understand more clearly why skipping meals isn't good for them.

Several criteria can help you decide when using an example would be most effective. Consider the following guidelines, all of which will help you answer in advance any questions your audience may have about your topic.

### Use Examples to Clarify Concepts

Identify the concepts in your speech that your audience might consider complex or unfamiliar, and then use an example to help you frame those concepts in terms your audience will understand. In other words, try to anticipate what parts of your speech might prompt your audience to ask, "What do you mean by that?" Examples frame abstract concepts and experiences in terms of concrete actions, events, people, and things. Thus, an example can make an abstract or complex point clearer.

In Clara's case, she anticipated her audience's question, "what does she mean by 'isn't good' for me?" Her detailed example about the physical and mental impacts of skipping breakfast clarified what she meant.

### Use Examples to Reinforce Points

What parts of your speech might prompt the audience to say, "I don't see how this point matters"? Examples help an audience see your points in terms of the larger case you're making in your speech. Therefore, examples help audiences recognize the relevance and importance of your points as support for your claims. Kyle used an example of how hazardous exotic pets can be to reinforce his point that owning exotic pets is a dangerous hobby. By describing what happened to one owner of such pets, and then what happened to the animals after the owner died, Kyle encouraged his audience to consider the potentially deadly consequences of this hobby.

### Use Examples to Bring Concepts to Life or to Elicit Emotions

When someone says, "I'm not affected by that issue," an example helps bring a concept to life by providing specific images an audience can picture in their minds. When they're able to create a mental picture, one that is filtered through their own thoughts and experiences, they can better understand how an issue affects them or someone they know. Eileen's example of the sheer amount of alcohol consumed by her friend brought the reality of binge drinking to life for her audience. Specifically, Eileen's reference to drinking that "stopped only when [her friend] ran out of alcohol, time, or money" highlighted just how out of control and self-destructive binge drinking can become, adding emotional weight to her claim. Similarly, Kyle's example of the exotic pets being euthanized brought out emotions in his audience. No longer were the exotic pets curiosities; they became real animals that died through no fault of their own.

### Use Examples to Build Your Case or Make Credible Generalizations

When someone says, "It's not as common or prevalent as you say," using a number of examples helps them see that it is. A series of examples can help you build a case or help you make a plausible generalization. For example, if Eileen cited numerous examples of binge drinking on college campuses throughout the country, those in her audience who think binge drinking is an isolated problem might be compelled to reconsider their views and see the issue as a nationwide concern.

## Guidelines for Using Examples Ethically and Effectively

Not all examples are equal. Some don't illustrate your point well, and others won't resonate with your audience. To evaluate an example for its strengths and weaknesses, consider the following questions.[2]

*Is the example relevant and appropriate?* Does your example refer to the point you are making or to something else? In her speech about binge drinking, if Eileen offers an example of treatment programs for older adults as her "success story solution," her example won't be relevant because her target population consists of students in their teens and early twenties, not older adults. It's a great example of a solution, but not the solution to her specific problem. Similarly, some examples are too graphic, emotional, detailed, or personal for an audience. Use caution with examples that contain violent details, the manipulation of emotions, overly technical material, or the use of explicit personal details. For example, when Judy Sheperd speaks about the 1998 murder of her son Matthew, killed in a hate crime in Laramie, Wyoming, she describes his body wrapped in bandages with tubes coming out from everywhere. She shares that his ear had been reattached by surgeons and continued to bleed as she and her family stayed with him in his final days of life. These details give her speech emotional power for her audience. However, she does not offer more graphic details of her son's physical condition, recognizing that these would prevent her audience from listening to her message.

*Is the hypothetical example ethical?* When you offer a hypothetical example, make sure it represents events or information grounded in fact. Your hypothetical example should be plausible; it really could be true or could have happened. You also should tell your audience the example is hypothetical. Don't mislead your audience into believing that a made-up example, however plausible, is real when it isn't.

*Are there enough examples to support your claim?* Is one example enough, or do you need several? If you can't find more than one example to support your point, perhaps your claim is unfounded. If you want to suggest something is common but you can't find examples of it, it may not be as common as you thought. One example suggests an isolated incident, not a trend, so avoid generalizing from a single example. When you are making a case for the extent of something, like the problem of binge drinking, you'll need quite a few examples. However, if you are only illustrating what something is, as in what constitutes binge drinking, one example should suffice.

*Have you accounted for the counterexamples?* Counterexamples are specific instances that contradict your claims; they make your assertions appear false or at least weaken them. If Kyle found that

**SPEECH Checklist**

### When to Use Examples

- [ ] To clarify concepts
- [ ] To reinforce points
- [ ] To bring concepts to life or to elicit emotions
- [ ] To build a case or make credible generalizations

To use an example ethically and effectively, make sure

- [ ] it is relevant and appropriate
- [ ] it is grounded in fact if it is a hypothetical example
- [ ] it is not an isolated example if you want to use it to support a claim
- [ ] you take counterexamples into account

many exotic pets were safe to own, he'd have to explain why this is so. If he can't explain these counterexamples, he has to adjust his claim to "some exotic pets, such as poisonous snakes, are dangerous to own." He can't ethically claim that *all* exotic pets are dangerous because he has counterexamples that refute this claim.

Using examples is an excellent way to support your claims and develop or clarify your information. Examples are important parts of speeches, and when used appropriately, they can help make your points clear and compelling.

## Narratives

A **narrative** is a story that recounts or foretells real or hypothetical events. Narratives help us explain, interpret, and understand events in our lives or the lives of others.[3] Speakers can use **brief narratives,** sometimes called *vignettes*, to illustrate a specific point or **extended narratives** to make an evolving connection with a broader point. Whatever their length, narratives can be valuable aids to public speakers. When used in speeches, stories can give historical context to events, make strong connections between ideas and experiences, add emotional depth to characterizations, and describe subjects, settings, and actions with sensory details that can captivate an audience.

Because narratives are so appealing to audiences, always search for stories you can use in your speech as you gather your supporting material. A carefully selected and well-told story can add a personal touch, make a point, or move an audience in significant ways. There are several criteria to follow when you are thinking about incorporating a narrative into your speech.

### Use Narratives to Personalize a Point

Former U.S. President Ronald Reagan was an expert at using stories to make his point in personal ways. An advocate of private initiative rather than government assistance, he told the story of Jose Salcido, whose wife had died of cancer.

> [Her death left Jose] both father and mother of thirteen children. In an accident only the Lord can explain, one day the brakes on his truck didn't hold and he was crushed against a brick wall as he walked in front of the vehicle. The children who had lost their mother now had lost their father. But even they were not orphaned.

Reagan went on to tell of extended family, neighbors, members of their church parish, and even strangers who stepped in to help the Salcido children in the absence of their parents. He finished his story by reading a letter from one of the people who assisted the children: "This is for the children of Jose Salcido. It is for them to know there are always others who care; that despite personal tragedy, the world is not always the dark place it seems to be." In this one story, Reagan drew his audience personally into his argument. As they listened to his story, they actually could see themselves assisting the children.[4]

### Use Narratives to Challenge an Audience to Think in New Ways

A narrative can challenge an audience to think differently or to understand the world in new ways. Curtis began his speech on the various kinds of racism in the following way: "Let me tell you the story of Ishmael."

> Ishmael was sitting at a restaurant in town, minding his own business, eating dinner with some of his friends. At another table nearby, he and his friends heard snickering and laughter but ignored it because they didn't think it related to them. Pretty soon, the laughter got louder, and two guys from that table began to address Ishmael and his friends. At first, they thought it was going to be a friendly exchange but soon realized they were the butt of the jokes being told—racist jokes, about the shape of Ishmael's eyes and the color of his skin. The so-called jokes soon turned to taunts and verbal abuse, with the

> girlfriends joining in. Not sure what to do, Ishmael and his friends were saved, so to speak, by the owner of the restaurant, who asked Ishmael and his friends to leave.

Curtis paused here to let the story sink in. He began again: "You think I might be making this up? It happened to my best friend a couple of years ago while he was a student at this very university."

With his narrative, Curtis compelled any listeners in his audience who might have believed that racism no longer exists to rethink their views. As we tell a story, we share our perspectives with an audience in personal, yet organized, ways. In listening to our story, an audience may find a commonality not recognized before or gain a new or deeper understanding of an issue.

***Speaking across DIFFERENCES***

**Using a narrative in a speech is a popular and effective way to share a perspective your audience might be unfamiliar with.**

### Use Narratives to Draw an Audience in Emotionally

Facts, statistics, and examples can prove the claims you make in your speech, but they lack the emotional appeal of a story. If your listeners can't connect with your speech on an emotional level, they may not feel that its subject is important enough for them to care whether you prove your claims or not. Use a story, then, when you want to draw your audience into the speech emotionally. Josiah used this brief story, found as he gathered materials for his speech on the history of battles portrayed in theatrical productions:

> Planned stage combat reduces the level of danger that is part of any battle scene in a play. According to William Hobbs in *Fight Direction for the Stage and Screen*, in early sixteenth-century Stockholm, the actor who played the part of Longinus in *The Mystery of the Passion*, and who had to pierce the crucified Christ, was so carried away with the spirit of the action that he actually killed the other actor. The king, who was present, was so angry that he leapt onto the stage and cut off the head of Longinus. And the audience, who had been pleased with the actor's zeal, were so infuriated with the king that they turned upon him and slew him.

Josiah could have made his point by offering statistics on the number of deaths and accidents in stage fights over some period of time, but instead, he drew his audience in emotionally with a brief story about the implications of unrehearsed fights in theatrical battle scenes.

**Skills & Confidence** Video Activity 13.1

## Use Narratives to Unite with Your Audience

Speaking across DIFFERENCES

Narratives can also help you establish common ground with an audience.

Stories can describe common, profound, or dramatic experiences that you can use to create unity between yourself and your audience. When you share a story about an experience that is just like everyone else's, you establish common ground with your audience. When you relate a powerful moment in your life, you reveal a personal aspect of yourself that allows your audience to identify with you more fully. When you tell dramatic or exciting stories, you can connect with your audience by sharing a way of thinking about the world that may be new to them. Stories, because of their human element and the personalized way they are told, can create a sense of togetherness between speakers and their audiences.

## Guidelines for Using Narratives Ethically and Effectively

In speeches, narratives are more than stories that entertain: They convey something specific to an audience. Use the following questions to determine whether the narrative you want to use in your speech does more than simply "tell a good story."

*Does your narrative make a specific point?* When you tell a story in a speech, you must tell it for a specific reason. The purpose of the story might be to reaffirm values, challenge perspectives, remind your audience of important events and beliefs, or teach ways of being and thinking. Examine the narrative you want to tell in your speech to be sure it has a clear point. Remember, many great stories are available, but not every story makes your point well. Reagan told the story of the orphaned children in such a way that his point could not be missed—without assistance from everyday people, the children would have suffered more than they already had.

*Is the length appropriate?* Speeches often have time limits, and stories—especially extended ones—take time to tell. Brief stories allow you to make your point quickly and often fit better into speeches, as did Josiah's story about stage fighting, but don't discard an extended story without considering how it might fit in your speech. An extended story offers more detail and, if handled appropriately, can draw the audience into your speech more fully. To use an extended story in a speech, open with part of the story, add pieces of it as you develop your speech, and then conclude with the remainder of the story. This use of an extended story can keep the audience listening throughout the speech to "hear how the story ends."

*Is the language vivid and the delivery appropriate to the story?* The language you use to present a story must do more than relate the story's details. It should also bring the story's message to life. This doesn't mean that you should use flowery or complicated language to present your story or that you can exaggerate or change a story to meet your needs. Rather, think about the language you choose and the images and messages it conveys and creates. Notice how language facilitates the story's message in some of the examples we've already seen in this chapter: In Josiah's example, the audience "turned upon him and slew him," and in Reagan's speech, the "world isn't always a dark place."

You also have an ethical obligation to tell the truth with your story. The language you use reflects your desire to tell the story accurately and, thus, ethically. Similarly, the manner in which you tell the story is significant. Practice telling your story several times until you get your pauses, emphasis, gestures, and expressions the way you want them.

*Is the story appropriate for my audience?* You can apply the same criteria to narratives that you use to determine the appropriateness of examples. Is your story too graphic, too personal, or simply inappropriate for a particular audience? As you do for examples, make sure the stories you tell ring true for your audience. Remember that not all listeners respond to stories in the same way and that how listeners do respond depends on many factors, including their cultural background. Some stories simply don't tell a familiar tale or recount a common experience. If you suspect certain parts of your story will be culturally unfamiliar to many in your audience, make sure you explain those parts. Or choose a different story if you anticipate that too much of the story will not be appropriate.

Similarly, stories often reference other stories or rely on parts of other stories to be complete. This process, called **intertextuality,** is very common in television programs, movies, and computer games. For example, one TV show refers to another or relies on part of a narrative from another show to make its point. Because today many of our stories come from entertainment media, intertextuality in everyday communication is becoming very common. Make sure your audience has the references necessary to follow these types of intertextual narratives.

**Speaking across DIFFERENCES**

**Narratives are most effective when they recount a common experience. It's perfectly fine to use stories from various cultures—just be sure to explain the parts of a story that an audience may not be culturally familiar with.**

**SPEECH Checklist ✓**

## When to Use Narratives

- [ ] To personalize a point
- [ ] To challenge your audience to think in new ways
- [ ] To draw your audience in emotionally
- [ ] To unite with your audience

To use a narrative ethically and effectively, make sure

- [ ] it makes a specific point related to your speech
- [ ] it is an appropriate length (a long narrative can divided among parts of the speech)
- [ ] it has vivid and memorable language
- [ ] it does not distort the truth
- [ ] you practice it enough times to tell it expressively
- [ ] it is appropriate—not too graphic, personal, or unfamiliar—for your audience

# Statistics

**Statistics** are numerical summaries of facts, figures, and research findings. They help audiences understand amounts (100 individuals participated), proportions (that's almost half the people in this organization), and percentages (fully 50 percent said they'd participate again). Numbers summarize and help audiences make sense of large chunks of information (eight glasses of water a day, every day of the year, is the equivalent of almost 3,000 glasses of water a year), and they help people see where something is in relation to other things (he's the third fastest runner in the world). See Figure 13.1 for a visual representation of statistics that could help an audience understand how the U.S. government classifies people who immigrate to the United States.

Numbers and statistics may seem less glamorous than a story or a clever example, but relevant, surprising, or little-known statistics can grab an audience's attention. Statistics can help you synthesize large amounts of data, point out exceptions to trends or generalizations, or express the magnitude or impact of an event or issue. Statistics can also help you make and refine your claims, and they can highlight

**FIGURE 13.1 Visual representation of statistics**
Visual representations of statistics help an audience understand complex or abstract information. This graph shows the number of immigrants admitted to the United States in 2004 and 2005 by class of admission.

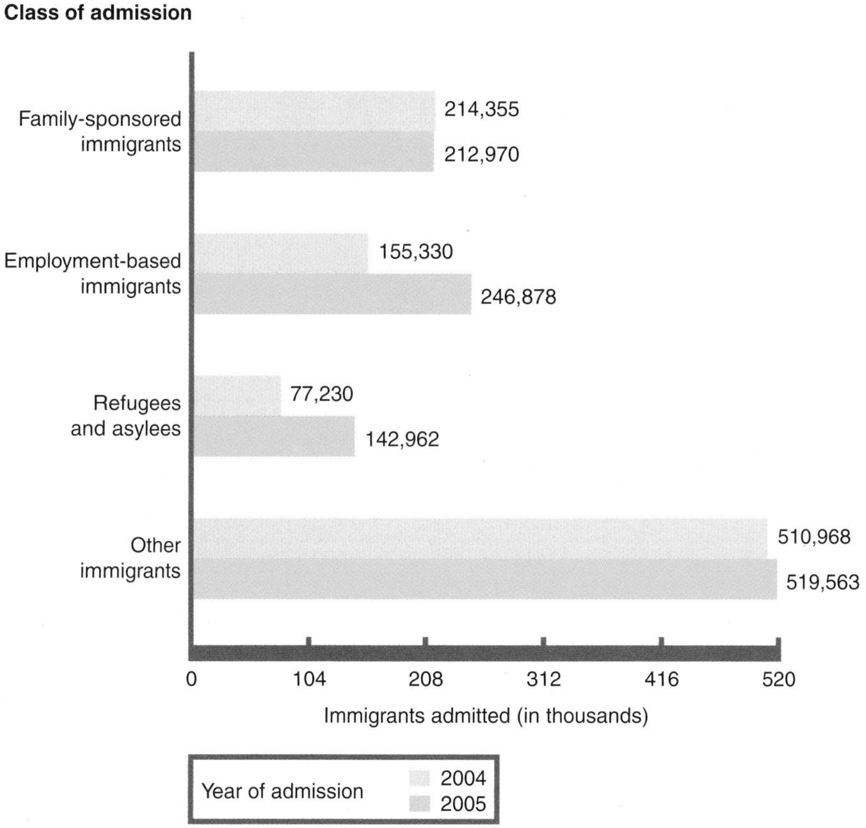

**Class of admission**

Family-sponsored immigrants
214,355
212,970

Employment-based immigrants
155,330
246,878

Refugees and asylees
77,230
142,962

Other immigrants
510,968
519,563

0
104
208
312
416
520

Immigrants admitted (in thousands)

Year of admission
2004
2005

**Source:** U.S. Census Bureau, Statistical Abstract of the United States, 2007.

certain aspects of your topic that other types of evidence cannot. According to Cynthia Crossen, author of *Tainted Truth: The Manipulation of Fact in America*, 82 percent of people surveyed said statistics increase a story's credibility.[5] One of the best sources of statistics is the *Statistical Abstract of the United States.*

Skills & Confidence Web Connect 13.1

## Types of Statistics

Common statistics include totals and amounts, costs, scales and ranges, ratios, rates, dates and times, measurements, and percentages. Other more technical statistics are the *mean, median*, and *mode*: numbers that summarize sets of numbers. When you use them correctly, they can be an important source of evidence, but why, how, and when to use them isn't

**FIGURE 13.2 Visual representation of mean, median, and mode**
The mean, median, and mode are numbers that summarize other groups of numbers. This figure shows the mean, median, and mode of the range of rents for fifteen one-bedroom apartments in the Boston area, September 2007.

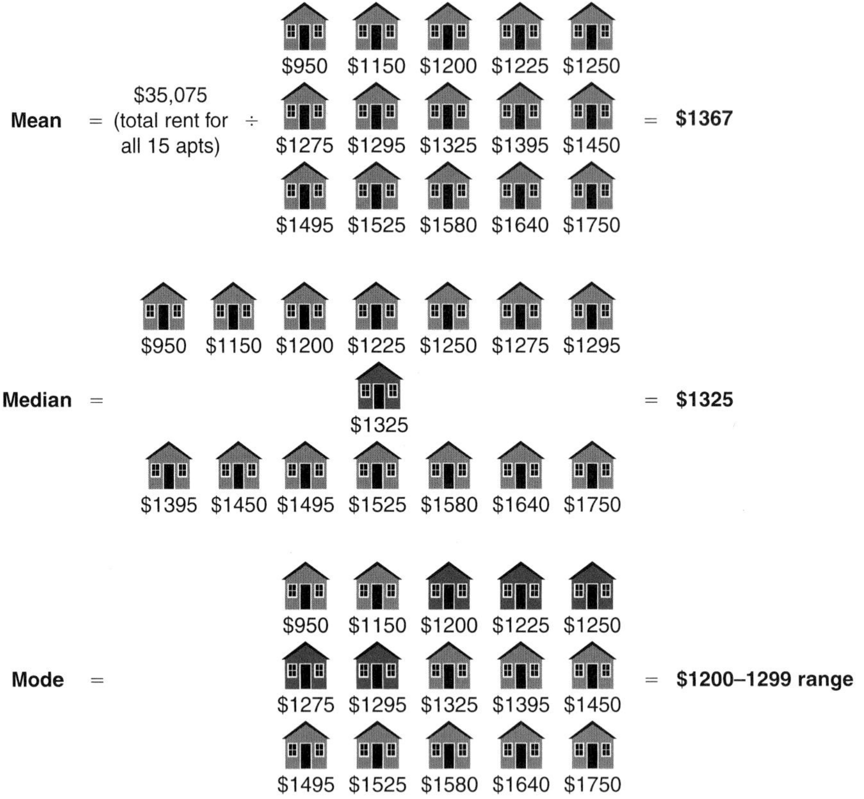


**Source:** craigslist.com

always clear. The descriptions that follow will help you determine the type of statistics you need in your speech. Also see Figure 13.2 for a visual representation of the differences between mean, median, and mode.

The **mean** tells you the average of a group of numbers. Find it by adding all the numbers in your data set and then dividing by the total number of items. Use the mean when you want to describe averages, patterns, tendencies, generalizations, and trends, especially for large groups of data. For example, the mean is what you need if you want to find the average weight of a group of teenagers, like Clara did in her speech to the after-school youth in our earlier example. To find the mean, Clara added the weight of each of the teens in her audience (they weighed 115, 121, 126, 132, 154, 159, 163, 167, and 170) and then divided that number (1,307) by the total number of teens she had weighed (9). This gave her the mean, about 145 pounds, as the average weight of her audience. She used that average, or mean, to compare her audience's average to the average weight of teenagers fifty years ago and then to teen athletes and nonathletes. She and her audience then entered into a discussion about average weights of teenagers in general.

However, when the data set includes extreme values, or what are called *outliers*, using the mean to generalize about the data is misleading.[6] A group of students speaking to county commissioners about affordable housing illustrates why this is so. The students presented information about the average cost of housing in their area. Most of the houses rented for $900 to $1,100 a month, but one home rented for $2,250 a month. In this case, the students couldn't have used the mean because the outlier in this set of data ($2,250) would have distorted the picture of housing costs in their area. To provide a more accurate statistic, the students need to use the median or the mode or leave out the $2,250 rental and explain why.

The **median** is the middle number in a series or set of numbers arranged in a ranked order. A median tells you where the midpoint is in your set of data. It shows you that one-half of your observations will be smaller and one-half larger than the midpoint. Use the median when you want to identify the midpoint and make claims about its significance or about the items that fall above or below it. For example, the median weight of Clara's teens is 154. This means that half the teens weighed more than 154 and half weighed less. Both Clara and her audience now have more information than simply the average weight of the teens (145 pounds). For example, they can begin to explain weight in relation to body type or height (those below the median ranged in height from four feet eleven inches to five feet eight inches, and those above the median ranged from five feet six inches to six feet one inch).

The students speaking about affordable housing used the median to explain that one-half of the homes they assessed rented for less than $950 a month and one-half rented for more than $950. They then explained that once the housing that rented for less than the median had been rented, families looking for rentals in their area had to pay more than $950 a month. They discussed the monthly income necessary to support such housing costs. Using the median in this way helped them make a case for building Habitat for Humanity homes in a particular neighborhood so more families could afford to live there.

The disadvantage of using the median is that significant numbers below and above the midpoint might not be discussed. For example, is it significant for a teen to weigh 39 pounds less than the median weight, as the lightest person does, or 16 pounds more than the median, as the heaviest does? Similarly, if the students failed to explain that below the median rent of $950, houses rented for no less than $875, their audience might assume that some housing was much more affordable than that. And if they didn't note that above the median, homes rented for as high as $1,300, their audience might not understand that about half of the housing in the area was too expensive for most families. Thus, their audience might get the impression that families could easily afford to live in a certain neighborhood, when actually they could not.

The **mode** is the number that occurs most often in a set of numbers. Use the mode when you want to illustrate the most frequent or typical item in your data set to establish the occurrence, availability, demand, or need for something. For example, if Clara found that of the nine teenagers in her group, seven ate five times a day and the other two ate four times a day, then the modal rate of food consumption is five times a day—that's the most common number of meals her audience eats in a day. She could then talk about metabolism during growth spurts and the need for many teens to eat more than three times a day as they are growing. Similarly, if the students showed that the most common monthly income for people looking for rental homes was $1,200, they could use the mode to show that most of the homes for rent in their area were priced too high for these people. Thus, they could argue that Habitat for Humanity homes were crucial.

Numbers help you make claims and establish the importance of your ideas. Because audiences give numbers so much credibility, consider the following guidelines when you want to use statistics ethically and appropriately.

SPEECH **TIPS**

### USING THE MEAN, MEDIAN, AND MODE

- Use the mean (unless there are outliers in your data set) to describe averages, patterns, tendencies, generalizations, and trends.
- Use the median to make claims about the midpoint in a data set or about figures that fall above or below it.
- Use the mode (the most common number in a data set) to make claims about the availability, demand, or need for something.

### Use Statistics to Synthesize Large Amounts of Information

Statistics allow you to present large amounts of data in a very precise way. For example, in a speech on the process of newspaper production, Josh explained that in his hometown of approximately 1 million people, 31,000 copies of the local paper were printed each weekday, and 37,000 copies were printed on Sunday. And he explained, "if you took one average-sized newspaper and cut it into the size of a paperback book, you have a book about 350 pages thick." Use statistics when you want your audience to appreciate the numerical force behind something or when you want them to understand the size or quantity of an event.

### Use Statistics When the Numbers Tell a Powerful Story

In a speech on cradle-to-grave marketing, Jess could have told the story of a child heavily influenced by television advertising. Instead, he chose to use statistics:

> The average twelve-year-old spends four hours a day watching television—the equivalent of two months of nonstop TV watching per year. The result is what marketers call the "nag factor," children badgering their parents to buy products, culminating in 188 billion children-influenced dollars spent on products in 1997. So powerful is the nag factor that advertisers spend $2 billion annually on advertising directed specifically at children.

The story Jess told with these numbers—two months total television watching that resulted in enormous costs for parents and increased focus on this market by advertisers—is far more powerful than the story of one child begging a parent to buy products on a shopping trip.

### Use Statistics When Numerical Evidence Strengthens a Claim

Statistics can strengthen a claim, especially one made in an example or a story, because they quantify or measure the impact of an event. They also allow you to make the same claim in a new way. After Tasha used verbal and visual examples to describe the damage done by the *Exxon Valdez* oil spill, she used statistics to strengthen her claim that the spill caused an enormous amount of damage: "You can see why this spill is known as the worst oil spill in history. The oil from the *Exxon Valdez* spread over a total of 10,000 square miles in Alaska. It covered 1,500 miles of shoreline and traveled as far as 600 miles from the original spill." Tasha's description and examples affected the audience on one level, her visual aids influenced them on another, and her dramatic statistics reinforced her claims about the impact of the spill.

### Guidelines for Using Statistics Ethically and Effectively

There are many ways to misuse statistics. Recall from our housing example that the mean rent misrepresented the affordability of housing in a particular neighborhood. Similarly, if Clara suggested that the modal number of meals for teens is five per day, we can easily overlook the thousands of teens who go without food each day because of poverty or eating disorders. Because statistics can be manipulated, the following guidelines will help you use them responsibly and accurately.

*Evaluate your statistics carefully.* In Chapter 8, you learned some guidelines for evaluating your supporting materials. You can use the same guidelines to assess the strength of a statistic. Be certain the source is credible, the data are current, and the statistic represents what you claim it does. It is easy to manipulate a statistic to say what you want. For example, when only 10 percent of those surveyed say they would try a product again but only twenty people were sampled, you don't have a very strong statistic. Similarly, be wary when a source that is overly invested in a particular outcome provides a statistic. For example, data on global warming compiled by the petroleum industry are likely to be influenced by the industry's views on the issue. To remain ethical, see if you can find other sources that confirm your statistic, or if that isn't possible, present statistics from various perspectives to make your claim more accurately.

*Use statistics sparingly.* Audiences will remember most of the stories you tell, but they will have a harder time remembering the numbers. In fact, the more numbers you use, the fewer your audience is likely to remember. How difficult do you think it would be to remember the numbers in the following example?

> Based on these 2005 figures, we can say that of the 1,393 males between the ages of eighteen and twenty-one with incomes above $24,000 a year and less than two years of training who attended this event more than three times but less than five, 743 drove their own vehicles, 259 rode with friends, 128 took the bus, and 11 walked. This leaves 252 unaccounted for. Now, let's look at the 2007 data. These figures change slightly.

Although this is a hypothetical example, it illustrates how beginning speakers sometimes tend to use too many numbers and use them randomly. The result is more information than audience members can remember, presented without a systematic structure to help them.

*Help your audience understand your statistics.* To help your audience grasp large or complicated statistics, try the following tactics:

- Display statistics visually on an overhead, in a PowerPoint slide, in a handout, or on a board or flip chart. Displaying statistics visually reinforces your verbal presentation by helping your audience keep track of the statistics.
- Round your numbers up or down wherever possible. Notice how Tasha rounded her numbers about the *Exxon Valdez* oil spill to whole numbers. She spoke of 10,000 and 1,500 and 600 rather than 10,143 and 1,485 and 621. When you want to emphasize general size rather than the exact amount, round your numbers.
- When you must present a lot of numbers to make a point, find ways to group them together so your audience can digest them more easily. Although your audience will still have to keep

track of quite a few numbers, "chunking" makes them easier to follow. Certain kinds of data can be grouped together easily. For example, in our hypothetical example, demographic data, mode of transportation, and insignificant data could be grouped so the audience could remember numbers that are related to one another.

- Translate your statistics for the audience. How big is 1,500 miles of shoreline? Show them that it's the distance between two familiar points, say, New York City to the southern tip of Florida. What does it mean to say "one in ten"? Represent that number by asking one in ten of your audience members to stand up. How large is a protected wilderness area of 10,000 acres? Ten thousand acres are equal to just over 7,500 football fields, including the end zones.[7]

You will find that you can use statistics in almost every type of speech you give.

**SPEECH Checklist**

## When to Use Statistics

- ☐ To grab an audience's attention (with a startling but relevant statistic)
- ☐ To synthesize large amounts of data
- ☐ To point out exceptions to trends or generalizations
- ☐ To express the magnitude or impact of an event or issue
- ☐ To help your audience understand the size or quantity of something
- ☐ To emphasize a point or highlight an aspect of your topic
- ☐ To make and strengthen claims
- ☐ To increase a story's credibility

To use statistics ethically and effectively, make sure

- ☐ the source is credible
- ☐ the data are current (or from the appropriate period for your topic)
- ☐ the data represent what you claim they do
- ☐ the data can be confirmed by other sources
- ☐ you do not use more statistics than necessary
- ☐ you help your audience understand your statistics by using visual aids, round numbers, categories of data, and translations into familiar quantities

## Ethical Moment

### What Evidence Should a Speaker Use to "Provoke a Debate"?

Speaking at a 2005 conference titled "Diversifying the Science and Engineering Workforce: Women, Underrepresented Minorities, and Their Science and Engineering Careers," Lawrence Summers, who was then the president of Harvard University, argued that "innate differences," "innate ability," and "natural ability" could explain why there were fewer women than men in the fields of science and engineering. The sources cited for these "innate" differences and abilities were his daughter's "inclination to treat her toy trucks as if they were dolls," the "fact" that "women with children were not willing or were unable to work 80-hour weeks," and newspaper reports that more "boys than girls in late high school had superior test scores in science and math."

LAWRENCE JACKSON/AP PHOTO

One of MIT's most prominent woman scientists walked out in the middle of his speech, and the faculty members of a Harvard committee on women wrote Summers a letter telling him he had done grave damage to the university's reputation. Summers apologized, maintaining that he was only trying to "stimulate various kinds of statistical research" and provoke debate. He assured the committee he was dedicated to increasing the number of female scientists at Harvard. Nevertheless, in 2007, Harvard replaced Summers with its first woman president, Drew Gilpin Faust, after Summers received a vote of no confidence by the faculty and resigned in 2006. Indeed, Summers's "facts" were grounded in little more than personal opinion and myth. According to an editorial in the *Pittsburgh Post-Gazette*, "the word *innate* has grown a little stale . . . [W]hen the president of a prestigious university presents a theory at a conference, he (or she) should rely on valid scientific evidence to back it up."[8]

## Ethical Moment

WHAT DO YOU THINK?

1. Do you think speakers should "provoke a debate"? Why our why not? How might provoking a debate contribute to the public dialogue? How might it detract from the public dialogue?
2. If a speaker wants to provoke debate, what types of evidence should he or she use? What obligations to accuracy does a speaker have when stimulating conversation?
3. When reasoning, how much personal opinion is acceptable? How much evidence should a speaker provide to support that personal opinion?

## Testimony

When speakers use the opinions or observations of others, they are using **testimony** as a source of evidence. Testimony is sometimes called "quoting others" or "citing the words of others." We usually think of testimony as coming from an authority, an expert, or a person who has professional knowledge about a subject. This is often true, but testimony can also come from average people who have relevant experience with your topic. Speakers sometimes also provide their own testimony—their own words and experiences as sources of evidence.

Testimony often takes the form of a **direct quotation,** an exact word-for-word presentation of another's testimony. At other times, speakers **paraphrase** the words, or provide a summary of another's testimony in the speaker's own words. Direct quotations are often seen as more credible than paraphrasing, but sometimes a person's words or stories are too long, too complex, or contain inappropriate language for a particular audience, making paraphrasing a better option.

Generally, use someone else's testimony when his or her words make your point more clearly, powerfully, or eloquently than your own. When you use the testimony of someone considered an authority in a particular field, you are using **expert testimony.** When you use the testimony of someone who has firsthand knowledge of a topic, you are using **peer testimony,** sometimes called *lay testimony.* You can also use your own testimony to convey your point. This is called **personal testimony.** To use each type of testimony ethically, always give credit

**SPEECH TIPS**

### USING DIRECT QUOTATIONS OR PARAPHRASES

- Use a direct quotation only when the source's exact words are brief and would lose meaning or emotional effect if worded in some other way.
- Use a paraphrase or summary if a direct quotation would be more than a few sentences and if you need only the major ideas. Paraphrasing is useful for technical or specialized sources unfamiliar to your audience.
- Always identify the source of both direct quotations and paraphrases.

to the person you are quoting or paraphrasing, including his or her name and credentials. (Chapter 8 discusses how to cite your sources in your speech.) Let's look at some more specific guidelines for using testimony in a speech.

## Use Testimony When You Need the Voice of an Expert

Sometimes, an audience may be interested in our descriptions of an issue or event, but we might not have enough credibility to make our claims believable. Expert testimony can give our ideas an extra boost. Phrases like "according to the surgeon general" add the voice of authority to a speech. Darian enhanced his credibility by using expert testimony in his speech on the shortage of qualified schoolteachers:

> "We have good people coming in," said Sandra Feldman, president of the American Federation of Teachers, "but we lose almost 50 percent of them in the first five years." Why? The reason is money, according to Ms. Feldman: "If someone lasts four or five years, they see that they can teach, but they can't support themselves or their families."[9]

Incorporating the testimony of recognized experts lends credibility to your own testimony and helps you build a stronger case.

## Use Testimony to Illustrate Differences or Agreements

Speakers often use testimony when they want to illustrate the range of opinions about a topic. Testimony from several different sources gives an audience a sense of the diversity—or lack of it—on opinions circulating in the public dialogue. If you can cite a variety of expert opinions on your subject, you illustrate the complexity of an issue. Or if all the experts agree and offer a unified voice, you illustrate the strength of a particular opinion.

Consider statements like these: "In my review of the minutes for the planning commission meetings from January to September of this year, I found only one person on the nine-member city planning commission who disagreed. Let me share what Joel Phillips, the dissenting voice, said and then tell what the other eight individuals had to say." Or "There seems to be incredible diversity on this issue. Of the five professors I interviewed, none offered the same solution to the problem I posed. Here are some of their suggestions." When used in these ways, testimony sheds light on agreements or disagreements over issues that affect your audience.

### Use Your Own Testimony When Your Experience Says It Best

Although the words of an expert can lend credibility to a speech, sometimes your own experiences make a stronger impression. In a speech on the peer pressure that contributes to the prevalence of eating disorders in young women, Rachael used her own testimony. She said to her audience, "No one has ever come up to me and said, 'Wow, Rachael, you look great! Have you gained ten?' It's always the opposite, isn't it? 'Have you lost ten?'" She could have used the testimony of a doctor or a psychologist, but her personal testimony about her own experiences with peer pressure strengthened her point about the peer pressure many young women encounter.

### Paraphrase Testimony to Improve Listenability

The exact words of an expert may not always be appropriate for an audience because they may be too complex or too vulgar. However, you can still use that person's words if you paraphrase, summarizing statements rather than repeating them exactly. For example, when Joel Phillips, the dissenting commissioner, explained, "residential zoning factors historically have an inverse effect on the growth this sector of the community can feasibly accommodate," Shatanna paraphrased his words by saying, "Mr. Phillips, the dissenting commission member, explained that, historically, zoning ordinances have a negative effect on the growth of our community." Her paraphrasing allowed her to use the commissioner's testimony without confusing her audience by using his specialized terminology.

Similarly, try paraphrasing when your source uses profanity or vulgar language that may not be appropriate for a particular audience. But note that if your source feels strongly enough about an issue to use profanity, or if the use of profanity is an important part of that person's personality, your paraphrase should reflect this without actually repeating his or her words. Tell your audience that your source feels strongly enough about an idea to swear about it or that the person uses profanity liberally in discussing the idea. Remember, paraphrasing is a summary of what was said, not a recasting of someone's feelings or beliefs. Also note that although profanity may not *always* be inappropriate in a speech, you should still think carefully about your reasons for including it and your audience's possible reactions to hearing it.

## Guidelines for Using Testimony Ethically and Effectively

Testimony enhances a claim or adds to a position much like a second opinion would. It brings in outside voices, adds other perspectives, and illustrates what others are thinking and saying about your issue. But to use testimony ethically and effectively, it must meet certain criteria.

***Is the source of your testimony credible?*** To be credible, testimony must come from people who are knowledgeable about your subject, have been trained in its particular area, and have earned the respect of other experts in their field. When you select testimony, ask yourself if the people you are quoting have the proper credentials or experiences and if your audience will find them sufficiently credible.

Advertisements often provide excellent examples of the unethical use of testimony. Advertisers frequently use the testimony of celebrities to promote products, yet these celebrities may know very little about the products. In your speeches, make sure your testimony comes from someone who actually knows about your subject, not just from someone people might like or find interesting. Similarly, testimony from a nonexpert, such as "my neighbor said . . . ," will not help your case unless your neighbor has some legitimate connection to the issue you are speaking about.

***Is the testimony biased?*** In the public dialogue, **bias** is an unreasoned distortion of judgment or prejudice about a topic, and a biased source will have an unreasoned personal stake in the outcome of an issue.[10] In contrast, an **objective** source is someone who does not have a personal stake in an issue and can provide a fair, ethical, and undistorted view of a topic. Although objective sources certainly have preferences and feelings, they are not so strongly influenced by their own stake in an issue that they distort information.

Obviously, no one can be completely objective. In fact, sometimes we *want* to use the testimony of someone who has a personal stake in an issue because that person understands the issue as an insider. For example, in his persuasive speech on transportation options for people who are legally drunk, Eric cited DUI officer Kirsten Innes as stating, "After 10 o'clock on a weekend evening, almost 50 percent of drivers are alcohol impaired." However, more often it's preferable to use testimony from sources who are not personally invested in an issue and do not stand to gain from a particular outcome. To determine whether a source is biased or objective, ask the following questions:

- What is this person's connection to the issue? How does that connection affect her or his perspective? Does he or she have a personal stake in the issue?
- Are this person's ideas about this topic so firmly rooted that she or he would be unable to speak credibly on another aspect of the topic?
- Are this person's words informed and reasoned? Is he or she making claims based on adequate exposure to the issue?

Answering these questions can help you determine how to use the testimony you have ethically and how to introduce it to your audience so they see it as credible.

***Have you paraphrased accurately?*** When you paraphrase another person's testimony or change some of the language so it is more suitable to your audience, do so carefully. Make sure you've retained the essential meaning of the testimony and haven't changed its tone. For example, one of the commissioners Shatanna interviewed said, "It's very complicated. Let me outline some of the issues for you." He then described seven distinct issues. Shatanna's paraphrasing reflected this complexity. In her speech, she said, "Commissioner Fields presented seven different issues. The issue that most directly affects my topic today is the first one he mentioned, the conflict between what residents and retailers want." Note that it is unethical to change the intended meaning of testimony or to place it in a context that your source did not intend. Although it can be tempting to use a great quote in a way your source did not intend, it is deceptive.

***Is the testimony connected to your point?*** In the public dialogue, we use testimony to strengthen a speech, not simply to share perspectives and experiences. This is important to consider when you use anyone's testimony, but especially when you use your own. When you use personal testimony, make sure it enhances your speech and that you're not using it simply because you want to tell your story. If you think testimony about your own experience—or the testimony of another person—fits into your speech perfectly, connect it to the larger issue you are speaking about.[11] Rachael's testimony about the pressure

**SPEECH Checklist** ✓

### When to Use Testimony

- ☐ To add credibility with the voice of an expert
- ☐ To illustrate a range of opinions
- ☐ To share your personal experience
- ☐ To improve listenability, paraphrase instead of directly quoting

To use testimony ethically and effectively, make sure

- ☐ your source is credible
- ☐ your source is objective and not biased
- ☐ you paraphrase accurately
- ☐ the testimony is connected to your point

to be thin followed this guideline. She used her experiences not to draw attention to herself but to illustrate a common experience for many young women. Rachael didn't just tell her own story; she also told the story of other women.

## Definitions

Definitions are essential to public speaking. Without them, the common language shared by speaker and audience breaks down quickly. A **definition** is a statement of the exact meaning of a word or phrase. Definitions can make terms, whether simple or complex, clear and meaningful for your audiences. Provide a definition of a word in a speech when its meaning may be ambiguous and confusing to your audience.

Every word has both a denotative and a connotative definition. The **denotative definition** is the objective meaning you find in a dictionary, the definition of a word on which most everyone can agree. In contrast, a **connotative definition** is the subjective meaning of a word or a phrase based on personal experiences and beliefs. Be aware that providing the dictionary definition of a word may not always be enough to get your point across—definitions come from personal experiences as well as from the dictionary.

An example illustrates how powerful a connotative definition can be. Abolitionist Sojourner Truth, born a slave in New York in approximately 1797 and freed in 1827, focused one of her most famous speeches on the definition of the word *woman*. In "Ain't I a Woman?" she repeatedly questioned the definition of this word, asking her audience to decide whether or not she actually was "a woman."

> That man over there says that women need to be helped into carriages, and lifted over ditches, and to have the best place everywhere. Nobody ever helps me into carriages, or over mud-puddles, or gives me any best place. And, ain't I a woman? Look at me, look at my arm. I have plowed and planted and gathered into barns, and no man could head me—and ain't I a woman? I could work as much and eat as much as a man (when I could get it) and bear the lash as well—and ain't I a woman? I have borne thirteen children and seen them most all sold off into slavery, and when I cried out with a mother's grief, none but Jesus heard. And ain't I a woman?[12]

As this example illustrates, connotative definitions can move an audience in a way that denotative definitions sometimes can't. However, because connotative definitions are based on emotions and personal experiences, they can cloud an issue or confuse an audience. Therefore, be sure to identify the connotative definitions you use in your speech and take into account the varying connotations one word may have. Truth did this when she questioned the audience's connotative definitions of *woman*.

Although some speeches are built around a definition, as in Truth's example, others incorporate definitions to clarify words for audiences. The guidelines for using definitions in your speeches are as follows:

### Use Definitions to Clarify and Create Understanding

Use a definition when you anticipate your audience will say, "I don't know what that word means" or "I've never heard that word used that way before." For technical terms, a denotative definition often suffices. For familiar words used in new ways, connotative definitions are a must. For example, in a speech to students at Moscow University, Ronald Reagan defined the word *freedom* as the recognition that no single authority has a monopoly on truth. At the time, democracy was new to the Soviet Union, so Reagan's definition helped his audience see more clearly what he believed are the benefits of a democracy.

## Use Definitions to Clarify an Emotionally or Politically Charged Word

Many words in our language have become emotionally and politically charged. Words like *race, sexism, disability, discrimination, equality, liberal,* and *conservative* have become hotbeds of dispute. When you use words like these, provide a definition. Explain how you are using the word so you can minimize some of the emotions and politics associated with it. Otherwise, your audience may not be able to understand or even listen to you.

## Use Definitions to Illustrate What Something Is Not

Definitions also explain to an audience what something isn't. In a student speech on the hostile environment created by sexual harassment, Hillary defined *hostile environment* and *harassment* first by what they are and then by what they are not:

> According to the *Webb Report: A Newsletter on Sexual Harassment*, behavior is sexual harassment if it (1) is sexual in nature, (2) is unwelcome by the person it is directed at, and (3) is sufficiently severe or pervasive that it alters the conditions of that person's employment and creates an abusive working environment. This means it's not sexual harassment nor is it seen as creating a hostile environment if the behavior (1) isn't sexual in nature, (2) is welcomed by the person it's directed at, and (3) doesn't negatively affect that individual's working environment and create an abusive climate. The behavior may be offensive, unproductive, or even harmful, but if it doesn't meet all three criteria, then it's not considered sexual harassment.

Hillary defined what sexual harassment is by illustrating for her audience what it isn't.

## Use Definitions to Trace the History of a Word

The history of a word, called its **etymology,** allows you to trace the original meaning of a word and to chart the changes it has undergone over time. The etymologies of two words are traced in this text: *audience* in Chapter 6 and *claim* here in Chapter 13. In speeches, tracing the history of words offers your audience insight into the words' origins and the ways those origins affect our understanding and use of the words today. Etymologies, then, can help you build an argument for a position or tell a more comprehensive story about an issue. Many dictionaries provide the etymology of words, but the

Skills & Confidence Web Connect 13.2

*Oxford English Dictionary* is a particularly good source for tracing a word's origins.

## Guidelines for Using Definitions Ethically and Effectively

Using definitions seems fairly straightforward and simple, and it usually is. But as with all forms of evidence, you must consider the credibility, clarity, and accuracy of your definitions to ensure that they are ethical and effective. When you define a word, keep the following questions in mind.

*Is the source of the definition credible?* Where does your definition come from? Consider whether the dictionary or other source you are using is credible. Some sources are far more extensive than others, offering recent definitions as well as a comprehensive history of a word. Examples of these sources include encyclopedias, textbooks, and books about specific topics such as music, law, or engineering. If you are tracing the etymology of a word, consult credible sources. Finally, if you are using a particular person's definition of a word, make sure that person is a credible and qualified source.

*Have you avoided "proper meaning superstition"? Proper meaning superstition* is a term that was coined by I. A. Richards and C. K. Ogden in the late 1920s. Proper meaning superstition is the belief that everyone attaches the same meaning to a word and that you are using that meaning. With proper meaning superstition, speakers use words believing that their audiences will have exactly the same referent, which isn't always the case. If you decide to use a term without defining it, be sure your listeners have the same understanding of the term that you do.[13]

**Skills & Confidence**
Web Connect 13.3

*Have you truly defined the term?* Avoid using a term to define itself. This happens when we say, "By *younger* I mean people who aren't very old—they're still young." With this definition, the audience still won't know what you specifically mean by "young." Is it five years of age, twenty years, or something else? Also avoid using unfamiliar words in a definition. This happens when we say something like "By *septifragal*, I mean dehiscing by breaking away from the dissepiments." This may be clear to scientists, but not to very many other people. Finally, avoid circular definitions, such as "By *masculine*, I'm referring to those traits not feminine, and by *feminine*, I mean those not masculine." With this definition, the audience still won't know what is meant by either "masculine" or "feminine." To ensure a fair and ethical public dialogue, our definitions must clarify our arguments rather than confuse our audiences.

**Skills & Confidence**
PPD Activity 13.1
Speech Studio 13.1

**SPEECH Checklist ✓**

## When to Use Definitions

- ☐ To clarify and create understanding
- ☐ To clarify an emotionally or politically charged word
- ☐ To illustrate what something is not
- ☐ To trace the history of a word and build an argument or give more background about an issue

To use definitions ethically and effectively, make sure

- ☐ the source of the definition is credible
- ☐ you have avoided "proper meaning superstition"
- ☐ you have truly defined the term in simple, familiar words

CHAPTER 14

# Introduction to Reasoning



*In this chapter, you will learn to*

- Identify logos, pathos, and ethos, Aristotle's three modes of proof
- Describe five common patterns of reasoning used to construct sound arguments
- Test the strength of your claims with Toulmin's model of reasoning
- Apply guidelines for reasoning ethically

Whether your speaking goal is to inform, invite, or persuade, sound reasoning plays a central role in your preparations to enter the public dialogue. Only through sound reasoning can you ensure that you have fully and ethically supported your claims with convincing evidence. Speakers accomplish sound reasoning when they use the three forms of proof that the Greek philosopher Aristotle labeled *logos, ethos*, and *pathos.* **Logos** refers to the logical arrangement of evidence in a speech, **ethos** to the speaker's credibility, and **pathos** to the emotional appeals made by a speaker.[1]

Skills & Confidence Web Connect 14.1

In the public dialogue, we share our knowledge and views most effectively when we reason with our audience. When we reason, we use logos, ethos, and pathos to justify the connections between our evidence and our claims. In other words, we arrange our evidence logically, establish and build our credibility, and appeal to emotion to show that our evidence supports our idea, position, or perspective. Reasoning helps audience members make **inferences,** the mental leaps they make when they recognize that a speaker's evidence supports his or her claims.

When you reason logically, you offer evidence that you think most people in your audience would accept as legitimate and appropriate.[2] As you learned in Chapter 13, evidence is the material you use to support your ideas, and it consists of the examples, narratives, statistics, testimony, and definitions you gather through research and interviews. This evidence helps you develop what is often called an *argument.* Although the term may bring to mind an angry dispute, in the public dialogue an **argument** is a set of statements that allows you to develop your evidence to establish the validity of your claim.[3]

Each time you develop a main point or link ideas together logically in a speech, you use evidence and reasoning to develop a sound and ethical argument for your perspective. Just as you use organizational patterns to arrange your main points in a speech, you use patterns of reasoning to help you organize your evidence and claims.

## Patterns of Reasoning

Although scholars have developed more than twenty-five different patterns of reasoning, here we discuss only five of the most useful for beginning public speakers: reasoning by induction, deduction, cause, analogy, and sign.[4] These patterns can help you develop logical arguments in all of your speeches, whatever their goals. You probably already use most of these patterns without giving them much thought. In public speaking, however, speakers consciously employ the patterns to arrange their evidence and develop the logic of their main points and subpoints.

### Induction, or Reasoning from Specific Instances

James is an excellent basketball player.

His brother Jeff is an excellent swimmer.

Their sister Julia is the star of the track team.

Jenny, the youngest of the family, will be a fine athlete too.

We often observe regularities, patterns of behavior, and trends, and we point to these repeating patterns to make a claim about something we

**FIGURE 14.1 Inductive reasoning**

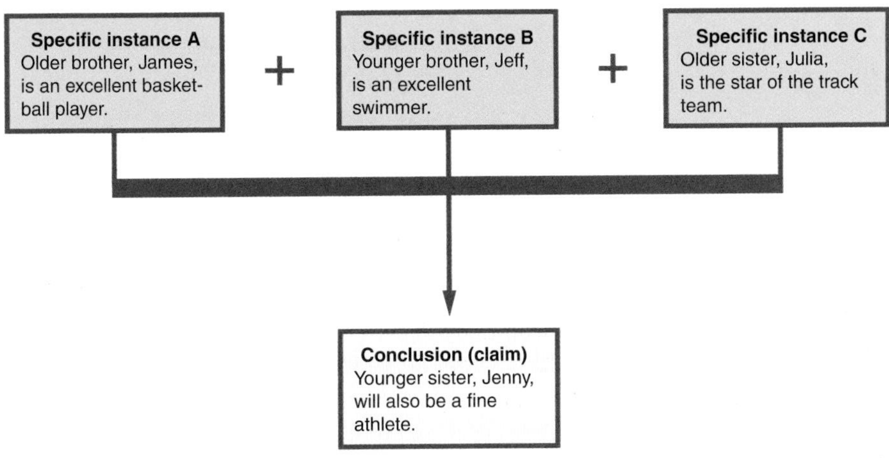


**Source:** Cengage Learning

expect to happen or be true. When we do so, we reason inductively. **Inductive reasoning** is a process of reasoning that uses specific instances, or examples, to make a claim about a general conclusion (Figure 14.1).[5]

Inductive reasoning, sometimes called *argument by example*, is best used when you can identify patterns in evidence that indicate something is likely to happen again or should hold true based on previous experience.[6] For example, in the scenario at the beginning of this section, the claim that Jenny, the youngest in a family of athletes, is likely to be a talented athlete is based on the trend her siblings have established.

Let's look at how inductive reasoning can be used in a speech. In her invitational speech on becoming a vegetarian, Karyl used inductive reasoning to describe her switch from eating meat to avoiding it. She gave examples from six slaughterhouses to illustrate the treatment of the animals and the reasons she chose to stop eating meat. This series of examples allowed Karyl to reason as follows:

> Animals in the six slaughterhouses I researched experience harsh conditions and unnecessary cruelty (*her series of specific examples*). Animals in slaughterhouses throughout the United States are treated inhumanely (*her generalization based on her examples*), and I decided not to support this treatment by not eating them (*her personal decision based on her inductive reasoning*).

When you reason from specific instances, you can state your claim (general observation) first and then offer your supporting instances, or you can present the instances first and then make your claim. In the following example, Ruby stated her claim first and then provided specific instances:

> The amount of privacy we are allowed to keep is under siege every day (*claim*). Beverly Dennis, an Ohio grandmother, completed a questionnaire to get free product samples. Instead, she got a sexually graphic and threatening letter from a convict in Texas who was assigned the task of entering product data into computers for the company (*specific instance*). Similarly, the dean of the Harvard Divinity School was forced to resign after downloading pornography to his home computer. He asked a Harvard technician to install more memory to his computer at home, and in the process of transferring files, the technician discovered, and reported, the pornography (*specific instance*).

Ruby used inductive reasoning again later in her speech. In the following example, she withheld her claim until after she had described her specific instances. Also notice how she used statistics to reinforce the pattern in her specific instances:

> Like many of you, I thought my own life was safe because I do not download pornography or request free product samples. But as I continued to do research for my speech, I learned that my medical records, phone calls, and faxes to my doctor aren't as private as I thought. Nor are my e-mails at work. Medical records are passed along to numerous individuals and recorded or filed electronically—accessible to any determined employee or computer hacker (*specific instance*). And phone calls and faxes can be monitored or picked up by anyone from the office staff to the other doctors (*specific instance*).
>
> And according to this year's report by the American Management Association, nearly three-quarters of U.S. companies say they are monitoring employees electronically. In fact, according to *The Unwanted Gaze*, some companies even use computer software that monitors and records every keystroke an employee makes. Using this software, called Spector, an employee at a Nissan dealership was fired after her employer opened one of her e-mails, a sexually explicit note to her boyfriend (*specific instance*). Can you imagine your boss reading your e-mails to your boyfriend? Our privacy has gone public in ways we are only beginning to imagine (*claim*).

Expressed as a formula, an inductive argument looks like this:

| | | |
|---|---|---|
| Specific instance A | or | Claim you want to establish |
| Specific instance B | | Specific instance A |
| Specific instance C | | Specific instance B |
| Specific instance D | | Specific instance C |
| Claim based on the specific instances | | Specific instance D |

***Guidelines for inductive reasoning.*** There are three guidelines for reasoning from specific instances:

- Make sure you have enough examples to make your claim.
- Make sure your generalizations are accurate.
- Support your inductive arguments with statistics or testimony.

Let's take a closer look at each of these guidelines. First, be sure you have enough examples to make your claim. For instance, if only one person in Jenny's family is a fine athlete, you cannot claim she also is likely to be, because you do not have enough specific instances to back that claim. Similarly, if only one or two slaughterhouses treat animals inhumanely, you cannot claim that most of them do.

To reason ethically, you need to avoid *anomalies.* Anomalies are exceptions to a rule, unique instances that do not represent the norm. When speakers rely on anomalies or use too few examples to make a claim, they may be guilty of making **hasty generalizations,** or reaching a conclusion without enough evidence to support it. To support your claim, find more than three instances before you make any inferences about larger patterns. However, your audience probably needs no more than four specific instances, even if you have identified far more than that.

Second, make sure your generalizations are accurate. Although it can be tempting to make a claim about only a few instances, be careful not to overgeneralize. For example, if warmer winters have been the trend for your region over the past decade, you can predict a warmer winter next year. But you probably can't extend that prediction to other parts of the country unless you have specific examples to support your claim. Don't be too hasty in extending examples from one area or group to another unless your data support that claim.

Third, support your inductive arguments with statistics or testimony. Although an endless list of examples would bore your audience, you can develop your case by supplementing your examples with statistics or testimony. For example, if you want to explain that organic farms produce competitively priced, high-quality crops, offer examples of two or three farms that do so. Then strengthen your inductive process with statistics showing that organic farmers are successfully competing with nonorganic farms at a county, state, or national level. You could also support your examples with testimony from the head of the Department of Agriculture, validating the profitability of organic farming. Statistics and testimony help your audience better understand the validity of the larger trend you are describing.

### Deduction, or Reasoning from a General Principle

> Grade inflation negatively affects all college students.
> Jody is a college student.
> Jody is affected negatively by grade inflation.

When speakers reason from general principles to specific instances (the opposite of inductive reasoning), they reason deductively. **Deductive reasoning** is a process of reasoning that uses a familiar and commonly accepted claim to establish the truth of a very specific claim (Figure 14.2). The first statement above, "Grade inflation negatively affects all college students," is called the **major premise,** or the *general principle,* and states a familiar, commonly accepted belief. The combination of the major premise with the second statement, " Jody is a college student," called the **minor premise** or the *specific instance,* establishes the truth of the third statement, "Jody is negatively affected by grade inflation," called the **conclusion.**

**FIGURE 14.2 Deductive reasoning**

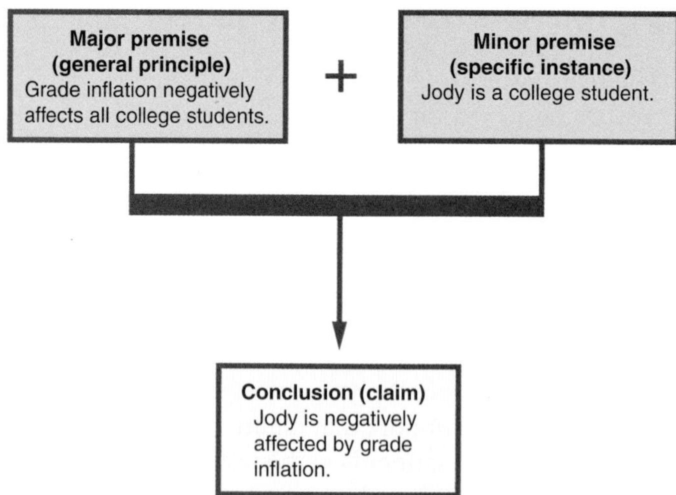


**Source:** Cengage Learning

Expressed as a formula, a deductive argument looks as follows:

Major premise, or general principle
Minor premise, or specific instance of the general principle
Conclusion based on the combination of the major and minor premises

*Guidelines for deductive reasoning.* Reasoning from general principles to specific instances is an effective way to build a case for your claims. When your general principle is firmly established or commonly accepted, your reasoning should unfold smoothly. For example, some general principles that are clearly established and commonly accepted are that asbestos causes lung cancer, driving drunk is dangerous, and elected officials should act with integrity.

Sometimes, audiences won't accept your general principle. When they don't, you will need to strengthen it with additional evidence or reasoning. This process is called *establishing the validity of the major premise.* For example, if you assert that raising cattle for beef consumption is cruel and unethical, juvenile crime is out of control, or pornography is a violation of women's rights, your audience is more likely to need proof. If your audience does not accept your major premise, they are less likely to accept your conclusion. You will need to use careful reasoning to develop your case.

We often enter the public dialogue precisely *because* we want to establish the truth of a general principle. Let's see how one very famous speaker, Susan B. Anthony, worked from a controversial general principle. Anthony spoke in favor of women's right to vote in the 1870s. She built her reasoning for women's right to vote on the premise that the U.S. Constitution guarantees all citizens the right to vote. Her full line of reasoning looked as follows:

| | |
|---|---|
| **Major premise** | The U.S. Constitution guarantees every citizen the right to vote. |
| **Minor premise** | Women are U.S. citizens. |
| **Conclusion** | The U.S. Constitution guarantees women the right to vote. |

Although this deductive argument does not seem controversial today, Anthony's major and minor premises were open to dispute more than 130 years ago. People did not agree that the Constitution guaranteed all citizens the right to vote, nor did they agree about who was a citizen. Anthony and many other suffragists devoted much of their speeches to trying to convince their audiences of their major and minor premises. Despite their passionate efforts, women did not get the right to vote in the United States until 1920.[7]

## Causal Reasoning

If I don't study, then I'll do poorly on my exam.

If I use recreational drugs, then I'll eventually turn to more addictive ones.

If I study self-defense, then I'm less likely to be hurt if someone attacks me.

**Causal reasoning** is a process of reasoning that supports a claim by establishing a cause-and-effect relationship. Causal reasoning identifies an "if-then" relationship that suggests that "if" one factor is present, "then" another is sure to follow.[8] The three statements at the beginning of this section are examples of causal relationships. Each of them establishes a cause-and-effect relationship: lack of preparation (the cause) results in poor grades (the effect); use of recreational drugs (the cause) leads to the use of addictive ones (the effect); and learning self-defense (the cause) lessens the risk of harm in the event of an attack (the effect).

Speakers often use causal reasoning to develop their ideas with great success. In the following example, Kameron uses causal reasoning to develop his argument that zebra mussels, native to the Caspian Sea in Europe but not to the waters of the United States, are seriously damaging the aquatic environment:

> Zebra mussels cause damage to every aspect of any aquatic ecosystem they encounter. They destroy the natural balance of the ecosystem by filtering the food from water at an insane rate of one liter of water each day. Not much you think? Well, these mollusks can live in colonies of up to 70,000 mussels. That's 70,000 liters of water cleared of all food each day. This means the zebra mussels consume all the food usually eaten by animals lower in the food chain. The result is catastrophic repercussions on down the line. For example, a body of water whose food is filtered away cannot support any kind of life. The larger fish then have nothing to eat, resulting in fewer fish for anglers.

Kameron's causal reasoning allows him to argue compellingly that zebra mussels (the cause) lead to aquatic devastation (the effect).

*Guidelines for causal reasoning.* Causal reasoning is an effective form of reasoning because it allows you to link two events together. But because causal relationships are sometimes difficult to prove, select your causal evidence carefully. Consider the following three guidelines:

- Avoid false causes.
- Avoid assuming an event has only one cause.
- Cite supporting evidence to strengthen your cause-and-effect relationships.

Let's take a closer look at each of these guidelines. First, avoid false causes.[9] A **false cause** is an error in reasoning in which a speaker assumes that one event caused another simply because the first event happened before the second. It can be easy to assume a false cause. You pick up your "lucky" pen from your desk, and five minutes later, you get a creative brainstorm for the project you are working on. Did the lucky pen cause the creative brainstorm? Perhaps, but it's hard to tell.

Similarly, your nephew watches two hours of violent cartoon programming in the morning. When he sits down to lunch, he points his hot dog at his sister and makes shooting noises. Did the violence in the cartoons cause the behavior? Perhaps his behavior was prompted by the game he played with neighbors the day before or the joke his father told while making similar gestures. Again, the connection is not certain.

Although it is tempting to assume direct causes when one event happens shortly after another, the two events may not be directly related. When one event happens *immediately* after another, there may be a link, but you would have to investigate further to be sure. To remain ethical, if you make a causal claim in a speech, you must be certain one event did in fact cause the other.

Second, avoid assuming that an event has only one cause. Events often have many causes, especially those that become topics in the public dialogue. For example, it is unrealistic to try to pin the cause of teen suicide on one factor. It is far more appropriate to address the multiple factors that contribute to teen suicide: the home and school environment, social pressures, individual personality traits, and the teen's support system and friendships. Similarly, it is inaccurate to suggest that watching violent television is the sole cause of violence in children. Many other factors contribute to violent behaviors, and a speaker's reasoning must address all these causes.

Third, strengthen your cause-and-effect relationships by citing strong supporting evidence. For example, in his informative speech about zebra mussels, Kameron identified a very strong connection between the overpopulation of zebra mussels and the damage done to boats, buoys, docks, and anchors. He was able to support his connection by providing testimony from local fishers who had seen buoys sink from the weight of too many mussels.

In contrast, in a persuasive speech about the relationship between power lines and cancer in people who live close to them, Christina could make only a very weak connection: Her father, who died of cancer, had lived near power lines for years. The scientific evidence she provided to establish a link between cancer and proximity to power lines was sketchy and inconclusive. Thus, no matter how hard she tried, her audience would not accept her claim that power lines caused her father's cancer.

## Ethical Moment

### Free Speech and Reasoning

When parishioners of the Westboro Baptist Church attend the funerals of U.S. soldiers killed in Iraq, they hold up signs that say God kills the soldiers because he's angry that the United States tolerates homosexuality. Shirley Phelps-Roper, a spokesperson for the Kansas-based church (with no affiliation to mainstream Baptists), explains: "Our goal is to help the nation connect the dots. You turn this nation over to the fags, and our soldiers come home in body bags." The church's signs feature slogans such as "God Loves IEDs" (improvised explosive devices) and "Thank God for Dead Troops."

EVAN E. PARKER/TIMES OF NORTHWEST INDIANA/AP PHOTO

Members of another group, the Patriot Guard Riders, also attend the funerals, but only at the request of the families of the deceased. This organization of approximately 10,000 members, both hawk and dove, form a protective shield with their motorcycles and American flags around grieving families, protecting the families from seeing and hearing the church protestors. When speaking of the group's presence at the funeral of a solider killed by a roadside bomb in Iraq, Richard Wilbur, state captain of the group's Indiana chapter, summed up the Riders' purpose—to afford families some privacy and to honor what the soldiers died for, the right to protest. The Riders recognize the irony in the situation—that the members of the Westboro Baptist Church are also exercising their right to protest—but they feel their methods reflect respect and the church's do not. As Kurt Mayer, a founding member of the Patriot Guard Riders, explains, "We show families in grieving communities that America still cares."[10]

WHAT DO YOU THINK?

1. What does free speech mean to you? Should speech that relies on flawed reasoning be protected as free speech or should it be restricted? What about speech that relies on sound reasoning but is offensive to others? Why do you think as you do?

## Ethical Moment

2. Do you think the members of the Westboro Baptist Church are ethical in their actions and words? Why or why not?
3. Do you think the Patriot Guard Riders are ethical in their actions and words? Why or why not?

## Analogical Reasoning

> Obama—the self-described "skinny kid with a funny name" and first African American male Democrat elected to the U.S. Senate—is . . . already in a different category of fame. A Tiger Woods category. A David Letterman and *Will & Grace* category. . . . A Robert F. Kennedy or Hillary Clinton comes-to-the-Senate category where the national publicity upon their election exceeds that received by most senators in their entire careers.[11]

When we compare two similar things and suggest that what is true for the first will be true for the second, we are reasoning analogically. **Analogical reasoning,** or reasoning by way of comparison and similarity, implies that because two things resemble each other in one respect, they also share similarities in another respect. For example, in 2005 when a *Newsweek* writer compared newly elected Senator Barack Obama's fame to that of such cultural icons as Tiger Woods, David Letterman, and *Will & Grace*, the writer argued that Obama, like the cited examples, had achieved a rare form of early popularity.

We also reason analogically when we contrast differences in two similar conditions or events and draw inferences about what should be true for both but isn't. Consider how Stephanie used analogical reasoning to inform her audience about the differences in the way crimes against minorities are treated in contrast to those against whites:

> I was living in Oak Harbor, Washington, when JonBenet Ramsey was killed. . . . Like everyone else, I was appalled and followed the coverage of her death for three months. Then, in my town of Oak Harbor, a seven-year-old girl named Deborah Palmer disappeared while walking to school one morning. . . . Her lifeless body was found washed up on a local beach, six miles from her house. Do you know who Deborah Palmer was? Well, JonBenet's murder ran as a cover story in almost every national newspaper and magazine. Her little face looked back

> at me for over a year every time I went into a grocery store. Deborah's story ran in the *Seattle Times*, the *Skaggit Valley Herald*, and the *Whidbey Island News* for a total of nine articles. In a very short period of time, Deborah's story disappeared completely.
>
> Why the difference when the crimes were so similar and neither murderer was ever found? JonBenet was a crowned beauty queen with blond hair and blue eyes. Deborah was the child of an African American father and a Filipino mother.

The analogy Stephanie used to draw her audience into her compelling speech is that JonBenet Ramsey and Deborah Palmer had much in common. They were little girls who died brutally and tragically within three months of one another. Police have yet to find either murderer. If one child received extensive news coverage, shouldn't the other one have too?

Although Stephanie held the audience's attention as she developed her analogy, analogies can also be short and straightforward. For example, when speaking to her audience about the importance of more than direct care, physician Deborah Prothrow-Stith used this simple and effective analogy: "We were just stitching them up and sending them back out on the streets, back to the domestic equivalent of a war zone."[12]

*Guidelines for analogical reasoning.* To increase the effectiveness of analogical reasoning, be sure the things you are comparing are truly alike. When you compare two things that don't share characteristics, your analogy is invalid and will seem illogical to your audience. Most of us have heard invalid analogies and thought to ourselves, "That's like comparing apples to oranges." For example, it is invalid to suggest that proposed nonsmoking ordinances will succeed in Kentucky, North Carolina, and South Carolina because they succeeded in California, Oregon, and Washington. This analogy is invalid because the public attitudes toward smoking in the three tobacco-growing southern states are different from those in the three western states whose economies do not depend on tobacco. If you make an analogy between two things, they must share true similarities for the analogy to be valid.

### Reasoning by Sign

> Even watching their seismographs jump—even if they could have measured the height of the waves at their origin—geologists couldn't have predicted with any certainty that the sea would rise up in Sri Lanka, a thousand miles away from the fault line.[13]

A **sign** is something that represents something else. It is one of the most common forms of reasoning: Dark clouds are a sign of a storm rolling in; a decrease in the number of applications for a certain academic program is a sign of declining interest; the bailiff's command "all rise" is a sign that the judge is about to enter the courtroom.[14] Signs have an important function in the reasoning process because they prompt us to infer what is *likely* to be. They help speakers establish relationships and draw conclusions for their audiences based on those relationships. However, as the example about the tsunami that struck Sri Lanka in 2004 suggests, sometimes the connection between a sign (the movement on a seismograph or the height of waves at their origin) that is needed to infer the likelihood of an event (a devastating tsunami in Sri Lanka) can't be made or just isn't there. **Reasoning by sign** assumes something exists or will happen based on something else that exists or has happened.

Signs, like causal relationships, can have strong or weak relationships. Reasoning by sign is strengthened when you can point to the repetition of one example to build a case. For example, *every* time the Richter scale registers above a certain level for an undersea earthquake, a tsunami occurs. Scientists have accurately predicted all five of the significant ocean-spanning tsunamis since 1950, but they also predicted fifteen that turned out to be false alarms.[15] Few signs are infallible, and most are open to question.

*Guidelines for reasoning by sign.* Because signs are fallible, consider three guidelines before using a sign to support your argument:

- Think about whether an alternative explanation is more credible.
- Make sure a sign is not just an isolated instance.
- If you can find instances in which a sign does not indicate a particular event, you do not have a solid argument.

Let's take a closer look at these guidelines. First, is an alternative explanation more credible? In a speech on the standards for licensing teachers, Seogwan suggested that the low test scores in the nation's public schools were a sign of poorly trained teachers. He reasoned that low scores represented, or signaled, poor teaching. However, when his audience questioned him, they raised a number of equally credible explanations. Could the lower scores be a sign of outdated or biased tests? Of overcrowded classrooms? Of the need to restructure our classrooms? Of poor testing skills? Each of these cxplanations is as likely as the one Seogwan offered, and much evidence supports each of them. As a result, his audience thought Seogwan's reasoning was flawed. To avoid this pitfall, be sure that when you claim one thing is a sign of another, an alternative explanation isn't equally valid or better.

Second, when you reason by sign, make sure the sign is not just an isolated instance. Speaking in favor of pornography, Mark argued that all of his friends, women included, had no problems with pornography. This, he claimed, was a sign that most people now accept pornography. He ignored the nationwide debate over pornography and the many people who are offended by it and campaign against it. He mistakenly assumed that one instance (his friends' support of pornography) represented a larger pattern.

Third, when you reason by sign, you are suggesting that the sign almost always indicates a particular event. If you can find instances in which the sign does not indicate that event, you do not have a solid argument. In his speech on our ability to predict natural disasters, Tim offered the evidence that not every undersea earthquake of a certain magnitude results in a tsunami. He added that, in fact, a few quakes of a lesser magnitude did. Thus, blaming scientists for not notifying authorities in the countries affected by the 2004 tsunami was unreasonable. However, Tim argued, the occurrence of that tsunami and the tragedies left in its wake are signs that warning systems, regardless of their overprediction rates, are imperative.

**Skills & Confidence**
PPD Activity 14.1
Video Activity 14.1

**SPEECH Checklist**

## When to Use the Different Patterns of Reasoning

- ☐ Use inductive reasoning—specific examples to make a claim about a general conclusion—when something can be expected to happen again or to hold true based on previous experience. Be sure there are enough examples to support your claim.
- ☐ Use deductive reasoning when there is a commonly accepted principle you can use to make a claim about a specific instance. Deductive reasoning can also be used to establish the truth of a controversial general principle.
- ☐ Use causal reasoning to show a cause-and-effect relationship between two factors. Strengthen your claim by avoiding false causes and by citing supporting evidence.
- ☐ Use analogical reasoning to compare or contrast two similar people, events, or conditions.
- ☐ Use reasoning by sign to establish a relationship and draw a conclusion about two people, events, or conditions. Be sure that an alternative explanation is not more credible.

## A Map of Reasoning

By now, you are familiar with the various types of evidence introduced in Chapter 13 (examples, narratives, statistics, testimony, and definitions). You can use the patterns of reasoning you've explored in this chapter to assemble your evidence into a logical argument. One way to help you assemble ideas logically and construct your argument is to develop a map of your reasoning process. A solid argument should follow this map of reasoning, which is adapted from Stephen Toulmin's model of a sound argument (Figure 14.3).[16]

| | |
|---|---|
| **Claim** | What do you think or want to propose? |
| **Grounds** | Why do you think this or want to propose it? |
| **Warrant** | How do you know the grounds support the claim? |
| **Backing** | How do you know the warrant supports the grounds? |

This model of a sound argument helps you both as a speaker and as an audience member. As a speaker, you can use these questions to double-check the logic of your assertions, making a map of your own reasoning. As a listener, you can use the map to assess the reasons speakers give in support of their own claims.

Let's look at a map of the reasoning in Damon's persuasive speech on teen suicide to understand how this model works in an actual argument:

**FIGURE 14.3 Toulmin's model of reasoning**

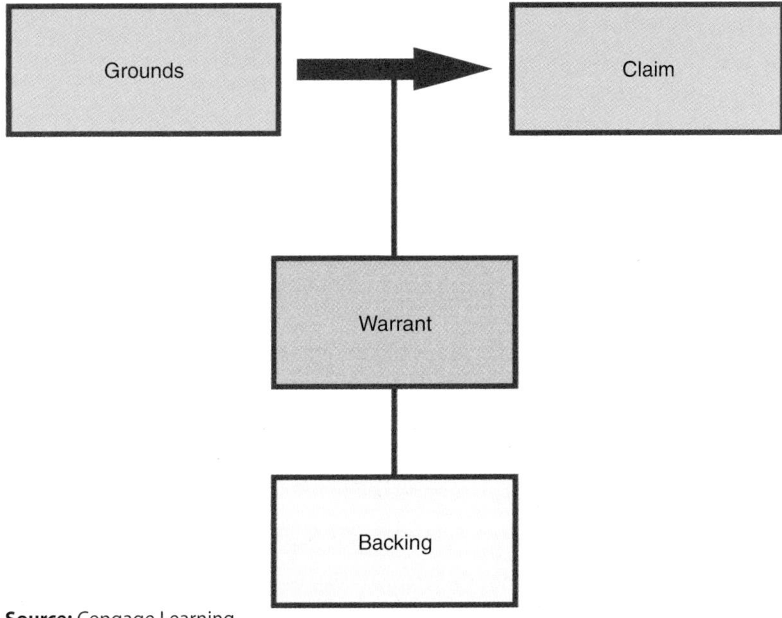


**Source:** Cengage Learning

| | |
|---|---|
| **Claim** | *What do you think or want to propose?* |
| | The high rate of teen suicide for males is now a part of our community. |
| **Grounds** | *Why do you think this or want to propose it?* |
| | Three boys have committed suicide in our community in the past two months. |
| **Warrant** | *How do you know the grounds support the claim?* |
| | Three suicides in two months represent a high rate of suicide for male teens in a community of our size. |
| **Backing** | *How do you know the warrant supports the grounds?* |
| | Research indicates that three suicides in two months are above the average rate for male teens in a community of our size. |

This map—a bit like a child's continually asking "why?"—helps speakers and audiences track a line of reasoning and find any flaws or loopholes. The reasoning in Damon's speech is solid, and the map helps us see this. He has acceptable grounds, warrant, and backing for his claim.

This map can also be used to test your reasoning in other types of speeches. In Stephanie's informative speech, she argued that crimes against minorities are treated differently from those against whites (*claim*). She used the murder of Deborah, a child with African American and Filipino heritage, and the murder of JonBenet, a white child, as her examples (*grounds*). Stephanie described the extensive coverage of JonBenet's murder and the minimal coverage of Deborah's murder (*warrant*), using an implied argument to say that what was true of the coverage of JonBenet's murder (it was extensive and gained a lot of attention) should also have been true of Deborah's murder (*backing*). With this backing, Stephanie relied on the common belief in the United States that all people should be treated equally, regardless of their master statuses.

Now let's use the model to uncover flaws in Christina's causal arguments about power lines and cancer. Notice that after the warrant, her backing breaks down:

| | |
|---|---|
| **Claim** | What do you think or want to propose? |
| | Living near power lines increases the risk of cancer. |
| **Grounds** | Why do you think this or want to propose it? |
| | My father died of cancer and we lived near power lines. |
| **Warrant** | How do you know the grounds support the claim? |
| | The reason my father had cancer was because of the power lines. |

**Backing** How do you know the warrant supports the grounds?

Scientific research has yet to confirm the connection between cancer and power lines.

Her causal reasoning fell prey to several problems: circular reasoning, overgeneralizing, and claiming only one cause. Using Toulmin's model, we see that Christina used a circular form of reasoning (you'll learn more about circular reasoning in Chapter 24):

**Grounds** My father died because of power lines.

**Warrant** Power lines caused my father's death.

Additionally, her backing discredits her argument; she produced no scientific evidence to support her claim. Her research turned up only speculation and inconclusive evidence as backing, rather than the definitive connection she needed. Mapping her grounds, warrant, and backing clearly illustrates the weakness of her argument.

How could Christina have improved her argument? If she had reasoned inductively, offering several examples of people who lived near power lines and died of cancer, her warrant would have been acceptable. She could also have offered statistics to support her claim, showing her audience the numerical correlation between power lines and cancer.

**Skills & Confidence**
PPD Activity 14.2
Web Connect 14.2

**SPEECH Checklist**

## Mapping an Argument with Toulmin's Model

As a speaker, tracing each step of your argument with Toulmin's model helps you find flaws in your reasoning and fix them. As an audience member, when you have trouble following a line of reasoning, ask the four questions of Toulmin's model to spot invalid claims and poorly developed arguments.

- ☐ What is being claimed or proposed? What is the thesis?
- ☐ What are the grounds, or reasons, for this claim?
- ☐ What are the warrants, or assumptions, that support the claim?
- ☐ Does any backing, or additional data, support the warrants?

## Guidelines for Reasoning Ethically

Evidence, reasoning, logic, and arguments are powerful tools in the public dialogue. With them, we can share information, express our perspective and invite dialogue on an issue, make a case for a certain position, and even celebrate someone's accomplishments. However, we can also manipulate, confuse, and misrepresent events, issues, and people. Thus, we must carefully consider the ethics of reasoning. Speaking ethically requires a commitment to giving speeches that are accurate and well reasoned. The following tips will help you reason ethically in your speeches.

### Build Your Credibility

The reasoning in your speech helps build your credibility with your audience. **Credibility** is the audience's perception of a speaker's competence and character. **Competence** is the audience's view of a speaker's intelligence, expertise, and knowledge of a subject. As a speaker, you express your competence through the reasoning, organization, and delivery of your speech. **Character** is the audience's view of a speaker's sincerity, trustworthiness, and concern for the well-being of the audience. You show your character through honesty and regard for your audience.[17]

Through ethical reasoning, as discussed throughout this chapter, you communicate to an audience that you are competent and that you care about them. You convey to the audience that you have thought about the best way to express your ideas and that you want others to understand them. In short, a careful reasoning process communicates an audience-centered stance that enhances your credibility. This credibility is a critical component of the ethical reasoning process. (For more about credibility, especially in regard to persuasive speaking, see Chapter 24.)

### Use Accurate Evidence

Because speakers are adding to the ongoing discussion of issues that affect us all, they want to use accurate evidence. Recall from Chapter 13 that it is just as easy to find examples, statistics, and testimony from unreliable sources as it is to find them from credible sources. It is also possible to misrepresent or alter any statistic, example, narrative, or testimony you do find. However, a healthy public dialogue depends on legitimate evidence to build sound reasoning.

As a speaker, you are ethically obligated to use accurate evidence in all of your reasoning, no matter what pattern you use to present it. Although you may be able to present a fully developed inductive argument based on fabricated examples or a compelling analogy that is false, you would be deceiving your audience.

**SPEECH Checklist**

## Ethical Reasoning

- [ ] Demonstrate your credibility with a well-reasoned, well-organized, and well-delivered speech and with honesty and concern for your audience.
- [ ] Use accurate evidence from reliable sources, and do not alter or misrepresent any statistic, example, narrative, or testimony.
- [ ] Verify your reasoning by applying Toulmin's model, and be sure you have adequate evidence to support your claims.

### Verify the Structure of Your Reasoning

Applying Toulmin's model of reasoning to your arguments is the final way you can ensure the ethical nature of your reasoning. (In fact, Toulmin developed this framework to assist average people in discovering weaknesses in their reasoning processes.) By using this model as you develop your speech, you can check the warrants, grounds, and backing for your claims and ensure their accuracy. Note that it is unethical to assert a claim is true if you do not have evidence to support the claim. Similarly, it is unethical to make unfounded arguments that could alarm audiences (recall Christina's speech about power lines and cancer). When you correct weaknesses and potentially disturbing claims before presenting them to your audiences, you are acting ethically.

**Skills & Confidence**
Speech Studio 14.1

CHAPTER 15

# Audience-Centered Language

- Language Is Ambiguous
- Language and Culture
- Language and Gender
- Language and Accuracy
- Language and Public Speaking

*In this chapter, you will learn to*

**Use clear and accurate language in your speeches**

**Use culturally inclusive and gender-inclusive language**

**Explain the differences between spoken and written language**

Language, the system of verbal or gestural symbols a community uses to communicate, is central to the speechmaking process. However, as the first opening quote states, we often take language for granted, failing to realize how much of our knowledge comes from language rather than from direct experience. Some would say that objects exist in the world around us and people use language to describe those objects as they truly are. But most experts now believe that the way we know something is through the words we use to describe it.[1] For example, even though a dog may sit directly in front of a group of people, one person may describe the dog as a large, clumsy, furry, lovable animal; another as an unpredictable, aggressive, frightening nuisance; and another as a hairy, smelly extra mouth to feed. Language, it seems, can be a tool we use to shape and describe the world around us. Communication scholars agree that language, the systematic code of a group of people, is central to establishing and maintaining societies.

In the public dialogue, language allows us to share our thoughts, question the ideas of others, and invite our audiences to consider our positions. In Chapter 4, we discussed language as it relates to listening. In this chapter, we explore language as it relates to speaking. Specifically, we discuss the ambiguity of language, culture and language, gender and language, the accurate use of language, and the importance of language in public speaking.

## Language Is Ambiguous

If a speaker never utters a word but instead communicates through mime and gesture, how well do you think you would understand the speech? What if a speaker delivered the speech in a different language? Could you grasp the intricacies of the message? Obviously, understanding others when we do not share a common language is difficult. But if we share a common language with our audience, shouldn't communication be easier? Isn't it enough to use the same labels for things to communicate a message? How much attention must we give to the language in our speeches if we speak the same language as our audience? Consider the semantic triangle of meaning, created in 1923 by C. K. Ogden and I. A. Richards,[2] as shown in Figure 15.1.

On the left corner of the triangle is the **symbol,** the word or phrase spoken by the speaker. For example, when a speaker says "freedom," as did Martin Luther King Jr. in his "I Have a Dream" speech, that word is the symbol. On the right corner of the triangle is the **referent,** the object, concept, or event the symbol represents. In our example, the referent is the actual experience of freedom. You might also think of this as the denotative definition of a word or event, as discussed

**FIGURE 15.1 Semantic triangle of meaning**

The line at the bottom of the triangle is broken, reflecting the arbitrary nature of language. There is not necessarily a connection between a symbol and a referent because the words (symbols) we use to name things (referents) are human inventions. For example, the symbol "freedom" is just a word English speakers came up with to name its referent, the state in which someone lives without undue restraints and restrictions.

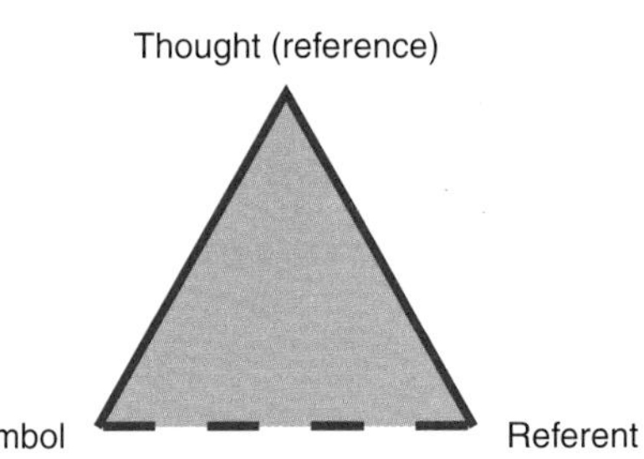


**Source:** Cengage Learning

in Chapter 13. This is the commonly held definition of a word or the actual object or event named by the speaker.

At the top of the triangle is the **thought,** or *reference*. This is the audience members' memory and experiences with an object, concept, or event. When a speaker offers a word or phrase, audience members recall their own experiences relating to that word or phrase. These are our connotative definitions (Chapter 13), our personalized, subjective interpretations of words, objects, or events. So the symbol "freedom" calls to mind a variety of connotative experiences and memories for the members of an audience.

The semantic triangle of meaning shows us that even though all the audience members might understand the symbol and even have a similar referent for it, they do not have the same thoughts, or references, for the symbol. This difference is what makes language ambiguous. The experience of freedom (or any referent) differs among people and groups, depending on their culture, geographical location, and master statuses (Chapter 6). For some, freedom is a given. For others, freedom is something that has been fought for over the centuries.

When speakers forget that words do not have the same meaning for everyone, they unintentionally create ambiguity for their audiences. When they forget that people may share symbols but not experiences with those symbols, they run the risk of confusing or alienating their audiences. One way to clear up some of this ambiguity is to use concrete language. **Concrete language** refers to a tangible object—a person, place, or thing. For example, rather than talking about "politicians," name specific ones so your audience knows exactly which politicians you are referring to. Undoubtedly, audience members have many different points of view about politics and politicians. Your audience is more likely to understand the points you are making if you try to avoid unnecessary **abstract language,** or general ideas and concepts.

***Speaking across DIFFERENCES***

**The same word may mean different things to different people. Help audience members understand what *you* mean by an ambiguous word by using concrete language, examples, and illustrations.**

To evaluate whether the language you plan to use in your speech is concrete or abstract, use Ogden and Richards's semantic triangle of meaning. Consider whether audience members may assign a variety of meanings to any of your words or phrases. If the language you plan to use is not as specific as you think it is, search for ways to represent generalized concepts or ideas with specific examples. And if you must use abstract language, define key concepts or ideas for your audience so your listeners will understand your intended meaning. Review the discussion of definitions in Chapter 13 to familiarize yourself with some of the ways speakers can define words for their audiences to eliminate the ambiguity created by connotations.

## Language and Culture

In its most basic sense, language is an organized and learned symbol system. It is used to represent human experiences and to transmit messages. Language allows us to describe, label, and share events with others and to understand each other's perspectives and experiences. However, people in different cultures have different life experiences and thus name and define the world differently.

For example, in American Sign Language, which is a visual rather than spoken language, signs are often subtly altered to reflect the visual aspects of objects and events. The concepts "modest home" and "mansion" begin with the same basic sign for "home" but differ in their execution. In contrast, in spoken English, words are only occasionally modified to emphasize some aspect of appearance (for example, "huuuge house"). Usually, to emphasize some visual aspect in spoken language, we add more words to the description or choose a different word.

Subcultures, or groups within a larger culture that share its language, may also use the language differently. For example, the language of rap music, which has roots in the African American tradition of "signifying," has clear differences from Standard English. Signifying is governed by its own rules of grammar, semantics, and syntax. It allows people to make statements that have double, and often even multiple, meanings that are not understood by people outside the subculture.[3] The topics of rap music, the words it uses, and the ways those words are put together and delivered reflect these multiple meanings, as well as the experiences and perspectives of members of this subculture.

The culturally bound nature of language requires us to be aware of obvious, as well as subtle, differences. As speakers, we can adapt our language choices to the culture of the people we are addressing, or, if we do not know their culture well enough to do so, we can acknowledge the differences as we speak. If we can identify which words our audience might not understand because of cultural or regional differences, then we can offer clarification for those words and promote understanding rather than confusion.

***Speaking across DIFFERENCES***

**Language is closely tied to culture. As an audience-centered speaker, do what you can to adapt your language to the cultures of your audience members, such as using appropriate labels for cultural groups and avoiding potentially confusing idioms.**

Idioms are especially difficult for people of other cultures to understand. An **idiom** is a fixed, distinctive expression whose meaning is not indicated by its individual words. "I was in stitches" and "they kept me in the dark" are examples of English idioms. In American Sign Language, "the train is gone" is an idiom that means you missed the joke or the point. We use the idioms of our native language without realizing it: "I don't get it," "it's way over my head," and "go figure" are three common English examples. Idioms are difficult for nonnative speakers. To be fully understood, speakers must "unpack the meanings" (another idiom) of potentially confusing phrases and words.

**Skills & Confidence** Web Connect 15.1

Cultural differences can interfere with communication in other ways too. If we do not know how a cultural group prefers to identify itself, we may accidentally offend some members of our audience. Table 15.1 lists some of the preferred labels for different cultural groups. Because these labels change as society changes, try to stay current with the ways different groups label themselves.

Although the use of appropriate labels is sometimes called "politically correct speech," appropriate labels are really about respecting others. Labels shape our perceptions of others, and our perceptions affect how we treat other people. Thus, inappropriate labels, such as those that perpetuate stereotypes, can cause audience members to feel disrespected and stop listening. The names groups use for themselves emphasize aspects of their lives that are important to them. Audience-centered speakers are aware of how cultures and subcultures name themselves and the characteristics or histories they are honoring. We show respect for our audience when we use appropriate labels.

## Language and Gender

In Chapter 4, you learned that it's important to use gender-inclusive language so your speeches address both women and men. To help you do this, consider the guidelines in Table 15.2 on page 269 for translating some common gender-biased language into gender-inclusive language. These guidelines are from the American Psychological Association.

***Speaking across DIFFERENCES***

**Using gender-neutral and gender-inclusive language helps you effectively address audiences that include both men and women.**

Increasingly, speakers are using gender-inclusive words and phrases in their speaking. In his speech to the American people after the terrorist attacks on the World Trade Center and Pentagon in 2001, President George W. Bush referred to the "business men and women, mothers and fathers..."

**TABLE 15.1 Appropriate Labels for People of Different Cultures**

| | |
|---|---|
| **Ethnicity** | African American or black<br>Asian American, or identify the country of heritage: Chinese American, Japanese American, Korean American. (Note that *Oriental* refers to the style of an object, like a rug, and not a person.)<br>Hispanic, Latina or Latino, or identify the country of heritage: Cuban American, Mexican American<br>Native American or American Indian, or identify the specific nation: Sioux, Navajo, Hopi. (Note that *Indian* usually refers to people from India.)<br>European American or white |
| **Physical ability** | A person with [name of disability]<br>A person living with [name of disability]<br>A person who has [name of disability] |
| **Age** | Boy or girl (a person eighteen years old or younger)<br>Young woman or young man (junior high or high school age)<br>Man or woman (a person nineteen years old or older)<br>Older person or senior (rather than *elderly*) |
| **Sexual orientation** | Bisexual man or woman<br>Gay man or lesbian<br>Straight or heterosexual man or woman<br>Transgendered person (a general term to describe those who have gender identities not traditionally associated with their birth sex)<br>Transvestite (someone who adopts the dress of the opposite sex)<br>Transsexual (a person who wants to change, or has changed, his or her anatomical sex) |

who lost their lives in the attack, acknowledging the professional as well as the personal roles of the women and men who died. Using gender-neutral and gender-inclusive language reflects your awareness of both men and women as valued and active participants in the world.

## Ethical Moment

### Did Don Imus Go Too Far?

On April 4, 2007, shock jock Don Imus referred on air to the Rutgers University women's basketball team, comprised largely of African American players, as "nappy-headed hos" during a discussion about the NCAA Women's Basketball Championship. Imus initially dismissed the incident as "some idiot comment meant to be amusing." But two days later, amid mounting calls for his firing, Imus issued a statement of apology: "It was completely inappropriate, and we can understand why people were offended. Our characterization was thoughtless and stupid, and we are sorry." A few days later, Imus appeared on Al Sharpton's syndicated radio talk show to address the controversy and said, "Our agenda is to be funny and sometimes we go too far. Here's what I've learned: that you can't make fun of everybody, because some people don't deserve it." However, his apology was too little, too late for his employer, MSNBC—Imus was fired April 11.[4]

RICHARD DREW/AP IMAGE

WHAT DO YOU THINK?

1. Do public figures have more or less responsibility to speak ethically than the general public? Why or why not?
2. Some critics charged that Imus provided a valuable public service by using his radio show as a forum for speech about politics and social issues and that firing him curtailed his right to free speech. What do you think? What is MSNBC's ethical responsibility for promoting free speech, even if some of it is offensive?
3. Is a public apology enough to absolve someone of using racist and sexist language in a public forum? Why or why not?

**TABLE 15.2 Guidelines for Gender-Inclusive Language**

| Problematic | Preferred |
|---|---|
| Man, mankind | People, humanity, human beings, humankind, human species |
| To man a project | To staff a project, hire personnel, employ staff |
| Manpower | Workforce, personnel, workers, human resources, staff |
| Man's search for knowledge | The search for knowledge |
| Chairman | Chair, chairperson, moderator, discussion leader, facilitator |
| Foreman, mailman, fireman | Supervisor or superintendent, postal worker or mail carrier, firefighter |
| Salesmanship | Selling ability |
| Sportsmanship | Teamwork, cooperation, conduct, respect for others, graciousness |
| He, his, him (universal "he" as a pronoun that refers to both women and men) | They (used with plural nouns), she or he, his or her, him or her |
| Dear Sir: | Dear Sir or Madam, To whom it may concern, Dear members of the ______ [name of the specific group] |
| Mr. and Mrs. John Smith | John and Jane Smith |
| Doctors and their wives | Doctors and their partners or significant others |
| Woman doctor, lady lawyer, woman driver | Doctor or physician, lawyer or attorney, driver |

## Language and Accuracy

Consider the following lists of words:

| | |
|---|---|
| persecution | prosecution |
| simple | simplistic |
| good | well |

What are the differences between the words in each column? If someone is *persecuted*, is that the same as being *prosecuted*? If you look in the dictionary, you'll see that to be persecuted is to be subjected to cruel or unfair treatment, whereas to be prosecuted is to be tried in a court of law for a criminal offense. The words have different meanings, yet they are often confused. Similarly, many speakers add

*-istic* to the ends of words because they think it makes a concept sound more complex. Yet *simple* means "easy," "straightforward," or "effortless," and *simplistic* means "lacking complexities." How about *good* and *well*? Do you know the difference between the two? Does your favorite band play good or do they play well? (They should play well and sound good.)

Knowing the correct definitions and usage of words is important because accurate language affects not only your meaning but also your credibility. Three simple steps will help you improve the accuracy of your language. First, check the definitions of the words you are using. When a word is central to the meaning of a sentence or a claim, look it up in the dictionary (in print or online) to be sure you have the correct word. Looking up words can save you embarrassment. In a commemorative speech, a student described her sister, saying, "She's kind, generous, and always thinks of others; she's notorious for this in my hometown." Although her sister was remarkable, *notorious* means to be well known for undesirable features, not desirable ones.

Second, if your use of language is not as strong as you'd like, work with someone who has strong language skills as you develop and practice your speech. Most colleges and universities have writing and tutoring labs, where people are ready to help students with clarity and grammar. (Ask your instructor about the resources available on your campus if you aren't familiar with them.) If you take time to seek this kind of help, you will find that not only will your speeches be clearer and your credibility enhanced, but your writing will improve as well.

**Skills & Confidence**
PPD Activity 15.1
Web Connect 15.2
Web Connect 15.3

Third, study the language. American civil rights leader Malcolm X copied the dictionary word by word to improve his language skills, but there are other ways. Read more books, magazines, and newspapers; take courses that focus on language skills; and practice with language and vocabulary workbooks from the library, bookstores, and teaching supply stores. You can even study a foreign language, which will teach you about your own language in the process. Studying the language systematically not only will increase your vocabulary but also will help you develop your arguments and ideas more clearly.

## Language and Public Speaking

Because of the complexities of language, we may be tempted to write out our entire speech beforehand to get every word right. And then we may be tempted to read the speech to our audience to avoid the ambiguities and errors discussed in this chapter. However, when we speak, we want to use language meant to be spoken, not read. Writing out a speech is appropriate only when speaking from a manuscript (see Chapter 17). Even though every speaker makes a mistake now and then, with care and attention to language, you can learn to address your audience with clarity and vividness most of the time.

The most effective speakers use what is called an **oral style,** a style that reflects the spoken rather than the written word. They "talk" their speeches rather than read them. The differences between the spoken word and the written word are significant: Spoken language is more interactive, more casual, and more repetitive than written language.[5]

## Spoken Language Is More Interactive

When we write to someone, we produce a steady stream of words. However, when we speak to others, we interact with them: We make adjustments as we speak, monitor their interest and understanding, and ask or respond to questions. When we speak publicly, our language reflects the shifts, pauses, and adjustments we make for our audience. We carry on a conversation with our audience in ways that we do not when we write to someone.

Our nonverbal communication also reflects this interactive mode. Our expressions and gestures reinforce our words, giving spoken language a different tone than written language. Written prose doesn't lend itself to this spontaneous nonverbal interaction. Speakers who read written-out speeches usually sound like they're delivering something the audience should be reading rather than listening to. Although speakers might feel more confident delivering a memorized speech, audiences get restless and irritated with this style. Remember to stay audience centered and use an interactive style of language and delivery.

## Spoken Language Is More Casual

Written language tends to be more formal than spoken language, although there are exceptions. If you open almost any book or magazine and read the text out loud, you will notice that the words sound a little formal. Written language and spoken language differ in formality because writing tends to be more rule governed than speaking. When we speak, we use more contractions (for example, "can't" instead of "cannot") and colloquialisms ("No way!" instead of "That simply is not possible"). We also run our words together when we speak (we read, "I'm going to ask" but say, "I'm gonna ask"). A speaker who delivers a speech in a written style sounds more distant and formal than one who talks to the audience.

Skills & Confidence Video Activity 15.1

### Spoken Language Is More Repetitive

In oral cultures, speakers communicate information primarily through narratives, or stories. Repetition is necessary to help audiences remember the details of spoken stories. Public speaking audiences also need help remembering what they hear, so public speakers use more repetition than writers do.

Skills & Confidence
PPD Activity 15.2
Web Connect 15.4
Speech Studio 15.1

Public speakers intentionally repeat main ideas and arguments. They summarize their main points and restate important arguments to help their audiences remember them. Recall from Chapter 12 that in your speeches, you present an overview of your ideas (introduction), state those ideas (body), and then summarize them (conclusion). You also use repetitive tools like transitions, internal summaries, and internal previews to help audiences remember your ideas (Chapter 10). This need for repetition is another reason to speak rather than read to audiences.

CHAPTER 16

# Language and Style

- Language That Creates Memorable Imagery
- Language That Creates a Pleasing Rhythm

Speech Checklist: **Imagery and Repetition**

*In this chapter, you will learn to*

**Describe three ways to use language to create memorable images**

**Describe at least four ways to use language to create a pleasing rhythm**

Because much of what we know comes to us through language rather than direct experience, we want to pay careful attention to the images we create with our words. As you put together the final touches of your speeches, listen to your words and phrases. Do they inspire you? Do they create a picture in your mind of what you are describing? Are they pleasing to your ears? Do they make you want to hear more? If your language draws you into your speech, then it will likely draw in your audience as well. By carefully choosing the words in your speech, you can use language to create rich images and sensations.

In this chapter, you will read about a number of verbal techniques you can use to draw your listeners into your ideas. These tools can be divided into two general categories: language that creates memorable imagery and language that creates a pleasing rhythm.

## Language That Creates Memorable Imagery

Our language can call to mind sights, smells, tastes, and sounds. With language, we can bring an idea to life and make abstractions seem concrete. Figures of speech—such as similes, metaphors, and personification—can create powerful images for our audiences, making our speeches appealing, interesting, and memorable. In the examples that follow, notice how these devices blend with the words around them. They call up the images without calling attention to themselves.

### Simile

When we use **similes,** we are making an explicit comparison of two things with the word *like* or *as.* Although the two things we are comparing are different, they are similar in a way that we want to highlight to make a specific point. Consider the following examples of similes from speeches given by Patrick and Haley:

***Patrick:***

> Although he stands only five feet ten to my six feet two, my *father seems like a giant* to me and probably always will. But he's a gentle giant, for the most part, and I look up to him and appreciate many of the lessons he taught me.

***Haley:***

> From the time you first begin to consume it, the sugar in your body scratches the lining of the arteries leading to your heart. *The process is like sandpaper on wood,* and it never reverses itself.

Through similes, Patrick emphasized his respect for his father, and Haley dramatized the hazards of consuming sugar. Patrick could simply have said he respected his father, and Haley could have said sugar is bad for your arteries. However, by using similes, their audiences could "see" Patrick's respect for his father and the damage sugar does to arteries.

### Metaphor

A **metaphor** is a comparison of two things that describes one thing as being something else. The word *metaphor* comes from a Greek term meaning "transference."[1] When we use metaphors, we are transferring the qualities of one thing to another, illustrating their similarities. Aristotle described having a command of metaphors as "the greatest thing by far."

Many metaphors create associations that are obvious, such as "the war on drugs"—which means the government is responding to drug trafficking in a warlike manner. Other metaphors are subtler, such as Guatemalan human rights advocate Rigoberta Menchú's "we are not myths of the past, ruins in the jungle, or zoos."[2] By comparing the Mayan people to myths, ruins, and zoos, Menchú is arguing for the rights of the Mayan people today by comparing them to what they are not. In both examples, the metaphors make the comparisons memorable.

Two student speakers, Silas and Brooke, used metaphors quite successfully in the following ways:

***Silas:***

> Melanoma is one of the most common cancers in Americans between the ages of twenty-five and twenty-nine. If it is caught early and removed, a person lives a normal life. Well, maybe it's normal. According to Matthew Brady, now nineteen, after summers on his boogie board and at the age of only fourteen, "they *cut a steak out of my back.*"

***Brooke:***

> As I ate, my mouth got hotter and hotter... and hotter. I took a sip of water. It kept right on heating up. The source of this *fire in my mouth*? The fairly well-known habanero chili.

Like similes, metaphors bring ideas to life with rich associations and comparisons. However, they can sometimes go astray in awkward ways. A **mixed metaphor** makes illogical comparisons between two or more things. When speakers mix their metaphors, they begin with one metaphor and then switch to another midstream. The humor, if not confusion, that results from mixed metaphors is apparent in the following examples:[3]

> It appears as though the *Achilles heel* of the Eagles' defense is about to *rear its ugly head.*
>
> I wanted all my *ducks in a row*, so if we did *get into a posture*, we could pretty much *slam dunk* this thing and *put it to bed.*

In the first example, the speaker asks the audience to associate the metaphors of an Achilles heel (a weak point) with the rearing of an ugly head (something unwelcome becoming a problem). However, heels cannot raise their heads. In the second example, the speaker associates a slam dunk (a high-probability shot in basketball) with putting something to bed (finishing a task). Combined with the metaphor of ducks in a row (everything in order) and getting into a posture (bluffing), the audience has trouble deciding which image to focus on. In short, mixed metaphors bring together too many or contradictory associations and are difficult to visualize.

### Personification

When we use **personification,** we attribute human characteristics to animals, objects, or concepts. Personification assigns sight, speech, hearing, thought, emotion, action, or sensation to objects (such as trees, rocks, buildings) or to concepts (such as love, bravery, sadness). "Confusion spoke," "the trees listen," and "the voice of democracy" are examples of personification. In the following examples, notice how easy it is to accept the traits assigned to things we don't typically see as having these human qualities.

> My *bones are tired.* Not tired of struggling, but tired of oppression. (Audley "Queen Mother" Moore, civil rights leader)[4]

With personification, the ideas expressed here come to life. Bones, which can break or weaken, can't become tired. However, the image of deep fatigue stays with the audience long after the words are said.

In a speech about losing his job, Carl used personification to describe the letter he received and his reaction to it:

> Those words just sat there staring at me. They wouldn't leave and they wouldn't explain themselves. "You're fired," they said. And they refused to tell me anything else.

Carl's image conveys the shock of being fired without explanation or recourse. Personification, like metaphor and simile, can call up vivid images and sensations for your audience.

## Language That Creates a Pleasing Rhythm

We can strengthen the images we create by focusing on the way the words sound when put together. Some of the most effective public speakers in history have used rhythm to strengthen the presentation of their ideas; Jesse Jackson, John F. Kennedy, and Barbara Jordan are examples. In speeches, **rhythm** is the arrangement of words into patterns so the sounds of the words together enhance the meaning of a phrase. Parallelism, repetition, alliteration, and antithesis are four ways to emphasize your ideas with rhythm.

### Parallelism

When we arrange related words so they are balanced or arrange related sentences so they have identical structures, we are using **parallelism.** The saying "*beauty is* as *beauty does*" is a simple but effective use of parallelism. Because of its rhythm and symmetry, parallelism helps an audience remember a statement. Here are more complex examples of parallelism:

> *Rich and poor, intelligent and ignorant, wise and foolish, virtuous and vicious, man and woman*—it is ever the same, each soul must depend wholly on itself. (Elizabeth Cady Stanton, nineteenth-century suffragist)
>
> My parents shared not only an improbable love, they shared an abiding faith in the possibilities of this nation. They would give me an African name, Barack, or "blessed," believing that *in a tolerant America* your name is no barrier to success. They imagined—they imagined me going to the best schools in the land, even though they weren't rich, because *in a generous America* you don't have to be rich to achieve your potential. (Illinois Senator Barack Obama, 2004 keynote address to the Democratic National Convention)

### Repetition

When we use **repetition** in a speech, we repeat keywords or phrases at the beginnings or endings of clauses, sentences, or paragraphs. President Franklin D. Roosevelt's "I see one-third of the nation ill-housed, ill-clad, and ill-nourished" is an example of repetition. The repetition of the word *ill* creates a rhythm that helped his audience remember his claims.

Representative Barbara Jordan used repetition in her 1976 keynote address to the Democratic National Convention:

> *We are a people* in a quandary about the present. *We are a people* in search of our future. *We are a people* in search of a national community.

In the next example, poet Nikki Giovanni used repetition to create a memorable message in her speech "We Are Virginia Tech," given at the close of the memorial ceremony for the 2007 Virginia Tech shooting victims. Notice that in the fourth sentence, "we are" is implied.

> *We are* Virginia Tech. *We are* strong enough to stand tall tearlessly. *We are* brave enough to bend to cry. And sad enough to know we must laugh again. *We are* Virginia Tech.

Repetition is one of the easier verbal techniques for beginning speakers to use. Consider these examples from student speeches:

> Let me talk about my experiences as a first-year teacher. I'll tell you now, I loved it, but *I was not prepared.* For the endless energy of the students? *I was not prepared.* The demands on

> my time outside the classroom? *Not prepared.* Angry parents? *Not prepared.* Learning disabilities? *Not prepared.* Language differences? Personal tragedies? Trusting faces staring up at me? You got it: *I was not prepared.*

> *As students, we need* to respond. *As students, we need* to care. *As students, we need* to step forward and share our positions.

Speakers often combine repetition with parallelism to reinforce messages rhythmically and ensure that their words stay with us long after a speech is over. In the following example, former Massachusetts Congressman Joe Moakley repeats "it is never a crime" and then uses parallelism to end with "It is always a duty."

> *It is never a crime* to speak up for the poor, the helpless, or the ill; *it is never a crime* to tell the truth; *it is never a crime* to demand justice; *it is never a crime* to teach people their rights; *it is never a crime* to struggle for a just peace. *It is never a crime. It is always a duty.*

### Alliteration

**Alliteration** is the repetition of the initial sounds of two or more words in a sentence or phrase. We can use alliteration to emphasize an idea, to create a humorous tone, or as a **mnemonic device** (a verbal device that makes information easier to remember).[5] Alliteration is not just for children's rhyming games (such as *P*eter *P*iper and his *p*ickled *p*eppers). Consider these common phrases: the *W*ild *W*est, *f*east or *f*amine, the *b*allot or the *b*ullet, *c*ompassionate *c*onservatism, *s*trong and *s*ilent, and the *M*illion *M*an *M*arch. These phrases have become familiar, in part because alliteration has made them more memorable. When used sparingly, alliteration can give a rhythm to your words that audiences find engaging and easy to remember. Consider these examples of alliteration and the ways the repetition of sounds make it easier to remember the ideas in a speech.

> We are in a transitional period right now—fascinating and exhilarating times, learning to adjust to *changes* and the *choices* we—men and women—are facing. (Barbara Bush, former first lady)

> Now is the time for *repentance, restitution*, and *reconciliation*, and I honor those three functions in the light of the great ethnic, racial diversity in our world today. (Maggie Kuhn, founder of the Gray Panthers)

### Antithesis

The word *antithesis* means "opposite." In a speech, you use **antithesis** when you place words and phrases in contrast or opposition to one another. One of the most famous uses of antithesis comes from John F. Kennedy's inaugural address in 1961: "And so, my fellow Americans: *Ask not what your country can do for you—ask what you can do for your country.*" With this simple phrase, he caused those listening to think about their personal responsibility for preserving the freedoms many Americans had begun to take for granted. Kennedy offered a second example of antithesis in that same speech:

> Let us never negotiate out of fear. But let us never fear to negotiate.

Other speakers have also used antithesis with great impact:

> We can do no *great things*—only *small things* with great love. (Mother Teresa, humanitarian and Nobel Peace Prize laureate)

> Words cannot *be remote from reality* when they *create reality.* (John Cowper Powys, English novelist)

Antithesis is perhaps more complex than alliteration and parallelism, but it can be used with great success. As you put together the ideas in your speeches, see if you might be able to phrase any of them using antithesis. Here's how Werner used antithesis in his speech:

> Some say that people with developmental disabilities only *take from us*, but I say they actually *give to us.*

Antithesis draws an audience into your speech, adding force and rhythm to your ideas.

**Speaking across DIFFERENCES**

**No matter what linguistic devices you use to enhance your speech, remember to use respectful and appropriate language.**

These seven devices for engaging your audience in your ideas—simile, metaphor, personification, parallelism, repetition, alliteration, and antithesis—can help you create memorable images and appealing rhythms in your speech. Used thoughtfully, they can help your audience recall sensations and experiences and remember your ideas.

As you use these linguistic devices, remember the importance of respecting cultural differences and speaking with gender-inclusive language (Chapter 15). Similarly, remember that language can be ambiguous, and your linguistic devices should clarify your ideas, not confuse your audience. If you create appropriate and engaging images with your language, you will enhance the public dialogue.

**Skills & Confidence**
PPD Activity 16.1
Video Activity 16.1
Speech Studio 16.1

**SPEECH Checklist ✓**

## Imagery and Repetition

To make your descriptions vivid, use imagery.

- ☐ A simile compares two unlike things with *like* or *as* ("Like a school kid waiting for the spring, I'm just sitting here waiting for you"—Nora Jones). Avoid stale similes or clichés, such as "I slept like a log," "he was busy as a bee," "it was cold as ice."
- ☐ A metaphor describes one thing by relating it to a different thing ("You're a cryptic crossword, a song I've never heard"—Sia). Avoid mixed metaphors ("Anyone who gets in the way of this cunning steamroller will find himself on a card index file and then in hot—very hot—water"—Len Deighton, *Winter*).
- ☐ Personification gives a human trait to a nonhuman object ("While my guitar gently weeps"—George Harrison).

To make important points memorable, use rhythm.

- ☐ Parallelism uses the same structure for related phrases or sentences ("There are not enough jails, not enough policemen, not enough courts to enforce a law not supported by the people"—U.S. Vice President Hubert Humphrey).
- ☐ Repetition uses a keyword or phrase two or more times ("We have nothing to fear but fear itself"—Franklin D. Roosevelt).
- ☐ Alliteration is the repetition of the initial sounds of two or more words ("This beat be bumpin' bumpin', this beat go boom boom"—Black Eyed Peas).
- ☐ Antithesis is the pairing of words or phrases with opposite meanings ("Injustice anywhere is a threat to justice everywhere"—Martin Luther King Jr.)

# PART VI

# DELIVERY AND VISUAL AIDS

## CIVIC ENGAGEMENT IN ACTION

### Food for Peace

Can creating and selling tasty snacks lead to a lasting peace in some of the most troubled regions of the world? Daniel Lubetzky thinks it can. In 1996, Lubetzky founded the PeaceWorks Foundation, an organization that supports efforts to "foster understanding, tolerance and co-existence in regions of conflict." Having long been passionate about both business and trying to resolve the Israeli-Palestinian conflict, he decided to combine the two, creating a vehicle for speaking out against the violence in the Middle East.

REED SAXON/AP PHOTO

PeaceWorks began by bringing Israelis and Palestinians together in the creation of "spratés," a combination of savory sauces and pâtés. Sporting labels of the characters Moshe (an Israeli chef) and Ali (an Arab magician), these products quickly became a popular symbol of Arab-Israeli cooperation. The duo, according to an invented legend, "averted war by creating a spraté whose aroma left soldiers in a rapture, causing swords to be melted into tablespoons." Now called Meditalia™, these spreads are truly an international effort. They're produced in Israel with olives grown in Palestinian villages and sun-dried tomatoes from Turkey, and they're bottled in jars made in Egypt. PeaceWorks has grown to also include a number of foods that foster peace in other regions, such as a line of Indonesian foods made by Muslims, Christians, and Buddhists. Lubetzky's approach is not wholly altruistic—calling PeaceWorks a not-only-for-profit company, he is clear that he wants to make a profit in addition to promoting peace. In fact, he feels that the two support each other: Economic cooperation between Arabs and Israelis can create a shared interest in peace.

### You Can Get Involved

If you'd like to learn more about PeaceWorks and OneVoice, access **Web Connect P.VI.1: OneVoice**. For information about two other non-profit, nonpartisan organizations that combine business and social activism, access **Web Connect P.VI.2: Business Council for Peace** and **Web Connect P.VI.3: Social Entrepreneurship.** The Business Council for Peace helps women in areas

(continued)

## CIVIC ENGAGEMENT IN ACTION continued

Skills & Confidence
Web Connect P.V1.1
Web Connect P.V1.2
Web Connect P.V1.3

In 2002, Lubetzky expanded his peace-building activities to include OneVoice, a grassroots movement intended to create a space for conversation between Israelis and Palestinians and to empower them to take an active role in resolving the conflict. Thus far, people from all over the world have joined 210,000 Palestinians and Israelis in committing to support OneVoice. "The vast majority of Israelis and Palestinians want nothing more than to end the conflict," Lubetzky says, and "if people are interacting on a daily basis, then hopefully it will shatter cultural stereotypes. People will realize that [it] is in their interest to work together and to humanize what formerly could have been an absolute enemy." The goal of OneVoice is to reframe the conflict in the Middle East and to communicate that the "moderate majority can prevail over the absolutist vision of an extremist minority, which so often succeeds in derailing the peace process."[1]

### You Can Get Involved (continued)

of conflict build businesses to sustain their families, create jobs in their country, and strengthen their ability to foster peace. Ashoka is an association of the world's leading social entrepreneurs, people who use their business skills to work for social change. Click the "Get Involved" and "Fields of Work" tabs from their homepages to see how you can become a part of the social entrepreneur movement.

# DELIVERY AND VISUAL AIDS

CHAPTER 17

# Methods of Delivery



***In this chapter, you will learn to***

**Identify and describe four different methods of delivering a speech**

**Describe how to respond to signs of disinterest, confusion, or disagreement in your audience**

If you look up the word *delivery* in the dictionary, you will discover the following definitions: (1) the carrying of something to a particular person or address; (2) the process of giving birth; (3) the action and manner of throwing or tossing a ball or punch; (4) the rescue of someone from hardship; and (5) the action or manner in which somebody speaks to an audience. Although this chapter focuses on the fifth definition of **delivery,** the action or manner of speaking to an audience, the other four definitions are also relevant.

When we deliver our speeches, we do carry something to others—our message. Our delivery also gives birth to our ideas as we bring them to life for our audience. Similarly, when we enter the public dialogue, we throw or toss our ideas out to our audiences, hoping they will catch them. Depending on the speaking environment, our passion and engagement, and the beliefs of our audience, our ideas may even feel like punches. Finally, when we share information with our listeners or encourage them to change, we can sometimes help them avoid hardship or confusion.

What these other definitions of *delivery* suggest is that delivery is more complex than simply "giving a speech." It is your way of connecting with your audience and sharing your ideas with them. In this chapter, you will learn about four methods of delivery and ways to listen to your audience and adapt to their needs, helping them listen to your speech more effectively. Chapter 18 covers the verbal and nonverbal components of delivery that will help you present your ideas in the most effective way.

## Methods of Delivery

The four types of delivery you use as a public speaker are

- extemporaneous,
- impromptu,
- manuscript, and
- memorized.[1]

Let's look at each of these methods of delivery and the reasons for using them.

### Extemporaneous Delivery

Most of your speeches will be extemporaneous. When you give an **extemporaneous speech,** you present a carefully prepared and practiced speech from brief notes rather than from memory or a written manuscript. Because extemporaneous delivery tends to be more natural than other deliveries, it is one of the more common methods.

An extemporaneous delivery evolves as your speech evolves. That is, as you work from your preparation outline to your speaking outline, you are getting ready to deliver your speech extemporaneously. Recall from Chapter 11 that when you work with your preparation outline, you organize all the material you've thoroughly researched. Therefore, you come to know your speech in full detail. You then summarize that detail in the speaking outline. When you practice giving your speech from the speaking outline, words and phrases remind you of the full ideas on the preparation outline. Thus, your speaking outline provides the brief notes you speak from. Because you don't need to read the full text of your speech to remember what you want to say, you can give your speech in a natural way.

The advantages of extemporaneous deliveries are many. The speaking outline or speaking notes prompt your ideas but do not allow you to read every word to your audience. Your eye contact and gestures are natural, and your tone is conversational. Finally, because extemporaneous deliveries encourage direct communication between the speaker and the audience, it is easier to stay audience centered.

***Guidelines for extemporaneous delivery.*** Beginning speakers sometimes find extemporaneous delivery intimidating because they fear they may forget their ideas. However, the way to overcome this fear isn't to write out every word of your speech and memorize the words or read them during your presentation. Instead, add more keywords and phrases to your outline (not full sentences) so you have more cues to aid your memory. Second, practice your speech often before you give it so you will feel more confident about what you will remember and want to say. Your goal isn't necessarily to eliminate your fear by reading your speech, but to give yourself tools so you can "talk" your speech.

The differences between an extemporaneous delivery and a speech read to an audience are striking. With an extemporaneous delivery, your language follows an oral rather than a written style (Chapter 15). An extemporaneous delivery has a **conversational style,** which is more formal than everyday conversation but remains spontaneous and relaxed.[2] Additionally, with a conversational style, your posture and gestures are relaxed, and you make frequent eye contact with your audience. In contrast, because reading requires your full attention, you're less able to make eye contact with your audience and gesture spontaneously. Imagine if Dr. Martin Luther King Jr. or Eleanor Roosevelt had read their most famous speeches to their audiences. Their charisma and power would have disappeared.

Skills & Confidence Video Activity 17.1

**SPEECH Checklist**

## Extemporaneous Speeches

- ☐ Create a detailed preparation outline based on your research.
- ☐ Use keywords and phrases from the preparation outline to create a speaking outline.
- ☐ Practice giving the speech from the speaking outline, adding keywords and cues to aid your memory with difficult spots.
- ☐ Use a conversational style when delivering your speech, making frequent eye contact with the audience and gesturing spontaneously.

### Impromptu Delivery

An **impromptu speech** is one that you have not planned or prepared in advance. Although you may be wondering why anyone would do this—especially in light of the importance of preparation, planning, and practice—impromptu speaking is quite common. It occurs in meetings or public gatherings when someone is asked to speak or feels the need to share her or his perspective. When you decide to speak, you have the advantage of having a moment or two to organize your ideas. If you are suddenly asked to speak, you may not be able to jot down notes, but you still can organize your ideas. Consider the following scenario:

> As a senior at the university, José was having trouble registering for the courses he needed to graduate. Enrollment on his campus was at an all-time high, and the number of majors in his own department had grown enormously. As a result, classes filled early. He expressed his frustration to his adviser, who suggested José attend a campus open forum on graduation requirements. José's adviser facilitated the discussion, and during the question-and-answer session, he asked José if he would share his frustrating experiences with the audience. José paused and quickly organized his thoughts about his frustrations and how they related to the discussion. His speech was a success not only because it addressed the discussion directly but also because he was candid about his experiences.

José entered the public dialogue through impromptu speaking. He took a few seconds to organize his thoughts and then began. That quick organization gave him confidence and helped him deliver

**SPEECH Checklist**

## Impromptu Speeches

- ☐ Stay calm and rely on the fundamentals of public speaking that you have learned.
- ☐ Mentally identify your main points, and jot them down if there's time.
- ☐ Preview your main points.
- ☐ Support each main point with subpoints, such as examples, narratives, statistics, testimony, and definitions. Indicate their connections with verbal signposts.
- ☐ Summarize your main points in a brief conclusion.

an audience-centered speech that was easy to follow. If you decide to give an impromptu speech, you may have time to make a quick speaking outline and jot down key ideas and points before you begin. However, if you have no time to make a few notes, as in José's case, you can quickly organize your ideas in your head before you begin to speak.

***Guidelines for impromptu delivery.*** Although you never have much time to prepare an impromptu speech, you can practice impromptu deliveries. In fact, your speech instructor will likely ask you to give several impromptu speeches during the semester. When you deliver an impromptu speech, use the following guidelines:

1. Quickly but calmly decide on the main points you want to make.
2. Introduce your main points as you would in a speech you had prepared in advance: Offer a preview such as "the three things I'd like to cover are" and use signposts such as "first."
3. Support your main points with subpoints and sub-subpoints.
4. Summarize your main points in a brief conclusion.

If you find yourself in an impromptu situation, stay calm. The skills you learn in your public speaking course are invaluable for such situations. Even though you may be nervous, you have learned to organize ideas and relate them to the audience. Remember, too, that when you give an impromptu speech, your audience does not expect elaborate source citations, fancy visual aids, or creative introductions. They are looking for immediate information or guidance. If you rely on the fundamental skills you have learned in your public speaking course, you can handle impromptu speeches successfully.

## Manuscript Delivery

When you give a **manuscript speech,** you read to an audience from a written text. Although most speeches are best delivered extemporaneously, some speeches require a manuscript delivery:

- When detailed and exact information must be reported carefully, such as to a professional board or a formal committee
- When your speech will be scrutinized word by word, archived, and referred to later (for example, the president's address to the nation)
- When your speech text will be used later for some other purpose (for example, a keynote address at a conference, which is often published)

A manuscript speech is one of the most challenging forms of delivery. Contrary to what most beginning public speakers think, speaking effectively from a manuscript requires more preparation and skill than extemporaneous or impromptu speaking. Two problems are likely when a speaker reads from the full text. First, the speech often sounds like a written text and not an oral text, or it sounds like one that "reads" well but doesn't "talk" well. (Recall the differences between spoken and written language explained in Chapter 15.) Second, the speaker may be inclined to read to the audience rather than talk with them, which isn't conducive to a healthy public dialogue. Let's look at some solutions to these problems.

**Speaking at Work**

*Manuscript delivery is particularly well suited for "official" workplace speeches, especially those that will be archived, evaluated, distributed, or that include information that must be reported carefully*

***Guidelines for manuscript delivery.*** For an oral style in a manuscript speech, talk the speech aloud as you write it. Working from your preparation outline, speak the words as you write them on your computer or paper. If you find yourself thinking the speech rather than saying it aloud, go back and speak the part you have just written. You will usually notice that you've slipped into a writer's style instead of a speaker's style. Change the language in these sections to reflect spoken ideas rather than written ideas. Remember, your goal is to write a speech, not an essay.

The second challenge with manuscript speeches is the temptation to read the manuscript to the audience. This will greatly reduce your eye contact with the audience because you are focusing on the manuscript and not your listeners. Also, your words may sound wooden because you are more concerned about reading your words accurately than how your words might sound to your audience. Finally, your delivery may be too fast because you are more focused on getting the words out than paying attention to how the audience is reacting to you.

The way to overcome the challenges associated with delivering a manuscript speech is to practice speaking from the manuscript again and again. As you become familiar with your manuscript during practice, you will find your natural rhythm and conversational style. You will notice where you can make eye contact with your audience easily and for extended periods. Like your extemporaneous speeches, you will be able to deliver full ideas or subpoints without reading. You will also discover that you'll want to slow down because, even though the words are in front of you, you feel comfortable enough to speak the words with feeling rather than rush through them.

**SPEECH Checklist**

### Manuscript Speeches

- ☐ Talk the speech aloud as you write it from your preparation outline so that it will have an oral style.
- ☐ Practice speaking from the manuscript many times in order to become familiar with it so that you will be able to deliver full ideas without reading them.
- ☐ As you speak, make eye contact with your audience as often as possible and speak your words slowly and with feeling.

## Memorized Delivery

A **memorized speech** is written out, committed to memory, and given word for word. With a memorized delivery, you give the speech without any notes. Orators 2,000 years ago prided themselves on their ability to memorize speeches that were hours long. Today, memorized speeches are usually used only for toasts, blessings, acceptance speeches, introductions, and sometimes in forensics. Use a memorized delivery in these situations:

- When your speech is very short
- When you want to say things in a very specific way
- When notes would be awkward or disruptive

The trick to a memorized delivery is to speak as naturally and conversationally as possible. Rather than focusing on remembering your words, focus on communicating your words to your audience. When you deliver a memorized speech, don't recite it but rather deliver it as though you were talking to your audience.

***Guidelines for memorized delivery.*** To commit a speech to memory, follow these steps:

1. Write a manuscript of the speech using an oral style, not a written one.
2. Begin with the first line or first part of the first line and read it aloud over and over.
3. When you are familiar with that first line, deliver it, or parts of it, without reading it. Do this over and over until you can deliver the full line by heart.

4. Now, holding your manuscript but not looking at it, deliver the line by memory, looking out at an imaginary audience.
5. Once you've committed that first line to memory, deliver it again from memory and then read the second line aloud. Do this again and again until this line is familiar.
6. Repeat steps 3 through 5 for the remaining lines of the speech. Every few lines, set the manuscript aside and practice them until you can deliver them naturally and with confidence.
7. Once you've learned the full speech, practice it over and over, reminding yourself to listen to the meaning of your words. Remember, you want to bring the words to life and connect with your audience.

If you must deliver a long memorized speech, keep your manuscript nearby, if you can, so you can find your place if you get lost. If you can't keep your manuscript near you, someone else may be able to hold it and prompt you if you lose your place. If you lose your place and have no one to prompt you, continue extemporaneously or pause; then backtrack to the last line you remember, repeat it in your head, and you should be able to remember what comes next.

**Skills & Confidence**
PPD Activity 12.1
Video Activity 17.2
Web Connect 17.1
Web Connect 17.2

Table 17.1 on page 292 reviews the advantages and disadvantages of the four delivery methods.

**SPEECH Checklist**

## Memorized Speeches

- ☐ Use memorized delivery only for very short speeches.
- ☐ Talk the speech aloud as you write it so that it will have an oral style.
- ☐ Memorize the speech by repeating aloud part or all of the first line until you can deliver it by heart. Then deliver it without looking at the paper, and repeat until you can deliver it confidently. Repeat the process with the second line, and then the third, and so on.
- ☐ Practice groups of lines and then the entire speech over and over.
- ☐ When you deliver a memorized speech, focus on communicating the meaning to your audience in a conversational style.
- ☐ If you lose your place, continue extemporaneously or repeat in your head the last line you remember, which should remind you of the idea that comes next.

**TABLE 17.1 Advantages and Disadvantages of the Four Delivery Methods**

| | EXTEMPORANEOUS | IMPROMPTU |
|---|---|---|
| **Definition** | A speech that is carefully prepared and practiced from brief notes rather than from memory or a written manuscript. | A speech that is not planned or prepared in advance and uses few or no notes. |
| **Advantages** | Combines a conversational style with a speaking outline. Encourages careful organization. | Allows for a conversational style with few or no notes. |
| **Disadvantages** | Requires practice time. Speakers may be tempted to memorize the speech. | Requires thinking and organizing ideas quickly. No time for preparation. |
| | MANUSCRIPT | MEMORIZED |
| **Definition** | A speech that is written word for word and read to an audience. | A speech that is written word for word, memorized, and given word for word. |
| **Advantages** | Helps present very detailed or specific information exactly as the speaker wants. | Frees the speaker to move about the room. No need for notes. |
| **Disadvantages** | Requires a conversational style that can be hard to achieve because the speaker reads from a full text. | Requires careful memorization. Speaker must remember important points and details without notes. |

## Speakers as Listeners: Adapting to Your Audience

Although this chapter has focused on delivery, speakers are also listeners. Speakers must do more than produce a steady stream of words. They must listen to their audiences by monitoring their expressions, posture, feedback, and level of attention. Then they must use this information to adapt to audience needs throughout the speech by slowing down or speeding up, taking more time to explain, omitting information, or adding extra examples to clarify.

When you give a speech, remember that audience members bring with them many bad listening habits (see Chapter 4). What follows are some examples of problematic audiences and ways you can counter their bad habits to help them listen better. When you as a speaker listen to your audience, you make your message more listenable and memorable, and you make it easier for your audience to give you the attention and respect you deserve.

### Audiences Who Are Uninterested

Sometimes audience members appear uninterested in your speech from the start or seem to assume they already know what you will say. Address this behavior by making your introduction and first main points compelling, innovative, and responsive to your audience's particular biases.

For example, Genet began his speech by saying,

> You say you already know. You say, "There's nothing new here!" You might even be thinking, "This will never happen to me," and maybe—just maybe—you're right. But what if you're wrong? What if you're *probably* wrong? Are you willing to be the two out of three who didn't listen?

After this introduction, he had the full attention of the class and was able to maintain their attention throughout his speech on alcohol and drug addiction.

### Audiences Who Are Distracted or Disruptive

Some audience members may slouch, fail to make eye contact, and daydream. Others make or attend to distractions. To counter this behavior, you can try techniques to involve your audience:

- Ask questions of the entire audience or of particular members.
- Ask them to complete an activity related to your topic, such as making a list or jotting down what they already know about the topic.
- Bring particularly disruptive people into your speech verbally or by inviting them to the front of the audience for a legitimate reason (for example, to give a demonstration or to record discussion ideas on a white board).

Here's how Seth handled this situation:

> Noticing that several of his audience members were reading the newspaper during his speech, Seth paused midsentence to catch his audience's attention and said, "You know, I bet that whatever's in that paper isn't as current or relevant to our lives as my next point. Because, at this moment in time, our government is spending billions of dollars to cover up…," and he continued with his topic. At that point, he had the full and respectful attention of the audience.

Be careful about singling out audience members, however. Make sure the speaking environment is such that you won't embarrass those people or make the rest of the audience feel uncomfortable. Approaching inattention with good-natured humor can go a long way toward making your audience feel that you value them.

### Audiences Who Are Distracted by the Speaker

If your audience is staring at your unusual style of clothing or is straining to understand because of differences in speech styles, take a moment to explain what the distraction means to you and why it's there. Angelique, a student with a strong accent, shared with her audience that she was from the Dominican Republic. Shc cxplained that her husband kept trying to correct her accent, but she told him, "It's my accent and I like it." Sharing this story in the introduction of her speech helped reduce the focus on her accent and enabled her audience to listen to her message instead.

### Audiences Who Are Confused

You can use a number of strategies to help audience members who appear confused by the information in your speech:

- Slow down.
- Explain with more detail.
- Reduce the number of your main points.
- Alter your language.

In addition, even if you had not planned to use visual aids, you could use an overhead projector or a whiteboard or ask someone from the audience to demonstrate your ideas. Marilyn saw her audience looking confused, so she proceeded to outline her main points on the board and jot down keywords and phrases. The audience applauded her efforts and acknowledged that her speech was much easier to follow with a visual map.

### Audiences Who Plan Their Responses Rather Than Listen

Sometimes particular audience members appear to be planning responses to you during your speech. Acknowledge their eagerness to participate, and recognize it as a positive sign of interest. Acknowledging someone's interest can bring a listener into your speech and create an environment in which everyone feels they can express themselves.

Hallie watched a member of her audience react with dismay to one of her claims and then fidget and sit on the edge of his seat. She acknowledged his desire to respond by saying, "I see I've struck a chord with some of you. If you'll hang on to your questions and hear me out, I'd love to hear your reactions at the end of the speech." Her resister relaxed a bit and was able to put his opposition aside long enough to listen to her full arguments and reasons. The conversation at the end of the speech was lively and dynamic, and both Hallie and the audience member benefited from it.

**Skills & Confidence**
Video Activity 17.3
Speech Studio 17.1

CHAPTER 18

# Verbal and Nonverbal Components of Delivery

- Verbal Components of Delivery
  - Speech Checklist: Verbal Delivery
- Nonverbal Components of Delivery
  - Speech Checklist: Nonverbal Delivery
- Rehearsing Your Speech

*In this chapter, you will learn to*

- List and demonstrate the verbal components of delivery
- List and demonstrate the nonverbal components of delivery
- Identify effective strategies for rehearsing your speech

Delivery, the action of speaking to an audience, has many components. When we hear or give a "carefully honed and well-articulated speech,"[1] we realize that delivery is the art of clarifying issues and engaging audiences. This chapter discusses both verbal and nonverbal components of delivery and concludes with advice for effectively rehearsing your speeches.

## Verbal Components of Delivery

A speech's ring of truth comes not only from its words but also from how they are delivered. Speakers known for their delivery—for example, John F. Kennedy, Barack Obama, Ann Richards, and Martin Luther King Jr.—use **vocal variety,** or changes in the volume, rate, and pitch of the voice that affect the meaning of the words delivered. We achieve vocal variety by consciously using volume, rate, pitch and inflection, and pauses. The proper articulation and pronunciation of words and a consideration of dialect are also important components of delivery.

## Volume

**Volume** is the loudness of a speaker's voice. Common sense tells us that we want to speak loudly enough for our audiences to hear us but not so loudly that we make our listeners uncomfortable. Knowing just how loud to speak can be difficult because our own voice sounds louder to us than to the audience and because the appropriate volume varies with each situation. Culture also affects perceptions about appropriate speaking volume. For example, in some Mediterranean cultures, a loud voice signals sincerity and strength, whereas in some parts of the United States, it may signal aggression or anger. In some Native American and Asian cultures, a soft voice signals education and good manners.[2] However, in some European cultures, a soft voice may signal femininity, secrecy, or even fear.

> ***Speaking across DIFFERENCES***
>
> **Culture affects perceptions about appropriate speaking volume.**

Pay attention to nonverbal cues from your audience to help you adjust your volume. If you are speaking without a microphone, watch the faces and postures of people in the back of the room as well as those in front as you begin to speak. If the people in the back seem confused, straining to hear, or are frowning and leaning forward intently, it's a signal to increase your volume. If the people in front move back in their seats and look uneasy, you are likely speaking too loudly. This is a signal to lower your volume.

Even if you use a microphone, you still need to pay attention to your volume. Before you begin your speech, test your voice with the microphone. Make sure you are the proper distance from it (neither too far nor too close) so the audience can listen comfortably.

Don't turn off or avoid a microphone because it makes you nervous or you think people can hear you without one. Microphones exist to help audiences listen (and speakers speak) comfortably. Stay audience centered and use the microphone.

## Rate

**Rate** is the speed at which we speak. There is no formula for the proper rate at which to deliver a speech. For example, Dr. Martin Luther King Jr. began his "I Have a Dream" speech at a rate of 92 words per minute and finished at a rate of 145.[3] Different rates convey different feelings. When we speak quickly, we project a sense of urgency, excitement, or even haste. When we speak slowly, we convey seriousness or even uncertainty. Both a rapid rate and a slow rate have their place. However, too much of either one strains the audience's attention and may cause them to stop listening.

To check your rate, tape yourself for several minutes. Then play back the recording and assess your speed. If you are using a manuscript, each page (typed, double-spaced, in a 12-point font) should take two minutes to deliver. If you are much faster or slower, adjust your rate accordingly.

You can also use rhythm (Chapter 16) to help you monitor your rate. Arranging your words into patterns so the sounds of the words together enhance meaning can help you vary your rate in an appealing way. Remember, rate is an audience-centered concern. We want to engage our audience, and our rate of speaking helps us in this effort by communicating certain emotions or energies.

When members of your audience come from varied cultural backgrounds or are not native speakers of your language, try to slow your rate so accents and unfamiliar words are easier to follow. Adjusting your rate in this way communicates an audience-centered stance and adds to your credibility.

***Speaking across DIFFERENCES***

**Be audience centered and enhance your credibility by slowing your rate when speaking to an audience whose members are not native speakers of your language.**

### Pitch and Inflection

**Pitch** refers to the position of tones on the musical scale, and in public speaking, it reveals itself in the highness or lowness of a speaker's voice. **Inflection** is the manipulation of pitch to create certain meanings or moods. Together, pitch and inflection help us communicate more effectively with our audience. Consider the word *well* and its different meanings when used in spoken language. The control of pitch and inflection allows us to say "well" in ways that suggest joyful surprise or indecision or indignation or pity. All of us alter our pitch to ask a question, express satisfaction or displeasure, convey confidence or confusion, or even communicate threats or aggression. Variations in pitch during our speech clarify meaning and help catch and maintain our audience's attention.

Speakers who do not pay attention to their pitch and inflection risk losing their audience. Speakers who do not alter their pitch speak in what is called a **monotone.** Other speakers may say everything in too low or high a pitch. When a speaker says everything in a monotone or a low pitch, the audience senses a lack of interest or energy. When the pitch is too high for too long, every word is communicated with equal

## SPEECH TIPS

### VOCAL VARIETY

Tape the introduction to your next speech, listening for your vocal variety. Adjust your delivery as needed to make sure you will catch your audience's attention and communicate your message clearly.

enthusiasm, or "excessive zeal,"[4] and the audience begins to wonder which points are the most important.

There are solutions to these problems with pitch. First, tape yourself so you can hear your pitch. If your pitch is too high, practice breathing more deeply (from the abdomen rather than the throat) and relaxing your throat muscles as you speak. Speak from your diaphragm rather than your throat, and read aloud regularly to practice this technique until you can get your pitch to drop naturally. (Proper breathing also helps you increase the volume of your voice and project your voice farther.) If you speak in a monotone or in too low a pitch, practice delivering your speech (or reading something aloud) in an overly dramatic way, using inflection, exclamations, and vocal variation as much as possible. With practice, vocal variation will come naturally and carry over into public speaking situations.

### Pauses

**Pauses** are hesitations and brief silences in speech or conversation. In speeches, they are often planned, and they serve several useful functions:

- Pauses give us time to breathe fully and to collect our thoughts during a speech or before we answer a question from the audience.
- Pauses give audiences time to absorb and process information—they're like a rest stop, giving the audience a breather before continuing.
- Pauses before or after an important word or point reinforce that word or point.

Pauses can also add clarity. Read the passage here without pausing after any of the words.

> The back of the eye on which an image of the outside world is thrown and which corresponds to the eye of a camera is composed of a mosaic of rods and cones whose diameter is little more than the length of an average light wave.

Without pauses, it's hard to understand what's being said here, isn't it? Now read the passage again and note where you would naturally pause. Does the meaning of the passage become clearer?

The four pauses that make this passage easier to understand are after *eye, thrown, camera,* and *cones.*[5] These are places where we would add commas in written text to indicate meaning. In written text, pauses are often indicated by punctuation, but in speeches, audiences can't see the punctuation.

Pause to punctuate your words, as well as to establish mood, indicate a transition, take time to reflect, or emphasize a point. For example, in his speech on the pollution caused by fossil fuels, Preston used a pause to dramatize a point. "In fact," Preston argued, "according to the Southern California Edison Electric Transportation website, updated only last month, running for half an hour in urban air pollution introduces as much carbon monoxide into your lungs as [pause] smoking a pack of cigarettes."

Learning the art of the pause takes time and practice. Before you become comfortable with brief moments of silence in a speech, you may have the urge to fill the silence. Avoid **vocalized pauses,** or pauses that speakers fill with words or sounds like "um," "er," or "uh." Vocalized pauses are not only irritating, but they can also create a negative impression of the speaker. When a speaker uses so many vocalized pauses that they intrude into an audience's awareness, listeners may begin to question the speaker's knowledge and speaking capabilities.[6]

If you have a habit of vocalizing pauses, try the following process to eliminate them:

1. Listen for vocalized pauses in your daily speech.
2. When you hear one, anticipate the next one.
3. When you feel the urge to say "um" or "er" to fill space, gently bite your tongue and don't let the word escape.
4. Wait until your next word of substance is ready to come out and say it instead.

It may take time to eliminate vocalized pauses from your speech, and you may feel awkward with the silence, but the results are worth the effort.

## Articulation

**Articulation** is the physical process of producing specific speech sounds to make language intelligible to our audiences. Our clarity depends on our articulation—whether we say words distinctly or whether we mumble and slur. Articulation depends on the movement of our tongue, lips, jaws, and teeth. This movement produces, for instance, either "didjago?" or "did you go?" Scholars of performance and delivery argue that poor articulation has become a trend across all sectors of U.S. culture.[7]

Audiences expect public speaking to be more clearly articulated than private conversation. Speakers with an audience-centered focus care about clear articulation. Clearly articulated words communicate that you want your audience to understand you, and they can add to your credibility. For your audience to understand your ideas, they must be able to decipher your words.

To improve your articulation skills, try the following exercise:

1. Several days before your speech, select a part of your speech or a short written text you can read aloud.
2. Practice saying each word of your speech excerpt or text as slowly and clearly as possible, exaggerating the clarity of each word.
3. Repeat this exercise once or twice each day before you give your speech.

This exercise will help you recognize how much you slur or mumble and teach you to speak more clearly when you give your speech. Don't worry—you won't speak in this exaggerated way when you finally deliver your speech, but your words will be much clearer.

### Pronunciation

Just as you would not turn in an essay you knew was filled with spelling errors, never deliver a speech filled with pronunciation errors. **Pronunciation** is the act of saying words correctly according to the accepted standards of a language. Pronunciation refers to whether a word is said *correctly*, whereas articulation refers to whether a word is said *clearly*. For example, the correct pronunciation of the word *nuclear* is "nu-cle-ar" rather than "nu-cu-lar," and mumbling either pronunciation is a matter of articulation.

Pronouncing words correctly communicates to your audience that you have listened carefully to the public dialogue going on around you and that you have taken care to learn the common language. (Recall from Chapter 15 that it is also important to use language accurately, to use the appropriate words to express your thoughts.) In addition, correct pronunciation of terms and names in a language other than your native one communicates your respect for that culture and enhances your credibility.

### Dialect

A **dialect** is a pattern of speech shared by an ethnic group or people from a particular geographical region. Dialects include words as well as

**Speaking across DIFFERENCES**

**Consider how familiar members of your audience will be with your dialect. If you suspect they will have trouble understanding you, define unfamiliar terms and soften your accent.**

styles of pronunciation shared by members of the group. All people have a dialect, and your own dialect comes from your ethnic heritage as well as the place where you grew up. For example, do you say “wash” or “warsh” when you want something clean? How about “soda,” “pop,” or “coke” when you want a soft drink? Your choices reflect your dialect.

People who use a standard American dialect (the dialect newscasters use when they are on the air) often forget that they, too, have a dialect, and they sometimes view the dialect of others as inferior. For public speaking, dialect is important because of the

**SPEECH Checklist**

## Verbal Delivery

- ☐ **Volume:** Speak loudly enough that all audience members can hear you, but don’t yell. If you use a microphone, test it before your speech so you know how close it needs to be.
- ☐ **Rate:** The basic rate is two minutes for a typed, double-spaced manuscript page. Vary your rate to enhance the content. Speaking quickly implies urgency or excitement. Speaking slowly expresses seriousness or uncertainty. Speaking slowly is also helpful if many in your audience are not native speakers of your language.
- ☐ **Pitch and inflection:** Vary your pitch to clarify meaning and maintain audience attention. A monotone or a consistently low pitch conveys boredom and disinterest. Raise your pitch only occasionally for emphasis. Tape yourself to hear your pitch, and practice changing it if it is too low or too high.
- ☐ **Pauses:** Plan pauses in your speeches to add clarity and emphasize important points. Do not fill silence with vocalized pauses.
- ☐ **Articulation:** Say your words distinctly and practice saying every word in your speech slowly and clearly if articulation is a problem.
- ☐ **Pronunciation:** Be sure you know the correct pronunciation of every word in your speech, including people’s names and words in languages other than your native one.
- ☐ **Dialect:** If your dialect is not shared by many in your audience, acknowledge the difference, define terms that are unfamiliar to your audience, and soften your accent if it might hinder understanding.

effect it may have on audience members who do not share it. Speakers who ignore their dialect may use words that aren't familiar to their audience or may pronounce words in ways that sound odd.

If you know your dialect will be unfamiliar to your audience, try the following strategies:

**Skills & Confidence**
PPD Activity 18.1
Web Connect 18.1

1. Talk about how your region of birth or your ethnic heritage shapes your use of language by giving examples of differences between your dialect and those of your audience.
2. Define terms that are unfamiliar to your audience.
3. Soften the accent associated with your dialect if that accent is fairly strong and might hinder understanding.

# Nonverbal Components of Delivery

To enhance your verbal message, give consideration to the nonverbal components of your speech. These are the aspects communicated through your body and face. For public speakers, they include personal appearance, eye contact, facial expression, posture, gestures, and proxemics.[8]

Scholars of interpersonal communication recognize that nonverbal communication has a powerful impact on the meanings exchanged between people. Researchers suggest that between 65 and 93 percent of the total meaning of a message comes through nonverbal signals.[9] Additionally, when nonverbal signals contradict verbal signals (for example, you say you're glad to see someone but your facial expression and physical posture suggest you're not), people tend to believe the nonverbal signals more than the verbal ones.[10]

For public speakers, nonverbal communication is especially important because it conveys meaning and it can either enhance or detract from the overall message. Let's look at how the components of nonverbal communication affect a speech.[11]

## Personal Appearance

One of the ways that others assess us is by our **personal appearance,** or the way we dress, groom, and present ourselves physically. People deemed "more attractive" earn more money than their "less attractive" peers, and personal grooming plays a large part in perceptions of both men's and women's attractiveness.[12] Attractive characteristics are defined as "those characteristics that make one person appear pleasing to another."[13] Even though we may say people shouldn't be judged by their looks, it seems that is exactly what we do.

Standards for attractiveness and beauty change with generations as well as with cultures and subcultures, but there is a universal standard

**Speaking across DIFFERENCES**

**No matter what your culture or generation, wearing clothing that is appropriate for the speaking occasion will enhance your credibility.**

for acceptable personal grooming in public speaking situations.[14] The standard is that the speaker's dress should be appropriate to the occasion. If the occasion is formal, the speaker is expected to dress formally. If the occasion is casual, the speaker's clothing should be less formal. A speaker who shows up at a formal occasion in a T-shirt and shorts displays a lack of audience awareness and is likely to lose credibility. Similarly, wearing formal business attire to speak at a casual gathering is also inappropriate. In short, be sure your clothing matches the style and tone of the occasion.

Another standard for appropriate grooming in public speaking situations is attire that is neither too revealing nor too restricting. Today, many celebrities accept awards and make speeches wearing almost nothing at all. However, most of us aren't movie stars or pop stars, so when giving a speech in public, we want the audience to listen to our message and not be distracted by our appearance. Dressing simply and tastefully does more than help your audience pay attention to your message. It also helps you move about comfortably and freely as you give your speech.

Your personal appearance should match your objective as a speaker, which is to have your words and ideas taken seriously in the public dialogue. Delivery begins the moment the audience sees you, so pay careful attention to your personal appearance and present yourself appropriately for the occasion at which you are speaking.

### Eye Contact

The second essential component of nonverbal delivery is **eye contact**, visual contact with another person's eyes. Like personal appearance, appropriate eye contact is affected by culture and gender. Most North Americans and Western Europeans expect a speaker to make extensive eye contact. However, in Native American cultures, as in Japan and

**SPEECH TIPS**

#### PERSONAL APPEARANCE

When you give speeches in class, consider your appearance. Give some thought to what is appropriate to wear for a classroom speech and will give you credibility.

parts of Africa, extensive eye contact is considered invasive and disrespectful. Gender, too, affects the meaning of eye contact. For men, direct and extended eye contact with another man may be perceived as a challenge or threat. For women, direct and extended eye contact with a man may be interpreted as an invitation to flirt.

*Speaking across DIFFERENCES*

**Gender and culture affect the meaning of eye contact, particularly extensive direct eye contact.**

Even though the nuances of eye contact are complex, most cultures expect at least some eye contact during a speech. Eye contact has three functions:

- It is a way to greet and acknowledge the audience before the speech begins.
- It is a way to gauge and keep our audience's interest. We use it to monitor feedback from our audience and adjust our volume, rate, and pitch accordingly.
- It is a way to communicate sincerity and honesty.

Audiences rate speakers who make eye contact for less than half their speech as tentative, uncomfortable, and even as insincere and dishonest.[15] In contrast, speakers who make eye contact for more than half their speech are viewed as more credible and trustworthy.[16]

For eye contact to be effective, try to do two things as you look out at your audience. First, make eye contact with many people in the audience rather than a few friendly faces. Make eye contact with people in all parts of the room, not just those immediately in front of you. Gather information about the level of comprehension, interest, and agreement from as many people as you can.

Second, look with interest. Rather than scanning faces in the audience or looking over listeners' heads to the back of the room, really look at individual people. Slow down the movement of your eyes so you actually make a connection with people through your eye contact. Looking with interest communicates that you are pleased to be speaking to your audience and are interested in their responses.

### Facial Expression

Your face lets your audience know your attitudes, emotional states, and sometimes even your inner thoughts. Your **facial expression** is the movement of your eyes, eyebrows, and mouth to convey reactions and emotions. Actors are highly skilled at using their faces to communicate, and audiences appreciate this talent. Although you don't need to be as skilled as an actor, you do need to consider your facial expressions as you deliver your speech. A poker face, although useful in a card game, will not help you communicate your ideas.

You can use your facial expressions to communicate your interest in your topic, your agreement or disagreement with a point, your openness to an idea, and even your feeling about an issue. Take some time to decide which facial expressions might be useful to include in your speech. If these expressions aren't coming naturally to you, practice them until you are comfortable delivering them.

### Posture

**Posture** is the way we position and carry our bodies, and whether we realize it or not, people assign meaning to our posture. We are perceived as confident and relaxed or tense and insecure based, in part, on our posture. A confident speaker is often called "poised," possessing assurance, dignity, and a sense of calm. Nervousness can affect our posture, making us feel awkward and act in ways we never would in other situations: grip the podium with both hands, slouch over our speaking notes, pace back and forth, or stand stuck to one spot. These nervous reactions detract from our delivery and communicate a message we probably don't want to send.[17]

By paying attention during practice to the way you carry your body, you can eliminate some nervous postures. Practice your speech in the way you will actually give it. That is, if you will deliver your speech standing, practice while standing up. Devise a makeshift podium if need be. Or if you are to sit while giving the speech, practice the speech while sitting, with chairs beside you and your notes on a table in front of you. Similarly, if you will use a handheld or attachable microphone, practice with something resembling it so you get the feel of speaking with a microphone.

## SPEECH TIPS

### BEGINNING AND ENDING YOUR SPEECH

- Wait until you are at the podium or have the microphone in your hand before you begin talking.
- Don't start speaking until you are facing your audience and have made eye contact.
- Similarly, don't walk off the stage until you have finished the last word of your conclusion. Finishing your conclusion or your final answer before you leave the spotlight communicates confidence and a willingness to give every word the attention it deserves.

If you find during practice that you pace or grip the podium tightly, you can replace the bad habit with a better one. If you discover that you stand immobilized, you can add cues to your speaking outline to remind you to move during your speech. If you slouch, you can practice sitting up straight and looking out at your audience. In sum, your posture during your speech should improve if you pay attention to your body during practice.

### Gestures

**Gestures** are movements, usually of the hands but sometimes of the entire body, that express meaning and emotion or offer clarity to a message. Students of rhetoric in ancient Greece and Rome spent hours learning specific gestures to accompany transitions, main points, and other specific parts of their speeches. These choreographed gestures were used until the eighteenth century.[18]

Today, research on gestures in public speaking indicates that gestures should be as natural as possible rather than memorized. However, beginning public speakers don't always know what gestures will appear natural in a speech. With only minor variations, natural gestures in a speech are the same as those you normally use in personal conversations to complement your ideas and bring your words to life. Gestures make your delivery lively, offer emphasis and clarity, and convey your passion and interest.

Use these guidelines to help you with gestures:

- *Vary your gestures.* Try to use different kinds of gestures rather than repeating only one gesture. Some gestures emphasize (a fist on the podium); some clarify (counting first, second, third on your fingers); and others illustrate (drawing a shape with your hands in the air). Try to incorporate a variety of these gestures into your speech.
- *Use gestures that fit your message.* Sometimes a point needs an extravagant gesture; at other times a more subtle gesture is more effective. For example, use a relaxed hand movement as you explain a point but a larger, more vigorous movement when you are emphasizing something quite important.
- *Stay relaxed.* Your gestures should flow with your words. Try to keep your movements comfortable and effortless. If you find that a gesture makes you tense, replace it with something more casual and familiar.

You will find that as you gain experience speaking, you will stop thinking about your gestures and simply use them as you normally do in conversation.

### Proxemics

Effective speakers pay close attention to **proxemics,** the use of space during communication. Be mindful of how far away you are from your audience as well as how high above them you are (for example, on a platform or a podium). The farther away you are, the stronger the sense of separation. The higher up you are, the more the idea of power is communicated.

You can work with proxemics in your delivery. One of the strengths of speakers like Barack Obama and Bill Clinton is their ability to move close to their audiences at key points during their

**SPEECH Checklist**

## Nonverbal Delivery

- ☐ **Personal appearance:** Dress appropriately for the speaking occasion and in a way that will not distract from your message.
- ☐ **Eye contract:** To be viewed as a credible and trustworthy speaker, try to make eye contact with your audience for more than half your speech. Look at many different individuals in the audience.
- ☐ **Facial expression:** Vary your facial expression to convey agreement or disagreement with different points and your feelings about various issues.
- ☐ **Posture:** Practice your speech standing at a podium or sitting at a table or in whatever way you will be giving it. Notice nervous habits and try to replace them. If you will be standing, practice moving in ways that fit your speech. If you will be sitting, concentrate on sitting up straight and looking at your audience.

  Do not start speaking until you are facing your audience and have made eye contact. Do not walk away until you have finished your conclusion or the last answer in a question-and-answer session.
- ☐ **Gestures:** Use familiar gestures to emphasize, clarify, and illustrate points. Do not try to use gestures that feel staged or uncomfortable to you.
- ☐ **Proxemics:** If you are speaking from a lectern or podium, move closer to your audience for important points or during the question-and-answer session, if possible.

speeches. Similarly, recall from Chapter 6 that the Dalai Lama worked without a lectern, sometimes even sitting down on stage.

Although you don't want to remain too close to your audience throughout your speech, getting close to them at key points allows for greater connection and communicates a desire to be perceived as more of an equal. Try stepping from behind the lectern or down from the podium and moving closer to your audience. If you can't do this because you need a microphone or a place to put your notes, you might be able to move closer during a question-and-answer session. Doing so will help you communicate openness and a willingness to engage in conversation with your audience.

**Skills & Confidence**
PPD Activity 18.2
Video Activity 18.1
Web Connect 18.2
Speech Studio 18.1

## Rehearsing Your Speech

Although it may not seem logical, the more you practice, the more natural you will sound. This is because you will be familiar with your speech on many levels. You will know the ideas and have some of the wording worked out. You will also be comfortable with the verbal and nonverbal components of your delivery. And you'll feel more confident during your question-and-answer session, if your speech includes one, because you will have prepared and rehearsed the answers to questions you might be asked. (For information about how to handle question-and-answer sessions, see Chapter 26.)

The following guidelines for rehearsing your delivery will help you participate effectively in the public dialogue.

1. Practice giving your speech aloud using your speaking outline (Chapter 11).
2. Practice all stories, quotations, statistics, and other evidence until you can deliver them exactly as you want.
3. When you are comfortable with your material, practice your speech in front of a mirror. Monitor your nonverbal communication and make adjustments as needed so you communicate your message clearly.
4. Now tape your speech and listen for vocal variety. Check your volume, rate, pitch and inflection, pauses, and how you articulate and pronounce words. If you think your dialect will hinder your delivery, make adjustments.
5. Practice your speech again, incorporating the verbal and nonverbal changes you worked out in steps 1 through 4.

Skills & Confidence Web Connect 18.3

6. Now practice a few times in front of a friend. If your speech will end with a question-and-answer session, have the person ask you questions at the end of the speech so you can practice answering them. Incorporate any useful feedback your friend may offer.
7. Stage a dress rehearsal. Wear the clothing you will wear on the day you speak. Set up your practice area so it resembles the actual speaking situation as closely as possible. Consider proxemics and the space you want between you and the audience.

CHAPTER 19

# Visual Aids: Purposes and Contents



***In this chapter, you will learn to***

- Discuss the importance of using visual aids
- Determine what to show on a visual aid
- Identify the five guidelines for using visual aids

Although people once listened to music and speakers without accompanying images, now we are bored by performances that aren't stimulating to the eyes as well as the ears. What does our visual culture mean for beginning public speakers? In at least one of your speeches for your speech class, you will probably be asked to use some kind of visual aid. And in many of your speeches outside the classroom, you will want to display parts of your message visually. To help you as a public speaker, this chapter discusses reasons for using visual aids, what kind of information to show on visual aids, and guidelines for using them. Chapter 20 discusses specific types of visual aids and formats for designing them.

**Speaking at Work**
*Speakers in the workplace often use visual aids, particularly computer-generated presentations such as PowerPoint.*

## Why Visual Aids Are Important

You can certainly give an effective speech without visual aids. In fact, many of the speeches you've read about in this book were given without visual aids, including Martin Luther King Jr.'s famous "I Have a Dream" speech. Yet many types of speeches benefit from effective visual aids, especially those that describe a process, include complex information, or are intended to have great impact. Let's take a look at the important functions of visual aids in a speech.

### Visual Aids Help Gain and Maintain Audience Attention

In 1996, when attorney Johnnie Cochran famously displayed the glove said to belong to accused murderer O. J. Simpson and told the jurors, "If it doesn't fit, you must acquit," he had his audience's full attention. Although his words were compelling and he used a memorable rhyme, it was the visual aid that caught the jury's attention and kept them focused on his argument. A visual aid gives an audience something to focus on, and it reinforces your verbal message. If you want to capture your audience's attention, consider using a visual aid to complement your words.

### Visual Aids Help Audiences Recall Information

Another goal of visual aids is to help your audience remember the information in your speech. One of the best-known studies of visual aids in speeches assessed the amount of information the audience recalls because of visual aids. The researchers found that when a speech does not include visual aids, the audience recalls 70 percent of the information three hours after the speech. Three days later, they recall only 10 percent of the information. When the same message is delivered with visual aids only, the audience recalls 72 percent after three hours and about 35 percent after three days. When the message is delivered both in a speech and with visual aids, the recall after three hours is 85 percent and after three days is 65 percent.[1] Clearly, visual aids assist with recall.

In another study, researchers asked people to examine a group of photographs and identify those that were repeated. From a group of as many as 200 photographs, people could still pick out the repeat photographs.[2] However, when their recall was tested by listening to groups of numbers, people began to forget which numbers were repeated in groups of only six or seven numbers. Although common sense tells us that it is often more difficult to remember numbers, this study reinforces the finding of the one cited previously: Visual information greatly improves audience recall.

### Visual Aids Help Explain and Clarify Information

Research also suggests that visual aids can help you explain material and thus enhance the clarity of your information. Complex ideas and numbers can be hard to understand verbally but are much easier to sort out when displayed visually. Presenting an idea visually makes it more concrete. Visual aids such as handouts also increase the audience's continuity of thought, because people can go back and check their understanding.[3] So the third goal of your visual aids is to help you explain or clarify your ideas.

### Visual Aids May Increase Persuasiveness and Enhance Credibility

Research also suggests that visual aids may increase your persuasiveness and enhance your credibility.[4] Visual aids can help organize information, identify key points, and facilitate the reasoning process. In addition, images encourage audiences to make associations, so you can use both text and images to move your audiences toward a particular position.

Visual aids can also add to your credibility by bringing a visual dimension to your speech. Professional-looking and creative visual aids can energize your speech, making you appear more prepared, engaging, and lively. For example, a graph that displays a trend in people's attitudes is an excellent way to display the evidence you're using to back up a claim.

### Visual Aids May Reduce Nervousness

In addition to enhancing the content of your speech, visual aids may help reduce your nervousness in a number of ways.[5] When you prepare effective visual aids, you pay more attention to the effectiveness of your speech's organization. Being better organized increases your confidence that your ideas are logical and carefully planned. Visual aids can also direct audience attention away from you and give you something to

## SPEECH **TIPS**

### CONTENT OF VISUAL AIDS

Review the specific purpose, main points, and supporting evidence in the subpoints of your speech. Consider what visual aids could help you clarify them, help your audience remember your message, and enhance your credibility.

focus on other than your nervousness. Additionally, visual aids give you something to do with your hands, which can help you relax in front of your audience. For example, in her speech on fitness, Jemma used a fit ball (a large rubber ball used to stretch and strengthen muscles) as a visual aid. Jemma found that as she demonstrated how to use the ball, her attention was focused on explaining her ideas rather than on her nervousness. Not only was she more relaxed, but the audience learned a great deal from her demonstrations.

## What to Show on a Visual Aid

The purposes of visual aids are to clarify, enhance, and illustrate your ideas and make your key points more memorable. You can use visual aids that are based on text (lists), diagrams (charts and graphs), or images (drawings, photographs, and maps).

### Lists

A **list** is a series of words or phrases that organize ideas one after the other. Lists are text-based visual aids, meaning that they rely on the written word rather than on images to convey meaning.

Use lists when your material lends itself to itemizing a group or a series, such as names, key features, or procedures. Lists help audiences keep track of material and identify the main points of a speech or discussion. The types of visual media best suited to lists are chalkboards and white boards, flip charts, poster boards, and PowerPoint and other computer-generated presentations (see Chapter 20 for details about each type of visual media mentioned in this chapter).

When you use lists, consider the following guidelines.

***Make your list brief and balanced.*** A list is a synopsis, so keep your lists brief. Use keywords or phrases rather than full sentences. Your goal is to clarify information and help your audience members remember it, not to have them read every word of your speech. Here are some examples showing how to shorten sentences to words or phrases:

| Incorrect | Correct |
|---|---|
| Visual aids help audiences recall more information. | Recall |
| Visual aids help explain and clarify information. | Explain |
| Visual aids can enhance a speaker's persuasiveness. | Persuade |
| Visual aids can enhance a speaker's credibility. | Enhance credibility |
| Visual aids can reduce a speaker's nervousness. | Reduce nervousness |

Audiences recall lists best if the items are parallel (Chapter 10). As you develop your lists, try to find balance or symmetry in the wording.

## SPEECH TIPS

### LISTS IN VISUAL AIDS

Follow the six-word/six-line rule: Use no more than six words per line and no more than six items per list.[6]

For example, in a list of tips for using objects as visual aids, here's how you could balance your wording:

| **Incorrect** | **Correct** |
|---|---|
| Use objects that illustrate or clarify. | Illustrate or clarify |
| Illegal and threatening objects may harm or frighten your audience. | Legal and nonthreatening |

Remember, you goal is to cue your audience visually, not to overload them with text.

***Include a heading.*** Put a heading in boldface type at the top of lists. Because your audience can't go back to the words you spoke earlier in your speech, help them with recall by naming each list you use.[7] Here's an example:

**The Importance of Visual Aids**

- Recall
- Explain
- Persuade
- Enhance credibility
- Reduce nervousness

### Charts

Charts show steps in a process or parts of a concept. They can help speakers illustrate the relationship between the steps or parts and how each relates to the whole process or concept.

The two most common charts used as visual aids are the flow chart and the organizational chart. A **flow chart** illustrates direction or motion—for example, the unfolding of a process or the steps to a goal. An **organizational chart** illustrates the structure of groups, such as organizations, businesses, or departments.

Use a chart as a visual aid when you want to represent the parts of a whole or to simplify a complex process. Because charts are usually drawn in advance, the types of visual media best suited to them are handouts, poster boards, and PowerPoint and other computer-generated presentations.

If you select a chart as your visual aid, consider the following guidelines.

***Emphasize the visual image.*** When you create a chart, make the visual element primary and the text secondary. Use single words or short labels for titles and positions, and as few words as possible to describe the steps of a process. You want your audience to visualize a process or the parts of a whole quickly and clearly, so keep it simple. For example, in Figure 19.1, a flow chart, each row of boxes indicates a separate phase of a fire department's response to an emergency—before and after a rescue crew arrives on the scene. Figure 19.2 an organizational chart, depicts a loose pyramid that places the head of a fire department's operations unit (the fire chief) at the top of the chart. Each layer of the pyramid reveals the level of each employee's supervisory responsibility. Those with the highest levels of responsibility appear at the top layers and those with the least in the bottom layers.

***Use lines, arrows, shading, and color to show relationships and direction.*** Use lines, arrows, shading, and color to help the audience follow your points as you explain the steps in a process or the structure of an organization. For example, in Figure 19.1, the yellow boxes show the beginning and the end of a fire department's response to an emergency, the green boxes indicate each step of the response process, and the arrows indicate the progression of the steps from beginning to end.

## Graphs

When you want to compare numbers, quantities, or statistics, graphs are excellent visual aids. A **graph** is a visual comparison of amounts or quantities. Graphs help audiences see growth, size, proportions, or relationships.

**FIGURE 19.1 Flow chart**

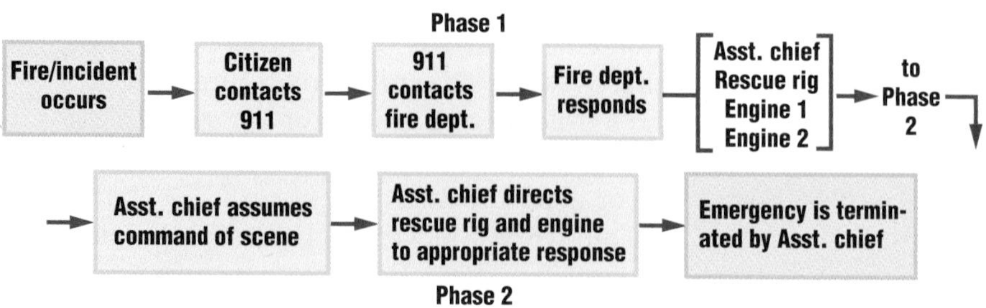


**Source:** Cengage Learning

**FIGURE 19.2 Organizational chart**

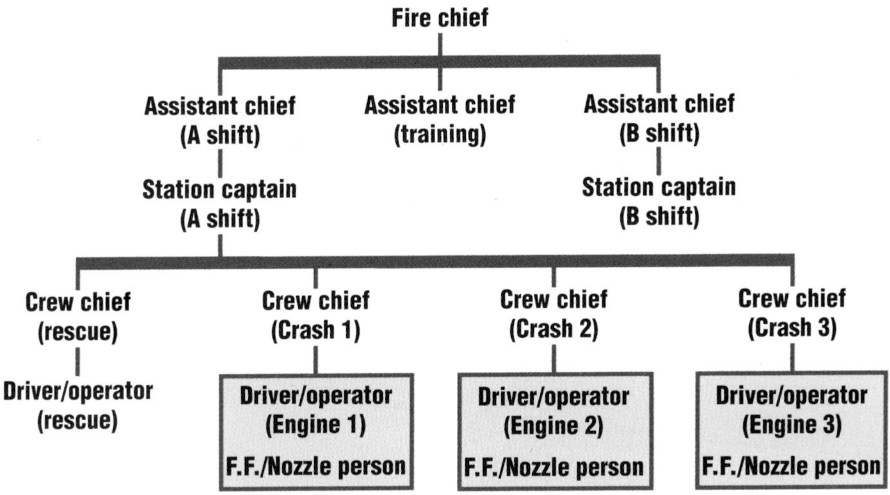


**Source:** Cengage Learning

You can use different kinds of graphs for different purposes:

- **Bar graphs** compare quantities at a specific moment in time.
- **Line graphs** show trends over time.
- **Pie graphs** show the relative proportions of parts of a whole.
- **Picture graphs** present information in pictures or images.

Figures 19.3, 19.4, 19.5, and 19.6 on pages 318 and 319 show how data from the U.S. Census of 2000 could be represented using different graphs.

Like charts, graphs are most effective when prepared in advance and used for handouts, poster boards, flip charts, and PowerPoint or other computer-generated presentations. When you decide to display figures in a chart, consider the following guidelines.

***Use clear and consistent labels.*** Use descriptive headings for graphs that contain horizontal and vertical axes—for example, "Year" and "Percentage." For line graphs, mark equal intervals in the graph's grid—for example, numbers by tens, hundreds, or thousands and dates by decades or centuries. Show the numbers of those intervals on the horizontal and vertical axes. This is illustrated in Figure 19.4, where the vertical axis indicates 1997 dollars earned in intervals of $4,000. The horizontal axis indicates time in intervals of ten years.

***Use a computer to design your graph.*** A computer can help you represent amounts, relationships, and proportions cleanly and precisely, drawing images to scale and marking points on a graph clearly. Using software such as Microsoft Graph or Microsoft Excel (or an equivalent), simply enter the numbers and labels into the program's

**FIGURE 19.3** Bar graph

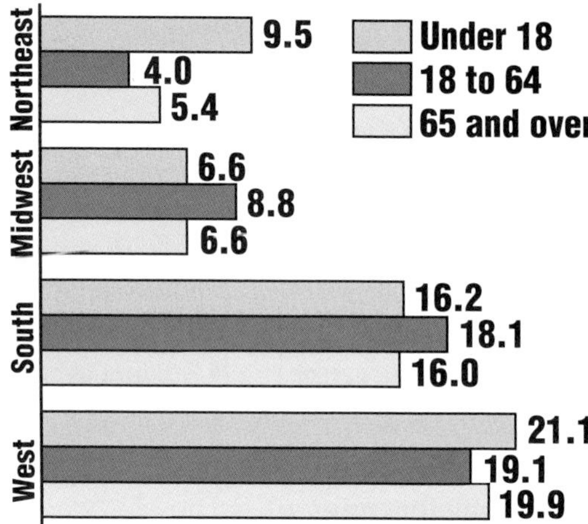


**Source:** U.S. Census Bureau, Population Division, Fertility and Family Statistics Branch. Maintained by Laura K. Yax (Population Division).

**FIGURE 19.4** Line graph

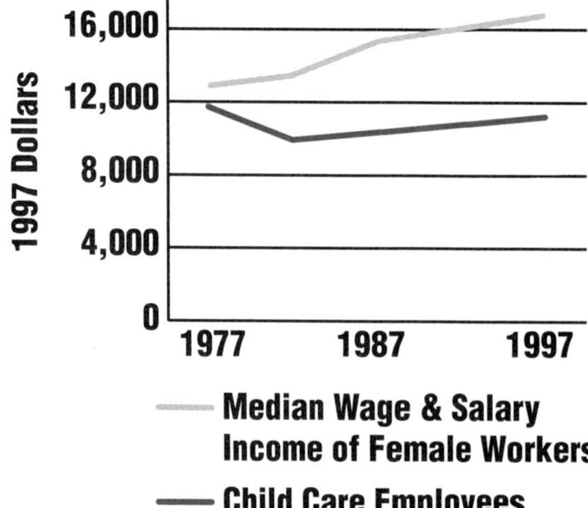


**Source:** U.S. Census Bureau 2000 Summary File 1; 1990 Census of Population, *General Population Characteristics, United States* (1990 CP-1-1).

**FIGURE 19.5** Pie graph

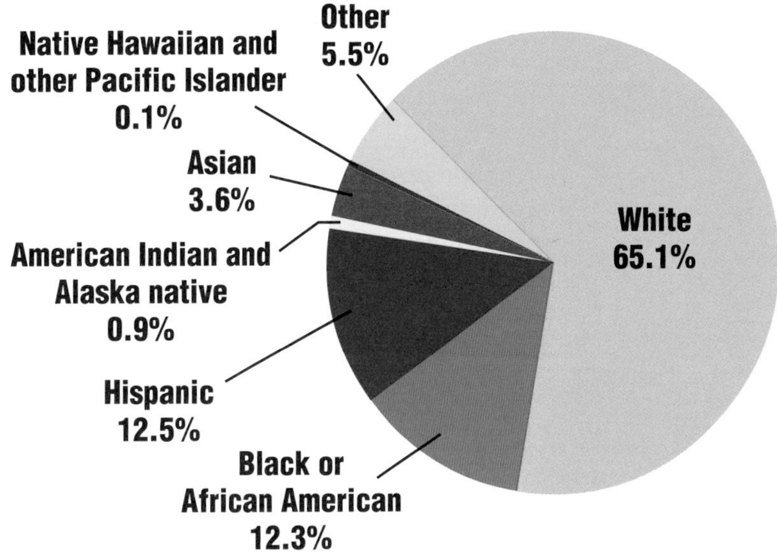


**Source:** U.S. Census Bureau, Census 2000.

**FIGURE 19.6** Picture graph

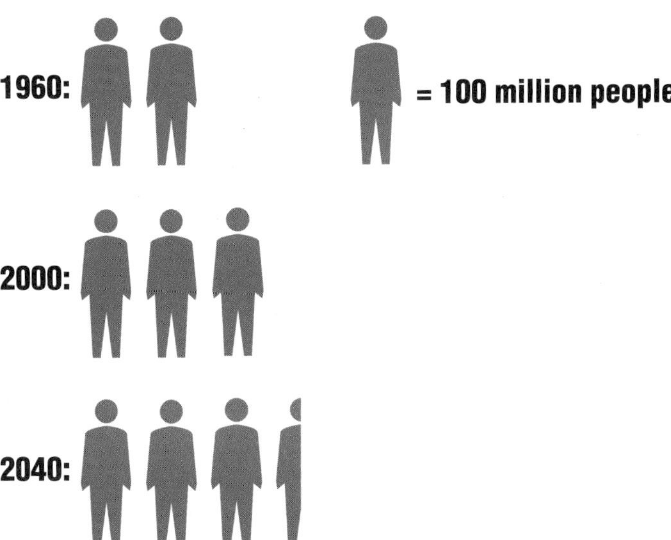


**Source:** U.S. Census Bureau, Census 2000.

data table and select the graph type you want to depict. You can even experiment with different kinds of graphs and how they display your information.

## Drawings

**Drawings** are diagrams and sketches of someone or something. They add clarity to your presentation because they help you show your audience what something looks like. You can create your own drawings, select them from computer or online resources (where they are often called *clip art*), or copy them from books, magazines, and other sources.

The best visual media for drawings are handouts, flip charts, poster boards, and PowerPoint or other computer-projected presentations. Simple drawings can also be rendered on a chalkboard or a white board. If you decide to use drawings in your speech, consider the following guidelines.

***Simple is best.*** According to many graphic arts texts, people seem to remember the outline of an image more than its details.[8] These texts advise you to keep your drawings simple. Use line drawings, symbolic representations rather than realistic drawings, simple clip art, and even children's art. When Cory gave a speech about the process of knitting a wool sweater, she used simple line drawings to illustrate how the wool from a sheep is processed into yarn. Remember, your goal is to represent your verbal message visually and not to use or create a great work of art (Figure 19.7).

***Make sure the drawing clarifies the verbal message.*** Although drawings can be used to set the tone or communicate emotion, more often you will use them to explain your ideas and articulate your message clearly. Use drawings to depict shapes (for example, animals, buildings, symbols, and patterns) or to show details (what someone with dyslexia sees or acupressure points on the body).

**FIGURE 19.7 Simple line drawing**

**Source:** From www.straw.com/clipart. Used with permission.

## SPEECH TIPS

### DRAWINGS

Before you add a drawing to your speech, think about how it helps communicate your message. Does it clarify a concept? Does it illustrate something your audience may not have seen before? Does it simplify something that is complex? Be sure the drawing will enhance audience understanding.

***Use audience-centered humor.*** You can use cartoons and funny or unusual drawings to make a humorous statement. However, first consider whether some audience members might have a different reaction to a drawing you find humorous. Consider the master statuses, standpoints, attitudes, beliefs, and values (Chapter 6) of your audience members. Be certain a humorous drawing will be funny to everyone. Reject drawings you think might offend or insult members of your audience. (For more on the topic of humor in speeches, see Chapter 25.)

***Speaking across DIFFERENCES***

**Be careful about using humorous cartoons and drawings. What's funny to one person may offend another. Consider the master statuses, standpoints, attitudes, beliefs, and values of your audience members.**

### Photographs

Photographs help you show your audience exactly what something looks like or what really happened. They can also add color and drama to your speech. Photographs are most often shown on PowerPoint slides projected onto a screen or a monitor, but you can also use them as handouts.

Unless everyone in your audience can easily see them, you shouldn't display actual photographs while delivering your speech. If a photograph will help clarify your ideas or make your point and you will be able to show it to the entire audience, consider the following guidelines.

***Describe the photograph.*** To use a photograph successfully, you need to tell the audience what they are seeing. Call their attention to the relevant aspects of the photograph by describing them or explaining the action. Don't be tempted to let the image speak for itself. Make sure your audience knows why you are showing it. For example, when Demetrious used photographs to describe the five villages of the

Cinque Terre (Chapter 10), he pointed out the unique aspects of each village to help the audience distinguish them.

***Don't pass out photographs.*** Rather than passing out original photographs to your audience during your speech, copy them and distribute them as handouts before the speech. When you are ready to refer to a photograph, call the audience's attention to the handout (in Chapter 14, Kameron did this to illustrate a zebra mussel colony on a buoy).

Passing out individual photographs poses several problems: Original photographs are much more expensive than photocopies, especially if you are reproducing them for a large audience. Your audience will be distracted by them and by the process of passing them around the room. And by the time the last rows get the photographs, you will probably have moved on to a new point.

***Do not display photos in a book.*** It might seem time and cost efficient to stand in front of your audience and show them photos from books. However, images in books are too small to be seen by anyone but those sitting right in front of you.

Instead of showing the picture in the book, reproduce it on a handout or use it to create a PowerPoint slide and project it onto a screen or a monitor. Your audience will appreciate your effort to include everyone in the presentation, not just those in the front rows. If for some reason you cannot reproduce images from a particular book or you want to show the entire book as well as the images it contains, display the book after the speech so the audience can get close to the images and even talk with you about them.

## Maps

**Maps** are visual representations showing the physical layout of geographical features, cities, road systems, the night sky, and the like. Maps can help you show your audience the geographical characteristics of a place, its location in relation to other places, and the route between locations.

Use a map to show your audience physical details that are best understood when presented both verbally and visually. The best visual media for maps are poster boards, handouts, and PowerPoint and other computer-generated presentations. If you decide to incorporate a map into your speech, consider the following guidelines.

***Include the most important details.*** When you copy a map or draw one yourself, follow the design principle for drawings: Simple is best. Eliminate unnecessary details so the most important features will stand out. This will help the audience focus on your points and not get

**FIGURE 19.8 Map of the Cinque Terre region in Italy**

**Source:** Cengage Learning

distracted by unrelated details. Just as you would when you draw a map for a friend, give your audience only the key points or markers to help them find their way or understand the path they should follow.

Mark the parts of the map you want to emphasize, using clear identifying features such as arrows, circles, or color. If you are giving directions or explaining movement, such as the migration of birds, mark the path with numbers or arrows. You can do this beforehand, or you can draw on the map with a highlighter or marker as you talk. For example, in Demetrious's speech about the Cinque Terre region in Italy, he could have circled each village on the map as he described it to help the audience see where the villages of the region are in relation to one another (Figure 19.8).

***Draw your map to scale.*** Because maps help audiences understand relationships, draw the map to scale so the relative distances are accurate. Put your scale of measurement on a corner of your map so your audience can gauge the actual distances. For example, in drawing a map of a your overall neighborhood in relation to the city you live in, you could use the scale of 4 inches = 1 city block. This kind of scale is appropriate for a map that doesn't require precise measurements. If you want to illustrate specific geographical or astronomical features, use a published map.

**SPEECH Checklist**

### Forms for Different Kinds of Information

- ☐ For a group or series of names, key features, or procedures: *list*
- ☐ For steps in a process: *flow chart*
- ☐ For the structure of a group: *organizational chart*
- ☐ For comparison of quantities at a specific time: *bar graph*
- ☐ For trends over time: *line graph*
- ☐ For relative sizes of parts of a whole: *pie graph*
- ☐ For comparison of quantities: *picture graph*
- ☐ For a thing or process unfamiliar to your audience: *drawing* or *photograph*
- ☐ For the physical layout of a place: *map*

***If you hand out a map, show a larger visual aid of that same map.*** Use a PowerPoint slide or poster board as you explain a handout map to your audience. This way, you can point to or mark areas of the map rather than trying to describe them with words alone. This technique is especially useful when you want to point out several areas of a map and a handout would help your audience follow your discussion.

Skills & Confidence PPD Activity 19.1

***Speak to the audience, not to the map.*** As you describe your map, maintain eye contact with the audience rather than looking at the map. This can be challenging because we usually want to follow the map with our eyes as we describe it. To prevent this, keep your notes in front of you and refer to places on the map by the number or color you used to highlight them or by pointing briefly to the map and then returning to your notes.

## Guidelines for Effective and Ethical Use of Visual Aids

No doubt you will use many different types of visual aids during your speech class and over the course of your speaking career. A few guidelines are common to all of them:

- **Prepare in advance.** By giving yourself adequate time to prepare your visual aids, you will avoid rushing to complete them at the last minute and can create visual aids that you can be proud of.
- **Practice in advance.** Practicing delivering your speech with your visual aids helps ensure that they will fit smoothly into your presentation. Practicing also lets you revise the visuals or change their order if necessary. Practice will also make it easier for you to maintain eye contact with the audience while you are presenting your visual aids.
- **Use your visual aids only when you discuss them.** When you're through discussing the point that relates to your visual aid, remove it from the audience's attention. This will help shift the audience's focus back to you and your next point.
- **Explain what is shown on each visual aid.** Take the time to explain each visual aid fully. Audiences will appreciate having an explanation and enough time to understand the relationship between your visual aid and your point.
- **Speak to the audience, not to the visual aid.** Because audiences look at visual aids briefly before turning back to the speaker, you want to be ready for them when their eyes return to you. By practicing your speech with your visual aids, you will be better prepared to return eye contact.

Another important consideration is the ethical use of visual aids. The goal of your visual aids is to clarify or illustrate your points so your audience will better understand them. The following guidelines will help ensure that your visual aids are appropriate for your speech and for your audience.

> ***Speaking across DIFFERENCES***
>
> **Using visual and audio media ethically will enhance your credibility and help you avoid alienating audience members.**

- **Avoid visual aids that might shock, disgust, or offend your audience,** particularly within the classroom. Sometimes, it may be tempting to jolt your audience with an extreme image or sound to gain their attention or make a point, but be careful not to jolt them too much.
- **Consider your audience's master statuses** when choosing your visual aids. Adapt your visual aids to your audience's needs as well as your speech goal.
- **Avoid misleading your audience.** Make sure your visual aids are accurate and do not distort or exaggerate your claims.

# PREPARATION OUTLINE

**with Commentary**

## *The Dun Dun Drum*

*by Joshua Valentine*

CENGAGE LEARNING

***Specific purpose:*** *To inform my audience about how and why the dun dun drum is used.*

***Thesis statement:*** *The dun dun is an African drum with an interesting history that is used both musically and linguistically.*

**Skills & Confidence**
Video Activity 19.1
Speech Studio 19.1

This informative speech makes good use of photographs and audio to illustrate and clarify points. Use your Premium Website for *Invitation to Public Speaking Handbook* to watch a video of Josh Valentine giving this speech and see his transcript and speaking outline. Josh gave this speech in an introductory public speaking class. The assignment was to give a four- to six-minute speech with visual aids. Students were also asked to create a preparation outline that indicated where in the speech the visual aids were to be displayed, that cited the sources of the visual aids, and that included a Works Cited section.

*Commentary*
*Josh, a drummer, takes his topic from his interest in music. He catches his audience's attention by asking them to imagine using a musical instrument to communicate language, something people in the United States don't typically do.*

*In the second main point of his introduction, he introduces his topic. He adapts his topic to his audience by using a familiar source, Webster's Dictionary,*

*INTRODUCTION*

I. Imagine that your friend asks you what you did over the weekend, but instead of using words, your friend beats a drum. *(catch attention)*

II. You will probably never have such an encounter, but in some cultures, music is used for purposes that are different from those we are accustomed to. *(reveal topic)*
   A. *Webster's Dictionary* defines language as "any system of symbols, sounds, or gestures used for communication."
   B. Our culture does not have instrumental sounds that represent English words, but in other cultures around the world, sounds have meaning.

III. I have been playing percussion since junior high, and I first learned about the dun dun while attending a percussion workshop two years ago. *(establish credibility)*

IV. Today, I will explain the history of the dun dun as well as its linguistic use and its musical use. *(reveal thesis statement and preview main points)*

*to define language, and then he explains that although Americans don't use music as language, other cultures do.*

*He establishes his credibility by indicating that he is a musician and that he learned about his topic in a percussion workshop.*

*The last point of his introduction previews the two main points of his speech.*

*BODY*

I. The Nigerian talking drum, dun dun (pronounced *doon doon*), actually does talk, in the Yoruba language. *[Display photograph of dun dun drum downloaded and used with permission from http://media.dickinson.edu/gallery/Sect5.html.]*

   A. The dun dun originated during the Oyo Empire of Yorubaland in the fifteenth century A.D. for the purposes of worship.

   B. Drums are constructed from trees located near roads where many people pass, which allows the tree to hear human speech.

   C. The Yoruba language is easily communicated on the dun dun.

      1. Yoruba is a tonal language.

      2. Yoruba speakers use three basic pitches or tones, connected by glides, as an essential element of pronunciation.

         a. Listen to this sound clip and try to identify the three main tones. *[Play a sound clip downloaded for one-time use from the Internet.]*

         b. If you have a sharp ear, you may also be able to pick out some glides essential to the Yoruba language.

      3. Melody is the basis for the Yoruba language since the same word pronounced with a different melody means something different.

*Because his audience is unfamiliar with his topic, Josh uses his first main point to explain what the dun dun drum is, where it originated, and what it is used for.*

*By showing photos and playing audio clips of dun dun drums, Josh helps his audience better understand his topic. In particular, the audio clips let the audience hear what is complicated to explain in words alone.*

*He kept a careful record of where he obtained his visual and audio aids so he could cite his sources accurately in his speech. Note that he downloaded copyrighted material according to the terms of use posted by the websites he accessed—he requested permission or agreed to use the material only for his speech in class.*

*The visual aid Josh used for subpoint D of his first main point clarifies how the drum works.*

D. The dun dun functions by changing the tension of two skin heads using the leather straps that hold the heads in place. *[Point out the straps on the PowerPoint slide.]*

*In his second main point, Josh explains how the drum is used to communicate. He continues to use visual and audio aids to enhance and clarify the information in his speech.*

II. The dun dun was originally created to communicate.

A. The Yoruba from southwestern Nigeria have used drums for spiritual communication throughout their history. *[Show photo of carved drum downloaded from www.hamillgallery.com...YorubaDrum01.html.]*

1. The dun dun was originally created as a tool for worship of the gods.
2. Songs and hymns of praise were created entirely on dun dun drums and are still recited today.
3. Listen to the intensity of this spiritual worship song played on talking drums. *[Play example downloaded for one-time use from http://www.world-beats.com/instruments/dundun.htm.]*

*In subpoint B, he provides details that his audience can relate to: "saying hi," "cracking jokes," "telling stories." Notice that he cites his sources simply but effectively.*

*Here Josh uses a specific example to explain how the Yoruba "talk" with the dun dun drum.*

B. The Yoruba also used drums for social communication.

1. The dun dun has been part of day-to-day casual conversation.
   a. According to the World Beats website, "A master drummer can maintain a regular monologue on a talking drum, saying hi to different people, cracking jokes, and telling stories."
   b. Dun dun drummers are often heard speaking the names of friends and family on their drums as a greeting and sign of respect.

C. The dun dun's secondary, yet most obvious, use is as a musical instrument.

1. It became a musical instrument because of its use in worship.

a. At first it was used mainly to communicate ideas, but since worship in the Yoruba culture is a corporate activity, people began coming together and music on the dun dun was born.

*In subpoint C, he adapts to his audience by explaining how the dun dun drum is used as a musical instrument, in a way that is familiar to people in the United States.*

b. Religious songs are still recited today, although often only for their musical value.

2. Even everyday speech becomes song when the Yoruba use the dun dun.
   a. According to the website Drum Talk, the word *kabo*, which means "welcome," is only a two-syllable word, so a more common phrase "spoken" on a dun dun is, "Welcome, we are happy that you arrived safely."
   b. "Speech" on the dun dun is always made rhythmic, even when the spoken word would not be rhythmic.
3. The dun dun's use as a musical instrument has spread far beyond Nigeria.
   a. Next to the *djembe*, the dun dun is the most well-known and recognizable African drum used in America.
   b. According to African American musician Francis Awe's drum clinic, "[It] fares well in jazz, blues, R&B, rock and roll, reggae, classical music, even choral music."
   c. This clip comes from a song by Francis Awe. *[Play sample clip downloaded from http://www.nitade.com/html/cd1.html.]*

*Josh ends the body of his speech with an audio clip that reinforces his final sub-subpoint, that the dun dun drum is now an international instrument.*

*CONCLUSION*

I. Whether in language or song, the dun dun's sound is always unusually beautiful. *(bring speech to an end)*

*Josh uses his conclusion to reinforce that the drum is used for both language and music. He then summarizes his main points.*

*He ends his speech with an intriguing statement that encourages his audience to remember what he's told them about a particular African drum*

II. Today we have seen the origins of the Nigerian talking drum (dun dun), its uses as a linguistic tool, and its uses as a musical instrument. *(reinforce thesis and summarize main points)*

III. So next time you hear music as simple as a beating drum, you might remember that the drummer may be communicating much more than you think.

**Works Cited**

Awe, Francis. (1999.) *Talking drum clinic by Francis Awe.* Retrieved March 20, 2007, from http://www.after-science.com/awe/clinic.html

BataDrum.com. (2002.) How bata drums talk and what they say. In *Understanding the purpose and meaning behind the rhythms.* Retrieved March 21, 2007, from http://www.batadrums.com/understanding_rhythms/talk.htm

DeSilva, Tamara. (1997.) Lying at the crossroads of everything: Towards a social history of the African drum. *Research, Writing, and Culture: The Best Undergraduate Thesis Essays, 1998–2000, 2.* Retrieved March 20, 2007, from http://www.artic.edu/saic/programs/depts/undergrad/Best_Thesis_Essay.pdf

Drum Talk Ltd. (2000.) *Background information.* Retrieved March 20, 2007, from http://www.drumtalk.co.uk/drum_background.html

Plunkett, A. (2002.) Nigeria (Africa) dun dun. *World Beats.* Retrieved March 21, 2007, from http://www.world-beats.com/instruments/dundun.htm

CHAPTER 20

# Visual Aids: Types and Formats



***In this chapter, you will learn to***

**Identify and describe different types of visual aids**

**Format visual aids effectively**

As Chapter 19 explained, visual aids have five purposes: to gain and maintain audience attention, aid audience recall of information, help you explain and clarify information, increase your persuasiveness and enhance your credibility, and aid your preparation and thereby reduce your nervousness. This chapter offers specific guidelines for a variety of visual and presentational aids:

- Objects, models, and demonstrations
- Handouts

- Chalkboards and white boards
- Poster boards and flip charts
- Overhead projectors
- Photographic slides
- Videotapes and audiotapes
- PowerPoint and other computer-generated presentations

When using keywords and phrases, charts, graphs, drawings, photographs, and maps on visual aids, pay careful attention to their formatting—font styles and sizes, color, and visual balance. This chapter explains basic design principles that will help you create audience-centered visual aids.

## Types of Visual Aids

There are various kinds of visual aids you may be required or choose to use. Every type of visual aid has different strengths and weaknesses, so don't settle on any one kind before you've decided what you want to accomplish with the visual aspect of your speech. Here we'll look at the most common visual and presentational aids for speeches. We also include two types of visual aid technology that are somewhat outdated but still used at times: slide projectors and overhead projectors.

### Objects, Models, and Demonstrations

An **object** is something that can be seen or touched, and a **model** is a copy of an object, usually built to scale, that represents that object in detail. Objects and models can help your audience understand certain ideas because they present the ideas visually.

If an object is impractical or impossible to bring to a speaking situation, a model can be ideal. A model can be smaller than the objects it represents (a model of a car engine), larger (a model of the mechanics of a wristwatch), or life size (a model of a human brain).

Displaying an object or a model can engage an audience immediately, and many speeches lend themselves to this type of visual aid. For example, several of the speakers in Chapter 10 displayed objects. Cindy displayed a flag in her speech on flag etiquette, Candice showed a scrapbook, and Martha displayed different batik patterns.

These speakers also used their objects to demonstrate a process. A **demonstration** is a display of how something is done or how it works. Cindy used her flag to demonstrate the process of folding a flag. Candice showed a scrapbook she'd created to demonstrate how to compile a scrapbook. Martha displayed various batik styles as she described how batik is produced. With the objects and the demonstrations, these speakers illustrated and clarified their topics and captured their audiences' attention.

When you display an object or a model or demonstrate a process, consider the following guidelines.

*Make sure your visual aids and demonstrations enhance understanding.* Some objects or models may be intriguing, but they might not enhance your speech. For example, when Lee gave a speech on the Vietnam Veterans Memorial, his only visual aid was a T-shirt he had purchased when he visited the memorial. Although the shirt was attractive, it did not help him clarify a point or illustrate the power of the memorial to evoke emotions. Lee would have been better off using an object (a replica of the item he left at the memorial, for example) to help him illustrate the power of the memorial on those who visit it.

Also try to avoid demonstrations that are too complex, require a lot of equipment, or might make you look awkward or unprofessional. If your process is complex, simplify it for your demonstration or show only a part of the process. When Brock gave his speech on emergency rescue services, he wanted to talk about the equipment used and the knowledge needed by rescue workers to use the equipment properly. To demonstrate some of the more complex knots rescue workers use, Brock brought in ropes with knots already begun. He finished tying the knots for his audience, demonstrating their strength as well as their complexity. Rather than make his audience sit through the entire process, he had a part of it prepared and set up before he began his speech.

*Choose objects that are legal and nonthreatening.* Avoid displaying weapons, chemicals, drugs, or animals—objects that may be interesting but can be illegal, dangerous, or difficult to handle. Although you may know how to handle these items outside a speech situation, you can't always predict what an animal, a dangerous substance, or other people will do during the speech. If you're not sure whether an object is appropriate for a classroom speech, check with your instructor.

## SPEECH **TIPS**

### DEMONSTRATING A PROCESS

To decide whether an entire process is too long or complex to demonstrate, compare the length of time for your speech and the amount of time the demonstration is likely to take.

**SPEECH Checklist**

## Showing an Object or Demonstrating a Process

- ☐ Show an object or demonstrate a process only if it helps to make a point in your speech.
- ☐ If you are speaking about an object or process unfamiliar to your audience, show it to your audience if at all possible.
- ☐ Use a model if the object cannot be easily brought to the classroom or auditorium.
- ☐ If the process you want to demonstrate is complex, simplify it or show only part of it.
- ☐ If you are not sure whether an object is appropriate for a classroom speech, ask your instructor.
- ☐ Before your speech, practice your demonstration or showing the object.

*Practice your demonstration before your speech.* Don't leave anything to chance with a demonstration. Rehearse it several times before the speech to be sure your equipment works correctly, your steps are smooth and effective, and your words explain what you are showing the audience. For example, for his speech on martial arts, Oscar practiced his demonstration in a small space so he knew he could show his audience his martial arts moves without hurting someone or knocking things over. He also practiced when and how he would speak as he demonstrated various moves.

### Handouts

**Speaking at Work**

*Speakers in the workplace often use handouts as visual aids because handouts are easy to distribute, are portable, and can include detailed information that audience members can refer to after a speech.*

Business speakers often use handouts as visual aids. Examples include bound copies of business plans or year-end summaries; agency or product brochures; maps and photographs; and photocopies of graphs, charts, or articles.

Handouts provide detailed information that the audience can refer to during a speech or read later and pass along to others. Handouts can elaborate on your message and help you spread it beyond your immediate audience.

Before you decide to use a handout, check with your instructor to see if you're allowed to use them in your course. If you can use handouts, consider the following guidelines.

*Mark the points you want to emphasize.* One of the problems with handouts is that the audience sometimes has trouble finding the point you want them to focus on. To prevent this confusion, mark the points you want the audience to locate. Use letters or symbols or a more visual device such as color-coded plastic tabs. For example, if you want your audience to pay attention to one area on a graph or map, identify it with an arrow, symbol, or number. If you want them to turn to specific pages in a report, place tabs on those pages.

Another way to help your audience locate specific spots in handouts is to show the page, chart, or map in a PowerPoint slide. Highlight the information or areas you will refer to, and direct the audience's attention to those places as you speak.

If you find an interesting image in a book or a magazine or on a website, do not simply photocopy the entire page and use that as your handout. Rather, isolate the image on a blank piece of paper or transfer it to a transparency or a PowerPoint slide. Showing only the image will help you focus your audience's attention and prevent them from getting distracted by extraneous information.

*Distribute the handout before or after a meeting.* To avoid the disruption of passing out material during your speech, distribute your

**SPEECH Checklist** ✓

## Using a Handout

- ☐ Check with your instructor if you're allowed to use handouts in your course.
- ☐ Use handouts especially for information you want your audience to refer to later and even pass on to others.
- ☐ Help the audience locate the relevant information in the handout by showing it on a computer-generated slide and highlighting the key points. Or highlight the information in the handout itself.
- ☐ Do not distribute a handout in the middle of your speech. Give it to your audience before or after.
- ☐ Do not read your handout to the audience. Just outline its key points in your speaking notes and refer to them.

handout, facedown, before your speech starts or the meeting begins. This helps ensure that your audience will listen to your speech rather than read your handout. Alternatively, distribute a handout after you've finished speaking if your speech includes information you'd like your audience to take away with them.

*Remember that the handout supplements the message.* A handout should add information to your speech and not become its text. Do not read lengthy passages from the handout aloud. Just refer to key points in it during your speech so your audience will be sure to note them when they read the handout after your speech.

To avoid depending on the handout too much, outline its key points in your notes. To keep your delivery extemporaneous, refer to your outline rather than to the handout itself.

## Chalkboards and White Boards

Available in many offices and classrooms, chalkboards and white boards are very convenient. They allow you to create a visual aid as you speak, clarify concepts during your speech, or keep track of ideas generated during discussions.

Although you'll want to prepare your visual aids before most speeches, a chalkboard or white board may come in handy when you need to respond immediately to audience confusion or questions. They also help you keep information in front of the audience rather than having to remove it to make space for new information. With some high-tech boards such as SMART Board, you can even duplicate what you write on them and make a handout for the audience at the end of your speech.[1] Used in these ways, chalkboards and white boards can help you stay audience centered throughout your speech.

If you use a chalkboard or white board during a speech, consider the following guidelines.

*Write neatly and legibly.* What you write on the board is not likely to be as neat as it would be on a prepared visual aid. It also hasn't been proofread for errors in spelling and grammar. So take care to write clearly, use a systematic organizational framework (such as an outline), and watch for spelling errors.

*Speak to the audience, not to the board.* We sometimes talk while we are writing on the board because we're trying to stay within our time limit and because we're involved in the speech and want to keep the momentum going. However, this means our back is to the audience while we're talking. To avoid this problem, stop speaking when you turn to the board to write. When you've finished writing, turn back to the audience and begin talking again. Although this pause may feel

**SPEECH Checklist ✓**

### Using a Chalkboard or a White Board

- ☐ Because you create these visual aids as you speak, they are best suited to clarifying concepts during your speech and keeping track of ideas generated during audience discussions.
- ☐ Take extra care to write neatly and legibly and watch for spelling errors.
- ☐ Stop talking when you turn your back to the audience to write on the board.

awkward the first few times, your audience will appreciate the care you take to speak to them directly.

### Poster Boards and Flip Charts

Poster boards and flip charts are a good choice for speeches you will deliver more than once (such as sales presentations) because they are durable and can be reused. If you want, you can write or draw your information lightly in pencil beforehand and then trace over your words and images as you speak, creating the visual as you go but ensuring neatness and correct spelling. In addition, you can use flip charts like chalkboards and white boards to record information during your speech, which is convenient for speaking in groups when brainstorming is a part of your process.

Because of their size (about twenty-four by thirty-six inches), poster boards and flip charts are not suitable for large audiences. Use them for small groups where everyone will be sitting near enough to read them. If you use a poster board or flip chart as a visual aid, consider the following guidelines.

*Make the design as professional as possible.* Take time to display your ideas neatly and professionally. Think carefully about what you want to include on the poster board or flip chart. Use color and images to attract interest and attention. Use rulers and guides to ensure straight lines for words and sentences. Print neatly and clearly. If your writing isn't suitable, find someone who can do the lettering for you, or use stencils or stick-on letters for a professional look. If you will be using the poster board or flip chart again and again, consider having it professionally designed and printed.

*Plan for and practice using your poster board or flip chart.* Before your speech, make sure you will have an easel or stand on which to place the poster board or flip chart. If you plan to hang your visual aids, bring pins or tape with you and think ahead about where you will display the poster board or flip chart so everyone can see it.

Avoid placing poster boards on the chalk tray of a chalkboard or white board. The poster boards tend to fall over, and because the chalk trays are usually behind you, you may block the audience's view of your posters.

Practice flipping the pages of your flip chart so you do not tear them or tip the stand over during your speech. Finally, think about where you will put poster boards when you've finished discussing them.

*Speak to the audience, not to the poster board or flip chart.* As with chalkboards or white boards, you may sometimes find yourself speaking to the poster board or flip chart rather than to the audience. To avoid this problem, practice your speech with the visual aid so you are able to glance at or point to it but talk to the audience. The students speaking on affordable housing (Chapter 13) not only prepared visual aids that looked professional, but they also worked in teams, with one student pointing to the visual aids while a second student explained the significance of the numbers, and they practiced using the poster boards so they were speaking to their audience rather than to the visual aid.

**SPEECH Checklist**

## Using Poster Boards or a Flip Chart

- ☐ These visual aids can be prepared beforehand, and you can also use them to record information during your speech.
- ☐ Do not use poster boards or flip charts for large audiences. They are too small for a large group to see.
- ☐ Plan in detail what you want on the poster boards or flip chart before you start writing.
- ☐ Before your speech, make sure there will be an easel or stand for the poster boards or flip chart.
- ☐ Practice flipping the pages of your flip chart so you do not tear them or tip the stand over.
- ☐ Practice speaking to the audience and only glancing at the poster board or flip chart.

### Overhead Projectors

Although some may think overhead projectors are old-fashioned, they continue to be used in many speech settings, including college classrooms. They are an excellent choice for incorporating visual aids into a speech because they require little technological expertise, you can move or reposition them easily, and the transparencies are inexpensive and easy to prepare and store. Overhead projectors are appropriate for large audiences because they display material on a screen or a wall so everyone can see it clearly. Overhead projectors have other advantages, too. Unlike chalkboards, white boards, poster boards, and flip charts, you can work with an overhead projector and transparencies without having to turn your back to the audience. And unlike some of the more sophisticated visual aid technology, less can go wrong with an overhead projector.

If you use an overhead projector, consider the following guidelines.

*Prepare your transparencies in advance.* Use a copy machine, printer, or professional copy service to prepare your transparencies. Design your visual message to enhance (not replace) your verbal message. For example, in her speech about locating stars in the night sky, Courtney used transparencies to add to her descriptions and show her audience how to identify the various constellations.

Proofread your transparencies for spelling and punctuation errors. Check for clarity of font and font size (see page 345). Check for consistency from transparency to transparency. For example, number your points consecutively or outline your points using the standard format for outlines.

*Check your equipment in advance.* Before your speech, turn on the overhead projector, position it where you want it, and adjust the focus. Then turn off the machine until you are ready to use it. This gives you a chance to troubleshoot before the speech, replacing light bulbs or cleaning dust from the machine.

Also note that most projectors run a fan to keep the projector from overheating; be sure to adjust your speaking volume as needed so your audience can hear you over any noise made by the fan.

*Speak to the audience, not to the overhead projector or screen.* When you use an overhead projector, your audience may be looking at the screen behind you rather than directly at you. You may be tempted to follow their gaze and turn around. Or you may be tempted to look down at the transparency rather than out at the audience. Keep your notes in front of you so you can speak from them rather than from the transparency or the material on the screen.

To prevent your audience or yourself from being distracted by the transparency, turn off the projector or remove or cover the transparency when you are finished discussing it.

### Photographic Slides

With the growing popularity of digital cameras, photographic slides and slide projectors are becoming obsolete. It can be difficult to find slide film and photo processors who will develop it, and in 2004, Kodak stopped manufacturing slide projectors. However, slides and slide projectors are still used occasionally. For example, photographic slides were popular in the 1960s and 1970s, and many families still have slides of family photos from that time. Today, you can buy stock slides of images (reproductions of fine art, for example), ask a professional to take photos for you and have them made into slides, or have slides made from your own photographs.

Photographic slides can be an excellent visual aid for large audiences because they allow you to display photographs that help you explain or reinforce a point. The biggest disadvantage of slides is that they require a darkened room, so be sure the room can be darkened, the audience does not need to take extensive notes, and you don't need to rely on your speaking outline or notes.

Slides take time to organize and you must practice to deliver effectively, so if you select this form of visual aid, consider the following guidelines.

*Prepare and organize your slides in advance.* Start preparing your slides early. Professional slides take time to produce, and you'll need time to take your own photographs and have them developed. In addition, you need time to organize and reorganize your images and possibly add new ones as you develop your speech, so that the sequence of slides will make sense to both you and your audience.

*Practice the wording of your descriptions.* Because your slides will help you tell a story, personalize an idea, describe a process, or illustrate an event, work out before your speech what you will say with each slide. This will help ensure a smooth delivery and help you remember when to advance to the next slide. Lots of practice will also give you confidence to laugh at the unexpected—like accidentally pressing the reverse button rather than the advance on the remote.

*Check the equipment.* Equipment failure is probably the most common problem for speakers using slides. Your slide carousel may not fit the projector, the projector bulb may have burned out, the remote control may be missing, or the plug may not reach the outlet without an extension cord. Many speakers (like Landon in Chapter 6) find they have to reload their slides into a different carousel moments before their speech or send people hurrying around to find a bulb or an extension cord. To avoid these last-minute stresses, check the equipment well before your speech so you have time to fix anything that isn't working. If you can, bring a replacement bulb and extension cord with you, and be sure the carousel in which you've assembled your slides fits the projector.

### Videotapes and Audiotapes

Videotapes and audiotapes allow you to support your speech with images and sounds of your topic. If your audience is unfamiliar with your topic, a videotape or audiotape can help bring it to life like no other presentational aid can. But if you rely too heavily on these visual aids, they can take over your presentation and diminish your own significance as a speaker.

If you decide to use a tape, consider the following guidelines.

*Keep your clip brief.* The longer your video or audio clip is, the less time you have to speak. For example, if you have five minutes for a speech, a one-minute video or audio clip would leave four minutes for your speech. After you subtract the time for your introduction and conclusion, you'll have less than three minutes to develop your main points. Consequently, the shorter your speech, the shorter your video or audio clip should be.

*Cue and edit your video or audio segment.* If you are using only one segment of a recording, cue up that segment before your speech. Then, when you deliver your speech, you only need to push "Play" to get the exact segment you want. If you are using more than one segment, make a master tape so that all of your clips are cued in the correct order on

**SPEECH Checklist**

#### Playing Videotapes and Audiotapes

- ☐ Try to use video and audio clips when your audience is unfamiliar with your topic.
- ☐ Video and audio clips should be no longer than necessary. They should not take over your speaking time.
- ☐ Cue or edit your video and audio clips. You do not want to spend time during the speech searching for the right segment.
- ☐ Do not talk during a video or audio clip.

a single tape, eliminating the need to switch tapes or find a segment by fast-forwarding. Or use the video feature on your home computer to create professional-quality clips, already cued and ready to go.

*Don't compete with your video or audio segment.* Avoid talking over a video or audio clip because this tends to distract audiences, who have to struggle to listen to both you and the clip.

### PowerPoint and Other Computer-Projected Presentations

**Speaking at Work**

*The use of PowerPoint and other computer-generated presentations is so widespread in the workplace that most audiences have come to expect speakers to include some sort of computer-generated presentation in almost every speech.*

Many speeches in the United States today, particularly those within the business world, include computer-generated presentations (commonly called *PowerPoint presentations* because of the popularity of the Microsoft program of the same name). This technology allows speakers to create slides containing text, diagrams, and images. The slides, in turn, can be arranged in any sequence, edited to include audio and video clips, printed on paper (to be used as handouts), and projected onto screens or monitors for viewing during presentations. This technology is excellent for large audiences but is also effective with small audiences.

**Skills & Confidence** Web Connect 20.1

Computer-generated presentations require the appropriate hardware and software, but if the technology is available, it can enhance your speech. However, as with all visual aids, you still need to think about what you want to display visually and the best format for that material. It may be tempting to use this technology because it has become so popular, but if it doesn't

**SPEECH TIPS**

**POWERPOINT**

Computer-generated presentations can be powerful, particularly when used to emphasize points and illustrate concepts that are difficult to describe in words. However, because this type of visual aid is so easy to create, it's easy to use it in a way that doesn't necessarily help you give a better speech.

help your audience understand and recall your message, there is no point using it in your speech.

When using computer-generated presentations, consider the following guidelines.

*Understand the purpose of a computer-generated visual aid.* Even though this technology offers a wide variety of design options (such as graphics, overlays, fadeouts, and sound), you don't need to use them all. Use only those that will help you focus, clarify, and organize your speech. Use this form of visual aid to enhance your message and build your arguments, not to impress your audience with the technology.

*Prepare and practice in advance.* As with any visual aid, take time to prepare your slides and the accompanying descriptions. Give yourself enough time to reorganize, add slides, and eliminate those that don't seem to contribute to your speech. Use your preparation time to decide which points (if any) lend themselves to fades, overlays, graphics, or sound. And don't forget to check for errors once you've designed your slides.

Practice using and describing your slides so your delivery is fluid and extemporaneous. Finally, familiarize yourself with the projection equipment prior to your speech so that you won't run into last-minute problems and can use the technology to its fullest.

**SPEECH Checklist ✓**

## Using PowerPoint or Other Computer-Projected Presentations

- ☐ Use this technology only if it will help your audience understand and remember your message.
- ☐ Do not be tempted to use all the available design options—such as fadeouts, graphics, and sound—unless they will help clarify your message and build your arguments.
- ☐ Give yourself time to prepare and edit your slides and to check for typos and errors.
- ☐ Practice using your slides so your delivery is extemporaneous. Do not read the slides to your audience.
- ☐ Before your speech, make sure you know how to use the projection equipment in the classroom or auditorium, and check that it is in working order.

## Formats for Visual Aids

Understanding a few basic design principles will help you develop professional-looking visual aids yourself or work with a graphic designer to create them. Don't underestimate the influence of these design principles. They have the power to enhance your visual aids and, by extension, your verbal message.

Note that if you decide to create visual aids with Microsoft PowerPoint, you have access to many templates that incorporate the ideas discussed in this section. However, some of these templates don't follow the formatting advice offered here and so can detract from your message. Be sure to review the templates provided by PowerPoint before you use them.

### Font Style and Size

A **font** is a type or style of print. Fonts range from simple to elaborate. As a rule, your text will be more readable if you choose a simple font over a fancy one. You will also need to choose between *serif fonts* and *sans serif fonts*. Serif fonts have small finishing flourishes at the ends of the strokes of the letters and so create a baseline for readers' eyes, leading them easily from letter to letter. (The font you're reading now is a serif font.) Most newspapers and books use serif fonts, and if your visual aid contains a lot of text, a serif font will be a good choice. To emphasize words, use a boldface version of your font to make the letters heavier and darker. Some common serif fonts are illustrated here, and you will find others on your computer.

| | |
|---|---|
| Times New Roman | **Times New Roman (bold)** |
| Bookman | **Bookman (bold)** |
| Palatino | **Palatino (bold)** |

Graphic artists suggest adding variety to your visual aids by using a contrasting font in your titles or headings. To do this, use a *sans serif font*, or a font without the finishing strokes at the ends of the letter strokes.[2] Because of their straight lines, sans serif fonts create a distinctive, crisp look. Thus, they tend to make titles or headings more prominent than the text that follows them in a serif font. Some common sans serif fonts are shown here, and you will find others on your own computer.

| | |
|---|---|
| Helvetica | **Helvetica (bold)** |
| Lucida Sans | **Lucida Sans (bold)** |
| Univers | **Univers (bold)** |

When you create your visual aids, avoid elaborate font styles, including shadow, embossed, engraved, and outline fonts. Although they look fun and interesting, they are more difficult to read and create extra work for your audience. Notice how your eyes have to slow down to identify each letter in the samples here:

| | |
|---|---|
| Mistral | CASTELLAR |
| Robotik | Handwriting |

**Font size** is the size of the letters measured in *points*. (A point is $\frac{1}{72}$ of an inch.) Guidelines for font size of headings, main points, and subpoints on visual aids are as follows:

| | |
|---|---|
| Headings: | 30- to 36-point font |
| Main points: | 24-point font |
| Subpoints: | 18-point font |

By using different font sizes, you help your audience tell the difference between main points and subpoints. Unless your audience will all be sitting close to the visual aid, don't use smaller fonts than these because they are hard to read from a distance. If people struggle to see your text, your ideas become difficult to follow. Note that in most classrooms, the first row of the audience is about two or three feet from the speaker, and it is farther if you are speaking, say, on a stage in an auditorium.

## SPEECH TIPS

### TEXT SIZE ON PROJECTED VISUAL AIDS

To test whether your audience will be able to read the text on a projected visual aid, view it from about fifteen feet away. If you have to strain to read it, you audience probably will too.

## Color

When you add color to your visual aids, you tap into design principles about the mood and meaning of colors and the combinations of colors for emphasis and legibility.

First, color helps an audience make associations. For example, soft tones tend to set a calm mood, whereas bright colors tend to set an exciting mood. In his speech about melanoma, Silas used Figure 20.1 when he discussed the dangers of spending too much unprotected time in the sun. The reds and oranges create an irritating, uncomfortable mood, implying the burning effects of the sun. He used Figure 20.2 with the same basic image, but with blues and greens to create a cooler, soothing mood implying shade and protection.

**Speaking across DIFFERENCES**

**The meanings of color vary across cultures. If your audience will include members from cultures other than your own, consider the cultural meanings of the colors you use in your visual aids.**

Note that the meanings of color, and the moods they evoke, vary across cultures. For example, in Western traditions, red can bring to mind anger or passion. But in China, red often symbolizes good fortune, and in ancient Mexico, red symbolized the sun and its awesome power.[3]

**FIGURE 20.1 Beach in hot colors**

**Source:** Cengage Learning

**FIGURE 20.2 Beach in cool colors**

**Source:** Cengage Learning

Second, different colors help your audience differentiate objects or items in a list. In addition, dark and light tones can show levels of importance, with the darkest being the most important. For example, Figure 20.3 on page 348 is a map that shows how intensely certain areas of Northern California are likely to shake during a major earthquake. The darker colors indicate more intense shaking, whereas the lighter colors indicate milder shaking.

To ensure that the words on a visual aid are legible, they should contrast with background color. But avoid combinations of colors that are hard to read, such as bright red on dark green or white on light beige. Also, be careful not to overwhelm your audience with too much color.

For effective use of color, follow these guidelines:

**Cool colors:** blue, purple, green. Cool colors are calm and relaxing for most people, and they tend to be easy on the eyes. Use no more than two of these colors per page. Use them for text or graphics (as alternatives to black and brown).

**Hot colors:** orange, red, fuchsia. Hot colors are stimulating and grab the audience's attention. Use them sparingly to identify keywords or bullet points, create emphasis, or draw attention to one particular item.

**FIGURE 20.3 Map that shows earthquake intensity with color**

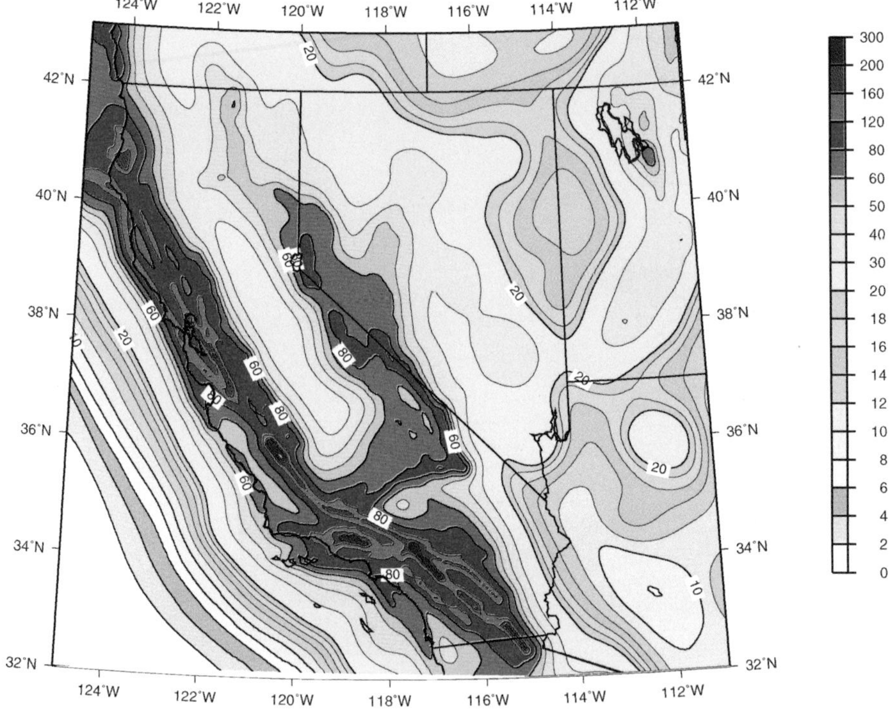


**Source:** Courtesy U.S. Geological Survey.

**Background colors:** soft yellow, light blue, lavender, light green, soft orange, beige. Use soft colors such as these to create backgrounds and borders. They can add interest without demanding the audience's attention. Background colors should help the audience better distinguish and focus on foreground elements such as letters or images.

## Balance

**Balance** is the visual relationship between the items on your visual aid. You establish balance by the way you use space to arrange your ideas. A balanced visual aid helps your audience find and understand information easily.

With text, it is easy to achieve balance by using bullets and indentation:

**Heading**

- First point
- Second point
- Third point

You can also achieve balance by dividing your page (or screen) down the center with an imaginary line. Then, on either side of the line, arrange your information in a visually pleasing way. Consider the placement of your information carefully. A balanced visual aid sets the audience at ease and makes listening easier. It also helps you communicate your message clearly.

**Skills & Confidence**
PPD Activity 20.1
Video Activity 20.1
Speech Studio 20.1

**SPEECH Checklist**

## Designing Visual Aids

- ☐ Use a serif font for text and a sans serif font for headings and titles. Avoid fancy fonts.
- ☐ For emphasis, use the boldface version of the font.
- ☐ All audience members should be able to read the visual aids.

    Headings should be 30 to 36 points.
    Main point text should be 24 points.
    Subpoint text should be 18 points.

- ☐ Use cool colors (no more than two per page) instead of black for text or graphics. Use hot colors to emphasize keywords, bullet points, and individual items.
- ☐ Soft background colors can add interest, but be sure that the text is easily readable against them.
- ☐ Group the words on visual aids so their relationships are clear. Use bullets before all the items in a list, and indent subpoints under main points or headings.

PART VII

# TYPES OF SPEAKING

## CIVIC ENGAGEMENT IN ACTION

### "To Care Is to Accept Responsibility"

DAVID LONGSTREATH, FILE/AP PHOTO

On August 8, 1988, several thousand unarmed civilians demonstrating for democracy in Burma (now called Myanmar) were gunned down by troops loyal to Ne Win, Burma's repressive leader. This event, known as the *Massacre of 8-8-88*, led pro-democracy activist Aung San Suu Kyi to realize that "I could not, as my father's daughter, remain indifferent to all that was going on."

Dr. Suu Kyi was only two when her father, General Aung San, was assassinated by political rivals. Revered as a national hero for negotiating Burma's independence from the United Kingdom in 1947, Aung San inspired not only his country but also his daughter, who as an adult decided to step forward and carry on his tradition of "selfless courage and his vision of a free and democratic Burma." In 1990, Dr. Suu Kyi and her party, the National League for Democracy, won 80 percent of the vote over the military regime that had called the election. But, having expected to win themselves, the regime refused to relinquish power and ordered Dr. Suu Kyi to leave the country. She refused, knowing that she would never be allowed to return to her country if she left. The military placed her under house arrest, and she remains imprisoned to this day, prevented from seeing her family and supporters.

In 1991, Aung San Suu Kyi was awarded the Nobel Peace Prize in recognition of her nonviolent struggle for democracy and human rights. She continues to speak out against oppression, despite the difficulties she has endured for over a decade. "It is undeniably easier to ignore the hardships of those who are too weak to demand their rights than respond sensitively to their needs," she says.

### You Can Get Involved

If you'd like to learn how you can get involved in the U.S. democratic process, access **Web Connect P.VII.1: E-Democracy**. This resource provides links to political news, unbiased information about candidates running in current elections, and resources that allow you to become part of our country's dialogue about politics and democracy. For information about how you can act in

(continued)

## CIVIC ENGAGEMENT IN ACTION continued

Skills & Confidence
Web Connect P.VII.1
Web Connect P.VII.2

"To care is to accept responsibility, to dare to act in accordance with the dictum that the ruler is the strength of the helpless." For her, the struggle for democracy is not simply about ideals; it is about what affects us in our everyday lives. It "is about your job and your children's education; it's about the house you live in and the food you eat; it's about whether or not you have to get permission from somebody before you visit your relatives in the next village; it's about whether or not you can reap your own harvest and sell it to the person you want to sell it to." And although the current government of Burma actively works against her efforts, Dr. Suu Kyi is committed to seeing democracy in Burma. "Running away is not going to solve any problems," she explains. "The nightmare of Burma must be resolved through dialogue with the Burmese government."[1]

### You Can Get Involved (continued)

support of democracy further afield, access **Web Connect P.VII.2: Freedom House**. Freedom House is an organization founded by Eleanor Roosevelt that works to promote democracy and freedom around the world. Both of these resources are nonprofit, nonpartisan organizations.

# TYPES OF SPEAKING

CHAPTER 21

# Informative Speaking

- Types of Informative Speeches
- Organizational Patterns for Informative Speeches
  - Speech Checklist: **Organizational Patterns for Each Type of Informative Speech**
- Guidelines for Giving Effective Informative Speeches
  - Speech Checklist: **Effective Informative Speeches**
- Ethical Informative Speaking
  - Speech Checklist: **Ethical Informative Speeches**
  - Ethical Moment: **When Must We Speak?**
  - Preparation Outline with Commentary: **Tap by Rachel Rota**

***In this chapter, you will learn to***

- Describe the five types of informative speeches
- Apply the four most common patterns of organization for informative speeches
- Apply three guidelines for giving effective informative speeches
- Identify three principles for giving ethical informative speeches

Although our days are often flooded with information—ideas, stories, data, statistics, and more—we don't always have enough to fully understand an important process, circumstance, or issue. If the part of the story we have is inaccurate or incomplete, our assumptions may be skewed. One public speaking student explained why this is a problem:

> Sometimes people just need more information. Like the time my friends asked me, "Why can't I just leave my trash here? Isn't that what the staff is paid for, to pick up my trash?" or when they said, "Why does it matter if we lose certain species? I'll never see that animal anyway." I knew then that they didn't need persuasion or invitation; they really didn't know why it mattered. They needed information.[1]

To fully understand the world we live in, we need a dependable flow of complete and accurate information. To meet that need, speakers in the workplace, in the classroom, and in our communities often speak informatively. An **informative speech** communicates knowledge and understanding about a process, an event, a place or person, an object, or a concept. Informative speakers share what they know or have researched to familiarize audience members with a topic they want or need to understand.

Informative speakers create **informative speaking environments** where they have expertise or knowledge that their audience needs but doesn't already have. When speakers create informative environments, their goal is not to invite (Chapter 22) or persuade (Chapter 23) but rather to illustrate for an audience the importance and relevance of a topic. Informative speakers attempt to enhance an audience's understanding of how some part of the world works.

As you enter the public dialogue, you will give informative speeches frequently.[2] In fact, across professions, demand is growing for employees with strong public communication skills and an ability to share information in a wide range of settings.[3] Informative speaking is an important skill because we need information every day—for example, to understand how a new medication will affect us, to learn how to parallel park, to deliberate over the governor's proposal for spending a budget surplus, or to complete the complex assignment our boss just gave us.

**Speaking at Work**
*Being able to impart and absorb information effectively is a crucial skill in every profession.*

## Types of Informative Speeches

The five types of informative speeches most common in public speaking classes and the workplace are speeches about:

processes
events
places and people

objects

concepts

Each type of speech has a different focus, and each is suited to a different occasion.

### Speeches About Processes

Commonly called *how-to* or *demonstration* speeches, **speeches about processes** describe how something is done, how something comes to be, or how something works. The fundamental goal of a process speech is to show your audience how to *perform* a process or how to better *understand* a process. Some sample topics for process speeches are:

how to get a passport

how to catch, land, and release fish without hurting them

how the Electoral College works

how trees are processed into the products we use every day

how women used different quilt designs to secretly give directions to runaway slaves along the Underground Railroad

Process speeches are common because people often need to learn how to perform new tasks. For example, your boss may ask you to explain to a colleague how to fill out and submit an expense report. Or you may be asked to explain to new staff how an employee incentive program came to be implemented, especially if you have a history with that particular program. In the classroom, you may be required to speak about a process that your classmates will benefit from learning more about.

**Speaking at Work**
*Process speeches are common in the workplace—they're often used to train employees on new procedures and policies.*

The following two examples illustrate process speeches about a familiar topic: coffee. In the first example, Tracee describes how coffee came to be a popular drink in North America.

| | |
|---|---|
| **Specific purpose:** | To inform my audience how coffee became one of the most popular drinks in North America. |
| **Thesis statement:** | Through a series of historical events beginning in the 1500s, coffee replaced tea as one of the most popular drinks in North America. |
| **Main points:** | I. Coffee found its way to North America in the 1500s when trade routes opened between coffee-growing countries and Europe, then expanded to North America. |

II. Coffee began to gain in popularity as tensions with England accelerated in the 1700s and imports of tea decreased.

III. By the 1900s, international commerce, marketing techniques, and individual lifestyles made coffee one of the most popular drinks in North America.

In the second example, Wynton describes the process of growing and harvesting a particular kind of coffee.

**Specific purpose:** To inform my audience how shade-grown coffee is grown and harvested.

**Thesis statement:** The process of growing and harvesting shade-grown coffee differs from the process used by coffee plantations in three significant ways.

**Main points:**

I. Shade-grown coffee is grown in small plots, quite unlike the more familiar coffee plantation method.

II. As the plants grow, these plots provide nonchemical forms of fertilizer and pest control.

III. When the coffee beans are mature, they are harvested and stored in ecologically friendly ways.

Notice how each of these speeches follows a progression of steps: from first to second to third. Because describing the steps is typical of process speeches, they are almost always organized chronologically. Recall from Chapter 10 that the chronological pattern traces a development or evolution over time. A chronological pattern of organization allows you to develop your speech from the first step to the last or from the earliest signs to the most recent examples. (Later in this chapter, organizational patterns for informative speeches are discussed more fully.)

### Speeches About Events

**Speeches about events** describe or explain significant, interesting, or unusual occurrences. These speeches help an audience understand what happened, why it happened, and what effect it had. Just as we often describe what happens in our personal lives so we can better understand how outside events influence us, public speakers share what happens with audiences to help them understand a significant event in the context of history or society or community. In some ways, speeches about events are mini history lessons that educate audiences about key moments. Some sample topics for speeches about events are:

the student protests at Tiananmen Square
Hurricane Katrina
New York's St. Patrick's Day Parade
the assassination of Dr. Martin Luther King Jr.
the discovery of penicillin

**Speaking at Work**

*Because it's not cost-efficient to send all employees to work-related events, such as conventions and trade shows, businesses send just a few people, who then report back about the event.*

People are often asked to speak about events—usually in professional settings. Consider Jackson, whose boss asked him to speak to his fellow employees about what he learned at a recent trade show.

| | |
|---|---|
| **Specific purpose:** | To inform our staff of last week's athletic equipment trade show. |
| **Thesis statement:** | The About Athletes trade show displayed the newest and most popular pieces of sporting equipment, promoted exercise as a part of a healthy lifestyle, and featured presentations about the latest trends in athletics. |

In a community setting, people may decide to speak about local events as a way of informing city councils, planning boards, or community service agencies and perhaps assisting them with the decisions they make.

| | |
|---|---|
| **Specific purpose:** | To inform the city council about the high rate of accidents at the corner of College and Elm Streets. |
| **Thesis statement:** | The intersection of College and Elm is the site of an unusually high rate of accidents during certain hours of the day. |

When you are required to speak about an event, select a topic your audience will find interesting and relevant. You might, for example, inform your classmates of an event that affects your campus (a public hearing to improve public transportation to the campus), the community around your campus (an annual jazz festival that showcases local musicians), or your state or region (a recognition ceremony for local volunteers who helped battle forest fires throughout the state).

SPEECH TIPS

### TOPICS FOR INFORMATIVE SPEECHES

Historical events are often interesting topics for informative speeches, especially if they relate somehow to an audience's current experience. What historical event do you think might make a good topic for an informative speech?

Most speeches about events, especially historical events, are arranged chronologically. However, if the way an event unfolds is not relevant to your speech, you can organize your speech topically. Or if you want to analyze why an event occurred and what effect it had, you can use a causal pattern.

## Speeches About Places and People

**Speeches about places and people** describe significant, interesting, or unusual places or people. These speeches can be fun to give in a classroom because you can share your experiences with places and people you've visited or have found fascinating. In the workplace or the community, these speeches can help audiences understand the importance or appeal of a particular place or person or the contributions a particular person has made to an organization or a community. Some sample topics for speeches about places and people are:

| | |
|---|---|
| service agencies in your community | Gabriel García Márquez |
| Ground Zero in New York City | Muhammad Yunus |
| Beijing | pro-democracy Buddhist monks of Myanmar |

Because you won't have time in a speech to discuss all there is to know about the place or person, the goal of this type of speech is to capture the *spirit* of that place or person. You want your audience to understand why this place or person is important or useful to them or their community, important historically, or just interesting and worth learning about. For example, Adrianna gave a speech about a historical area in her public speaking course.

**Specific purpose:** To inform my audience about the history and features of the Freedom Trail in Boston, Massachusetts.

**Thesis statement:** The Freedom Trail, which originated in the late 1950s, is a pedestrian path through downtown Boston that links sites of historical importance to the United States, such as our first public school and the site of the Boston Massacre.

Garrett informed his classmates about Captain Nicole Malachowski, the first woman selected to join the Thunderbirds, the Air Force's most elite team of pilots.

**Specific purpose:** To inform my classmates of Captain Nicole Malachowski, the first woman selected to fly with the Thunderbirds.

**Thesis statement:** In 2005, the Thunderbirds, a small eight-person team of the best pilots in the Air Force, selected its first woman pilot, Captain Nicole Malachowski, to join them in flying the most advanced aircraft in the world.

Speeches about places or people can be organized topically (how the Freedom Trail was conceived or the importance of the historical sites along the trail), chronologically (events in Captain Malachowski's life that led to her selection), or spatially (the recreational areas of Big Bend National Park in Texas in the mountains, the desert, and at the Rio Grande River).

### Speeches About Objects

**Speeches about objects** are about anything that is tangible, that can be perceived by the senses. When we speak informatively about an object, we describe its components or characteristics so an audience can better understand it and why it might be important or valued. Some sample topics for speeches about objects are:

| | |
|---|---|
| Stradivarius violins | albino leopards |
| hybrid automobiles | poisonous frogs |

Speeches about objects are common in the working world. For example, a product development coordinator is likely to speak

**Speaking at Work**
*Speeches about objects are common in the workplace; being able to inform effectively about, say, a new product is a useful skill.*

regularly to her colleagues about new products that come across her desk, describing their qualities, uses, and appeal. Similarly, tour guides often speak about local objects of importance or interest, describing buildings, sculptures, and pieces of art. For a required classroom speech about an object, you might describe something useful, rare, or interesting. For example, Jun Lee gave a speech about the *Mona Lisa*'s mysterious smile:

| | |
|---|---|
| **Specific purpose:** | To inform my audience about the *Mona Lisa* and the many theories about her famous smile. |
| **Thesis statement:** | One of the most famous paintings of all time, the *Mona Lisa* has inspired several theories about the reason behind her mysterious smile. |

A very popular topic for speeches about animate objects is animals, including their behaviors, habitats, and ways of interacting with humans and other animals. Here is a sample specific purpose and thesis statement for a speech about the communication patterns of African elephants.

| | |
|---|---|
| **Specific purpose:** | To inform my audience of the sophisticated communication behaviors of the African elephant. |
| **Thesis statement:** | African elephants are known to send messages to one another across great distances and to communicate deep grief at the loss of a member of their family or community. |

Many speeches about objects are organized topically (the characteristics of the poisonous frog). Others are organized spatially (the features of the Stradivarius violin), and sometimes a speech about an object can be organized chronologically (hybrid automobiles, from the first to the latest model). Select the pattern that helps you express your ideas most clearly and efficiently.

### Speeches About Concepts

**Speeches about concepts** are about abstractions (things you can't perceive with your senses), such as ideas, theories, principles, worldviews, or beliefs. The goal of a speech about a concept is to help your audience understand your subject, its history, its characteristics, and its effect on society or individuals. Some sample topics for speeches about concepts are:

| | |
|---|---|
| philosophies about reincarnation | social equality |
| adult literacy | theories of child development |
| principles of modern art | poverty in the United States |

When you give speeches about concepts, you help audiences more fully understand or appreciate issues, principles, or systems. Consider the specific purpose and thesis statement of Mallori's speech about the benefits of a sustainable design in housing.

**Specific purpose:** To inform my audience about the benefits of sustainable design in housing.

**Thesis statement:** Many people think a sustainable design will result in an unattractive or expensive home, but sustainable designs are often attractive and affordable.

Speeches about concepts can be challenging because it can be difficult to explain an abstraction clearly. However, this type of speech is important because sometimes audiences need to understand concepts before they can understand how something works or why a person is significant. For example, if Mallori had not first informed her audience about the nature and qualities of sustainable design, her listeners may not have

**Skills & Confidence**
PPD Activity 21.1
Web Connect 21.1
Web Connect 21.2
Web Connect 21.3

**SPEECH Checklist ✓**

## Organizational Patterns for Each Type of Informative Speech

- ☐ **Speech about a process:** chronological organization
- ☐ **Speech about an event:** chronological, topical, or causal organization
- ☐ **Speech about a place or a person:** spatial, topical, or chronological organization
- ☐ **Speech about an object:** topical, spatial, or chronological organization
- ☐ **Speech about a concept:** topical, chronological, or causal organization

appreciated her later discussion about how to build sustainably designed homes.

Speeches about concepts are often organized topically (the principles of modern art) or chronologically (from the earliest theories of child development to the most recent theories). Some speeches about concepts can be organized causally (the causes of poverty in the rural United States).

## Organizational Patterns for Informative Speeches

Informative speeches can be organized in a variety of ways, and you will probably use a wide range of organizational patterns as you become a proficient public speaker. As a beginning speaker, practice using the most common patterns, discussed in Chapter 10 generally and in this section specifically. These organizational patterns are:

chronological
spatial
causal
topical

Using these patterns, you can organize your main points logically.

### Chronological Pattern

With a chronological pattern, you can organize your main points to illustrate how a topic has developed over time or what steps an audience must take to complete a task. Most of us are familiar with the chronological pattern because it is the most common pattern for stories. The chronological pattern is especially effective for process speeches, but as you learned earlier in this chapter, it is also well suited for other kinds of informative speeches. Alan used a chronological pattern for his speech explaining how the Ford Mustang set the standard for the muscle cars of the 1960s.

**Specific purpose:** To inform my audience of the history of the Ford Mustang.

**Thesis statement:** The Ford Mustang, which quickly became the muscle car to beat in 1964 with its combination of high performance and low cost, continues to be the most popular car of that decade.

**Main points:**

I. Pontiac's GTO—which stands for "gas, tires, oil"—is credited as the first of the muscle cars of the 1960s.

II. Ford quickly took the top spot among muscle cars, releasing the high-performance, low-cost Mustang to the public on April 17, 1964.

III. Ford then added new makes with increasingly attractive features and options to maintain its popularity, among them the Fastback, the Grande, the Mach I, the Boss 302, and the Boss 429.

IV. The muscle cars of the 1960s remain some of the most popular cars of that decade, and the newer Mustangs give us a glimpse into why this is so.

Alan took his audience through the evolution of muscle cars in the 1960s, beginning with the Pontiac GTO. He then moved on to Ford's first Mustangs; the release of newer makes, features, and options; and the influence of those features on today's cars. By using the chronological pattern, he provided his audience with basic information they could build on as he progressed through his speech.

The next example illustrates how Joseph used the chronological pattern to trace the evolution of a concept. He described a spiritual belief system, its evolution, and the ways in which the system is integrated into every aspect of life.

**Specific purpose:** To inform my audience how the Kemetic civilizations of ancient Egypt created a holistic view of existence.

**Thesis statement:** Even though African civilizations are often thought of as pagan, the Kemetic civilizations of ancient Egypt created a holistic view of existence in which a monotheistic spiritual belief system was integrated into every aspect of life, including architecture and astronomy.

**Main points:**

I. This religious belief system began with the observation of heavenly bodies.

II. The Kemites began to integrate their knowledge of celestial cycles into their religious beliefs and identified many deities, each worshiped as different aspects of one God.

III. As the Kemites' body of knowledge increased, their society began to integrate their religious beliefs into every aspect of life.

Joseph takes the audience through an evolutionary process, tracing and describing the development of a belief system from its origins to its full development.

SPEECH TIPS

## ORGANIZING INFORMATIVE SPEECHES

Many topics of informative speeches can be organized in several different ways. For example, a speech about the devastation caused by extreme weather events could be organized chronologically (the evolution of a particular weather event) or spatially (the types of extreme weather events that occur in different parts of the world).

Depending on your topic and your purpose, the chronological pattern can be used for any type of informative speech.

### Spatial Pattern

The spatial pattern allows you to address topics logically in terms of location or direction. Recall from Chapter 10 that with this pattern you can arrange your main points by the position they represent within a physical space. You can use this pattern to inform your audience of the places that relate to your topic, the activities that occur in those places, or the activities that are necessary to the functioning of your topic. In the following example, Lehla used a spatial pattern to describe the animal shelter she works for.

**Specific purpose:** To inform my audience about the animal shelter and the various kinds of animals we care for there.

**Thesis statement:** Although we care for dogs and cats at the shelter, we also have the capability of caring for animals ranging from livestock to fish.

**Main points:**

I. Dogs and cats, which make up most of our clientele, are housed closest to the entrance for ease of care and visitation.

II. In the cages and containers behind the dogs and cats, we have birds, fish, and small reptiles.

III. Outside, in back of the shelter, we house the livestock, which need more space and open air.

IV. At the furthest border of the property, and under tight lock and key, we keep the large reptiles.

By addressing her topic spatially, Lehla guided her audience around the various parts of the shelter. They learned something about the shelter itself as well as about the animals, which was one of her primary speech goals.

In the next example, Scott used a spatial pattern to describe the different parts of a guitar and how each part works to produce sound.

**Specific purpose:** To inform my audience of how the different parts of the guitar work together to produce sound.

**Thesis statement:** The guitar has three main parts—the head, neck, and body—and all work together in intricate ways to produce the sounds we call music.

**Main points:**

I. The top of the guitar is the head, which houses the nut and the tuning pegs.

II. The next part is the neck, which contains three essential parts: the frets, the truss rod, and the fingerboard.

III. The bottom part is the body, which is made of a reinforced front, back, and side panels, a sound hole, and the bridge and saddle.

The spatial pattern is a clear and effective way to describe the different parts of an object or a place.

### Causal Pattern

The causal pattern highlights cause-and-effect relationships. A cause is an event that makes something happen, and an effect is the response or change that results from that cause. When you use a causal pattern, you inform your audience about what caused a certain event, place, object, or concept.

In the following example, Erin addressed the issue of school violence, particularly as it affected her. She was one of the students at Columbine High School in Colorado on April 20, 1999, when two students killed thirteen fellow students and one teacher. Erin's use of a causal pattern helped her explain why school violence is becoming more common.

**Specific purpose:** To inform my audience about some of the causes of school violence.

**Thesis statement:** Experts agree that school violence is caused by several factors: frustration, manipulation, retaliation, and the misconception that violence is an appropriate response.

**Main points:**

I. Some students turn to violence because they lack a constructive outlet to express their frustration.

II. Some students lash out when they are manipulated by other students.

III. Some students seek retaliation against perceived wrongs or insults.

IV. Some students have learned that responding to certain situations with violence is appropriate.

Erin did not try to persuade or to invite her audience into her world. Rather, she provided information about a difficult issue, helping her audience understand, as she had come to understand, how the violence at Columbine could have happened. By using the causal pattern, she helped her audience understand why some students resort to violence. In a later speech to the same audience, Erin discussed possible solutions to school violence.

The causal pattern is used most often for speeches about events or concepts.

### Topical Pattern

A topical organizational pattern allows a speaker to address different aspects of a topic. For example, the topic of elephants can be organized according to their habitats, favorite foods, and interactions with other elephants. The topical pattern works best for topics that can be easily and logically divided into subtopics. Using a topical pattern, you can highlight the aspects of a topic that are most useful and important for your audience to understand.

In Pia's speech about the Crossroads safe house, she used a topical pattern to discuss the organization's characteristics and services.

**Specific purpose:** To inform my audience about Crossroads, the safe house for battered women and children in our community.

**Thesis statement:** Crossroads shelters battered women and children so they feel safe as they begin to rebuild their lives.

**Main points:**

I. A "safe house" is a secret location where battered women and their children can live without fear of being found by their abusers.

II. The typical family at Crossroads is a woman and her children who are seeking respite from an abusive husband or boyfriend.

III. To help women and their children get back on their feet, Crossroads provides temporary housing, clothing, job placement services, counseling, and, above all, safety.

By using this organizational pattern, Pia highlighted the different features of Crossroads and educated an audience about the purpose of safe houses, the families that stay at Crossroads, and the services provided there.

Topical organization can work for speeches about events, objects, and concepts as well as about places and people.

**Skills & Confidence**
PPD
Activity 21.2

# Guidelines for Giving Effective Informative Speeches

In an informative speaking environment, you contribute to the public dialogue by sharing your knowledge with your audience and illustrating with clarity and detail the relevance of that knowledge to your listeners. Three guidelines will help you create an informative speaking environment and give an effective informative speech: (1) bring your topic to life, (2) tailor your information to your audience, and (3) use language that is clear and unbiased.

## Bring Your Topic to Life

Effective informative speakers bring a subject to life for an audience, engaging their listeners so that they appreciate the information they receive. Take careful stock of your topic and your audience so you can be sure to share information that is both *engaging* and *relevant.* Engaging material draws an audience in and excites or interests them. Audience members find material relevant if it is useful or something they must know for doing their job, participating in a community, or making an informed decision.

One of the ways to bring a topic to life is to stay audience centered. As you craft your speech, continually ask yourself how your overall topic, main points, and subpoints relate to your audience.

- What does the audience need to know?
- How will they use the information you present?
- How can you make the information clear to them?

If you keep your audience in mind throughout your preparation process, you will be more likely to present your material in an engaging and relevant way. For example, in her speech about school violence, Erin brought her second point, manipulation by other students, to life by asking her audience a rhetorical question: "Think back to high school. How many examples of manipulative behavior can you think of? Probably too many. In my junior year, I remember one group of students who constantly picked on my friends and me. It felt like no matter what we did, we were the brunt of their jokes and the focus of their hostility." By sharing her own experience of manipulation, she touched on an experience common to many members of her audience.

Another way to bring your topic to life is to share the human side of your topic. If you are presenting technical information, explaining intricate details, or carefully outlining a process, try to use examples, images, and descriptions that will help your audience connect to the topic personally. If you are presenting numbers or statistics, give the figures a human face. After hearing an informative speech about electromagnetic waves and their relationship to cancer, one student asked, "What do all those formulas and fancy names mean for me personally?" As you prepare your speech, anticipate this kind of question and look for opportunities to relate your information to your audience. For example, in a speech on modern art, you might personalize different techniques and styles by drawing parallels to skills learned in art classes at your school or by asking your audience to attempt the techniques on their own as you describe them.

### Tailor Your Information to Your Audience

Recall the discussion of information overload from Chapter 7. Just as you can feel overwhelmed by the abundance of information you find in your research, your audiences can be overwhelmed by the information you share with them in your speech—no matter how engaging and relevant you make that information. As an informative speaker, one of your most challenging tasks is to decide how much information to include in a speech and how much to leave out.

If you present too much information, of course, you run the risk of overwhelming an audience. However, if you present too little information, you run the risk of leaving them confused about your topic.

Similarly, if you present material that is too technical, detailed, and complicated, your audience will have a hard time following it. On

**SPEECH TIPS**

#### USING A DEMONSTRATION

Demonstration speeches are often very engaging because they provide audiences with relevant, useful information. When you give this type of speech, remember to avoid overwhelming your audience with too much information. Think carefully about the most important information your audience will need.

the other hand, if the information in your speech is too simple, your audience will become bored or feel that you are talking down to them.

The best way to tailor your information to your audience is to stay audience centered throughout the speech process. As you develop and present your speech, continually reflect on the needs and interests of your audience. Include information that you think would be of the greatest educational value for your audience, and adjust your presentation of this information so that it matches your audience's level of knowledge, expertise, and experience.

The decisions about what information to include or exclude can seem very subjective, but if you follow the principles of effective listening (Chapter 4), audience centeredness (Chapter 6), and organizing your speech for clarity (Chapter 10), you will find it easier to determine how much information to include in your speech.

### Use Language That Is Clear and Unbiased

Because informative speeches primarily describe, define, and explain, use language that is descriptive and instructive. To ensure your audience can follow you,

- Define all new terminology.
- Break complicated processes into steps.
- Explain language specific to a particular field or activity.

For example, when Wynton spoke about shade-grown coffee, he defined the terms *shade grown*, *fair trade*, *organic*, and *sustainable*. Similarly, when Jackson spoke to his colleagues about the About Athletes trade show, he made sure his audience understood the jargon used to discuss marketing strategies and the competition.

In addition, explain familiar words that you use in new ways. For example, the terms *safe*, *house*, and *client* are common terms used in various industries and circumstances, but they had a specific meaning when Pia was talking about the Crossroads shelter for battered women.

Make informative language as objective as you can. Focus on presenting your information clearly and accurately, and avoid expressing your own views (as in invitational speaking) or trying to sway your audience (as in persuasive speaking). Remember that the goal of informative speaking is to pass along information your audience needs or wants.

Make sure the language of your speech is fair and unbiased. Use phrases like "my research indicates that" or "according to the experts" rather than "I hope I've convinced you that this is the best way." Similarly, when you incorporate personal knowledge into an informative speech, which is common when you describe or explain

**SPEECH Checklist ✓**

### Effective Informative Speeches

- ☐ What does your audience need to know about your topic?
- ☐ How will your audience use your information?
- ☐ How much does your audience already know about the topic? What do you need to explain? (Techniques to ensure understanding include defining unfamiliar terminology and jargon and breaking complicated processes into steps.)
- ☐ How can you engage your audience with your topic and show its relevance? (Techniques include sharing personal experiences, using anecdotes and examples to give numbers and facts a human face, and involving your audience through rhetorical questions and activities.)
- ☐ Are you presenting the information objectively?

something you have experience with, make sure the language you use reflects your *experience*, not your biases or preferences. For example, phrases like "after seven years with these machines, I'd recommend the following steps" and "I've been involved with this issue since I began with this agency, so I can give you some background and details" are informative and do not express an opinion or try to persuade.

The distinctions here may seem slight, but they are important because they set informative speaking apart from invitational and persuasive speaking (Chapters 22 and 23). For more information on the effective use of language, see Chapter 4 (how language affects listening) and Chapter 16 (language style).

## Ethical Informative Speaking

Ethical informative speakers make sure their speeches are based on:

careful research

unbiased information

the honest presentation of information

Let's take a look at each of these components of ethical informative speaking.

First, when we present information to audiences, they expect that we have taken the time to find information that is accurate and complete. Thus, we must carefully research the details of our topic so we can share the full story with our audiences. You will lose credibility and do a disservice to your audience if you present inaccurate or incomplete information. (See Chapter 7 for tips on how to gather accurate and complete supporting materials for your speech.)

Second, as an informative speaker, strive to present unbiased information to your audience. Recall from Chapter 6 that although we all hold biases, we can take steps to minimize them. Minimize biases by presenting your examples, statistics, testimony, and other materials as fairly and as neutrally as possible, regardless of your own personal positions. You can express your preferences in your persuasive speeches; use your informative speeches to help your audiences gain a full understanding of your topic.

Finally, present your information honestly. Don't distort your evidence or make up supporting material as you need it. A healthy public dialogue depends on accuracy. If you misrepresent your speech topic, your audience will come away with an inaccurate view of important issues and situations. Ethical informative speaking relies on the honest and accurate distribution of information, which can happen only if speakers present that information truthfully.

**SPEECH Checklist**

## Ethical Informative Speeches

- ☐ Is your information carefully researched, complete, and accurate?
- ☐ Is your information as neutral and unbiased as possible?
- ☐ Is your evidence and supporting material presented fairly and without distortion?

## Ethical Moment

### When Must We Speak?

In 2003, as part of a federal case against the Bay Area Laboratory Co-Operative (BALCO) for distributing illegal "designer steroids" to professional athletes, baseball great Barry Bonds told a grand jury that he had not taken steroids during his career. Bonds provided this information because he and other athletes were offered immunity if they testified in the case, which targeted Victor Conte, the founder of BALCO, and Greg Anderson, Bond's trainer and longtime friend. Bonds explained that he trusted Anderson and used the creams and gels Anderson supplied because he thought they were simply flax seed oil and arthritis pain relievers. His testimony, which was supposed to be secret, was leaked to outside sources, and prosecutors, believing Bonds had lied under oath, began a perjury investigation. Bond's attorney, Mike Raines, responded by claiming that the federal government was persecuting Bonds and "going after his client because of his name and notoriety, not the allegations leveled against him." He said, "You offer immunity and you get him in there and then you ask them questions and you get them on lying to federal officers. That's the trap. That's exactly what they got Martha [Stewart] for."[4]

DAVID ZALUBOWSKI/AP PHOTO

WHAT DO YOU THINK?

1. Both Barry Bonds and Martha Stewart were required to speak in a court of law about cases that were not about them specifically. Do you think people should be required to speak in this way? Why or why not?
2. Whether Bonds was telling the truth or not, do you think that people should always be completely forthcoming about what they are required to speak about? Should some information be kept private and immune from punishment? Why or why not?
3. When potentially damaging information that is supposed to be private is leaked, as in Bonds' case, is it ethical to use that information against the person? Why or why not?

# PREPARATION OUTLINE

**with Commentary**

## *Tap*

*by Rachel Rota*

CENGAGE LEARNING

***Specific Purpose:*** *To inform my audience about the art of tap dancing.*

***Thesis Statement:*** *Tap dancing, one of the oldest forms of dance, is based on just a few basic steps and was popularized in modern times in part by the great tap dancer and choreographer Gregory Hines.*

*You may have already given an informative speech in your class. Whether you have or whether this is the first time you've spoken informatively, you can use the following outline as a model. Use your Premium Website for* Invitation to Public Speaking Handbook *to watch a video of Rachel Rota giving this speech and see her transcript and speaking outline. Rachel gave this speech in an introductory public speaking class. The assignment was to give a four- to six-minute speech, with a minimum of four sources cited. Students were also asked to create a preparation outline that included a Works Cited section and to use at least one visual aid in their speech. (Remember that you can use your Premium Website to access videos of several other informative speeches, including Chung-yan Man's "Chinese Fortune Telling," Elizabeth Lopez's "The Three C's of Down Syndrome," and Josh Valentine's "The Dun Dun Drum.")*

**Skills & Confidence**
Video Activity 21.1
Speech Studio 21.1

*INTRODUCTION*

(Begin by doing a short tap routine) *(catch attention)*

I. Tap dancing is a vibrant art that is popular around the world and continues to appeal to people. *(reveal topic)*

   A. According to performingarts.net, tap artist Gregory Hines once said, "Tap is here, now."

*Commentary*
*After catching her audience's attention by tap dancing, Rachel begins her speech with a quotation pertaining to her speech topic, and she cites the source of the quotation.*

B. The art of tap dancing can be found all around our nation, with style variations around the world.

C. Public interest in tap is growing, and tap can be seen in many forms of entertainment, such as films and theatrical Broadway shows.

II. Still alive today, tap is one of the oldest styles of dance.

*After Rachel reveals the topic of her speech, she proceeds by asking her audience to think about their experiences with her speech topic. Rachel uses this strategy to connect the audience to her topic.*

A. Many may think tap went out with performers like Gene Kelly and Fred Astaire, but it is still thriving.

B. Have you encountered tap dancing? *(connect to the audience)*

III. I am interested in this topic because I have been dancing since the age of four and have found tap quite enjoyable. *(establish credibility)*

*Rachel clearly establishes her credibility as a speaker by revealing her personal experience as both a student and teacher of tap.*

A. Not only have I been a student of tap, but I have also taught tap to young dancers.

B. I also enjoy watching entertainment that includes tap dancing.

IV. Today I will tell you about the beginnings of tap dancing, some basic techniques of tap, and I will also discuss a tap great, the late Gregory Hines. *(reveal thesis statement and preview main points)*

*Rachel briefly previews the main points of her speech, revealing her topical organizational pattern. She will elaborate on each main point in the same order provided in the internal preview statement.*

*BODY*

I. According to performingarts.net, tap is a combination of elements of African drumming and dancing and European clog and step dancing.

*Rachel's first main point, the evolution of tap, provides her audience a brief overview of the history of her topic. Within her explanation of how tap evolved, Rachel cites the websites that contain the information provided in her speech. Notice that she cites them in her speech as well as in her outline.*

A. The core of all forms of tap is percussive footwork, but the unique rhythms of jazz distinguish American tap dance from other types of tap.

B. From the 1600s to the early 1800s, tap evolved from European step dances (for example, clog and jig) and African religious dances (for example, juba and ring shout).

C. These dances were performed mostly by African slaves.

1. Around 1828, the juba and the jig evolved to dances performed on the minstrel stage.
2. Later these dances were polished into what is now American tap dance.

D. The article "The History of Tap" from performingarts.net outlines the evolution of modern tap.
1. Vaudeville talents like Bill "Bojangles" Robinson and John Bubbles helped define the rhythm of tap dance.
2. Hollywood popularized tap in films starring Fred Astaire and the Nicholas Brothers.
3. According to offjazz.com, Gene Kelly became a star in the 1950s and created his own style of tap by adding movements from ballet and modern dance.
4. Although tap lost some popularity in the 1950s, it became known as an art form as well as a form of entertainment in the 60s.
5. In the 70s, tap returned to film, the concert stage, and the theater in the United States, Europe, and Japan.
6. Tap still flourishes in the entertainment industry today and can be seen on stage, TV, and in the movies.

*Transition:* In light of the early beginnings of tap, the steps that created the history are just as important.

*Rachel provides a clear transition from her first to her second main point to signal that she has finished discussing the history of tap and will move on to discuss tap steps. She also performs the steps she describes in her first subpoint. This demonstration adds clarity to her speech.*

II. Tapdance.org lists a few basic movements and steps in tap dance.

A. The shuffle, flap, heel drop, brush, tip, step, stomp, and stamp create the basis of all the steps and sounds of tap.

B. These basics create steps like the cramp role, time steps, Maxi-ford, and the rolling pullback.

C. To successfully create these sounds, tap shoes have hard leather soles with metal "taps" screwed into them.

D. Although there are many variations of tap shoes, the sounds and steps of American tap dancing remain the same.

*Between her second and third main points, Rachel provides a short internal summary and then transitions to her third point.*

*Transition:* We've heard about the history and the basics of tap. Now, let's take a deeper look into the life of a tap dancing great.

III. According to an article at the website cigaraficionado.com, one famous modern tap dancer, Gregory Hines, led an interesting life and became a highly acclaimed dancer and choreographer.

*Notice how her three main points are fairly balanced, providing approximately the same amount of information. Also notice how each point, subpoint, and sub-subpoint in her outline includes only one complete sentence.*

A. When he was five years old, he was in a tap group called the Hines Kids with his older brother, Jake.

1. When the boys reached adolescence, they were called the Hines Brothers, and they spent much of their time performing at the Apollo Theatre.
2. In 1954, Gregory debuted on Broadway at the age of eight in the musical *The Girl in Pink Tights.*
3. In 1963, the family group became Hines, Hines, and Dad, and they performed in New York nightclubs and on television.
4. In 1992, Gregory was awarded a Tony for his role in *Jelly's Last Jam.*
5. He showcased his dancing talent in movies such as *The History of the World*, *The Cotton Club*, and *White Nights.*

B. Gregory has left his mark on the world of tap, and his technique and style continue to be studied.

C. His untimely death in August 2003 from liver cancer has been a great loss not only for the tap community but also for the entire entertainment industry.

*CONCLUSION*

I. As we have seen today, tap is a very old form of dance, and the steps and sounds of tap have been performed by many talented people throughout its history. *(reinforce thesis and summarize main points)*
   A. The basic steps of tap remain about the same as they have throughout tap's history.
   B. The work of Gregory Hines contributed greatly to tap.

II. If any of you desire to be a tap dancer, I hope I have equipped you with enough information to get you started.

III. Just go and screw some metal taps into the bottom of your shoes and start tapping! *(end memorably)*

*Rachel signals that she is concluding her speech by saying, "As we have seen today." She provides a clear internal summary, briefly recapping her three main points. Her conclusion is short, and she ends memorably.*

**Works Cited**

"The History of Tap." Accessed April 30, 2005. http://www.performingarts.net.

Rothstein, Mervyn. "The Man in the Dancing Shoes: Gregory Hines Scores Big on Broadway with *Jelly's Last Jam*." *Cigar Aficionado.* Autumn 1992. Accessed April 30, 2005. http://www.cigaraficionado.com/Cigar/CA_Archives/CA_Show_Article/0,2322,863,00.html.

"Tap Steps." Accessed April 30, 2005. http://www.tapdance.org/tap/steps/index.html.

"Top of the Taps." Accessed March 19, 2005. http://www.offjazz.com/tap-stars.htm.

CHAPTER 22

# Invitational Speaking



*In this chapter, you will learn to*

- Identify the three conditions for an invitational speaking environment
- Describe the two types of invitational speeches
- Apply the four most common patterns of organization for invitational speeches
- Apply three guidelines for giving effective invitational speeches
- Identify two principles for giving ethical invitational speeches

The diversity of people and perspectives we encounter in our daily lives is both a gift and a challenge. On the one hand, the variety of perspectives people have about the world enriches our communities, workplaces, and schools, helping us learn new things and see situations in new ways. On the other hand, all of these different perspectives can sometimes make finding common ground on important issues difficult.

We have probably all encountered people whose positions on social and political issues are not at all like our own. We've probably also learned that we're not likely to change their views nor are they likely to change ours, no matter how hard we both try. In fact, in many situations (such as business meetings and community forums), trying to persuade someone that our view is the best is not only unrealistic, but it can be inappropriate, especially if mutual problem solving is the goal.

**Speaking at Work**
*Invitational speaking is common in the workplace, where it's not always realistic or appropriate to try to persuade others that our view is best.*

Trying to persuade other people to change their views on a subject can be inappropriate when we do not have enough information to know what is best for them or when their positions are so personal that it is not our place to ask them to change. For example, issues such as the death penalty, animal rights, and stem cell research are tied to deeply held personal beliefs about politics, economics, and religion that are far beyond any one speaker's area of expertise.

As public speakers, do we simply give up when our audience sees things differently than we do? Or do we forge ahead with our attempts to persuade them even though we do not really understand their perspectives? Or could we try a different kind of interaction, one that encourages the audience to share their perspectives with us? Could we avoid stereotypes (for example, "Republicans see Democrats as naive," and "Democrats see Republicans as greedy"), asking instead, "What are the different ways of viewing this issue?" Could we try to understand the various positions more fully, without necessarily arriving at a single clear-cut solution or course of action?

This chapter suggests that even though we may not be able to change the attitudes of our audience or even want to change them, we can still enter the public dialogue. We can engage in **invitational speaking,** a type of public speaking in which a speaker enters into a dialogue with an audience to clarify positions, explore issues and ideas, or articulate beliefs and values. To speak invitationally is to do something other than inform or persuade. To speak invitationally is to continue the public dialogue and seek mutual recognition despite firm differences in opinions, values, and beliefs.

Let's look at an example that illustrates the difference between informative, invitational, and persuasive speaking. An informative speaker might inform an audience that ethical hunting can help control wildlife populations, and he would stop there. He wouldn't ask the audience to accept his position on the topic. An invitational speaker might explain why he supports ethical hunting, ask the audience to understand his position as one viable opinion, and then lead a discussion with the goal of understanding opposing or differing opinions raised by the audience. A persuasive speaker might ask the audience to support ethical hunting and possibly take a course of action, such as supporting a local initiative to extend the hunting season. Although a persuasive speaker might also be interested in opposing opinions, his goal as a speaker would be to advocate his own position over others.

In summary, to speak invitationally is to engage an audience in a civil and open investigation of a topic and give voice to its complexities.[1]

## The Invitational Speaking Environment

**Speaking across DIFFERENCES**

**Creating an environment of respect for differing viewpoints is important in all types of speaking. However, it's especially important in invitational speaking because encouraging dialogue is an essential component of this type of speaking.**

To speak invitationally, you must try to create an **invitational environment** in which your highest priority is to understand, respect, and appreciate the range of positions on an issue, even if some positions are quite different from your own. Creating an environment of respect is important in all types of speaking, but it is especially important in invitational speaking because promoting dialogue between the speaker and audience is essential. In this dialogue, you offer your position as one viable stance and encourage your audience to express their positions so that everyone can come to a fuller understanding of the different positions on your subject. Because invitational speaking needs dialogue, it is best suited for situations in which the speaker has some time with an audience to allow for the fullest expression of the various positions. (For specific techniques on leading discussions and encouraging dialogue with audiences, see Chapter 26. Chapter 6's advice on adapting to audience expectations may also be useful.)

As an example, let's look at the invitational environment created during the process of soliciting ideas for rebuilding the World Trade Center site.[2] The events of September 11, 2001, created an atmosphere of chaos and conflict. The attacks on New York City and Washington, D.C., and the failed attack leading to the plane crash in Pennsylvania seemed unimaginable to many in the United States. Similarly, when government agencies began to talk about replacing the fallen World Trade Center buildings and providing a memorial to the victims of the attacks, many people could not imagine what the new site would look like. The organizations responsible for rebuilding the site, the Lower Manhattan Development Corporation (LMDC) and the Port Authority of New York and New Jersey, recognized the public's need to provide input about the project. So twice the LMDC held public meetings, linking Long Island and New York's five boroughs via video conferencing to explore the issue of redeveloping the World Trade Center and Lower Manhattan. Furthermore, an LMDC website gave the public the opportunity to observe and participate in additional meetings. This unprecedented move invited thousands of citizens to participate in a dialogue.[3]

When the first round of designs for the memorial failed to inspire the citizens of New York, officials initiated a second design competition, receiving a record 5,201 entries from forty-nine U.S. states and sixty-three nations. Further public forums solicited input from the community, and a thirteen-member jury reviewed the submissions. When the jury—which included a family member of one of the attacks, victims, architects, public officials, and a historian—finally reached its decision, its statement illustrated the invitational approach taken to select the finalists:

> We understand the obligation we have to the victims, to their families, to society—indeed, to history—to serve the mission given to us; to remember and honor those who died, to recognize the endurance of those who survived, the courage of those who risked their lives to save the lives of others, and the compassion of all those who supported the victims' families in their darkest hours.[4]

The jury admitted that the task was not an easy one. Coming to a consensus "entailed hours of frank discussions, agreements and disagreements, always with the goal of arriving at common ground." When selecting the finalists, the jury consulted with many members of the community, including New York City Mayor Michael Bloomberg, New York Governor George Pataki, people who lived and worked in Lower Manhattan, and representatives of the victims' families. In a final invitational move, the jury exhibited all 5,201 submissions, allowing the public to consider the meaning of each submission. When the final design, *Reflecting Absence*, was displayed, the jury avoided suggesting how the audience should think, feel, and react to the memorial. Instead, they acknowledged "that memory belongs primarily to the individual."

As the jury noted, "*Reflecting Absence*... evolved through months of conversation between the jury and its creators,"[5] making the process of selecting a memorial to the victims of the September 11 attacks on the World Trade Center a truly invitational one. Port Authority Executive Director Joseph J. Seymour stated: "The rebuilding of Lower Manhattan has been the most open and accessible process in history."[6]

This example illustrates one of the keys to creating a successful invitational environment: The traditional roles of the speaker and the audience must be altered. Rather than taking on the role of "expert" and assigning the role of "listener" to the audience, invitational speakers consider both themselves and the audience as the experts and the listeners. They not only express their views, but they also listen carefully to their audience's views. They then facilitate a discussion of ideas, and the speaking environment becomes more than a speech given by one person to an audience. As the example about the World Trade Center memorial shows, the traditional relationship between the speaker and the audience is replaced with one that encourages the exchange of views without risk of attack or ridicule.

To build an invitational environment, you must create three conditions:

- equality
- value
- self-determination

These conditions allow you and your audience to see one another as knowledgeable and capable, although perhaps in different ways. These three conditions are interrelated, but they are presented separately here to clarify each condition and its goal. However, all of these conditions help you create an atmosphere of mutual respect, understanding, and exploration. They help you communicate effectively with people who hold positions quite different from your own.[7]

Skills & Confidence Video Activity 22.1

## The Condition of Equality

When you create the **condition of equality,** you acknowledge that all audience members hold *equally valid* perspectives worthy of exploration. You use language, delivery, and the presentation of ideas to let your audience know that you recognize that their knowledge, experiences, and perspectives are as valid for them as yours are for you. Because you and your audience are equal participants in a dialogue (although you still give the speech and lead the discussion), your audience is able to offer their perspectives, share their experiences, and even question you—in the same way you do with them. A condition of equality creates a sense of safety and welcome that encourages audience members to share their perspectives. The jury who selected the World Trade Center memorial created the condition of equality by making every effort to recognize all community members as equals and to solicit their input.

### The Condition of Value

You create the **condition of value** by recognizing the *inherent value* of your audience's views, even though those views might be different from yours. In creating the condition of value, you let your audience know that when they express differing views and opinions, the differences will be explored in a spirit of mutual understanding, without judgment or any effort to change them. In fact, in creating the condition of value, you communicate that you will try to step outside your own standpoint (Chapter 6) to understand other perspectives and see the world as your audience sees it. So when disagreement on an issue arises, you and the other participants in the dialogue try to understand the opposing positions and the reasons why people hold their views.

### The Condition of Self-Determination

As a speaker, you can create a **condition of self-determination** by recognizing that the members of your audience are experts in their own lives—that they know what is best for themselves and have the right to make choices about their lives based on this knowledge. Although their choices may not be the ones you would make, the members of your audience are free to decide for themselves how to think, feel, and act. The condition of self-determination means you won't close off conversation or try to persuade your audience to do something they may not feel inclined to do. Rather, you will create an atmosphere in which the members of the audience feel in control of their choices and are respected for their ability to make them.

Skills & Confidence Video Activity 22.2

## SPEECH TIPS

### INVITATIONAL SPEAKING

In our increasingly diverse and complicated world, invitational speaking is a useful tool in some of the most difficult public conversations. When you choose to speak invitationally, you are seeking a full and open exchange of ideas. Creating the conditions of equality, value, and self-determination helps you succeed in this exchange.

Invitational speaking goes beyond informing and avoids any effort to persuade. When you speak invitationally, your goal is to explore issues in a spirit of openness.

**SPEECH Checklist**

### Establishing an Invitational Environment

- ☐ Be sure there will be time both for your speech and for audience members to explain their positions.
- ☐ Show by your language and delivery that you believe audience members' knowledge, experiences, and perspectives are as valid as yours. (condition of equality)
- ☐ Encourage audience members to explain the reasons for their perspectives. (condition of value)
- ☐ Ensure that audience members do not feel they are being persuaded to change their minds or do something they don't want to do. (condition of self-determination)

## Types of Invitational Speeches

The two types of invitational speaking are to articulate a position and to explore an issue. In the first, you hold a fairly well-defined position, and your goal is to explain your position and then discuss it with your audience so they can understand you and your position more fully. In the process, you may better understand the positions of your audience members as well. In the second type, you have some tentative thoughts about an issue or a plan, but you want to discover and understand what your audience thinks about the issue too. In this way, you can understand your own position more fully or develop a course of action that more fully accounts for differing positions. Let's take a closer look at these two types of invitational speaking.

### Speeches to Articulate a Position

When you hold a fairly well-developed perspective on a subject and want to explore your perspective with others, you may want to give an invitational speech to articulate your position. When you deliver a **speech to articulate a position,** you invite an audience to understand an issue from your perspective. This type of invitational speaking is similar to informative speaking in that you share information with your audience, but it differs because you are also open to conversation with the audience about *their* views on a topic. The result is that both you and your audience leave the exchange with a richer understanding of a complex issue.

Let's look at two examples of invitational speeches to articulate positions and how they differ from informative and persuasive speeches. In the first example, Avery asked her audience to consider standardized testing in public schools. Standardized tests are given to students nationwide in an attempt to measure student and school performance. If Avery had given an informative speech on these tests, she could have organized it so the audience learned something about the tests, their history, and the reasons they are controversial. In a persuasive speech, she might have attempted to convince her audience to support or oppose standardized testing. However, because Avery decided to give an invitational speech, she provided information about both the pros and cons of the current tests, as well as balanced information about two alternatives. Her position was that some types of standardized testing are appropriate, yet she wanted to explore the two alternatives and remain open to their possible flaws and weaknesses. Her specific purpose, thesis statement, and main points looked like this:

**Specific purpose:** To invite my audience to understand the advantages and disadvantages of standardized testing and to explain two promising alternatives.

**Thesis statement:** Standardized testing has a long and controversial history in our educational system, and two alternative methods of evaluating schools and students have caught the attention of both educators and parents.

**Main points:**

I. Many education experts believe that standardized testing is an effective way to measure the success of students and schools.

II. Other education experts argue against standardized tests, suggesting that the tests compromise school funding and don't accurately assess students' performance.

III. An alternative to standardized testing, the portfolio-based assessment method, which collects work from students throughout a school year, has caught the attention of many educators and parents.

IV. A second alternative, the performance exam, also has the potential to replace the familiar standardized test because it measures a student's performance through writing samples and public speaking skills.

V. I do favor some form of standardized test, and I'd like to discuss the benefits of the two proposed alternatives with my audience to learn their views on all these methods.

Avery provided information not only to educate her audience but also so they could respond with full, well-informed expressions of their own views. She invited her audience to see the issue as she did and then asked her audience to share their perspectives on the issue with her.

In the second example, from a speech on gun control, Martin could have chosen to persuade his audience to support his position that the United States does not need stricter gun control laws. Instead, he chose an invitational approach because he knew that many in his audience strongly supported stricter regulations. Martin knew that changing their minds was not only unrealistic but could lead to angry interactions. So he chose to invite the audience into his world to see the issue of guns from another perspective. In doing so, he created an atmosphere of openness so people could voice their concerns, frustrations, and even their anger without judgment. Martin's specific purpose, thesis statement, and main points were as follows:

**Specific purpose:** To invite my audience to consider some of the positive lessons that can be taught with the ethical use of guns.

**Thesis statement:** Although many people fear guns, two hunting experiences in my childhood taught me to use guns responsibly and ethically, and I believe the lessons I learned have been invaluable in my life.

**Main points:**

I. People fear guns for a number of reasons.

II. I had two memorable hunting experiences during my childhood, one positive and the other negative.

III. Those experiences have proved to be invaluable in my life and shaped my current views on the responsible and ethical use of guns in our society.

IV. I'd like to explore with my audience ways in which the ethical use of guns could be a healthy part of our lives.

In a persuasive speech, Martin would have tried to convince the audience that guns actually aren't as bad as some people think. However, in this invitational speech, he was more interested in sharing positions than changing minds. His goal was to facilitate understanding and the exchange of ideas on gun control, a very controversial topic.

When you articulate a position, you try to develop your position as fully and openly as possible. You invite your audience to see the issue from your perspective and return the gesture by asking for their perspectives. Your primary goal is not to provide information or to persuade anyone to change, although both of these things might happen.

Instead, you seek to promote a deeper understanding of the issue by exploring different views on it so that both you and your audience will be able to frame it in more complete, inclusive ways in the future.

## Speeches to Explore an Issue

When you give an invitational **speech to explore an issue,** you attempt to engage your audience in a discussion about an idea, a concern, a topic, or a plan of action. Your goal is to gather different perspectives from your audience so you can understand the subject more fully. Quite often, you use what you have learned from your audience to find a solution or plan a course of action that will appeal to a broad range of perspectives.

**Speaking at Work**

*Speeches to explore an issue are often used in the workplace, where finding solutions and courses of action that will appeal to a broad range of perspectives is important.*

You often begin this type of invitational speech by stating your intent to explore the issue. Then you might lay out the positions on the issue. Or you may share your opinions, even if they are tentative, about the issue. With either approach, you are laying the groundwork for an open dialogue, one rooted in equality, value, and self-determination and one in which people feel heard and respected by one another.

The following two examples illustrate invitational speeches to explore issues. In the first example, David spoke invitationally about the federal minimum wage. His goal was to get his audience thinking about the amount of money someone earning the minimum wage makes, the way of life of the working poor, and possible ways to address this issue.

**Specific purpose:** To invite my audience to explore, and to explore for myself, the federal minimum wage and whether there are better approaches to assisting the working poor.

**Thesis statement:** A federal minimum wage of $7.25 per hour leaves many working people dependent on public assistance agencies like our county's food bank, but raising the minimum wage creates many problems and may not be the best approach to helping the working poor.

**Main points:**

I. The minimum wage of 25 cents per hour set in 1938 has risen to $7.25 per hour, providing a full-time worker a little over $14,000 annually.

II. In recent years, food banks and other public assistance agencies have seen huge growth in the number of working families seeking their aid.

III. Experts suggest that raising the minimum wage may decrease employment opportunities for entry-level employees.

IV. Other options exist, but all have their own limitations.

V. An open discussion about the minimum wage can help us gain more insight into this complex issue.

In this speech, David provides some history regarding the federal minimum wage, debunks some of the myths surrounding the working poor, and presents a few of the existing approaches to this issue. He then opens the discussion, knowing that his audience will have strong views. However, throughout his speech, he set the stage for an invitational discussion so that his audience felt free to share their views.

In the next example, Amanda explored the issue of funding HIV/AIDS research and support in both Africa and the United States. She compared and contrasted the AIDS epidemic in both regions, inviting her audience to explore the topic of prioritizing funding and support efforts when there is too little money to fully fund research and support in both parts of the world.

**Specific purpose:** To invite my audience to explore, and to explore myself, the issues involved in funding HIV/AIDS research and support in Africa and the United States.

**Thesis statement:** Because my volunteer efforts this semester have shown me that the HIV/AIDS epidemic significantly affects both the United States and Africa, that funding is a problem for both, and that people are divided over where federal funding should go, I'd like to explore with my audience possible ways to prioritize relief efforts in both regions.

**Main points:**

I. Both Africa and the United States are dealing with an AIDS epidemic.

A. Sub-Saharan Africa has less than 11 percent of the world's population but is home to 70 percent of those living with HIV.

B. Approximately 1 million people currently living in the United States have HIV/AIDS.

II. Funding is inadequate for both Africa and the United States.

A. The budget the U.S. Agency for International Development (USAID) set aside for Africa is $15 billion for the next five years, but that barely scratches the surface of the HIV/AIDS problems in Africa's fifteen most affected countries.

B. The federal HIV/AIDS budget for the United States is $11 billion this year, but that also falls short of the goal of adequate assistance.

III. People are conflicted over where funds to alleviate the HIV/AIDS crisis should go.

A. Some argue that our money is being wasted on Africa and we should just support the United States.

B. Others believe that we should give more money to Africa because the problem there is so large.

C. Yet others believe that we are spending just the right amount of money in both regions.

D. And some believe that not enough is being spent in either region.

IV. Prioritizing relief funding for HIV/AIDS in Africa and the United States requires careful discussion, and I'd like to now open up the floor to my audience so we can discuss this important issue.

Here, Amanda presented the controversy fairly and openly. Because she did not have a firm position on the issue, she asked her audience to share their views with her as she sorted out her own perspectives. Using an invitational approach, she created an environment in which both she and her audience felt free to express their views openly.

**Skills & Confidence**
PPD Activity 22.1
Video Activity 22.3
Web Connect 22.1

Speaking invitationally, like any form of speaking, has its challenges and rewards. People are more likely to feel free to share their positions when the conditions of equality, value, and self-determination are met, but these conditions can take time to develop, especially among strangers or when issues are hotly contested. You can create the conditions from the very beginning

**SPEECH TIPS**

## TOPICS FOR INVITATIONAL SPEECHES

Invitational speeches are well suited to exploring topics related to complex ethical issues. An example of such a topic would be the pros and cons of new technologies whose ethical implications may still be controversial, such as cloning and stem cell therapies.

**SPEECH Checklist**

### Outlines for Invitational Speeches

- [ ] Does your specific purpose include a phrase like "to invite my audience to..."?
- [ ] Does your thesis statement and/or your last main point include an invitation to your audience, such as "I'd like to explore with my audience...," I'd like to hear my audience's view on this problem," or "I'd like to now open up the floor to my audience"?
- [ ] In your introduction or main points, do you explain the reasons for your own position?
- [ ] In your main points, do you identify problems or alternative points of view so that audience members are encouraged to speak about them?

of a speech (Chapter 12) and through your delivery (Chapter 18). You can also create them through the organizational patterns you choose for your invitational speech, which are discussed next.

## Organizational Patterns for Invitational Speeches

As with informative and persuasive speaking, many organizational patterns are suitable for invitational speaking. The easiest for beginning speakers are the familiar chronological, spatial, and topical patterns, as well as a new pattern that is especially appropriate for speeches to explore an issue, multiple perspectives. As your skill at invitational speaking develops, you can modify these patterns and adapt to your audiences and speaking situations as needed.

### Chronological Pattern

Recall from Chapter 10 that a chronological pattern of organization allows you to trace a sequence of events or ideas. This pattern works well for invitational speeches, both to articulate a position and to explore an issue. In the next example, Eric uses the chronological pattern to explore an issue. He develops the issue and his position on that issue as they have changed over time.

**Specific purpose:** To invite my audience to consider the damage done to trails by mountain bikers and to explore possible solutions to this problem.

**Thesis statement:** An avid mountain biker, I've recently discovered the damage that mountain bikers can do to trails, and I'd like to hear my audience's view on this problem and explore possible solutions with them.

**Main points:**

I. An avid mountain biker since I was a teenager, last year I began to research the damage often done to trails by bikers like me.

II. In addition, just recently, I returned to my early routes and saw with new eyes the impact of mountain bikers on these trails.

III. I'm not willing to give up riding, but I wonder if there are solutions to the problems caused by mountain bikers.

Eric used the chronological pattern to trace his evolution as a mountain biker as well as his evolving consciousness about the trail damage caused by mountain biking. In the discussion with his audience, he considered such suggestions as completely closing trails to mountain bikers, encouraging bikers to adopt different riding practices, and finding ways to increase the maintenance of existing trails. Eric's audience learned about the attraction of mountain biking, and he learned of their concerns for the environment and frustrations with mountain bikers. Together, they explored solutions that could work for the whole community rather than just one group.

The next example illustrates how the chronological pattern might work in a business setting. In this example, Shalon addressed colleagues about proposed changes in a parental leave policy to explore whether those changes would work for the employees.

**Specific purpose:** To invite my audience to work with me to develop a parental leave policy that benefits all employees.

**Thesis statement:** A discussion with my coworkers could help us develop a parental leave policy that may be more comprehensive, and thus more advantageous, to more employees than the company's original policy, current policy, and the new policy proposed by our employer.

**Main points:**

I. Our company's original parental leave policy, which reflected the demographics and politics of the office at the time that it was created, had both strengths and weaknesses.

   A. The policy's strengths lay in the fact that it reflected the demographics and politics of the workplace at the time it was created.
   B. However, the nature of the workplace has changed over the years, highlighting the policy's weaknesses.

II. Our current policy reflects the fact that the company made changes to the original policy as a result of employee need.
   A. The changes affected women in certain ways.
   B. The changes affected men in certain ways.
   C. The changes also affected our company as a whole.

III. The new parental leave policy proposed by our employer is both similar to and different from previous policies.

IV. Given the history of the plan and the new proposal, I'd like to explore with my coworkers the changes we might want to suggest to the proposed plan.

Shalon described past parental leave policies, not to bias or sway her colleagues nor simply to educate them, but rather to collect information, stimulate open discussion, and foster self-determination. With this history, her audience could see more clearly how the proposed changes might affect them and could thus develop an alternative proposal to present to management.

A chronological pattern allows you to share history and offer background information that may help audience members enter a discussion. In the first example, the background information helped Eric's audience understand his position more fully and explore possible solutions. In the second, it helped Shalon's audience propose changes that would be in their best interests. By tracing your perspective on an issue over time, you establish common ground and an openness to seeing how the perspective or issue might continue to evolve.

### Spatial Pattern

Recall from Chapter 10 that the spatial pattern of organization can help you organize your ideas according to location or geography. You can use this pattern to articulate your position or explore an issue. This pattern is helpful when you want to discuss what a topic has in common, or how it differs, across nations, states, or cities. Riley used a spatial pattern to describe the ways communities have responded to hate crimes and to explore how his community might begin to heal from such a crime.

**Specific purpose:** To invite my audience to visit the scenes of several hate crimes committed across the country so we might know how to begin to heal from what happened in our own town.

**Thesis statement:** Trying to understand the response to the many hate crimes that have been committed in other communities across the United States might help my own community heal from our recent tragedy.

**Main points:**

I. The response of a Texas community to the hate crime against James Byrd Jr. involved both public and private actions.

II. Similarly, the response of a Wyoming community to the hate crime against Matthew Shepard was both private and public, bringing in the surrounding areas as well.

III. The response of a California community to the hate crime against a church with a largely Middle Eastern congregation was far more public in nature.

IV. With these responses in mind, I'd like to invite the audience to discuss ways in which we might respond to our own recent tragedy.

By describing how other communities responded to hate crimes, Riley stimulated and encouraged discussion with his audience about the needs of the community and how audience members felt they might respond to their own tragedy. By exploring this issue, both he and his audience began to formulate a plan of action that helped the community come to terms with a painful event.

You can use a spatial pattern to invite your audience to see how other localities have dealt with many types of public issues such as transportation, health, poverty, crime, education, and pollution. You can also use this pattern in business speeches to compare how other businesses have dealt with a problem. The spatial pattern allows you to connect your position to others or to help your audience explore an issue using information from other places.

Skills & Confidence Video Activity 22.4

### Topical Pattern

When you articulate a position, the topical pattern is effective. Recall from Chapter 10 that this pattern allows you to discuss the aspects of your topic point by point. Martin's speech on gun control, discussed earlier in this chapter, used the topical pattern. In that speech, Martin addressed audience fears about guns, his own experiences with guns, and the lessons he learned from those experiences. He then initiated a discussion with the audience about his position. Here is an example of the topical pattern from Phillip's speech, where he articulates his position about sentencing people who commit serious crimes to death or to life in prison.

**Specific purpose:** To invite my audience to consider that the death penalty is not as just and efficient as keeping an inmate in prison for life.

**Thesis statement:** Although the death penalty is commonly accepted as a just form of punishment, keeping inmates in prison without the possibility of parole may be a better solution, but both approaches present ethical dilemmas.

**Main points:**

I. Life sentences may be a better option than the death penalty, primarily because there have been cases of innocent people being placed on death row and subsequently executed.

II. The death penalty does not seem to deter people from committing murder—the United States is one of a few first-world countries to practice corporal punishment, yet it still has the highest rate of murder.

III. Surprisingly, a life sentence is cheaper for taxpayers than an execution.

IV. However, the suffering caused by a lifetime spent in prison cannot be overlooked.

V. Because each approach presents moral dilemmas, I'd like to invite my audience to discuss what they think about sentencing people who commit serious crimes to life in prison compared with sentencing them to death.

Using the topical pattern, Phillip shared what he had learned from his research about corporal punishment and life sentences. However, he did more than inform his audience about these aspects of our penal system; he shared the ethical dilemmas of each and remained open to alternatives, new information, and concerns from his audience.

**Speaking across DIFFERENCES**

**The multiple perspectives approach allows both the speaker and the audience to consider a wide diversity of viewpoints in a respectful way.**

### Multiple Perspectives Pattern

Although you can use this organizational pattern in other types of speeches, it is particularly well suited for invitational speeches. The **multiple perspectives pattern** allows you to systematically address the many sides of an issue before beginning a dialogue with the audience. You can go beyond dividing an issue into only two opposing sides and illustrate multiple perspectives on it. This approach not only respects a diversity of opinions but also invites your audience to consider even more views than those you have covered, making room for additional perspectives from your audience.

This organizational pattern works well when you want to speak to explore an issue with an audience. In the next example, Cara invited her audience to explore what to teach in U.S. schools about the creation of the universe. She used the multiple perspectives pattern for her speech, inviting her audience to consider how views from different cultures might fit into an elementary or high school education. The basic outline of her speech was as follows:

**Specific purpose:** To invite my audience to explore the many theories of creation and their role in U.S. education.

**Thesis statement:** Perhaps some of the many theories throughout time and across cultures that explain how the universe was created—including creationism, the big bang theory, intelligent design, ancient Egyptian and African theories, and Native American theories—could be taught in U.S. schools.

**Main points:**

I. One of the modern theories of how the universe was created, that God created the universe, comes from the Judeo-Christian tradition.

II. A second theory, proposed by the Greek philosopher Democritus in 400 B.C., set the stage for the big bang theory of creation proposed by most scientists today.

III. A third theory, known as the intelligent design theory, accounts for the origins of RNA and DNA and could add yet another perspective to our children's education.

IV. A fourth theory, offered by ancient Egyptian and African civilizations, presents a holistic view of existence in which many deities are worshiped as different aspects of God.

V. Yet another theory, advocated by many Native American peoples, suggests that the creator of all, sometimes known as Thought Woman, has both female and male aspects and "thinks" all things into being.

VI. I'd like to discuss with my audience the possibility that all of these creation theories be taught in U.S. schools to create a more inclusive curriculum.

The next example illustrates how the multiple perspectives pattern can be used in community presentations. In this example, Marko addressed businesspeople and articulated his perspective on donating to the United Way.[8]

**Specific purpose:** To invite my audience to consider the various benefits of donating to the United Way and to value the ways they already give back to their community.

**Thesis statement:** The United Way, with its overarching view of the community and its needs, is but one of many excellent ways to give back to a community.

**Main points:**

I. Because of its holistic view, contributing to the United Way is a great way to give back to the community.
   A. The United Way brings together key public and private entities to address many of the social ills of our community.
   B. One contribution to the United Way supports forty-one different agencies and projects in this community.
   C. Those who donate can feel confident that their contributions will be wisely distributed, because the advisory committee that determines the distribution formula is composed of volunteers from our own community.

II. The United Way also supports other avenues of giving to the community.
   A. Donations to individual agencies and projects are excellent ways to give to the community.
   B. Volunteering is yet another way to support these agencies and projects.
   C. When time or money is tight, simply speaking highly of the United Way and other forms of giving is a third positive act.

III. I'd like to discuss with my audience the idea of donating to the United Way and to other community-based agencies.

Although a persuasive speech might seem most appropriate to solicit donations, Marko uses an invitational approach with great success. He uses the multiple perspectives pattern in a unique way. Not only does he articulate his position on why he believes the United Way is a fine charitable organization worthy of support, but he also addresses other ways to contribute to one's community, thereby examining his topic from different perspectives. By doing this, Marko validates the various perspectives audience members may hold on his topic, encouraging their self-determination. Audience members will appreciate Marko's efforts to examine his topic from so many perspectives and likely be more open to dialogue about the numerous possibilities for giving back to one's community.

To use the multiple perspectives organizational pattern, you must follow three guidelines:

- Do your research so you can explain the various sides to your audience.
- Present each perspective fairly so audience members can make their own assessment of them all.
- Make room for even more perspectives to be offered from the audience when you open your speech up for dialogue.

In this diverse world, invitational speaking is an option that allows you to continue the public dialogue, even about the most controversial issues. With effort and respect, you can establish the conditions of equality, value, and self-determination even when you disagree with someone. These three conditions become increasingly important because, as cultural critic bell hooks explains, if "a person makes a unilateral decision that does not account for me, then I feel exploited by that decision because my needs haven't been considered. But if that person is willing to pause, then at that moment of pause there is an opportunity for mutual recognition because they have at least listened to and considered, honestly, my position."[9]

**Skills & Confidence**
PPD Activity 22.2
Web Connect 22.2

**SPEECH Checklist**

## Organizational Patterns for Invitational Speeches

- ☐ Use the **chronological pattern** to explore how an issue or your position on the issue has changed over time. It is also useful for providing background information.
- ☐ Use the **spatial pattern** to compare similarities or differences in approaches to an issue across countries, states, cities, or businesses.
- ☐ Use the **topical pattern** to identify the pros and cons of a policy or your reasons for your point of view.
- ☐ Use the **multiple perspectives pattern** to go beyond an either/or approach to an issue and present several alternatives for discussion.

## Guidelines for Giving Effective Invitational Speeches

Three guidelines can help you give effective invitational speeches and create a speaking environment of equality, value, and self-determination:

- Know your position.
- Use invitational language.
- Allow time for discussion.

### Know Your Position

For an invitational speech, especially when articulating a position, it is essential to take time before you begin putting your speech together to figure out how you really feel about the issue and why you feel as you do. An invitational speech must be researched as thoroughly as any other type of speech, because you must support your main ideas with evidence as well as personal opinion. To articulate your position fully and with respect for your audience, you cannot just ramble. Your attempts to create conditions of value and self-determination will be enhanced if you speak with accuracy, clarity, and detail about your views and why they are correct for you.

### Use Invitational Language

A second guideline for creating an effective invitational speaking environment is to use invitational language. Invitational language offers your view as one possible view but not as "the best" view. Phrases like "you should," "the correct position is," "anyone can see," which advocate your position over others, reduce your chances of creating the condition of equality. *Equality* means that all positions have merit and that they are viable for the people who hold them, even if they may not be right for you.

To communicate to your audience that you are trying to explain your view without imposing it on anyone else, use phrases such as these:

"I came to this view because..."

"For me, this position makes sense because..."

"Because of that experience, I began to see this issue as..."

"Although this may not work for all of you, this is the position I hold."

Try to use language throughout your speech that implies respect for and openness to other positions.

Invitational language is also important during discussions with your audience. In discussions, people may offer views different from yours or even the opposite of yours. Rather than silencing or censoring those views, encourage dialogue about those differences and disagreements. In an invitational setting, you are asking your audience to articulate their positions as fully as you do your own. Offer positive reinforcement to the ideas of others so the dialogue can develop openly and freely. Instead of responding with "that's not a good idea" or "I doubt that would work," ask questions like these:

"Can you elaborate on that idea?"
"How might that work?"
"Why do you think so?"
"Can you explain why you prefer that solution?"
"What benefits do you see with that policy?"

As you engage audience members in exploring an issue, get them to talk about their views. When the discussion gets heated, keep track of ideas you want to return to later by writing notes on a white board or flip chart (Chapter 20).

If you encounter a hostile audience member, your language can help manage, and even reduce, some of that hostility. When an audience member responds with anger, the reason usually is that the speaker has touched a sensitive nerve. But your language can defuse the situation and reestablish value. Use words and phrases that acknowledge your audience member's position, express your desire to understand that position more fully, and even apologize for upsetting the person. Rather than responding with angry words or denying that the person has reason to be angry, use language that communicates your respect for him or her as someone with views that may be different from yours.

**Skills & Confidence**
Web Connect 22.3

### Allow Time for Discussion

Articulating positions and exploring ideas with an audience take time. This means you must not rush through your presentation or hurry the discussion with your audience. If we are to create the conditions of equality, value, and self-determination and make a space for others in the public dialogue, we must be willing to take the time necessary to do so. Sometimes, this can seem inefficient. Western culture encourages us to get things done quickly and to make decisions without delay. Efficient presentations are often considered brief, to the point, and tightly organized. However, in invitational speaking, brevity and efficiency may work against you if you become overly controlling and

**SPEECH Checklist**

### Effective Invitational Speeches

- ☐ Fully research your topic so that you can clearly articulate your position—as well as alternative positions.
- ☐ Use invitational language with such phrases as "I came to this view because..." and "that is why I support..." (instead of "you should" or "the right thing to do is...").
- ☐ During the discussion period, invite audience members to share their views. Encourage dialogue and reinforce diversity of opinion with questions such as "Can you elaborate on that idea?"
- ☐ If an audience member expresses anger or hostility, realize that you have touched a sensitive spot and refrain from responding in anger. Instead, acknowledge that person's point of view and the right to feel strongly about the issue.

unwilling to explore someone else's position. Invitational speakers must allow time for a dialogue about ideas.

Where the time for speeches is limited, in classrooms and other settings, finding the time for invitational speeches can be challenging. If you are required or choose to speak invitationally, there is a solution to time constraints. First, consider your time frame carefully. If you have only a small amount of time, decide what you can address in that amount of time and restructure your invitation. For example, instead of covering five different cultural views of creation, Cara could have named all the different theories of creation she had discovered and then explained two of those views in detail. By reducing the scope of her presentation, she could still respect the opinions of the audience and make it possible to engage in a discussion of the larger issue.

These three guidelines—know your position, use invitational language, and allow time for discussion—will assist you in creating an invitational environment and giving an effective speech. They will also help you organize your ideas and keep your focus on inviting an audience to understand and explore an issue with you.

## Ethical Invitational Speaking

Ethical invitational speakers must be sure they are open to discussing their topic and that their purpose is mutual understanding. Let's look at these two components of ethical invitational speaking.

If you are not able to listen to perspectives that are incompatible with your own or to grant them value, then it would unethical for you to give an invitational speech. Ethical speakers stay true to their beliefs and values, and they do not pretend they are open to views when they are not. Being open to other views doesn't mean you have to be willing to change your view, but it does mean you have to be willing to listen with respect to other views. If you cannot grant value and self-determination to someone who disagrees with you on a topic, then give an informative or a persuasive speech on that topic. Religion, sexuality, and instances of oppression are three topics that may be especially difficult for invitational speeches, because people have such strong beliefs about them.

Your second ethical responsibility as an invitational speaker is to stay true to your purpose. It is tempting to try to invite an audience to consider your perspective with the underlying goal of persuading them that your view really is best. To speak ethically, you must truly have invitation as your goal. Although you can create the three conditions of equality, value, and self-determination in other types of speaking, in invitational speaking, you create these conditions because your fundamental goal is the exchange and appreciation of perspectives, not persuasion. If you really want to change your audience, do not pretend you are offering an invitational approach; give a persuasive speech instead.

**SPEECH Checklist ✓**

## Ethical Invitational Speeches

- ☐ Be truly willing to listen with respect and grant value to other views on your topic. Do not pretend to be open to other views if you have very strong beliefs about the topic and your opinion cannot be swayed.
- ☐ Do not use an invitational speech if your real goal is persuading your audience to share your point of view. Be true to the goal of inviting a variety of solutions and points of view.

## STUDENT SPEECH

with Commentary

# *Funding for HIV/AIDS in Africa and the United States*

*by Amanda Bucknam*

CENGAGE LEARNING

***Specific Purpose:*** *To invite my audience to explore, and to explore myself, the issues related to funding for HIV/ AIDS in the United States and in Africa.*

***Thesis Statement:*** *I'd like to describe the difficulty of deciding whether the United States should continue to fund HIV/AIDS relief in Africa or reserve those funds for HIV/AIDS relief here in the United States and then explore where it would be best to direct those funds.*

*Are you ready to give an invitational speech? You can use the following speech as a model. You can use your Premium Website for* Invitation to Public Speaking Handbook *to watch a video clip of this speech, see the accompanying outline, and read the discussion that followed the speech. Amanda Bucknam gave this speech in an introductory public speaking class. The assignment was to give a five- to seven-minute invitational speech, manage a five- to seven-minute dialogue with the audience, and wrap up with a one-minute conclusion. Amanda was also asked to provide at least four sources, meet the objectives of an effective introduction and conclusion, and provide relevant information. Notice how she created the conditions of equality, value, and self-determination and remained invitational throughout her dialogue with the audience. (You can use your Premium Website to access videos of other invitational speeches, including David Barworth's "Federal Minimum Wage" and Cara Buckley-Ott's "Creationism Versus the Big Bang Theory.")*

**Skills & Confidence**
Video Activity 22.5
Speech Studio 22.1

Picture this: You have a distant relative who is pretty much a stranger to you, who lives very far away. You never see him, but you've heard that he is in desperate need of help. He is suffering. He is experiencing pain, loss, anguish, hunger, and much more. You can help him, but there is another factor to consider. You also have a very close family member you see every day, and she is also in need of help. She is struggling and suffering, but not as much as the distant relative.

In these two situations, who do you help? Who do you give your time, money, and compassion to? Do you help the person who needs it most? Do you help the person whose life you can realistically improve? Do you help the familiar face or the face you never see? Think about it. Who, honestly, would you help?

Over the past couple of weeks, I have been researching the story I just told you. Only, at the heart of it, this isn't just a story; this is real life. If you haven't caught on yet, our distant relative is Africa, and our dear, close family member is the United States, and the problem each one is facing is the HIV/AIDS epidemic. You all are the United States government, and you must decide who to assist and where the relief money will go. Today I want to invite you to explore, and to explore myself, the issues relating to the U.S. funding that goes to Africa versus the amount of funding being offered here in the United States.

Because I am currently volunteering at NCAP, the Northern Colorado AIDS Project, I personally see the problems they face regarding lack of funding. They are just not getting enough money. The U.S. government is supplying aid and relief overseas, yet there is still a funding problem for U.S. agencies like NCAP. Is this right? Should we fund Africa at all? Should we give them more? Should we give them less? What about the problems with HIV/AIDS right here in the United States? I am not sure what we should do, so I am offering the information to you so that all of you can help me decide what an effective approach to this issue might be.

*Commentary*

*Amanda begins with a hypothetical story to capture her audience's attention, asking her audience to imagine two suffering relatives, one who is close and the other who is distant. She then proceeds to ask her audience how they would respond to the difficult decision of who to help. Amanda is able to draw her audience into her speech by making them feel connected to the situation.*

*Amanda establishes credibility by telling her audience that she has not only researched the story she just shared but has also investigated a broad range of information on her speech topic, the HIV/AIDS epidemic in Africa and the United States. She then draws her audience in with two techniques: (1) She asks them to put themselves in the place of the U.S. government and imagine having to decide how funding should be distributed, and (2) she poses some tough questions for her audience to consider.*

*She does a nice job of previewing the main points of her speech. Notice how she has arranged the main points of her speech into a spatial pattern of organization by comparing and contrasting the AIDS epidemic in the United States and Africa.*

*Because Amanda is still unsure of how U.S. HIV/AIDS relief funds should be spent, she invites her audience to explore, as she herself explores, the issues related to this topic. Note that she uses invitational language like "I am not sure what we should do" and "I will open up the floor to all of you, allowing you to voice your opinions."*

Today I will compare and contrast the AIDS epidemic in the United States and Africa to give you an idea of the severity of the problem. I will then give you the facts and figures about the amount of funding given to each region. I will present numerous sides of the issue to give you an idea of its different aspects and the opinions the U.S. public has about it. Finally, I will open up the floor to all of you, allowing you to voice your opinions on this issue and the obstacles we face.

*Amanda begins by citing information from the UNAIDS website to support her first main point. Note the importance of using current statistics to build credibility and keep the speech relevant.*

Both the United States and Africa are dealing with an AIDS epidemic. The magnitude of the problem is different in each area. According to the UNAIDS website, sub-Saharan Africa has more than 10 percent of the world's population but is home to 70 percent of all people living with HIV. An estimated 25 million people live with HIV/AIDS. In 2003 alone, an estimated 3 million people became newly infected, and 20 million people have died of complications related to AIDS since the epidemic started. That's a lot of people. In contrast, the Kaiser Family Foundation website states that in the United States, around 1 million people are currently living with HIV/AIDS. There are 40,000 new cases of HIV/AIDS every year, and 500,000 people have died of complications related to AIDS.

*In her second point, Amanda provides her audience with detailed and relevant information on how funds are currently spent in both Africa and the United States. Here and throughout her speech, she remains audience centered by presenting multiple perspectives carefully and with excellent detail.*

Funding is the main issue here. Africa is the continent that the United States supplies with the most aid. According to USAID Africa, in 2003, the President's Emergency Plan committed $15 billion over five years to combat HIV/AIDS in fifteen African countries. In 2004, the Emergency Plan gave $2.4 billion to Africa. The Emergency Plan is providing treatment to at least 2 million HIV-infected individuals, preventing 7 million new infections, and providing care and support to 10 million people living with and affected by HIV/AIDS in these fifteen countries.

In the U.S., there is also a plan to combat the problem. According to the Kaiser Family Foundation, the total federal spending on HIV/AIDS care in the United States was $11 billion in 2004. Forty-nine percent of that, or $5.4 billion, went to Medicaid. Twenty-four percent, or $2.6 billion, went to Medicare. And 19 percent, or $2 billion, went to the Ryan White CARE Act. Medicare and Medicaid provide the basic health care services people need. However, these programs don't cover long-term care or prescription drugs. That's where the Ryan White CARE Act comes in. According to the U.S. Department of Health and Human Services, the Ryan White CARE Act funds primary care and support services for people living with HIV who lack health insurance and financial resources for their care. CARE Act programs reach more than 500,000 people each year. It also funds organizations like the Northern Colorado AIDS Project.

According to their website, NCAP is funded by a lot of local sponsors, plus the United Way and the Ryan White CARE Act, but this still isn't enough. This organization is struggling to make ends meet. Lucas Walker, NCAP's events, office, and volunteer coordinator, told me that they are just not getting enough money, and he is hoping they won't have to close their doors. He said that a similar organization like NCAP in Boulder, Colorado, has already had to lay off some of its staff because of lack of funding. Should we continue to fund other countries like Africa when we need funds right here?

*Amanda adapts to her audience by describing a local organization's need for additional funding. Throughout her speech, she hints at her own opinion about where to focus relief efforts by asking whether we should fund African relief efforts. However, since she is exploring the issue of HIV/AIDS funding, she states a variety of facts and opinions about the issue and refrains from taking sides or persuading her audience to agree or disagree with her about how funds are spent.*

*She also presents a range of public opinion about her topic, prompting her audience to consider their own opinions. This approach reinforces her invitational position—that each person must sort out for herself or himself what she or he believes and that, as a group, they can help one another do just that.*

Coming to a close, I would like to present a few sides of the issue and tell you how the U.S. public feels about this topic. There are some people who think that we should just support our own country. They feel that there is no point in giving money to Africa, that we really can't make a difference there. However, we really can help out people here so that organizations like NCAP won't be struggling as much as they are now. A Kaiser Family Foundation poll taken in June 2004 shows the public opinion on whether or not we can make a difference in Africa: 48 percent say our spending is not making much of a difference; 41 percent say we're making meaningful progress; 5 percent say it depends on the volume or amount we give; and 6 percent don't know.

*In discussing public opinion on the subject of HIV/AIDS funding, Amanda uses current statistics from credible sources to support her claims.*

Others believe that we should give *more* money to Africa because the problem is so large, they need more money and more funds to help them, and the problem is more severe there than it is here. According to a public poll taken by *Newsweek* in January 2000, 48 percent are in favor of more money for Africa; 43 percent are opposed; and 9 percent don't know.

In addition, there are those people who feel we are spending too much money on HIV/AIDS and that we should worry about other health problems, that this is not the number one problem in the U.S. And there are other people who feel we are spending just the right amount of money on important health causes. They say we should continue doing what we are doing. Lastly, there are people who believe that we are just not giving enough money to the HIV/AIDS cause compared to the other things the U.S. budget is spent on. To illustrate this last point, in 2002 HIV/AIDS funding made up only 0.7 percent of the total federal budget.

*She concludes the main portion of her speech by inviting her audience to discuss what they think should happen with funding in the United States and Africa. She poses four questions for her audience to consider as they begin to dialogue.*

Now that you have heard all of the facts and opinions, I want to open up the floor to all of you to discuss what you think we should do about HIV/AIDS funding here in the U.S. and in Africa. Who do we help? Are we making a difference in Africa? What should we do about the funding shortages here in the United States? How can we help organizations like NCAP?

*Stating the benefits she feels came from the discussion of her topic with her audience, Amanda closes by voicing her hope that her audience now has a better understanding of the issues they've discussed. She ends with a question that reinforces her invitation to consider who should receive HIV/AIDS relief funding from the U.S. government.*

*Amanda and her audience discussed the issues related to HIV/AIDS funding in Africa and the United States. When the discussion was over, Amanda concluded her speech.*

I want to thank everyone for their time, attention, and opinions. I feel that we were able to discuss several different approaches to this issue. I hope you leave here with a little more information on the problems we are dealing with down the street at NCAP, here in the United States, and overseas in Africa. Just keep asking yourself, who would you help?

CHAPTER 23

# Persuasive Speaking



***In this chapter, you will learn to***

- Describe the three types of persuasive speeches
- Apply the most common patterns of organization for persuasive speeches
- Use three guidelines for giving effective persuasive speeches
- Identify the principles for giving ethical persuasive speeches

Throughout history, people have given persuasive speeches in political arenas, courtrooms, workplaces, community settings, social gatherings, and classrooms.

Today, just as our ancestors did, we use persuasive speech in the public dialogue to influence and alter the perspectives, the positions, and even the lives of others. When you understand the principles of persuasive speaking, you too can add your voice to the public dialogue as a persuasive speaker, whether you decide to speak, are asked to speak, or are required to speak.

Persuasion, the act of influencing people's thinking, feelings, or behavior, is so common that few of us go through a day without encountering some sort of persuasive communication. For example, as you drive to school in the morning, a radio advertisement tries to convince you that you'll have the time of your life if you attend an upcoming concert. Before lunch, you try to convince your friends to eat at the campus cafeteria because it's cheaper than eating at a restaurant off campus. And in the evening, your roommate tries to convince you to go out to a campus demonstration even though you have to get up early for work the next morning. Thus, the study of persuasion continues because this subject is such an integral part of our lives.

A **persuasive speech** is one whose message attempts to change or reinforce an audience's thoughts, feelings, or actions. To ask an audience to see things the way we do is quite different from speaking informatively (Chapter 21) or invitationally (Chapter 22). When we speak to inform, we share our knowledge or expertise with an audience, helping them better understand a topic by providing information. When we speak to invite, we set the stage for exploration of a topic, encouraging an open discussion that welcomes different perspectives. In contrast, when we speak to persuade, we ask an audience to think as we do about a topic, to adopt our position, or to support our actions and beliefs. In that sense, we act as advocates for a particular issue, belief, or course of action.

This chapter discusses the three major types of persuasive speeches, the organizational patterns best suited to persuasive speeches, some strategies for gaining audience support, and some of the common challenges and ethical considerations that persuasive speaking presents.

## Types of Persuasive Speeches

Attempts at persuasion generally address questions of fact, questions of value, or questions of policy. Each category concerns a different type of change sought from an audience. Knowing which type of change you want to request from your audience members helps you develop a listenable message for them.

### Questions of Fact

When we want to persuade an audience about a debatable point, we are speaking about questions of fact. A **question of fact** addresses whether something is verifiably true or not. For example, the winner of last summer's Boston marathon is not a debatable fact; we can determine the name by consulting a yearbook or looking up marathon records online. But no one can know with certainty what training schedule will produce the fastest marathon runners in the future. Any claim to such knowledge is speculative and therefore open to dispute. An audience can be persuaded to accept one opinion or another about the best training method for marathon runners by a speaker's use of arguments, evidence, and reasoning (Chapters 14 and 24).

Our understanding of many topics today derives from theories that have not yet been conclusively proven. Whether it is the reason dinosaurs became extinct, the original purpose of Stonehenge, the techniques used to construct the Egyptian pyramids, the way to end the global HIV/AIDS crisis, or the most effective methods of improving student reading skills, the facts about these issues leave room for competing theories. Therefore, such topics are well suited to speeches in which you try to persuade an audience that you have the most plausible answers.

### Questions of Value

When we want to persuade an audience about what is good or bad, right or wrong, we are speaking about questions of value. A **question of value** addresses the merit or morality of an object, action, or belief. Are old-growth forests worth saving from logging? Is it moral to punish certain crimes with death? Is it ethical to require all children to say the Pledge of Allegiance in school? These are questions of value, as are debates over what constitutes "good" and "bad" art, music, or theater.

When you attempt to persuade your audiences about questions of value, you move from asserting that something is true or false to advocating that one thing is better or worse than another. Questions of value cannot be answered simply by analyzing facts. Rather, they are grounded in what people believe is right, good, appropriate, worthy, and ethically sound. Thus, it can be difficult to persuade audiences about questions of value. This is because when we speak on questions of value, we must justify our claims. We must provide suitable reasons for accepting a particular action or view. When we justify a claim, we set *standards* and we argue that our view satisfies certain principles or values generally regarded as correct and valid by most people. So when we try to persuade an audience that old-growth forests are worth saving, we justify that claim by arguing that a stand of old-growth trees meets a certain standard for protection. Or when we attempt to persuade our audience that it is moral to punish certain crimes with death, we try to justify our claim on the basis of a particular standard: that certain actions fall into a specific category that warrants this kind of punishment.

### Questions of Policy

When we want to persuade an audience about the best way to act or solve a problem, we are speaking about questions of policy. A **question of policy** addresses the best course of action or solution to a problem. What form of support should employers provide for veterans with disabilities? How should the federal government implement mandatory drug testing? How many credits for graduation should the university require? At what age should people legally be allowed to drink alcoholic beverages? Each of these questions focuses on an issue that cannot be resolved solely by answering a question of absolute fact or debating its morality.

Although questions of policy might address the facts about the contributions veterans with disabilities make in the workplace or the morality of mandatory drug testing, they go beyond these questions to offer solutions and plans of action. In sum, speeches about questions of policy present audience members with a specific solution to or plan for a problem and try to persuade them that the solution or plan will eliminate the problem satisfactorily.

**Skills & Confidence**
PPD Activity 23.1
Video Activity 23.1
Web Connect 23.1

Because each type of persuasive speech—questions of fact, value, or policy—focuses on different issues and goals for change, each requires a different type of organizational pattern to be most effective. Many persuasive speeches can be organized according to the patterns discussed in Chapter 10, particularly speeches about questions of fact and value. However, speeches about questions of policy often call on an audience to take a specific action, so they sometimes require unique organizational patterns.

## Organization of Speeches on Questions of Fact

Speeches on questions of fact can be organized chronologically, spatially, or topically. To help you decide which organizational pattern is best to use, ask yourself this question: Can I achieve my goals best by describing the issue as it developed over time, by describing a spatial arrangement, or by covering distinct topics? The following example shows how Kendra built a case for the benefits of aerobic exercise by tracing fifty years' worth of data.

**Specific purpose:** To persuade my audience that regular aerobic exercise can enhance their quality of life.

**Thesis statement:** Research over the past fifty years indicates that regular aerobic exercise significantly enhances a person's quality of life in ways that other forms of exercise do not.

**Main points:**

I. Recognition of the importance of aerobic exercise and its impact on the quality of life began in the 1950s.

II. In the 1970s, "new" findings on aerobic exercise and its impact on the quality of life prompted the aerobics craze most of us are familiar with.

III. In the 1990s, additional research on the link between aerobic exercise and the quality of life revealed that this form of exercise is more beneficial than other forms, such as strength training.

IV. Sports scientists continue to recognize the superior benefits of aerobic exercise and to tinker with the "perfect" aerobic workout for the current era.

Occasionally, questions of fact can be organized spatially. In a speech about campus lighting, Thomas traced the layout of the campus from its center to its perimeter to make the case that it was not adequately lit for safety.

**Specific purpose:** To persuade my audience that the lighting on campus is not adequate.

**Thesis statement:** From the library to the farthest parking lot, the lighting on campus is not adequate to ensure safety after dark.

**Main points:**

I. Lighting near the center of the campus casts many shadows in which someone can hide.

II. Around the perimeter of this center, the lighting is spaced too far apart to offer adequate protection.

III. The lighting in the parking lots that border the campus should be much brighter than it currently is.

In the next example, Cody used the topical pattern to develop his speech about the increasing problem of obesity among America's children.

**Specific purpose:** To persuade my audience that childhood obesity is becoming a serious problem in the United States.

**Thesis statement:** Levels of childhood obesity have increased steadily since the 1960s, resulting in serious health and social problems for these young people.

**Main points:**

I. Obesity levels among children have increased since the 1960s, and the trend is not slowing down.

II. Obese children have a range of health problems such as asthma, type 2 diabetes, hypertension, orthopedic complications, and sleep apnea, placing a strain not only on the children but also on our medical system.

III. The self-esteem of obese children is damaged by the negative assumptions of their peers, including that obese children are lazy and lacking in self-control.

By organizing his speech topically, Cody was able to use his main points to persuade his audience of the problem of childhood obesity and the negative consequences of this escalating problem.

## Organization of Speeches on Questions of Value

Like speeches on questions of fact, speeches on questions of value can be organized chronologically, spatially, or topically. In the following example, Eiji used the chronological pattern to develop her speech about the value of encouraging girls to participate in the sciences.

**Specific purpose:** To persuade my audience that encouraging girls to participate in the sciences is of value to us all.

**Thesis statement:** Throughout history, when women have been encouraged to participate in the traditionally male-dominated world of science, they have made significant contributions that have benefited all of us.

**Main points:**

I. In the late 1700s, Caroline Lucretia Hershel's father and brother encouraged her interest in astronomy, and she developed the modern mathematical approach to astronomy.

II. In the late 1800s, with the support of her husband and colleagues, botanist Elizabeth Knight Britton built impressive botanical collections and is said to be the first person to suggest the establishment of the New York Botanical Gardens.

III. In the early 1900s, Maria Goeppert-Mayer was encouraged by her university professors to pursue her interest in science, which led to her winning the 1963 Nobel Prize in Physics for her groundbreaking work in modeling the nuclei of atoms.

The next example illustrates a speech about a question of value organized spatially. In his speech, Trevor's main points were about different areas in and around a city.

**Specific purpose:** To persuade my audience that the preservation of open space within and between communities should take priority in city planning.

**Thesis statement:** Open space both within and along the perimeter of a city is crucial for a healthy community.

**Main points:**

I. Open space in the heart of a city creates a friendlier, more relaxed city center.

II. Open space in identifiable areas or districts within a city brings people together, resulting in more familiarity with one's neighbors and safer neighborhoods.

III. Open space between two cities reduces urban sprawl and strengthens people's attachment to their own city.

Liza used the topical pattern to organize her speech about the unethical practice of producing veal.

**Specific purpose:** To persuade my audience that the veal industry is a highly unethical industry.

**Thesis statement:** The veal industry grew out of the dairy industry as a way to make use of bull calves, and unethical practices keep these animals confined and nutrient-deficient to please the palates of people who enjoy eating veal.

**Main points:**

I. The veal industry is a by-product of the dairy industry.

II. Although heifers grow into dairy cows, bull calves are sentenced to a different fate: They become veal.

III. Bull calves are confined to small crates and kept inactive to keep them tender.

IV. These calves are also fed an iron-deficient diet to maintain the pale pink color people who eat veal have come to expect.

When we give persuasive speeches on questions of fact or value, we may ask our audience to change their view or agree on what is right or wrong, but we do not ask them to do anything. Therefore, the chronological, spatial, and topical patterns work well for these types of speeches. However, for persuasive speeches about questions of policy, we also ask our audience to agree on what must be done to solve a problem. Thus, we must rely on different types of organizational patterns.

## Organization of Speeches on Questions of Policy

Persuasive speeches about questions of policy usually require organizational patterns that clearly define a problem and then offer a well-developed solution. Determining the best pattern for your speech depends on the kind of change you are hoping to get from your audience: *immediate action* or *passive agreement*. The differences between the two are simple, yet the impact they have on a speech is significant.

**SPEECH TIPS**

### ORGANIZING SPEECHES ON QUESTIONS OF VALUE

Persuading an audience on a question of value can be a challenge, especially if audience members have different opinions about what is good or moral. You need to consider their perspective when selecting an organizational pattern. For example, would it be more effective to persuade a group of teenagers that smoking is dangerous by discussing the diseases that smokers typically die of (topical) or by discussing the debilitating progression of a particular disease (chronological)?

When you attempt to **gain immediate action,** your goal is to encourage an audience to engage in a specific behavior or take a specific action. You want to move beyond simply asking your audience to alter a belief. When you seek immediate action, you want to be as specific as possible in stating what you want your audience to do. You need a clear **call to action,** an explicit request that an audience engage in some clearly stated behavior. For example, rather than asking audience members to simply agree with you that the lighting on campus is inadequate, you ask them to contact the school administration and urge it to provide the funds needed to improve campus lighting in next year's budget.

In contrast, when you want to **gain passive agreement,** your goal is to ask an audience to adopt a new position without also asking them to act in support of that position. When you seek passive agreement, you still advocate a solution to a problem, but you don't call your audience to action. Instead, you simply encourage them to adopt a new position or perspective.

Consider the differences between requesting immediate action and passive agreement in the following specific purpose statements:

**Immediate action**

To persuade my audience to stop eating veal.

To persuade my audience to vote against placing vending machines in our public schools.

To persuade my audience to adopt my aerobics training program.

**Passive agreement**

To persuade my audience that open space in a city benefits that city and its residents by making it more attractive and livable.

To persuade my audience that childhood obesity is a serious problem.

To persuade my audience that aerobic exercise is fun and significantly enhances a person's quality of life.

Notice how the requests for immediate action focus on asking an audience to do something specific, whereas the requests for passive agreement simply ask an audience to alter a belief. Let's look at some organizational patterns that will help you meet your speech goals whether you request immediate action or passive agreement.

## Problem-Solution Organization

Speeches that follow a **problem-solution organization** focus on persuading an audience that a specific problem exists and can be solved or minimized by a specific solution. These types of persuasive speeches are generally organized into two main points. The first point specifies a problem, and the second proposes a solution to that problem. In the problem component of your speech, you must define the problem clearly, and the problem must be relevant to your audience. In the solution component, you must offer a solution that really does help solve the problem and that your audience can reasonably support and implement.

Consider the following examples of problem-solution speeches given by Courtney and Jacinta. Both speakers used their thesis statement to state the problem clearly and then communicated that problem to their audiences in their first main point. They also related the problem to their audiences directly and personally. In the first example, Courtney spoke about the issue of light pollution.

**Specific purpose:** To persuade my audience that although light pollution is a problem that affects us increasingly every day, we can implement simple solutions to reduce the effects of this pollution.

**Thesis statement:** Light pollution disrupts ground-based astronomy, is a costly energy waste, and affects our health and safety, but there are simple solutions to the problem of light pollution.

**Main points:**

I. Light pollution poses three significant problems.

A. In cities, light pollution causes urban sky glow, which disrupts ground-based telescopes.

B. Light pollution represents an extreme waste of energy, and that waste is costly to all of us.

C. Light pollution causes mild to severe medical conditions and so is unsafe for our communities.

II. The problem of light pollution can be alleviated in two ways.

A. Light pollution can be controlled through government regulations, such as light codes, which are similar to noise codes.

B. Light pollution can be reduced through personal actions, such as using less unnecessary light and purchasing equipment that reduces light directed toward the sky.

Courtney's first main point clearly defined the specific problems created by light pollution, and her second main point offered reasonable solutions. Also note that she asked for passive agreement when she stated that supporting government regulations is a good idea, and she asked for immediate action when she suggested her audience modify the lights in their homes.

In the next example, Jacinta urged immediate action: She wanted her audience to stop requesting plastic bags when they go grocery shopping.

**Specific purpose:** To persuade my audience to stop using plastic bags when they shop.

**Thesis statement:** Because plastic bags are harmful to the environment, wildlife, and marine life, shoppers should choose paper or cloth bags instead.

**Main points:**

I. Plastic bags are made from ethylene, a by-product of oil, gas, and coal production, and they emit harmful gases that should be prevented from entering the atmosphere.

II. Plastic bags are prone to blowing out of our landfills, littering our towns and countryside, and negatively affecting wildlife.

III. India, Ireland, and other countries are "sacking" the plastic sack because of an infestation of these bags in their waterways.

IV. Each time they shop, shoppers can bring cloth bags or select paper bags when asked "paper or plastic?"

Jacinta illustrated the damages caused by plastic shopping bags. She also offered a viable solution that suited the problem and that her audience could easily implement.

Skills & Confidence Video Activity 23.2

Because problem-solution speeches pose a problem and offer a solution for it, they are excellent vehicles for persuading an audience to support a cause or take an action.

## Problem-Cause-Solution Organization

The problem-cause-solution pattern of organization is a slight variation of the problem-solution pattern. Speeches that follow a **problem-cause-solution organization** identify a specific problem, the causes of that problem, and a solution to the problem. This type of speech is especially effective if explaining how a problem came about will help you be more persuasive. Explaining the causes of a problem can sometimes help your audience better see the merits of a proposed solution. Describing causes can also allow you to explain how people came to believe what they do and to clarify misconceptions your audience may have about a topic.

Problem-cause-solution speeches generally have three main points: The first identifies a clear and relevant problem, the second identifies the relevant causes of that problem, and the third details a clear and appropriate solution to the problem. Brandi's speech about feeding wild animals illustrates this pattern of organization:

**Specific purpose:** To persuade my audience that the problems caused by feeding big game wildlife can be easily solved.

**Thesis statement:** The problems of wildlife overpopulation, the spread of disease, and other negative consequences caused by feeding big game wildlife can be solved by keeping human food away from wild animals.

**Main points:**

I. In many areas where people and big game wildlife live near each other, there is overpopulation in certain species, outbreaks of disease, and a decrease in our acceptance of hunters and hunting.

II. These problems are caused by well-meaning people leaving food out for wildlife in the winter and by campers who are not careful to keep their food and food smells away from wild animals.

III. These problems can be solved by simply not feeding wildlife; by protecting our food, washing our dishes, and washing our faces and hands when camping; and by putting our garbage in sealed containers.

Skills & Confidence Video Activity 23.3

Notice how Brandi was able to make a stronger case for her solution by identifying the specific causes of wildlife overpopulation, the spread of disease, and other wildlife-related problems. Once her audience knew the reasons for the problems, they could see the merits of a solution that might have seemed too simple to be effective.

Tony's speech about wildfires illustrates a different purpose for addressing a cause of a problem:

**Specific purpose:** To persuade my audience that wildfires should be allowed to burn because they are an important and natural part of the ecosystem.

**Thesis statement:** By letting wildfires burn, supporting prescribed burns, and allowing clear-cutting, we can prevent unnecessary forest fires caused by a century-long policy of fire suppression.

**Main points:**

I. Aggressively suppressing or putting out fires interferes with a necessary environmental cycle and leads to an unnatural state in the forest.

II. A century-long policy of "fight all fires" has created this imbalance and has confused the public about the purpose of fire in forests.

III. Letting fires burn themselves out, prescribing burns in certain safe areas, and thinning forests manually could help right the imbalance we now face.

In this example, Tony addressed the cause of the forest fire problem so his audience could better understand their beliefs about wildfires and how they start. By addressing this cause, Tony illustrated some of the unintended outcomes of the fire suppression campaign and helped people adjust their beliefs about fire and its effects.

### Comparative Advantages Organization

When your audience agrees with you about a problem but feels the solution is up for debate, a comparative advantages speech is often an excellent choice. Speeches that follow a **comparative advantages organization** illustrate the advantages of one solution over others. In this type of speech, use each main point to explain why your solution is preferable to other possible solutions. If you must criticize alternative solutions to strengthen your explanations, simply explain why the alternatives will not work, taking care not to degrade or belittle them.

Consider Angela's situation. Her coworkers and bosses already knew a problem existed: Sales were down and they were beginning to

**SPEECH TIPS**

#### THE PROBLEM-CAUSE-SOLUTION PATTERN

The problem-cause-solution organizational pattern is useful when you think that information about the cause of a problem will help persuade your audience to change their views or beliefs.

lose what had once been faithful customers. Therefore, Angela chose to give a comparative advantages speech so she could focus on illustrating the strengths of her proposed training program.

**Specific purpose:** To persuade my coworkers that my new training program will increase our sales and enhance our public profile.

**Thesis statement:** My proposed training program—which includes a longer initial training period, a more detailed assessment and understanding of the strengths of our products, and a stronger mentoring component than our current program—will turn our sales around.

**Main points:**

I. A longer initial training program will give our staff more time than our current program allows to develop a working knowledge and appreciation of the company and its mission.

II. A more detailed knowledge of our products and their value will enable our staff to work with our clientele more expertly than our current training allows.

III. A stronger mentoring program will improve the communication style of our new sales staff and help them respond to unfamiliar situations more effectively than our current mentoring program does.

Angela did not spend time describing the problem, because her audience already knew the training program needed improvement. Instead, she compared the advantages of her proposed program to the weaknesses of the company's current program. She was careful to avoid criticizing the current program too heavily, because her boss had been instrumental in bringing that model to the company. Rather, she simply said, "Our current program is no longer meeting our needs. If we make a few changes, we'll be back on top."

**SPEECH TIPS**

### THE COMPARATIVE ADVANTAGES PATTERN

The comparative advantages pattern is useful when your audience agrees about the problem and you want to focus on your proposal for the solution.

### Monroe's Motivated Sequence

Another organizational pattern helps us address an audience's motives and how those motives could translate to action. Developed in 1935 by Alan Monroe, **Monroe's motivated sequence** is a step-by-step process used to persuade audiences by gaining attention, demonstrating a need, satisfying that need, visualizing beneficial results, and calling for action. Monroe maintained that this pattern satisfies an audience's desire for order and helps a speaker focus on what motivates an audience to action. Monroe's motivated sequence organizes the entire speech, not just the body, and takes listeners through a step-by-step process of identifying a problem and resolving to help solve that problem.[1]

1. **Attention.** In this step, you catch the audience's interest so they take notice of an issue. Your goal is to motivate the audience to listen and to see the personal connection they have to a topic.
2. **Need.** In this step, you identify the need for a change, meaning a problem that can be solved. You define the problem and how it directly or indirectly affects the audience. Your goal is to encourage your audience to become invested in the problem, feel affected by it, and want to find a solution.
3. **Satisfaction.** In this step, you define what the specific solution is and why it solves the problem. In doing so, you show the audience how their "need" is "satisfied."
4. **Visualization.** In this step, you describe the benefits that will result from the audience's need being satisfied. You can describe what life will be like once the solution is in place, or you can remind the audience what it would be like if the solution

**Skills & Confidence**
PPD Activity 23.2
Video Activity 23.4
Web Connect 23.2

## SPEECH TIPS

### MONROE'S MOTIVATED SEQUENCE

Use this organizational pattern when you want to be very clear about what will motivate your audience to take action to solve a problem. This pattern's step of visualization can motivate your audience by appealing to their self-interest.

**SPEECH Checklist**

### Organizational Patterns for Persuasive Speeches

- [ ] To persuade an audience that your perspective on a topic is the most accurate one (a speech about **questions of fact**), use chronological, spatial, or topical organization.
- [ ] To justify your claim that one view is better, more appropriate, or more moral than another (a speech about **questions of value**), use chronological, spatial, or topical organization.
- [ ] To persuade your audience about the best solution to a problem (a speech about **questions of policy**), use problem-solution, problem-cause-solution, comparative advantages, or Monroe's motivated sequence organization.

were not implemented. Either way, you help the audience visualize how the solution will benefit them.

5. **Action.** In this final step, you outline exactly what the audience should do. This is your call to action, your plea for the audience to take immediate action or make a personal commitment to support the changes you're advocating.

## Guidelines for Giving Effective Persuasive Speeches

Consider the many times you've wanted to convince others to join with you, think like you, or support you. You may have wanted them to do something as simple as eat a new kind of food or as complicated as join a particular organization. It's natural to want others to share our commitments and beliefs, and most of us can think of many times we wanted to convince others to think, feel, and act as we do. The following guidelines will increase your chances for successful persuasion: (1) Be realistic about changing your audience's views, (2) use your evidence fairly and strategically for the best results, and (3) use language that respectfully motivates your audience to change.

### Be Realistic About Changing Your Audience's Views

Researchers generally agree that for persuasion to succeed, an audience must be open to change. If an audience is not open to change, even your best persuasive efforts are likely to fail. This means you must consider your audience's perspectives carefully and frame your persuasive attempts around issues that your audience will be open to considering. If you know your audience isn't open to change (views on religion often fall into this category), you probably won't be successful in convincing them to change no matter how well reasoned or researched your speech is. However, if your audience may be open to considering an alternative perspective (for example, that our society should allow different religious practices), your persuasive efforts are more likely to be successful.

It is often tempting to ask an audience to change their views completely, especially if you don't agree with those views. However, successful persuasion involves advocating a position or some *aspect* of a position that your audience can be open-minded about. For example, it may be unrealistic to think you can change your audience's views on legalizing certain drugs if your audience has had bad experiences with drugs or people who use drugs. But you may be able to persuade them to see the benefits that some of these drugs offer in medical treatments. In other words, you may be able to persuade them to reconsider some part of their position rather than reverse their position entirely.[2]

Your attempts at persuasion will likely be more successful if you take a realistic, audience-centered approach to changing others. Rather than asking for radical changes, approach your speech goals and your audience with some restraint. People hold particular beliefs and positions because of their experiences and worldviews. If you respect those positions and experiences as you ask your audience to change, you'll be more likely to give a successful speech.

### Use Evidence Fairly and Strategically

Research on evidence and persuasion suggests that besides carefully researching, organizing, and delivering your speech, there are some strategies you can use to help construct effective persuasive arguments. These strategies include two-sided messages, counterarguments, and fear appeals.

Because persuasive speakers advocate one position over others, they often frame an issue as two sided, even if there are multiple perspectives on the issue (Chapter 22). A **two-sided message** addresses two sides of an issue, refuting one side to prove the other is better. Research suggests that when speakers discuss two sides of an issue, they are more persuasive if they actively refute the side they oppose rather than simply describing it without providing evidence for why the audience should share the speaker's views.[3]

Similarly, addressing **counterarguments,** or arguments against the speaker's own position, enhances the speaker's credibility. For example, when Tony advocated a policy of controlled burns to prevent forest fires, he increased his believability when he discussed the counterargument that controlled burns can get out of control and cause major damage. By doing so, Tony illustrated why those concerns are unfounded, strengthening his position that controlled burns prevent other fires from burning out of control.

Note, however, that you must use two-sided messages and counterarguments with care. In persuasion, credibility is important (Chapters 14 and 24), and you must take care that your opposing comments are not too judgmental or inflammatory. If you unfairly attack someone else's view or refute an opposing position too harshly, your audience may perceive you as less likable—and audiences find unlikable speakers less persuasive. Additionally, audience members are likely to focus their attention on assessing the merits of your judgmental claim rather than attending to the rest of your message.[4] When Tony described the counterargument against controlled burns, he did not say, "That's stupid. Anyone knows that the fear of out-of-control prescribed burns is as ridiculous as fearing you'll burn down your house by lighting your barbecue!" Instead, he clearly and directly illustrated why the fear is unfounded—but not stupid—and why his policy is preferable.

Speakers can also use fear appeals to persuade audiences to change or take action. A **fear appeal** is the threat of something undesirable happening if change does not occur. In political ads, politicians frequently employ fear appeals as a way to motivate voters. Research suggests that fear appeals may motivate audiences who are not initially invested in your topic to *become* invested.[5] A fear appeal causes audience members to take notice of an issue and see how it relates to them personally. When audiences already feel connected to the topic, fear appeals simply reinforce that connection. However, if a fear appeal is so extreme that audience members feel immobilized, imagining that there is nothing they can do to solve the problem, they may simply avoid or deny the problem.[6] Thus, if you use fear appeals, temper them so your audience feels there is a solution to the problem that will actually work. For example, if your speech is about the risk of violent crime in your community, speak honestly about it but do not exaggerate it. Then offer practical steps your audience can take to reduce their risk so they feel hopeful and empowered rather than defeated.

## Ethical Moment

### How Graphic Is "Too Graphic"?

The Animal Liberation Front (ALF), founded in 1976, is an international group known for its militant and often illegal actions designed to "free animals from abuse (i.e., laboratories, factory farms, fur farms, etc.) and place them in good homes where they may live out their natural lives, free from suffering." In fact, they are so militant that the FBI placed the ALF on its domestic terrorism list in 1987 after the ALF burned down a veterinary lab in California.

LEFETRIS PITARAKIS/AP IMAGES

To persuade others to stop the abuse of animals, they attack butcher shops, retail furriers, and medical and scientific research laboratories. They also acknowledge participation in theft, vandalism, arson, and the destruction of research records and equipment. Two of the ALF's goals are "to inflict economic damage to those who profit from the misery and exploitation of animals, and to reveal the horror and atrocities committed against animals behind locked doors."

In the FAQ section of its website, the ALF states, "each day we *butcher* millions of other sentient beings because we like the taste of their *flesh*," and asks, "Imagine the anguish caused by an oxyacetylene torch applied, if only for a few seconds, to your child's face. Unspeakably appalling? Yet each day we pay—by our choice in food purchases—to have other living creatures treated no less abominably." The ALF's website also includes graphic images depicting the torture and mistreatment of animals, to encourage people to join their cause and support their goal of "forcing animal abuse companies out of business."[7]

WHAT DO YOU THINK?

1. Do you think the graphic language and images used by the ALF are appropriate and persuasive? Why or why not?
2. Given your answer to question 1, describe the ethical principles that allow you to believe as you do.

*(Continued)*

## Ethical Moment

3. Do you think the destruction of property is an ethical persuasive tool? Why or why not?
4. Make a list of the ethical and persuasive strategies you might use to convince an audience to prevent harm to someone or something.

### Use Language That Encourages an Audience to Change

Just as informative speaking relies on language that is clear and unbiased, and invitational speaking relies on language that fosters openness and a desire to explore an issue, persuasive speaking relies on language that will motivate an audience to think or act differently. The most obvious examples of persuasive language are words and phrases that indicate what an audience "should do," what the "best" solution would be, or how something is "better than" something else. Persuasive language often appeals to emotions, as in "Wouldn't it be tragic if we failed to respond appropriately to this situation?" (See Chapter 24 for more about emotional appeals.) Additionally, audiences should hear strong calls to action such as "I'm asking each one of you to attend the rally tonight" or appeals such as "Imagine what our national park would look like with power lines running through it." However, research indicates that the more invested people are in a position, the less effective phrases such as "Today, I'll persuade you that" or "I'm here to convince you that" are, especially in your introduction.[8] When you tell an audience you will persuade them, they tend to hold more firmly to their positions.

Research on persuasion in conversations suggests that speakers who use words and phrases that show they understand the feelings and motivations of others are generally more persuasive than speakers who don't.[9] This means your language should reflect an appreciation for the positions audience members hold. Use language that helps you clarify your position and its merits without casting a negative light on the views of others. Although persuasive speeches are sometimes used to attack or argue, avoid this tactic when you enter the public dialogue by using respectful language, even if you and your audience disagree.

Using respectful language does not mean you should not try to motivate your audiences to change. On the contrary, the goal of persuasive speaking is to encourage an audience to think or act differently, and your language should reflect this challenge. Phrases like "Perhaps you've never thought about the impact of…," "I encourage

**SPEECH Checklist**

### Effective Persuasive Speeches

Be realistic about what you can or cannot persuade an audience to think, feel, or do. For very personal or controversial issues, respect your audience's views and focus on some aspect of the issue that audience members could reasonably consider.

- ☐ Use evidence to refute the opposing point of view (a **two-sided message**).
- ☐ Describe and refute **counterarguments** objectively. Making fun of them or criticizing them unfairly will cost you audience support.
- ☐ If you feel you need to use a **fear appeal**, also give your audience a realistic solution to the problem so they will not feel powerless.
- ☐ Use language that will motivate audience members by appealing to their emotions and making strong calls to action that challenge them to think in new ways.
- ☐ Use language that shows you understand positions different from yours and respect people's reasons for holding them.

you to consider this evidence carefully," and "How can we let this kind of damage continue?" do not attack or demand but instead urge audiences to reevaluate their positions. Some of our best efforts at persuasion have resulted in speeches that respectfully challenge an audience to think in new ways.

## Ethical Persuasive Speaking

Have you ever noticed that sometimes when you try to change someone, that person regularly resists your attempts?[10] Can you recall when your parents tried to persuade you to do (or not do) something, like dress a certain way, date a certain kind of person, or attend a certain function? For many people, as soon as the persuasion began, so did the resistance. Why does this happen when our parents likely had our best interests at heart?

Research and personal experience tell us that when others try to persuade us, we feel our freedom to choose our own path is threatened. In the United States especially, the freedom to choose is often basic to our sense of self. When someone tries to convince us to think, feel, or do something new or different, we are likely to dig in our heels and hold on to our position even more firmly. The issues we try to persuade others about are often complicated, making the process of persuasion even more challenging. Questions of fact, value, and policy are rarely simple or clear cut. And when beliefs, preferences, experiences, and habits come into play, these questions can get clouded and emotional, and people often invest in particular outcomes.

Given these characteristics of persuasion, be sure you request change ethically. To persuade ethically is to persuade others without threatening or challenging their sense of freedom to choose what is best for them. When you persuade, you are an advocate for a particular position, not a bully who tries to force or threaten an audience to see things your way. Ethical persuasion also requires you to recognize the complexity of the issues you speak about and the possible impact of your proposed solutions on your audience.

As you prepare your persuasive speech, keep the following four questions in mind. The first three address the complexity of audiences and issues, and the fourth helps you consider the effect of the changes you request.

- What is my position on this topic, and why do I hold this position?
- What are my audience's positions on this topic, and why do they hold these positions?
- Why am I qualified to try to persuade my audience on this issue?
- Is my request reasonable for my audience, and how will they be affected by the change?

As an ethical persuasive speaker, you must understand your own position and the positions of your audience. Acknowledge your own master statuses, standpoints, and unique experiences, as well as those of each member of your audience.

Similarly, ethical persuasive speaking requires you to *present information* in an ethical way. This means you must tell the truth, avoid distorting or manipulating evidence, and present information accurately and completely. To ensure that you present your evidence ethically, review the research tips in Chapter 7. Audiences dislike being manipulated and mislead. Even if a speaker gains support through the unethical manipulation of evidence or ideas, that support is usually lost when the audience discovers the deceit. Gaining support through ethical means will increase your credibility.

***Speaking across DIFFERENCES***

**You will be a more ethical persuader if you keep in mind that people don't like to feel that their sense of freedom to choose what is best for them is threatened. Acknowledging the differences between you and the members of your audience will help you craft a persuasive message that advocates, rather than forces, a position.**

**SPEECH Checklist**

## Ethical Persuasive Speeches

- ☐ Be sure you thoroughly understand your position and your reasons for holding it.
- ☐ Be able to explain why you are qualified to try to persuade your audience of your point of view.
- ☐ Consider what positions members of your audience are likely to hold and why they hold them.
- ☐ Think about the possible impact of your proposed solution on your audience and be sure you are making a reasonable request of them.
- ☐ Avoid making your audience feel you are threatening their sense of freedom to choose what is best for them.
- ☐ Present information accurately and completely. Avoid distorting or manipulating your evidence.

# PREPARATION OUTLINE

**with Commentary**

## *No Child Left Behind: Addressing the School Dropout Rate Among Latinos*

*by Dana Barker*

CENGAGE LEARNING

***Specific Purpose:*** *To persuade my audience that our nation must address the high dropout rate among Latinos.*

***Thesis Statement:*** *The dropout rate among Latinos in high schools and colleges, caused by low economic status and lack of family support, is too high, and this problem must be addressed with increased funding and teacher training.*

**Skills & Confidence**
Video Activity 23.5
Speech Studio 23.1

*Are you ready to practice your powers of persuasion by giving an effective persuasive speech? Use the following speech as a model. Use your Premium Website for* Invitation to Public Speaking Handbook *to watch a video clip of this speech and see Dana's transcript and speaking outline. Dana gave this speech in an introductory public speaking class. The assignment was to give a four- to six-minute speech with a minimum of four sources cited. Students were also asked to create a preparation outline that included a Works Cited section. (You can use your Premium Website to access videos of other persuasive speeches, including "The U.S. and the World Peace Crisis" by Renee DeSalvo.)*

*Commentary*
*Dana begins her speech by sharing an inspiring story about Mabel, a young Latina high school dropout.*
*With this story, she reveals the topic and problem of her speech: Latino dropout rates.*

*INTRODUCTION*

I. I'll begin with a story from the *Santa Fe New Mexican* about Mabel Arellanes. *(catch attention)*
   A. After becoming pregnant and dropping out of school at sixteen, Mabel has reenrolled in high school and is the junior class president.

B. Her change in attitude has led her to the hope of becoming a lawyer.
C. But Mabel's story is not representative of the current trends among Latinos.

II. I have researched trends in Latino socioeconomic status, graduation rate, and population in the U.S. *(establish credibility)*

III. Today I will discuss the problem of a high Latino dropout rate and suggest a solution. *(preview main points)*

*She then establishes her credibility by explaining that she has conducted extensive research on her topic. She completes her introduction by previewing the main points of her speech.*

*Transition:* Let me begin by discussing the problem.

*BODY*

I. The dropout rate among Latinos in secondary schools and colleges is too high and must be addressed.
   A. The dropout rate is excessive.
      1. Statistics and firsthand accounts attest to the high dropout rate.
         a. According to the *News & Observer*, one in twelve Latino students dropped out of high school in North Carolina during the 2003–2004 school year.
         b. This statistic does not account for the 47.5 percent of Latino students who have not graduated in four years since the beginning of the 1999–2000 academic year.
         c. Gamaliel Fuentes, who dropped out of school at fifteen, said, "We have no money; that's why I dropped out of school. [My father] asked me, but I decided. Now, if I could go back in time, I would stay still in school."
      2. The tendency for Latinos to drop out is triggered by low socioeconomic status and a lack of family support.
         a. The *Hispanic Outlook in Higher Education* explains that students coming from families of lower

*Dana begins the body of her speech by clearly stating her argument: The dropout rate for Latinos in secondary schools must be addressed.*

*She supports her proposition by citing recent statistics about the North Carolina school system. Additionally, she uses peer testimony to explain why Latino students are dropping out of high school and to establish pathos.*

socioeconomic status are less likely to succeed in college because high schools do not prepare them well.

b. Latino families expect their young people to contribute economically, and work schedules often conflict with studies.

*Transition:* Next, I will discuss the importance of addressing the Latino dropout rate.

*To support her point that dropout rates contribute to the generally low economic status of U.S. Latinos, Dana provides a source that describes the discrepancy of income levels between high school dropouts and university graduates. She also provides statistics to highlight the low number of Latinos graduating from college.*

B. Addressing the dropout rate will keep Latinos from remaining at a generally low economic status.
   1. Income is heavily dependent on education level.
      a. According to the *Daily Evergreen* newspaper, a person with a bachelor's degree can earn almost one million dollars more over the course of their lifetime than someone with no college education.
      b. A census report in the *San Antonio Express-News* found that Latinos earned merely 6.2 percent of the bachelor's degrees awarded in 2001.
      c. Yet the U.S. Census Bureau found that Latinos made up 12 percent of the national population in 2000 and 13.3 percent in 2002.
      d. In her essay "Canto, locura y poesía," Olivia Castellano of California State University, Sacramento, writes, "They [Latinos] carry a deeply ingrained sense of inferiority, a firm conviction that they are not worthy of success."

*Next, Dana uses expert testimony to explain why such low graduation rates exist for the Latino population.*

   2. Ultimately, all who hold the belief that our country is the "land of opportunity" are affected by the Latino dropout rate.

a. The U.S. Census Bureau states that in 2001, two out of ten Hispanics lived below the poverty line, while only one out of four earned a yearly salary of $35,000 or more.
b. Comparatively, around 50 percent of non-Hispanic whites earned $35,000 or more that year.
c. These figures are far from exemplifying opportunity for Latinos.

*Dana also provides statistics from a highly credible source to illustrate the typical disparity between the income level of Hispanics and non-Hispanic whites.*

*Transition:* But what will happen if the problem is not solved?

C. Since the percentage of Latinos in our population is still climbing, ignoring this issue will lead to a greater gap between the life of the typical American and the life of the Latino-American.

*Dana's transition between points B and C tells her audience that she is about to explain the consequences of not addressing the problem of Latino dropout rates.*

*Transition:* As I proceed to discuss the solutions for this problem, are you beginning to sense the urgency of the situation?

II. To solve the problem of a high dropout rate, we must fund teacher sensitivity training and programs that help Latinos succeed in education, and Latinos must change their perspective on the importance of education and their ability to succeed.
   A. Programs that educate teachers about Latino culture and beliefs and that help Latino students succeed in education will have the most impact on the dropout rate.
      1. Properly educated teachers will become aware of how they are able to meet the needs of Latino students.
      2. The *Santa Fe New Mexican* reported on the success of a program called AVID, which boasts a 95 percent college entrance rate among its Latino students.

*Before moving to her solution, Dana draws her audience in personally by asking them to consider the urgency of the problem. Then Dana presents her solution, explaining that teacher training and educational success programs will help Latinos succeed in school and will help change the Latino mind-set about education.*

*She uses an example of a successful program, AVID, to support her claim. Note how with this example Dana uses analogical reasoning (Chapter 14) to convince her audience that her solution will be successful, suggesting that the success of this program could be repeated with similar programs. Additionally, in point B, she succinctly states how her solution could be implemented.*

*Transition:* What can we expect from this solution?

B. This solution, which can be implemented at the national, state, and local levels, is dependent on increased funding and the efforts of educators with experience in Latino culture.
   1. Increased funding will help reform educational budgets for Latino communities and fund college success programs like AVID.
   2. This solution also requires the collective efforts of highly knowledgeable professionals with experience in education and Latino culture who can train other educators.

*Dana explains the potential results of implementing her plan. She informs her audience that the results will take time, but the plan could produce a newfound sense of accomplishment and pride among the U.S. Latino community.*

C. Given proper attention and execution, the plan to address the Latino dropout rate will help the dropout rate begin to fall and will instill pride in the Latino community.
   1. Although it will take at least a decade before results are fully apparent, perhaps even a generation, ideally the plan will result in an increase in Latinos earning bachelor's, master's, and doctoral degrees.
   2. The sense of accomplishment gained by furthering education will change the typical Latino mind-set regarding education and instill an overall sense of pride in the U.S. Latino community.

*CONCLUSION*

*Dana completes her speech with a brief conclusion that summarizes her main points and reinforces her thesis.*

I. I have discussed the problem of the high dropout rate among Latinos, and I have discussed a possible solution for addressing the issue. *(summarize main points)*

II. Hopefully, you can clearly see that the high Latino dropout rate is an issue of great concern, one that requires prompt and thorough attention. *(reinforce thesis)*

**Works Cited**

Castellano, O. (1997). Canto, locura y poesía. In M. L. Andersen (Compiler) & P. H. Collins (Ed.), *Race, class, and gender: An anthology.* Belmont, CA: Wadsworth.

Ferry, B. (2005, February 15). High school program gives students a fighting chance. *Santa Fe New Mexican,* p. B1.

Hannah-Jones, N. (2005, February 18). School an elusive dream: For Latino students, desire for diploma often clashes with needs of families. *News & Observer,* p. A1.

McGlynn, A. P. (2003). Improving completion rates for Hispanic students: "Best practices" for community colleges. *Hispanic Outlook in Higher Education, 14*(4), 21–25.

Ramirez, R. R. & de la Cruz, G. P. (2003, June). *The Hispanic population in the United States, March 2002* (Current Population Reports no. P20-545). Washington, DC: U.S. Census Bureau. Retrieved from http://www.census.gov/prod/2003pubs/p20-545.pdf.

Silva, E. (2004, June 6). Latino grad rate still lags across U.S.: Finances often hinder earning a four-year degree. *San Antonio Express-New,* p. 1K.

Turner, D. (2005, January 10). Four-year degree worth the wait. *Daily Evergreen.*

*Dana's bibliography of the specific research she references in her speech shows the currency of her sources. She relies on a variety of sources, including books, newspapers, and the Internet.*

CHAPTER 24

# Persuasion and Reasoning

- Evidence and Persuasion
  - Speech Checklist: **Persuasive Evidence**
- Credibility and Persuasion
  - Speech Checklist: **Your Credibility as a Persuasive Speaker**
- Emotion and Persuasion
  - Speech Checklist: **Appealing to Emotions**
- Mythos and Persuasion
  - Ethical Moment: **What Are Good Reasons?**
- Fallacies
  - Speech Checklist: **Avoiding Fallacies**
  - Preparation Outline with Commentary: **You Have My Deepest Sympathy: You Just Won the Lottery by Maria DiMaggio**

***In this chapter, you will learn to***

- Use evidence effectively in a persuasive speech
- Enhance your credibility before, during, and at the end of your speech
- Use emotional appeals effectively and ethically to persuade your audience
- Appeal to mythos effectively and ethically to persuade your audience
- Avoid five of the most common fallacies in persuasive arguments

The last thing Charlotte expected after being physically abused by her husband was to be victimized a second time by health insurance companies. But that's exactly what happened when the twenty-five-year-old Pennsylvania woman sought medical care after her husband shoved her into some furniture during an argument, injuring one of her hips. After a battered women's group urged Charlotte to report this injury and others before it, two national health insurance companies denied her coverage, citing the single episode of abuse. As one company representative said, covering battered women is like "covering diabetics who refuse to take their insulin"—the analogy being that battered women who remain in relationships in which they are repeatedly injured bear as much responsibility for their plight as do people with serious health problems who refuse to take their medications.

Responding to such arguments, U.S. Representative Constance A. Morella (D-MD) told a Senate committee hearing on insurance discrimination, "domestic violence has now become a preexisting medical condition"—that is, another justification to deny coverage to policyholders.[1] Although some insurance companies find the analogy valid and use it as a way to keep costs down, other groups, especially those that offer services to women battered by their spouses or partners, do not. Is the reasoning of the analogy accurate or, as Congresswoman Morella argued, are insurance companies treating the victims of crimes unfairly, as if they had preexisting medical conditions, to save money? Whatever your reaction to this true story, it is a powerful example of the use of an analogy and the way we reason to justify claims.

The arguments in this story, and the ones you will use in your speeches, are based on reasoning. Recall from Chapter 14 that speakers accomplish sound reasoning when they use logos, ethos, and pathos. **Logos** is the logical arrangement of evidence in a speech; **ethos** refers to the speaker's credibility; and **pathos** refers to the emotional appeals made by a speaker.[2] In this chapter, you'll learn more about these three components of reasoning as well as a fourth: *mythos*. Speakers appeal to mythos when they want to tap into common cultural beliefs and attitudes to persuade their audience. This chapter also examines fallacies, which are errors in logic and reasoning commonly made in persuasive speaking.

In persuasive speeches, your logical use of evidence, your appeals to credibility, and your appeals to emotion determine the strengths or weaknesses of your arguments. When used effectively, evidence, credibility, and emotion work together to help you move an audience toward a particular position. They help you introduce an issue and increase the audience's awareness of its implications. They also help you secure your audience's agreement and encourage them to take action. Finally, the effective use of reasoning helps your audience integrate their new awareness into their daily lives.[3] The next three sections discuss how you can successfully incorporate evidence, credibility, and emotion in your persuasive speeches.

## Evidence and Persuasion

When you speak persuasively, you use evidence in much the same way you use it in other types of speeches. However, for persuasive speeches, three aspects of the effective use of evidence are especially important. These are the use of:

- specific evidence
- novel information
- credible sources

### Use Specific Evidence

When you want to convince your audience that something is true, good, or appropriate, you will be more successful if you use evidence that is *specific* rather than *general*.[4] Your evidence should support your claims as explicitly as possible. For example, in a speech persuading her audience not to smoke, Shannan used the following specific evidence to describe the toxic ingredients in cigarettes:

> You want to make a cigarette? According to Dr. Roger Morrisette of Farmington State College, a single cigarette contains over 4,000 chemicals. If you want the recipe, well, this is what you'll need. You'll need some carcinogens, or cancer-causing agents; some formaldehyde, or embalming fluid; some acetone, which is paint stripper or nail polish remover; benzene or arsenic; pesticides such as fungicides, herbicides, and insecticides; and toxins like hydrogen cyanide, ammonia, and nicotine.

Shannan could have argued "Cigarettes are toxic and contain thousands of poisonous chemicals," but that is far less specific than her list of ingredients. She is more persuasive because she uses specific evidence rather than simply making a general claim.

### Present Novel Information

When we seek to persuade our audiences, we are trying to get them to change their views. Research indicates that you will be more persuasive when you present new rather than well-known information to your audience.[5] When you go beyond what your audience already knows, you capture their attention and cause them to listen more carefully to your ideas.

In a speech on pet overpopulation, Malachi produced new information that was quite persuasive. His audience already knew that unspayed animals are the cause of pet overpopulation, so he presented some novel information on this familiar topic: "According to the Humane Society of the United States," Malachi stated, "in seven years, one unspayed female cat and her unspayed offspring can theoretically produce 420,000 cats. In six years, one unspayed female dog and her offspring can produce 67,000 dogs." Malachi used information that was new to his audience as well as specific evidence (the exact figures).

### Use Credible Sources

In research, credibility relates to the potential bias of a source, but in reasoning, it relates to the trustworthiness of the source. When you want to persuade your audience, you must use evidence that comes from dependable sources.

There are two guidelines for using credible sources persuasively. First, provide enough information about your source so that your audience can assess its credibility.[6] Cite as much specific information as you can, such as date of publication, author credentials, and organizational affiliation. In the following example, Brian's credibility is weakened because he does not provide this information: "Numerous articles have been published explaining the benefits of laser eye surgery. According to one, this procedure is the safest of all available." How many is "numerous"? Who wrote these articles? When were they written? Who made the claim that laser surgery is the safest? Although the evidence might be legitimate, the audience is less likely to be persuaded than if Brian had offered concrete information about dates, publications, and authors' names and credentials (see Chapter 8 for citing sources in speeches).

Second, select sources your audience will see as trustworthy and fair. Although every source has a perspective, use sources your

**SPEECH Checklist** ✓

### Persuasive Evidence

- ☐ Use specific, detailed support for your arguments.
- ☐ Use supporting information that will be new to your audience.
- ☐ Give your audience specific information about your sources, such as name and date of publication, author name and credentials, and organizational affiliation.
- ☐ Select sources that your audience will see as fair, trustworthy, and knowledgeable.

audience will see as relatively unbiased. For example, even though the Humane Society has a position on animal overpopulation, it also has a reputation for being credible and fair. To be persuasive, choose sources that are reliable and known for expertise in your subject. Avoid sources that may be seen as extreme or overly biased.

Your audience is more likely to consider your persuasive arguments when you strengthen your reasoning with specific evidence, novel information, and credible sources. However, you must go beyond using evidence effectively in a persuasive speech. You must also make appropriate use of ethos, or your credibility as a speaker.

## Credibility and Persuasion

Credibility, like evidence and emotion, is one of the linchpins of persuasive speaking. Without it, you'll have a hard time persuading an audience of anything, regardless of what other appeals you make. Audiences might be entertained or even informed, but they will not be persuaded if you lack credibility. Recall that a speaker's **credibility** comes from the audience's perception of a speaker's competence and character. As you learned in Chapter 14, the most important aspect of credibility is that it be attributed to the speaker by the audience. No matter how talented, prepared, or polished you are as a speaker, if the audience does not see you as credible, you simply aren't credible.[7]

Politicians are perhaps the most obvious examples of the effect of weak credibility on persuasive appeals. Voters who perceive a politician as lacking competence and character will not be persuaded by her or his arguments, regardless of the claims and appeals used. Factors that cause an audience to perceive a speaker as credible include sociability (are you friendly and pleasant?), dynamism (are you energized and expressive?), physical attractiveness (are you well groomed and well dressed?), and similarity (does your audience perceive your values and views as similar to theirs?).

However, the two most important factors in credibility are the audience's perception of your competence and character. As you learned in Chapter 14, **competence** is the audience's view of a speaker's intelligence, expertise, and knowledge of a subject, and **character** is the audience's view of a speaker's sincerity, trustworthiness, and concern for the well-being of the audience.[8]

You express your competence through your research, your organization, and your delivery. If you have taken time to prepare and practice your speech, you are more likely to be viewed as competent. Competence also comes from your personal talents and your expertise, the experience and knowledge you bring to the speech before your research.

You communicate your character by taking the time to analyze your audience and tailor your speech to meet their needs, using inclusive language and convincing logic to express your integrity, values, principles, and attitudes toward others. These actions let your audience know you care about them and can be trusted to give a speech that is thoughtful and worth listening to.

### Types of Credibility

Three types of credibility exist in any speech: initial, derived, and terminal. **Initial credibility** is the credibility a speaker has before giving a speech, **derived credibility** is the credibility a speaker develops during a speech, and **terminal credibility** is the credibility given to the speaker at the end of a speech. The following scenario illustrates how these three types of credibility develop:

> You've been assigned to speak to a group of high school students and persuade them to volunteer in their community. When you arrive at the high school auditorium to speak, you've brought your *initial credibility* with you—what the students think about you before you even begin your speech. Their impression might be based on very little information (you're some college student) or on some specific information (their teachers told them who you are, why you're coming to speak, and what you'll be talking about).
>
> You begin your speech. It's well researched and you've thought carefully about your audience and how your topic is relevant to them. You've developed a style of delivery that you think the students will appreciate. You've worked hard on your introduction, knowing you need to catch their attention right away. You've also decided to share your own volunteer experiences with them. As you give your speech, you are establishing *derived credibility*—what you say and do throughout your speech to cause students to see you as competent and trustworthy.
>
> You finish your speech and open up the floor for questions and discussion. At the end of your time with the students, you close your presentation and say good-bye. When the students leave their interaction with you, they've assigned what's called *terminal credibility*; they walk away with some conception of your level of knowledge, expertise, sincerity, and trustworthiness.

As you can see from this scenario, credibility is a process. You may start your speech with high initial credibility, but if you don't follow through by building derived and terminal credibility throughout your speech, your overall credibility with your audience will drop. Or you may begin with low initial credibility because an audience does not know you but wind up with excellent overall credibility because you worked diligently to build your derived and terminal credibility during your speech.

### Enhancing Your Credibility

If you begin a speech with little initial credibility because the audience does not know you, you can build credibility during the speech in three ways:

- Explain your competence as you begin your speech.
- Establish common ground with your audience.
- Deliver your speech fluently, with expression and conviction.

Your introduction (Chapter 12) is an ideal place to establish your competence. Here you can reveal credentials, training, or experiences that make you competent to speak on your topic. Or you can explain that although you may not be specifically trained, you have done extensive research on the topic. Throughout the speech, you can increase your credibility by citing sources, sharing your experiences, and offering your insights based on your background and research.

In her speech on teen suicide, Chelsey enhanced her credibility right away by citing statistics and credible sources. Throughout her speech, she used narratives and visual aids to increase her credibility. And at the end of her speech, she used personal testimony to great effect:

> I've been a member of the Yellow Ribbon Organization [a suicide prevention program] for three years now and a survivor for five years. I found this organization at the worst stage of my life when I had completely hit rock bottom. With their help, I recovered and have now made it one of my missions in life to speak out about youth suicide.

At first, Chelsey seemed to be just another speaker with the usual amount of initial credibility. But as she spoke, her research, evidence, and preparation increased her credibility quite effectively. Her startling personal testimony at the end of her speech enhanced her terminal credibility, bringing a personal note to the speech that moved her audience and made her speech memorable.

A second way to build your credibility is to establish common ground with your audience. To establish **common ground** is to identify similarities, shared interests, and mutual perspectives with an audience. You can establish common ground by showing the audience you share values, experiences, and group memberships with them.[9] You can also establish common ground when you explain your views and positions and why they are in harmony with those held by audience members. When you take time to establish a friendly bond (often called *rapport*) with your audience, they will begin to like, trust, and respect you. Audiences attach higher credibility to speakers they see as similar to themselves.

**Speaking across DIFFERENCES**

**Establishing common ground with your audience members encourages them to like, trust, and respect you, regardless of the differences among you.**

Barbara Bush is a speaker who is well known for establishing common ground in one notable speech. In 1990, Bush was asked by the senior class of Wellesley College to give the commencement speech when they found their first choice, author Alice Walker, could not attend. About a quarter of the graduating class protested, claiming that because Bush was famous not for her own accomplishments but because of the man she married, she was not a good role model for the career-oriented students of Wellesley. Knowing how her audience perceived her, Bush established common ground by acknowledging their interest in Walker and relating that interest to their college experience.

> Now I know your first choice today was Alice Walker, known for *The Color Purple*. Instead you got me—known for the color of my hair! Alice Walker's book has a special resonance here. At Wellesley, each class is known by a special color. For four years the class of '90 has worn the color purple. Today you meet on Severance Green to say good-bye to all of that, to begin a new and a very personal journey to search for your own true colors.

A third way to enhance your credibility is through your delivery. Research indicates that speakers who are prepared, are energetic, speak moderately fast, and appear comfortable in front of their audience are seen as credible.[10] If you practice your speech and work on your delivery (Chapters 17 and 18), your credibility should increase. Here's how one student enhanced his credibility by preparing his speech with effective delivery in mind:

> Kip knew his initial credibility for his speech would be low. He'd blown his first speech for the class and this was the second round. Not only that, he was a member of the football team and he'd missed some classes because of travel to games. He knew the other students thought he was just a "dumb football player" who didn't care about the class.
>
> However, Kip wanted to get his degree and teach history at a high school. He knew the importance of public speaking

and communication skills in his future profession. So he chose a topic he felt really connected to, worked hard on putting his speech together, and practiced delivering his speech as many times as he could before the speaking day. He worked on his speaking rate because he knew he talked too fast when he was nervous. He worked on his eye contact so he could connect with his classmates nonverbally as well as verbally. He was enthusiastic about the topic and found ways to convey that enthusiasm in his delivery and his language. He also wanted to appear comfortable (even though he was really nervous), so he worked on his introduction until he had it just perfect.

On the day of the speech, Kip appeared confident, prepared, and quite engaged with his material and the audience. He went from being a "dumb football player" in the eyes of his classmates to a very credible speaker.

**Skills & Confidence**
PPD Activity 24.1
Video Activity 24.1

Remember that the audience assigns credibility to a speaker. Speakers with high credibility tend to be more persuasive than those with low credibility, so give this component of your speech careful consideration. You can also strengthen your persuasive message by making appropriate use of pathos, or appeals to emotion.

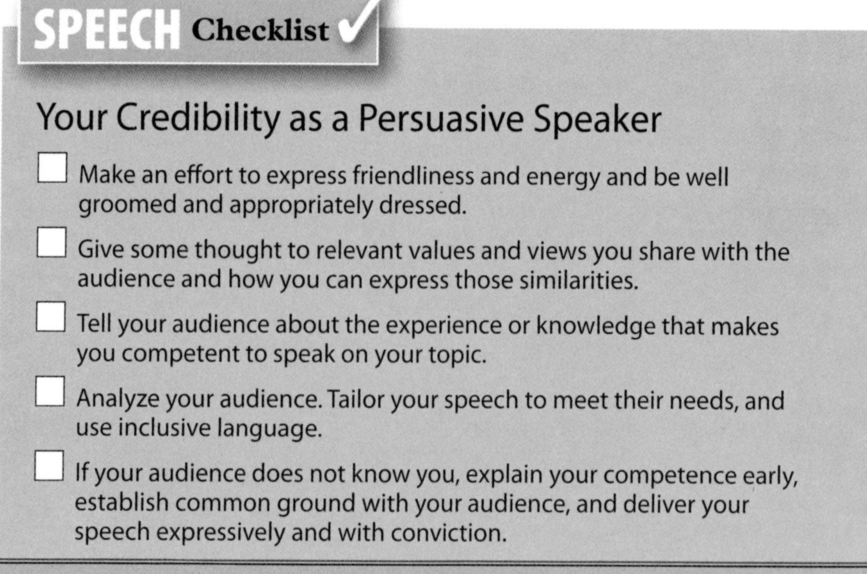

**SPEECH Checklist**

## Your Credibility as a Persuasive Speaker

- ☐ Make an effort to express friendliness and energy and be well groomed and appropriately dressed.
- ☐ Give some thought to relevant values and views you share with the audience and how you can express those similarities.
- ☐ Tell your audience about the experience or knowledge that makes you competent to speak on your topic.
- ☐ Analyze your audience. Tailor your speech to meet their needs, and use inclusive language.
- ☐ If your audience does not know you, explain your competence early, establish common ground with your audience, and deliver your speech expressively and with conviction.

## Emotion and Persuasion

Emotional appeals, or pathos, can be one of the most challenging aspects of persuasion. On the one hand, research suggests that speakers persuade only if they appeal to emotions. Appeals to emotions can be powerful because they encourage your audience to relate to an issue on an internal, personal level. On the other hand, because emotions are so personal and powerful, research also suggests that an inappropriate appeal to emotions can cause your audience to shut down in an instant.[11]

Appeals to emotions can be complicated, so it's useful to understand something about emotions. Emotions are internal mental states that focus primarily on feelings. Research distinguishes emotions (internal states such as fear, anger, sadness) from bodily states (tiredness, hunger), cognitive states (confusion, uncertainty), and behavioral states (timidity, aggressiveness).[12] Communication research has identified six primary emotions that tend to be expressed similarly across cultures and three secondary emotions that are expressed differently depending on age, gender, and culture.[13] The primary emotions are:

- *Fear:* an unpleasant feeling of apprehension or distress; the anticipation of danger or threat
- *Anger:* a feeling of annoyance, irritation, or rage
- *Surprise:* a feeling of sudden wonder or amazement, especially because of something unexpected
- *Sadness:* a feeling of unhappiness, grief, or sorrow
- *Disgust:* a feeling of horrified or sickened distaste for something
- *Happiness:* a feeling of pleasure, contentment, or joy

The secondary emotions are:

- *Pride:* an appropriate level of respect for a person, character trait, accomplishment, experience, or value; feeling pleased or delighted
- *Guilt:* an awareness of having done wrong, accompanied by feelings of shame and regret
- *Shame:* a feeling of dishonor, unworthiness, and embarrassment

***Speaking across DIFFERENCES***

**When considering the emotional appeals you will use in your persuasive speech, remember that the primary emotions (fear, anger, surprise, sadness, disgust, and happiness) tend to be expressed similarly across cultures and that the secondary emotions (pride, guilt, and shame) are expressed differently depending on age, gender, and culture.**

Another emotion common to persuasive speeches but not identified among the primary or secondary emotions is

- *Reverence:* a feeling of deep respect, awe, or devotion

In persuasive speaking, you make appeals to emotions to accomplish the following goals:

*Gain attention and motivate listening:* You often catch an audience's attention and motivate them to listen by appealing to their emotions with a compelling short story, testimony, or examples.

*Reinforce points:* You can use emotional appeals to reinforce main points or subpoints. For example, when you support a point with a statistic and then reinforce the statistic with an example of how some aspect of the statistic has affected a specific person, an audience can understand your point on a more personal level.

*Express personal commitment:* When you care deeply about an issue and want your audiences to recognize this depth of commitment, you may appeal to emotions by shifting your delivery to a more passionate or intense tone, or you may personalize your claims and arguments.

*Make a call to action or conclude memorably:* You can often move an audience to action by asking them to envision the result of that action and how it could affect them personally. You might end your speech with a compelling story or quote and so conclude memorably.

Because emotional appeals engage an audience personally, you'll want to consider a few aspects of emotional appeals to use them effectively: audience centeredness, vivid language, and a balance of emotion and reason.

**Speaking across DIFFERENCES**

**Remember that almost every one of our master statuses influences how we respond to emotional appeals. Carefully consider the master statuses of each member of your audience and choose appeals that they will accept.**

### Stay Audience Centered

Perhaps the most important component of a persuasive emotional appeal is its appropriateness for the audience. Consider your audience very carefully before you decide what kinds of appeals to use. For example, almost every one of our master statuses (Chapter 6) affects how we respond to the emotional side of an issue; our age, gender, physical ability, religion, ethnicity, and culture greatly influence how we see an issue and thus the acceptability of an emotional appeal.

As you consider the emotional appeals you want to make to your audience, ask yourself the following questions:

- Will the members of my audience have firsthand experience with my topic, or will it feel distant to them?
- What kinds of experiences will they have had?
- What emotions might be associated with those experiences? If they haven't had direct experiences, why not?
- In what ways could I draw them into my topic emotionally without offending anyone?

Although no one can predict with total accuracy how an audience will respond to an emotional appeal, you can consider your audience carefully and select those appeals to emotions that seem most appropriate. When speakers misjudge the appropriateness of an appeal to an emotion, they generally make one of the following three errors:

- *Overly graphic and violent appeals:* An overly graphic visual or verbal appeal is one that describes wounds and injuries, deaths, attacks, or harm to another being in extensive detail. The speaker is probably hoping to impress the audience with the horror of an act but carries the description too far and causes the audience to shut down or feel overwhelming revulsion.
- *Overly frightening or threatening appeals:* When a speaker describes something so frightening or threatening that the audience feels helpless or panicked, they will stop listening or they will feel immobilized. A common overly frightening appeal is the assertion that if the audience doesn't prevent something from happening or stop some behavior, they or someone they care about will die. This kind of appeal tends to stay with audience members long after a speech is over and causes them to feel unnecessarily fearful. In contrast, an appropriate fear appeal is one that moves the audience to act but does not immobilize or terrorize them (Chapter 23).
- *Overly manipulative appeals:* An appeal to an emotion, either positive or negative, that relies on theatrics, melodrama, and sensation rather than on fact and research is overly manipulative. Such appeals encourage the audience to feel pity, shame, guilt, or humiliation about something or to become overly excited or enthusiastic. Speakers may make overly manipulative appeals when they want their audience to see a person in a certain way, donate time or money to a cause, or act in a particular way. For example, in a speech asking an audience to give to a charitable organization, Jade showed images of children with cerebral palsy. She asked her audience

> questions to engage them and then created sad stories about the children based on the answers they gave. Although she received donations, she manipulated her audience's emotions with hypothetical stories rather than relying on true stories or research.

By staying audience centered, you will recognize which appeals are appropriate for your audience and which ones aren't. An example of a speaker who made appropriate appeals to emotions in a speech is Mary Fisher, who addressed the 1992 Republican National Convention as a person with AIDS. In her moving speech, she appealed to the emotions that accompany illness, loss, death, HIV/AIDS, conceptions of evil, risk and safety, and love and care for one another. Although her appeals were powerful, they were appropriate to her audience and not overly graphic, frightening, or manipulative. Fisher is an example of an audience-centered speaker who used pathos to make compelling emotional appeals without misusing the audience's feelings.

### Use Vivid Language

Appeals to emotions ask an audience to recall some of their most profound experiences. Using vivid descriptions and examples will help your audience connect with those experiences. One of the reasons Martin Luther King Jr. is considered one of the most influential speakers of the twentieth century is that he used vivid language to create images for his audiences. In his "I Have a Dream" speech on the steps of the Lincoln Memorial, his language helped his audience "see" his vision and connect to it emotionally as well as rationally. When he spoke of freedom, he described the "chains of discrimination" and the "manacles of segregation" that "crippled." He used evocative words and phrases such as "languishing" and "exile," the "magnificent words of the Constitution," and a "promise to all" for the "riches of freedom."[14]

The world's most profound speakers have been trained to make the most of vivid language, but even novice speakers can use language to move and inspire. In a speech on American veterans that was both persuasive and commemorative, Darrin created the following emotional appeal through his vivid language:

> Imagine sitting down to a peaceful meal with your wife, husband, or children. A "ring, ring, ring" is heard, interrupting you like an unwanted guest. The distinct sound of this ring suspends all talk. It's like this illusionary figure drifts across the room, touching the souls of those dear to you. Even before you pick it up, you know your country has gone to war, and this is your call to duty.

**SPEECH TIPS**

### PERSUADING AUDIENCES WITH LANGUAGE

Images that appeal to the senses can help your audience see what you're talking about and make an emotional connection to your topic.

Vivid language helps your listeners create images that are rich with feeling. When you speak persuasively, try to find words and phrases that tap into your audience's memories. If you do so, you will have an easier time drawing your audience in emotionally to your claims and arguments.

### Balance Emotion and Reason

When you speak persuasively, seek a balance between reason and emotion. An extremely emotional speech may stimulate your audience members, but without sound reasoning, they are less likely to be persuaded by your arguments.

Use appeals to emotion to elaborate on your reasons or to show the more personal side of your evidence. If you make a claim with statistics

**SPEECH Checklist**

### Appealing to Emotions

- ☐ Consider using an emotional appeal to gain attention, motivate listening, reinforce an important point, express your commitment to an issue, issue a call to action, or conclude memorably.
- ☐ Before you use an emotional appeal, consider whether your audience has had experience with your topic and what emotions might be associated with their experiences.
- ☐ Avoid appeals that your audience may regard as overly graphic or violent, overly frightening or threatening, or overly manipulative.
- ☐ Use vivid language to help your audience share experiences you are describing.
- ☐ Balance factual information and well-reasoned arguments with appeals to emotion, such as personal stories.

or offer an example of the impact of a plan, support it by drawing out the emotional aspects—for example, with an anecdote about an affected individual. Similarly, if you make an appeal to emotions, back it up with sound reasoning. When you balance emotion and reason, your audience will see more than one dimension of your persuasive appeals and can be persuaded on more than one level.

Appeals to emotion are necessary parts of persuasive speeches. If you avoid overly graphic, frightening, or manipulative appeals, you can tap into powerful emotions. By staying audience centered, paying careful attention to your language, and balancing reason and emotion, you will be able to craft persuasive arguments that encourage your audience to think differently about issues.

## Mythos and Persuasion

"No one is immune to the folk knowledge of their culture," state Marian Friestad and Peter Wright, marketing and psychology researchers at the University of Oregon.[15] The folk knowledge of a culture is **mythos,** the interrelated set of beliefs, attitudes, values, and feelings held by members of a particular society or culture. Friestad and Wright explain that we learn mythos not through any formal training but rather through the "whisperings of Mother culture."[16] We listen to these whisperings as children, adolescents, young adults, and adults. They come through anecdotes and customs as well as through events and accepted norms for behavior.

Whether you have grown up in the United States or another country, you're likely familiar with some of the cultural myths of the United States. These cultural narratives stress the importance of freedom and democracy. They describe the United States as the land of opportunity and tell of journeys from rags to riches. They emphasize the value of progress and the exploration of new frontiers. They celebrate heroes and heroines who have made the United States a world leader. The mythos of any culture communicates who its people are and what values it holds most important.

Mythos and persuasion are tightly interconnected. When we appeal to mythos, we call to mind history, tradition, faith, feelings, common sense, and membership in a community or culture. In doing so, we tap into a rich reservoir of emotions, attitudes, and values. We encourage our audience to accept our claims based on stories told over generations. We personalize an argument beyond making an appeal to an emotion, tapping into larger stories about "the way things are" and "the way things should be." Because mythos is an important part of the persuasive process, consider a few guidelines when you use this appeal in your speeches.

## A Part of the Story Can Tell the Whole Story

To tap into the mythos of a culture, you rarely need to tell the full story to the audience. In the 1960s, John F. Kennedy referred to the mythos of the American frontier in many of his speeches, calling forth the complete myth with just a few words:

> The New Frontier of which I speak is not a set of promises—it is a set of challenges. It sums up not what I intend to offer the American people, but what I intend to ask of them.

With these few words, Kennedy was able to call to mind the stories of settling the West, of overcoming odds, and of hard work. With the phrase "New Frontier," he transferred the myths of the "old frontier" to his presidency and drew people into the adventure and its challenges.

Similarly, when Martin Luther King Jr. spoke of freedom in his "I Have a Dream" speech, he did not detail the complete story of freedom in the United States. Instead, he referred to elements of that story to call forth for his audience the full mythos of freedom in a democratic society:

> In a sense we've come to our nation's Capital to cash a check. When the architects of our republic wrote the magnificent words of the Constitution and the Declaration of Independence, they were signing a promissory note to which every American was to fall heir. This note was a promise that all men—yes, black men as well as white men—would be guaranteed the unalienable rights of life, liberty, and the pursuit of happiness.

When speakers rely on mythos, they don't tell just any story. They refer to an intensely familiar story, one that has been repeated over the years and is part of the common sense of a culture.

## Mythos Has a Logic

Although a culture's myths may be as much legend as fact, they do contain a logic that rings true for that culture. They're like the fairy tales, folklore, and science fiction we grow up with. Although these myths are filled with larger-than-life heroes and villains, incredible adventures, death-defying feats, and supernatural powers, they reflect the logic, or common sense, of their culture. For example, consider the story of George Washington and the cherry tree. Washington probably never chopped down a cherry tree, but the logic of the story rings true: It is wrong to tell lies.

The power of mythos in a persuasive speech is that it allows you to tap into the logic of a culture. When you use mythos, think carefully about what logic you are appealing to and how that logic "makes sense" to your audience.[17]

## Ethical Moment

### What Are Good Reasons?

After twenty-four-year-old Army Specialist Casey Sheehan was killed in an ambush in Baghdad in 2004, his mother, Cindy Sheehan, became known as the "public face of the peace movement" in the United States. In August 2005, Sheehan camped near President George W. Bush's Texas ranch for a month, demanding that he explain the cause for which her son died. Her actions drew national media attention and galvanized the U.S. grassroots peace effort. Sheehan devoted herself to antiwar activism, making public speeches and attending protests and demonstrations across the country.

DUANE A. LAVERTY/WACO TRIBUNE-HERALD/AP PHOTO

Many criticized Sheehan for her work, arguing that she was exploiting her son's death and that her political stance hurt the troops and their families. Others were outraged that she called President Bush a "bigger terrorist that Osama Bin Laden" because his war policies had resulted in the deaths of thousands of Iraqi men, women, and children. Still others praised Sheehan for her efforts and for the sacrifices she made to bring attention to what she and others saw as an unjust war.

On Memorial Day 2007, the day her son would have turned twenty-seven, Sheehan announced that she had "resigned" as the "leader of the movement." She explained that she had sacrificed a twenty-nine-year marriage, her health, and her finances to fight against the war and that the devastating conclusion she had reached "was that Casey did indeed die for nothing." In her online diary, Sheehan wrote, "Good-bye America . . . you are not the country that I love and I finally realized no matter how much I sacrifice, I can't make you be that country unless you want it. It's up to you now." However, in July 2007, she was back in the public arena, running for Congress as an independent with a multi-issue platform against House Speaker Nancy Pelosi. Although she lost the race, she continued to take part in the public dialogue through a blog and a radio show.[18]

## Ethical Moment

WHAT DO YOU THINK?

1. Do you think Sheehan was unethical in her reasoning that President Bush was as much a terrorist as Osama Bin Laden? Does the loss of her son in the war make her statement more reasonable or acceptable? Why or why not?
2. Do you think Sheehan was justified in "resigning" from the antiwar movement? Why or why not? What kinds of sacrifices should we expect of someone who chooses to enter the public dialogue?
3. Do you think Sheehan exploited the death of her son, as some say she did, for her peace efforts? Why or why not?
4. What would cause you to enter the public dialogue, as Sheehan did, and to speak out so strongly about an issue? If you did, what ethical issues would you have to consider to persuade others to agree with you?

### Different Cultures Have Different Myths

Because each culture has a unique history, they all have unique myths. When you appeal to mythos in a speech, stay audience centered and keep in mind that members of your audience may have different cultural myths.

For example, Native Americans recognize communication with nonhuman entities, such as the rivers or the wind, as completely normal and even necessary for human survival. However, people from other traditions may have difficulty understanding this perspective. Similarly, many African Americans tell a story of two worlds, the one in which African Americans live and another inhabited by white people. In contrast, many white people tell a story of only one world, inhabited equally by all, in which all are equally free to move about and make choices. Each culture has a different mythos, and you must recognize these differences or risk alienating rather than persuading your audiences.

**Speaking across DIFFERENCES**

**When you appeal to mythos, keep in mind that members of your audience may have different cultural myths than your own. Refer to cultural myths that will resonate most effectively with your audience.**

**Skills & Confidence**
PPD
Activity 24.2
Video
Activity 24.2
Web
Connect 24.1

Using evidence effectively and appealing to credibility, emotion, and mythos will help you build a strong case for your position. Another strategy that will help you craft persuasive messages is to build sound arguments. By avoiding the five common fallacies in reasoning discussed next, you can make sure that your arguments are accurate and strong.

## Fallacies

Whether you intend to or not, you can make inaccurate arguments, called fallacies. A **fallacy** is an argument that seems valid but is flawed because of unsound evidence or reasoning. Fallacies are a problem in persuasive speeches not only because they undermine speakers' arguments but also because, despite their factual or logical errors, they can be quite persuasive. Fallacies can seem reasonable on the surface, but when we analyze them, we see that their logic is flawed. (Toulmin's model of reasoning from Chapter 14 is an excellent tool for analyzing arguments.) Although there are more than 125 different fallacies, a discussion of the five most common types is adequate for beginning public speakers. These are ad hominem, bandwagon, either-or, red herring, and slippery slope.[19]

### Ad Hominem: Against the Person

*Ad hominem* is a Latin term that means "against the person." An **ad hominem fallacy** is an argument in which a speaker attacks a person rather than that person's arguments. By portraying someone with an opposing position as incompetent, unreliable, or even stupid, you effectively silence that person and discredit her or his arguments or ideas. The story that opens this chapter contains an ad hominem argument. Here is another example of an ad hominem fallacy:

> Let me be clear: Saddam Hussein is a brutal, ruthless dictator who has repressed his own people, attacked his neighbors, and remains an international outlaw. The world would be a much better place if he were gone.[20]

Ad hominem fallacies are persuasive because they turn the audience's attention away from the content of an argument and toward the character and credibility of the person offering that argument. They cloud an issue, making it hard for an audience to evaluate the ideas the speaker challenges. But more important, ad hominem fallacies make erroneous claims. The argument against Hussein's character clouds the issue of whether it is ethical to go to war.

Listen carefully for arguments against a person's character and avoid them in your own speeches. They do little to build your credibility or help your audience see that your ideas are preferable to someone else's.

### Bandwagon: Everyone Else Agrees

When you fall prey to the **bandwagon fallacy,** you are suggesting that something is correct or good because everyone else agrees with it or is doing it. In public speaking, this translates to making statements like these:

> Many other communities are adopting this nonsmoking ordinance in restaurants. It's a perfect solution for us as well.
>
> How can we allow gays and lesbians in our organization? They've not been allowed in the military or scouting organizations, so why should we accept them in ours?

The bandwagon fallacy is like group pressure: It's hard to say no to something everyone else is doing. But the logic of the bandwagon is flawed for two reasons. First, even though a solution or a plan might work well for some, it might not be the best solution for your audience. You need to do more than argue "it will work for you because it worked for others." You need to explain exactly why a plan might work for a particular group of people, community, or organization. Second, just because "lots of others agree" does not make something "good." Large groups of people agree about many things, but those things aren't necessarily appropriate for everyone. To recognize a bandwagon fallacy, ask yourself two questions:

- If it is good for them, is it good for *me*?
- Even if many others are doing something, is it something I support?

### Either-Or: A False Dilemma

A dilemma is a situation that requires you to choose from options that are all unpleasant or that are mutually exclusive. In persuasive speeches, an **either-or fallacy,** sometimes called a *false dilemma*, is an argument in which a speaker claims our options are "either A or B," when actually more than two options exist. To spot a false dilemma, listen for the words *either* and *or* as a speaker presents an argument. Consider these two examples:

> Either we increase access to our before- and after-school meal programs or our students will continue to fail.
>
> Either we increase our candidate's appeal to women or we don't get elected.

In both examples, the audience is presented with a false dilemma. Intuitively, we know there must be other options. In the first example, there are other ways to respond to poor student performance—better nutrition is only one part of the solution. In the second, there likely are a number of ways to increase a candidate's appeal and chances of success. Sometimes it's hard to see the other options immediately, but they are usually there.

Either-or arguments are fallacious because they oversimplify complex issues. Usually, the speaker has created an atmosphere in which the audience feels pressured to select one of the two options presented. Even if those options may be good choices, an either-or argument prevents us from considering others that may be as good or even better.

## Red Herring: Raising an Irrelevant Issue

The term *red herring* comes from the fox hunting tradition in England. Before a hunt began, farmers often dragged some smoked herring around the perimeter of their fields. The strong odor from the fish masked the scent of the fox and threw the hounds off its trail, keeping the hounds from trampling the farmers' crops. Although this worked well for the farmers, trailing the equivalent of a red herring around an argument is not such a good idea. The **red herring fallacy** is the introduction of irrelevant information into an argument to distract an audience from the real issue. The following are examples:

> How can we worry about the few cases of AIDS in our town of 50,000 when thousands and thousands of children are dying of AIDS and AIDS-related illnesses around the world?

> Admittedly, women are beaten by their husbands. But what about those men who are battered by their wives or girlfriends? With the code of masculinity and toughness in today's society, we should be working toward assistance for the men, not more money for women.

In the first example, the speaker turns the argument away from her own community and toward the international problem of AIDS. Undoubtedly, this is an important issue, but it is not the one under discussion. Because of the red herring, the audience is less inclined to move toward a solution for the local situation. In the second example, the speaker brings up the issue of battered men to deflect the audience's attention from the issue of inadequate assistance for battered women. Although violence against anyone is a serious issue, the red herring of violence against men diverts the conversation from focusing on women and the need for increased assistance.

Red herring arguments are fallacious because they turn the audience's attention from one issue to another. This type of fallacy can be hard to spot because both issues are usually important, but the audience feels pulled toward the most recently raised issue. As an audience member, listen carefully when a speaker introduces a new and important topic in a persuasive speech; you might be hearing a red herring fallacy.

### Slippery Slope: The Second Step Is Inevitable

A **slippery slope fallacy** is an argument in which a speaker claims that taking a first step in one direction will inevitably lead to undesirable further steps. Like tripping at the top of a steep hill and tumbling to the bottom, a slippery slope fallacy suggests that the momentum of one decision or action will cause others. Here are two examples of slippery slope fallacies:

> If we allow our children to dress in any way they want for school, they will soon be wearing more and more outrageous clothing. Then it'll be increasingly outrageous behaviors inside and outside the classrooms. Soon they'll turn to violence.
>
> Our government says it will drill for oil in just one small portion of the Alaska National Wildlife Refuge. However, the only test to find oil in the refuge was performed in 1980, and the finding that oil was present was speculation, not the result of hard evidence. What if our government finds no oil when it drills? It will most likely be embarrassed and begin drilling all over the refuge to save face.

Each of these speakers suggests that if one unwanted thing happens, others certainly will follow. The audience gets caught up in the momentum of this "snowball" argument. Slippery slope arguments can be persuasive because the speaker relates the first claim (for example, the dress codes) to something frightening that is unrelated (violence). Before you accept the full claim made with a slippery slope argument, stop and consider whether the chain of events really is inevitable.

As you listen to speeches, and as you put your own arguments together, keep in mind that a fallacy is an error in logic. When we persuade others, we want to be sure our logic is sound and not based on error or deception. The fallacies that commonly occur in persuasive speeches are easy to spot if you understand how they work. Those presented in this chapter, as well as the errors in reasoning identified in Chapter 14, are easy to avoid if you take time to lay out your arguments carefully. By avoiding fallacies, you will enhance your persuasive efforts, increase your credibility, and contribute positively to the public dialogue.

**Skills & Confidence**
PPD Activity 24.3
Web Connect 24.2

**SPEECH Checklist**

## Avoiding Fallacies

- ☐ Argue against opposing points of view, but do not discredit or make fun of the people who hold them (**ad hominem fallacy**).
- ☐ Avoid arguing that a solution will work for your audience because it worked somewhere else (**bandwagon fallacy**).
- ☐ Do not try to pressure your audience into making a decision by falsely claiming that they have only two choices (**either-or fallacy**).
- ☐ In the public dialogue, do not try to divert an audience from consideration of one issue by raising an equally important but irrelevant one (**red herring fallacy**).
- ☐ Be careful not to argue against a decision or action by claiming that it will start a series of increasingly undesirable but imaginary consequences (**slippery slope fallacy**).

# PREPARATION OUTLINE

**with Commentary**

## *You Have My Deepest Sympathy: You Just Won the Lottery*

*by Maria DiMaggio*

CENGAGE LEARNING

**Specific Purpose:** *To persuade my audience that winning the lottery is not as great as it's perceived to be and that they should invest their money in alternative ways.*

**Thesis Statement:** *Lottery participants could avoid the financial and personal problems that often accompany lottery winnings by finding alternatives to this form of gambling.*

*Now that you've explored how to use logos (evidence), ethos (credibility), pathos (emotion), and mythos (cultural beliefs) in persuasive speaking, how to avoid some common fallacies, and how to persuade audiences effectively and ethically, create your own persuasive speech. Use the following speech as a model. Go to your Premium Website for* Invitation to Public Speaking Handbook *to watch a video clip of this speech and see Maria's transcript and speaking outline. Maria gave this speech in an introductory public speaking class. The assignment was to give a five- to seven-minute persuasive speech with a minimum of four sources cited. Students were also asked to create a preparation outline that included a Works Cited section. (You can use your Premium Website to access videos of other persuasive speeches, including "Colorado Prison Reform: A Solution to Reduce Recidivism and Overcrowding" by Jessica Fuller, "Fat Discrimination" by Carol Godart, and "Stop Animal Testing" by Amanda Konecny.)*

**Skills & Confidence**
Video Activity 24.3
Speech Studio 24.1

*INTRODUCTION*

I. You have my deepest sympathy; you just won the lottery. *(catch attention)*

II. Most of us would be shocked if someone said we'd won $20 million and then offered us condolences; however, hundreds of lottery winners have discovered the downside of winning big.

*Commentary*
*Maria begins her speech by combining antithesis with an intriguing statement that makes her audience want to hear more. She also uses the words "shocked," "condolences,"*

*and "downside" to draw her audience in emotionally.*

*She creates common ground with her audience by telling them that she used to think she'd be happy if she won the lottery, a common dream in the United States. She also establishes her credibility by letting her audience know that she's researched her topic.*

*Maria is hoping to persuade her audience to immediate action ("I hope you'll follow my example"). She alludes to her solution throughout her introduction and states it explicitly here: People should seek happiness in other ways and find alternative ways to spend their money.*

III. I used to think I'd be the happiest person in Brooklyn if I could just win a million dollars, but my research about the lottery winners convinced me to spend my money elsewhere—and I hope you'll follow my example. *(establish credibility)*

IV. Lottery participants can avoid problems that often accompany lottery winnings by finding alternatives to this form of gambling.

V. Today I'll explain that the lottery is a form of gambling that raises money for good causes; however, winners often end up with financial and personal problems, and you are better off spending your money elsewhere. *(preview main points)*

*Maria uses her first main point to describe the evolution of lotteries. In subpoint I.A, she explains why lotteries exist and how they are played. Notice that she defines lotteries as a form of gambling, evoking a negative connotation. However, this definition does not just reflect her opinion—she takes her definition from a highly credible source. In her sub-subpoint I.A.2, she cites an interesting statistic to reinforce that lotteries are a form of gambling unlikely to yield a big payoff.*

*In her sub-subpoint I.A.4, Maria uses historical evidence to add credibility to her argument that lotteries were viewed as a*

*BODY*

I. Lotteries are a form of gambling that raises money for good causes.
   A. The *World Book Encyclopedia* identifies lotteries as a popular form of gambling.
      1. Winners pay to participate, generally by purchasing tickets at a uniform price.
      2. According to a 2002 article in *The Detroit News*, winners are determined by random drawings; unfortunately, you are sixteen times more likely to get killed driving to buy the ticket than you are to win a record amount.
      3. Lotteries were popular in the United States in the 1700s.
      4. However, several states made them unconstitutional in the 1880s due to fraud by lottery companies and pressure from social reformers.
      5. New Hampshire reinstated the lottery in 1963; now, more than half the states have state-run lotteries.
   B. Lotteries generate revenue for good causes.
      1. The earliest lottery, organized in London in 1680, raised money for a municipal water supply.

2. A French lottery helped pay for the Statue of Liberty.
3. Closer to home, a national lottery helped support the American Revolutionary War.
4. In 1772, one lottery's proceeds were divided among a Presbyterian church, a German Lutheran church, the Newark Academy, and three Philadelphia schoolmasters.
5. Current lotteries in New Hampshire and Oregon, among other states, provide educational funding.

*Transition:* Now that we know a bit about the history of lotteries, you'd think your life would be great if you could only win big. Right? Well, there can be major problems for winners and their heirs.

II. Unexpected problems arise for lottery winners.
   A. First, their dreams of instant riches are not always fulfilled.
      1. Unless winners take a much lower lump sum, funds are distributed over twenty to twenty-five years.
      2. A lottery "millionaire" is really a "thousandaire" who gets about $50,000 annually before taxes, delinquent taxes, past-due child support, and student loans are taken out.
      3. Winners cannot draw cash from winnings, use them as collateral for loans, or liquidate future payments.
   B. In addition, many suffer personal loss and rejection.
      1. William "Bud" Post won $16.2 million but watched his brother go to jail, convicted of hiring a hit man to kill him.
      2. Debbie won $6.58 million but lost contact with her sisters, who stopped speaking to her when she declined to pay their debts.

*harmful form of gambling. In her sub-subpoint I.A.5, she brings her audience up to date on the numbers of state-run lotteries.*

*The examples she uses not only call attention to important historical moments, but also bring to mind treasured American values such as supporting our troops during wartime, supporting faith-based endeavors, and funding education for children.*

*Her examples also touch on two iconic American events: our receipt of the Statue of Liberty from the French and the American Revolution. These examples and Maria's acknowledgment that lotteries are used for good causes set the stage for her appeal to mythos later in the speech.*

*Reasoning deductively, Maria makes a broad claim (dreams of instant riches are not always fulfilled) that supports her thesis: "Unexpected problems arise for lottery winners." Her supporting examples establish her claim as viable (lottery winners do not necessarily become instant millionaires, some lottery winners experience pain and loss as a result of their winnings, and having money doesn't guarantee personal fulfillment).*

*Organized according to the problem-solution pattern, Maria's speech focuses on a question of policy. In her second main point, she states a portion of the problem she is identifying: Winning the lottery often causes misery rather than happiness. Citing statistics and examples from her research, she establishes the scope of the problem.*

*In her subpoint II.B, she continues to reinforce her point that the lottery can cause unhappiness, by using examples that appeal to emotions.*

*In her subpoint II.C, Maria continues to use evidence to support her claim that lottery winnings do not guarantee happiness. However, she cites a study that is almost thirty years old; her evidence would be stronger if it were more recent.*

3. Bernice took a day off work to claim her $1 million; her job was given to someone else.
4. Daisy won $2.8 million but went through a painful lawsuit.
    a. Her son's friend sued for half the winnings because she asked the friend to pray that she'd win.
    b. He prayed and she won, so he thought he was entitled to some of her money.
    c. The court ruled against him, saying he couldn't prove his prayers caused her to win.

C. Lottery winnings don't necessarily bring happiness.
    1. A study conducted by the *Journal of Personality and Social Psychology* of people with the best of luck and those with the worst of luck supported this conclusion.
    2. Accident victims weren't as unhappy as expected; however, lottery winners were unhappier and took less pleasure in life than expected.

D. Finally, heaven help the heirs if a lottery-winning relative dies and leaves them with a fortune.
    1. They must immediately pay estate taxes on the unpaid total, with monthly penalties added after nine months.
    2. According to the book *Lottery Players and Winners*, Johnny Ray Brewster won $12.8 million, taking it in annual payments. His sister Peggy inherited the payments, but upon inheritance, she immediately owed $3.5 million in taxes.

*In this transition, Maria reminds her audience of the nature of the problem and then lets them know that she has some possible*

*Transition:* Given the low probability of winning and the many problems winners face, there surely must be other solutions if you have money to burn.

III. Use your extra money in far more profitable expenditures.
   A. Invest in the stock market; investing just $10 to $20 monthly can pay off immensely by the time you retire.
   B. Donate your extra money to a charitable organization and claim a tax deduction.
   C. Indulge yourself: buy cable, eat lobster occasionally, buy season tickets to a sporting or a cultural event, or get an exotic pet.
   D. Finally, if you like to think your lottery money supports education, you can donate to my college fund!

*CONCLUSION*

I. I hope I've convinced you that playing the lottery is not all it's advertised to be.
II. I've explained what the lottery is, the problems it can cause, and some alternative ways to get rid of the money.
III. So the next time you see a new lottery millionaire, consider sending your sympathies rather than your congratulations.

**Works Cited**

Associated Press. "Compare the Odds." *The Detroit News*. [Electronic version]. 2002. Retrieved June 2, 2005, from http://www.detnews.com/2002/metro/0204/16/b01-446437.htm.

Beyer, G. W. and Petrini, J. *Lottery Players and Winners: Estate Planning for the Optimistic and the Lucky*. 2002. Retrieved June 2, 2005, from http://www.professorbeyer.com/Articles/Lottery.htm.

Brickman, P., Coates, D., and Janoff-Bulman, R. "Lottery Winners and Accident Victims: Is Happiness Relative?" *Journal of Personality and Social Psychology*, 36(8), 1978: 917–927.

Findlay, J. M. *People of Chance*. New York: Oxford University Press, 1986.

Goodman, E. *8 Lottery Winners Who Lost Their Millions*. November 18, 2004. Retrieved June 2, 2005, from http://moneycentral.msn.com/

*alternatives to buying lottery tickets. Thus, she begins to develop her solution.*

*In her third main point, Maria explicitly proposes her solution: Invest your disposable income in endeavors that will generate a greater return or that will be more personally fulfilling. Her suggestions are reasonable, and her audience will probably be open to considering them. Notice how she uses language that asks her audience to take immediate action: "invest," "donate," "indulge."*

*Also notice that she makes an indirect appeal to mythos by asking her audience to spend money on pursuits that define the American way of life: endorsing capitalism by investing in the stock market, supporting altruism by donating to charity, and indulging in little luxuries that we've earned through our hard work.*

*Maria could have strengthened this portion of her speech by spending as much time discussing her solutions as she did discussing the problem. For example, she could have provided statistics and examples to reinforce her suggestion about investing in the stock market, and she could have provided examples of charities that depend on donations.*

*Overall, she could have provided much more evidence to convince her audience that her solutions would result in happiness.*

*She uses a common phrase to signal the end of a speech. She then provides a nice, succinct summary of her main points, and she reinforces her thesis.*

*Maria concludes her speech by circling back to the intriguing statement she made in her introduction.*

content/Savinganddebt/Savemoney/P99649.asp.

Sanford, R. *Jackpot! What to Do before and after You Win the Lottery*. 1996. Retrieved June 2, 2005, from www.note.com/note/pp.jackpot.html.

Von Herrmann, D. *Their Big Gamble: The Politics of Lottery and Casino Expansion*. Westport, CT: Praeger, 2002.

PART VIII

# SPEAKING IN SPECIFIC CONTEXTS



## CIVIC ENGAGEMENT IN ACTION

### A Few Citizen Activists with Buckets

When activist Erin Brokovich and attorney Edward Masry, both made famous by the movie *Erin Brokovich*, became ill in 1995 from fumes emitted by an oil refinery Masry was suing, the Bucket Brigade movement was born. Bucket brigades are community-based groups that use specially designed buckets, commissioned by Masry, to gather and test air samples in neighborhoods near state-owned oil refineries, chemical plants, and similar facilities that emit toxins into the environment. When people in these neighborhoods experience health problems they suspect are caused by pollution, they form bucket brigades to help crack down on facilities that are violating environmental laws.

LOUISIANA BUCKET BRIGADE

The Bucket Brigade movement achieved one of its most important successes in 1999, when a Louisiana brigade successfully monitored emissions from more than fifty industrial facilities around Mossville, Louisiana, including vinyl plastic manufacturers, chemical production facilities, oil refineries, and a coal-fired power plant. Mossville residents had long complained of numerous illnesses but were repeatedly told by industry representatives that the facilities' emissions were not harmful. "I've asked [the refinery officials] to solve their problems, but they deny, deny, deny," explained Ken Ford, President of St. Bernard Citizens for Environmental Quality.

Fed up with the companies' total lack of response to their complaints, the community decided to make their problem a "national issue," says Anne Rolfes, director of the Louisiana Bucket Brigade. Mossville residents formed their own bucket brigade and began taking samples of air

#### You Can Get Involved

Check out **Web Connect P.VIII.1: Social Issues from Multiple Perspectives.** You can use this link not only to brainstorm and research persuasive speech topics but also to see how you can get involved with numerous local and national organizations dedicated to a wide variety of social issues.

## CIVIC ENGAGEMENT IN ACTION continued

Skills & Confidence
Web Connect P.VIII.1

around the facilities, which revealed extraordinarily high levels of contaminants. Those levels were verified by the Environmental Protection Agency, and offending companies were forced to pay fines and upgrade to state-of-the-art monitoring equipment. In addition, other towns in Louisiana's "cancer alley" took Mossville's cue and formed their own bucket brigades, leading to the establishment of the Louisiana Bucket Brigade. As a result, reports the Louisiana Bucket Brigade's website, "Pollution has been significantly reduced, all of which stemmed from a few citizen activists with their buckets."[1]

# SPEAKING IN SPECIFIC CONTEXTS

CHAPTER 25

# Speaking on Special Occasions



*In this chapter, you will learn to*

- Describe the four types of special occasion speeches
- Apply at least four guidelines for giving effective special occasion speeches

People give special occasion speeches when they come together to celebrate, reflect, remember, or establish a common purpose or goal. We give these speeches when we want to acknowledge someone's accomplishments or celebrate events or transitions. We also give them when we come together after difficult events. Special occasion speeches are given at weddings, awards ceremonies, banquets, and funerals. These speeches often bring an audience together and remind people of what they have in common. They also mark certain occasions as special, as different from the familiar events of our lives.

This chapter introduces four types of special occasion speeches: speeches of introduction, speeches of commemoration, speeches of acceptance, and speeches to entertain. Chapter 2 introduced the first three types of speeches: introduction, commemoration, and acceptance. Here you will learn more about these speeches, and you'll be introduced to speeches to entertain. Each of these speeches recognizes a different kind of special occasion; therefore, each has a slightly different goal. You will learn about these different goals as well as specific guidelines to help you prepare and deliver effective special occasion speeches.

## Speeches of Introduction

When you give an **introductory speech,** you provide an audience with a unique perspective on the person you are introducing. Introductory speeches are given for two reasons:

- To introduce yourself, such as at a job interview or in a newly formed group.
- To introduce someone else, usually at a formal event before that person gives a speech.

**Speaking at Work**

*Speeches of introduction are given routinely in the workplace and at professional events, such as company meetings and conferences. The most common type is the brief speech of introduction you give about yourself at job interviews.*

Regardless of whom you're introducing, introductory speeches tend to be brief and tightly organized. The principle of "less is more" applies because the audience is often more interested in what follows the introduction than in the introduction itself. Listeners want you to be brief and to give them specific, interesting, and useful information. Introductory speeches are organized around three goals:

- Acquaint the audience with a person.
- Establish the person's credibility.
- Generate enthusiasm for the person.

To accomplish these goals, include the following in your speeches of introduction:

***Introducing Yourself***

- State your name and any of your credentials or titles.
- Identify qualifications, experiences, or expertise you possess that directly relate to why you're giving your speech. ("I've worked in the insurance business for four years as a . . . , during which I learned . . . ").
- State your pleasure at being invited to speak or for the opportunity to participate in the task at hand.

***Introducing Another Person***

- State your own name and credentials. ("Hello, I'm Mary Brown, director of the Office of Volunteer Programs.")
- Indicate that you are introducing another person. (For example, "It is my privilege tonight to introduce our speaker, Dr. Robert Gonzales.")
- Provide accurate, relevant details about the person, including credentials, accomplishments, activities, personality traits, personal stories, or even a quote from something the person has said. ("Dr. Gonzales holds a Ph.D. from Harvard University and is currently working as a consultant for . . . He also has experience in . . . He has received numerous awards, some of which include . . . He describes his life as . . . ")
- Identify the topic of the person's speech by describing the general topic or simply giving the title of the presentation. ("The title of Dr. Gonzales's presentation this evening is . . . He plans to share with us some highlights of his most recent research in . . . ")
- Provide closure to your remarks and welcome the person to the podium or the front of the room. ("Please join me in welcoming Dr. Robert Gonzales.")

When you introduce yourself or another person, your goal is to create in your audience a sense of respect, an eagerness to hear more, and an understanding of what to expect. To give an effective speech of introduction, consider the following guidelines.

## Be Brief

When you introduce yourself, be concise. A successful introductory speech rarely lasts more than three to four minutes. It can be tempting to share a lot of details about yourself, recount past experiences, and tell personal stories, but doing so can take a lot of time. If you do opt to share a past experience or personal story, make sure you can tell it within a minute or two and that it clearly relates to the subject of the introduction.

When you introduce another person, remember that you are giving an introduction, not a full-length speech. Avoid lengthy stories and drawn-out explanations. Try instead to share enough information so that the audience is eager to hear from the speaker, but not so much information that they feel overwhelmed.

### Be Accurate

Introductory speeches can require background information on the person being introduced. If you're introducing someone else, there's a good chance you will need to do some research on the person. To conduct research on a person, you have a number of options. You can do your research on the Internet or at the library, interview the person you are introducing, or obtain a copy of his or her résumé or biography to get the information you need.

Being accurate in your speech means that you correctly state all titles and awards the person has received and their dates, and that you cite the sources of all quotes and personal stories. Being accurate also means that you pronounce all information correctly, including the speaker's name. If you take time to get your details correct, you not only show respect for the person you are introducing, but you also enhance your own credibility.

### Be Appropriate

Use your skills at analyzing an audience to present a speech that is appropriate to the occasion. Remember, your goal is to enhance your own or another person's credibility and build enthusiasm for what's to come. If your remarks are too personal, irrelevant to the occasion, or too informal, you will affect not only your own image but damage the credibility of the person you are introducing. Share only information that fits the occasion.

## SPEECH TIPS

### INTRODUCING A SPEAKER

Acquaint your audience with the speaker you are introducing and generate their enthusiasm for hearing his or her speech. Give some thought to what pieces of information will help this particular audience get excited about hearing what the speaker has to say.

**SPEECH Checklist**

## Speeches of Introduction

- [ ] The speech should not be longer than three or four minutes, so avoid long stories.
- [ ] Unless you are introducing yourself, do some background research so that you can provide information that will establish the person's credibility and interest your audience.
- [ ] Be sure every detail of your information about the person is accurate and that you know how to pronounce everything correctly, including his or her name.
- [ ] Before sharing any personal information about the person you are introducing, check with him or her. Share only information that is appropriate to the occasion.

Ask for permission before you share anything personal about the person you are introducing. What may seem like trivial details or interesting anecdotes to you may embarrass or disturb the person you are introducing. If the person asks you not to share that information, don't do so, even if it's one of your favorite stories.

# Speeches of Commemoration

**Commemorative speeches** praise, honor, recognize, or pay tribute to a person, an event, an idea, or an institution. Commemorative speeches are usually given in formal settings such as banquets, receptions, retirement parties, special birthdays, memorial services, and rallies. The two most common types of commemorative speeches are speeches of tribute and speeches of award. A **speech of tribute** is given to honor someone. A **speech of award** is given to present a specific award to someone and describe why that person is receiving the award. Both types of speeches highlight a person's exceptional value, qualities, contributions,

**Speaking at Work**

*Commemorative speeches are also common in the workplace, given at special events such as important company anniversaries, retirement parties, and meetings at which awards are presented.*

or accomplishments. Speeches of commemoration are organized around two goals:

- Help an audience appreciate the importance of a person, an event, an idea, or an institution.
- Illustrate for an audience a person's unique achievements or the special impact of an event, idea, or institution.

To accomplish these goals, a speech of commemoration should do the following:

- Identify who or what you are commemorating. Name the person, event, idea, or institution being celebrated.
- Describe the qualities or activities that make this person, event, idea, or institution special. Clearly state the unique characteristics or actions being commemorated.
- Describe the contributions made by the person, event, idea, or institution.
- Describe any obstacles the person, event, idea, or institution had to overcome to be successful.
- Describe your relationship to the person, event, idea, or institution being commemorated.

Effective commemorative speeches also include a specific kind of language. Commemorative speakers tell compelling stories and anecdotes, use rich language that brings to mind vivid images, and, when appropriate, express deep emotion. They also recite special phrases, sayings, or quotations used by the person being commemorated or attributed to the event, idea, or institution.

In the next example, note how South African activist Nelson Mandela uses the occasion of his release from prison in 1990 to pay tribute to those who assisted him. Although the second part of the speech (not included here) is a call to action, Mandela begins the speech by commemorating the people and institutions that supported him during his thirty-year imprisonment in South Africa:

> On this day of my release, I extend my sincere and warmest gratitude to the millions of my compatriots and those in every corner of the globe who have campaigned tirelessly for my release.
>
> I extend special greetings to the people of Cape Town, the city which has been my home for three decades. Your mass marches and other forms of struggle have served as a constant source of strength to all political prisoners.
>
> I salute the African National Congress. It has fulfilled our every expectation in its role as leader of the great march to freedom.

> I salute our president, Comrade Oliver Tambo, for leading the ANC even under the most difficult circumstances.
>
> I salute the rank-and-file members of the ANC. You have sacrificed life and limb in the pursuit of the noble cause of our struggle.[1]

Throughout this excerpt, Mandela uses vivid imagery to commemorate the specific contributions of those who assisted him in his long struggle for freedom. In the next excerpt, notice that he uses simple, yet deeply emotional, language to pay tribute to his family:

> My salutations will be incomplete without expressing my deep appreciation for the strength given me during my long and lonely years in prison by my beloved wife and family. I am convinced that your pain and suffering was far greater than my own.[2]

This simple use of emotional language ("deep appreciation," "long and lonely years," "beloved wife and family," "pain and suffering") allows Mandela to express his feelings clearly and appropriately.

The next example illustrates a speech of award. In 1999, Representative Bobby Rush, a U.S. Congressman from Chicago and a former Black Panther, encouraged his audience to support legislation to award the Congressional Gold Medal to Rosa Parks for her remarkable role in the civil rights movement:

> Mr. Speaker, I rise today in support of legislation to award a Congressional Gold Medal to Rosa Parks.
>
> Occasionally in our nation's history there are pivotal moments and indispensable individuals that move America away from its divisive past and closer to its imagined promise. December 1, 1955, produced such a moment and such a person.
>
> Rosa Parks grew up in segregation. Every day she was forced to deal with the violation of America's constitutional guarantees. On December 1, 1955, this American woman exacted of this country the freedom and equality the Constitution promises.
>
> Tired, like most citizens after a hard day's work, Rosa Parks refused to obey a shameful law that required her to sit at the back of a Montgomery, Alabama, bus. Her actions set the stage for the civil rights movement of a people who were unfairly and unjustly living under racist law.
>
> Because of this brave American woman, segregation laws around the nation began to crumble and our nation

> began to respond to the call for African-American equality. Because of her invaluable contribution to our nation, every American lives a better life today. For that reason, it is quite appropriate that Mrs. Rosa Parks receive the Congressional Gold Medal.
>
> But I must add, Mr. Speaker, that today, our nation continues to call for equality and freedom. There are still issues in our America that were issues in 1955. There are still Americans who do not enjoy the promises enumerated in the Constitution.
>
> So, if we are to truly honor this great woman, we must do so, not only with a Gold Medal, but also with actions that further her purpose. We must all become individuals working to end the discrimination and inequalities that exist in our great nation.
>
> I urge my colleagues to support this legislation and honor the mother of the civil rights movement, Mrs. Rosa Parks. Thank you.[3]

When you give commemorative speeches, you become responsible for conveying the significance of a person, event, idea, or institution to an audience. And if you're commemorating a person, you also want him or her to feel a sense of pride for having been praised and commemorated. To give an effective commemorative speech, consider the following guidelines.

### Share What Is Unique and Special

Do not assume the audience already knows the exceptional qualities of who or what you are commemorating. It is your job to inform your listeners of these qualities. Offer specific praise for your subject that consists of representative examples of successes, talents, accomplishments, special characteristics, and significant impacts. Be specific about the importance and meaning of who or what you are commemorating.

### Express Sincere Appreciation

Express sincere appreciation for all that a person, event, idea, or institution has given or made possible. Speeches of commemoration, whether tributes or awards, praise and honor some person or some thing. Include in your speech sincere recognition of the ways in which the person or thing you're commemorating has affected a community. Your words should be genuine and express respect and gratitude.

**SPEECH Checklist**

### Speeches of Commemoration

- ☐ Use vivid imagery and sayings or quotations to convey the significance of the person, event, or institution being commemorated.
- ☐ Provide specific examples to inform the audience why the person or institution is being commemorated, and express sincere respect and gratitude.
- ☐ Be certain your information is accurate and not exaggerated.
- ☐ Consider the specific characteristics of the person or institution being honored that will appeal to your audience.

### Tell the Truth

Be certain that the facts, stories, and traits you attribute to the subject of your commemoration are all accurate. Do not alter the truth to make a story more exciting. Instead, make an effort to find unique and special qualities and experiences that make your speech especially compelling.

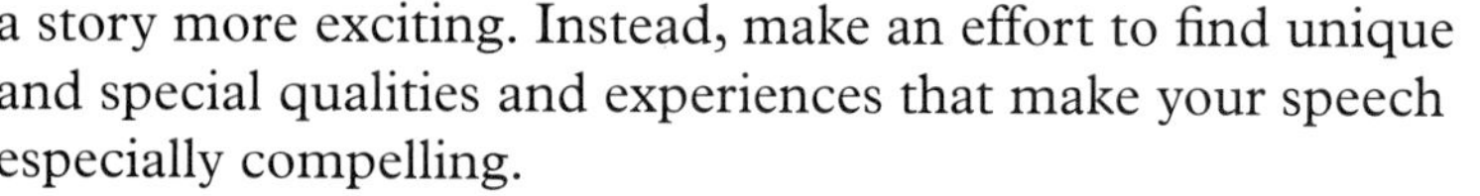

**Skills & Confidence**
PPD Activity 25.1
Video Activity 25.1
Video Activity 25.2
Web Connect 25.1

When you commemorate a person, share your personal experiences with that person so your audience can appreciate his or her exceptional qualities. When you commemorate an event, idea, or institution, share the characteristics that make your subject special in a way that appeals to your audience. When you give a commemorative speech, you want your audience to feel inspired and appreciative and to respect and admire the person or thing you are honoring.

## Speeches of Acceptance

In an **acceptance speech,** you express your gratitude, appreciation, and pleasure at receiving an honor or a gift. Speeches of acceptance are organized around three goals:

- Thank the audience and the organization that has presented you with the award.
- Show your awareness of the significance of the award.
- Acknowledge the people who helped you accomplish what you're being honored for.

In the next example, notice how Guatemalan human rights activist Rigoberta Menchú Tum conveyed her understanding of the significance of receiving the Nobel Peace Prize in 1992.

> Please allow me to convey to you all what this prize means to me. In my opinion, the Nobel Peace Prize calls upon us to act in accordance with what it represents and the great significance it has worldwide. In addition to being a priceless treasure, it is an instrument with which to fight for peace, for justice, for the rights of those who suffer the abysmal economic, social, cultural, and political disparities, typical of the order of the world in which we live.[4]

Sometimes speakers use the significance of an award to call attention to a larger issue. For example, Adam Horovitz, member of the hip-hop group Beastie Boys, included in his acceptance of the 1999 MTV Video Vanguard Award a call to address the serious problem of sexual assault at some large music festivals, particularly the 1999 Woodstock festival. "They [the sexual assaults at the festival] made me feel really sad and angry," he said as he accepted the award. "I'm talking to all the musicians here—I think we can talk to the promoters and make sure they do something about the safety of all the women and girls who come to all of our shows."[5]

Although the main focus of a speech of acceptance is to express your thanks for receiving an award or a gift, it has other purposes as well. To give an effective speech of acceptance, consider the following guidelines.

### Understand the Purpose of the Award

Be familiar with the background, history, and unique characteristics of the award. To receive an award is to receive an honor. Be certain you understand the honor you are receiving so you can speak intelligently about what the award means to you. You may even choose to organize your acceptance speech around the specific qualities of the award, as Menchú did. Similarly, you can use your understanding of the meaning and purpose of the award to encourage others to act, to remind the audience of larger social issues, or simply to reinforce shared values and principles.

### Recognize Others

Although you are being recognized as an outstanding individual, give credit and thanks to those who have contributed to your success. Verbally acknowledge their influence, support, and the ways in which they helped you succeed. Avoid the pitfall of trying to thank everyone to whom you are close. Thank only those people or groups who have been especially supportive, helpful, or pivotal to your success.

**SPEECH Checklist**

### Speeches of Acceptance

- [ ] Be sure you know the background and unique characteristics of the award you are receiving.
- [ ] Give thanks to the audience and the sponsoring organization and to those who contributed to your success related to this award—don't try to thank everyone in your life.
- [ ] Find out ahead of time how much time is being allotted for your speech so you can prepare a speech of the appropriate length.

### Respect the Time Limitations

The length of your acceptance speech will vary depending on the situation. Some acceptance speeches are quite short, lasting only a minute or two. Others, like Menchú's Nobel Peace Prize acceptance speech, last longer. When you are invited to receive an award and give a speech, ask how long your speech should be. If the award committee requests a short speech, plan to be brief. If they want a longer speech, respect this request. A longer speech suggests that your audience is interested in hearing a little more about you. For example, they may want to hear what you plan to do with a monetary award or what your future plans are.

Skills & Confidence
PPD Activity 25.2
Video Activity 25.3

## Speeches to Entertain

Sometimes called *after-dinner speeches*, speeches to entertain are often given after a formal meal—usually a dinner, but also after a lunch or a breakfast meeting.[6] Generally, those who give speeches to entertain are experienced speakers. However, even a novice speaker may be asked to deliver a speech to entertain at a luncheon for a service group or after a formal dinner at a club. A **speech to entertain** is lighthearted and addresses issues or ideas in a humorous way. But don't mistake these speeches for comedic acts. They do more than just provide the audience with a series of jokes, and they follow many of the basic principles of other special occasion speeches.

Speeches to entertain have a specific purpose, thesis statement, and main points. They may be informative, invitational, or persuasive and are organized in specific patterns, just like other speech types. Speeches to entertain have two goals:

- Entertain the audience.
- Make the audience think.

When you give a speech to entertain, you want to make the audience laugh and smile as you give your speech. You also want the audience to "entertain" the issue—to look at it carefully and explore its implications. This balance between humor and presenting issues can be a tricky one. Let's take a closer look at each of these components of a speech to entertain.

Humor is perhaps one of the most complicated communication phenomena. What is funny to one person isn't always funny to another. You might tell a joke or story to two people and only one laughs. Then there are times when you tell a joke in the right environment and everyone thinks it's funny. If you repeat that joke in the wrong context, no one will find it the least bit amusing. And if subjectivity and context weren't enough to consider, delivery is also a tricky matter. If you rearrange the wording of a joke just a bit or forget to tell a line, no one will understand what is supposed to be so funny. Predicting what will make people laugh is a bit like predicting the weather—we're often wrong. However, research tells us that what makes something funny is a combination of three elements:

- Timing
- Your objective in telling the joke
- The members of your audience

**Timing** is the way you use pauses and delivery for maximum effect. Research suggests that timing is a critical element in humor.[7] Personal experience also tells us that timing is integral to how a joke is received and understood. Pauses to set a mood, before punch lines, or before key phrases can make the difference between a successful joke and one that falls flat. In a now famous joke, Barbara Bush, in her 1990 speech to the graduating class of Wellesley College, told her audience, "Who knows, somewhere out in this audience may even be someone who will one day follow in my footsteps and preside over the White House as the president's spouse." She paused and added, "I wish him well."

The second aspect of successful humor is the objective of the joke. Appropriate jokes for speeches to entertain should strive to make light of something, remind us of our humanity, highlight the silly or the bizarre, tease others playfully, and even relieve tension in difficult times. Avoid negative humor that makes fun of others and puts them down.[8] This type of humor will likely offend audience members. Appropriate humor stands a greater chance of truly entertaining the audience.

The third component of successful humor is the audience. Of course, no two audiences will respond to the same joke in the same way. Still, when you know your audience well, you should have a better sense of what your listeners will find funny. One of the most common reasons a joke backfires is that the speaker has failed to consider the group memberships as well as the individual or collective experiences of the audience.[9] This can lead to you telling a joke that "isn't funny" or that "goes too far" for the members of your audience.[10] So before you select the amusing stories and jokes for your speeches to entertain, carefully consider the master statuses, standpoints, values, and backgrounds of your audience.[11]

***Speaking across DIFFERENCES***

**What we think is funny is heavily influenced by our master statuses. When incorporating humor into your speech, be aware of the master statuses of each member of your audience and use humor that is appropriate for your entire audience.**

Research over the past thirty-five years suggests a number of interesting differences related to master statuses. Although men often find humor that shows contempt for others to be funny, women are far less likely to appreciate jokes of this sort. In contrast, women tend to find self-directed humor funnier than do men—but not when it's too harsh. Additionally, ethnic minorities may enjoy in-group humor but often take offense at out-group humor. That is, when people from a particular group make jokes about their own group, those jokes may be seen as funny. However, when people outside that group make jokes about the group, those jokes are far less likely to be perceived as funny and may be considered offensive.[12] As a rule, then, when the master statuses of your audiences are quite varied, avoid jokes that make fun of people or groups in ways that can be perceived as harsh or mean-spirited.

Although funny, speeches to entertain are also about issues that are relevant to a particular audience or community. Some issues that might be relevant to audiences today are how the government spends, or doesn't spend, tax dollars; the environment; and family life in a recession. Speeches to entertain help an audience make sense of what is happening around them or come to terms with issues and dilemmas that affect their lives.[13] These speeches often put things into a new perspective and add humor to situations that may have been difficult or drawn out. They can also introduce new ideas, giving the audience something to think about that may not have occurred to them before.

**SPEECH TIPS**

**SPEAKING TO ENTERTAIN**

Carefully consider how your audience will receive your humor. When you are planning your speech, think about who your audience will be and what kind of humor appeals to them.

As you consider the issues you could address in your speech to entertain, identify those topics that may be particularly relevant to members of the audience. Once you've identified several possibilities, narrow these general topics and formulate a thesis statement. Check to be sure your approach has a humorous side to it and will appeal to your audience. From there, you can begin to develop the main points of your speech.

To balance the delivery of humor and relevant information to your audience and give a speech that entertains rather than offends or bores, consider the following guidelines.

### Use Humor Carefully

Always err on the side of caution when you use humor in your speech. Although it is easy to get caught up in the moment, don't let your jokes run away from you. Remember, jokes often have more than one interpretation—what may be funny to some can be offensive to others.[14] Most people don't find being made fun of publicly to be humorous. If you think a joke might offend or put someone down, leave it out of the speech. Your goal is to entertain, not to alienate, the audience. When you offend an audience, you lose credibility and respect, which are difficult to regain.

### Speak About Meaningful Issues

Remember that a speech to entertain is also about issues. Although it is meant to be funny, your goal is not to provide the audience with a continual stream of jokes. Rather, your goal is to develop an argument or an idea in an amusing way. As you select your topic and decide how you will frame it, consider your audience carefully. Although they do want to be entertained, they also want to hear a speech that is interesting and insightful. Before you finalize the topic of your speech, make sure it is truly relevant, appropriate, and will hold the interest of your audience.

## Pay Careful Attention to Your Delivery

Skills & Confidence
PPD Activity 25.3
Web Connect 25.3
Web Connect 25.4

Although delivery is a key component of any speech, a skilled delivery is paramount in a speech to entertain. Practice your speech many times so you can deliver your stories, jokes, and anecdotes smoothly and flawlessly. Work out the timing of your jokes well in advance, and practice them until they feel like second nature. Your words and ideas will be even funnier if you can deliver your humor eloquently, in a relaxed style, and with the appropriate timing.[15]

**SPEECH Checklist**

### Speeches to Entertain

- ☐ Give thought to who your audience will be, what they will think is funny, and the purpose of each joke or anecdote.
- ☐ What is the issue you want your audience to "entertain"? What new perspectives do you want them to explore?
- ☐ Avoid humor that makes fun of other people.
- ☐ Work out the timing of your jokes, and practice your speech over and over so that your delivery will be smooth and relaxed.

# PREPARATION OUTLINE

## with Commentary

## *My Grandfather, John Flanagan Sr.*

*by Tara Flanagan*

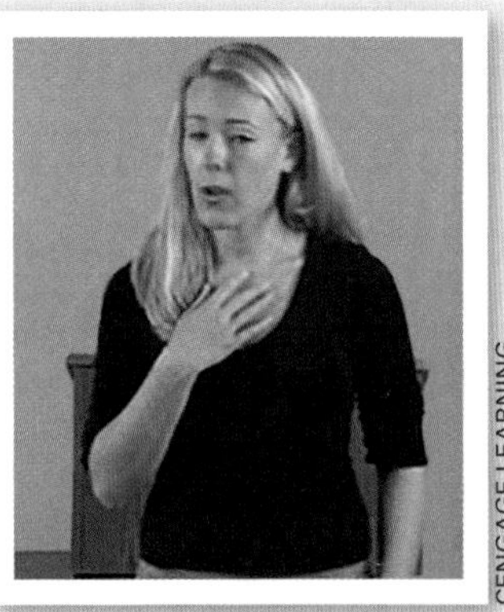

***Specific Purpose:*** *To commemorate my grandfather and the lessons he taught me.*

***Thesis Statement:*** *Although the day of my grandfather's funeral was the saddest day of my life, I was uplifted by my memories of him and by the stories that confirmed his compassion, humor, and courage.*

**Skills & Confidence**
Video Activity 25.3
Speech Studio 25.1

*Are you ready to give a special occasion speech? Use the following speech as a model. Use your Premium Website for* Invitation to Public Speaking Handbook *to watch a video clip of this speech and see Tara's transcript and speaking outline. Tara gave this speech in an introductory public speaking class. The assignment was to give a three- to five-minute speech commemorating a special person in the speaker's life.*

*INTRODUCTION*

I. As I wiped the streams that flooded down my face, I saw a group of homeless men enter the room.
   A. My sadness turned to anger as these uninvited guests interrupted my grandfather's funeral.
   B. They were like unwanted ants invading a family picnic.

II. After our pastor's eulogy, I approached them to ask them to leave.
   A. "Excuse me," I said, "but this is my grandfather's funeral, and only invited guests are allowed inside."
   B. One of the men looked at me and said, "You must be Tara. Your grandfather carried a picture of you in his wallet."

*Commentary*

*Tara begins her speech with a narrative that describes the strong emotions she felt at her grandfather's funeral, especially about a perceived intrusion. Notice how she uses descriptive language to express her feelings ("My sadness turned to anger," "uninvited guests," "like unwanted ants invading a family picnic"). She also provides interesting detail about her encounter with the homeless men who attended the funeral, and her expressive delivery gives a sense of how well the men knew her grandfather. Finally, the story's surprise ending reveals the special character of her grandfather.*

*Tara's speech is arranged in a rough chronological order. Throughout her speech, she provides interesting and detailed transitions to move her audience from one main point to the next.*

III. To my surprise, these homeless men were friends of my grandfather.
IV. My grandfather was never a good judge of people; he was just better at not judging them at all.

*Transition:* As I walked around the room, I saw many people that neither my family nor I recognized.

*BODY*

I. Each of the people at the funeral told a story about my grandfather's virtues.
  A. My grandfather had touched all of them with his love and kindness.
  B. He was a loving, brave man with an amazing sense of humor.
  C. These virtues never shone brighter for me than they did on the day of his funeral.

*In each of her main points, Tara shares what is unique and special about her grandfather. In her introduction and her first point, she talks about her grandfather's compassion and kindness, illustrating his impact not only on her own family but also on many other people. Note her use of personification in her subpoint I. C: "These virtues never shone brighter…"*

*In her second main point, Tara tells a story that illustrates how her grandfather's habit of telling jokes and pulling them on the family caused them to laugh rather than get upset during a mishap with the hearse. Again, note her use of vivid language: "terrible, white smoke" and "huge, immovable beached whale."*

*Transition:* From the funeral home, we headed to the cemetery. It was a hot July day, and the sun was just pounding down on our car.

II. We were following the white hearse to the cemetery when all of the sudden it stopped.
  A. Terrible, white smoke billowed out of the hood, and it lay there like a huge, immovable beached whale.
  B. My father laughed as the cars piled up behind us, and he said, "I bet your grandfather had something to do with this."
    1. My grandfather had an amazing sense of humor.
    2. This incident reminded us of the many jokes he told and pulled on our family.
  C. Making his own hearse break down on the day of his funeral to give us all a good laugh wasn't beyond him.
III. I remembered a time when my grandfather cheered me up when I was younger.
  A. I was visiting my father for the summer and was incredibly homesick.

B. All afternoon my grandfather told me silly knock-knock jokes and did random things to make me laugh, and my homesickness melted away.
C. My grandfather always had a way of making our family laugh and feel better, and the day of his funeral was no exception.

*She uses her third main point not only to further illustrate the impact of her grandfather's sense of humor but also to express her sincere appreciation of his using his humor to cheer her up when she was feeling down.*

*Transition:* When we finally got the white whale back on the road, we drove into the lush cemetery. There were flowers blossoming and a gentle stream that ran through the middle. It was like a scene out of the Garden of Eden.

*In her transition from main point III to main point IV, Tara again uses descriptive language, which is laden with peaceful imagery and appropriately describes her grandfather's final resting place.*

IV. At the cemetery to greet us were several gentlemen dressed in their Marine best.
  A. They carried with them large guns and gave my grandfather his twenty-one-gun salute.
  B. They told me of my grandfather's bravery while he served in World War II.
    1. One of the men had served with my grandfather.
      a. He told me a story about how my grandfather had saved his life.
      b. They ended up being the only two men out of the entire platoon to survive.
    2. At the end of the war, they saw the famous raising of the flag at Iwo Jima.

*In her last main point, Tara uses credible peer testimony to illustrate her grandfather's bravery when he served in World War II. Notice that she uses interesting, true stories from her grandfather's life to make her speech compelling to her audience. She doesn't need to exaggerate his virtues because they are evident in his deeds.*

*Transition:* Living, laughing, loving life.

*Tara's clever use of alliteration not only provides a nice transition to her conclusion but also summarizes her grandfather's character and life.*

CONCLUSION

I. My grandfather was an amazing man who taught me so much about humor, courage, and compassion.
II. Even though his funeral was the saddest day of my life, I was uplifted by all the lives that he had touched.
III. I hope that someday I can learn to love people more than I judge them, just like he did.

*Tara concludes her speech by restating her thesis statement and once again expressing her deep emotion at her grandfather's death. She leaves her audience with a touching and eloquent statement of hope that someday she can be as loving and compassionate as her grandfather.*

CHAPTER 26

# Speaking in Small Groups



***In this chapter, you will learn to***

- Explain what small groups are and why people speak in them
- Describe the six most common formats for small group speaking
- Use the reflexive thinking method to solve problems in a group
- Conduct a productive meeting
- Identify at least three tips for managing question-and-answer sessions
- Identify at least four tips for speaking effectively and ethically in small groups

In this chapter, we take a look at how speakers come together in small groups to create and organize presentations. A great deal of the public dialogue occurs in small group settings as people come together to discuss issues and dilemmas that affect them. Consider these examples:

- Local activist groups often start as small groups of people concerned about some aspect of their community. Through discussions, planning, and presentations, they use their voices to influence issues and policies.

- In business settings, teams of coworkers pool their abilities to complete projects. As they work together, they use their voices to communicate ideas and ways of implementing their ideas.
- Local city councils hear concerns from residents, discuss those concerns, and then make decisions they hope are in the best interests of the community.

As these examples indicate, small group speaking is an important part of the public dialogue. **Small group speaking** is speaking to give a presentation to a small collection of individuals or speaking as part of a small group of people. You can find yourself engaged in this form of speaking when you deliver oral reports, participate in panel discussions, present at symposiums, give team presentations, solve problems as a team, conduct meetings, or participate in question-and-answer sessions.

Your speaking goals in these situations may include informing, inviting, or persuading, but the unique setting of your speech requires that you give special consideration to your listeners and your interaction with them. When speaking to a small group, you must attend to group processes and dynamics, ethically moderate disagreements, promote inclusive dialogue, and accomplish whatever task you and the other members of your group have been asked to complete. In this chapter, we look closely at these dynamics, beginning with a discussion of small groups and why people speak in them. We then examine the six most common formats for small group speeches.

## What Are Small Groups?

A **small group** consists of three to fifteen people who must work together to achieve a common goal and who have the ability to influence one another through verbal and nonverbal communication.[1] Let's take a closer look at these characteristics of small groups.

The first characteristic of small groups is their size. Although not everyone agrees on the upper limit of small groups, three members is the minimum. And when a group has more than fifteen members, it usually isn't "small" any longer, and the interactions among the members change significantly.

The second characteristic of small groups is open verbal communication among group members. Small group dynamics require that all members must be able to express their ideas freely and communicate openly with one another. In small groups, even though a leader may guide the group's interaction, each group member should be able to participate easily in the group's dialogue.

The third characteristic of small groups is the importance of nonverbal communication. Gestures, facial expressions, and even a person's unique habits and styles are just as important as the words that are said. Group members sometimes get the wrong idea about another person's nonverbal communication, which can negatively affect a group's overall communication and performance. To complicate matters, much small group interaction today takes place through mediated channels, such as video conferencing, Internet chat, or satellite television. Thus, as technology is used more and more, groups will have to use more effective verbal communication to compensate for the lack of nonverbal communication.

Finally, the fourth characteristic of small groups is that group members are working together to achieve a common goal. This common goal binds group members together in a shared purpose, makes them interdependent, and keeps them communicating with each other. Ideally, members of a group must think of themselves as a group rather than as individuals. Thus, group members must recognize that they can achieve more working together as a group than if they act alone.

## Why Do People Speak in Small Groups?

As we discussed in Chapters 1 and 5, public speaking occurs in different contexts. Speakers decide to speak, are asked to speak, or are required to speak. These same contexts influence speaking in small groups.

### Deciding to Speak in Groups

Important issues can motivate us to speak as individuals (recall Lois Gibbs in Chapter 5), but they can also cause us to decide to speak in groups. Sometimes an issue is so important that we join with people who also have decided to speak out about an important matter. For example, Susan Love, Susan Hester, and Amy Langer joined together in 1991 to create the National Breast Cancer Coalition (NBCC).[2] Although each had been speaking about breast cancer alone, they found they had more influence by joining together, and they were successful in getting Congress to approve funding for breast cancer research. Love, Hester, and Langer have spoken on television shows, testified at congressional hearings, and addressed survivor and activist groups. Today, the NBCC oversees more than 600 organizations dedicated to breast cancer advocacy.

### Being Asked to Speak in Groups

You might be asked to speak as a member of a group because of your particular experiences or expertise. In the workplace, you might be asked to give a speech because you have experiences or training that others want to hear about. You might also be asked to speak in an informal group (for example, a club) to provide information or new insights. Similarly, members of Congress are often asked to join committees because they have experience in a particular area. For example, the U.S. Senate Committee on Agriculture, Nutrition, and Forestry includes members who come from agricultural states and have knowledge about agricultural issues. Senators who join this committee have experiences and expertise they wish to use to shape the nation's farming and forestry policies. They speak in small groups to other members of Congress, the media, and even their own constituents.

### Being Required to Speak in Groups

Finally, you might be required to communicate in a group context, especially for your job. In today's workplace, a great deal of work is done in small groups. In this setting, people frequently meet to give speeches about their ideas, research, or other findings. Additionally, today's workplace often involves teleconferencing and video conferencing, and workers often find themselves giving speeches via mediated communication.

**Speaking at Work**

*In the workplace, collaborating successfully in groups and teams is often more important than shining as an individual. Learning to communicate effectively in a group is a crucial workplace skill.*

## Formats for Small Group Speaking

There are six common formats for speaking in small groups: oral reports, panel discussions, symposiums, team presentations, problem-solving sessions, and meetings. These types of presentations are briefly described and summarized in Table 26.1 on page 492 and discussed in detail in this section.

### Oral Reports

An **oral report** is a speech given by an individual to present a group's findings, conclusions, or proposals to other members of the group or to a larger audience. When you present an oral report, use the skills you have learned in earlier chapters for giving a speech. Prepare your general purpose, specific purpose, and thesis statement. Outline your main points, and select your pattern of organization. Be sure your introduction will catch your audience's attention, reveal the topic of your report, establish your credibility, and preview your main points.

**TABLE 26.1 Common Formats for Small Group Presentations**

**Oral report**

- Speech given by one member of a group to present findings, conclusions, or proposals to an audience.

**Panel discussion**

- Informal discussion among group members in which they respond and react to one another's ideas.
- Often includes comments and responses from the audience.

**Symposium**

- Formal presentations on one topic by group members.
- Group members do not necessarily have the same goal or purpose. They may disagree with one another.

**Team presentation**

- Well-coordinated, formal presentations on one topic by group members.
- Each presentation builds support for the goal of the team presentation.

**Problem-solving session**

- Discussion among group members that uses the reflective thinking method to identify solutions to a problem.

**Meeting**

- A formal gathering of a group to discuss an issue or solve a problem.
- When you conduct a meeting, you facilitate communication among the group members attending the meeting.

Include transitions between the major sections of your report, and write a conclusion that reinforces your thesis statement and brings your presentation to a close.

## Panel Discussions

A **panel discussion** is a structured discussion among group members, facilitated by a moderator, that takes place in front of an audience. When you are part of a panel discussion, you not only share your ideas with the other members of your group, but you also share them with a larger audience. A panel discussion typically begins with brief opening statements by each of the panelists, followed by an informal discussion among them about their ideas. A moderator, who may be a member of the panel, facilitates the discussion. Usually, the discussion becomes more focused as group members learn from each other and the audience. Occasionally, the moderator or panel members may wrap up the discussion and summarize what has been said, but just as often, the discussion ends without resolution or summary.

Because the goal of a panel discussion is to react to the ideas of other people, it is an ideal setting for invitational speaking. Group members can present their current thinking on a topic, learn from each other and the audience, and refine their ideas for future decision making.

When you are going to be part of a panel discussion, prepare your opening remarks beforehand, thinking of them as a short informative speech to preview what you hope to discuss during the session. Then view your participation in the discussion as a series of short speeches in which you develop a particular idea, invite others to understand your perspective or explore an issue with the other panel members, or encourage others to adopt your views.

### Symposiums

A **symposium** is a public discussion in which several people each give speeches on different aspects of the same topic. Unlike panel discussions, which usually feature short opening statements by the participants, symposium speakers usually have fully prepared speeches that are presented formally. At a symposium, either the speakers are experts in a particular subject area or a topic may be divided into different areas so the audience can learn about many aspects of a single topic. If you are part of a symposium, a moderator usually introduces each speaker and his or her topic and facilitates audience questions and comments if appropriate. Symposiums usually feature three to five speakers, with each person speaking for ten to fifteen minutes. Typically, a symposium session lasts anywhere from one to two hours, with the time divided between the participants' presentations and audience questions.

If you are part of a symposium, follow the procedures for giving a speech outlined in this text. You will probably find that you use a manuscript for this presentation or that your speaking outline is quite detailed. Remember to stay within your time limit so other speakers can present their speeches and so enough time will be left for the question-and-answer session. Typically, a moderator will time the speeches and signal the speakers as they reach the end of their allotted time. Be sure to practice your presentation before you give the speech, and formulate answers to likely questions from the audience.

### Team Presentations

A **team presentation** consists of several members of a group, with each presenting a speech on a different aspect of a single topic. For instance, your group might use a team presentation to present a proposal for a new program or product you have developed as a team. Each of the speeches is formal, with each speaker addressing a different part of the proposal or product and all the speakers using a similar delivery style. The individual speeches in team presentations follow each other without interruption. To make sure the presentation flows smoothly, team presentations usually have one group member acting as the moderator.

If you give a speech in a team presentation, it should be well organized, using one of the organizational patterns discussed in this book. Typically, each group member gives a speech on a single main point, with one member presenting the introduction and conclusion. This person usually is the moderator, who may introduce each speaker and his or her topic.

## Problem-Solving Sessions

At times, you will speak as a member of a group to seek a solution to a problem your group faces. At other times, you may be asked to identify solutions to a problem faced by other people or groups. These tasks are typically performed in a **problem-solving session,** a discussion among group members that uses the reflective thinking method to identify solutions to a problem. The **reflective thinking method** is a five-step method for structuring a problem-solving discussion. Developed by philosopher John Dewey, the reflective thinking method is one of the most widely used methods of solving problems.[3] Reflective thinking involves taking a careful, systematic approach to a problem. This model has five steps:

1. Identify the problem.
2. Analyze the problem.
3. Suggest possible solutions.
4. Consider the implications of the solutions.
5. Reach a decision about the best solution.

Many researchers have added a sixth step, implementing the solution, which we'll discuss at the end of this section after we look at the five steps in detail.

*Identify the problem.* The first step of the reflective thinking model is problem identification. In this stage of the decision-making process, group participants identify

- the nature of the problem
- the extent of the problem
- who is affected by the problem
- the impact on those affected

Groups often research a problem extensively and may use an invitational approach at this stage to be sure that they identify and explore all aspects of the problem. Once the group identifies the problem, it moves on to the next step, problem analysis.

*Analyze the problem.* It can be tempting to jump to a discussion of solutions to the problem. Instead, effective group communication starts by discussing why the problem exists. Much like a physician who must diagnose a patient's illness, the reflective thinker must understand the causes of the problem before moving on to discussing solutions. Besides helping the group arrive at a more reasoned solution, this step helps the group present its findings more successfully. At this stage, groups often continue to use an open, invitational approach to ensure they understand the problem as fully as possible. After group members have thought carefully about the reasons the problem exists, they can move on to suggesting solutions.

*Suggest possible solutions.* A popular method for this stage is *brainstorming*. Recall from Chapter 5 that **brainstorming** is the process of generating ideas randomly and uncritically, without attention to logic, connections, or relevance. When groups brainstorm, they suggest as many ideas as they can think of without judging those ideas. After the group has listed as many ideas as possible, they can do two things. They can go through the list and eliminate ideas that are not suitable, until just a few options remain. Or the group may rank a longer list of options and then choose the solution that has the most support.

A potential pitfall for groups as they generate solutions is **groupthink,**[4] which occurs when the group conforms to a single frame of mind and chooses a solution without fully and objectively examining other possible solutions. Groups that fall victim to groupthink are often under a tight timeline, are pressured by the leader, or are afraid to question each other's ideas. They also tend to get along well and favor consensus over conflict. Groupthink can be avoided by having a group member play the role of devil's advocate and questioning everything that is said, by removing the group's leader from discussions, or by taking time to fully evaluate each potential solution.

*Consider the implications of the possible solutions.* After a group has arrived at potential solutions, it studies the implications of those solutions. The group should avoid immediately enacting a single solution and instead take time to fully examine each solution's disadvantages or impact on others. This stage requires a good deal of discussion about causes and effects.

*Reach a decision about the best solution.* Groups may use any of several methods to reach a decision about the best solution. For example, if the group has the time and resources to implement a pilot study, it can study the effects of the decision over a period of time. Groups can also use reasoning to choose the solution that has the fewest detrimental effects. Or groups can use a consensus model, which requires all members to agree on a single solution. Alternatively, they can vote on the best solution, letting the majority decide which solution to support.

*Implement the solution.* Researchers often add a sixth step to Dewey's reflective thinking model: implementing the solution. In this stage, the group determines how to carry out what it has decided. It is important for the group to consider who will be responsible for the different parts of the solution and when they should be implemented.

## Meetings

One of the most common forms of public speaking in groups is the **meeting,** a formal gathering of a group to discuss an issue or solve a problem. When you conduct a meeting, you facilitate communication among the group members. You prepare an agenda so people stay focused, and you manage the flow of conversation so people stay on track. Here are some guidelines for conducting a successful meeting.

*Provide an agenda in advance.* Several days before the meeting, provide participants with an agenda. The **agenda** lists what topics will be discussed and for how long. If possible, gather topics from group members before you prepare and pass out the agenda. To help the group stay focused, make sure the progression of items is logical (for example, follow a chronological pattern that moves from old business to new business). If you cannot distribute a copy of the agenda to the group before the meeting, pass it out at the start of the meeting so the participants can follow your plan.

*Specify the time and location of the meeting.* Clearly state the start time, end time, and location of the meeting. Include this information on the agenda or post it where group members will see it. Although it is sometimes difficult to specify an end time, meetings that have one typically stay on topic, and groups are more likely to solve problems within the time frame they are allowed. In addition, group members need to know approximately how long a meeting will last so they can schedule other meetings and events.

*Be prepared for the meeting.* The best meetings are those for which both you and other group members are prepared. When group members have not read meeting materials or have not thought about issues that will be discussed, an ineffective meeting often results. To avoid this, distribute important materials to group members beforehand. Be sure you read the materials ahead of time. Think

**SPEECH Checklist** ✓

## Small Group Formats

### Oral reports

- [ ] As for other kinds of speeches, have a general and a specific purpose and a thesis statement (Chapter 5). Organize and outline your main points (Chapters 10 and 11). Develop an introduction and a conclusion (Chapter 12).

### Panel discussions

- [ ] Prepare your opening remarks as a short informative speech (Chapter 21).
- [ ] Use an invitational approach for your contributions to the panel discussion (Chapter 22).

### Symposiums

- [ ] Prepare your speech (typically ten to fifteen minutes long) according to the procedures described in this text. Be sure it will not exceed the time you are allotted.
- [ ] Practice your presentation, whether a manuscript delivery (Chapter 17) or from a detailed outline (Chapter 11).
- [ ] Give some thought to questions the audience might ask you and how you will answer.

### Team presentations

- [ ] Discuss with your team who will present which main point, who will present the introduction and conclusion, and who will be the moderator.
- [ ] Prepare your speech according to the procedures described in this text, and choose an organizational pattern that suits your topic (Chapter 10).

### Problem-solving sessions

- [ ] Follow the steps of the reflective thinking method: identify the problem, analyze the problem, suggest possible solutions, consider their implications, decide as a group which is the best solution, and plan how that solution will be implemented.

### Meetings

- [ ] Prepare and distribute an agenda, which includes the start and end times of the meeting and its location.
- [ ] Distribute background materials ahead of time, and prepare any visual aids.
- [ ] Use an established procedure for conducting each meeting.
- [ ] Afterward, distribute the minutes of the meeting to participants.

carefully about the issues and how you will manage the discussion around them. Prepare any visual aids beforehand and check your equipment. Notify members in advance if you want them to report on their activities so they can prepare their presentations. Plan to follow the steps for reflective thinking to help the group solve problems and stay focused.

*Use an effective procedure for conducting meetings.* Group members must know the group's rules for conducting meetings, such as the rules for governing who may speak, how decisions will be made, and how votes will be taken. Many groups have an established procedure for conducting meetings that new group members are able to pick up after they attend a few meetings. Here's a general procedure for conducting a meeting:

- Open the meeting by stating what is to be discussed and what the group should try to accomplish by the end of the meeting.
- Appoint someone to take the minutes, or notes, of the meeting or ask a volunteer to do so.
- If any group members have been asked to present information to the group, ask them to do so.
- At this point, the group should have the information it needs to begin discussing the topics of the meeting. Open up the meeting to discussion, facilitating the conversation so that the group stays focused.
- When the group has concluded its discussion, summarize the main points that were raised and specify how the group should follow up on the meeting.

*Distribute the minutes of the meeting to group members.* After the meeting, provide copies of the minutes to group members. The minutes of a meeting should clearly identify what the group discussed and any action it took. Be sure to identify group members who are responsible for certain tasks and assignments. Provide reports of these actions at future group meetings.

## Question-and-Answer Sessions in Small Group Formats

Small groups are common and excellent formats for exploring issues with question-and-answer sessions. These sessions provide an opportunity for group members and their audiences to explore an idea or proposal in more detail, ask for clarity, and share their own perspectives.

### Expectations About Speaker-Audience Discussions

Responding to an audience when they ask questions or want to discuss the ideas you present is an important part of the public dialogue. Speakers are often expected to make time for question-and-answer sessions at the end of a speech or to manage brainstorming sessions and discussions. This sort of audience interaction can be challenging because when you share the floor with others, you lose some of the control you had when you were presenting, and you cannot always predict what will happen or what the audience will ask or say.

Despite the unpredictability of discussions and question-and-answer sessions, you can use several strategies to stay audience centered and manage this flow of information effectively. First, consider why people ask questions. They usually ask because they want to clarify points you raised, get more information about a position you advocate, satisfy their curiosity about an issue or an idea, identify or establish connections between ideas, or support or challenge you or the ideas you have presented.[5] Audience members participate in discussions for many of the same reasons that they ask questions. They may also want to share specific information with the group, restate information in a way that may be easier to understand, or even dominate the conversation.

Identifying which of these reasons motivates someone to participate in a speaking event can help you enormously. When audience members ask you for more information or to clarify a point, try to recognize that they are interested in your topic, not commenting on your ability to present information clearly. When audience members attempt to make connections between what they previously believed and the new information you've presented, help them make those connections rather than getting frustrated that they just don't "get it." Similarly, when audience members try to organize their thoughts about a complicated topic, work with them and perhaps incorporate their ideas into your plan for the discussion. To deal with audience members who try to dominate the conversation, set some time limits for each question and explain that, although their views are important, you want to hear from as many people in your audience as possible.

Recognizing what motivates an audience member to attack or challenge a speaker is a particularly valuable tool. Attacks or challenges from the audience during a question-and-answer session is often a speaker's greatest fear. When an audience member attacks or challenges you, it is usually because he or she doubts the validity of your information or your credibility as a speaker. When you recognize why audience members do these things, you are more likely to respond appropriately rather than feel intimidated or engage in unproductive sparring. Consider the following example:

> Ramón is a small, young-looking man with a graduate degree in communication. Fluent in both Spanish and English, he works as an interpreter for a health-care collective that serves migrant workers in his community. The collective consists of physicians, physician's assistants, nurses, and interpreters. Ramón is the only minority in the collective and the only one who has had extensive conversations with the migrant workers the collective serves.
>
> At a recent meeting, Ramón gave a presentation addressing some of the problems people on his staff were having managing cases. He offered a solution based on his experiences with the workers. He was immediately challenged by one of the physicians, who questioned his suggestions and labeled them "impractical." He told Ramón that there were factors at work he couldn't possibly recognize and then quickly moved the discussion in another direction. Although Ramón had the knowledge, education, and experience to make useful suggestions, he was challenged by someone who had more "credibility" than he did.

The challenge to Ramón's credibility was the result of his master statuses. As a small, young-looking minority, Ramón occupied a less authoritative position than the other people at the meeting, who were all older looking, white, and seen as having more credible credentials. Although Ramón's facts were correct, his audience could not see past his status, and so, however unconsciously, they labeled him as less knowledgeable than they. Ramón understood why his coworker challenged him and responded by saying, "You know, I often get overlooked as a source of ideas because of my age, and I realize that being a minority can sometimes throw people off. But I've lived in this community all my life and am quite familiar with the migrant and farming culture. I've also spoken with many of our clients outside the context of the clinic, and they've told me what they think would help them. I still think there might be ways to translate their suggestions into a feasible plan." Once Ramón explained how his experience and communication skills lent his ideas credibility, the other members of the group were able to move beyond their assumptions and work with his ideas and suggestions.

***Speaking across DIFFERENCES***

**Our master statuses can affect how credible we appear to others. If audience members view you as less credible because of your master statuses, you'll need to enhance your credibility so they can move beyond their assumptions.**

Despite the unpredictable nature of question-and-answer sessions, speeches that allow time for questions or incorporate discussion can be particularly rewarding for both audiences and speakers. In these speeches, speakers communicate to audiences that they're interested in the audience's thoughts, beliefs, and concerns. They also communicate that they want to interact with the audience to provide more information if necessary or perhaps learn something new themselves. They are engaging in a healthy public dialogue by making a space for conversation, confirmation, and the exchange of perspectives.

Even though you won't know for sure what to expect during question-and-answer sessions, there are ways you can prepare for them, and preparation can make the difference between a mediocre question-and-answer session and a stimulating one. Ensuring a good question-and-answer session has two steps: preparing for potential questions beforehand and managing the discussion during the session.

## Preparing for Questions

To prepare for the question-and-answer session, take time to identify the questions you think might be asked. Then prepare your answers to the questions.

*Identify potential questions.* As you think about the topic under discussion, keep a log of the questions you think group members or your audience might ask. To help you identify potential questions, pay attention to the controversies or disagreements raised by the issue you are discussing. If you can discuss the topic with others before the session, they can help you identify likely questions. Add these to your log of questions.

*Formulate and practice answers.* After you've identified the questions you might be asked, prepare your answers as thoroughly as you can. Write out your answers, outline them, and record pertinent quotes, statistics, examples, or other data that support each answer. Although this may seem like a lot of extra work, it can give you the confidence you need to respond to your audience in respectful and audience-centered ways.

Although you cannot always anticipate the exact questions you will receive, you will often come close. You should be able to answer a question that is similar to one you anticipated by making minor adjustments to the answer you formulated. If some of the questions are likely to be controversial, practice your answers in front of other people. They can help you with wording and organization as well as with adding or subtracting details.

As a rule, your answers to simple questions should be brief—between ten and sixty seconds in length. Answers to complex questions may take longer, but remember, you are answering questions, not giving a speech. Remember too that others are waiting to ask questions. If you spend all your time on one question, you will prevent others from raising important issues.

## Managing the Question-and-Answer Session

Several techniques will help ensure a productive question-and-answer session. They can help you manage the flow of conversation as well as keep an audience-centered perspective.

*Explain the format.* It's a good idea to establish the format of the question-and-answer session during the introduction of the session. You might want to establish a few rules, such as time limits for each question, the number of questions a person may ask, or rules to ensure that as many sides of an issue as possible are raised and discussed. Setting the rules will help all involved know what to expect and help you manage the flow of discussion ethically and effectively.

*Listen and clarify.* One of your most important tasks when managing a question-and-answer session is to listen thoughtfully to each question before answering in a respectful manner. This can be a difficult task if the question is unclear or hostile. When a group member asks you an unclear question, try to listen carefully for the keywords and important points. Then, using this information, restate the question so it is clear to you and ask the person if this is what he or she meant. Use such language as, "If I understand the question, you are asking... Is that correct?" or "I think what you're asking is... Am I right?" If you simply cannot make sense of the question, you can always ask the person to repeat it for you.

When you are faced with a hostile question, it can be hard to understand what the person is asking. Hostile questions usually come from someone who feels threatened or believes you have not addressed his or her needs and concerns. Sometimes, you can respond to the content of the question as well as acknowledge the emotion. This takes practice. Here are some tips:

1. Don't take the hostility personally. If you can, establish goodwill and common ground by identifying points of agreement, shared experiences, or common background with the members of your group.
2. Display an audience-centered perspective and communicate with civility as you respond. Responding civilly is more likely to decrease the hostility than an uncivil response.
3. Listen to the content as well as the emotional components of the question being asked. Separate out the emotions and determine the facts or information you are being asked to provide.

4. Address your answer to the content of the question, not the emotion. Offer information that will clarify your ideas or position. In responding, also strive to reinforce an invitational environment (Chapter 22) so you can explore an issue and get as many perspectives on it as you can. Try to explain rather than argue.
5. Offer evidence for your position. Use the skills you learned in Chapter 13 to present your ideas logically and reinforce your own credibility. Sometimes the hostility can be reduced when you respond with strong evidence to support your claims.[6]

After you have tried these strategies, if you feel confident enough to do so, you can acknowledge the emotion attached to the issue. You want to be careful here, though, because many people do not like to be told how they feel. If you say something like "I understand the anger attached to this issue," the person may either appreciate the recognition or snap back with a retort about not being angry. As a rule, use caution when answering emotionally charged questions.

*Keep a positive mind-set.* Some beginning speakers are uneasy about question-and-answer sessions. One way to feel more confident about this part of a speech is to frame it positively. Most questions are signs of interest and curiosity—your listeners genuinely want to know more about a subject. A question-and-answer session gives people a chance to ask for additional information and you the opportunity to provide it.

*Address the entire group.* Even though a specific person in the group has asked a question, keep your answer audience centered. First, restate the question so all in the room can hear it. Second, deliver the answer to the entire group, not just to the person asking the question. These two actions bring the full group into the conversation and help keep everyone interested. Usually, a question asked by one group member is a question that others have too. However, you occasionally receive a question whose answer applies only to the person asking it. When this happens, respond that the question seems to address the needs of only one person, and you will be glad to speak with him or her after the presentation. In doing so, you acknowledge the importance of the person, but not at the expense of the larger group.

*Answer with honesty.* At more than one point in your speaking career, you will be asked a question for which you do not have an answer. Rather than trying to fake an answer or justify why you don't have one, be honest. Admit that you don't know the answer. Then acknowledge the importance of the question, refer it to someone who may know the answer, or offer to try to find the answer after the session if it seems appropriate to do so.

*Stay focused.* Unlike a speech, which has a specific purpose and thesis statement, question-and-answer sessions can cover a wide range of ideas and perspectives, some of them only remotely related to the topic at hand. Additionally, with many people asking questions, keeping track of time and the flow of ideas can be difficult. However, you can do several things to keep the dialogue focused.

1. State how much time you have for the question-and-answer session. This will help group members and your audience gauge the number of questions that they can ask and the amount of detail you can provide in your answers.
2. You will occasionally get a few people who try to dominate the session. They either ask repeated questions or use their question to engage in an extended monologue. When you can regain the floor, thank those people for their interest and ideas, and explain that it's important to hear from a variety of group members. Then turn to other people with questions to keep the discussion moving.
3. Keep track of time, alerting the group and audience when the question-and-answer session has reached its midpoint as well as when the session is nearing its end. At these points, refocus the discussion, stating, "We've had a number of questions related to [this aspect of the topic]. Do we have any questions on topics we haven't covered yet?" In this way, you can make a space for people who have not yet been able to ask their questions.

**SPEECH Checklist**

## Question-and-Answer Sessions

- ☐ As you prepare your speech, develop a log of potential questions and their answers. For controversial topics, practice your answers.
- ☐ Start the question-and-answer session with ground rules to ensure that as many people get to ask questions as possible. State how long the session will last and urge people to limit the length of their questions.
- ☐ Keep your answers brief—between ten and sixty seconds.
- ☐ For hostile questions, address your answer to the content and not to the emotion. Try to maintain an invitational environment (Chapter 22).
- ☐ Address the entire group, and try hard not to be pulled into a back-and-forth dialogue with one or two audience members.
- ☐ At the midpoint and near the end of the session, ask if there are questions on any topic that hasn't been covered yet.

## Guidelines for Speaking Effectively and Ethically in Small Groups

Whatever type of small group speech you make, keep in mind some general tips. These tips will help you organize your ideas and work together with other group members so each of you can participate effectively and ethically in the group's dialogue.

### Consider the Group's Purpose and Audience When Selecting a Presentation Format

If the group is in the preliminary stages of identifying a problem, the problem-solving session or panel discussion may be the best format. Later, the group may wish to use the symposium format to air ideas for a more specific audience. When finished with the task, the group may choose to make a team presentation or an oral presentation to the audience that will enact the group's solution. Whatever format you choose, consider including a question-and-answer session if members of the group or the audience would benefit from the opportunity to engage in open dialogue.

Throughout your presentation—and your question-and-answer session, if you include one—remain faithful to the group's stated purpose and format. Switching to a new purpose or format during a presentation is unethical, conveys a lack of organization, and can communicate dishonesty and an unwillingness to listen to what audience members wish to say.

### Use Appropriate Delivery Style and Skills

Panel discussions, problem-solving sessions, and meetings usually consist of impromptu and extemporaneous speeches. Symposiums and team presentations are usually extemporaneous, delivered from a manuscript, or even memorized.

In addition, group members must remember that even when they are not speaking, they are still communicating with the audience. Facial expressions, gestures, or body language that contradict another speaker's message send confusing signals to the audience. Note that small group formats often foster invitational speaking, so make sure your nonverbal and verbal messages reflect this approach.

### Organize Your Presentation

For panel discussions, symposiums, and team presentations, one group member should introduce the speakers. Likewise, one group member should offer concluding remarks. Organize the rest of the presentation in a format consistent with the purpose of the presentation and the type of format used.

- Panel discussions have a looser organization than symposiums; remain ethical during these discussions and allow time for each presenter to speak.
- Team presentations and oral reports are highly structured so that the group can achieve its goal and present its information effectively.
- For meetings and problem-solving sessions, be sure to explain the format and, to stay ethical, follow the agenda or established rules throughout the presentation.
- If you include a question-and-answer session with any of these speaking formats, remember that the session is more likely to be successful if you prepare for questions likely to be asked.

**Skills & Confidence**
PPD Activity 26.1
Speech Studio 26.1

## Use Effective Visual Aids as Needed

If visual aids are used, all members of the audience should be able to see them, and they should reflect the guidelines for effective and ethical visual aids discussed in Chapter 19. For a team presentation in particular, coordinate visual aids between all of the team members so the style of the visual aids is consistent.

APPENDIX B

# RECORDING YOUR RESEARCH SOURCES

- Creating a Works Cited Page (MLA)
- Creating a References Page (APA)

To create the document listing your research sources, follow the guidelines given to you by your instructor or use one of the following guidelines based on the Modern Language Association (MLA) *Handbook for Writers of Research Papers*, 7th edition (2009), or the *Publication Manual of the American Psychological Association* (APA), 5th edition (updated with the *APA Style Guide to Electronic References* [2007]).

## Creating a Works Cited Page (MLA)

Start the works cited list on a new sheet of paper. Center the title "Works Cited" one inch from the top of the page.

Indent second and subsequent lines of each source half an inch (this is called *hanging indent*). Do not number or bullet the sources.

*Alphabetical order*: Put all the sources cited in the speech in alphabetical order by author names. For works with no author or editor named, start the entry with the title of the work.

*Author names*: If a work has more than one author, only the name of the first one is inverted (last name before first name). If a work has more than three authors, you can give the name of only the first one and abbreviate the rest as "et al." (the Latin abbreviation meaning "and others"), or you may give the names of all the authors.

*Titles of works*: Italicize the titles of books, magazines, newspapers, and other long works. Enclose titles of articles, poems, and short works in double quotation marks. Capitalize all major words (nouns, pronouns, verbs, adjectives, adverbs, and subordinating conjunctions).

*Medium*: End all entries by identifying the medium, such as Print, Web, Interview, CD, or Television.

### Books

Lastname, Firstname. *Title of Book*. Publisherplace: Publishername, year. Print.

#### Book with two or three authors

Adler, Ronald B., Russell F. Proctor II, and Neil Towne. *Looking Out, Looking In*. 11th ed. Belmont, CA: Wadsworth, 2005. Print.

#### Book with unnamed author

Begin with the title if no author or editor is named.

*Oxford Spanish Dictionary*. New York: Oxford University Press, 1997. Print.

### Book with an editor or anthology

Ravitch, Diane, ed. *The American Reader: Words That Moved a Nation.* New York: HarperCollins, 1990. Print.

### Selection from an anthology

End the entry with the first and last page numbers of the selection.

Hughes, Langston. "Let America Be America Again." *Against Forgetting: Twentieth-Century Poetry of Witness.* Ed. Carolyn Forché. New York: Norton, 1993. 12-34. Print.

### Pamphlet

World Conference Against Racism. *Racial Discrimination, Xenophobia, and Related Intolerance.* New York: United Nations Department of Public Information, 2001. Print.

## Magazines and Newspapers

Scholarly journals must have a volume number and an issue number; these are not necessary for general-interest magazines and newspapers. Month names are abbreviated.

Lastname, Firstname. "Title of Article." *Title of Magazine or Newspaper* day Month year: pagenumbers. Print.

Lastname, Firstname. "Title of Article." *Title of Scholarly Journal* volumenumber.issuenumber (year): pagenumbers. Print.

### Magazine article with author

McPherson, James M. "Commander in Chief." *Smithsonian* Jan. 2009: 38-45. Print.

### Magazine article with unnamed author

"Planning a Trip? 10 Ways to Save." *Consumer Reports* Feb. 2009: 12. Print.

### Newspaper article with author

Perlman, David. "Trees Dying in West at Record Rate." *San Francisco Chronicle* 23 Jan. 2009: A1. Print.

### Scholarly journal article with author

Keshishian, Flora. "Political Bias in Nonpolitical News." *Critical Studies in Mass Communication* 35.2 (1997): 332-343. Print.

## Electronic Sources

### Online article or Web page

The citation for an article on the Web is like that for a printed article but with the additions of the name of the publisher or sponsor of the site, Web as the name of the medium, and the date of access (after the publication date). End the entry with the URL *only* if the other information in the entry is not adequate to easily locate the source or if your instructor requires a URL.

Wheaton, Sarah. "Lasting Buzz over Aretha Franklin's Hat." *The Caucus: The New York Times Politics Blog.* New York Times. 23 Jan. 2009. Web. 2 Feb. 2009. <http://thecaucus.blogs.nytimes.com/2009/01/23/kits-aretha-post/?hp>.

If no publisher or sponsor name appears on the website, write "n.p." for "no publisher." If the site omits the date of publication or update, write "n.d." for "no date."

### Database

After the basic information about the article (author, article title, periodical, date, pages), add the title of the database in italics, the medium (such as Web or CD), and the date of access.

. . . . *LexisNexis.* Web. 2 Feb. 2009.

**E-mail**

Use the e-mail subject line as the title.

Griffin, Cindy. "Additional Techniques for Public Speaking Anxiety." Message to the author. 13 Feb. 2009. E-mail.

**Personal Interviews** Name the interviewee and identify the type of interview you conducted: Personal interview or Telephone interview.

Krasny, Michael. Personal interview. 2 Apr. 2009.

## Creating a References Page (APA)

Start the reference list on a new sheet of paper. Center the title "References" one inch from the top of the page.

Indent second and subsequent lines of each source half an inch (this is called *hanging indent*). Do not number or bullet the sources.

*Alphabetical order*: Put all the sources cited in the speech in alphabetical order by author names. For works with no author or editor named, start the entry with the title of the work.

*Author names*: For each author's first name, use initials rather than a full name. If a work has more than one author, invert the names of all authors (last name before initials). Use an ampersand (&) instead of *and* before the name of the last author. If a work has seven or more authors, give names of the first six and abbreviate the rest as "et al." (the Latin abbreviation meaning "and others").

*Titles of works*: Use italics or underlining for the titles of books, magazines, newspapers, and other long works. Do not enclose any titles in quotation marks.

Capitalize only the first word in titles and subtitles (as well as all proper nouns). The one exception is titles of magazines, newspapers, and other periodicals; in these, capit major words (nouns, pronouns, verbs, adjectives, and adverbs) and all words of four letters or more.

### Books

Lastname, A. B. (year). *Title of book*. Publisherplace: Publishername.

**Book by two or three authors**

Adler, R. B., Proctor, R. F., II, & Towne, N. (2005). *Looking out, Looking in* (11th ed.). Belmont: Wadsworth.

**Book by unnamed author**

Begin with the title if no author or editor is named.

*Oxford Spanish dictionary*. (1997). New York: Oxford University Press.

**Anthology or book with an editor**

Ravitch, D. (Ed.). (1990). *The American reader: Words that moved a nation*. New York: HarperCollins.

**Selection from an anthology**

End the entry with the first and last page numbers of the selection.

Hughes, L. (1993). Let America be America again. In C. Forché (Ed.), *Against forgetting: Twentieth-century poetry of witness* (pp. 12–34). New York: Norton.

**Pamphlet**

World Conference Against Racism. (2001). *Racial discrimination, xenophobia, and related intolerance*. New York: United Nations Department of Public Information.

### Magazines and Newspapers

Only the first word of an article title is capitalized, but all important words

...talized. ...ten out in ...nals usually ... number and an issue ...general-interest magazines ...ewspapers may not. The page ...umbers of newspaper articles are preceded by "p." or "pp." (for more than one page).

Lastname, A. B. (year, Month day). Title of article. *Title of Magazine, volumenumber*(issuenumber), pagenumbers.

Lastname, A. B. (year, Month day). Title of article. *Title of Newspaper,* pp. pagenumbers.

Lastname, A. B. (year). Title of article. *Title of Academic Journal, volumenumber*(issuenumber), pagenumbers.

Magazine article with author

McPherson, J. M. (2009, January). Commander in chief. *Smithsonian, 39*(10), 38-45.

### Magazine article with unnamed author

Planning a trip? 10 ways to save. (2009, February). *Consumer Reports*, 12.

### Newspaper article with author

Perlman, D. (2009, 23 January). Trees dying in West at record rate. *San Francisco Chronicle*, p. A1.

### Academic journal article with author

Keshishian, F. (1997). Political bias in nonpolitical news. *Critical Studies in Mass Communication,* 35(2), 332-343.

**Electronic Sources** Start with author, publication date, and title. Provide a retrieval date if there is no date of publication or update or if the document is likely to be updated or changed (such as an entry in Wikipedia or a blog). Do not put a period after the URL.

### Online article or Web page

The citation for an article on the Web is like that for a printed article but with all additional information available from the online host, especially the URL.

Wheaton, S. (2009, 23 January). Lasting buzz over Aretha Franklin's hat. *The Caucus: The New York Times Politics Blog*. Retrieved February 2, 2009, from http://thecaucus.blogs.nytimes.com/2009/01/23/kits-aretha-post/?hp

Plunkett, A. (2002.) Nigeria (Africa) dun dun. *World Beats*. Retrieved March 21, 2007, from http://www.world-beats.com/instruments/dundun.htm

### Database

To the information about the article, add the title of the database:

. . . Retrieved February 2, 2009, from LexisNexis database.

### E-mail

Do not make an entry in the reference list. Identify the author and date in your speech—for example:

In an e-mail on February 13 of this year, Cindy Griffin wrote that ". . . ."

**Personal Interviews** Personal communications—including personal interviews, telephone conversations, letters, and e-mail—are not included in the reference list in APA style because they are not publicly accessible.

# GLOSSARY

**abstract** Summary of the text in an article or publication.

**abstract language** Language that refers to general ideas or concepts but not to specific objects.

**acceptance speech** Speech that expresses gratitude, appreciation, and pleasure at receiving an honor or a gift.

**ad hominem fallacy** Argument in which a speaker attacks a person rather than that person's arguments.

**affirmations** Positive, motivating statements that replace negative self-talk.

**agenda** List of topics that will be discussed in a meeting and for how long.

**alliteration** Repetition of initial sounds of two or more words in a sentence or phrase.

**analogical reasoning** A process of reasoning by way of comparison and similarity that implies that because two things resemble each other in one respect, they also share similarities in another respect.

**antithesis** Placement of words and phrases in contrast or opposition to one another.

**argument** Set of statements that allows development of evidence to establish the validity of a claim.

**articulation** Physical process of producing specific speech sounds to make language intelligible.

**attitude** General positive or negative feeling a person has about something.

**audience** Complex and varied group of people the speaker addresses.

**audience centered** Acknowledging the audience by considering and listening to the unique, diverse, and common perspectives of its members before, during, and after a speech.

**balance** Visual relationship between the items on a visual aid.

**bandwagon fallacy** Argument that something is correct or good because everyone else agrees with it or is doing it.

**bar graph** Graph that compares quantities at a specific moment in time.

**behavioral objectives** Actions a speaker wants the audience to take at the end of a speech.

**belief** Person's idea of what is real or true or not.

**bias** Unreasoned distortion of judgment or prejudice about a topic.

**bibliographic database** Database that indexes publishing data for books, periodical articles, government reports, statistics, patents, research reports, conference proceedings, and dissertations.

**Boolean operators** Words can be used to create specific phrases that broaden or narrow a search on the Internet.

**brainstorming** Process of generating ideas randomly and uncritically, without attention to logic, connections, or relevance.

**brief narrative** Short story or vignette that illustrates a specific point.

**call to action** Explicit request that an audience engage in some clearly stated behavior.

**canon** Authoritative list, an accepted principle or rule, or an established standard of judgment.

**canon of arrangement** Guidelines for ordering the ideas in a speech.

**canon of delivery** Guidelines for managing your voice, gestures, posture, facial expressions, and presentational aids as you give your speech.

**canon of invention** Guidelines for generating effective content for a speech.

**canon of memory** Guidelines for your efforts to rehearse a speech and for the ways you prompt yourself to remember the speech as you give it.

**canon of style** Guidelines for using language effectively, appropriately, and ethically.

**careful listener** Listener who overcomes listener interference to better understand a speaker's message.

**causal pattern** Pattern of organization that describes a cause-and-effect relationship between ideas or events.

**causal reasoning** Process of reasoning that supports a claim by establishing a cause-and-effect relationship.

**channel** Means by which the message is conveyed.

**character** Audience's view of a speaker's sincerity, trustworthiness, and concern for the well-being of the audience.

**chronological pattern** Pattern of organization that traces a sequence of events or ideas.

**civility** Care and concern for others, the thoughtful use of words and language, and the flexibility to see the many sides of an issue.

**claim** Assertion that must be proved.

**closed-ended question** Question that requires the respondent to choose an answer from two or more alternatives.

**cognitive restructuring** Process that helps reduce anxiety by replacing negative thoughts with positive ones, called affirmations.

**colloquialism** Local or regional informal dialect or expression.

**commemorative speech** Speech that praises, honors, recognizes, or pays tribute to a person, an event, an idea, or an institution.

**common ground** Similarities, shared interests, and mutual perspectives a speaker has with an audience.

**communication apprehension** Level of fear or anxiety associated with either real or anticipated communication with another person or persons.

**comparative advantages organization** Organizational pattern that illustrates the advantages of one solution over others.

**competence** Audience's view of a speaker's intelligence, expertise, and knowledge of a subject.

**conclusion** Logical outcome of an argument that results from the combination of the major and minor premises.

**concrete language** Language that refers to a tangible object—a person, place, or thing.

**condition of equality** Condition of an invitational environment that requires the speaker to acknowledge that all audience members hold equally valid perspectives worthy of exploration.

**condition of self-determination** Condition of an invitational environment that requires the speaker to recognize that people know what is best for themselves and have the right to make choices about their lives based on this knowledge.

**condition of value** Condition of an invitational environment that requires the speaker to recognize the inherent value of the audience's views, even though those views may differ from the speaker's views.

**confirm** To recognize, acknowledge, and express value for another person.

**connective** Word or a phrase used to link ideas in a speech.

**connotative definition** Subjective meaning of a word or phrase based on personal experiences and beliefs.

**considerate speech** Speech that eases the audience's burden of processing information.

**context** Environment or situation in which a speech occurs.

**conversational style** Speaking style that is more formal than everyday conversation but remains spontaneous and relaxed.

**coordination** Process of arranging points into successive levels, with the points on a specific level having equal importance.

**counterarguments** Arguments against the speaker's own position.

**credibility** Audience's perception of a speaker's competence and character.

**critical listener** Listener who listens for the accuracy of a speech's content and the implications of a speaker's message.

**culturally inclusive language** Language that respectfully recognizes the differences among the many cultures in our society.

**database** Collections of information stored electronically so that they are easy to find and retrieve.

**decoding** Translating words, sounds, and gestures into ideas and feelings in an attempt to understand the message.

**deductive reasoning** Process of reasoning that uses a familiar and commonly accepted claim to establish the truth of a very specific claim.

**definition** Statement of the exact meaning of a word or phrase.

**delivery** Action or manner of speaking to an audience.

**demographic audience analysis** Analysis that identifies the particular population traits of an audience.

**demonstration** Display of how something is done or how it works.

**denotative definition** Objective meaning of a word or a phrase you find in a dictionary.

**derived credibility** Credibility a speaker develops during a speech.

**dialect** Pattern of speech that is shared by an ethnic group or people from specific geographical locations.

**dialogue** Interaction, connection, and exchange of ideas and opinions with others.

**direct quotation** Exact word-for-word presentation of another's testimony.

**drawing** Diagram or sketch of someone or something.

**either-or fallacy** Argument in which a speaker claims that our options are "either A or B," when actually more than two options exist. Sometimes called a false dilemma.

**empathy** Trying to see and understand the world as another person does.

**encoding** Translating ideas and feelings into words, sounds, and gestures.

**ethical listener** Listener who considers the moral impact of a speaker's message on one's self and one's community.

**ethical public speaker** Speaker who considers the moral impact of his or her ideas and arguments on others when involved in the public dialogue.

**ethnocentrism** Belief that our own cultural perspectives, norms, and ways of organizing society are superior to others.

**ethos** Speaker's credibility; the second of Aristotle's three types of proof.

**etymology** History of a word.

**euphemism** Word or phrase that substitutes an agreeable or inoffensive expression for one that may offend or suggest something unpleasant.

**evidence** Materials that speakers use to support their ideas.

**example** Specific instance used to illustrate a concept, experience, issue, or problem.

**expert testimony** Opinions or observations of someone considered an authority in a particular field.

**extemporaneous speech** Speech that is carefully prepared and practiced from brief notes rather than from memory or a written manuscript.

**extended narrative** Longer story that makes an evolving connection with a broader point.

**eye contact** Visual contact with another person's eyes.

**facial expression** The movement of eyes, eyebrows, and mouth to convey reactions and emotions.

**fallacy** Argument that seems valid but is flawed because of unsound evidence or reasoning.

**false cause** Error in reasoning in which a speaker assumes that one event caused another simply because the first event happened before the second.

**fear appeal** Threat of something undesirable happening if change does not occur.

**feedback** Verbal and nonverbal signals an audience gives a speaker.

**flow chart** Chart that illustrates direction or motion.

**font** Type or style of print.

**font size** Size of the letters in a particular font, measured in points.

**full-text database** Database that indexes the complete text of newspapers, periodicals, encyclopedias, research reports, court cases, books, and the like.

**gain immediate action** Encourage an audience to engage in a specific behavior or take a specific action.

**gain passive agreement** Ask an audience to adopt a new position without also asking them to act in support of that position.

**gender-inclusive language** Language recognizing that both women and men are active participants in the world.

**general purpose** A speech's broad goal: to inform, invite, persuade, introduce, commemorate, or accept.

**gestures** Movements, usually of the hands but sometimes of the full body, that express meaning and emotion or offer clarity to a message.

**global plagiarism** Stealing an entire speech from a single source and presenting it as one's own.

**graph** Visual comparison of amounts or quantities that shows growth, size, proportions, or relationships.

**group communication** Communication among members of a team or a collective about topics such as goals, strategies, and conflict.

**groupthink** Act of a group conforming to a single frame of mind and choosing a solution without fully and objectively examining other potential solutions.

**hasty generalization** Error in reasoning in which a speaker reaches a conclusion without enough evidence to support it.

**hearing** Vibration of sound waves on our eardrums and the impulses then sent to the brain.

**hypothetical example** Instance that did not take place but could have.

**idiom** Fixed, distinctive expression whose meaning is not indicated by its individual words.

**impromptu speech** Speech that is not planned or prepared in advance.

**incremental plagiarism** Presenting select portions from a single speech as your own.

**index** Alphabetical listing of the topics discussed in a specific publication, along with the corresponding year, volume, and page numbers.

**inductive reasoning** Process of reasoning that uses specific instances, or examples, to make a claim about a general conclusion.

**inferences** Mental leaps made when it is recognized that a speaker's evidence supports his or her claims.

**inflection** Manipulation of pitch to create certain meanings or moods.

**information overload** Taking in more information than can be processed and realizing there still is more information expected to be known.

**informative speaking environment** Environment in which a speaker has expertise or knowledge that an audience needs but doesn't already have.

**informative speech** Speech that communicates knowledge about a process, an event, a person, a place, an object, or a concept.

**initial credibility** Credibility a speaker has before giving a speech.

**interference** Anything that stops or hinders a listener from receiving a message.

**internal preview** Statement in the body of a speech that details what the speaker plans to discuss next.

**internal summary** Statement in the body of a speech that summarizes a point a speaker has already discussed.

**Internet** Electronic communications network that links computer networks around the world via telephone lines, cables, and communication satellites.

**interpersonal communication** Communication with other people that ranges from the highly personal to the highly impersonal.

**intertextuality** Process in which stories reference other stories or rely on parts of other stories to be complete.

**interview** Planned interaction with another person that is organized around inquiry and response, with one person asking questions while the other person answers them.

**intrapersonal communication** Communication within a person via the dialogue that goes on in that person's head.

**introductory speech** Speech that provides an audience with a unique perspective on the person introduced.

**invitational environment** Environment in which the speaker's highest priority is to understand, respect, and appreciate the range of possible positions on an issue, even if those positions are quite different from his or her own.

**invitational speaking** Type of public speaking in which a speaker enters into a dialogue with an audience to clarify positions, explore issues and ideas, or articulate beliefs and values.

**invitational speech** Speech that allows the speaker to establish a dialogue with an audience to clarify positions, explore issues and ideas, or share beliefs and values.

**jargon** Technical language used by a special group or for a special activity.

**language** System of verbal or gestural symbols a community uses to communicate.

**line graph** Graph that shows trends over time.

**list** Series of words or phrases that organize ideas one after the other.

**listenable speech** Speech that is considerate and delivered in an oral style.

**listening** Process of giving thoughtful attention to another person's words and trying to understand what you hear.

**logos** Logical arrangement of evidence in a speech; the first of Aristotle's three types of proof.

**main points** Most important ideas addressed in a speech.

**major premise** Claim in an argument that states a familiar, commonly accepted belief (also called the general principle).

**manuscript** conversational style. Speaking style that is more formal than everyday conversation but remains spontaneous and relaxed.

**manuscript speech** Speech that is read to an audience from a written text

**map** Visual representation showing the physical layout of geographical features, cities, road systems, the night sky, and the like.

**mass communication** Communication generated by media organizations that is designed to reach large audiences.

**master statuses** Significant positions occupied by a person within society that affect that person's identity in almost all social situations.

**mean** Average of a group of numbers.

**median** Middle number in a series or set of numbers arranged in a ranked order.

**meeting** Formal gathering of a group to discuss an issue or solve a problem.

**memorized speech** Speech that has been written out, committed to memory, and given word for word.

**message** Information conveyed by the speaker to the audience.

**metaphor** Figure of speech that makes a comparison between two things by describing one thing as being something else.

**minor premise** Claim in an argument that states a specific instance linked to the major premise.

**mixed metaphor** Metaphor that makes illogical comparisons between two or more things.

**mnemonic device** Verbal device that makes information easier to remember.

**mode** Number that occurs most often in a set of numbers.

**model** Copy of an object, usually built to scale, that represents an object in detail.

**monotone** Way of speaking in which a speaker does not alter her or his pitch.

**Monroe's motivated sequence** Step-by-step process used to persuade audiences by gaining attention, demonstrating a need, satisfying that need, visualizing beneficial results, and calling for action.

**multiple perspectives pattern** Organizational pattern that allows the speaker to address the many sides and positions of an issue before opening up the speech for dialogue with the audience.

**mythos** Interrelated set of beliefs, attitudes, values, and feelings held by members of a particular society or culture.

**narrative** Story that recounts or foretells real or hypothetical events.

**noise** Anything that interferes with understanding the message being communicated.

**object** Something that can be seen or touched.

**objective** Having a fair, ethical, and undistorted view on a question or issue.

**open-ended question** Question that allows the respondent to answer in an unrestricted way.

**oral report** Speech given by an individual that presents a group's findings, conclusions, or proposals to other members of a group or to a larger audience.

**oral style** Speaking style that reflects the spoken rather than the written word.

**organization** Systematic arrangement of ideas into a coherent whole.

**organizational chart** Chart that illustrates the structure of groups.

**panel discussion** Structured discussion among group members, facilitated by a moderator, that takes place in front of an audience.

**parallelism** Arrangement of related words so they are balanced or of related sentences so they have identical structures.

**paraphrase** Summary of another's testimony in the speaker's own words.

**patchwork plagiarism** Constructing a complete speech that is presented as the speaker's own from portions of several different sources.

**pathos** Emotional appeals made by a speaker; the third of Aristotle's three types of proof.

**pauses** Hesitations and brief silences in speech or conversation.

**peer testimony** Opinions or observations of someone who has firsthand knowledge of a topic (sometimes called lay testimony).

**personal appearance** Way speakers dress, groom, and present themselves physically.

**personal testimony** Speaker's opinions or observations that are used to convey a point.

**personification** Figure of speech that attributes human characteristics to animals, objects, or concepts.

**persuasive speech** Speech whose message attempts to change or reinforce an audience's thoughts, feelings, or actions.

**picture graph** Graph that presents information in pictures or images.

**pie graph** Graph that shows the relative proportions of parts of a whole.

**pitch** Highness or lowness of a speaker's voice.

**plagiarism** Presenting another person's words and ideas as one's own.

**posture** Way speakers position and carry their bodies.

**preliminary bibliography** List of all the potential sources collected as a speech is prepared.

**preparation outline** Detailed outline a speaker builds when preparing a speech that includes the title, specific purpose, thesis statement, introduction, main points and subpoints, connectives, conclusion, and source citations of the speech.

**preview** Brief overview in the introduction of a speech of each of the main points in the speech.

**probe** Question that expands upon or follows up an answer to a previous question.

**problem-cause-solution organization** Organizational pattern that focuses on identifying a specific problem, the causes of that problem, and a solution to the problem.

**problem-solution organization** Organizational pattern that focuses on persuading an audience that a specific problem exists and can be solved or minimized by a specific solution.

**problem-solution pattern** Pattern of organization that identifies a specific problem and offers a possible solution.

**problem-solving session** Discussion among group members that uses the reflective thinking method to identify solutions to a problem.

**pronunciation** Act of saying words correctly according to the accepted standards of a language.

**proxemics** Use of space during communication.

**public communication** Communication in which one person gives a speech to other people, most often in a public setting.

**public dialogue** Ethical and civil exchange of ideas and opinions among communities about topics that affect the public.

**public speaking anxiety (PSA)** Anxiety we feel when we learn we have to give a speech or take a public speaking course.

**question of fact** Question that addresses whether something is verifiably true or not.

**question of policy** Question that addresses the best course of action or solution to a problem.

**question of value** Question that addresses the merit or morality of an object, action, or belief.

**rate** Speed at which a speaker speaks.

**real example** Instance that actually took place.

**reasoning by sign** Process of reasoning that assumes something exists or will happen based on something else that exists or has happened.

**red herring fallacy** Argument that introduces irrelevant information to distract an audience from the real issue.

**referent** Object, concept, or event a symbol represents.

**reflective thinking method** Five-step method for structuring a problem-solving discussion: identify the problem, analyze the problem, suggest possible solutions, consider the implications of the solutions, and reach a decision about the best solution. A sixth step is often added: implement the solution.

**repetition** Repeating keywords or phrases at the beginnings or endings of clauses, sentences, or paragraphs to create rhythm.

**research inventory** List of the types of information collected for a speech and the types needed.

**rhetorical question** Question used for effect that an audience isn't supposed to answer out loud but rather in their own minds.

**rhythm** Arrangement of words into patterns so the sounds of the words together enhance the meaning of a phrase.

**sign** Something that represents something else.

**signpost** Simple word or statement that indicates where the speaker is in a speech or highlights an important idea.

**simile** Figure of speech that makes an explicit comparison of two things using the word like or as.

**slang** Informal nonstandard vocabulary, usually made up of arbitrarily changed words.

**slippery slope fallacy** Argument in which a speaker claims that taking a first step in one direction will lead to inevitable and undesirable further steps.

**small group** Three to fifteen people who must work together to achieve a common goal and who have the ability to influence one another through verbal and nonverbal communication.

**small group speaking** Speaking to give a presentation to a small collection of individuals or speaking as part of a small group of people.

**spatial pattern** Pattern of organization in which ideas are arranged in terms of location or direction.

**speaker** Person who stimulates public dialogue by delivering an oral message.

**speaking environment** Time and place in which a speaker will speak.

**speaking outline** Condensed form of a preparation outline used when speaking.

**specific purpose** Focused statement that identifies exactly what a speaker wants to accomplish with a speech.

**speech about a concept** Informative speech about an abstraction (something that can't be perceived with the senses), such as an idea, a theory, a principle, a worldview, or a belief.

**speech about a place or a person** Informative speech that describes a significant, interesting, or unusual place or person.

**speech about a process** Informative speech that describes how something is done, how something comes to be what it is, or how something works.

**speech about an event** Informative speech that describes or explains a significant, interesting, or unusual occurrence.

**speech about an object** Informative speech about anything that is tangible, that can be perceived by the senses.

**speech of award** Speech given to present a specific award to someone and describe why that person is receiving the award.

**speech of tribute** Speech given to honor someone.

**speech to articulate a position** Invitational speech in which the speaker invites an audience to understand an issue from her or his perspective and then opens up a conversation with audience members to learn their perspectives on the issue.

**speech to entertain** Lighthearted speech that addresses issues or ideas in a humorous way.

**speech to explore an issue** Invitational speech in which the speaker attempts to engage an audience in a discussion about an idea, a concern, a topic, or a plan of action.

**speech topic** Subject of a speech.

**spotlighting** Practice of highlighting a person's race or ethnicity (or sex, sexual orientation, physical disability, and the like) during a speech.

**standpoint** Perspective from which a person views and evaluates society.

**state, or situational, anxiety** Apprehension about communicating with others in a particular situation.

**statistics** Numerical summaries of facts, figures, and research findings.

**stereotype** Broad generalization about an entire group based on limited knowledge or exposure to only certain members of that group.

**subordination** Process of ranking ideas in order from the most to the least important.

**subpoint** Point in a speech that develops an aspect of a main point.

**sub-subpoint** Point in a speech that develops an aspect of a subpoint.

**summary** Concise restatement of the main points at the end of a speech.

**symbol** Word or phrase spoken by a speaker.

**symposium** Public discussion in which several people each give speeches on different aspects of the same topic.

**systematic desensitization** Technique for reducing anxiety that involves teaching the body to feel calm and relaxed rather than fearful during a speech.

**team presentation** Presentation consisting of several individual members of a group, with each presenting a speech on a different aspect of a single topic.

**terminal credibility** Credibility a speaker has at the end of a speech.

**testimony** Opinions or observations of others.

**thesis statement** Statement that summarizes in a single declarative sentence the main ideas, assumptions, or arguments the speakers want to express in a speech.

**thought, or reference** Memory and past experiences that audience members have with an object, concept, or event.

**timing** Way a speaker uses pauses and delivery for maximum effect.

**topical pattern** Pattern of organization that allows the speaker to divide a topic into subtopics, each of which addresses a different aspect of the larger topic.

**trait anxiety** Apprehension about communicating with others in any situation.

**transition** Phrase that indicates a speaker is finished with one idea and is moving on to a new one.

**two-sided message** Persuasive strategy that addresses both sides of an issue, refuting one side to prove the other is better.

**value** Person's idea of what is good, worthy, or important.

**verbal clutter** Extra words that pad sentences and claims but don't add meaning.

**visualization** Process in which a person constructs a mental image of oneself giving a successful speech.

**vocal variety** Changes in the volume, rate, and pitch of a speaker's voice that affect the meaning of the words delivered.

**vocalized pauses** Pauses that speakers fill with words or sounds like "um," "er," or "uh."

**volume** Loudness of a speaker's voice.

**World Wide Web** System that allows users to easily navigate the millions of sites on the Internet.

# NOTES

**Part I**

1. Compiled from http://www.convergingvoices.com/oband (accessed June 12, 2007).

**Chapter 1**

1. Harold Barrett, *Rhetoric and Civility: Human Development, Narcissism, and the Good Audience* (Albany: State University of New York Press, 1991), p. 147.
2. Deborah Tannen, *The Argument Culture: Moving from Debate to Dialogue* (New York: Random House, 1998), pp. 1–4.
3. See, for example, Shawn Spano, *Public Dialogue and Participatory Democracy: The Cupertino Community Project* (Cresskill, NJ: Hampton Press, 2001); William Isaacs, *Dialogue and the Art of Thinking Together* (New York: Currency, 1999); Stephen L. Carter, *Civility: Manners, Morals, and the Etiquette of Democracy* (New York: Basic Books, 1998); Linda Ellinor and Glenna Gerard, *Dialogue: Rediscover the Transforming Power of Conversation* (New York: Wiley, 1998); Jeffrey C. Goldfarb, *Civility and Subversion: The Intellectual in the Democratic Society* (Cambridge: Cambridge University Press, 1998); Josina M. Makau and Ronald C. Arnett, *Communication Ethics in an Age of Diversity* (Chicago: University of Illinois Press, 1997); Ivana Markova, Carl F. Graumann, and Klaus Foppa, eds., *Mutualities in Dialogue* (Cambridge: Cambridge University Press, 1995); Douglas N. Walton and Erik C. W. Krabbee, *Commitment in Dialogue: Basic Concepts of Interpersonal Reasoning* (Albany: State University of New York Press, 1995); Rob Anderson, Kenneth N. Cissna, and Ronald C. Arnett, *The Reach of Dialogue: Confirmation, Voice, and Community* (Cresskill, NJ: Hampton Press, 1994); Harold Barrett, *Rhetoric and Civility: Human Development, Narcissism, and the Good Audience* (Albany: State University of New York Press, 1991).
4. For an excellent discussion of the public dialogue, see Spano, *Public Dialogue and Participatory Democracy.*
5. Adapted from Kenneth Burke, *The Philosophy of Literary Form: Studies in Symbolic Action*, 3rd ed. (1941; reprint, Berkeley: University of California Press, 1973), pp. 110–111.
6. Melbourne S. Cummings, "Teaching the African American Rhetoric Course," in James W. Ward, ed., *African American Communications: An Anthology in Traditional and Contemporary Studies* (Dubuque, IA: Kendall/Hunt, 1993), p. 241.
7. Adapted from Janice Walker Anderson, "A Comparison of Arab and American Conceptions of 'Effective' Persuasion," *Howard Journal of Communications* 2 (Winter 1989–1990): 81–114; Larry A. Samovar and Richard E. Porter, eds., *Intercultural Communication: A Reader*, 10th ed. (Belmont, CA: Wadsworth, 2003); A. J. Almaney and A. J. Alwan, *Communicating with the Arabs: A Handbook for the Business Executive* (Prospect Heights, IL: Waveland, 1982), p. 79.
8. Bonnie Dow, "Ann Willis Richards: A Voice for Political Empowerment," in Karlyn Kohrs Campbell, ed., *Women Public Speakers in the United States, 1925–1993* (Westport, CT: Greenwood Press, 1994), p. 456.
9. Material for this section is from Ward, *African American Communications*; Mary Jane Collier, "A Comparison of Conversations among and between Domestic Culture Groups: How Intra- and Intercultural Competencies Vary," *Communication Quarterly* 36 (1988): 122–144; Larry A. Samovar and Richard E. Porter, *Communication between Cultures* (Belmont, CA: Wadsworth, 2007); Anderson, "A Comparison of Arab and American Conceptions of 'Effective' Persuasion"; Samovar and Porter, *Intercultural Communication*; Almaney and Alwan, *Communicating with the Arabs.*
10. Charmaine Shutiva, "Native American Culture and Communication through Humor," in Alberto Gonzalez, Marsha Houston, and Victoria Chen, eds., *Our Voices: Essays in Culture, Ethnicity, and Communication, 3rd ed.* (Los Angeles: Roxbury, 2000), pp. 113–117.
11. Bonnie J. Dow and Mari Boor Tonn, "'Feminine Style' and Political Judgment in the Rhetoric of Ann Richards," *Quarterly Journal of Speech* 79 (1993): 286–302; Julia T. Wood, *Gendered Lives: Communication, Gender, and Culture*, 6th ed. (Belmont, CA: Wadsworth, 2005); Marsha Houston, "When Black Women Talk with White Women: Why the Dialogues Are Difficult," in Gonzalez, Houston, and Chen, *Our Voices*, pp. 98–104.

**Chapter 3**

1. James C. McCroskey, "Oral Communication Apprehension: A Summary of Recent Theory and Research," *Human Communication Research* 4 (1977): 78.
2. Ralph R. Behnke and Chris R. Sawyer, "Milestones of Anticipatory Public Speaking Anxiety," *Communication Education* 48 (1999):

164–172; Amy M. Bippus and John A. Daly, "What Do People Think Causes Stage Fright? Naïve Attributions about the Reasons for Public Speaking Anxiety," *Communication Education* 48 (1999): 63–72; Thomas E. Robinson II, "Communication Apprehension and the Basic Public Speaking Course: A National Survey of In-Class Treatment Techniques," *Communication Education* 46 (1997): 190–197.

3. Michael J. Beatty, "Situational and Predispositional Correlates of Public Speaking Anxiety," *Communication Education* 37 (January 1988): 29–30; Bippus and Daly, "What Do People Think Causes Stage Fright?"
4. Murray B. Stein, John R. Walker, and David R. Forde, "Public-Speaking Fears in a Community Sample: Prevalence, Impact on Functioning, and Diagnostic Classification," *Archives of General Psychiatry* 53 (1996): 169–174.
5. John A. Daly, Anita L. Vangelisti, and David J. Weber, "Speech Anxiety Affects How People Prepare Speeches: A Protocol Analysis of the Preparation Processes of Speakers," *Communication Monographs* 62 (December 1995): 383–397.
6. See Karen Kangas Dwyer, *Conquer Your Speechfright: Learn How to Overcome the Nervousness of Public Speaking* (Fort Worth, TX: Harcourt, 1998); Karen Kangas Dwyer, "The Multidimensional Model: Teaching Students to Self-Manage High Communication Apprehension by Self-Selecting Treatments," *Communication Education* 49 (2000): 72–81; James C. McCroskey, "The Implementation of a Large Scale Program of Systematic Desensitization for Communication Apprehension," *Speech Teacher* 21 (1972): 255–264.
7. Michael T. Motley, "Public Speaking Anxiety qua Performance Anxiety: A Revised Model and an Alternative Therapy," *Journal of Social Behavior and Personality* 5 (1990): 85–104.
8. Joe Ayres and Theodore S. Hopf, "Visualization: A Means of Reducing Speech Anxiety," *Communication Education* 34 (1985): 318–323; Joe Ayres and Theodore S. Hopf, "Visualization: Is It More Than Extra-Attention?" *Communication Education* 38 (1989): 1–5; Joe Ayres and Theodore S. Hopf, "The Long-Term Effect of Visualization in the Classroom: A Brief Research Report," *Communication Education* 39 (1990): 75–78; Joe Ayres, Tim Hopf, and Debbie M. Ayres, "An Examination of Whether Imaging Ability Enhances the Effectiveness of an Intervention Designed to Reduce Speech Anxiety," *Communication Education* 43 (1994): 252–258; Robert McGarvey, "Rehearsing for Success: Tap the Power of the Mind Through Visualization," *Executive Female* (January–February 1990): 34–37.
9. Adapted from Ayres and Hopf, "Visualization: Is It More Than Extra-Attention?" p. 2–3.
10. Joe Ayres, "Coping with Speech Anxiety: The Power of Positive Thinking," *Communication Education* 37 (October 1988): 289–296.
11. William J. Fremouw and Michael D. Scott, "Cognitive Restructuring: An Alternative Method for the Treatment of Communication Apprehension," *Communication Education* 28 (1979): 129–133.

## Chapter 4

1. Lyman K. Steil, Larry L. Barker, and Kittie W. Watson, *Effective Listening: Key to Your Success* (New York: McGraw-Hill, 1993), p. 51.
2. Martin Buber, in Rob Anderson, Kenneth N. Cissna, and Ronald C. Arnett, eds., *The Reach of Dialogue: Confirmation, Voice, and Community* (Cresskill, NJ: Hampton Press, 1994), p. 23.
3. Michael P. Nichols, *The Lost Art of Listening* (New York: Guilford Press, 1995), p. 3.
4. This definition is adapted from Donald L. Rubin, "Listenability = Oral-based Discourse + Considerateness," in Andrew D. Wolvin and Carolyn Gwynn Coakley, eds., *Perspectives on Listening* (Norwood, NJ: Ablex, 1993), pp. 261–281.
5. Adapted from Amy Tan, *The Kitchen God's Wife* (New York: Putnam, 1991), pp. 71–72.
6. Dr. Seuss, *Oh, the Places You'll Go!* (New York: Random House, 1990), pp. 1–2.
7. Adapted from Arthur K. Robertson, *Listen for Success: A Guide to Effective Listening* (New York: Irwin Professional Publishing, 1994), pp. 25–26.
8. Geneva Smitherman, *Black Talk: Words and Phrases from the Hood to the Amen Corner*, rev. ed. (Boston: Houghton Mifflin, 2000), p. 118.
9. Julia Wood, *Gendered Lives: Communication, Gender, and Culture*, 7th ed. (Belmont, CA: Wadsworth, 2007), p. 114.
10. Diana K. Ivy and Phil Backlund, *Exploring GenderSpeak: Personal Effectiveness in Gender Communication*, 2nd ed. (Boston: McGraw-Hill, 2000), pp. 175–176.
11. Ivy and Backlund, *Exploring GenderSpeak*, p. 174.
12. Adapted from Amy Einsohn, *The Copyeditor's Handbook: A Guide for Book Publishing and Corporate Communications*, 2nd ed. (Berkeley: University of California Press, 2006), pp. 404–416.
13. U.S. Department of Labor, Bureau of Labor Statistics, Chart 2: Median usual weekly earnings of full-time wage and salary workers by sex, race, and Hispanic or Latino ethnicity, 2007 annual averages, *Highlights of Women's Earnings in 2007*. October 2008 [Online]. Available: http://www.bls.gov/cps/cpswom2007.pdf.

14. Andrew Wolvin and Carolyn Gwynn Coakley, *Listening,* 5th ed. (Madison, WI: Brown & Benchmark, 1996), p. 232.

### Part II

1. Compiled from http://www.un.org/Dialogue/heroes.html; http://www.messagestick.com.au/awareness/jbeetson/index.html; http://www.smh.com.au/articles/2002/09/20/1032054956049; and http://news.sbs.com.au/livingblack/index.php?action=proginfo&id=345, May 24, 2006, Series 5, Episode 12.

### Chapter 5

1. "The New Student Politics" [Online]. Available: http://www.actionforchange.org/getinformed (accessed May 7, 2007).
2. Lois Gibbs, *Love Canal: My Story* (Albany: State University of New York Press, 1982).
3. Lois Gibbs, *Dying from Dioxin* (Boston: South End, 1995).
4. "On the Cover: The Quiet Victories of Ryan White," http://www.elibrary.com/s/edumark/; Ryan White and Ann Marie Cunningham, *Ryan White: My Own Story* (New York: Dial, 1991), p. 256.
5. http://hab.hrsa.gov/history.htm.
6. Rebecca Vollelker, "Ryan White, 18, Dies After 5-Year Battle with AIDS," *American Medical News* (April 20, 1990): 11.
7. Thomas C. Reeves, *The Life and Times of Joe McCarthy: A Biography* (Lanham, MD: Madison Books, 1997).
8. Alfred Rosa and Paul Escholz, *The Writer's Brief Handbook,* 2nd ed. (Scarborough, Canada: Allyn & Bacon, 1996), p. 7.

### Chapter 6

1. Vincent Mosco and Lewis Kaye, "Questioning the Concept of the Audience," in Ingunn Hagen and Janet Wasko, eds., *Consuming Audiences? Production and Reception in Media Research* (Cresskill, NJ: Hampton Press, 2000), pp. 31–46.
2. For an excellent summary and discussion of the various theories that attempt to explain social development, see Julia T. Wood, *Gendered Lives: Communication, Gender, and Culture,* 7th ed. (Belmont, CA: Wadsworth, 2007), pp. 37–59.
3. Gordon Marshall, ed., *The Concise Oxford Dictionary of Sociology* (New York: Oxford University Press, 1994), p. 315.
4. See, for example, Angela Browne, "Violence against Women by Male Partners: Prevalence, Outcomes and Policy Implications," *American Psychologist* 48 (1993): 1077–1087; Angela Browne and Kirk R. Williams, "Gender, Intimacy, and Lethal Violence: Trends from 1976–1987," *Gender and Society* 7 (1993): 78–98; Bureau of Justice Statistics, "Violence against Women: A National Crime Victimization Survey Report," 1994 [Online]. Available: http://www.ojp.usdoj.gov; Eve Buzawa, Thomas L. Austin, and Carl G. Buzawa, "Responding to Crimes of Violence against Women: Gender Differences Versus Organizational Imperatives," *Crime and Delinquency* 41 (1995): 443–466; Leandra Lackie and Anton F. de Man, "Correlates of Sexual Aggression among Male University Students," *Sex Roles* 37 (1997): 451–457; Russell P. Dobash, R. Emerson Dobash, Kate Cavanagh, and Ruth Lewis, "Separate and Intersecting Realities: A Comparison of Men's and Women's Accounts of Violence against Women," *Violence Against Women* 4 (1998): 382–414; Federal Bureau of Investigation, *Crime in the United States. Uniform Crime Reports* (Washington, DC: U.S. Department of Justice, 1989); Federal Bureau of Investigation, "Violence against Women: Estimates from the Redesigned Survey," August 1995 [Online]. Available: http://www.ojp.usdoj.gov; U.S. Bureau of Labor Statistics, "The Employment Situation News Release," 1998 [Online]. Available: http://stats.bls.gov; "The Wage Gap," *Ms.* (March–April 1996): 36–37.
5. Compiled from *Bowling for Columbine* [Motion picture], dir. Michael Moore (United States: Alliance Atlantis Communications, 2002), and Gabriella, "Interview with Marilyn Manson: I Don't Hate Journalists, I Just Feel Better When They're Not Around," *NY Rock,* September 2000 [Online]. Available: http://www.nyrock.com/interviews/2000/mm3_int.htm (accessed August 10, 2007).
6. Alice A. Egly and Shelly Chaiken, "Attitude Structure and Function," in *Handbook of Social Psychology* 1 (1998): 323–390; James M. Olson and Mark P. Zanna, "Attitudes and Attitude Change," *Annual Review of Psychology* 44 (1993): 117–154.
7. Rushworth M. Kidder, *Shared Values for a Troubled World* (San Francisco: Jossey-Bass, 1994); Milton Rokeach, *Beliefs, Attitudes and Values: A Theory of Organization and Change* (San Francisco: Jossey-Bass, 1970); Milton Rokeach, *The Nature of Human Values* (New York: Free Press, 1973); Shalom H. Schwartz and Wolfgang Blisky, "Toward a Theory of the Universal Content and Structure of Values: Extensions and Cross-Cultural Replications," *Journal of Personality and Social Psychology* 58 (1990): 878–891.
8. His Holiness the Dalai Lama and Howard C. Cutler, *The Art of Happiness: A Handbook for Living* (New York: Riverhead Books, 1998), pp. 1–2.

9. Kenneth Burke, *Counter-Statement* (Berkeley: University of California Press, 1968), p. 31.

### Part III

1. Compiled from http://www.un.org/works; "Angelina Jolie on Her UN Refugee Role," *National Geographic News*, June 18, 2003 [Online]. Available: http://news.nationalgeographic.com/news/2003/06/0618_030618_angelinajolie.html and "UNHCR Goodwill Ambassadors" [Online]. Available: http://www.unhcr.org/help/3f8d07664.html (accessed August 2, 2007).

### Chapter 7

1. Alvin Toffler, *Future Shock* (New York: Random House, 1970), p. 350.

### Chapter 8

1. Adapted from Myrtle S. Bolner and Gayle A. Poirier, *The Research Process: Books and Beyond*, 2nd ed. (Dubuque, IA: Kendall/Hunt, 2002), pp. 144–145; Shirley Duglin Kennedy, *Best Bet Internet: Reference and Research When You Don't Have Time to Mess Around* (Chicago: American Library Association, 1998), pp. 144–145.
2. Patricia Senn Breivik, *Student Learning in the Information* Age (Phoenix, AZ: Oryx Press, 1998), p. 2.
3. Adapted from Bolner and Poirier, *The Research Process*, p. 168; Christine A. Hult, *Researching and Writing across the Curriculum* (Boston: Allyn & Bacon, 1996), pp. 28–29.

### Chapter 9

1. Adapted from Charles J. Stewart and William B. Cash Jr., *Interviewing: Principles and Practices*, 11th ed. (Boston: McGraw-Hill, 2006), p. 1.
2. Larry King, *The Best of Larry King Live: The Greatest Interviews* (Atlanta: Times, 1995). Review this book and notice the depth of knowledge King possesses over a wide range of subjects and topics. His preparation beforehand enables him to ask relevant, informed questions of each of his interviewees.
3. Adapted from George Killenberg and Rob Anderson, *Before the Story: Interviewing and Communication Skills for Journalists* (New York: St. Martin's Press, 1989).

### Part IV

1. Compiled from CTV Television, Inc., "CANADA AM," April 18, 2007; *The Record* (Ketchener-Waterloo, Ontario), April 18, 2007, p. B1; *The Globe and Mail* (Canada), April 14, 2007, p. F3; *The Globe and Mail* (Canada), March 3, 2007, p. D6; *National Post* (f/k/a *The Financial Post*, Canada), February 6, 2007, p. A12.

### Chapter 10

1. For a historical overview of the research on organizing speeches, see Ernest Thompson, "Some Effects of Message Structure on Listeners' Comprehension," *Speech Monographs* 34 (1967): 51–57; James C. McCroskey and R. S. Mehrley, "The Effects of Disorganization and Non-Fluency on Attitude Change and Source Credibility," *Communication Monographs* 36 (1969): 13–21; Arlee Johnson, "A Preliminary Investigation of the Relationship between Organization and Listener Comprehension," *Central States Speech Journal* 21 (1970): 104–107; Christopher Spicer and Ronald E. Bassett, "The Effect of Organization on Learning from an Informative Message," *Southern Speech Communication Journal* 41 (1976): 290–299. For more recent discussions of the importance of organization in speeches, see Patricia R. Palmerton, "Teaching Skills or Teaching Thinking," *Journal of Applied Communication Research* 20 (1992): 335–341; Robert G. Powell, "Critical Thinking and Speech Communication: Our Teaching Strategies Are Warranted—Not!" *Journal of Applied Communication Research* 20 (1992): 342–347.

### Chapter 12

1. Bas A. Andeweg, Jaap C. de Jong, and Hans Hoeken, "'May I Have Your Attention?' Exordial Techniques in Informative Oral Presentations," *Technical Communication Quarterly* 7 (1998): 281.
2. Mark L. Knapp, Roderick P. Hart, Gustav W. Friedrick, and G. M. Shulman, "The Rhetoric of Goodbye: Verbal and Nonverbal Correlates of Human Leave-Taking," *Speech Monographs* 40 (1973): 182–198.

### Part V

1. Compiled from http://www.actionforchange.org/getinformed and *The New Student Politics: The Wingspread Statement on Student Civic Engagement*, 2nd ed. (Providence, RI: Campus Compact, Brown University, 2002).

### Chapter 13

1. Adapted from James Crosswhite, *The Rhetoric of Reason: Writing and the Attractions of Argument* (Madison: University of Wisconsin Press, 1996), pp. 51, 55, 56.
2. Adapted from Edward S. Inch and Barbara Warnick, *Critical Thinking and Communication: The Use of Reason in Argument*, 3rd ed. (Boston: Allyn & Bacon, 1989), pp. 194–197.
3. Walter R. Fisher, *Human Communication as Narration: Toward a Philosophy of Reason, Value, and Action* (Columbia: University of South Carolina Press, 1987), p. 58.

4. Kathleen Hall Jamieson, *Eloquence in the Electronic Age: The Transformation of Political Speechmaking* (New York: Oxford University Press, 1988), p. 140.
5. Cynthia Crossen, *Tainted Truth: The Manipulation of Fact in America* (New York: Simon & Schuster, 1994), p. 42.
6. Reza Fadaei, ed., *Applied Algebra and Statistics* (Needham Heights, MA: Simon & Schuster, 2000), pp. 544, 545.
7. Phillip H. Taylor, Philip F. Rice, and Roy H. Williams, *Basic Statistics* (Cincinnati, OH: Thompson Learning, 2000), chap. 2, pp. 1–4. The author would like to thank the reference librarians at the Fort Collins Public Library for their help with this example.
8. Compiled from Valerie Strauss and Susan Kinze, "Woman Chosen to Lead Harvard: Collegial Historian to Follow Summers's Stormy Tenure," *The Washington Post,* February 10, 2007, p. A1; Cathy Young, "Women, Science, and the Gender Gap," *The Boston Globe,* October 2, 2006, p. A11; Suzanne Goldenberg, "Harvard Chief Resigns Amid Rifts and Rebellion," *The Guardian* (London), February 22, 2006, p. 15; Editorial, "Big Foot: Harvard President Says a Dumb Thing," *Pittsburg Post-Gazette,* p. J6; Victoria Griffith, "Summers Releases Transcript in Effort to Calm His Critics," *Financial Times* (London), February 18, 2005, p. 2; Mary Dejevsky, "Women's Brains, Men's Brains, and the Fraught Sexual Politics of America," *The Independent* (London), p. 37; Derrick Z. Jackson, "Summers's Tortured Logic," *The Boston Globe,* January 19, 2005, p. A15; Suzanne Goldenberg, "Why Women Are Poor at Science, by Harvard President," *The Guardian* (London), January 18, 2005, p. 1.
9. Barbara Kantrowitz and Pat Wingert, "Teachers Wanted," *Newsweek,* October 2, 2000, p. 40.
10. Adapted from Inch and Warnick, *Critical Thinking and Communication,* p. 154.
11. Adapted from bell hooks, *Talking Back: Thinking Feminist, Thinking Black* (Boston: South End, 1989), pp. 3, 107, 109, 110.
12. The discussion over the type of language used by Truth, and whether or not she actually did repeat the phrase "ain't I a woman," is nicely summarized in Suzanne Pullon Fitch and Roseann M. Mandziuk, *Sojourner Truth as Orator: Wit, Story, and Song* (Westport, CT: Greenwood Press, 1997).
13. I. A. Richards, *The Philosophy of Rhetoric* (New York: Oxford University Press, 1965) (original work published 1936); C. K. Ogden and I. A. Richards, *The Meaning of Meaning: A Study of the Influence of Language upon Thought and of the Science of Symbolism* (New York: Harcourt, Brace & World, 1923).

### Chapter 14

1. For a discussion of the importance of maintaining Aristotle's distinction between logos and logic, see Joseph Little, "Confusion in the Classroom: Does Logos Mean Logic?" *Journal of Technical Writing and Communication* 29 (1999): 349–353. Aristotle suggested that logos refers to the process of reasoning as well as establishing credibility, or ethos, and using emotional appeals, or pathos. See also George Kennedy's translation of *Aristotle: On Rhetoric: A Theory of Civic Discourse* (Oxford: Oxford University Press, 1991), p. 37.
2. See Chaim Perelman and Luce Olbrechts Tyteca, *The New Rhetoric: A Treatise on Argumentation,* John Wilkinson and Purcell Weaver, trans. (Notre Dame, IN: University of Notre Dame Press, 1969), pp. 31–35, for a discussion of the universal audience, or that group of imagined listeners to whom we submit claims and test their "logic."
3. Adapted from Stephen Toulmin, Richard Rieke, and Allan Janik, *An Introduction to Reasoning* (New York: Macmillan, 1979).
4. Perelman and Olbrechts-Tyteca identify approximately twenty-two different argument schemes in *The New Rhetoric,* and Douglas N. Walton offers twenty-five different argumentation schemes in *Argumentation Schemes for Presumptive Reasoning* (Mahwah, NJ: Erlbaum, 1996). Although all of these schemes are important, students in a beginning public speaking course do well to rely on the five basic schemes or types discussed in this chapter and in most other public speaking texts.
5. The material in this section and the section on deductive reasoning is from Lester Faigley and Jack Selzer, *Good Reasons* (Needham Heights, MA: Allyn & Bacon, 2000); Howard Kahane and Nancy Cavender, *Logic and Contemporary Rhetoric: The Use of Reason in Everyday Life,* 8th ed. (Belmont, CA: Wadsworth, 1998); Stephen Toulmin, *The Uses of Argument* (London: Cambridge University Press, 1969).
6. See, for example, David Vancil, *Rhetoric and Argumentation* (Boston: Allyn & Bacon, 1993), p. 134, who suggests that argument by example is "one of the archetypal forms of the inductive process"; David Zarefsky, *Public Speaking: Strategies for Success* (Needham Heights, MA: Allyn & Bacon, 2002), pp. 153–154.
7. For an excellent compilation of women's speeches related to their right to vote, as well as other rights, including Anthony's speech, see Karlyn Kohrs Campbell, ed., *Man Cannot Speak for Her: Key Texts of the Early Feminists* (New York: Praeger, 1989).

8. See Faigley and Selzer, *Good Reasons*; Kahane and Cavender, *Logic and Contemporary Rhetoric;* Edward S. Inch and Barbara Warnick, *Critical Thinking and Communication: The Use of Reason in Argument*, 3rd ed. (Boston: Allyn & Bacon, 1998).
9. False causes are also known by their Latin name, *post hoc, ergo propter hoc*, which means "after this, therefore because of this." For a succinct discussion of false causes, see Inch and Warnick, *Critical Thinking and Communication*, pp. 208–209.
10. Many thanks to Wayne Webster, Patriot Guard Riders Southeast Wyoming Ride Captain and U.S.A.F Retired, for bringing this example to my attention. Compiled from http://www.patriotguard.org; Ann M. Simmons, "Biker Group Escorts Fallen Troops; Patriot Guard Riders, an Informal Organization of Motorcyclists, Attends Funerals to Pay Tribute to Military Personnel," *Los Angeles Times*, October 1, 2007, Part B, p. 1; Jennifer Harper, "Riders Shield Mourners: Patriot Guard Offers 'Corridor of Honor' for Troops," *The Washington Times*, March 24, 2006, p. A9; Francis Harris, "Bikers on Guard at War Funerals; Volunteer Army of Patriots Shields Grieving Relatives from Anti-Gay Pickets," *The Daily Telegraph* (London), March 9, 2006, p. 18.
11. Jonathan Alter, "Who's Next 2005," *Newsweek*, December 27, 2004–January 3, 2005, p. 76.
12. Cited in Paul Rogat Loeb, *Soul of a Citizen: Living with Conviction in a Cynical Time* (New York: St. Martin's Griffin, 1999), pp. 68–69.
13. Jerry Alder and Mary Carmichael, "The Tsunami Threat," *Newsweek*, January 10, 2005, p. 42.
14. Inch and Warnick call reasoning by sign "coexistential" reasoning, suggesting "an argument from coexistence reasons from something that can be observed (as a sign) to a condition or feature that cannot be observed." See Inch and Warnick, *Critical Thinking and Communication*, p. 201.
15. Alder and Carmichael, "The Tsunami Threat," p. 42.
16. Toulmin, *The Uses of Argument*; Toulmin, Rieke, and Janik, *An Introduction to Reasoning*. See also Mary M. Gleason, "The Role of Evidence in Argumentative Writing," *Reading & Writing Quarterly* 14 (1999): 81–106.
17. For a discussion of the characteristics of credibility, see James B. Stiff, *Persuasive Communication* (New York: Guilford Press, 1994), pp. 89–98.

### Chapter 15

1. The debate over the role of language in constructing or reflecting reality is centuries old, beginning with Plato and Aristotle. For a summary of this debate and the implications of the many positions, see Gill, *Rhetoric and Human Understanding*. James L. Golden, Goodwin F. Berquist, and William E. Coleman offer an anthology of some of the primary texts in this debate in their book *The Rhetoric of Western Thought*, 6th ed. (Dubuque, IA: Kendall/Hunt, 1997).
2. C. K. Ogden and I. A. Richards, *The Meaning of Meaning: A Study of the Influence of Language upon Thought and of the Science of Symbolism* (New York: Harcourt, Brace, 1930) (original work published 1923).
3. For an excellent discussion of signifying, see Henry Louis Gates, *The Signifying Monkey: A Theory of Afro-American Literary Criticism* (New York: Oxford University Press, 1988); Geneva Smitherman, *Talkin and Testifying: The Language of Black America* (Boston: Houghton Mifflin, 1977).
4. Compiled from David Carr, "Networks Condemn Remarks by Imus," April 7, 2007, *The New York Times* [Online]. Available: http://www.nytimes.com/2007/04/07/arts/television/07imus.html?hp (accessed August 2, 2007); Deepti Hajela, "Imus Takes His Lumps on Sharpton's Show," April 9, 2007, ABC News [Online]. Available: http://abcnews.go.com/Entertainment/wireStory?id=3023239 (accessed August 2,2007); "MSNBC Pulls 'Imus in the Morning'," April 12, 2007, CNN.com. Available: http:// edition.cnn.com/2007/SHOWBIZ/TV/04/11/imus.rutgers/index.html (accessed August 2, 2007).
5. The material in this section is from Khosrow Jahandarie, *Spoken and Written Discourse: A Multi-Disciplinary Perspective* (Stamford, CT: Ablex, 1999), pp. 131–150; Eckart Scheerer, "Orality, Literacy, and Cognitive Modeling," in Boris M. Velichkovsky and Duane M. Rumbaugh, eds., *Communicating Meaning: The Evolution and Development of Language* (Mahwah, NJ: Erlbaum, 1996), pp. 211–256; M. A. K. Halliday, "Spoken and Written Modes of Meaning," in Rosalind Horowitz and S. Jay Samuels, eds., *Comprehending Oral and Written Language* (New York: Harcourt Brace Jovanovich, 1987), pp. 55–82; Wallace Chafe and Jane Danielewicz, "Properties of Spoken and Written Language," in Horowitz and Samuels, eds., *Comprehending Oral and Written Language*, pp. 83–113.

### Chapter 16

1. Eric Partridge, *Usage and Abusage: A Guide to Good English* (New York: Norton, 1995), p. 182 (original work published 1942).
2. Rigoberta Menchú, "Five Hundred Years of Sacrifice Before Alien Gods," *Interview*, 1992 [Online]. Available: http://www.indigenouspeople.net/menchu2.htm.

3. Richard Lederer, *The Bride of Anguished English: A Bonus of Bloopers, Blunders, Botches, and Boo-Boos* (New York: St. Martin's Press), pp. 33, 44.
4. Audley "Queen Mother" Moore, in Toyomi Igus, ed., *Book of Black Heroes: Vol. 2, Great Women in the Struggle: An Introduction for Young Readers* (Orange, NJ: Just Us Books, 1991), p. 12.
5. Partridge, *Usage and Abusage*, p. 14.

### Part VI

1. Compiled from http://www.onevoicemovement.org; http://peaceworks.net; "Creating Mideast Peace with Food?" Eyewitness News' Lauren Galsberg, September 8, 2006, 7online.com New York City and Tri-State News from WABC-TV, http://abclocal.go.com/wabc (accessed June 12, 2007); and "Mideast Peace Recipe? Ask Moshe, Ali," *Christian Science Monitor* (Boston, MA), January 8, 1998, p. 7.

### Chapter 17

1. Herbert W. Hildebrant and Walter W. Stevens suggest that no one method is better than another. Rather, "it is the ability of the individual speaker in using a particular method" that is influential. See Hildebrant and Stevens, "Manuscript and Extemporaneous Delivery in Communicating Information," *Speech Monographs* 30 (1963): 369–372.
2. Robert J. Branham and W. Barnett Pearce, "The Conversational Frame in Public Address," *Communication Quarterly* 44 (1996): 423.

### Chapter 18

1. Patsy Rodenburg, *The Need for Words: Voice and the Text* (New York: Routledge, 1993), pp. 5–6.
2. Peter A. Andersen, Michael L. Hecht, and Gregory D. Hoebler, "The Cultural Dimension of Nonverbal Communication," in William B. Gudykunst and Bella Moody, eds., *Handbook of International and Intercultural Communication* (Thousand Oaks, CA: Sage, 2002), pp. 89–106; Larry A. Samovar and Richard E. Porter, *Communication between Cultures* (Belmont, CA: Wadsworth, 1991), pp. 205–206.
3. Stephen E. Lucas, *The Art of Public Speaking*, 7th ed. (New York: McGraw-Hill, 2001), p. 290.
4. Paul L. Soper, *Basic Public Speaking*, 2nd ed. (New York: Oxford University Press, 1956), p. 151. Soper also cites Ambrose Bierce as suggesting, with regard to too high a pitch, that positive is "being mistaken at the top of one's voice." See Soper, *Basic Public Speaking*, p. 150.
5. Adapted from Soper, *Basic Public Speaking*, p. 143.
6. Nicholas Christenfeld, "Does It Hurt to Say Um?" *Journal of Nonverbal Behavior* 19 (Fall 1995): 171–186. Christenfeld's study also found that audiences prefer no pauses to empty pauses.
7. See, for example, Stephanie Martin and Lyn Darnley, *The Teaching Voice* (San Diego, CA: Singular Publishing Group, 1996), p. 60; Rodenburg, *The Need for Words*; Linda Gates, *Voice for Performance* (New York: Applause, 2000); Richard Dowis, *The Lost Art of the Great Speech: How to Write One, How to Deliver It* (New York: American Management Association, 2000).
8. Many communication scholars define nonverbal communication as all aspects of communication other than words. In a public speaking course, the distinction between vocalized communication as verbal and nonvocalized communication as nonverbal seems pedagogically useful.
   A similar distinction is made in many other public speaking texts.
9. Ray Birdwhistell, *Kinesics and Context* (Philadelphia: University of Pennsylvania Press, 1970); Albert Mehrabian, *Silent Messages: Implicit Communication of Emotion and Attitudes*, 2nd ed. (Belmont, CA: Wadsworth, 1981).
10. See, for example, April R. Trees and Valerie Manusov, "Managing Face Concerns in Critics: Integrating Nonverbal Behaviors as a Dimension of Politeness in Female Friendship Dyads," *Human Communication Research* 24 (1998): 564–583; James C. McCroskey, Aino Sallinen, Joan M. Fayer, Virginia P. Richmond, and Robert A. Barraclough, "Nonverbal Immediacy and Cognitive Learning: A Cross-Cultural Investigation," *Communication Education* 45 (1996): 200–211; Mary Mino, "The Relative Effects of Content and Vocal Delivery during a Simulated Employment Interview," *Communication Research Reports* 13 (1996): 225–238. See also Julia T. Wood, *Interpersonal Communication: Everyday Encounters*, 2nd ed. (Belmont, CA: Wadsworth, 1999),p. 148.
11. For an excellent discussion of variations in nonverbal expectations across cultures, see Gudykunst and Moody, eds., *Handbook of International and Intercultural Communication.*
12. For example, see "Good-Looking Lawyers Make More Money, Says a Study by Economists," *Wall Street Journal*, January 4, 1996, p. A1; Patricia Rozell, David Kennedy, and Edward Grabb, "Physical Attractiveness and Income Attainment among Canadians," *Journal of Psychology* 123 (1989): 547–559; Tracy L. Morris, Joan Gorham, Stanley H. Cohen, and Drew Huffman, "Fashion in the Classroom: Effects of Attire on Student Perceptions of Instructors in College Classes," *Communication Education* 45 (1996): 135–148.
13. Arthur J. Hartz, "Psycho-Socionomics: Attractiveness Research from a Societal Perspective,"

*Journal of Social Behavior and Personality* 11 (1996): 683.

14. Paula Morrow writes that even though physical attractiveness is difficult to "quantify," "people within a given culture tend to agree with each other regarding whether a person's facial appearance is physically attractive or not and they tend to be consistent in their judgments over time." See Morrow, "Physical Attractiveness and Selection Decision Making," *Journal of Management* 16 (1990): 45–60, esp. p. 47. See also Ruth P. Rubinstein, *Dress Codes: Meanings and Messages in American Culture*, 2nd ed. (Boulder, CO: Westview, 2001); C. Peter Herman, Mark P. Zanna, and E. Tory Higgins, *Physical Appearance, Stigma, and Social Behavior open: The Ontario Symposium, Vol. 3* (Hillsdale, NJ: Erlbaum, 1986).
15. Mark T. Palmer and Karl B. Simmons, "Communicating Intentions through Nonverbal Behaviors," *Human Communication Research* 22 (1995): 128–160.
16. Steven A. Beebe, "Eye Contact: A Nonverbal Determinant of Speaker Credibility," *Speech Teacher* 23 (1974): 21–25; Steven A. Beebe, "Effects of Eye Contact, Posture and Vocal Inflection upon Credibility and Comprehension," *Australian Scan Journal of Nonverbal Communication* 7–8 (1979–1980): 57–70; Martin Cobin, "Response to Eye Contact," *Quarterly Journal of Speech* 48 (1963): 415–419.
17. See, for example, Peter E. Bull, *Posture and Gesture* (New York: Pergamon, 1987).
18. See, for example, Gilbert Austin in Mary Margaret Robb and Lester Thonssen, eds., *Chironomia or A Treatise on Rhetorical Delivery* (Carbondale: Southern Illinois University Press, 1966) (original work published 1806); John Bulwer, in James W. Cleary, ed., *Chirologia: Or the Natural Language of the Hand, and Chironomia: Or the Art of Manual Rhetoric* (Carbondale: Southern Illinois University Press, 1974) (original work published 1644).

### Chapter 19

1. Will Linkugel and D. Berg, *A Time to Speak* (Belmont, CA: Wadsworth, 1970), pp. 68–96. See also Elena P. Zayas-Bazan, "Instructional Media in the Total Language Picture," *International Journal of Instructional Media* 5 (1977–1978): 145–150; Emil Bohn and David Jabusch, "The Effect of Four Methods of Instruction on the Use of Visual Aids in Speeches," *Western Journal of Speech Communication* 46 (1982): 253–265.
2. Raymond S. Nickerson, "Short-Term Memory for Complex Meaningful Visual Configurations: A Demonstration of Capacity," *Canadian Journal of Psychology* 19 (1965): 155–160.
3. Bohn and Jabusch, "The Effect of Four Methods of Instruction on the Use of Visual Aids in Speeches," p. 254.
4. William J. Seiler, "The Effects of Visual Materials on Attitudes, Credibility, and Retention," *Speech Monographs* 38 (1971): 331–334.
5. Joe Ayres, "Using Visual Aids to Reduce Speech Anxiety," *Communication Research Reports* 8 (1991): 73–79.
6. Wilma Davidson and Susan J. Klien, "Ace Your Presentation," *Journal of Accountancy* 187 (1999): 61–63.
7. For a nice discussion of using lists as visual aids, see Margaret Y. Rabb, *The Presentation Design Book: Tips, Techniques and Advice for Creating Effective, Attractive Slides, Overheads, Multimedia Presentations, Screen Shows and More* (Chapel Hill, NC: Ventana, 1993).
8. For example, see Lynn Kearny, *Graphics for Presenters: Getting Your Ideas Across* (Menlo Park, CA: Crisp, 1996); Claudyne Wilder, *The Presentations Kit: Ten Steps for Spelling Out Your Ideas* (New York: Wiley, 1994); Rabb, *The Presentation Design Book.*

### Chapter 20

1. Myles Martel, *Before You Say a Word: The Executive Guide to Effective Communication* (Upper Saddle River, NJ: Prentice Hall, 1984).
2. For example, see Margaret Y. Rabb, *The Presentation Design Book* (Chapel Hill, NC: Ventana, 1993); Claudyne Wilder, *The Presentations Kit* (New York: Wiley, 1994); Russell N. Baird, Duncan McDonald, Ronald H. Pittman, and Arthur T. Turnbull, *The Graphics of Communication: Methods, Media and Technology* (New York: Harcourt Brace Jovanovich, 1993).
3. Hans Biedermann, *Dictionary of Symbolism: Cultural Icons and the Meanings behind Them*, trans. James Hulbert (New York: Facts on File, 1992).

### Part VII

1. Compiled from Alan Clements, *The Voice of Hope: Aung San Suu Kyi; Conversations with Alan Clements* (New York: Seven Stories, 1997); Michael Aris, Ed., *Freedom from Fear and other Writings* (London: Penguin, 1991).

### Chapter 21

1. Conversation with Jennifer McMartin, student at Colorado State University, June 6, 2001.
2. John R. Johnson and Nancy Szczupakiewicz, "The Public Speaking Course: Is It Preparing Students with Work Related Public Speaking Skills?" *Communication Education* 36 (1987): 131–137.
3. See, for example, Deanna P. Dannels, "Time to Speak Up: A Theoretical Framework of Situated Pedagogy and Practice for Communication across the Curriculum," *Communication Education* 50 (2001): 144–158; Sherwin Morreal, Michael Osborn, and Judy Pearson, "Why

Communication Is Important: A Rationale for the Centrality of the Study of Communication," *Journal of the Association for Communication Administration* 29 (2000): 1–25; and Andrew D. Wolvin, "The Basic Course and the Future of the Workplace," *Basic Communication Course Annual* 10 (1989): 1–6.

4. Compiled from Lance Williams, Mark Fainaru-Wada, "What Bonds told BALCO Grand Jury" *San Francisco Chronicle*, Friday, December 3, 2004, http://sfgate.com/chi-bin/article.cgi?file; Ted Rowlands, CNN.com Law Center, "Grand Jury Looking at Whether Bonds Lied about Steroid Use, April 14, 2006, http://www.cnn.com/206/bonds.steroid/index.html; T. J. Quinn, *New York Daily News*, "Jury's in on Bonds: Feds Eye Fall Indictment," July 21, 2007, http://www.nydailynews.com/sports/baseball/2007/07; and Paul T. Rosynsky, "Bonds Threatens to Sue Detractors," *Mercury News*, August 13, 2007, http://www.mercurynews.com. Accessed August 22, 2007.

**Chapter 22**

1. The theory of invitational rhetoric was initially proposed by Sonja K. Foss and Cindy L. Griffin in "Beyond Persuasion: A Proposal for an Invitational Rhetoric," *Communication Monographs* 62 (1995): 1–18. That theory has been modified here so that it is applicable to public speaking practices.
2. This example comes from Jennifer Emerling Bone, Cindy L. Griffin, and T. M. Linda Scholz, "Invitational Rhetoric: Myths, Misunderstandings and the (Re)Making of Theory," unpublished manuscript, 2005. Thanks go to Jennifer Emerling Bone for her work on this portion of the manuscript.
3. "World Trade Center Site Memorial Competition Jury Statement," *New York Times*, November 19, 2003 [Online]. Available: http://www.nytimes.com/2003/11/19/nyregion/19WTC-JURY-TEXT.html.
4. "Memorial—*Reflecting Absence*: WTC Memorial Jury Statement for Winning Design," Lower Manhattan Development Corporation, January 13, 2004 [Online]. Available: http://www.renewnyc.com.
5. "Memorial—*Reflecting Absence*: WTC Memorial Jury Statement for Winning Design."
6. Lower Manhattan Development Corporation, January 2, 2003 [Online]. Available: http://www.renewnyc.com.
7. For more discussion on the conditions of equality, value, and self-determination, see Harold Barrett, *Rhetoric and Civility: Human Development, Narcissism, and the Good Audience* (Albany: State University of New York Press, 1991); Seyla Benhabib, *Situating the Self: Gender, Community, and Postmodernism in Contemporary Ethics* (New York: Routledge, 1992); Linda Ellinor and Glenna Gerard, *Dialogue: Creating and Sustaining Collaborative Partnerships at Work* (New York: Wiley, 1998); William Isaacs, *Dialogue and the Art of Thinking Together* (New York: Currency, 1999); Paul Rogat Loeb, *Soul of a Citizen: Living with Conviction in a Cynical Time* (New York: St. Martin's Griffin, 1999); M. Scott Peck, *The Different Drum: Community—Making and Peace* (New York: Simon & Schuster, 1987); Carl R. Rogers, "The Interpersonal Relationship: The Core of Guidance," *Harvard Educational Review* 32 (1962): 416–429; M. U. Walker, "Moral Understandings: Alternative 'Epistemology' for a Feminist Ethics," *Hypatia* 4 (1989): 15–28.
8. My thanks to Marko Mohlenhoff, former campaign associate at the Fort Collins Area United Way, for sharing his approach to public speaking and working with me on this example.
9. bell hooks, *Outlaw Culture: Resisting Representations* (New York: Routledge, 1994), p. 241.

**Chapter 23**

1. Adapted from Bruce E. Gronbeck, Raymie E. McKerrow, Douglas Ehninger, and Alan H. Monroe, *Principles and Types of Speech Communication*, 11th ed. (Glenview, IL: Scott, Foresman/Little, Brown Higher Education, 1990), pp. 180–205.
2. Numerous scholars, beginning with Aristotle, define persuasion as a process, as something that takes place over time. For example, see Gerald R. Miller and Michael E. Roloff, eds., *Persuasion: New Directions in Theory and Research* (Beverly Hills, CA: Sage, 1980); Kathleen Kennedy Reardon, *Persuasion in Practice* (Newbury Park, CA: Sage, 1991); James B. Stiff, *Persuasive Communication* (New York: Guilford Press, 1994) for three examples of this processual definition of persuasion.
3. See Stiff, *Persuasive Communication*, pp. 117–119.
4. Bryan B. Whaley and Lisa Smith Wagner, "Rebuttal Analogy in Persuasive Messages: Communicator Likeability and Cognitive Responses," *Journal of Language and Social Psychology* 19 (2000): 66–84.
5. Connie Roser and Margaret Thompson, "Fear Appeals and the Formation of Active Publics," *Journal of Communication* 45 (1995): 103–121.
6. Patricia A. Rippetoe and Ronald W. Rogers, "Effects of Components of Protection-Motivation Theory on Adaptive and Maladaptive Coping with a Health Threat," *Journal of Personality and Social Psychology* 53 (1987): 596–604.
7. Compiled from "Animal Liberation Front (ALF) Frequently Asked Questions," the North American ALF Supporters Group, http://www.hedweb.com/alfaq.htm; "Animal Liberation

Front.com: Worldwide News and Information Resource about the ALF" http://www.animal-liberationfront.com; "North American Animal Liberation Press Office," http://animalliberationpressoffice.org; and "MIPT Terrorism: A Comprehensive Databank of Global Terrorist Incidents and Organizations," http://www.tkb.org/Group.jsp?groupID=14. Accessed, August 22, 2007.

8. Hong Chyi Chen, Richard Reardon, Cornelia Rea, and David J. More, "Forewarning of Content and Involvement: Consequences for Persuasion and Resistance to Persuasion," *Journal of Experimental Social Psychology* 28 (1992): 523–541.
9. Vincent R. Waldron and James L. Applegate, "Person Centered Tactics during Verbal Disagreements: Effects on Student Perceptions of Persuasiveness and Social Attraction," *Communication Education* 47 (1998): 55–56.
10. Jack W. Brehm, *A Theory of Psychological Reactance* (New York: Academic Press, 1996); Patricia Kearney, Timothy G. Plax, and Nancy F. Burroughs, "An Attributional Analysis of College Students' Resistance Decisions," *Communication Education* 40 (1991): 325–342.

**Chapter 24**

1. Deborah L. Shelton, "Twice a Victim: Battered Women and Insurance," *Human Rights: Journal of the Section of Individual Rights and Responsibilities* 23 (1998): 26–28.
2. For a nice discussion of the importance of maintaining Aristotle's distinction between logos and logic, see Joseph Little, "Confusion in the Classroom: Does Logos Mean Logic?" *Journal of Technical Writing and Communication* 29 (1999): 349–353. Aristotle suggested that logos refers to the process of reasoning as well as establishing credibility, or ethos, and using emotional appeals, or pathos. See also Aristotle, *On Rhetoric: A Theory of Civic Discourse*, George Kennedy, trans. (Oxford: Oxford University Press, 1991), p. 37.
3. Awareness, understanding, agreement, acceptance, and enactment are based on William J. McGuire's phases describing the process of persuasion. See William J. McGuire, "Attitudes and Attitude Change," in Gardner Lindzey and Elliot Aronson, eds., *Handbook of Social Psychology, vol. 1* (New York: Random House, 1985), pp. 258–261.
4. See John C. Reinard, "The Empirical Study of the Persuasive Effects of Evidence: The Status after 50 Years of Research," *Human Communication Research* 15 (1988): 3–59.
5. Donald Dean Morely and Kim B. Walker, "The Role of Importance, Novelty, and Plausibility in Producing Belief Change," *Communication Monographs* 54 (1987): 436–442.
6. See Edward S. Inch and Barbara Warnick, *Critical Thinking and Communication: The Use of Reason in Argument*, 3rd ed. (Boston: Allyn & Bacon, 1998),p. 159.
7. See, for example, Peter A. Andersen and Laura K. Guerrero, eds., *Handbook of Communication and Emotion: Research, Theory, Applications, and Contexts* (San Diego, CA: Academic Press, 1998), esp. chaps. 16 and 17; Kathleen Kelley Reardon, *Persuasion in Practice* (Newbury Park, CA: Sage, 1991), pp. 108–110; James B. Stiff, *Persuasive Communication* (New York: Guilford Press, 1994), pp. 119–131.
8. See, for example, Andersen and Guerrero, eds., *Handbook of Communication and Emotion*, esp. chaps. 16 and 17; Reardon, *Persuasion in Practice*, pp. 108–110; Stiff, *Persuasive Communication*, pp. 119–131.
9. Richard E. Porter and Larry A. Samovar, "Cultural Influences on Emotional Expression: Implications for Intercultural Communication," in Andersen and Guerrero, *Handbook of Communication and Emotion*, p. 452.
10. For a sample of speakers who possess these traits, see "Top 100 American Speeches of the 20th Century," News and Public Affairs, University of Wisconsin–Madison [Online]. Available: http://www.news.wisc.edu/misc/speeches/.
11. See Richard M. Perloff, *The Dynamics of Persuasion* (Hillsdale, NJ: Erlbaum, 1993), pp. 136–155; Stiff, *Persuasive Communication*, pp. 89–106.
12. Stiff, *Persuasive Communication*, pp. 102–104.
13. Perloff, *Dynamics of Persuasion*, pp. 170–179.
14. "Top 100 American Speeches of the 20th Century."
15. Marian Friestad and Peter Wright, "Everyday Persuasion Knowledge,"*Psychology & Marketing* 16 (1999): 185.
16. Friestad and Wright, "Everyday Persuasion Knowledge," p. 188.
17. For a nice discussion of the logic of mythos, see Glenn W. Most, "From Logos to Mythos," in Richard Buxton, ed., *From Myth to Reason? Studies in the Development of Greek Thought* (Oxford: Oxford University Press, 1999), pp. 25–47.
18. Cindy Sheehan, "Good Riddance Attention Whore," *Daily Kos*, May 28, 2007 [Online]. Available: http://www.dailykos.com/story/2007/5/28/12530/1525 (accessed August 23, 2007). Evelyn Nieves, "Cindy Sheehan, the 'Peace Mom,' Now a Candidate," *San Francisco Chronicle*, October 7, 2008. Cindy Sheehan, *Cindy's Soapbox*, n.d. Available: http://www.cindysheehanssoapbox.com/CINDY_S_SOAPBOX.html (accessed March 22, 2009).
19. See Frans H. van Eemeren and Rob Grootendorst, *Argumentation, Communication, and Fallacies: A Pragma-Dialectical Perspective*

(Hillsdale, NJ: Erlbaum, 1992); Howard Kahane and Nancy Cavender, *Logic and Contemporary Rhetoric: The Use of Reason in Everyday Life*, 8th ed. (Belmont, CA: Wadsworth, 1998).

20. Paul Wellstone, "Senate Floor Speech Regarding Military Action in Iraq, 2002." Wellstone: The Paul and Sheila Wellstone Online Archive [Online]. Available: http://www.wellstone.org/archive.article_detail.aspx?itemID=5423&catID=3605.

### Part VIII

1. Compiled from http://www.labucketbrigade.org; The Smiley Group, *The Covenant with Black America*, (Chicago: Third World Press, 2006); "Watchdog Group to Protest Refinery: Activists to Mix with Exxon Stockholders," *Times-Picayune* (New Orleans), May 24, 2005, p. 1; "Two Groups Suing Refinery: They Claim Plant Violates Clean Air Act," *Times-Picayune* (New Orleans), February 13, 2004, p. 1; "Group Plans to File Suit Against Refinery: They Allege Pollution Violations," *Times-Picayune* (New Orleans), December 5, 2003, p. 1: "Refinery Emissions Too High, Groups Say: Chalmette Residents Fear for their Health," *Times-Picayu*ne (New Orleans), September 24, 2003, p. 1; "Residents to Learn to Test Air Quality: Devices to Check for Chemicals on Display," *Times-Picayune* (New Orleans), October 18, 2002, p. 1; and, "Neighbors Seeking Proof of Pollution," *Times-Picayune* (New Orleans), July 20, 2000, p. 1.

### Chapter 25

1. Nelson Mandela, "Now Is the Time to Intensify the Struggle," in Steve Clark, ed., *Nelson Mandela Speaks: Forging a Democratic, Nonracial South Africa* (New York: Pathfinder, 1993), pp. 23–28.
2. Mandela, "Now Is the Time to Intensify the Struggle," p. 25.
3. Congressman Bobby Rush, "Tribute to Mrs. Rosa Parks," April 20, 1999 [Online]. Available: http://www.house.gov/rush/pr42099s.htm.
4. Available: http://nobelprize.org/nobel_prizes/peace/laureates/1992/tum-lecture.html.
5. Joal Ryan, "Rock Throws Stones at MTV Video Music Awards," *E! Online*, September 9, 1999 [Online]. Available: http://aol.eonline.com/News/Items/0,1,5285,00.html.
6. Stephen E. Lucas, *The Art of Public Speaking*, 7th ed. (Boston: McGraw-Hill, 2001), p. 445.
7. Jerry Palmer, *Taking Humor Seriously* (London: Routledge, 1994), p. 161.
8. See, for example, Charles R. Gruner, "Advice to the Beginning Speaker on Using Humor—What the Research Tells Us," *Communication Education* 34 (1985): 142–147; Christie McGufee Smith and Larry Power, "The Use of Disparaging Humor by Group Leaders," *Southern Speech Communication Journal* 53 (1988): 279–292; Elizabeth E. Grahm, Michael J. Papa, and Gordon P. Brooks, "Functions of Humor in Conversation: Conceptualization and Measurement," *Western Journal of Communication* 56 (1992): 161–183; Frank J. MacHovec, *Humor: Theory, History, Applications* (Springfield, IL: Charles C Thomas, 1988); Palmer, *Taking Humor Seriously*.
9. Jeffrey H. Goldstein, "Theoretical Notes on Humor," *Journal of Communication* 26 (1976): 104–112. See also Barry Alan Morris, "The Communal Constraints on Parody: The Symbolic Death of Joe Bob Briggs," *Quarterly Journal of Speech* 73 (1987): 460–473.
10. Even experienced comedians can go too far for their audiences. Consider the example of Joe Bob Briggs in Morris, "The Communal Constraints on Parody."
11. For an interesting discussion of gender differences in humor, see M. Alison Kibler, "Gender Conflict and Coercion on A&E's *An Evening at the Improv*," *Journal of Popular Culture* 32 (1999): 45–57.
12. See Joan B. Levine, "The Feminine Routine," *Journal of Communication* 26 (1976): 173–175; Lawrence La Fave and Roger Mannell, "Does Ethnic Humor Serve Prejudice?" *Journal of Communication* 26 (1976): 116–123; Dolf Zillmann and Holly Stocking, "Putdown Humor," *Journal of Communication* 26 (1976): 154–163.
13. See Palmer, *Taking Humor Seriously*; Joseph Alan Ullian, "Joking at Work," *Journal of Communication* 26 (1976): 129–133.
14. Victor Raskin, *Semantic Mechanism of Humor* (Dordrecht, The Netherlands: D. Reidel, 1985).
15. Sylvia Simmons, *How to Be the Life of the Podium: Openers, Closers and Everything in Between to Keep Them Listening* (New York: AMACOM, 1991).

### Chapter 26

1. Sherwyn P. Morreale, Brian H. Spitzberg, and J. Kevin Barge, *Human Communication: Motivation, Knowledge, and Skills* (Belmont, CA: Wadsworth/Thomson Learning, 2001), p. 295.
2. Karen Stabiner, *To Dance with the Devil: The New War on Breast Cancer* (New York: Delacorte Press, 1997).
3. John Dewey, *How We Think* (Boston: D. C. Heath, 1910).
4. Irving L. Janis, *Groupthink*, 2nd ed. (Boston: Houghton Mifflin, 1982).
5. Lyman K. Steil, Larry L. Barker, and Kittie W. Watson, *Effective Listening: Key to Your Success* (New York: McGraw-Hill, 1993), p. 91.
6. Adapted from Herbert W. Simons, *Persuasion: Understanding, Practice, and Analysis*, 2nd ed. (New York: Random House, 1986), p. 138.

# INDEX